The QuickStudy Guide for Sage ACT!

Susan Clark

Cornerstone Solutions Inc.
Houston

Sage ACT!

The QuickStudy Guide for Sage ACT! 2012

Author: Susan Clark, ACT! Certified Consultant, Swiftpage Certified Consultant
Cornerstone Solutions, Inc. (clark@cornerstonesolutions.com)

© 2011 Cornerstone Solutions, Inc. and QuickStudy Guide Series - All rights reserved. This product and related documentation are protected by copyright and are distributed under licenses restricting their use, copying, distribution, and decompilation. No part of this product or related documentation may be reproduced in any form by any means without prior written authorization of Cornerstone Solutions, Inc.

Printed in the United States of America

Trademarks: Cornerstone Solutions is a trademark of Cornerstone Solutions, Inc. Sage, the Sage logos, ACT!, and the Sage product and service names mentioned herein are registered trademarks or trademarks of Sage Software, Inc., or its affiliated entities. Microsoft SQL Server, Windows Vista, Windows 7 and associated logos are trademarks or registered trademarks of Microsoft Corporation in the United States and/or other countries. All other trademarks are the property of their respective owners.

Disclaimer: All statements, technical information, and recommendations in this Guide are believed reliable, but the accuracy and completeness thereof are not guaranteed or warranted, and they are not intended to be, nor should they be understood to be, representations or warranties concerning the products described. Cornerstone Solutions, Inc does not assume any responsibility or liability for errors or inaccuracies with respect to this publication or usage of information. Further, Cornerstone reserves the right to make changes to the information described in this Guide at any time without notice and without obligation to notify any person of such changes.

The QuickStudy Guide for Sage ACT!

Using ACT! Everyday — 1

The Basics — 3

- How Did "Quick" Get Included in the Book Name?........ 4
  - Using This QuickStudy Guide…Hey, Don't Skip This........ 4
- What's Contact and Customer Management Software?........ 5
- Anytime, Anywhere Access 6
- ACT! Pro vs. ACT! Premium 7
  - ACT! on the Web (Premium Only) 7
- Starting Your ACT! Software 7
- ACT! Setup Assistant 8
- Log on 8
- Opening a Database 9
  - Setting Up for Your Self-Study 9
  - Returning to Real Life 10
- ACT! Screen Elements 12
- Welcome View 12
  - Changing Your Startup View 13
- The Navbar 13
  - View Toolbar 14
  - Layout Tabs 15
- Layouts 16
  - Sizing the Contacts: Detail View Window 17
- Contact Record Basics 18
  - The "My Record" Contact Record 18
  - Our Practice Database 19
  - An Overview of Security Roles 19
  - Contact Fields 20
- Inserting a New Contact Record 22
  - Drop-down Fields 22
  - Duplicating Contacts 27
  - Assigning Security 28
  - Limited Access (Premium Only) 29
  - Assigning Limited Access by Default (Premium Only) 30
  - Deleting Contacts 31

Working with Your Contacts — 33

- Locating Contacts 34
  - Browsing Records 34
- Detail View and List View 35
  - Sorting the List View 36

- Related Task Pane – Another Sort Option ... 37
- Adding and Removing Columns ... 38
- Navbar Lookup Pane ... 39
- Lookup ... 40
  - Wait, We Didn't Tell ACT! the Last Name ... 45
  - Fixing a Problem Contact Name ... 46
- Lookup Variations ... 47
  - Adding to Lookups ... 47
  - Narrowing Lookups ... 48
  - Previous Lookups ... 49
  - Back (and Forward) Buttons ... 50
  - Universal Search ... 51
  - Using Special Characters in Search ... 52
  - Lookup, Any fields ... 54
  - Lookup Annual Events ... 55
  - Working In List View Edit Mode ... 57
  - Tag Mode ... 57
  - Lookup and Omit Tagged Records ... 58
  - Printing Lookups ... 60
- Secondary Contacts ... 60
  - Lookups on Secondary Contact Fields ... 62
  - Promoting from Within ... 63
- Documents Tab ... 64
  - Opening and Editing Files ... 67
  - Removing Files from the Documents Tab ... 67
- Relationships ... 68
- Your Contact's Website ... 71
- Web Info Tab ... 71
  - Web Info tab - User Links section ... 72
  - Attaching Web Pages From Internet Explorer® ... 74
- Web Info tab - ACT! Business Info section ... 76
  - Accessing Key Business Info for a Contact or Company ... 78
  - Company Profile ... 79
  - Importing Companies ... 80
  - Company Alerts ... 81
  - Importing Contacts ... 82
  - Build a List ... 83

Scheduling Your Day   87

- ACT! vs. a PIM ... 88
- Activity Types ... 88
- Simple Scheduling ... 89
- Adding an Outlook Meeting Request to Your Calendar ... 95
- Scheduling Activities Using the Calendar ... 96
- Viewing Your Calendar ... 97

Sage E-marketing For ACT! — 219

- Sage E-marketing For ACT! Features — 220
- How Is E-marketing Different from Outlook? — 220
  - View Some Tracking Examples — 221
- Creating an E-marketing Account — 222
- Creating E-mail Templates — 224
  - Creating your first basic Swiftpage e-mail template — 224
- Basic Template Editor Window — 225
  - What is [[SpePersonalMessage]] ? — 226
- Sending the Template — 226
- Creating a New Template Using Your Base — 228
  - What are SwiftWindows? — 228
  - Editing text — 229
  - Saving your SwiftWindow edit — 230
  - Saving your template changes — 230
  - Add a signature — 232
- Getting Results — 232
  - Scoring — 233
- Marketing Results Tab — 235
- Call Lists — 236
- What is Drip Marketing? — 236
- Surveys and Web Forms — 239
- E-marketing and Swiftpage Help — 242

Advanced Lookups — 243

- Activity Data Mining — 244
- Queries — 245
- Lookup By Example — 246
- Advanced Queries — 248
  - Operator Options — 250
  - And/Or — 254
  - Grouping — 256
  - Deleting Query Files — 257

Groups & Companies — 259

- Groups — 260
  - Displaying a Group Lookup — 260
  - Manually Adding a Contact to a Group — 261
- Companies — 263
- Creating and Populating a Group or Company — 265
  - Adding Multiple Contacts to a Group or Company — 267
  - Using Criteria for Your Groups — 271
  - Linking Contacts and Companies — 272
  - Create a Company from a Contact — 272
  - Link…Associate…What's the Difference? — 273

   Create a Contact from a Company 275
   Disabling a Company Link 275
   Pushing Company Changes Back to Contacts 277
   Pulling Changes from the Company Record 278
   Convert a Group to a Company 280
  Divisions and Subgroups 280
   What's the Up Button? 281
   Move or Promote a Division 282
  Cumulative Views of Notes, History, etc. 282
   Company Note or History 282
   Manually Sharing Items with a Company (or Group) 283
   Changing Companies 285
   Filtering Tabs 286
  Lookup Companies or Groups 287
   Advanced Queries for Companies and Groups 287

Opportunities   289

  Creating Opportunities 290
   Opportunities tab 295
  Updating an Opportunity 296
  Creating a Quote 297
  Closing the Deal 299
  Opportunity Management 300
   Opportunity List View 300
   Lookup Opportunities 302
   Export to Microsoft Excel 304
  Opportunity Reports 306
   Opportunity Pipeline 308
   Opportunity Graph 310

Viewing Dashboards & Reports   311

  Using Dashboards 312
   Displaying Dashboard Views 312
   Working in the Dashboard Views 313
   Other Dashboards 318
  ACT! Reports 319
  The Anatomy of an ACT! Report 322
   Favorite Reports 324

Customizing ACT! — 325

Database Design & Layouts — 327

- Creating a New Database 328
  - Customizing Fields 329
- Field Attributes 331
  - Enter field name and type 331
  - One-to-Many Tables 334
  - Customize field and list behavior 335
  - Customize field behavior 335
  - Set field triggers 339
- Manage Drop-down Lists 340
  - Creating Drop-down Lists for Importing 342
  - Importing the Drop-down List 343
  - Minor Changes to the Drop-down List 345
- Editing the Database Structure 346
- Field Security 347
- Creating New Fields for Other Entities 351
- Defining and Modifying Layouts 352
  - Designing Layouts 352
  - Saving Layouts 354
  - The Tool Palette 355
  - Formatting Toolbar 355
  - Modifying Layouts 356
  - Renaming the Field Labels 358
  - Moving Objects 358
  - Aligning Objects 360
  - Adding New Fields to Your Layout 362
  - Layout Tabs 364
  - Adding Other Objects 366
  - Formatting 367
  - Changing Background Tab Color 368
  - Make Same Width or Height 369
- Testing Your Layouts 370
  - Field Entry Order 370
- Customizing the Product View 372

Feature Customizations — 373

- Customizing Menus and Toolbars 374
  - Adding an Object to the Menu/Toolbar/Keystroke ... 376
  - Resetting Toolbars, Menus, and the Keyboard 378
  - Modifying the Navbar 379
- Creating Custom Web Info Links 379
- Priorities 381

> Customizing Priorities 381
Creating New Activity Types 383
Events 385
Creating a Custom Opportunity Process 386
> Creating Defined Product Lists 388
> Editing the Quote Template 388

Activity Series & Smart Tasks — 391

Activity Series 392
> Scheduling an Activity Series 394
What are Smart Tasks? 397
Creating a Smart Task 398
> Adding Steps to the Smart Task 399
> Manually running a Smart Task 404
> Pending Smart Task Steps 405
> Status of Smart Tasks 406
> Editing a Smart Task 408
> How Does A Smart Task Run Automatically? 408
> Enabling a Smart Task 411
Smart Tasks vs Activity Series 412
> Criteria for when to use Activity Series 412
> Criteria for when to use Smart Tasks 412
> Keep These Suggestions in Mind 413
Drip Marketing vs. Smart Tasks 414

Designing Dashboard & Reports — 415

Creating Your Own Dashboards 416
> Custom Components 419
> Alternative Dashboards 421
Report Templates 422
> The Report Designer Screen 423
> The Report and Page Header Sections 424
> The Detail Section 424
> The Report and Page Footer Sections 424
Adding Report Objects 425
> Formatting 426
> Is it a Field or a Label? 428
> Sizing Sections 429
> Using Group By for Sorting or Subtotals 432
> Section Behavior 433
> Summary Fields 434
> Subreports 436
Report Filters 441
Using Custom Reports 442
Using Scripting in Your Reports 443

Removing Blank Space Between Fields 444
Using Checkmarks for Yes/No Fields in Reports 446
Make Your Label Choose Home or Business on Print 448

Administering ACT!   451

Setting Up   453

Using Available Documentation 454
    Using the ACT! Knowledge Base 454
Enabling Your Database for Multiple Users 454
Examining Structure 455
    File Structure 455
    Directory Structure 456
    Moving the Database to the Server 457
    Enable Share for an Existing Database 458
    Opening the Shared Database 459
Pre-Install Checklist 460

Database Security   461

Database Security 462
Understanding Security Roles 462
    Custom Permissions for Manager or Standard Roles 463
Creating New Users 464
    Making Users Inactive 466
Password Management 467
    Defining a Global Password Policy 467
    Setting a Password for Yourself 470
Team Management (Premium Only) 471
    Limiting Contact Access   (Premium Only) 472
    Assigning Limited Access to a Lookup (Premium Only) 473
    Lookup Contacts by Access (Premium Only) 476
    "Managers" Team 477
Field Security 478

Database Maintenance   479

Database Preferences 480
    Disabling Notes and History Editing 480
    Disabling E-mail History on User Records 481
    Disabling File and/or E-mail Attachments 481
    Changing ACT!'s Default Duplicate Checking Criteria 482
File Locations for a Multi-user Database 483
General Database Maintenance 484
    Automatic Update Notification 484
    Back Up 485
    Automatically Backing Up Your Database 486

Sage ACT!

- Manually Backing Up Your Database 488
- Restoring a Backup 490
- Restore As 491
- Deleting a Database 493
- Check and Repair 494
- Scheduling Database Maintenance 496
- Checking the ACT! Scheduler Log 497
- Importing an Excel File 498
- Cleaning Up the Data 501
  - Duplicates 501
  - Tips for Dealing with Duplicates 502
  - Combine Duplicate Records 503
  - Edit, Replace 505
  - Remove Old Data 506

Synchronization   507

- Synchronizing Databases 508
- Administrator Tasks – Setting Up the Sync Environment 509
  - Determine and Setup the Connection Method 509
  - Define Remote User(s) 509
  - Restore the Database to Its Final Location 510
- Administrator Tasks – Creating the Sync Databases 510
  - Enable Synchronization 510
  - Manage Sync Sets 511
  - Create Remote Databases 513
  - Prepare the Remote Database(s) for Delivery 516
- Administrator Task – Turning On Synchronization 516
  - Setting Up Application Sync 516
  - Setting Up the Network Sync Service (Premium Only) 516
  - Setting Up Internet Sync (Premium Only) 518
- User Tasks – Restoring and Syncing Your Database 520
  - Changes for Remote Internet Sync 522
  - Synchronizing the Remote Database 522
  - Set Up a Sync Schedule with the ACT! Scheduler 523
  - Using the Subscription List in a Remote Database 524
- Administrator Task – Territory Realignment 525
- Synchronization Troubleshooting 525

Appendix   527

- User Roles and Permissions 528
- Converting an Older ACT! Database-Custom Conversion 530
  - Standard vs. Custom Conversion 531
- Using the OLE DB2 Provider 533

Index   535

Introduction

Thank you for investing in **The QuickStudy Guide for Sage ACT! 2012**. I hope you'll gain a better understanding of ACT! ... and that a better understanding benefits your business. In addition to giving you step-by-step instructions, I've tried to offer reasons why you would even want to use each feature or enable specific options.

While you can go through the guide chapter by chapter, or jump around to those topics you specifically want to know more about, I've divided the book into 3 logical groupings.

- **{Using ACT! Everyday}** is ideal for the normal end users.
- **{Customizing ACT!}** is for those who really want a custom look and feel to their database.
- **{Administering ACT!}** is great for those users who are responsible for the health and security of the database.

I welcome your feedback about **The QuickStudy Guide for Sage ACT!**. Tell me what was valuable and where I could improve: clark@cornerstonesolutions.com.

About the Author

Susan Clark is an ACT! Certified Consultant and a Swiftpage Certified Drip Marketing Consultant. Her company Cornerstone Solutions, Inc. has one of the larger teams of ACT! Certified Consultants in the world and is one of the top ACT! and Swiftpage resellers in the nation.

This is the tenth QuickStudy Guide she has written for ACT! (she's been writing it since version 5/2000). She has also written The E-marketing/Swiftpage QuickStudy Guide for ACT! (www.MarketingWithYourDatabase.com).

Susan is also a Sage Authorized Premiere Trainer and her courseware is used by many consultants in their training classes nationwide. In addition, Sage (ACT!'s corporate parent) has hired her when they needed to train and certify new ACT! Consultants. She served over six years on ACT!'s Advisory Board. She also facilitates the Houston Area ACT! Users' Group.

As impressive as her technical credentials are, Susan has that remarkable ability to conjure her genius from both the left <u>and</u> right sides of her brain. She has just as many qualifications on the applied marketing side of the desk, having served 10 years as Director of Marketing for a Fortune 500 oilfield service company before starting Cornerstone in 1987.

Susan holds a BA in Public Relations and Advertising and an MBA. On a lighter side, she lives in Houston with her husband of 30+ years and 2 grown sons (who are responsible for getting her involved in Karate and Scuba Diving over the years.)

QR Code Bonus Materials and Discounts

Throughout the book you will notice square bar codes like the one you see here. These are called Quick Response codes or QR Codes. They are essentially a hyperlink from this printed book to a specific online web page.

I've included many QR Codes throughout the book to give you more value for your book purchase, as well as help you understand the chapter material better.

To access these ACT! bonuses and discounts, use your smart phone or tablet QR Code Reader App. If you don't have one, they are fun and easy to use. You can download a free reader from your App Store or Marketplace on your device. The reader uses your device camera to take a picture of the bar code and then redirects you to more online information.

Try it now to get a free keyboard template that you can print out
or go to:
http://www.cornerstonesolutions.com/downloads/ACT2012-KBTemplate.pdf

Using ACT! Everyday

Sage ACT!

The Basics

To become acquainted with the basics of working in ACT!, you will:

☑ Explore the concept of Contact and Customer Management Software.

☑ Start your ACT! software.

☑ Familiarize yourself with the ACT! program window.

☑ Add new Contact records to the ACT! database.

How Did "Quick" Get Included in the Book Name?

How can a book with close to 600 pages include the word "quick" in the title? While it does seem a bit contradictory, the idea was to create a guide where each topic (and associated procedures and exercises) could stand on its own. That way, you can stop and start where you like or skip around. While you can read from start to finish… if you need to learn something fast, then the "QuickStudy" allows you to easily jump to that section to pick up what you need to know.

Using This QuickStudy Guide…Hey, Don't Skip This

This self-paced QuickStudy Guide has a very simple and straightforward flow. A **description** of each topic appears first. Following each description is a step-by-step "**Procedure**:" In this way you can also use this QuickStudy Guide as a reference tool.

Procedure: To understand the QuickStudy Guide

1. This column displays the commands, like…

    Choose **F**ile, **O**pen/Share Database…,
    or
    click the **O**pen/Share Database… toolbar icon.

    This column is used for **comments** or more complete descriptions. All of our procedures are clearly displayed in a numbered format with comments for clarification.

2. Select the database.

    We never miss a step.

3. Click **O**pen Database.

    Any command references are in **Bold** with the appropriate character <u>underlined</u> for quick recognition.

After you have reviewed the basic steps outlined in the "**Procedure:**" section, you can "**Practice:**" what you have learned. Don't skip the Practice sections. The comments have even more tips on things you should know to be more effective in your use of ACT!.

Practice: Topic to Try	
What to do	**How to do it/Comments**
1. The "**What to do**" column of each Practice gives the instructions on what is to be accomplished.	If you need help, this column provides **step-by-step keystroke instructions**. Try covering this column to see if you can perform the practice on your own. Then read for even more tips.

 *These notations indicate that a valuable, **tried-and-true tip** is being offered. Pay particular attention to these.*

 This icon gives information on how to accomplish the same thing if you are using the Windows Vista® or Windows 7® operating system.

Oh…by the way…our QuickStudy Guide also contains a bit of tongue-in-cheek humor. Its style fits with the easy-to-understand, straightforward ACT! software. We hope you'll forgive us and not groan too loudly.

What's Contact and Customer Management Software?

Contact and Customer Management Software helps you manage all of the data and activities associated with developing and maintaining relationships with the people (contacts) and companies you do business with…or would like to do business with. Managing relationships using ACT! can help you convert your prospects into customers and your customers into life-long relationships as part of a successful, long-term business strategy. ACT! is still the number one selling Contact and Customer Management Software in the world.

Not only does it keep track of names, addresses, and phone numbers, but it also performs countless other important tasks:

- Provides **easy ways to look up contacts** by not only their name and address information, but also by other key details about them.
- Creates **personalized letters or e-mails** and remembers when it was sent, who sent it, and what was said. Sending correspondence to individuals or groups of people is quick and easy.
- **Keeps a record of each "touch" with your contacts**, all in one easy-to-view place…on the contact's record (not just with yourself as in Microsoft® Outlook® or in an iPad® or Android™ applications). You can see the last time you or anyone in your company called, wrote, e-mailed, or met with them, what you talked about, and so on. ("When did I last have lunch with JP and what did we talk about?")
- Allows easy input and viewing of extensive Notes and Histories.
- Provides **one-click access to scheduling new appointments** or keeping track of currently scheduled meetings, phone calls, and important tasks. Displays or prints appointment calendars so you can keep an eye on your schedule.
- Synchronizes your ACT! Contact and Calendar data with Outlook or with your Gmail™ account.
- Synchronizing your Calendar and Contacts with Outlook or Gmail makes it incredibly easy to **keep your data on your smart phone** (Blackberry®, iPhone®, iPad®, Android™ OS phone, etc), so you don't have to take your PC everywhere.
- **Automate some of your follow-up tasks** to help you keep important things from slipping through the cracks.
- Helps you define and remember **Relationships** between contacts.
- **Tracks Opportunities** that you hope to close, those that did close, and (gulp!) the ones that got away. **Exports your list to Microsoft Excel®** for further slicing and dicing.
- Offers a **customizable Dashboard view of key business indicators** using data pulled from different areas of ACT! to help you manage your business.

Sage ACT!

- Provides a **view of all contacts linked or associated to a specific Company** record, including a view of their combined Notes, History, Activities, and Opportunities. Now, you really can view the big picture of what is going on with a specific company.
- **Generates reports** on the information you keep about your contacts: summaries of meetings, notes taken, opportunities, or activities.

To be successful in most businesses, you need to know the people you do business with. Besides name and address information, you want to know when you talked to them last, what you said, what *they* said, what their spouse's name is (do they *have* a spouse?), what their interests are, when you are supposed to call them again, and so on, and so forth, ad infinitum.

ACT! understands that the more you know about your customers, the more effectively you can do business with them. Keeping track of all these details could be a daunting task, especially if you deal with hundreds or even thousands of people. However, that is one of the reasons why ACT! has become so popular. With everything linked to the Contact record, these details are only a mouse-click away. ACT! is a powerful, flexible, and above all, **EASY TO USE** software program that has one goal in mind:

To turn your contacts into relationships,
and your relationships into results.

Anytime, Anywhere Access

If you sit at your desk all day and never leave the office, the desktop version of ACT! may be all you ever need. However, if you have appointments outside the office, travel to other locations, or even work in a remote office, you may want to look at the different ways you can always have ACT! with you so you can be productive, whether you are in the office or on the road!

- If you are a remote employee, travel a great deal, or just like to take your work home with you, you could **synchronize the database to your laptop** for complete offline access when out of the office.
- ACT! also has a **web version** that allows your remote, traveling, or office-based users to access their information in real time though a Web browser…and you can host it on your own IIS server…so no monthly fees.
- You could access your ACT! database using **Citrix®** or Terminal Services.
- Synchronize your ACT! calendar and contacts to your smart phone (Blackberry, iPhone, Android phone, etc) or tablet device (iPad, Xoom, etc) using the Outlook or Google sync model or with a third-party application.
- If you just can't give up that Day-Timer® or FranklinCovey® Planner, then you can **print your calendar** to over 20 popular paper organizers so you always have your schedule with you.

ACT! Pro vs. ACT! Premium
ACT! comes in several versions...

Sage ACT! Pro – can be used by up to 10 named users per database.

Sage ACT! Premium – designed for companies with a larger base of users who will share data. The Premium version provides additional security and workgroup features. This version also offers the ability to host the data on your own Web server, so your end users can access the data locally or over the Web... you choose.

ACT! on the Web (Premium Only)
ACT! Premium delivers anytime, anywhere access to your data. So you can choose how you want to deploy ACT! throughout your organization... with different options for different users... some on the Web... some on the desktop.

You can install ACT! Premium for Web on your own servers for an easy roll-out to users. Since you are hosting the database on your own equipment, there are no monthly charges....and your desktop users and your Web users are accessing the exact same database...no syncing. You can access your ACT for Web database using Internet Explorer or Firefox® 4.

Web users have similar functionality to the desktop product. In fact, with only a few exceptions, you could use this book to train yourself how to use ACT! on the Web if you focus on the Menu commands and Toolbar icons (ACT! Web users cannot use any of the right-click or Function Key options).

The primary features that are not available in the web products are:
- Accounting integration
- Sage E-marketing for ACT!
- Add document shortcuts (but you can add files)
- Attach URLs to contacts
- Availability tab in calendar
- Contact creation from Outlook
- Customizable menus
- Edit an advanced query
- Edit mode (edit fields in Contacts: List View)
- Lookup indicator at lower left
- Quick print

Starting Your ACT! Software
Now that we've talked a bit about how this QuickStudy Guide is set up and about Contact and Customer Management software, let's start ACT! and see what the world's leading Contact and Customer Manager can do for you.

When normal installation is performed, the program icon is created in a program group called **Sage ACT!** (or **Sage ACT! Premium**). Installation may also create a desktop icon that you can click to run the program.

ACT! Icon

8 | Sage ACT!

Procedure: To start ACT!

1. Click the **Start** button, point to **All Programs**.

   Click the **Start** button (usually on the lower left of your screen) and point to **All Programs**. A menu opens.

2. Click on **Sage ACT!**.

   Click the program group that contains ACT!. Your group might have a slightly different name.

3. Click the **ACT!** icon.   ACT! starts.

 Depending on the options you selected during the ACT! software installation, you can also double-click the icon on the desktop or single-click the icon on the Quick Launch Toolbar to the right of the Start button.

ACT! Setup Assistant

When you start ACT! for the first time, it runs the ACT! Setup Assistant. This program guides you through creating a new (or converting an existing) database, selecting the e-mail system to use with ACT!, (if using Outlook, you are prompted to add your ACT! database(s) as an address book in Outlook), set your e-mail preferences, define your Outlook calendar integration and meeting invitation settings and select your default word processor. This is a great way to get started with a new ACT! installation. If you cancel the **ACT! Setup Assistant**, you can run it at any time by choosing **Help**, **Setup Assistant...** from the menu.

 *This QuickStudy Guide assumes you have already set up ACT!, therefore, should the **ACT! Setup Assistant** show its face, click the **Cancel** button. You can return to it any time you wish.*

Log on

You may be asked to log on to your database when you start ACT!. If this happens, don't worry about it. ACT! is just asking who you are, so it knows what information to display (it may also ask you to input your password, if you have one).

The Basics | 9

Practice: Start Your Engines

What to do	How to do it/Comments
1. Start ACT!.	**Start**, **All Programs**, **Sage ACT! Premium**, **Sage ACT! Premium**.
2. If the **ACT! Setup Assistant** appears, click **Cancel**.	Observe the screen.

 At the completion, you either see a blank window, or a database is open and visible in the ACT! window. It does not matter which appears.

Opening a Database

When ACT! software is installed, a copy of the **ACT2012Demo** database is also installed and is perfect for our practice exercises. ACT2012Demo is a sample database for a company called CH TechONE, which is run by **Chris Huffman**. Chris has grown this company (since the early days of ACT!) from a small import/export company to a multi-national company.

 If you have installed previous versions of ACT!, you may have several copies of the demo database floating around, each with an embedded number indicating which version of the software it was created with. For this QuickStudy Guide, we use the ACT2012Demo.

Setting Up for Your Self-Study

We are assuming that you have already installed ACT!, so you can easily find the ACT2012Demo database files on your PC.

Procedure: To open the ACT2012Demo

1. With ACT! open on your PC, choose **File, Open/Share Database…**	If you are in a different database, ACT! automatically closes it before opening our practice database.
2. Click **ACT2012Demo** and click **Open Database**.	If you don't see the ACT2012Demo listed, click **The database I want is not listed** and navigate to your "\My Documents\ACT\ ACT Data\Databases" folder.
	or \Users\Public\Public Documents\ACT\ACT Data\Databases.
3. If prompted to roll over your activities in our practice database, click **Cancel**.	If prompted for a logon name, use: Chris Huffman (no password).

Sage ACT!

☞ *If the ACT2012Demo has been deleted from your system, you can download a copy of the database from www.actmanual.com.*

Returning to Real Life

You can easily move back and forth from the ACT2012Demo to the one you use every day. Remember, in this QuickStudy Guide, review the "**Procedure**" section to understand the procedure, and then, go to the "**Practice:**" section to try it out.

Procedure: To open a different database

1. Choose **File, Open/Share Database...**

2. Select the database you wish to open.   If you don't see the database listed, click "The database I want is not listed" hyperlink.

3. Click **Open Database**.   The database opens in ACT!.

☞ *ACT! can only have one database open at a time. If you have a database open and choose to open another, the first one closes automatically before the second one opens.*

If you constantly move between two or more databases, you can change quickly by selecting the database from the "Recent Files" list at the bottom of the **File** menu. The names of the last four databases you have opened appear immediately above the Exit command.

If you have not yet started using a working database for your business, you can skip this practice (moving back and forth between the practice database and your real one) and go straight to the "ACT! Screen Elements" section on the next page.

☞ *We'll cover creating your own custom database starting on page 328.*

The Basics | 11

Practice: Open Another Database

What to do	How to do it/Comments
1. If you just opened the ACT2012Demo database, then switch back to your working database.	**File**, click option **2** at the bottom of the menu. This should be the database that you were in before you opened the class database.
2. Enter your name, if prompted. *[screenshot: Log on to CornerstoneSusan dialog box showing "Enter your user name for this database:" with "Chris Huffman" ← Replace with your name, "Enter your password for this database:", Remember password checkbox, OK and Cancel buttons]*	If you share your company database with other users, you need to enter your name (instead of Chris Huffman) in the **Enter your user name for this database:** area.
3. Enter your password, if necessary, and click **OK**.	**[Tab]** to or click in the password area and enter your password. Click **OK**.
4. Now re-open the practice database called… **ACT2012Demo**.	**File**, click option **2** at the bottom of the menu, or you can try, **File**, **Open/Share Database…**, click ACT2012Demo, and click **Open Database**.
5. If you are prompted to roll over activities, click **Cancel**.	

 Since the ACT2012Demo has only one active log-on user and the password feature has not been enabled (by default), you should not be prompted to enter a user name or password.

Sage ACT!

ACT! Screen Elements

The first time you open ACT!, the **Welcome** view displays with options to help you learn more about, and better utilize, ACT!.

Title bar displays the name of the program, (e.g., ACT! by Sage Premium) and the currently open database name.

Menu bar displays the commands that are available for the active window. Menu options change depending on the view you are in.

The **Global Toolbar** with the large easy-to-read (and most commonly used) buttons sits below the menu bar.

The **Current View** name displays at the left below the global toolbar.

Welcome View

The Welcome View is full of hyperlinks to help you better use ACT!. Some links will display help files and feature tour videos. Some are actually shortcuts to common ACT! commands. The options that are available will depend on how you log into ACT! (For example, if you are not an Administrator, the "Add/Modify Fields" option will not be available for you.) There are also separate options for new users (Getting Started) and more experienced users (Do More With ACT!).

Practice: ***Welcome, Bienvenidos, Willkommen, Howdy***	
What to do	*How to do it/Comments*
1. Display the Welcome view, if necessary.	Click the Welcome button on the Navbar.
2. Under Try It (in the Do More With ACT! column), click **Manage Users**. (This link only displays if you are a Manager or Administrator user.)	Clicking this link is the same as clicking **Tools, Manage Users…**. We will talk about creating new users later on so click **Close** for now.
3. Under **Learn About It**, click the **Organizing Contacts into Groups** link.	An ACT! by Sage Help dialog displays with steps for adding contacts.
4. Check out one of the Featured Video tutorials.	Click on one of the links to view a quick tutorial on the selected item.

The Basics   13

Changing Your Startup View

When you start the ACT! program, the default initial view is the Welcome view. While this is a handy view for locating resources to help you become more efficient in using ACT!, you may want to change your startup view to one that gets you working with your ACT! data. ACT! provides you with four options for a startup view: Welcome, Contacts, Contact List, or Dashboard. We will be looking at all of these views as we go through the book.

Procedure: To change your startup view.

1. From the Welcome Page, under **Try It**, click **Change the Default View**,

   or click **Tools**, **Preferences…**, click the **Startup** tab.

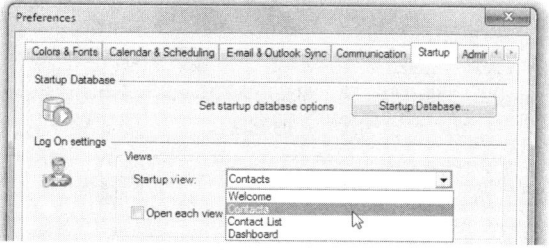

2. Change the **Startup view:** to your choice.

   The next time you log into ACT!, your selected view will be the first one you see.

3. Click **OK**.

The Navbar

The **Navbar** appears at the left of the ACT! window. It contains a list of **Related Tasks** to help you be more productive in your current view, and the **Navigation** buttons.

ACT! has so much to offer, you can't see everything on one screen. Clicking a Navigation button will show a different view of your ACT! database. When you click the Calendar icon, the display switches to the last Calendar view you selected (the Day, Week, Work Week or Monthly view). When you click the Contacts icon, you are returned to the Contacts view.

We'll review each of these functions as we go through the QuickStudy Guide.

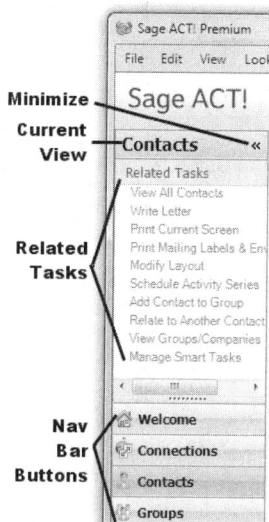

 You can easily collapse the Navbar by clicking on << (minimize) next to the Current View label.

14 Sage ACT!

Practice: Playing with the Navbar

What to do	How to do it/Comments
1. Notice how clicking on the Navbar buttons at the left, changes your views.	
2. Drag the separator bar between Related Tasks and the Navigation buttons down. Notice how the Navigation icons fall into place on the bottom bar.	
3. Collapse the Navbar by clicking on the << at the top of the Navbar.	
4. Drag the separator bar back up so that you can see all of the Navbar icons.	
5. Expand the Navbar and drag the separator bar to the location that works best for your PC.	

View Toolbar

In all views (except Welcome), a **View toolbar** displays directly beneath the Global toolbar. View toolbars change as you work in the different ACT! views.

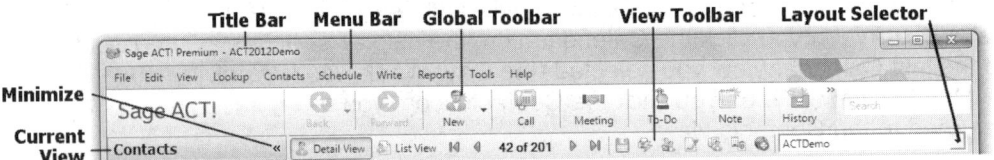

When the meaning of a toolbar button is unclear, just *point* to the icon (don't click it). After a moment, a **tool tip** appears, and identifies the button for you.

The Basics 15

Practice: What the Heck Is This Button!?!

What to do	How to do it/Comments
1. Click on the **Contacts** button in the Navbar at the left.	This switches from Welcome page to Contacts view in your database.
2. Notice that there is now a second row of smaller icons (under the Global toolbar).	The View Toolbar changes depending on which view you have selected.
3. What's the name of this icon?	Point to the icon, but *don't* click it. The tool tip appears telling you that it's the **Duplicate Contact** icon.
4. Find out the names of several other icons on the View toolbar.	

Layout Tabs

Running across the middle of the screen are the Layout Tabs. You can track lots of information about your contacts (far more information than can comfortably fit on your screen at once). Each notebook-style tab provides you with a "page" where you can record additional data about your contacts. Click a tab to display the information stored on it. The names on the tabs describe the type of information stored on them.

 If your screen is not wide enough to display all of the available tabs, they may wrap around to a second row.

Practice: View Layout Tabs

What to do	How to do it/Comments
1. What layout tab is displayed now?	If you look carefully, one tab appears to be in front of the others and displays with a highlighted background. The contents of its "page" appear in the bottom part of the window.
2. Display the **Secondary Contacts** tab.	Click the **Secondary Contacts** tab to see if any additional Contacts are listed for the current Contact.
3. Display the **History** tab.	Besides clicking on the **History** tab, you can also press **[Shift+F9]** to display the **History** tab for the current Contact.
4. Click some additional tabs to view their contents.	What kind of information do you think you will find there?

Sage ACT!

What to do	How to do it/Comments
5. When finished browsing, click the **Notes** tab.	Let's all be on the same page, shall we?

Layouts

At times, you may find it advantageous to see less (or more) information or to see it ordered in a different way. Screen layouts allow you to arrange the information stored in your database in many different ways (the same data, just arranged differently).

ACT! has two default Basic Contact Layouts: one for a smaller screen resolution (800x600) and one for a larger screen resolution (1024x768). The Layout button is used to switch between available layouts: ones that come with ACT! or ones that you design.

Procedure: To change to a different layout

1. Click the Layout selector drop-down arrow.

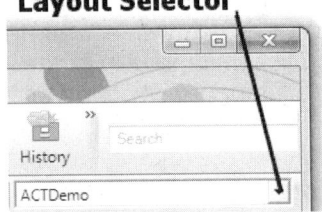

Layout Selector

The button appears at the upper-right of the window. When you click the Layout drop-down, a list of choices appears. The name of the currently selected layout is displayed.

2. Click the desired layout.

The screen changes to the new layout.

☞ *The numbers to the right of the default layout names (800x600 or 1024x768) indicate that the layout is optimized for that screen size. If you don't know your PC's screen resolution, just find a layout that seems to fill up your screen, but that doesn't require you to scroll to see the information.*

Procedure: To change your theme color between green and silver

1. **Tools, Customize, Color Scheme, Sage Green** or **Sage Silver**, or

   Tools, Preferences, Colors & Fonts tab.

   This changes the background color of the menu and the active color in the Navbar.

The Basics | 17

Practice: Admire the Views

What to do	How to do it/Comments
1. Switch to the **Basic Contact Layout – 800x600** layout (if necessary) and notice the location of the ID/Status and Referred By fields.	Click the Layout button at the upper right of the window and choose **Basic Contact Layout – 800x600** from the drop-down menu (if it is not already selected).
2. Switch to the **Basic Contact Layout – 1024X768 Default**.	Click the Layout button again and click the **Basic Contact Layout – 1024X768 Default**.
Notice the location of the ID/Status and Referred By fields now. Also notice that more fields have been moved to the top panel of the layout.	Some fields moved to the top panel.
3. Switch to the **ACTDemo** layout.	We will use this layout as we go through the QuickStudy Guide.
4. Determine your favorite theme color.	**T**ools, **C**ustomize, C**o**lor Scheme, Sage **G**reen or Sage **S**ilver

Sizing the Contacts: Detail View Window

The Contacts: Detail View is divided into two panes. The top contains the Company, Contact name, address, and phone number information. The bottom half displays the information contained in the tabs.

Procedure: To resize the panes of the Contacts: Detail View

1. Place the mouse pointer on the bar that divides the top and bottom of the layout.

   When positioned properly, the mouse pointer turns in to a double-headed arrow.

2. Click and hold the left mouse button and drag the bar up or down to resize the two window parts relative to each other.

   The two parts of the screen stay the size that you make them, until you change them again.

Sage ACT!

Practice: Size the Parts

What to do	How to do it/Comments
1. Change the size of the bottom portion of the Detail View. Adjust the size so you can see the maximum information in both the top and bottom of the window.	Place your mouse pointer on the bar that divides the top and bottom of the screen. Look for the double-headed arrow that indicates the pointer is positioned properly, click and hold the left mouse button, and drag up or down to resize the bottom half of the window.

 If you have a computer with a large Screen Area setting, you may want to adjust the bar tightly to the top half of the screen (so that you can just see all of the fields in the top half) with all of the extra room in the bottom half. That way, as you continue to enter Notes and History, you can see more of them without scrolling.

Contact Record Basics

Now that you have a feel for the ACT! screen, we need to look around. All related information about each Contact in your database is called a **Contact record**.

- The Detail View displays information about the current record.
- Each bit of information appears in its own text box. These boxes are called **fields**.
- To the left of each text box is a **label** that describes the data stored in that box.
- There are many more fields than can be displayed easily on your computer monitor, so they are divided among the tabs in your layout.

The "My Record" Contact Record

The first contact you always see in your database is the one that contains information about the person you logged in as…usually yourself. This record contains your "My Record" information.

Since more than one person can have access to an ACT! database, each person should have a logon user name created for them.

- Creating a logon user name automatically creates an associated "**My Record**" (yes that is its official designation).
- My Record information is used for signatures at the end of letters and e-mails and for information on the Fax cover sheet. However you input your title (Supreme Commander?), your fax number, your e-mail address, etc., that is how the information appears in your correspondence.

The Basics | 19

- The My Record logon is also used to track, and separate, all of the activities each user is planning in a separate calendar.
- Any Contact, Note, History, or Opportunity entered in the database is marked with the My Record name of the user who entered it.

☞ *While you may be the only user of your database now, it's good to know that ACT! can grow with you.*

Our Practice Database

For the purposes of this QuickStudy Guide, you will be logging on as a fictitious character…Chris Huffman. As CEO of CH TechONE, you spend your days managing a multi-national company (with employees on three continents) supplying TechONE systems for a discriminating clientele.

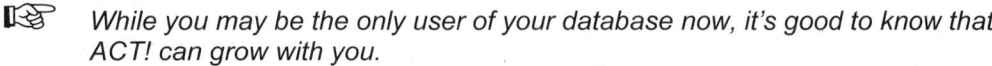

The TechONE system is available for small offices to large facilities. It can improve your profitability. Make you more "green." The major piece of the system is the "ONE Component."

- ONE Component, many possibilities.
- It is the ONE thing that you need to accelerate your company's growth.
- It's the ONE thing you can't live without.
- Everyone needs ONE.

We also offer the "TWO Component," which is two times more powerful than the ONE. Service contracts and replacement parts are also available. Use your imagination. ;-)

An Overview of Security Roles

ACT! includes five levels of security called **roles**. When you log into the ACT2012Demo database as Chris Huffman, you have been assigned to an Administrator role in the database. Your security role determines which features you can access and the functions you can perform.

Since users with an Administrator role can do anything in the database, using the ACT2012Demo is perfect for going through this QuickStudy Guide. You can play, test, try out, and destroy all you like, while your real company data remains safe. You can read more about security roles in the Appendix on page 528.

☞ *You can verify your current security Role by pointing to your Logon name at the lower-right corner of the ACT! window.*

Contact Fields

The purposes of most of the fields are fairly evident. The top half of the layout has "business card" information (data found on almost everyone's business card). However, a couple of fields in each area of the screen are worth discussing. (They may be displayed in a different order depending on the layout that you are using. We are using the ACTDemo layout.) The fields discussed below can be found in all ACT! databases.

Salutation: By default, the Salutation field is automatically populated with the Contact's first name. You can always change it (from Robert to Bob or to Dr. Smith). The contents of this field will be used in your correspondence: Dear <Salutation> or Dear Bob. You can modify Preferences to indicate how this field gets populated…with a first or last name or no name.

ID/Status: ID/Status field can be used to segment your database into Customers, Prospects, Vendors, Friends, etc. Don't ignore this field. It is a quick way to group your database for mailings or other quick look ups. **ID/Status** is one of the options on the **Lookup** menu. This field is also what is known as a "history" field. Anytime you alter something in this field, the change is automatically posted to the **History** tab with the current date and time, along with the user name that entered the new information.

Referred By: Keeping track of how new leads reach you can help you decide how to spend your marketing dollars next year. It can also help remind you to thank your friend for the lead that turned into a client. ACT! has a built-in report (**Reports**, **Source of Referrals**) that sorts and counts the number of Contacts by referral source.

Web Site: If you enter the Contact's Web site information, you can click the field to display the client's Web site in your browser window…handy to refresh your memory about services or products the company provides.

"System" fields: As you work in ACT!, system date fields are automatically updated by ACT! and cannot be changed by the user. They indicate the date of the… **Last Edited** (the last date that a field was changed, an activity was entered or cleared, a history or note or opportunity was entered.. well… any time the record was changed in any way) along with the name of the last user to make a change to the record (**Last Edited By**). Other system fields are **Last Reach** (the most recent call to this Contact), **Last E-mail** (the last e-mail history created), **Last Meeting** (the date of the last meeting held), and **Last Letter** (the date of the most recent letter that you printed),.

[Contact Access]

Access Level: Public or Private: No, this isn't asking whether it is a publicly- or privately-held company. It's about who can see the record. All Contacts by default are marked as **Public**. If you share the database with other users in your company, you can opt to change this field to Private for certain records. After a Contact is marked as **Private**, only the listed "Record Manager" can see it.

Not even the Administrator can see it, unless they log on to the database as that Record Manager. This also affects the total number of Contacts displayed in the record counter. Private records are included in your count, but not in anyone else's count. All changes to Contact Access are recorded to the Contact's History tab using an "Access Changed" history type.

The **Create Date** indicates when the record was originally created by the listed **Record Creator**. **Import Date** indicates if (and when) the record was imported.

If you are using the ACT! Premium, you have a third level of Contact Access…**Limited Access**. The Limited Access feature allows you to select a user(s) or a defined team of users that can access the current record. Only users with Administrator or Manager roles can create Teams. More about this later.

 My Record/User records must remain Public and CANNOT be assigned to Private or to Limited Access.

User Fields

User 1 – User 10: ACT! provides you with some "blank" fields so you can begin to enter other information about your contacts. Perhaps you would like to keep an "Industry" field so that you can focus your marketing efforts on specific groups. We'll learn to change the field names later in this guide.

Personal Info

Personal E-mail: Some of your contacts may have a personal e-mail address that they would prefer you use for non-work correspondence. While you can click this field to open an e-mail window addressed with the contact's e-mail address, you cannot use it in an e-mail merge.

Messenger ID: The ID you would use to set up this contact in your Instant Messaging program.

Spouse: All things being equal, people do business with people they like. The next time your client mentions their spouse's name, record it here. How impressive is it if you remember their name and ask about them? Very!

Birthday: Birthday allows you to keep track of your clients' birth dates. While it is a date field, you don't have to be that precise here (unless you are in the insurance business). Just the month and day will do (who cares if it fills in the current year). This field is also an **Annual Event** field, meaning that you can look up all Contacts that have a birthday in the current week, month or other specified time period (regardless of the year entered).

Some of the fields that you see were created just for the ACT2012Demo database and are not automatically created for new ACT! databases (e.g. Key Contact, Last Year's Purchases, First Purchase, Customer ID, and Twitter.) There are also more tabs displayed in our layout. We'll be getting to all of these features… just keeping it simple to start.

Inserting a New Contact Record

The list of people you know and do business with is in a constant state of change. As you make new contacts, you will need to add them to the database.

Procedure: To add a contact to a database

1. Choose Contacts, New Contact,   A blank Contact record appears.

   or press the **[Insert]** key on your keyboard,

   or right-click anywhere on the background of the Contact layout screen and choose **New Contact** from the shortcut menu.

   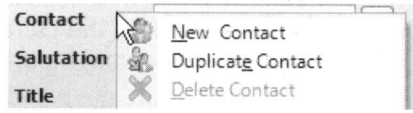

2. Enter the information for the new contact. Press **[Tab]** to move from field to field. **[Shift+Tab]** returns you to the previous field.

☞ *The information entered into ACT! is saved as you go.*

Drop-down Fields

Certain fields in your database can display drop-down lists. These lists often contain common or required entries for that field. Using these drop-down fields can help speed your data entry, but if you need to enter something not in the list, you can usually do that as well. **Title**, **ID/Status**, **City**, and **State** are some examples of drop-down fields.

Procedure: To use a drop-down field

1. Click in the desired field. Fields with associated drop-down lists have a downward pointing arrow at the right.

2. Click the drop-down arrow to display the list, A list "drops down" from the field box.

   or press **[F2]** to open the list.

3. Click the desired entry. The list closes and your selection appears in the field.

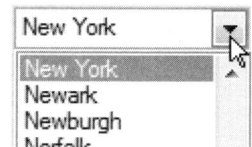

☞ *If the field allows multiple selections from the drop-down, a checkbox appears to the left of each value. Click the items you want to insert in the current field (or click again to remove the check), then **[Tab]** or click out of the field. You can also click the drop-down arrow again to collapse the list.*

The Basics | 23

There are several ways to enter data from a drop-down list. You can display the list using the mouse (as described above), or you can just type the entry. If the item you are typing is in the list, ACT! displays it as you type the first few letters. Once you see the appropriate entry, even if you haven't finished typing, you can move on to the next field and the displayed item is entered. If the item you are entering is not in the list, just finish typing it and move to the next field.

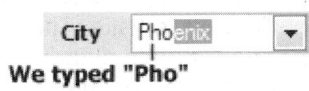
We typed "Pho"

 Use semi-colons to separate multiple items.

Practice: Adding a Contact

What to do	How to do it/Comments
1. Add a new record to the database. **William Wonderful**	**Contacts**, **New Contact...** or press **[Insert]**. Use **[Tab]** to move from the **Salutation** field. Notice the **Salutation** field automatically filled in after you entered the Contact name.
2. Change the Salutation to **Bill**.	No one calls him William.
3. He works for: **Captains of Industry**	Tab to the Company field and fill in the information.
4. His **Title** is **Director**. Start typing and notice how it finishes the word for you.	Click in the field and then type **di**. Notice that, even if you started in lower case, when you exit the field, the word is capitalized.
5. In the **ID/Status** field, select **Prospect** and **Vendor**. Notice how easy it is to select multiple values (or unselect them).	**[Tab]** to or click in the **ID/Status** field and click the drop-down arrow or press **[F2]**. Click **Prospect** and then click **Vendor**. Click the drop-down arrow again to close the list.
6. Phone numbers next: Phone (713) 661-5091 Mobile (713) 661-5096	**[Tab]** to or click in the Phone field to enter the phone number. Notice that ACT! formats it for you.

What to do	How to do it/Comments
7. E-mail is bill@captainsoi.com Web site = www.captainsoi.com Notice that both the Web site and the E-mail fields are hyperlinked. Click the Web site name to display that Web site in your default Internet browser. If you have set up your e-mail system to work with ACT!, you can click the e-mail address and write an e-mail to Bill.	Once you have entered and clicked out of the field, it is active. Click the Web address that you entered to display the Web site. Then close your browser and return to entering data. Click the e-mail address to launch a new message window to send a note to Bill. ☞ *If you make a mistake entering a Web site or e-mail address, right-click the field and then edit as necessary.*

8. The company address is:
   555 Patton Way
   Houston, TX 77005
   United States	

9. Click the **Contact Access** tab and note who created this record and when it was created.	If you haven't moved off of the record, the record hasn't been "created" in ACT! yet…it has only been started.
10. Use the Forward arrow on the Toolbar to move off of the record and then the Backward arrow to return to the record. Now look at the **Contact Access** tab again to verify the Create Date.	Notice that you didn't have to do anything to save the data. Once you move off of a record, everything is saved. ☞ *There is a Save icon on the toolbar if you want to save the information for any reason without having to move off of the record.*
11. Click the **User Fields** tab and notice the 10 fields that are just waiting to be customized to your needs.	Users with Administrator or Manager roles can customize fields in the database.
12. Click the **Personal Info** tab and review the fields there. It's not likely that you will get many home addresses, but sometimes it's nice to have a place to put them.	If your clientele is consumer-based and you contact them through their home address, use the regular address fields (not the home address). All of the letter templates, labels, and envelopes used in mail-merges are designed around the main address fields…not Home.

The Basics 25

What to do	How to do it/Comments
13. While talking to Bill, he mentioned his wife **Helen**. Enter her name in the Spouse field.	The Spouse field is on the **Personal Info** tab.

☞ We added a few fields to the ACT2012Demo. These fields are not found in the default design when you create a new database. However, we wanted to demonstrate some of the power available for customizing the database to your business. Keep reading, and we'll teach you how to incorporate any of these custom designs in to your database.

You must be using the ACT2012Demo and viewing it using the "ACTDemo" layout to view these custom fields.

What to do	How to do it/Comments
14. Mark Bill as one of the key contacts for Captains of Industry.	(Custom field) Click in the **Key Contact** field (below the Company name) to place a checkmark in the field.
15. Enter today's date in the **First Purchase** field. When you **[Tab]** out of the field, the Schedule Activity Series dialog box pops up. Notice the activities that are about to be scheduled, and then click the **Schedule** button.	(Custom field) The drop-down arrow at the left of a date field displays a calendar to help you choose today's date. (Custom feature) This field was designed to automatically launch the New Customer Activity Series which schedules five activities with various people in our organization whenever a prospect becomes a customer. We'll talk more about Activity Series later.
16. Enter an eight-character **Customer ID** with some lower-case alpha characters and some numbers. Notice that you can't enter more than eight characters.	(Custom field) We created the Customer ID field to allow up to 8 numbers and/or uppercase letters. If you enter an alpha character in lowercase, when you **[Tab]** out of the field, it changes to uppercase.
17. Notice above the First Purchase field, there is an empty **Last Year's Purchases** (hey, he's new… he won't have any yet). But also notice that you can't enter or modify any numbers in this field. You can only view data in this field.	(Custom field) We plan to use the Customer ID field as a basis for importing those numbers at the beginning of each year. ☞ ACT! Premium allows you to define which users have rights to change the data…or to even view it.

What to do	How to do it/Comments
18. Go back and change his **ID/Status** to remove Prospect and add Customer.	Click the drop-down arrow for ID/Status, add a check next to Customer, and uncheck Prospect. ID/Status is a "history" field. When the field is modified and the record is saved, a **Field Changed** entry is created in the **History** tab.
19. Display the **History** tab. Click the Save icon on the Toolbar at the top of the window and notice the new entry.	The history entry indicates which field was changed, the previous value in the field, the new value entered into the field, the date on which it was changed, and the Record Manager who changed it. Now you can see the date that the Prospect became our customer.
20. Enter some **Trivia** about Bill. Type as much as you want. As the content fills the field, a scroll bar appears to the right to allow you to enter and review as much as you like.	(Custom field) Trivia was created as a memo field, which allows virtually unlimited data entry. You might like a Trivia field to give your team a place to store data not related to any field choices.
21. Did you notice the square on the right of the **Personal Info** tab? It's a place for a photo. Some of the contacts in our database already have photos added to their record. Sometimes you can grab a photo of a client from their company Web site or a social media site. William's photo can be found on his Web site.	(Custom field) Click the Web site link for Captains of Industry and locate Bill's photo under Staff. Right-click his photo, click **Save Picture As...**, change the location to "Desktop" and click **Save**. Close the Web site. In the photo square on the **Home Address** tab, right-click, select **Choose Image**, click the "Desktop" icon at the left, click the file you just saved, and click **Open**.

 We don't need the photo on the desktop anymore. After you have exited ACT!, delete the image of Bill from the desktop. The photo will still be in the database.

The Basics | 27

Duplicating Contacts

ACT! isn't just about the companies you do business with, it is about the people who work for those companies. It is very possible you will have more than one Contact for any given company.

Example: You leave a meeting clutching three business cards. All three are important people, and all three work for the same company, so the **Company**, **Address**, **Web site**, and **Phone** information are the same on all the cards. This could mean a lot of repetitive data entry.

ACT! can duplicate data from certain fields in the currently displayed record and place them in a new record. All you have to do is fill out the name of the contact and those items that are different.

Procedure: To enter a duplicate (almost) Contact

1. Display the Contact to duplicate.

   This is the Contact that has the basic information you want to duplicate.

2. **Contacts, Duplicate Contact**…

   or click the **Duplicate** icon on the toolbar or

   or right-click the background of the Contact Detail screen and choose **Duplicate Contact**….

   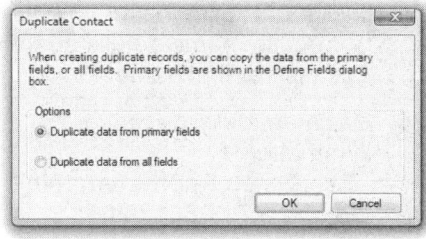

3. Click the **Duplicate data from primary fields**,

   or the **Duplicate data from all fields** option, click **OK**.

   Duplicate data from primary fields duplicates only fields that are likely to be the same. The default primary fields are **Company**, **Address 1**, **Address 2**, **Address 3**, **City**, **State**, **Zip**, **Country**, **Phone**, **Fax**, and **Web Site**. Other fields are left blank.

   Duplicate data from all fields duplicates everything (including fields like Spouse) from the current record… *except* the contact's name.

4. Make necessary entries or changes.

   Change whatever fields need to be changed.

Sage ACT!

Practice: Duping a Contact

What to do	How to do it/Comments
1. Let's enter another employee for the same company. (You should still be on Bill's record.) After you duplicate the record, notice that Company name and address fields were duplicated	Choose **Contacts**, **Duplicate Contact...**, click the Duplicate Contact icon, or right-click the layout background and choose **Duplicate Contact... OK**., ID/Status, Mobile Phone, or Spouse were not duplicated.
2. Enter the following information. Contact: **Sue Ellen Mix**	When you enter a contact with more than two names, ACT! automatically displays the **Contact Name** dialog box to verify that it has correctly parsed the names.
3. Notice in the background that ACT! entered "Sue" in the Salutation field. Also notice that ACT! erroneously thinks that "Ellen" is the middle name. Correct the name details so that **Sue Ellen** is her first name.	Use the drop-down arrow to the right of **First name:** and select Sue Ellen. Change the **Middle name:** to nothing. Click **OK**.

4. Finish entering the rest of the information.
  Title: **Sales Representative**
  Phone: **(713)661-5200**
	Notice that ACT! corrected the Salutation field with the revised first name of the contact.

Assigning Security

All records added to the database are automatically assigned to a Public status, meaning that anyone who has access to the database can view the contact's information. If you share your database with other users and would like to restrict who can see one of your contacts, you can mark the record as Private. You might assign a setting of Private to friends, family, personal physicians, etc.

☞ *Log-on Users must remain Public. You cannot change their Contact Access.*

Procedure: To restrict access to a Contact record

1. Click the **Contact Access** tab of the Contact's record.

2. Click access level...

   Public – All users may view the record.

   Private – Only the current Record Manager can access the record in ACT!.

Records marked as private can only be viewed in ACT! by the current Record Manager.

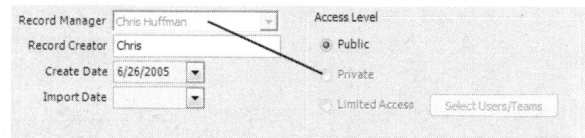

 The current Record Manager is the only user that will be granted access to the current record if it is marked Private.

Limited Access (Premium Only)

ACT! Premium has a third level of security called Limited Access, which limits access to the record by one or more Users or Teams (a collection of pre-defined users). For example, you may have a Western Team that is made up of Sales Reps from the West Coast, along with an Inside Sales Rep, Customer Support personnel, and Regional and Executive-level management.

Once a Team has been defined, then you only have to grant a specific Team access to instantly allow everyone on that Team access to the record. If a Sales Rep is reassigned from the West Coast to the East Coast, simply removing the user from the Western Team and adding them to the Eastern Team instantly updates all records to reflect the change in security.

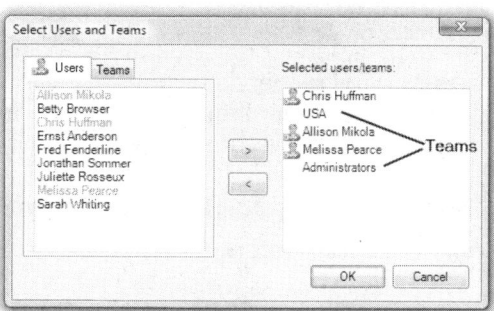

Procedure: To limit access to a Contact record (Premium Only)

1. Click the **Contact Access** tab of the Contact's record.

   The Contact Access area may have been moved to a different tab.

2. Click **Limited Access**.

3. Click the **Select Users/Teams** button.

   The current Record Manager is automatically granted access, as well as all Administrator users in the database.

4. Double-click users in the left pane to grant them access to the record.

   You can also single-click a name from the Users list and click the **Add** button in the middle of the dialog box to add the name to the list of users on the right that have access to the Contact record.

5. Click the **Teams** tab and add the Team that will have access to the record.

    You can right-click a team name to display a list of its members.

6. Click **OK**.

☞ *Teams can only be created and populated by a user with Manager or Administrator-level access. However, any user can assign Team membership (using the Limited Access feature) to records that they create or manage.*

Practice: Assigning Limited Access

What to do	How to do it/Comments
1. Restrict access to the record you just entered to only yourself and another user in the database.	Click on the **Contact Access** tab of the Contact's record. Click **Limited Access**. Double-click a user's name in the left pane to grant them access to the record. Click **OK, OK**.

Assigning Limited Access by Default (Premium Only)

If you are a sales rep that works with only a portion of the database (using the Limited Access feature), then you can assign your Team or only your name by default each time you create a new Contact in the database. Changes to your ACT! preferences will determine how ACT! responds on your PC without affecting anyone else using ACT! in your company. However, rather than go through every Preferences option now, we'll return to this area off and on to make changes relating to the topics at hand.

Procedure: To assign Limited Access by default (Premium Only)

1. **Tools, Preferences…**, click the **Startup** tab.
2. Click the **Record Creation Options…** button.
3. Change "Make new contacts:" to **Limited Access**. — Review the other options as well.
4. Click **Select Users/Teams** button.
5. Double-click Users in the left pane to grant them individual access to the record.
6. Click on the **Teams** tab and add the default Team that will have access to the record.

   You can also single-click a User or Team name from the list and click the **Add** button in the middle of the dialog box to add the name to the **Selected users/teams:** list on the right.

7. Click **OK, OK**.

Deleting Contacts

ACT! takes pains to make sure you won't lose data accidentally. You can delete individual Contacts or an entire lookup, but it requires more than one confirmation step. That's a good thing.

Procedure: To delete a Contact record or lookup

1. Display the record you want to delete, or perform a look up that displays all of the records you wish to delete.

   If you are going to delete a lookup, review the records to make sure you really want to delete all of them.

2. Choose **Contacts**, **Delete Contact** from the menu,

   or press **[Ctrl+Delete]**,

   or right-click on the layout background and choose **Delete Contact**.

   A warning message appears. *Read the warning carefully!*

3. Click **Delete Contact** to delete the current Contact record *only*, or click **Delete Lookup** to delete *the entire lookup*.

    View the Lookup indicator at the lower left of your screen to verify your last lookup type.

   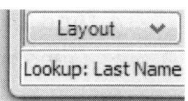

4. A confirmation message appears. *Read this one carefully.* If the described action is really what you want to do, click **Yes**.

   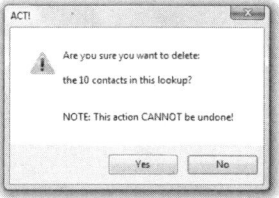

Sage ACT!

5. If you were deleting a lookup, you receive a final information message indicating that no more records match the search criteria.

   Click **OK**.

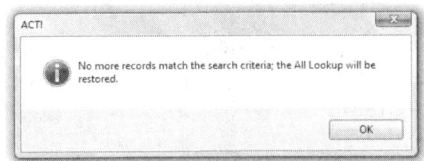

Of course…you just deleted everything you looked up.

Practice: Happy Trails to You

What to do	How to do it/Comments
1. You should still be on **Sue Ellen Mix's** record.	
2. It turns out that Sue Ellen has taken an offer in another part of the country. She no longer works here. Let's delete her.	Choose **Contacts**, **Delete Contact**, and click **Delete Contact**.

Review: The Basics

1. What record do you see every time you open a database in ACT!?
2. Display the **Activities** tab for the current record.
3. Change your Preferences so that Contacts List is the default open view in ACT!. Exit and restart ACT! to verify your changes.
4. Add yourself as a Contact record, including your e-mail address.
5. Duplicate the primary fields in your record and add a co-worker.
6. Never mind…delete your co-worker.

Working with Your Contacts

To get a feel for how ACT! can be put to work for you every day, you will:

- ☑ Work with your Contacts in the List View.

- ☑ Learn to locate Contacts in your database.

- ☑ Create and work with Secondary Contacts.

- ☑ Create Relationships between your Contacts.

- ☑ Research your Contacts over the Internet using the Web Info tab.

Sage ACT!

Locating Contacts

Let's continue by using some ACT! features that you'll use every day. One thing you'll do over and over is lookup people and companies in your database. The better you are at finding names, the more valuable ACT! becomes.

Browsing Records

Most of what we have seen up to now involves the My Record Contact record and the one contact we added to the database. Located at the upper-left side of the toolbar are four buttons that help you to move from record to record using the mouse.

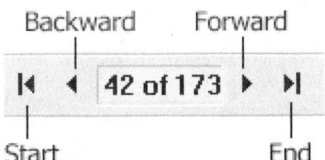

- Click the inside buttons to go forward to the next or back to the previous record; click the outside buttons to go to the start or the end of the list.
- The record counter between the browse buttons indicates the current position in the database. You see a phrase such as 42 of 173, which means you are looking at record number 42 of 173 available records.

To Move:	Keyboard	Mouse
To the previous record	[Ctrl+PageUp]	◀
To the next record	[Ctrl+PageDn]	▶
To the start of the list	[Ctrl+Home]	◀◀
To the end of the list	[Ctrl+End]	▶▶
To the next alpha Company name	[Alt+PageUp]	
To the previous alpha Company name	[Alt+PageDn]	

Practice: Moving Around

What to do	How to do it/Comments	
1. What is the number of the current record? How many records are available to view?	The Record counter displays the information. ◀◀ ◀ 41 of 198 ▶ ▶▶	
2. View the next four or five records.	Press **[Ctrl+PageDn]** or click Forward button.	▶
3. Display the first record.	Press **[Ctrl+Home]** or click the Start button.	◀◀
4. View the last record.	Press **[Ctrl+End]** or click the End button.	▶▶
5. View the previous four or five records.	Press **[Ctrl+PageUp]** or click Backward button several times.	◀

Working with Your Contacts | 35

Detail View and List View

When you view Contacts in the **Detail View** (your current view), you can review the information for *one Contact at a time*. There are times when you would like to see several Contacts in a spreadsheet type of list view.

The **List View** displays the current records in list form. Field names appear at the top of the columns, and the list is usually sorted by company name. It is very easy to move back and forth between the views.

Procedure: To toggle between Detail View and List View

1. Click the **List View** button on the toolbar,  or press **[F8]** to display Contacts: List View.

   The List View for Contacts displays the current lookup in a list view. The current record is highlighted.

2. Click the **Detail View** button on the toolbar to return to viewing details about the last record you were viewing.

   You can also press **[F11]** to display the Contacts: Detail View.

3. Double-click a Contact in the List View to display the selected record in Detail View.

- Watch the scroll bar at the right side of the window. If the scroll box is not at the top of the bar, you are not viewing the first item in the list.
- You can click on or drag the scroll bar to browse the list. You can also use the **[UpArrow]**, **[DownArrow]**, **[PageUp]**, or **[PageDn]** keys on your keyboard if you wish.
- In any of the ACT! list views, you can use a **wheel mouse** to scroll up and down the list.

Sage ACT!

 By default, ACT! displays two columns at the beginning of the List View. The first column (the icon with a key at the bottom) identifies any Contact in the database that also has logon rights. The second (the icon that looks like a lock) identifies Contacts that you have marked as Private. Pointing to one of the icons displays its name.

Practice: Display the List View for Contacts

What to do	How to do it/Comments
1. Display the **List View**.	Press **[F8]** or click the **List View** button.
2. Observe the list.	The record you were viewing when you displayed the list is highlighted. This may not be the top record in the list.
3. Try all the different ways to move up and down in the list.	• Click or drag the scroll bar. • Use the mouse scroll wheel. • Use the **[Up Arrow]**, **[Down Arrow]**, **[PageUp]**, and **[PageDn]** keys on your keyboard. • Use the Forward, Back, Start and End buttons.
4. Double-click one of the Contacts to display it in **Detail View**.	You can see more details of the record in this view, including Notes, History, Opportunities, and scheduled Activities.
5. Return to the **List View**.	

Sorting the List View

When the List View displays, it is a bit easier to see how the database is sorted. Normally it is sorted by the Company field. When you are browsing the list, looking for someone by name, it would be better if you could sort the list by the Contact name column, don't you think?

Procedure: To sort using the List View

1. Observe the column headings in the list. One heading contains a triangle. The triangle points either up or down. 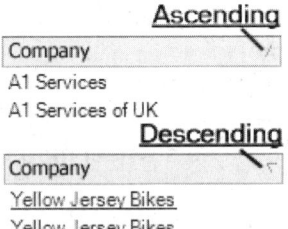 This triangle is the sort indicator. When it appears in a column heading, the list is sorted by that column. When it points up, the sort is ascending (0-9, A-Z). When it points down, the sort is descending (Z-A, 9-0).

Working with Your Contacts | 37

2. Click once on any column heading you want to sort by. 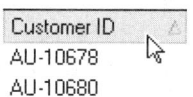 The list sorts in ascending order by that column.

3. Click again on the same column to sort in descending order.

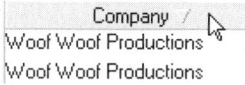

 *When you sort the **Contact** column, it is assumed that you wish to sort by **Last Name**.*

 You cannot view Notes, History, Activities, Opportunities, Relationships, or Secondary Contacts while displaying the List View. Once you have found the desired record, you can double-click the record to display the regular Detail View for that Contact.

Practice: Sorting the List

What to do	How to do it/Comments
1. Sort the List View by the **Contact** column.	You should be viewing your Contacts in List View. Click the **Contact** column heading once to sort the list in ascending order.
2. Sort the list by **City** in descending order.	You may have to scroll right to display the **City** column. Click the **City** column heading twice to sort in descending order.
3. Sort by **Contact** again.	Click the **Contact** column heading.
4. Double-click any row to view that record in Detail View.	Be careful not to click a Company hyperlink (which takes you to the Companies: Detail View, which we will talk about later).
5. Return to the List View.	Press **[F8]** or click the List View button on the Toolbar.
6. Leave the list displayed.	

Related Task Pane – Another Sort Option

Notice as you switch views between Detail View and List View, that the Related Tasks pane, at the left in the Navbar, displays different options for you to select from. In each of the views that we learn about, you will find a list of tasks (or commands) relevant to the current view. Most of these tasks we have yet to talk about, but we'll point them out as we go along to help you find the quickest way to get things done in ACT!. To perform one of these tasks… just click on it.

Sage ACT!

Practice: Sorting on More Than One Field

What to do	How to do it/Comments
1. Notice the different options offered in the Related Tasks pane for Detail View and List View.	Click the Detail View and List View buttons to view the differences.
2. Note that when you sort on the City field by clicking the column header, that the Company field is not in any particular order.	In List View, click on the City column header to sort the list. Look at New York, for example, to see that Companies are not in alpha order.
3. While in List View, use the **Sort List** option in the Related Tasks pane and sort by City, then by Company, then by Contact.	Click "Sort List" task, fill in, and click **OK**.

Adding and Removing Columns

The List View displays a default selection of fields that will probably suit most users. However, you may find you would like to see a piece of information that is not currently displayed in the list. You can add columns to the List View (and remove them) quite easily.

Procedure: To add, remove, or move a column in the List View

1. **Right-click** anywhere inside the List View and choose **Customize Columns...**,

   or click the **Customize Columns** icon.

   You could also click the Options button or select **Change Columns** in the Related Tasks pane.

2. All Contact fields in the database appear in alphabetical order at the left. Fields currently displayed as columns are shown at the right.

   Select a field and use the middle arrow buttons to add or remove fields for column display.

   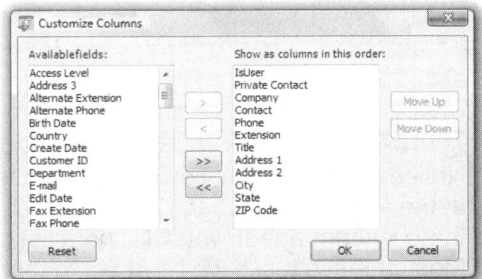

   You can also double-click a field in either pane to add or remove a field from display.

Working with Your Contacts | 39

3. Select a field in the right pane and click the **Move Up** or **Move Down** buttons to organize your display.

4. Click **OK**.

 Columns are only removed from the List View. They are not removed from the database. You can always add them back to the view.

Practice: Adding the E-mail Field

What to do	How to do it/Comments
1. Add the field named **E-mail** to your List View. Display it to the right of the Phone Extension field.	Right-click anywhere in the List View and choose **Customize Columns...**, and then double-click **E-mail** in the left pane. Now, select E-mail in the right pane and use the **Move Up** button to display it next to the Extension field. Click **OK**.
2. Sort the list on the **E-mail** column.	Click the E-mail column header (blanks are always displayed first).
3. Sort the list by the Contact name.	Notice that the list displays alphabetically by Last Name.
4. Double-click any name to return to Detail View.	

Navbar Lookup Pane

Once you have some names in your database, you'll need to have a quick way to look them up. At the top of the Navbar at the left, is a quick Lookup pane that gives you a way to search your database (particularly handy if you are in List View). By default, it searches for a Contact name in most views (except for Groups, Companies and Opportunities views). It is very handy for looking up contacts while in other views in your database.

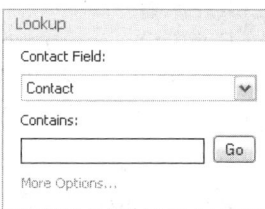

Note that the lookup uses "Contains". That means when you are searching for a Contact name, you can enter any part of the name (first, middle, last or partial) and ACT will search the specified field for matches. It works the same way for other fields selected from the drop-down.

 *If you don't see the Lookup Pane at the left in the Navbar, click the Startup tab, click the "Display Lookups in navigation bar" option. Click **OK**.*

Procedure: To look up a record using the Lookup pane

1. In the Lookup pane at the top of the Navbar, use the drop-down to select a field to search on.

    The last field you selected (during your current ACT! session) will be displayed.

   If you are displaying a Contacts, Calendar, Task List, Reports, or Dashboard view, drop-down lists will display fields you can search on that are specific to Contacts. Groups, Companies, or Opportunities view drop-down lists will display fields you can search on that are associated with those entities.

2. Enter a value to search for under the word "Contacts:"

   Not case-sensitive. No drop-down options will be offered. This option will find records that contain the entered value.

3. Click **Go**.

 *Click **More Options...** to display the Lookup dialog with your selections so far (handy if you want to change from "Contains" to another operator).*

Practice: Using the Navbar Lookup Pane

What to do	How to do it/Comments
1. Use the Navbar pane to find any contact with Van in their name.	Verify that "Contact" is the selected field, type "van" in the text box, and click Go. Note ACT! also found Ivan.
2. Search for a Company that contains the word "Restaurant".	Use the drop-down to select the Company field. Type "restaurant" in the text field and click Go.

Lookup

But wait... there are even more ways you can look up a record in your database. A few common lookup fields are available with the Lookup menu, but when you are in Detail View you can right-click inside any field to generate a quick look up on the selected field.

Procedure: To look up a record

1. While in Detail View, right-click any field and select **Lookup <current field>** from the shortcut menu.

   You can also choose **Lookup** from the menu and click the appropriate item, but the menu options are more limited. However the menu option is one way you can Lookup "First Name" or "Last Name".

Working with Your Contacts | 41

Note: The **Lookup** dialog box confirms the field you chose (**Contact** in this case). You can also use the drop-down arrow to change the field to search on.

2. Change the operator (the middle field), if desired.

    If you point to the "operator" field, the tool tip displays "Select how to find information."

   If you are searching in a field that has a multi-select drop-down list, the operator will be "Contains".

   For all other character fields, the operator will usually be "Starts With".

   Numeric and date fields will start with the operator of "Equal to".

    See a list of operators starting on the next page.

3. Type part or all of the name or number you wish to look up.

    *If available, you can select an option from the associated drop-down list (**City** is an example of this).*

   The more you type, the more specific the lookup.

4. Click OK.
   - If only one record matches your criteria, it appears in **Detail View**.
   - If more than one record matches your criteria, the results are displayed in **List View**.

   ACT! scans all available records and displays only those records that fit the lookup. The record counter reflects the resulting number of records and indicates which of those Contact records you are currently viewing. You may use normal navigation keys or the mouse to browse these Contact records.

   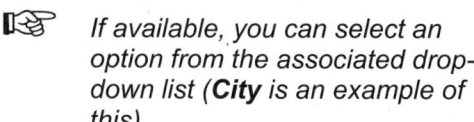

   Seven contacts matched the lookup example

   If necessary, double-click the Contact you want to display in Detail View.

 *If no contacts match your search criteria, then ACT! offers you the option of... **Lookup again** or **Create new contact**.*

The most common operators you might use in a lookup are listed below *(some options are only available for specific field types). A more complete list can be found in the Advanced Lookups chapter on page 250.*

Starts With – The value you type must be at the very beginning of the field.

Contains – The value you specify can appear anywhere in the field.

Contains Data – The field is not empty.

Does Not Contain Data – The field is empty.

Equal To (=) – The value you type must match the field exactly.

Greater Than or Equal To – The number or text in the field must be greater or the same as what you type. For a date field, use On or After.

On or After – The date in the field is the same as or later than the date you enter.

Less Than or Equal to – The number or text in the field must be less than or the same as what you type.

On or Before – The date in the field is the same as or earlier than the date you enter.

Lookup Tips

- You can right-click any field to perform a look up on that field.
- Lookups are not case-sensitive - all you have to do is spell it right!
- If the field has a **simple drop-down** list or **no drop-down** list, then ACT! only returns records where the data in the field you are searching on "**Starts with**" the search criteria you input (e.g., searching for a city "Cleveland" finds "Cleveland" and "Cleveland Heights," but not "East Cleveland.")
- If the field **allows multiple selections** from the drop-down (i.e., drop-down lists that display a ☐ to the left of the options, as in the ID/Status field), then ACT! returns records where the field you are searching in "**Contains**" the criteria you input anywhere in that field (e.g., "Lead" finds "Hot Lead", "Qualified Lead", "Lead", as well as "Leader" or "Pleading Innocent" – not a likely ID/Status – but you get the point).

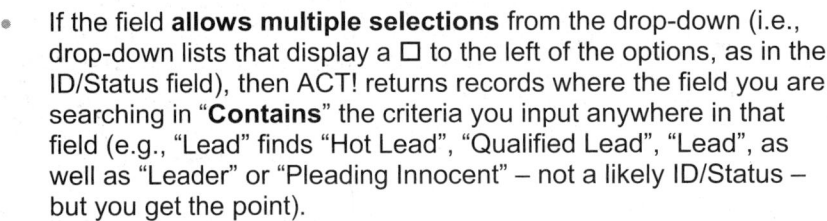

- The more you type, the more specific the lookup is. The less you type, the less specific it is.

    Example: You are looking up a Last Name. Type "**h**" to look up all Contacts that begin with the letter **H**. Type **Hal** to locate all Contacts with last names that begin with **Hal**. Type **Hall** to look up only the last name of **Hall**. (There could be a Hallmark and Hallman and…)

Working with Your Contacts | 43

Example: Right-click the **Phone** field and type the area code only. The result is all those Contacts whose phone number starts with that area code.

- The Lookup Indicator in the lower left corner of the screen lets you know which filters are in place.
- To return to viewing all Contact records, choose **Lookup**, **All Contacts**. Your results will display in Contacts: List View. However, every time you perform a lookup, ACT! scans all records available to you, not just those currently displayed (unless you change the options). It is **not** necessary to look up all Contacts before performing a new Lookup.
- ACT! remembers the last five search strings that you used for looking in each field. If the field contains a drop-down list, the pre-defined values display below the most recently used list.
- You can look up the full Contact name (really handy for common names like Susan Clark – lots of last names "Clark" and lots of first names "Susan"). However, be aware that you must enter the name exactly as it displays in the Contact field...down to any periods or commas. For example, John D Rockefeller...not John D. Rockefeller or John Rockefeller. However, John D Rock will display records for both Jr. and Sr.
- If you typed too many characters in the Search for area, the most recently used feature can sometime make it difficult to enter the correct text. Use the spacebar to "white out" any incorrect characters. The spaces will be ignored in the lookup.
- Greater than and Less than options are available for numeric or date fields.

Practice: Simple Lookups

What to do	How to do it/Comments
1. Find the company that starts with the word **Yale**.	Right-click the Company field, select **Lookup Company**, type **yale**, **OK**.
2. How many records did ACT! find to match your entry?	Should have only found one record.
3. Try to move to another record.	Click the Previous button or press **[PageUp]**. It doesn't do much good, does it? It's because you are currently displaying 1 of 1 records.
4. Display all records in the database.	Choose **Lookup**, **All Contacts** from the menu or click **View All Contacts** in the Related Tasks pane. Notice that the list displays in Contacts: List View.
5. What record displays? What number is it?	It's still Mr. Yale! His record is still displayed, but now it shows the total number of records in the database.

What to do	How to do it/Comments
6. Double-click his name to display it in Contact Detail view. Now, try to move to another record.	You can move to other records because the lookup is **All Contacts**.
7. How many Contacts have an **ID/Status** of "Influencer"? ☞ *ID/Status allows multiple selections, so the lookup finds contacts that **Contain** "Influencer" anywhere in the field.*	Right-click the ID/Status field and select **Lookup ID/Status**, type **influencer** and click **OK**. More than one Contact will match your criteria, so ACT! will display the results in List View.
8. Return to Detail View to browse the records. Notice that "Influencer" is not always the first word in the field. ☞ *Notice Detail View displays the same number of contacts.*	Double-click the first Contact to go to Detail View. Use the Browse buttons at the top of the page to review the other ID/Status listings on other contacts.
9. How many Contacts in the database **Contain** the word "President" in the Title field? We want to include President, Vice-President, Founder, and President, etc.	Right-click the Title field and select **Lookup Title**, type "president", change the operator from "Starts With" to "Contains", and click **OK**. In List View, click on the Title header to sort the list by Title.
10. How many Contacts in our database have an e-mail address?	In Detail View, right-click the E-mail field and select **Lookup E-mail**. Change the operator from **Starts With** to **Contains Data** and click **OK**.
11. How many of our contacts made at least $3,000 in purchases from last year?	In Detail View, right-click the **Last Years Purchases** field and select **Lookup Last Yrs Purchases**. Change the operator from "Equal To (=)" to "Greater Than or Equal To". Enter 3000 for the information to find and click **OK**.
12. Look up Ernst Anderson's record by searching for any last name that **Starts With** "and." How many records does ACT! find?	We have to use the menu option here since there is no Last Name field to right-click. Choose **Lookup**, **Last Name...**, type **and**, and click **OK**. Ernie is not the only Anderson in the database. Double-click his name to display it in Detail View.

Working with Your Contacts | 45

Wait, We Didn't Tell ACT! the Last Name

We just finished searching for a Contact by his last name. Do you see a First Name or Last Name field in ACT!? How does ACT! do that?! We're glad you asked. ACT! looks at the first word you entered in the Contact field and designates it as the First Name. It looks at the last word you entered and assigns it to the Last Name. That works great for Tom Mix, but what about Dr. John Henry Holliday Jr.? We certainly don't want Dr. to be labeled as the first name and Jr. as the last name. That's OK. ACT! knows how to handle more complicated names as well. Let's go back to the Preferences dialog box.

Procedure: To edit name preferences

1. **Tools, Preferences…**, on the **Admin** tab, click the **Name Preferences** button. Click the arrows at the top right to display the Admin tab.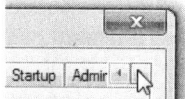

2. **First name prefixes** are a list of words that ACT! ignores if they are the first word typed (e.g., Doctor, Dr., Mrs., Ms., Mr., etc.). So if you type Mrs. Jane Doe, ACT! ignores the first word "Mrs." and uses the second word that you type as the first name…pretty smart!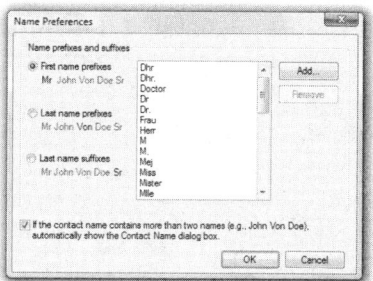

3. **Last name prefixes** are words that, if found immediately to the left of the last name, should be included *with* the last name (e.g., Jolly Old St. Nicholas…his last name would be St. Nicholas, not just Nicholas).

4. **Last name suffixes** are a list of words that ACT! ignores if they are the last word typed in the Contact field (Jr., Sr. PhD, CPA, etc.). If you work with Contacts that have a common certification after their name, you should verify that their certification is listed here so that ACT! will ignore the title and use the next-to-last word for the Last Name.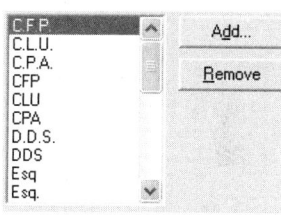

5. Click **OK, OK**.

Sage ACT!

Fixing a Problem Contact Name

If you have worked with a database for a while, you may have some names where ACT! could not correctly identify the first and last names. As you find these problematic names, they are easy to fix.

Procedure: To fix a problem name

1. Click the button to the right of the Contact name or press **[F2]**.
2. Use the drop-down arrows to correct the name.
3. You may have to correct the **Middle name** as well.
4. If necessary, click the **Automatically show this dialog if the contact name contains more than two names** to avoid this problem in the future.
5. Click **OK**.

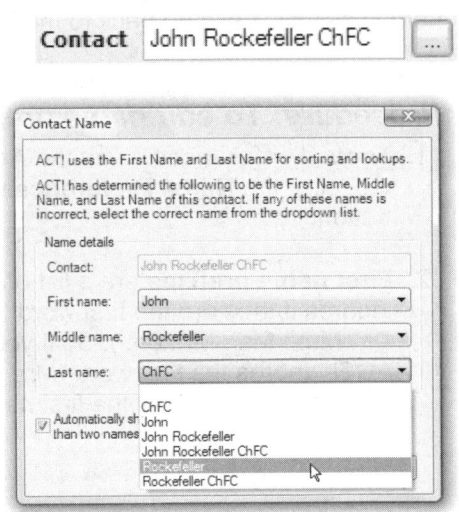

Practice: Fixing Names

What to do	How to do it/Comments
1. Find Van Johnson by looking up his *first* name.	**Lookup**, **First Name**, Van, **OK**. Sorry, can't find him. Select **Cancel**, **Cancel**.
2. Look him up using the **Contact Name** feature and fix his "first" name.	Right-click the **Contact** field and select **Lookup Contact**, van johnson, **OK**. There he is! Click the button beside his name and select Van from the drop-down list for his first name. Correct his last name as well.
	Since "Van" is a Last name prefix, ACT! thought his **last name** was Van Johnson (as in Rip Van Winkle).

OK, we digress…back to more Lookups.

Lookup Variations

The simple lookups, like those we have just performed, will serve most of your lookup needs. However, there will be times when you need to look up more than one city, or more than one last name. There are also times when a simple lookup displays too many matching Contacts and you want to "whittle it down" to a more manageable size. You can refine your lookups in several ways.

You can:

- Add to the current lookup.
- Narrow the current lookup.
- Use the Universal Search feature.

Adding to Lookups

It's pretty easy to look up all Contacts from a given city. But what if you want to see all Contacts from two cities, or three? Easy! All you need to know is how to add to an existing lookup.

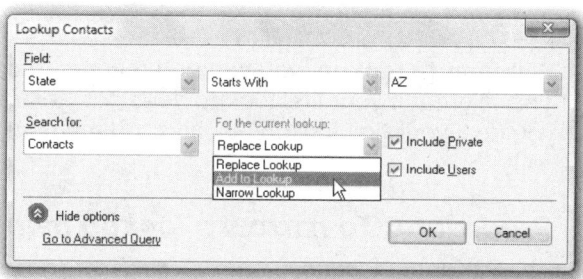

Procedure: To add to a lookup

1. Perform the first lookup.

   You can't add to something you don't have yet.

2. To add to the first lookup, right-click in the desired field and choose **Lookup** once again.

   You do not have to choose the same field used in the previous lookup.

3. Complete your next lookup options, but don't click **OK** yet.

4. Click the drop-down list **For the current lookup** and choose the **Add to Lookup** option.

   ☞ *If necessary, click **Show more options** to expand the Lookup dialog. If **Hide options** is displayed, then you are seeing everything.*

5. Click **OK**.

   All records that fit your new criteria are added to your previous lookup.

6. Repeat steps 2 through 5 as desired.

   You can add multiple lookups together.

☞ *You may exclude Private records by clearing that option. You may also exclude Users (people who have been given logon rights to the database).*

Sage ACT!

Practice: Lookup, Then Lookup More

What to do	How to do it/Comments
1. So you have to make a trip to Phoenix. Look up all Contacts from the city of **Phoenix**.	Choose **Lookup, City...**, type **pho**, and click **OK**.
2. Scottsdale is only a few miles away. Let's see how many Contacts are in Scottsdale.	Choose **Lookup, City...**, type **scotts**, select **Add to Lookup**, and click **OK**.
3. Can you add **Tempe** to the current lookup?	You're on your own on this one. It should add four more records to your list.

Narrowing Lookups

With **Add to lookup**, you can add records to create a complex lookup one step at a time. This is great if your first lookup does not yield all of the Contacts, you wanted. But what do you do if your first lookup displays too many records? Simple! Narrow the lookup.

Procedure: To narrow a lookup using another field

1. Perform a lookup.
   This first lookup should display more records than you can easily use.

2. Use the Lookup menu or right-click inside the field that you want to use to narrow the list and select **Lookup <fieldname>**.
   Determine a *different* field to use to narrow the lookup and right-click the field or click the **Lookup** menu commands to display the **Lookup** dialog box for that field.

3. Type desired lookup criteria.

4. Click the drop-down list **For the current lookup** and choose the **Narrow Lookup** option.
   Don't forget to choose **Narrow Lookup** or this lookup will replace the previous lookup instead of narrowing it.

5. Click **OK**.
   The current lookup is narrowed to display only those records that fit the new criteria *and* the original criteria.

6. Repeat steps 2 through 5 as desired.
   You can continue to narrow the lookup until only the records you want are displayed.

Working with Your Contacts | 49

Practice: Lookup, Then Lookup Less

What to do	How to do it/Comments
1. Start with the lookup we created from the previous exercise or just Look up all Contacts in the state of AZ.	If necessary, choose **Lookup**, **State...**, type **AZ** and click **OK**.
2. Since we have limited time in Arizona, let's display a list of our "Prospects" (ID/Status) in that area. Narrow the lookup to only those records?	Choose **Lookup**, **ID/Status...**, type **pr**, select **Narrow Lookup**, and click **OK**.
3. Can you add records with an ID/Status of Customer to the current lookup?	Yes, but it would add all Customers from the entire database to your already narrowed lookup. Probably not what you want. Always use the **Add** commands first, and then use the **Narrow** option.

Previous Lookups

What if you are compiling a list using **Add to Lookup** and **Narrow Lookup** when the phone rings and you have to look up some information in ACT!. Bummer! You just lost the list that you were working on.

Just kidding! You can quickly return to any of the past nine lookups (since you logged into your database). Any time you perform a Lookup or click Go To, the query is remembered and added to the top of the previous lookup list.

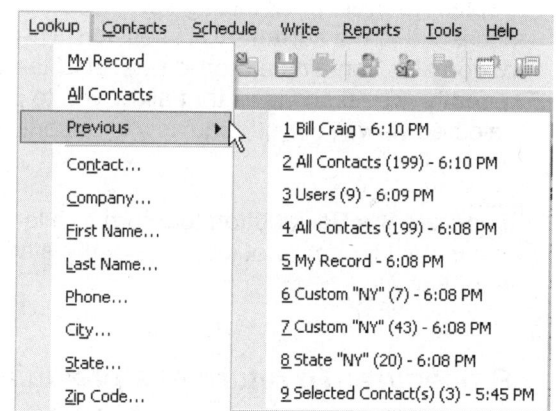

The Previous list displays chronologically with the most recent listed first. Each lookup is preceded by a number for keyboard access. A brief description of the lookup displays to the right of the number and may include the lookup type and/or value, the number of contacts (#) returned by the lookup, and a date/time stamp. (Well it usually only displays a time stamp, but if you are working late into the night or you never exit ACT!, you will start to see the dates as well.)

Procedure: To return to a previous lookup

1. Click **Lookup, Previous,** select a lookup from the list.

   The lookup runs immediately without displaying any lookup dialog.

☞ *Selecting a previous lookup item will copy that lookup to the top of the list, update the count if it needs to, and update the date/time stamp.*

Practice: Lookup Previous	
What to do	**How to do it/Comments**
1. If you've been performing the lookups we've been doing in our practice sessions, you should have several that you can return to.	Click **Lookup, Previous**. Notice how the previous lookups have been named.
2. Select a previous lookup from the list.	Select a previous lookup from the list.

Back (and Forward) Buttons

Lookup Previous is not the only way to go back in time. You can also use the Back button on the Global Toolbar to cycle back through previous views accessed in the current ACT! session. The Back button also contains a drop-down list of the 9 most recently accessed views that allow you to jump to the selected view. Your current view is underlined and bold in the list.

If you use the Back button to return to a lookup, it will re-run the lookup... not just display the static data you were viewing.

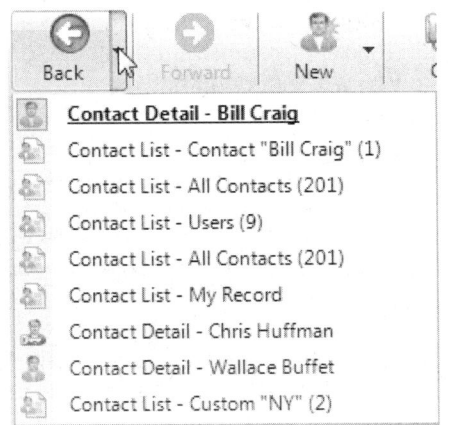

Procedure: To return to a previous View

1. Click the Back button to return to the previous view, or...

   Click the drop-down button at the right of the Back button and select the desired view.

   Notice that the drop-down options look similar to the Lookup, Previous menu options... except that may be mixed with views like the Calendar view or Groups view... that had nothing to do with a previous lookup.

☞ *Once you have used the Back button (or the drop-down option to skip to a previous view), then the **Forward** button is enabled and you can use it to come back to the future.*

Working with Your Contacts | 51

Practice: Return to a previous View

What to do	How to do it/Comments
1. Click on the **Groups** button at the left in the Navbar.	
2. Now click on the **Calendar** button and then the **Task List** button	We are just moving around.
3. Click the **Back** button to return to the previous view.	
4. Click the **Back** button drop-down to jump to a selected view.	
5. Use the **Forward** button to move forward.	Enough moving… let's move on… so to speak.

Universal Search

Looking in specific fields is great… if you remember where you added an item to your ACT! database. The **Universal Search** feature works similar to the way you might search for something on the web. You enter the word (or words) you want to search for, and ACT! can help you quickly locate that key document or piece of info that you added to your database over a month ago. You can also filter your search criteria by all dates, last 24 hours, last week, and last month.

Example: When you spoke with someone last year about the "Greenway" project, who was it? Where did you input the information? Was it in a field or a note or an appointment?

 These lookups may take more time, since all fields, as well as all notes, histories, activities, opportunities, and relationships are searched (instead of specific fields as with other lookups).

Procedure: To perform a universal search

1. Enter your search term(s) in the Search box at the right of the Global toolbar and click **Go**,

   or to start with the Search View, click the **Search** button in the Navbar at the left,

   or click **Lookup, Search...** or **View, Search**.

Sage ACT!

2. In the Search view, under **Show Only:**, you can narrow your search to specific entities by clicking only the ones you want to search in. (**Show Only:**).

   Be as specific or as general as you need. Lookups are not case-sensitive (all you have to do is spell it right). The default is to search all ACT! entities.

3. Narrow the time frame under **Last Edited:** by selecting the appropriate option.

   The default is all dates.

4. Click **Go**.

   ACT! searches the specified area(s) of the database for your word or phrase and displays a list of the items containing those criteria in the **Search view**.

5. Click the item you want to view.. If it is not the correct item, click the **Back** button on the Global toolbar.

☞ *Your search results may be limited to the first 50 entities. You can narrow the search using the **Show Only** options to help you locate just the information that you are looking for.*

Practice: *Performing a Search*

What to do	How to do it/Comments
1. We've met someone who played tennis at Yale. Unfortunately, can't remember where we entered the data. So start by doing a Search to find the word "yale."	In the Search box at the top right, type in **yale**, and click **Go**.
2. Click a few of the items to see the results. Use the **Back** button to return to the **Search** view.	The word "yale" was found in several items: a Contact records, an activity detail, some Opportunity records, and, some notes.

Using Special Characters in Search

You can use special characters and operators with your search term to help you expand or narrow your search.

Operators

* Enter an asterisk in front of, or at the end of, your term(s) to search for the listed word with any number of characters before or after the word. For example, *yale* would locate all items containing at least the letters "yale", such as Bayale.

? Use the question mark to substitute any character in the listed word at the inserted location. For example "C?O" would find "CEO" and "COO" and "CFO".

Working with Your Contacts | 53

or   Use the word "or" to connect words where you want to search for either term. For example, "green or plastics" would find any item that contained either of the listed words.

and   Use the word "and" between your terms to include both words in the search. For example "yale and tennis" would find any item that contained both words..

w/[x]   Use this operator to narrow the search where the second term appears within X words of first term. For example, "green w/10 plastics" would display all items containing the term "plastics" within 10 words of the word "green".

w/[x] xfirstword   This operator limits the word to within the first few words in the item. For example, "green w/5 xfirstword" would find all items that have the term "green" within the first five words.

and not   This operator finds only the first word and excludes any item that includes the second word. For example, "green and not plastic" would display all items referencing the word "green", but did not contain the word "plastic".

not w/[x]   Use this operator to narrow the search where the second term, if found, would eliminate the item from the search results. The second term must not appear within X words of first word. For example, "plastic not w/2 green" would eliminate any item where the words plastics and green were separated by two words or less.

w/[x] xlast word   This operator limits the word to within the last few words in the item. For example, "green w/5 xlastword" would find all items that have the term "green" within the last five words.

Practice: Using Special Characters in Search

What to do	How to do it/Comments
1. Try searching for all instances where both "yale" and "tennis" are used.	In the Search term area, enter: yale and tennis and click **Go**.
2. Click the hyperlink for the note (or double-click the item).	The reference was in a note on Tommy Morgan's record. There is currently no easy way to go to Tommy's record. You'll have to look him up if you want to get his phone number.
3. Are there any additional items that *include* the term yale?	In the Search term area, enter: *yale* and click **Go**. Yes, Bruce Baker has an Address on Bayale Dr.
4. Find all CFO's and CEO's in the database.	In the Search term area, enter C?O and click **Go**. Notice that in addition to contact names, it also includes some notes, history, and attachments where the reference was to Chris Huffman as the CEO of CH TechOne.

Sage ACT!

What to do	How to do it/Comments
5. Find all CFO's and CEO's in the database that do not include the name Chris	In the Search term area, enter "C?O and not Chris" and click **Go**.
6. Search Attachments only for the term: ROI	In the Search term area, enter: ROI In the **Show For** column, click Attachments. Click **Go**. Note that you cannot see the name of the contacts where these two Attachments are found. ;-(

 *The Universal Search feature replaced the **Lookup, Advanced, Search on Keywords**. Universal Search will search more items (Secondary Contacts, Attachments and Products for example) and has the ability to narrow the search by a given time frame. However, Keyword searches will create a list that allows you to do a Lookup of all records found. So it may be a good alternative for you if a Lookup is required.*

Lookup, Any fields

ACT! can also search through all available phone, address, or e-mail fields. This is a handy feature, for example, if you have identified some new Address fields such as Physical Address or a new Phone field such as Main Phone.

Procedure: To look up a Contact's address, phone, or e-mail fields

1. **Lookup, Other Fields….**

2. Click on the **Look in this field** drop-down arrow to scroll to and select one of the "Any <field>" choices.

3. Fill in the Search criteria.

4. Click **OK**.

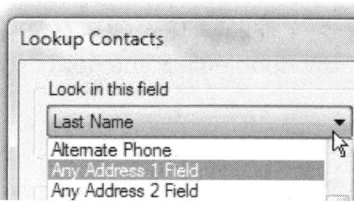

Displays the Contacts that match your search criteria.

Working with Your Contacts | 55

Practice: Who Was That Missed Call From?	
What to do	**How to do it/Comments**
1. You can see a missed call on your phone from: 832-661-5200 Looks familiar…who does it belong to?	**Lookup**, **Other Fields…** Click on the **Look in this field** drop-down arrow to select **Any Phone Field**. Search for 832-661-5200 and click **OK**. Oh yeah, your friend at Captains of Industry.

Lookup Annual Events

Missing a contract renewal (or a birthday for that matter) is serious stuff. You may have an activity scheduled to take care of this, but sometimes you just need to get a list of all contracts that come up for renewal next month or next quarter.

If a date field in your database is defined as an Annual Event field, ACT! searches those dates based on the month and day only (ignoring the designated year). After creating a lookup on the Annual Event type of field, you could then use the ACT! Mail Merge feature to generate birthday announcements, contract renewal letters, etc.

   *To convert a regular Date field in your database to an Annual Event field type, click in the field and select **Tools**, **Define Fields…**. Change the field type to **Annual Event**. Click **OK**.*

New databases in ACT! contain one pre-defined Annual Event field (Birth Date); however, you can add as many Annual Event fields as you like.

Procedure: To look up annual events

1. **Lookup, Annual Events…**

   or press **[Ctrl+Shift+A]**.

2. Select an event using the drop-down arrow in the **Search for:** list.

3. Select a time frame.

   *For **Date Range:**, the year makes no difference (as long as you use the same year for both fields). Only the month and day are considered.*

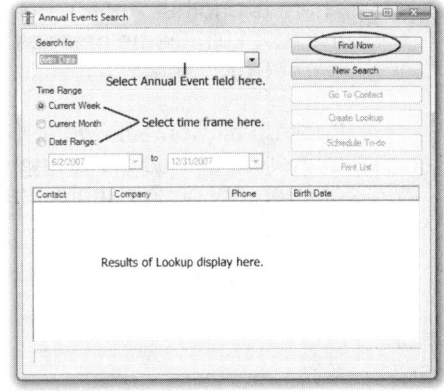

Sage ACT!

4. Click **Find Now**.

   New Search clears the list so that you can start another search.

   Go To Contact displays the record of the selected Contact and minimizes the **Annual Events Search** dialog box for later use.

   Create Lookup creates a lookup of the Contacts that matched your search criteria (great for mail merges or printing address labels!).

   Schedule To-do starts the scheduling of a to-do for the selected Contact only.

   Print List prints the results of the lookup with the same four columns.

6. Click **Close**.

Practice: Generating a Birthday Call List

What to do	How to do it/Comments
1. Look up all birthdays for the current month.	**Lookup, Annual Events…**, click **Current Month**, and click **Find Now**.
2. Look up the birthdays for July.	**Lookup, Annual Events…**, click **Date Range**, and enter an ending date of 7/31 and starting date of 7/1. Click **Find Now**.
3. Look up the Contacts with the July birthdays.	Click **Create Lookup**. Notice that the **Annual Events Search** dialog box is minimized at the lower-left of your screen.
4. Restore the Annual Events dialog box and look up Bill Willis' record.	Click the Restore button and then double-click Bill Willis or select his name and click **Go To Contact**.
5. There is another Annual Event field in the ACT2012Demo database named "**First Purchase**." Look up all Contacts we might send a thank you to anytime during the month of February on the anniversary of their first purchase.	While still in the "Annual Events Search" dialog box, change the **Search for** criteria from Birth Date to First Purchase (uncheck Birth Date and check First Purchase). Select **Date Range** and 2/28 in the ending date and then enter 2/1 in the start date. Click **Find Now.** Click **Create Lookup**.
6. Close the Annual Events dialog box.	Click the **Close** button.

Working In List View Edit Mode

List View may end up being your favorite view to work in. There are several controls you should know about to be sure you are taking advantage of this valuable feature.

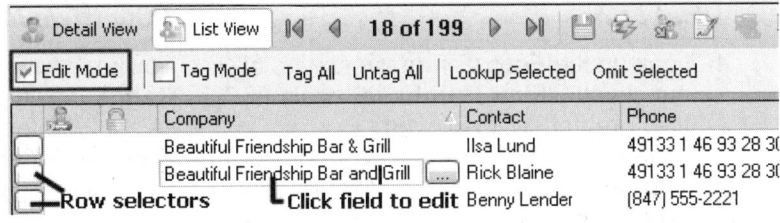

There are specialized controls at the top of the List View. When you put a check in the **Edit Mode** option, you can easily enter and edit records while still in List View.

While **Edit Mode** is enabled on your PC, you can modify the contents of any of the fields in the record by just clicking in the field you wish to change and entering the updates. Edit Mode is a "sticky" option and will remain enabled as you move from view to view (or even close and reopen the database) until you clear the option.

 You can also use [Ctrl+E] to toggle Edit Mode off and on. You can use [Tab], [Shift+Tab], [Enter], and [Shift+Enter] to move around in the view. [F2] will open any drop-down list associated with a field. [Esc] highlights the entire row as if the user clicked on the Row Selector to the left of the record. When the entire row is selected, you can use the [UpArrow] and [DownArrow] keys to move from record to record.

Tag Mode

Tag Mode allows you to easily select individual records, so that you can perform an action on the selected record(s). For example, if you tag 10 Contacts and click **Lookup Selected**, you could write them all a letter, or export their names to Excel, or press **[Ctrl+Delete]** to delete all 10 records.

Procedure: To tag records in the List View

1. Click the checkbox to **Enable Tag Mode**.
2. Click on the record anywhere to tag or untag it. You can also use the arrow keys to move to different records, pressing the **[Spacebar]** to tag or untag.

The entire row appears selected (displayed in a dark color with white text) when it is tagged.

Sage ACT!

Practice: Editing and Tagging Stuff

What to do	How to do it/Comments
1. Look up the February anniversaries of our clients' "**First Purchase**" again (if they are not still displayed). You can then close the Annual Events dialog box.	**Lookup**, **Annual Events…**, click **Date Range**, select 2/1 for the starting date, and select 2/28 for the ending date. Click **Find Now**. Click **Create Lookup**. Close the Annual Events dialog box.
2. Liz just got a promotion to Vice President. While still in List View, make the change.	Put a check in the "Edit Mode" checkbox. Click on Liz's current title of Manager. Use the drop-down to select Vice President (or type it in manually if you like).
3. Add an Extension number for some phones if you like.	Click in the Extension field and add the number.
4. Enable **Tag Mode**.	Remove the check from **Edit Mode** and put one in the **Tag Mode** checkbox.

5. Locate and Tag the following records.
    Liz Dittmeier
    Bill Craig
    Mary Nara
    George Agen
    Andy Bosson
	Locate each record and click it to tag it.

6. Leave the five records tagged. Leave the list displayed.	

Lookup and Omit Tagged Records

Once you have Contacts tagged, you can create a lookup from the tagged records. There are two variations of this process.

- Create a lookup consisting only of those Contact records you have tagged. This is a "**Lookup Selected**" action.
- Create a lookup consisting of those Contact records that are not tagged. This is an "**Omit Selected**" action.

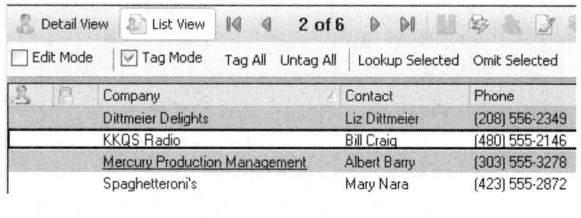

☞ *Note that there are buttons for these actions at the top of List View.*

Working with Your Contacts | 59

Procedure: To lookup or omit tagged Contacts

1. Tag the records you wish to Lookup/Omit.
2. Click **Lookup Selected** to display only the tagged records. [Lookup Selected] This performs a real lookup. If you return to the Contacts window, only the remaining records are available.

   Click **Omit Selected** to display only those Contact records that are not tagged. [Omit Selected]

 You can also right-click any record to O<u>m</u>it Selected Contacts, <u>L</u>ookup Selected Contacts, <u>T</u>ag All, or Untag <u>A</u>ll.

Practice: Lookup and Omit

What to do	How to do it/Comments
1. Look up the currently tagged Contact records. (You should still have the five Contact records tagged from the previous exercise.)	Click the **Lookup Selected** button at the top of the List View, or right-click and select **Lookup Selected Contacts**. [Lookup Selected]
2. Observe the list. Display the **Detail View**.	Only the tagged records are displayed. Click the **Detail View** button. [Detail View]
3. How many records display?	Five records should display in the Detail View as well.
4. Return to the **List View**. Are the records still tagged?	Click the **List View** button. The Contacts are still highlighted. [List View]
5. Untag all records.	Click **Untag All**.
6. Omit Liz from the lookup (she already renewed her contract). Now you have a lookup of Contacts to call to remind them of their contract renewal dates.	Tag Liz Dittmeier, and then click (or right-click) **Omit Selected**. [Omit Selected]
7. Look up all Contact records. Disable **Tag Mode**. Leave the **List View** displayed.	Choose **Lookup**, **All Contacts**. Uncheck **Tag Mode**.

Printing Lookups

Once you have your list just the way you like it, you sometimes need a quick print out to work with. You have a few options.

Procedure: To print your lookup

1. Perform a lookup as desired

2. Add fields that you want displayed as columns.

    Right-click, **Customize Columns…**

3. Click the **Export to Excel** icon and print,

    You may not have rights to Export to Excel based on permissions assigned to your log on name (read about custom permissions and setting up users starting on page 463).

    or **File, Quick Print Current Window** (the same as clicking **Print Current Screen** in the Related Tasks pane),

    or **File, Quick Print Selected** will only print the selected row(s).

Secondary Contacts

Secondary Contacts are alternate Contacts that have some relationship to the current (or primary) Contact. They are maintained on their own tab on the Contact's record. While you may have an unlimited number of Secondary Contacts, generally these Contacts are maintained only for information purposes. Usually, they would have no impact on the decision-making process to use your company's products or services. However, it is sometimes useful to maintain a list of associates that could be helpful to you…the Contact's assistant, a person in accounts payable who has helped you get your bills paid in the past, shipping personnel who can check on status of packages delivered, etc.

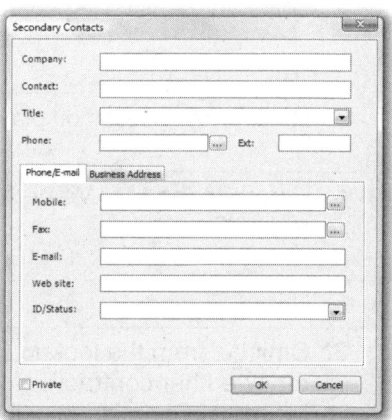

You can maintain basic information on each Secondary Contact, including their title, phone, mobile, fax, e-mail, and Web address. You need not fill in the company name and business address unless it is different from the main Contact's information.

 Keep in mind that all notes, histories, and scheduled activities are associated with the primary Contact only (not with specific Secondary Contacts). In addition, you cannot mail merge to Secondary Contacts (although you can send a single e-mail from the dialog box).

Working with Your Contacts | 61

Procedure: To add a Secondary Contact

1. On the Contact's record, click the **Secondary Contacts** tab.

2. Click **New Secondary Contact** button on the tab, or right-click in the Secondary Contacts tab and select **New Secondary Contact**.

3. Fill in the data as desired.

4. Click **OK**.   Secondary Contacts display in alphabetical order by last name.

 The display of Secondary Contacts is a list view. If you would like different columns of information to display for these Contacts, you can customize the list the same way that you customized the List View. See page 38.

Double-click a Secondary Contact to display the complete information. Both the E-mail address and the Web site are hyperlinked when displayed in the dialog box. That means you can click the e-mail address and it will open a new message window for sending e-mail. The Web site is also hyperlinked and when clicked, opens the site in your default Internet browser.

 We've also used the Secondary Contact feature to store site-specific Web addresses for quick access to a customer logon.

Procedure: To delete a Secondary Contact

1. On the Contact's record, click the **Secondary Contacts** tab.

2. Select a Secondary Contact, right-click it and select **Delete Secondary Contact**.

3. Click **Yes** to confirm the deletion.

 Unless you have a Manager or Administrator role, you can only delete a Secondary Contact that you have created.

Sage ACT!

Practice: Assistants	
What to do	**How to do it/Comments**

1. Thomas Andrews hired a new assistant. Add her as a Secondary Contact.
 	
    Jane Boxer
    Administrative Assistant
    (727) 555-4572
 	
Delete the old assistant.
	Lookup, **First Name**, thomas, **OK**. Click the **Secondary Contacts** tab and click the **New Secondary Contact** button on the tab header bar. Add her name, title, and phone and click **OK**.
	
	Select Connie Lawrence. Right-click, **Delete Secondary Contact**.

Lookups on Secondary Contact Fields

You can also perform lookups on any of the fields you have entered for a Secondary Contact. This is a great feature for those times when you know you entered a Contact on someone's record, but can't remember who.

Procedure: To look up data contained in Secondary Contacts' records

1. **Lookup, Other Fields….**

2. Click the **Look in this field** drop-down arrow to select one of the Secondary fields.

3. Fill in the Search criteria.

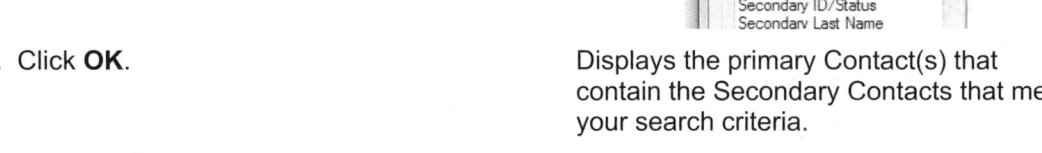

4. Click **OK**. Displays the primary Contact(s) that contain the Secondary Contacts that met your search criteria.

5. Click the Secondary Contacts tab, if necessary. You will still have to search the **Secondary Contacts** tab to locate the Secondary Contact that you searched for.

Working with Your Contacts 63

Practice: Locating Chase

What to do	How to do it/Comments
1. You met an interesting chef named Chase last week at a dinner party, but you can't remember who he worked for. Look up his name in the Secondary Contact listings.	**Lookup**, **Other Fields…** Click the **Look in this field** drop-down arrow to select **Secondary First Name**. Look for Chase, and click **OK**. He works for Sierra's Cafe.

Promoting from Within

Sometimes a Contact that you have entered as a Secondary Contact turns out to be more important than you originally thought. You may need to upgrade one of these associates to their own record so that you can schedule activities, record histories, enter notes, and mail merge to them. You can easily promote a Secondary Contact to a primary Contact.

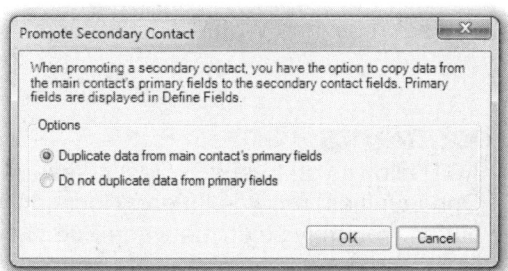

Procedure: To promote a Secondary Contact to its own record

1. Select the Secondary Contact to promote.
2. Click the **Promote** button,  or right-click and select **Promote Secondary Contact…**.
3. Select the desired option.
   - **Duplicate data from main contact's primary fields** – fills in missing company and address information as this new record is created.
   - **Do not duplicate data from primary fields** – creates a new record from the selected Secondary Contact using only the information entered for the Contact on this tab.
4. Click **OK**.

Primary fields are usually Company name, the main address information (not home address), phone, fax, and Web site, along with any other fields that are defined as primary.

If different address or phone information has been entered for this Contact, it will not be overwritten when the Duplicate data option is selected. Only missing fields are filled in.

 Once the Secondary Contact is promoted, there is no longer any association with the primary Contact.

Practice: *Promote*

What to do	How to do it/Comments
1. Chase Thomas is a Secondary Contact on Brandon Sloan's record.	If necessary, **Lookup**, **Last Name** Sloan, and display the **Secondary Contacts** tab.
2. We need to develop a relationship with this up-and-comer. Let's promote him to his own record in ACT!. Go ahead and duplicate the data from Sloan's record.	Click Chase Thomas' name to select it. Click **Promote**, select **Duplicate data from main contact's primary fields** and click **OK**.
3. Notice how Chase's new record already has the Company name, phone, fax, address, and Web site information filled in.	

Documents Tab

ACT! allows you to attach files in several places on Contact (or Company or Group or Opportunities) records. In each location where you find the **Attach** or **Add Document** button, you may select between **File...** or **Shortcut...**.

- **Selecting "File..."** copies (not moves) the selected file to the \Attachments folder and places a link on the record. When you manually add a file as an attachment (either in the History tab or the Documents tab...or to any tab for that matter), ACT! creates a copy of the file and places it in the \Attachments folder. The original file (the one you selected when you attached the file) still exists in its original location. When you double-click the attachment icon on the History or Documents tab, you will be viewing or editing the copy and not the original. In fact, you may want to consider deleting the original to avoid confusion.

    ☞ *It is possible to set up remote synchronization databases to receive copies of attachments in their syncs.*

- **Selecting "Shortcut..."** creates a link to a file on your PC or network. The shortcut file command is also maintained in the \Attachments folder and displays with a shortcut icon to the left of the attachment. The files referenced by shortcuts will not sync. However, remote users may access the file using the shortcut if they have a VPN connection allowing them to open files on the network.

Five kinds of ACT!-related attachments are maintained in the **History** tab:

- an attached file that was created and linked to the Contact when you printed any correspondence that was initiated from the Write menu command, and
- an attached file that was created when you sent an e-mail from ACT! or from Outlook, for which you selected the option to attach a copy to history, and
- an attached file that was created when you generated and printed a Quote from the Opportunities tab, and

Working with Your Contacts | 65

- any file or shortcut to a file that was attached to a scheduled or completed activity, and
- any file or shortcut to a file that was manually attached to the History tab.

If you have created a file for a client outside of ACT! (such as a Microsoft PowerPoint® presentation or Microsoft Project file) and want to attach it to a specific record, you can choose to attach the file (or a shortcut to the original file) either in the **History** or the **Documents** tab.

Since attachments that are automatically generated by ACT! are displayed in date order along with other history entries (letters and e-mails sent, completed activities, field changes, Contacts deleted, etc.), it is not always easy to find previous attachments without scrolling through or filtering the list on the **History** tab.

Adding non-ACT! types of files to the **Documents** tab keeps them at your fingertips for quick retrieval. You can open and edit any file type from the **Documents** tab (assuming the program that can read that file type is installed on your computer).

 *Files and Shortcuts added to the **Documents** tab are listed in reverse alpha order by file name only. You cannot sort the list by date. In addition, there is no area to add notes about the document (as in a History entry). However, it is a great place to quickly store and find files that you created for a specific contact.*

Procedure: To add files (or shortcuts) to the Documents tab

1. Display the Contact, Company, or Group record you wish to attach the file to. Display the **Documents** tab.

   Click the tab to display its contents.

   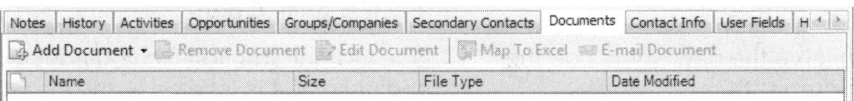

2. Click the **Add Document** button, and select **File…** or **Shortcut…**.

   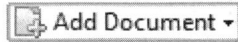

   Selecting **File…** copies (not moves) the file to the \Attachments folder and its file name displays alphabetically in the **Documents** tab. Selecting **Shortcut…** creates a link to a file on your PC or network. The path to the file displays alphabetically in the **Documents** tab.

3. Browse to locate and select the file you wish to add, and click **Open**.

   We can't help you here. If you don't know where the file is located, you're just out of luck.

Sage ACT!

The tab shows the file size, the file type (if it can be determined), and the date it was last modified.

	Name	Size	File Type	Date Modified
	GoogleTip for Phones.doc	29 KB	Microsoft Office Word 97 -...	5/21/2007
	C:\Program Files\ACT\Act for...	2 KB	Bitmap Image	5/21/2007

Add Document ▼ | Remove Document | Edit Document | Map To Excel | E-mail Document

 *You can also add a file (not a shortcut) by dragging a file from the Windows Explorer or browser window directly to the **Documents** tab.*

Practice: Adding Files to the Documents Tab

What to do	How to do it/Comments
1. Look up UR Powerful again.	**Lookup**, **Last Name**, type **pow** and click **OK**.
2. Add any document you like to the record.	Display the **Documents** tab and click the **Add Document** button and select **File…**. Browse to your My Documents folder and select any file. Click **Open**.
3. Add an attachment to a file.	Display the **Documents** tab, click the **Add Document** button, and select **Shortcut…**. Browse to your My Documents folder and select any file. Click **Open**.
4. Observe the new entries on the **Documents** tab.	Don't forget, the first file you added is a copy of the original and it is located in the current database's **\Attachments** folder. The second one is an shortcut to the original file.

 It is possible to disable the ability for users to attach any files to the database (only shortcuts to files can be used). See page 481 for more information.

Working with Your Contacts | 67

Opening and Editing Files

As long as the application that created the files is on your computer, you can open the files from your **Documents** tab and edit them.

Procedure: To open a document

1. Display the **Documents** tab (if necessary). — All documents for the current entity (Contact, Company, and Group) display.

2. Select the file you wish to open. — Click anywhere on the row to select the file.

3. Click **Edit Document** on the **Documents** tab toolbar. — You can also double-click the attachment's row to open the file for editing.

4. Edit…or just admire. — The file opens in its native application.

5. Save changes and exit the program.

Practice: Editing

What to do	How to do it/Comments
1. View the **Documents** tab for Chris Huffman.	Choose **L**ookup, **M**y Record.
2. This tab has several documents. Double-click the Canadian Provinces file (a Notepad document) to edit it.	Select the **Canadian Provinces.txt** from the **Documents List**. Click **Edit Document** (or just double-click the filename).
3. Newfoundland has changed to "Newfoundland and Labrador" and the abbreviation is now "NL".	Make the changes, save, and close Notepad. ☞ *You may need to click View Refresh to update the Date Modified field.*

Removing Files from the Documents Tab

At some point you may wish to remove a file from the **Documents** tab (or from the **Notes**, **Activities**, or **History** tab). When you remove an attached file from any tab, it is deleted from the \Attachments folder as well.

Procedure: To remove files from the Documents tab

1. On the **Documents** tab, select the document to remove.

   Click the row for the desired document to select it.

2. Click the **Remove Document** button.

   On the **Documents** tab toolbar.   [Remove Document]

3. Click **Yes** to remove the document.

   The document is removed from the list *and* from \Attachments folder.

☞ *You can also right-click the file in the Documents tab and select Remove Document. If you are in the History tab, right-click and select Delete Selected.*

Practice: Cleaning Up	
What to do	**How to do it/Comments**
1. Delete the: **WorkshopInvoice** from Lance's record.	Display the **Documents** tab on Lance's record. Select the WorkshopInvoice and click **Remove Document** button. Answer **Yes** to confirm the deletion.

Relationships

Defining and viewing relationships between two or more contacts in your database can help you (and your team mates) keep track of (and maybe leverage) the links they all have to one another. The Relationship tab displays those defined links, as well as allow you to create a Lookup (or printout) of the related contacts.

While similar to the Secondary Contacts feature, Relationships are defined between contacts and provide much more flexibility. You might define standard relationships of "Boss" and "Employee" or "Friend". However, you can also use the Relationships feature to track other connections. For example, if you are in Placement you might create a relationship between your client and a potential employee. When the client hires the contact, you can change the relationship from "Sent resume" to "Hired", or…. "Rejected". Perhaps you can create a contact record for a project and create relationships with all players: "Consultant", "Architect", "Lawyer", "Decision Maker", etc.

☞ *If a logged-in user does not have rights to see one of the contacts in the relationship, then the relationship will not display (even though it will continue to exist).*

You can determine which fields you want to display on the Relationship tab by right-clicking inside the tab and selecting **Customize Columns…**. Contact specific fields, as well as Relationship specific fields, can be added to the Relationship tab list view.

Working with Your Contacts

Procedure: To create a relationship between contacts

1. Lookup the first contact.

2. Display the Relationship tab and click the **Relate Contact** button,

   or click **Contacts, Relate Contacts**.

3. Select the contact(s) you wish to link to the current record from the drop-down list,

   or begin typing the last name of the contact to scroll to the desired contact.

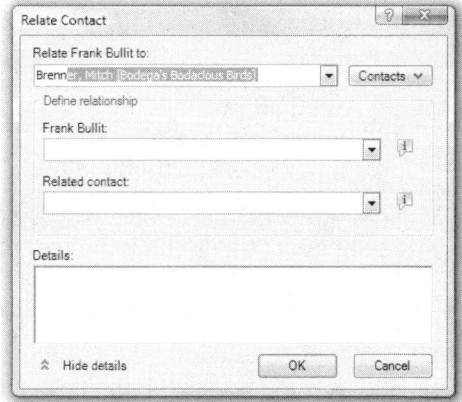

☞ *If you want to select multiple contacts, click on the **Contacts** button to the right and click **Select Contacts...** Select the contacts and click **OK**. When multiple contacts are selected, a separate relationship is created for each contact using the same relationship type for each.*

4. Select or enter the relationship for the first contact.

   In defining the Relationship, you can select one or more options from a defined drop-down list or create your own relationship type on the fly by just typing the description.

5. Select or enter the relationship for the second contact.

6. Add **Details:** if necessary to further describe the relationship.

   You may need to click **Show details** to see the input screen for this data element. You can enter URLs or e-mail addresses in this area as well.

7. Click **OK**.

☞ *Double-click or right-click, Edit Relationship to modify anything about the relationship.*

So now you have the relationship defined. What can you do with it? Click the contact name to quickly lookup the related contact. You can also right-click inside the Relationship tab and select **Create Lookup**.

Practice: Relationships

What to do	How to do it/Comments
1. Lookup Lance Parker. Jean Louise Finch is his lawyer. Create that relationship where Lance is the "Client" and Jean Louise is the "Attorney".	Lookup, Last name, Parker, OK. On the Relationships tab, click **Relate Contact** button at the top of the tab. In the first text box, type Finch and notice that Jean's name appears. In the **Define Relationships** section, type "Client" under Lance's name and "Attorney" under Jean Louise's name.
2. Add details to the relationship – "She took over the account from her father."	In the **Details** section, enter the indicated text and click **OK**.
3. Note how the relationship displays on Lance's record. Click on the record (not Jean Louise's name) so that you can see the Details displayed in the preview pane at the right.	
4. See how the relationship displays on Jean Louise Finch's record.	Click on Jean Louise's name (it displays as a blue hyperlink). ACT! will quickly display her record and you can view a list of her clients that are also in your ACT! database.
5. Change the column display on the Relationships tab to include the Phone number. Notice you can display any contact fields. Better yet, when any of the data (like Phone number) is updated, it is immediately reflected on this tab.	Right-click anywhere in the Relationships tab and select **Customize Columns…**. Scroll to locate the Phone field among the Available fields: list and double-click it to move it to the list at the right. Use the **Move Up** button to rearrange the display if you like.
6. Return to Lance's record.	Click on Lance's name to display his record.
7. Kirby York of Duke Industries is the frame supplier for Yellow Jersey. In addition, Kirby is also Lance's Golfing Buddy. Create that relationship.	Click the Relate Contact button. Type York to start the relationship. Under Lance's name, type or use the drop-down to select "Client". Since Golfing Buddy is not on the drop-down list, enter semicolon after the word Client and type "Golfing Buddy". Under Kirby's name enter "Golfing Buddy;Vendor." In details, enter "frame supplier." Click **OK**.

Working with Your Contacts | 71

What to do	How to do it/Comments
8. Create a Lookup of the contacts related to Lance.	Right-click in the Relationships tab and click **Create Lookup**.
9. Notice that both Jean Louise and Kirby have an ID/Status of "Prospect" and they both have open opportunities. Perhaps we can leverage our relationship with Lance to help us close that business.	Hmm.

 *To remove an existing relationship, right-click the relationship and select **Remove Relationship** to delete the relationship from both records.*

Your Contact's Website

The Internet is an integral part of most of our business lives. In an age where information is key, accessing more information about our clients and prospects could make the difference between being awarded the next deal and missing out because we didn't realize that the company offices had moved since we last spoke with them.

As a very basic method of fact finding, if the Contact has a URL entered in their **Web Site** field, when your mouse pointer moves over the field, it 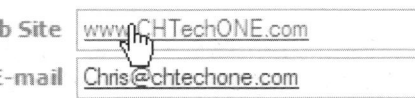 displays as a hand and the link changes color. If you click the address, the Web site opens in your default Internet browser window.

Web Info Tab

But wait, there's more. You don't even have to leave ACT! to view the contact's Web site. There are several options for doing Internet research on your contacts inside the Web Info tab.

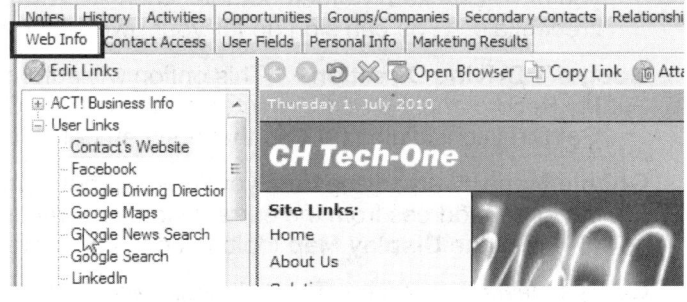

There are two main categories of search on the Web Info tab: ACT! Business Info and User Links.

The pane to the right acts as a mini browser window inside of ACT! that displays relevant information for the current contact, with respect to the link that you click.

Sage ACT!

Procedure: To use the Web Info tab

1. Look up the Contact you wish to research.

2. Click the desired research link at the left. (See a description of the options on the following pages.) — The corresponding Web site displays in the browser window to the right.

3. If you'd like to open the current Web site in its own window, click the **Open Browser** icon. 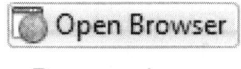 Opens the current URL into your default Internet browser window.

4. Click the **Copy Link** icon to paste the current URL into a document or e-mail.  Since you can't see an Address bar, this is a handy way to access the current Web link.

5. To take a snapshot of the current Web site, click the **Attach Web Page** icon.  This option attaches a static view of any Web page that you think might change over time to the History tab.

6. Click the **Increase Tab Size** icon on the tab's toolbar to maximize the tab.  To return the tab to its regular half-size, click the **Decrease Tab Size** icon.

Web Info tab - User Links section

Let's look at the options under the User Links section first.

Contact's Website – Clicking this link displays the URL found in the Web Site field in the browser window in the Web Info tab.

Facebook – Searches all profiles in www.Facebook.com for the current Contact. In order to view a selected profile you will need to log on to your Facebook account the first time. If you have checked "Remember Me", then ACT! will remember your Facebook logon credentials. (You can sign up for your own account at www.Facebook.com.)

Google™ Driving Directions – This option will automatically enter the address found on the My Record and the address listed on the current Contact's record into a Google map's Get Directions dialog box, so that you can get … driving directions.

Google Maps™ – If driving from your office is not a good option, Google can grab the street address from the current Contact's record and display a map. You can also click the **Display Map** toolbar icon shortcut to this option.

Google News™ Search – This link searches Google for stories containing the company name of the current Contact.

Google Search – This link searches Google for items concerning the contact name of the current Contact.

Working with Your Contacts | 73

LinkedIn® – Searches all profiles in www.LinkedIn.com for the current Contact. You must log into your LinkedIn account before you can use this search option. If you have checked "Remember Me", then ACT! will remember your LinkedIn logon credentials. (You can sign up for your own profile at www.LinkedIn.com.)

Plaxo - Searches all profiles in www.Plaxo.com for the current Contact. You must log into your Plaxo account before you can use this search option. As with the other options, ACT! remembers your log-on credentials.

Weather – This weather.com link provides the weather forecast for the current Contact's city-state-zip location.

Yahoo!® Local Info – This link provides a link to the Yahoo! City Guide for a quick look at what is going on in the current Contact's city.

Yahoo! Person Search – This menu command passes the current Contact's name to Yahoo! to search their white pages to access phone and address information on the Web. The information comes from telephone companies, so is likely to only find head of household names. It also returns a general Internet search on the name as well.

☞ *You can use **Edit Links** to add URLs to the User Links section. The links can be created to use database fields (for example the Weather link uses the current contact's Zip Code to display the local weather). For creating custom links, see the Database Design & Layouts chapter.*

☞ *You must have access to the Internet to complete the next exercise.*

Practice: Check Out Your Contact on the Web

What to do	How to do it/Comments
1. Lookup Lance Parker.	Type "Lance Parker" in the Lookup pane in the Navbar and click Go.
2. View his company Web page.	Click the Web Info tab, and select **Contact's Website** from the links at the left.
3. Enlarge the tab so you can see more of the Web site.	Click the **Increase Tab Size** button.
4. Click the Personal Info tab (in the ACT! Demo layout) and notice his photo.	You don't have to change the size of the tab to view another tab in the layout.
5. Return to the Web Info tab and see if Lance has a profile in Facebook.	Click the Facebook link on the Web Info tab. Scroll until you see his photo. You will have to sign in to your Facebook account to see more about Lance.
6. Get driving directions. Well, it may be a bit far to drive from New York to San Diego.	Click on the Google Driving Directions. Notice that it entered Chris Huffman's address as the starting location and Lance's address as the ending location.

Sage ACT!

What to do	How to do it/Comments
7. Try out some of the other links at the left. Open at least one of them in their own browser window.	Select one of the links and click the **Open Browser** button on the tab toolbar.
8. Close the browser window, return to ACT! and return the Web Info tab to its regular size.	Click the **Decrease Tab Size** button on the tab toolbar.

Attaching Web Pages From Internet Explorer®

While you can attach a Web page from within the Web Info tab (maybe you will want to attach Google Driving Directions for later review or printing), it is more likely that one day you will come across a Web page whose content has a great deal of relevance to one of your Contacts. Perhaps it's a news article about one of your clients or their organization. Perhaps it is a competitor's Web page.

Procedure: To attach a Web page to a Contact record

1. In Internet Explorer, display the Web page you wish to attach.

   Other browsers are not supported at this time.

2. Look up the contact in ACT!.

   You don't have to do this, but it makes attaching quicker.

3. Click the **Attach Web page to ACT!** contact icon on the Internet Explorer toolbar.

   The **Attach Web Page to the Following Contact(s)** dialog box displays.

☞ *If you are using Internet Explorer 7, you may need to click the more button at the end of the toolbar to display the Attach Web page to ACT! icon.*

Working with Your Contacts | 75

The current Contact in ACT! is automatically added to the **Selected contents** pane.

If you didn't look up the contact first or ACT! is not open…

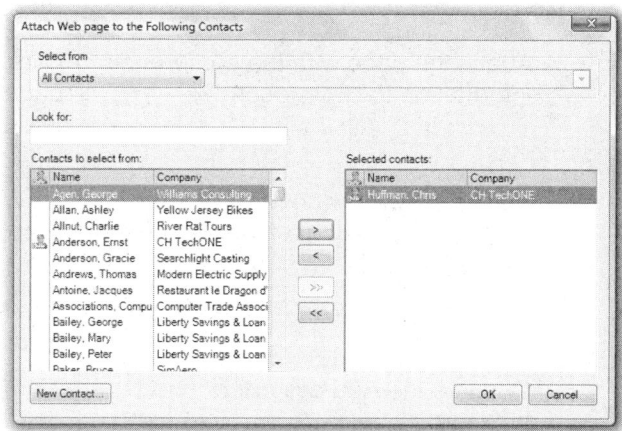

4. Use the drop-down arrow to "Select from" **All Contacts**, the **Current Lookup**, or existing **Groups** or **Companies**. Then locate the Contact to attach the page to. You may specify multiple Contacts if you want to attach the page to all of them.

To select a range of Contacts, click to select the first one, then hold **[Shift]** and click the last one. All Contacts in between are selected. To select random Contacts, click to select the first Contact, and then hold the **[Ctrl]** button as you click each additional one.

5. Click the **Add** button.

All selected Contacts are added.

6. Repeat as necessary and click **OK**.

A copy of the Web page is attached to the **History** tab of specified record(s).

 When you attach a Web page to a Contact, it is usually saved using the Mime HTML format (with an .mht file extension). This file is self-contained; you do not need to be connected to the Internet to view it.

Practice: Attach UR's Page	
What to do	**How to do it/Comments**
1. Look up UR Powerful.	Click **Lookup**, **Last Name**, type **pow** and **OK**.
2. Captains of Industry is sponsoring a conference that you are interested in next January. Find the conference information. www.captainsoi.com	Click the Web site in UR's record.

What to do	How to do it/Comments
3. Attach the page with the conference information to UR's record.	Click on Conference at the top of the page. Click the **Attach** button on the Internet Explorer toolbar. It looks like UR's name is already selected, so you can just click **OK**.
4. Close the Web page and return to ACT! and display the **History** tab on UR's record.	View the **History** tab to see the newly attached Web page at the top of the list.
5. Single-click the icon for the attached page.	The same page that previously appeared is still displayed, or is it?
6. Observe the Address bar on the browser.	This page is not on the Web. It is stored on your hard drive so it is always accessible to you.

Web Info tab - ACT! Business Info section

Sage Business Info Services for ACT![1] allows you to connect your ACT! database to the online Hoover's™ database of more than 65 million public and private companies and 85 million executives. With this tool at your disposal you can...

- Easily locate information to fill in the gaps of information about a company or contact in your database.
- Find new prospects by creating targeted lists that meet your specific criteria.
- Import contact and company lists directly into your database (level 2 subscription).
- Subscribe to alerts to notify you when key changes occur for the company or contact.

In short, ACT! Business Info makes it easy to do research and learn more about your contacts than ever before. And you can get this data all before you ever pick up the phone.

To get started, you need to create a Sage Business Info Services account. The amount of information that you can view is determined by your current Service level.

Feature	Depth of Info	Free	Reference	+Leads
Contact Profile	Basic	X	X	X
Company Profile	Basic	X	X	X
	Full Description		X	X
	Alerts		X	X
	Import Company			X

---

[1] The first level is free. The Reference levels require additional subscription.

Working with Your Contacts

Feature	Depth of Info	Free	Reference	+Leads
Co Financials	Basic	X	X	X
	Expanded		X	X
Co Contacts	Import Key People		X	X
Industry Info	Competitors-Top 3	X	X	X
	Overview		X	X
	Competitors-Full List		X	X
Co News	News & Timeline		X	X
Leads	Build-A-List			X
	Keyword Search			X
	Purchase Add Leads			X

The first level is **Free** and allows you to gain access to basic company headquarters information such as name, address main telephone and website. It provides limited Company financials and competitor information.

The **Reference** level (by subscription only) offers full company information, all available contact information, and additional competitor information. This level also allows you to import Contacts and Companies.

The **Reference + Leads** level (by subscription only) increases the number of contacts and companies you can import into your database at a fixed monthly rate.

You can easily create your own Business Info Services Account.

Procedure: To set up a Sage Business Info Services account

1. In the Navbar, click the **Connections** button. Setup your account using the links under the **Sage Business Info Services for ACT!** panel.

2. If you are already using the Sage E-marketing services for your mass e-mails, then you will add this service to your existing account But you can start out with the free version.

   You will receive a single combined bill if you decide to also subscribe to the Business Info Services.

   Select "Use Free Version" and click **Activate Selected**.

3. Fill in your existing Sage E-marketing or Swiftpage account information or create a new Account, UserID and Password and click **Submit**.

   They don't even ask for a credit card number to sign up for this level… so go ahead. You have nothing to lose. Tell them I told you so under the Resellers, if you like (Cornerstone Solutions, Inc.).

Sage ACT!

4. Once you have entered your account information, you can click **Activate Selected** to start your new account.

Accessing Key Business Info for a Contact or Company

You probably already figured this out, but all of the contacts in the ACT2012Demo database are bogus, so you won't be able to link any company information.

You can access key business information for a contact or company from the Web Info tab in ACT! using the links in the ACT! Business Info section. So let's start by adding a real company to the database that we can play with (it can be one of your own if you prefer).

Practice: Sign up already and look up a company	
What to do	**How to do it/Comments**
1. If you haven't already signed up for your Sage Business Info Services account… do so now.	Click the **Sage Business Info Services for ACT!** icon on the toolbar. If you are not working with a reseller, you can enter Cornerstone Solutions, Inc.
2. Close the IE Window that opens after you activate your account and return to ACT!.	
3. Create a new contact in ACT!	Press the **[Insert]** button on the keyboard to create a new blank record.
4. Enter a contact for: 　　Michael S. Dell 　　Dell, Inc.	Let's find out more about this company.
5. Click the **Save** icon on the toolbar.	Normally you don't have to save contact data. When you move off of a record everything is saved automatically. But we aren't going anywhere yet.

Working with Your Contacts | 79

Company Profile

To start your research on the current contact in your database, click the Company Profile link on the Web Info tab. ACT! will search the Hoover's database using the Company name and Web Site information found on the current record. If an exact match is not found, then a list of potential companies is displayed.

Click on the company that you wish to view.

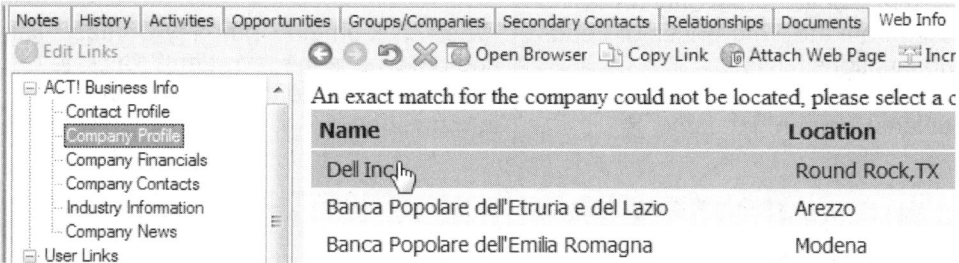

The Company Profile will display. f you selected the wrong company or the wrong one displays, click the **(wrong company?)** link to return to a list of options.

Practice: Review their information

What to do	How to do it/Comments
1. While still in the contact record you just created for Dell, Inc., click on the **Company Profile** link (under ACT! Business Info) to find out more about the company.	Click on the **Increase Tab Size** icon if necessary.
2. If there is more than one company that displays, click on the company that seems most likley. The Company Profile should now display.	If you selected the wrong company or the wrong one displays, click the **(wrong company?)** link to return to a list of options. Scroll to see the Phone and address information.
3. Click on the **Contact Profile** link to find out more about this contact.	
4. Click on the **Company Financial** and **Industry Information** links to view the company data.	You can find information here to fill in address, phone, and financial information.

Sage ACT!

What to do	How to do it/Comments
5. Who else could we call on? (Click on the **Company Contacts** link.) Click the **Company News** link to see what is up. Both of these options can only be accessed from the References or Leads teir subscriptions. Well at least we can get some	If you have a subscription, and there is any news found, the posts will display below the timeline. You can use your mouse to drag the timeline Click on any of the hyperlinked stories to catch up with what is going on with this company. When click on the Company Contacts link, find out who is the president? Click on the hyperlinked name to find out more information.

Importing Companies

When you are displaying the Company Profile in the Web Info tab, the toolbar has two buttons that allow you to **Import Company...** or **Subscribe to Alerts**.

 You must have a Reference or Reference + Leads service level account to use this feature.

Procedure: To import a Company

1. Lookup a contact in the database. In the Web Info tab, under ACT! Business info, click on the **Company Profile** Link. If this company is not currently in the Companies list in your database, click the **Import Company...** button.

    The **Import Company...** button will create a **Companies** record in your database (it does not create a Contact record or fill in missing data for the current Contact).

2. Click **Open**.

3. Select **Custom import** to control what data is imported into your database and click **Next>**.

    Select **Typical import** if you want to import only the Basic fields and you are sure that all data will go to the correct fields in your ACT! database.

Working with Your Contacts | 81

4. The data fields available for importing are displayed at the left. Your ACT! database fields display at the right.

   Some of the fields will already be mapped. Use the drop-down to the right to map any remaining desired fields. If a specific field is not available in your database (and you are an Administrator), you can select the <Create new ACT! field> option.

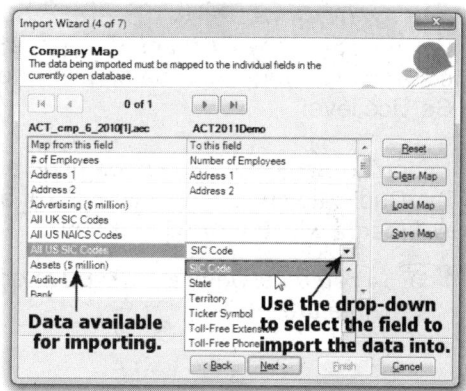

 Once all of the fields have been mapped, click the **Save Map** button. The next time you import a Company, click the **Load Map** button to quickly return to your field mapping.

5. Click **Next>**.

6. If you used the <Create new ACT! field> option, modify the Field Name or Field Length as desired, and click **Next>**.

7. Click **Next>** and **Finish**.

   If you added a field you will be prompted to add the newly created field to your layout.

Company Alerts

Put your clients and prospects on a watch list and have Hoover's send you important business information on selected companies as the news breaks.

 You must have a Reference or Reference + Leads service level account to use this feature.

Procedure: To subscribe to a Company alert

1. Lookup a contact in the database.

2. On the Web Info tab, under ACT! Business Info, click the **Company Profile** Link.

3. Click the **Subscribe to Alerts** button.

   Not all companies are supported for the alerts feature.

4. Click **OK** to acknowledge that the alert was created.

Importing Contacts

On the **Company Contacts** link pane, there is an option to allow you to import selected contacts into your ACT! database. The ability to import is based on your Business Info Service level.

Importing Business Info Leads uses an abbreviated version of the Import wizard which uses the Duplicate checking setting. So, if a new lead matches the duplicate checking settings, it will merge with the existing record.

> *You must have a Reference or Reference + Leads service level account to use this feature.*

Procedure: To import selected contacts

1. In the Web Info tab, under ACT! Business info, click on the **Company Contacts** Link.
2. Select the contacts you are interested in importing into your database.
3. Click the **Import Selected Contacts...** button.
4. Click **Open**.
5. Select **Custom import** to control what data is imported into your database and click **Next>**.

   Select **Typical import** if you want to import only the Basic fields and you are sure that all data will go to the correct fields in your ACT! database.

6. The data fields available for importing are displayed at the left. Your ACT! database fields display at the right.

   Most of the fields will already be mapped (including First Name and Last Name). Use the drop-down to the right to map any remaining desired fields. If a specific field is not available in your database (and you are an Administrator), you can select the <Create new ACT! field> option.

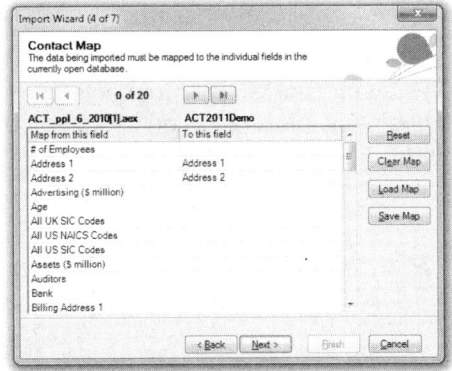

> *Once all of the fields have been mapped, click the **Save Map** button. The next time you import a Company, click the **Load Map** button to quickly return to your field mapping.*

7. Click **Next>**.

Working with Your Contacts | 83

8. If you used the <Create new ACT! field> option, modify the Field Name or Field Length as desired, and click **Next>**.

9. Click **Next>** and **Finish**.

   If you added a field you will be prompted to add the newly created field to your layout.

Build a List

It's great to be able to get more information on your current contacts but sometimes you just need a new list of leads. Using your Sage Business Info link to Hoover's, you can build a list based on Location, Company Size, Industry, Company Type, People (Job Functions or Compensations packages), Financial data, or other Specialty Criteria.

Procedure: To build a prospect list

1. Click the **Sage Business Info Services for ACT!** icon on the toolbar.

   You could search for a specific company here, but let's focus on building a list.

2. Click the + to the left of the criteria that you want to use in building your list.

3. As you select your criteria, notice that the **Total Results** at the bottom of the page reflects the number of contacts that match your currently selected criteria.

4. When you've narrowed the list to your preferences click the **View Results** hyperlink

5. Select the Companies that you want to import into your ACT! database.

   Companies will be imported to your currently open database.

6. Click the **Export** hyperlink at the bottom of the screen.

7. Click **Open**.

8. Select **Custom import** to control what data is imported into your database and click **Next>**.

   Select **Typical import** if you want to import only the Basic fields and you are sure that all data will go to the correct fields in your ACT! database.

9. The data fields available for importing are displayed at the left. Your ACT! database fields display at the right.

   Some of the fields will already be mapped. Use the drop-down to the right to map any remaining desired fields. If a specific field is not available in your database (and you are an Administrator), you can select the <Create new ACT! field> option.

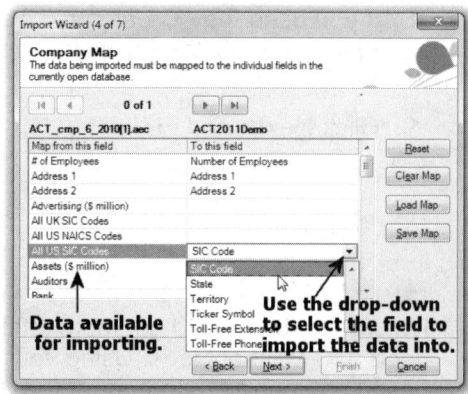

 *Once all of the fields have been mapped, click the **Save Map** button. The next time you import a Company, click the **Load Map** button to quickly return to your field mapping.*

10. Click **Next>**.

11. If you used the <Create new ACT! field> option, modify the Field Name or Field Length as desired, and click **Next>**.

12. Click **Next>** and **Finish**.

If you added a field you will be prompted to add the newly created field to your layout.

Procedure: To lookup the Companies that you just imported

1. Click on the **Companies** button in the Navbar at the left.

2. Click the **Company Info** tab so that you can see the Create Date for the Company record.

3. Right-click the Create Date field, and select **Lookup Create Date.**

4. If necessary change the lookup to be **Equal To (=) Today** and click **OK**.

Working with Your Contacts | 85

Procedure: To flesh out the leads with contacts

1. In the Companies Detail View, click on the Web Info tab.

   Click on the Companies button in the Navbar at the left.

2. Click on the Company Contacts link under the ACT! Business Info.

3. Click on the company in the right pane to select it.

4. Select the contacts that you might be interested in pursuing and click **Import Selected Contacts…**

5. Follow the rest of the procedure from page 82.

Practice: *Find a Prospect to follow up with*

What to do	How to do it/Comments
1. Use the previous procedures to locate a few prospects that you should be calling up on.	
2. Try looking up data for your favorite contact. Then build a list of companies with the SIC code in your metropolitan area.	

Review: Working with Your Contacts

1. Find everyone that plays tennis.
2. Can you figure out how to look up everyone in the database who has a Secondary Contact?
3. Which month has more birthdays…May or September?
4. Delete the Secondary Contact on Bill Willis' record. Lorraine is an old Contact and doesn't work for him anymore.
5. Create another Vendor/Client Relationship between Lance Parker and Ben Braddock.

Scheduling Your Day

To understand how to get your day and your life organized with ACT!, you will:

- ☑ Learn to schedule simple activities.

- ☑ Review all of the features packed in the Calendar view windows.

- ☑ Print your calendar (sometimes you just have to have it on paper).

- ☑ Use the Task List view to organize your day.

- ☑ Learn to make changes to activities that have already been scheduled.

- ☑ Understand how you can use the History feature to document your conversations.

- ☑ Create a note for a Contact.

ACT! vs. a PIM

If you are thinking that you could continue to use Outlook (or Google Calendar™ or some other simple calendar) to schedule your activities, maybe you should consider the advantages of scheduling your appointments in ACT!. The Outlook types of calendars (called PIMs or Personal Information Managers) are fine for tracking your own time, but not that good at tracking your relationships.

For example, if you wanted to see when was the last time that you met with Lance Parker... in a calendar like Outlook, you would have to scroll back and search for the approximate time... because a PIM is focused on managing your time... not your contacts. Once you clear an activity in ACT!, it becomes a permanent part of your Contact's history. You can electronically search through all old activities to almost instantly find who you spoke with last year about a specific project. (Try doing that from a paper calendar!)

For example, lookup Lance Parker's record in ACT! and view the history tab to see that you last met with him in August (that might have taken some time to locate in another software).

In addition, if your company does not have a way to share calendars, if someone else on your team met with Lance, there would be no way to know that. (Ernst was the first person to open an opportunity with this account years ago.)

Even if the rest of your company is using a corporate calendar like Outlook, scheduling and completing activities in ACT! ensures that you are keeping good notes on the contact's record. Besides... we can sync the ACT! calendar to Outlook so the rest of the company knows what you are up to. How could you not love something that could help you stay so organized and on top of your business and personal life?

Feeling more convinced? Keep reading.

Activity Types

ACT! starts with five basic activity types for you to use in your scheduling.

- Calls
- Meetings
- To-do's
- Personal Activities
- Vacations

 It is also possible to create custom activity types to better manage your day. It is an administrative type of task which you can read more about starting on page 383.

Scheduling Your Day | 89

Activities will appear on any of several Calendars or the Task List views. You can update the Microsoft Outlook calendar with your scheduled ACT! activities, and vice versa. Your ACT! calendar can even display on your smart phone (e.g. iPhone, Blackberry, or Android). No smart phone? Then ACT! can print out your calendar on plain paper or on paper that fits in your Day-Timer®, FranklinCovey®, Day Runner®, At-A-Glance®, or Time/System® planners.

Simple Scheduling

You will only rarely schedule activities with yourself (with your My Record) except maybe to call your Mom...no wait...that's on her record. OK then, perhaps a To-Do to make travel arrangements for vacation...no, that's on the travel agent's record. Maybe...to pick up the cleaning?

So start by looking up the Contact that you will schedule the activity for; scheduling anything is very straightforward and easy. All activities are scheduled in exactly the same way using the same dialog box. The only difference is which menu, keystroke, or icon you use to begin them.

Menu Option	Keyboard	Toolbar Icon
Schedule, Call	[Ctrl+L]	📞
Schedule, Meeting	[Ctrl+M]	🤝
Schedule, To-Do	[Ctrl+T]	✋
Schedule, Other, Personal Activity		
Schedule, Other, Vacation		

 Vacation and Personal Activities can only be scheduled through the menu. They do not have a keyboard shortcut equivalent (by default) or an icon on the Standard toolbar.

Let's start with creating a simple activity (we'll review the more advanced options in the next chapter).

Procedure: To schedule a simple activity

1. Look up the Contact the activity concerns.   You may associate some activities with your My Record, but most will be related to specific Contacts in your database.

2. Click one of the scheduling icons on the toolbar,
   or
   choose **S̲chedule**, and select the appropriate action from the menu,
   or
   press **[Ctrl]+** the corresponding key on the keyboard (see previous page).

The **Schedule Activity** dialog box appears.

☞ *Right-click anywhere on the background of the Contact layout, select **Schedule**, and then click **C̲all...**, **M̲eeting...**, or **T̲o-do...** or **O̲ther**.*

The activity type you chose appears under **Activity Ty̲pe:**. If you wish, you can click the drop-down arrow and change to a different type of activity.

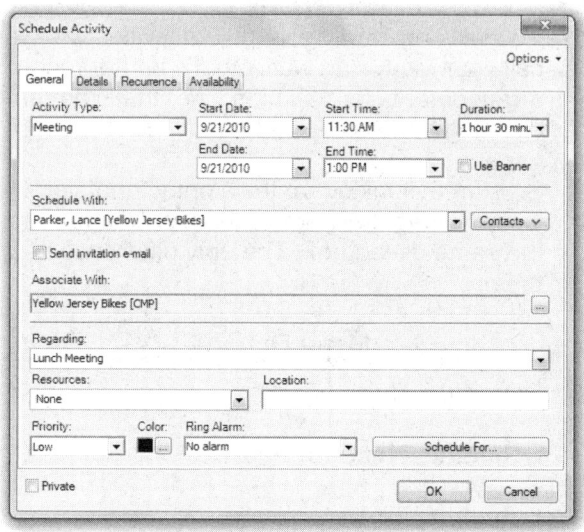

3. Select a **Start Date:**

Normally, the current date displays. You can manually type any date you like or choose a different date by clicking the drop-down list button, and clicking the desired date.

To view a different month in this calendar, click the arrows to the left or right of the month indicator as shown in the illustration at left.

When the drop-down "Mini-Calendar" displays, right-click and drag on the Calendar Header to quickly display a calendar up to three months in either direction.

Scheduling Your Day | 91

4. **End Date:**, while not used very often, it is great for multi-day activities like Conferences or Vacations or Flight Arrival Times.

5. Select a **Start Time:**

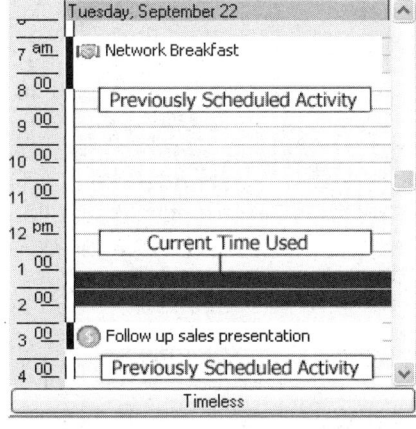

The Duration automatically displays the number of days included in the activity.

By default, the current time is used with a default **Duration:** selected. To choose a different **Start Time:**, click the drop-down arrow. The default time is highlighted on the time line and any previously scheduled activities also appear here.

☞ *If you don't want to assign a particular time for the activity, click the **Timeless** button at the bottom of the list. To-do's and calls are often timeless activities.*

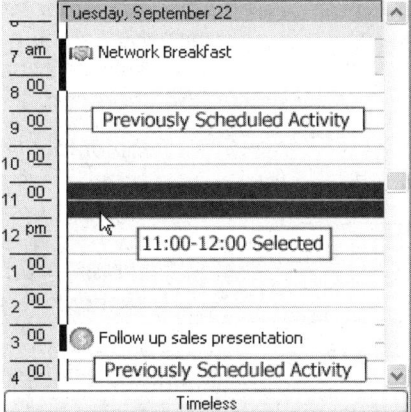

Each hour is divided into two 30-minute intervals. Click the bar next to the time when the activity is to begin.

If you like, you can drag over the appropriate number of bars to block off the duration of the activity (for example, drag over four bars for a two-hour meeting).

6. Either enter an **End Time:** or specify a **Duration:**.

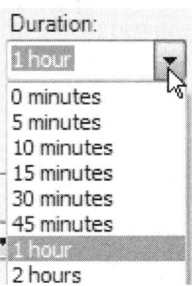

You can also type your duration into the box. If, for example, a meeting is scheduled to last exactly two hours and 17 minutes (hey, it could happen!), you would type **2 hrs 17 min** into the **Duration:** text box.

For airline reservations, you could enter a starting and ending time for the flight. The **Duration** is automatically calculated.

7. Click **Use Banner** if desired.

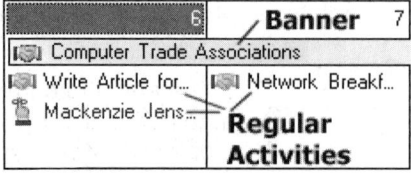

The full-day banner displays as a bar across the box in the **Calendar** view, as illustrated here.

8. Put a check in "**Send invitation e-mail**" to send the activity as a Meeting Request/Invitation (iCalendar format.)

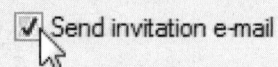

Since not everyone uses ACT! (so sad), this option sends the scheduled activity in a format that other calendars can accept. iCalendar file format works with products like Outlook, Lotus Notes®, Google, Yahoo or Windows Live™ Calendars... even Apple® iCal®, and Facebook.

9. Specify what the activity is **Regarding:**.

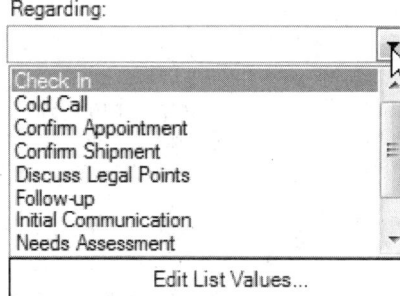

You may select from the options in the drop-down list, or you can type anything you like. The list of commonly used options changes with each **Activity Type:** you select. If you choose to type into the field, you can enter a maximum of 256 characters.

 *If a particular activity you often schedule is not on the list, click the **Edit List Values...** button at the bottom of the drop-down list, choose **Add...**, type the activity description, **OK**.*

10. If appropriate, specify a **Lo_c_ation:** for the meeting.

This is a free-form field in which you can enter the location of the activity.

11. Click the **Details** tab to enter any details that relate to the activity. You can enter as much as you like or cut and paste text from another application into this box (e.g., information the contact sent you in an e-mail).

 *If you would like to attach a related file (or a shortcut to a file) to the activity, use the **Attach...** button to browse to and select the desired file.*

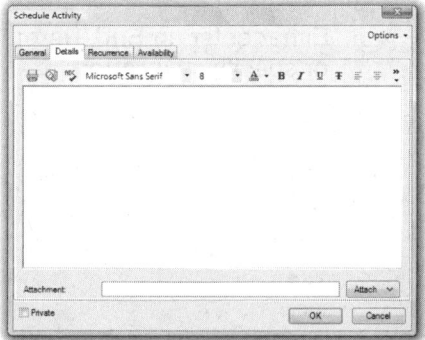

Scheduling Your Day | 93

12. Click OK.

13. If you selected to send an invitation via e-mail, a new Meeting Request dialog will prompt you for additional details prior to sending the Invitation.

    Specifics of the activity are included in the Invitation, as well as anything you included in the Details tab. In addition, any file you attached to the activity in ACT! will also be attached to the Invitation.

    Modify as desired and click **Send**.

We know there are other features, but let's keep it simple for now.

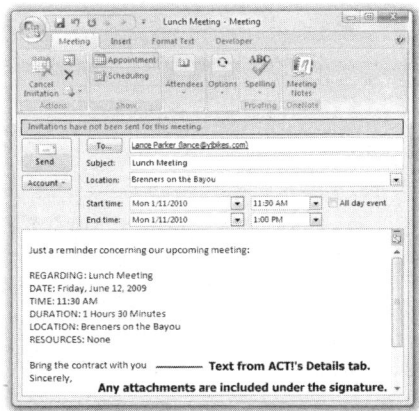

 *If you accidentally schedule an activity that conflicts with an existing activity, the **Conflict Alert** dialog box appears. Click **Accept** to schedule the activity anyway or **Reschedule** to reset the time or date of the new activity.*

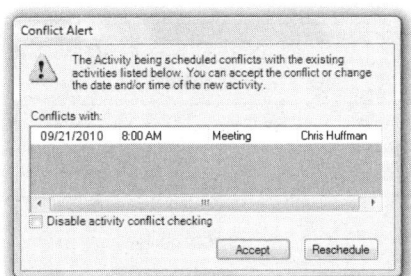

When you schedule an activity, it appears in the **Activities** tab of the Detail View. Activities appear sorted by date.

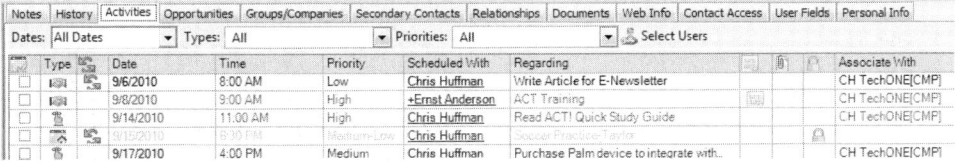

When Details have been entered for an activity, an icon appears in the Details column on the **Activities** tab. To view the details only, double-click this "Details" icon. The **Schedule Activity** dialog box opens, with the **Details** tab displayed. The same icon displays on the Calendar and the Task List to indicate the presence of details in that activity.

Sage ACT!

Practice: Simple Scheduling

What to do	How to do it/Comments
1. Look up the record for **Jackie Jorgensen**.	Right-click the Contact field, choose **Lookup Contact**, enter **jackie j**, and click **OK**.
2. Schedule a meeting.	Choose **Schedule**, **Meeting**, or click the Meeting toolbar button, or press **[Ctrl+M]**.
3. Schedule the meeting for this next Friday.	Click the drop-down button for the **Start Date:** and click next Friday's date. If you need to view next month, click the next-month arrow at the top right of the calendar.
4. The meeting is to last from 2:00 until 3:00 PM.	Click the drop-down button for **Start Time:** and select **2:00**. Click the drop-down button for **End Time:** and select **3:00**.
5. Select **First Meeting** as the reason for the meeting.	Click the drop-down arrow for **Regarding:** and select the phrase.
6. In **Location:**, type: **Meeting at Jackie's office.**	Enter the phrase in the **Location** text box.
7. On the **Details** tab, enter: **Bring crumpets.**	Click the **Details** tab and enter the text.
8. If you are using Outlook, have ACT! send an Invitation.	Put a check in "Send invitation e-mail" to send the activity as a Meeting Request/Invitation.
9. Finish the activity.	Click **OK**.
10. Complete the Outlook Meeting invitation as desired and click Send.	Jackie does not have a valid e-mail address, but by clicking send, the meeting will be added to your Outlook Calendar. Verify that it did add the activity to your Outlook Calendar.
11. View the meeting on the Contact's record.	If necessary, display the **Activities** tab. The meeting should display there.
12. View the meeting Details.	Double-click the icon in the Details column.
13. Close the **Schedule Activity** dialog box.	Click **OK**.

Adding an Outlook Meeting Request to Your Calendar

Not only can you send Meeting Requests, but you can also receive them and add them to your ACT! calendar. When you open and accept a Meeting Request in your Outlook Inbox, the activity is automatically added to your Outlook Calendar. ACT! can add that same meeting to your ACT! calendar…scheduled with all contacts included on the Meeting Request.

Procedure: To add an Outlook Meeting Request to your ACT! Calendar

1. Open the Meeting Request in Outlook and Accept the invitation.

   The meeting is added to your Outlook calendar.

2. When ACT!'s **Schedule Activity** dialog displays, verify that ACT! has selected the correct contact(s) in the **Scheduled With:** area.

   ACT! adds all contacts in the Meeting Request to the Scheduled With: area. If ACT! can't locate a contact's e-mail in your default database, then the Activity will be scheduled with your My Record. You can manually add/remove anyone by clicking the **Contacts** drop-down and choosing **Select Contacts…**.

3. Complete any details of the activity that you like and click **OK**.

   A copy of the meeting invitation is also added to your ACT! calendar.

 Accepting a meeting request from someone else will add an activity to your ACT! calendar. However, creating (or editing) a new Meeting Request in Outlook will not create (or edit) an activity in ACT!. If you want to create a Meeting Request to appear in both your ACT! and Outlook calendars, you need to start the activity in ACT! (put a check in "Send invitation e-mail" in the Activity dialog).

Preferences for this feature are maintained in the E-mail Setup Wizard and will allow you to set which program will display the activity alarm and determine how ACT! creates (or doesn't create) the activity in the ACT! calendar. The Invitation options are discussed more in detail starting page 168 along with setting up how ACT! interfaces with the Outlook Inbox.

 This is a difficult one to try out, since it requires that someone send you a Meeting Request in Outlook… and besides that, most likely the meeting will be added to your REAL database… not the ACT! demo database.

Sage ACT!

Scheduling Activities Using the Calendar

When you need to schedule an activity for a particular day, you might find one of the Calendar views more convenient than the Detail View.

Procedure: To schedule an activity from the calendar

1. Look up the Contact first.

   This step is not necessary, but it makes the scheduling go faster.

2. Display your preferred Calendar view and select the date for the activity.

   Display the desired day in the calendar. You can use any calendar view.

3. If you chose Daily or Work Week view, select the time and duration.

   The default Activity Type is Meeting.

   If the activity is short, double-click the desired time slot. For longer activities, drag over the appropriate number of bars on the calendar.

   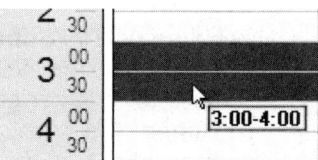

   The **Schedule Activity** dialog box appears. Time and duration are already set for you because you selected them in the calendar.

   ☞ *The* **Schedule With:** *box displays the name of the Contact that is currently displayed in the Detail View. Remember, you can use the drop-down list to change the Contact, if necessary.*

3. The correct **Start Date:**, **Start Time:**, and **Duration:** should already be displayed (if you selected them).

   You can change any of this information as necessary.

4. Fill out the remaining options as desired and click **OK**.

   Change the activity type, priority, alarm options, etc., as with any activity.

Practice: *Scheduling Activities from the Calendar*

What to do	How to do it/Comments
1. Display next week in the **Work Week** Calendar view.	Display the calendar, if necessary. Click the **Work Week** button at the top of the calendar. Click Monday of next week in the Mini-calendar.
2. Select the hour from 4:00 to 5:00 PM on Monday.	Click the **4:00** bar, drag to **5:00**, and release the mouse button. The **Schedule Activity** dialog box appears.

Scheduling Your Day

What to do	How to do it/Comments
3. We will be scheduling a meeting.	Notice that Meeting is already selected for the Activity Type. The date and time are also correctly filled in for you.
4. Select **Morgan Kennedy** as the Contact. (We forgot to look up Morgan's record first.)	Click the drop-down list button to the right of the **Scheduled With:** box, locate, and select **Kennedy**, **Morgan**. *(Hint: Drag over the current name to select it and type **ken** on your keyboard to jump to the first Contact whose last name begins with **ken**.)*
5. Note that the meeting is to be a discussion of contract negotiations.	Display the drop-down list for **Regarding:** and choose **Contract negotiations**.
6. Finish scheduling.	Click **OK**.

Viewing Your Calendar

A good way to start each day is to check your Calendar. When you schedule activities in ACT!, they are added to the Contact's **Activities** tab, but also display in the ACT! Calendar and Task List views. You can view your calendar by clicking the Calendar button on the Navbar. Once a Calendar view appears, you can select the display type from the toolbar at the top of the window.

Procedure: To view the Monthly calendar

1. If you are not viewing the calendar already, click the Calendar button on the Navbar, then click the **Monthly** button on the calendar toolbar,  or

    press [Ctrl+F5].

    The Monthly Calendar view appears.

The Month view of the Calendar shows... well, the *month*. Activities (other than timeless) appear (with very little detail) on the day they occur.

All the selected day's activities (including timeless) appear in the List Pane at the right under the mini-calendar.

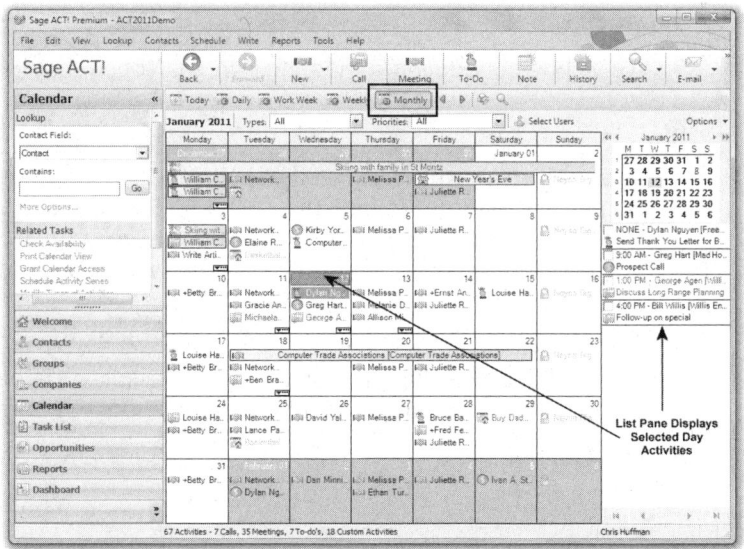

 At the bottom of each Calendar window, the Status Bar displays the total count of scheduled activities for the time period displayed. (If the month displays, the totals are for the month...if the week displays, the totals are for the week, etc.)

Calendar Pop-ups

If you move the mouse pointer over an activity in the Calendar window (or the activity icon in the List Pane), a pop-up window displays showing the basic activity information. Not only does the Regarding and Contact information appear, but you can also see the company name, the actual start Time, Duration, the first few words from the **Details** tab, and any Location you have listed for the meeting.

Note in the example above, you can see that the appointment is scheduled for 3:15. You can only see the first 30 or so characters of the Details section. The ellipsis (...) at the end of the phrase lets you know that more details can be found when you double-click the activity to open it. If a Location has been entered, it will also display.

Practice: The Big Picture View

What to do	How to do it/Comments
1. Display the Monthly Calendar.	Click the Calendar view. If necessary, click the **Monthly** icon on the toolbar. 
2. Notice activities scheduled for the current month. How many are there?	Look at the status bar at the bottom of the calendar.
3. Do you see the meeting that you scheduled with **Jackie Jorgensen** for next Friday?	Point to the activity that you scheduled in the previous exercise to see the details of the meeting.

Navigation Tips for the Calendar Views

In the upper-right corner of all calendar views is a small calendar displaying the current month (unless you change it, of course). Today's date is enclosed in a box. The selected time period on the calendar appears in reverse video (grey number, shaded background). Days on which activities are scheduled are boldfaced.

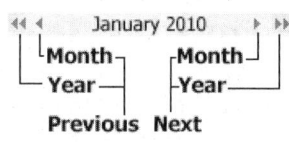

- You can change the current date in any of the calendar views by clicking the desired date in this one-month Mini-calendar.

- You can also view the next or previous month or year by clicking the navigation buttons at the top of the one-month Mini-calendar.

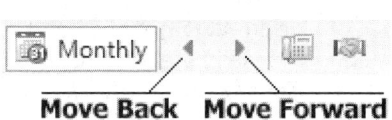

- When in a calendar view, buttons on the toolbar at the top of the screen can also assist your movements through time. These buttons are sensitive to the type of calendar you are viewing (admit it, we could all stand a little more sensitivity in our lives). In the Daily Calendar view, click a button to see the next or previous day. In the Weekly Calendar view, the buttons move to the next or previous week and so on.

- You can also change the current Calendar View. Double-click any day to display that day in the Daily Calendar view. Double-click the month name on the Mini-calendar to display the Monthly view. Single-click the week number (at the left of each week) to display that week in Weekly view.

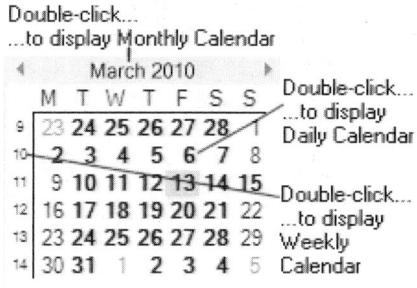

Sage ACT!

The Today Button

The Calendar has four views buttons on the toolbar at the top of the calendar. There is also a **Today** button. This handy button does not change your Calendar view; it simply brings you to today in whatever calendar view you happen to be in. If you jump around in the calendar a lot, this is a very handy feature to bring you back to what is on your plate for today.

Practice: Moving Around a Bit

What to do	How to do it/Comments
1. While still in the Monthly calendar view, click next Friday to see what else is on the calendar for that day.	Click the date in the Mini-calendar.
2. Notice the Mini-calendar. Today's date is enclosed in a box and the date you just clicked appears in a grey shaded box. What do the bold days mean?	Days on which activities are scheduled are in bold.
3. What day of the week is your birthday on this year?	Use the navigation tools.
4. Return to Today.	Click the **Today** button.

Procedure: To view the Daily calendar

1. In Calendar View, click the **Daily** view button on the Calendar toolbar,

    or press **[Shift+F5]** to display the Daily view and the Schedule Activity dialog box.

    The **Daily Calendar** shows your schedule in two ways. A "time line" view appears at the left of the window and a **List Pane** displays on the right under the Mini-calendar.

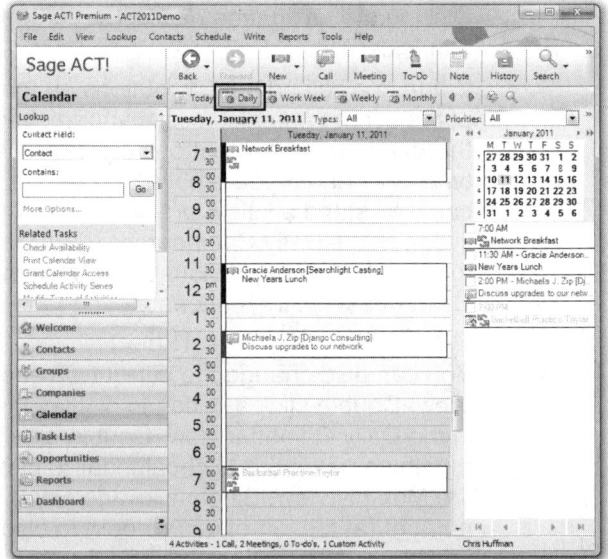

Scheduling Your Day | 101

 Timeless activities do not display on the Calendar time line… only in the List Pane at the right.

Procedure: To view the Work Week calendar

1. In Calendar view, click the **Work Week** button on the calendar toolbar,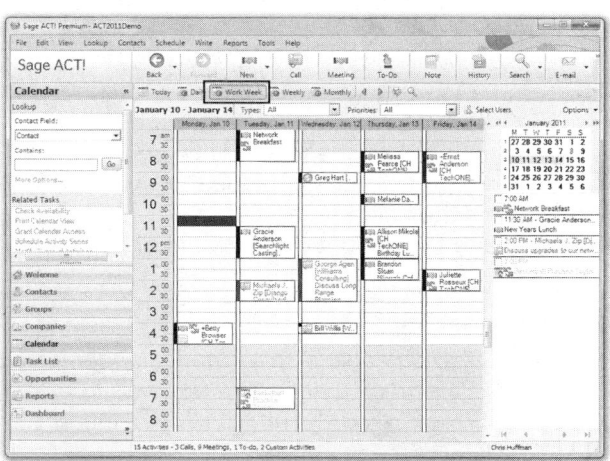

    or press **[Shift+F3]** to display the Work Week view (and the Schedule Activity dialog).

    The **Work Week** calendar shows the defined week (Monday through Friday by default). Timeless tasks do not appear on the actual calendar, but all tasks (for the selected day) appear in the **List Pane** to the right of the calendar.

 *If your work week is other than Monday through Friday, you can change which days display in this view. Choose **Tools**, **Preferences…** from the menu, display the **Calendar &***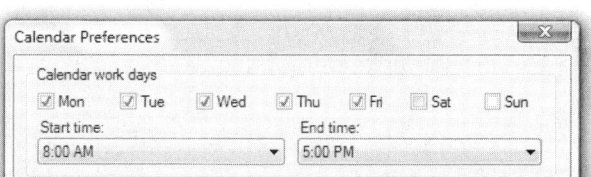
***Scheduling** tab, and click the **Calendar Preferences…** button. Now check or uncheck the days, to define your workweek. You can also define what time the day begins and ends (for those of you who are early risers or late workers… you know who you are!).*

Sage ACT!

Procedure: To view the Weekly calendar

1. If you are in the Calendar view, click the **Weekly** button on the calendar toolbar,

   or press **[F3]**.

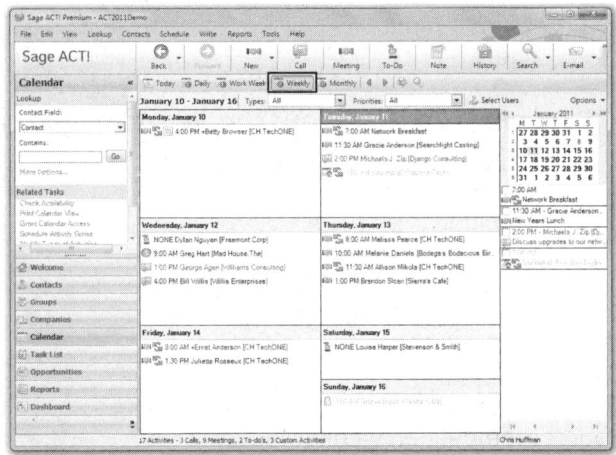

   The Weekly Calendar shows you the whole week Monday through Sunday. All scheduled tasks (including Timeless) appear in both the calendar and the **List Pane** to the right of the calendar.

☞ You can also display the Calendar window from the menu by choosing **View**, **Calendar**. A submenu appears from which you can choose to view the **Daily**, **Work Week**, **Weekly**, or **Monthly** calendars.

Practice: Viewing the Calendar(s)

What to do	How to do it/Comments
1. View the calendar for this week.	In calendar view, click Weekly Calendar icon.
2. Switch to the Day calendar.	Click the Daily Calendar icon or press **[Shift+F5]**.
3. Display the daily calendar for yesterday.	Click yesterday's date on the Mini-calendar.
4. View next month's calendar.	Click the Monthly Calendar icon and then click the **Next Month** navigation button.
5. Return to today.	Click the **Today** button. Notice that the Calendar view does not change to the Daily Calendar view. It only displays Today on the current Calendar view.
6. View the December 2009 Calendar and look up all the Contacts that were scheduled for the month.	Navigate to the December 2009 calendar. Right-click anywhere and select **Create Lookup** or click the icon.

Scheduling Your Day | 103

What to do	How to do it/Comments
7. Display the week of December 3rd in the Weekly Calendar view.	Click the **Calendar** button to return to the Calendar. Click December 3 in the Mini-calendar. Then click the **Weekly Calendar** view icon.
8. Point to several of the appointments to view the calendar pop-ups.	Let your mouse hover over the activities in the calendar to display the pop-ups.
9. Change to the Daily View and test the Calendar pop-ups.	Click the **Daily Calendar** view and navigate to a day with activities on the Calendar time line. 

Filtering the Calendar

It is easy to use the filter area at the top of the Calendar view

 You can also right-click the list and select **Filter Calendar** to display a dialog box with the same filter options all in one place.

The **Types:** filter allows you to control what type(s) of activities display in any of the Calendar views. For example, to only work with your to-do activities, you can uncheck all but **To-do** on the filter list. In fact, you can show (or hide) any combination of activity types.

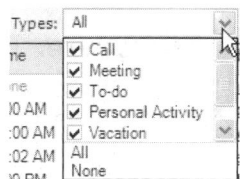

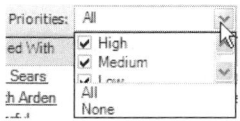 The **Priorities:** filter can also be useful. If you are a very structured person and have set High, Medium, or Low **Priorities** for your activities, you can choose to display only the High priorities for days when your time is at a premium.

The **Options** button, located at the far right of the filtering area allows you to display (or hide) several different activity classes. When an item displays a checkmark to its left, it is active. (You may need to click the **>>** to the right of Select Users button to display the Options button.)

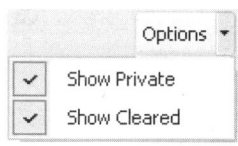

- **Show Private** shows or hides private activities.
- **Show Cleared Tasks** displays cleared tasks. Cleared tasks are designated by a check mark in the box at the start of the row and a line through the text.

No matter which Calendar view you are using, you can create a lookup of all Contacts associated with the filtered calendar by right-clicking anywhere on the list and choosing **Create Lookup** from the shortcut menu or by clicking the **Lookup** icon in the Calendar toolbar. The Contacts display in List View where you can work with each Contact one at a time as you move through your list.

Sage ACT!

Practice: Filtering Your Calendar

What to do	How to do it/Comments
1. Select any Calendar view you like. Filter to display only Meetings.	In the **Types**: drop-down, click **None**. Then click **Meetings** to add it back to the list.

Printing the Calendar

There may be times when you need to have a printed version of your calendar. Whether you carry a brand-name paper calendar like FranklinCovey, Day Runner, or Day-Timer around with you, or you just want something printed on plain paper, ACT! has a terrific printing feature that allows you to take your on-line calendar with you, even if your computer stays behind when you travel.

- The calendar print feature offers dozens of popular calendar layouts for the major paper planning calendars. All you have to do is print using the appropriate format, punch the pages, put them in your book, and you're off.
- Many companies offer pre-printed, pre-perforated calendar inserts designed for just this purpose.
- There are also plain paper options, if all you need is a basic printout.

Procedure: To print a calendar

1. View the calendar you want to print (day, week, or month).

   You can change your mind in the next step, but if you select the view you want, you won't need to change the options and your current calendar filters will be used.

2. Choose **File**, **Print...**,

   or click the **Print** icon,

   or press **[Ctrl+P]**.

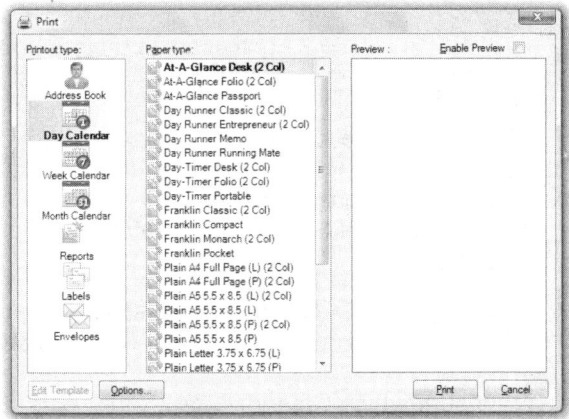

Scheduling Your Day

3. Select a **P**rintout Type:, if necessary (the active calendar view is assumed).

   If you want to change to a different calendar view, choose it from the **P**rintout Type: list. For each printout type, a different list of layouts is listed in the **P**aper Type: column.

4. Select the desired **P**aper type:.

   Click one of the choices in the list. A preview of the page appears on the right. If necessary, click the **Enable Preview** checkbox to see how your activities will look on the selected page type.

5. If you wish to customize your printout, click the **Options...** button. The Calendar **Options** dialog box displays several customization options.

   Click **Print text in black** if some of your calendar entries are displayed in a light color that might not display well in black and white.

6. From the Calendar **Options** dialog box, you can also click the **Filter...** button to filter users, dates, activity types, priorities, etc.

   The filters you selected for your calendar view will be displayed for you to modify.

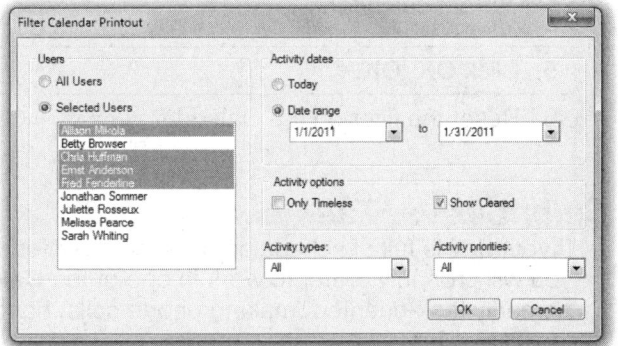

7. After setting desired calendar and filter options, click **OK** until you return to the initial **Print** dialog box, then click **OK** once more.

   Another **Print** dialog box appears. This Print dialog box allows you to control the printer itself, number of copies, etc.

8. Set print options as desired and click **OK**.

   It always helps to be sure that your printer is on, properly connected, and loaded with the appropriate paper before you print.

 *You can also quickly print the current **Calendar** by clicking **F**ile, **Quick Print Current Window**, or by clicking the **Quick Print** icon on the Task List toolbar. This printout is similar to a screen print.*

Sage ACT!

Practice: Printing a Calendar

What to do	How to do it/Comments
1. View next week's calendar, if necessary.	Click the **Weekly** calendar icon and click any date next week on the Mini-calendar at the upper right.
2. Display the **Print** dialog box.	**File**, **Print...**, or click the Print icon.
3. Select **Plain Letter Full Page (P) (2 Col)**.	Scroll down in the list to find the plain paper option and click it.
4. Before printing, check the filter options. Notice that filters set in the previous exercise (only Meetings) are used as your default filter for printing the current calendar.	Click **Options...** to display some basic choices. Click **Filter...** to display a filter dialog box. **Meeting** is selected for both **Activity types:**.
5. Click **OK**, **OK**.	
6. Reset the filter on the Calendar view.	Change the Types back to **All**.

Calendar vs. Task List

If your day is full of scheduled meetings, conference calls, and other time-scheduled events, you will probably prefer to work in one of the **Calendar** views. However, if your day is primarily task-oriented (making phone calls, handling to-do's, etc.), you will want to work in the **Task List** view.

The **Task List** is a different way of looking at the same activities that appear in the **Calendar** (and vice versa). The choice of which to use depends on how you prefer to see the data (as a list or arranged in calendar format).

The Task List

When you schedule an activity with one or more Contacts, that activity appears on the **Activities** tab of their record, along with any other activities scheduled for them. The **Task List** is similar to the **Activities** tab in the Detail View, but it displays a listing of pending activities for *every Contact* in your database.

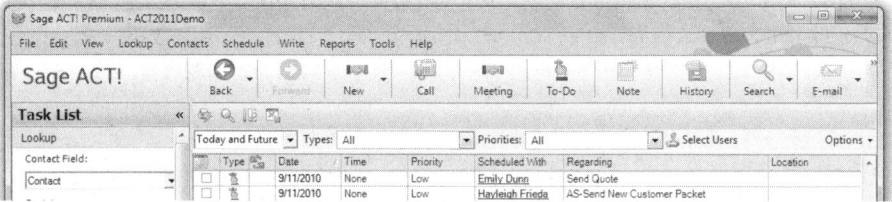

Scheduling Your Day | 107

Procedure: To view the Task List

1. Choose **V**iew, **T**ask List, The Task List view appears:

   or click **Task List** icon,

   or press **[F7]**.

2. Filter as desired.

If you are syncing the ACT! and Outlook or Google calendars, displaying these tasks in the Task List is NOT the default. Click **Options** at the upper right. Click **Show Tasks from other Applications**.

Filtering the Task List

Filtering the Task List is similar to filtering the Calendar views with a few additional options. The Filter area displays at the top of the Task List and contains options for **Dates:**, **Types:**, and **Priorities:**.

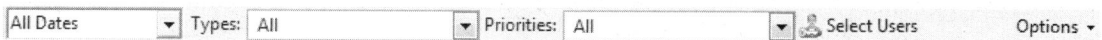

 *You can also right-click the list and select **F**ilter Task List... to display a dialog box with the same options all in one place.*

The **Dates:** filter allows you to display tasks based on pre-defined time frames. You can choose from **Today** (for focusing on what you have to handle today), **Past** dates (for catching up on old items), or **Today and Future** (for getting an overview of things to come). You can also try the **Custom...** option, which allows you to choose specific **From:** and **To:** dates and see the range you *really* want to see. Of course, there is always **All dates** (if you enjoy feeling overwhelmed).

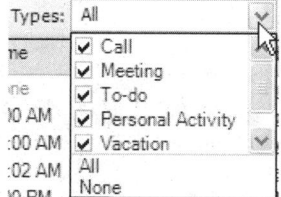 The **Types:** filter provides the same filter options here that are available in the Calendar views. For example, you might want to use the Calendar for your meetings and the Task List for your To-do's and Calls. (Changes in the Task List filter do not affect their display in the calendar.)

The **Priorities:** filter options here are the same as those in the Calendar views. You can choose to display only the High priorities for days when your time is at a premium or only Low priority activities when you feel like procrastinating on the important stuff.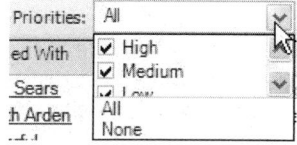

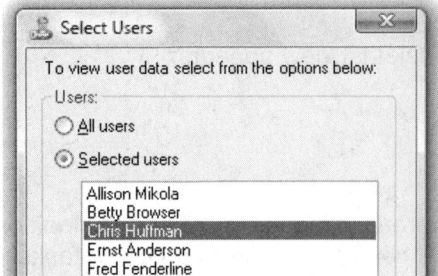

The **Select Users** options is also the same as the Select users button in the Calendar views. Click **All users** to show everyone's activities. Click **Selected users** and click one or more names to select or click a selected name to unselect it. When you click **OK**, your Task List will update to include activities for the selected user(s).

 ACT! remembers your User list selections until you change them to something else.

The **Options** button, located at the far right of the filtering area allows you to display (or hide) several different activity classes. When an item displays a checkmark to its left, it is active. (You may need to click the **>>** to the right of Select Users button to display the Options button.)

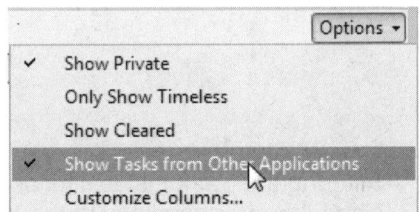

- **Show Private** shows or hides private activities.
- **Only Show Timeless** shows only those activities that do not have a specifically scheduled time.
- **Show Cleared Tasks** displays cleared tasks. Cleared tasks are designated by a check mark in the box at the start of the row and a line through the text in each column.

        ☑ 🏢   10/21/2010   None   Low   Dan Minnick   AS Change ID/Status to Customer
        ☐ 📧   10/21/2010   2:00 PM Low   Michaela J. Zip   Discuss Electronic Catalog

- **Show Tasks from Other Applications** shows tasks imported from the Microsoft Outlook calendar or from the Google calendar.

        ☐ 🏢   9/25/2012   12:00 PM Medium   Chris Huffman   Staff Luncheon - Catered
        ☐ 📧   9/25/2012   1:00 PM   Low   Merkin Muffley   Presentation

- **Customize Columns** allows you to add additional columns to the display, such as the **Company** and **Phone** fields next to the Contact name.

Since the Task List is a list view, you can click on any of the column headers to sort the list. For example, you could group all of your Prospect Calls. If you have a list of scheduled mail-merge Thank You letters, click on the first activity and **[Shift+click]** on the last item. Then right-click and select **Go to Contact** to create a lookup ready for mail-merging.

You can create a lookup of all Contacts associated with the filtered list by right-clicking anywhere on the list and choosing **Create Lookup** from the shortcut menu or by clicking the **Lookup** icon in the Task List toolbar. The Contacts display in List View where you can work with each Contact one at a time as you move through your list.

Scheduling Your Day | 109

You can see all the filtering options in one place, if you wish. Choose **View**, **Filter Task List...** from the menu bar, or right-click anywhere on the list and choose **Filter Task List...** from the shortcut menu.

For each activity, the name of the Contact that each task is **Scheduled With** is underlined. Click the hyperlinked name to "jump" to that Contact in Detail View. If the activity is scheduled with more than one Contact, a plus sign will appear in front of the name in the **Scheduled With** column. When you click a Contact with a + in front of the name, a lookup of all the Contacts scheduled for that activity will appear in the List View.

☞ *If multiple contacts are scheduled for an activity, the names are arranged in alphabetical order by last name. Only the first name (alphabetically) will display on the Calendar, Task List, Activities tab, etc.*

Scheduled with multiple contacts
+Ernst Anderson   USA Sales Meeting
Julie Britton   Follow-up to First Order

You can also export the filtered Task List to Excel by clicking on the icon in the Task List toolbar.

You can print the current **Task List** by first selecting all of the activities and then clicking **File**, **QuickPrint Current Window**, or by clicking the **Quick Print** icon at on the Task List toolbar. The filter options that you have selected will be used as the default for printing your Task List.

Practice: Viewing the Task List

What to do	How to do it/Comments
1. Use the Filter area to view the activities scheduled for Today only.	Select **Today** from the **Dates:** list.
2. View the activities for all past dates.	Display the **Dates:** list and choose **Past**.
3. Create a lookup of all Contacts with these overdue activities.	Right-click anywhere in the Task List view and select **Create Lookup**, or click the icon.

What to do	How to do it/Comments
4. Return to the Task List, display everything, and experiment with some of the other filter options to hide or show certain types and priorities of activities.	Click the Task List icon. Select **All** from the **Dates:** list. Play with some of the other filter lists.
5. Select two activities and display only the Contacts associated with those two activities.	Click the first activity to select it, hold the **[Ctrl]** key down while you click the second, right-click, and select **Go to Contact**.
6. Display the Task List in Excel.	Click the Export to Excel icon.

Printing Your Task List

Want to take your To-do list with you? Click the Export to Excel icon on the toolbar to export the filtered Task List to Excel.

You can also print the current **Task List** by selecting all of the activities and then clicking **File**, **QuickPrint Current Window**, or by clicking the **Quick Print** icon at on the Task List toolbar. The filter options that you have selected will be used as the default for printing your Task List.

Display the Mini-calendar Any Time!

The Mini-calendar is always displayed when you are viewing the calendar. You may find there are times you would like to glance at the calendar without having to leave the Task List or Detail View. Choose **View**, **Mini-calendar**, or press **[F4]**. A three-month Mini-calendar displays on the screen, regardless of what view you are in.

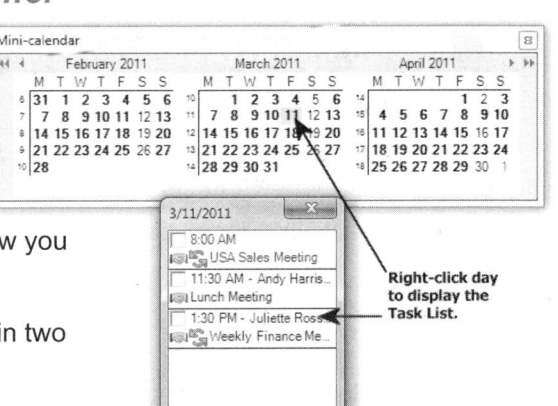

This little pop-up Mini-calendar can be handy in two ways...

1. It gives you a quick view of the calendar in case you want to know what date next Tuesday is.
2. Right-click a bold date to pop open a list displaying your activities. Let your mouse hover over an activity, and a pop-up displays with more activity information. Click a checkbox, and you clear its activity.

Scheduling Your Day | 111

  In other words, you could manage your calendar without leaving the Detail View.

Practice: Mini-Calendar

What to do	How to do it/Comments
1. While in Task List view, display the Mini-calendar.	Press **[F4]**.
2. Right-click a date that is bold to see what you are scheduled for that day. Close the Mini-calendar.	Press **[F4]** again.

Modifying Scheduled Activities

Schedules change. Sometimes a change is a good thing (your tax audit has been canceled). Sometimes it's not so good (the initial meeting with a new client has been set back a week). You can change an activity a number of ways.

Procedure: To modify an activity

1. Select the scheduled activity that you wish to modify in the **Calendar**, the Contact's **Activities** tab, or in the **Task List** view.

   Usually activities are sorted by date.

2. Double-click the activity,

   or **S**chedule, Res**c**hedule Activity,

   or press **[Ctrl+Shift+D]**,

   or right-click and choose **Res**c**hedule Activity...** from the shortcut menu.

   The Schedule Activity dialog box appears for the selected activity.

3. Make your change and click **OK**.

  *If you **modify a recurring activity** (we will discuss these starting on page 146), ACT! displays a dialog box asking if you want to change just this occurrence or all of the originally scheduled occurrences. Click **Edit this occurrence** to change just this one activity or **Edit all occurrences** to change all of the future occurrences of the recurring activity as well.*

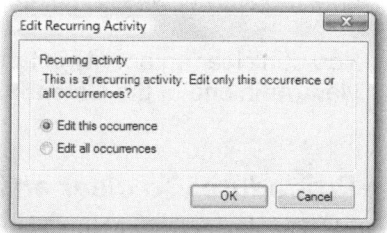

Sage ACT!

 *If you **modify a Meeting Request** that was created in ACT! (and you are using Microsoft Outlook), then be sure to check the Send Invitation E-mail before clicking OK so that changes will be made to the Outlook Calendar and e-mails will be sent to all who have responded to the original request.*

Practice: Ch.. Ch.. Changes

What to do	How to do it/Comments
1. Display the Task List.	**View**, **Task List**, or click the Task List icon.
2. On **Thomas Andrew's** record, change the date of the planned Prospect Call to next Monday.	Right-click the Prospect Call Meeting and choose **Resc**h**edule Activity…**. Click the **Start Date:** button, then click the Today button and then change to next Monday's date in the calendar.
3. Look up **Emma Francis** and edit the phone call we had scheduled with a Regarding of Send international pricing. Change the "Call" to a "To-do" for tomorrow at 1:00PM. Add to the details section: "Include a company brochure as well."	Look up Emma's record. On her **Activities** tab, double-click the row containing the scheduled call. Click the drop-down for **Activity type:** and select **To-do**. Change the date to tomorrow and the time to 1:00PM. Click the **Details** tab. Type the new text and click **OK**.

Clearing Activities

When an activity has been completed, you should "clear" it. Clearing an activity is marking it as complete. After you mark the activity as completed, it is removed from display in the **Activities** tab (unless told otherwise) and recorded in the **History** tab where the date and time the activity was completed displays along with other information about its completion.

You can clear an activity in three places: in the Contact's **Activities** tab, in the **Task List** view, or in one of the **Calendar** views.

Procedure: To clear an activity

1. Display activity in the **Task List** view, on the Contact's **Activities** tab, or in Calendar view.

Scheduling Your Day | 113

2. Click the check box at the left of any activity you wish to clear,

   or select the activity, then right-click, and choose **Clear Activity...**,

   or press **[Ctrl+D]**.

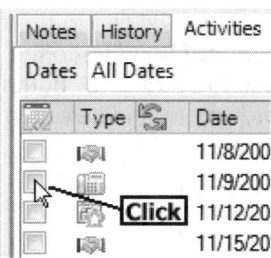

   The **Date:**, **Time:** and **Duration:** that was originally scheduled displays. If this is not correct, you can change it before clearing the activity (in case it didn't go off as planned).

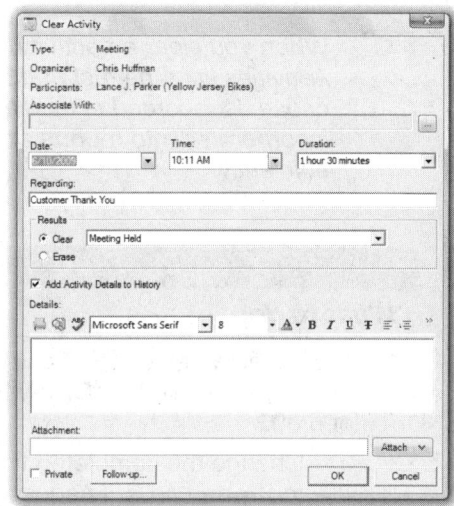

3. Specify the **Results** of the activity.

   If the activity is being cleared, choose the appropriate option from the drop-down list to the right of the **Clear** radio button. If you choose **Erase**, the activity is removed, and no history is recorded.

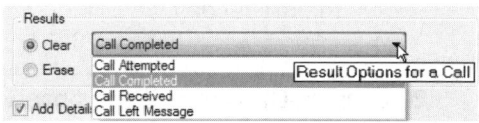

   Options in the Results list depend on the type of activity.

4. If you want any **Details** to appear in the History for the Contact, verify that the **Add Details to History** option is checked, and enter or modify the **Details** section of the dialog box.

   Type any new details of the customer Contact or modify existing details, if necessary. You can type as much as you like here. "I said this and he said that and promised to do this…"

5. To schedule a follow-up activity, click **Follow-Up...** and a new activity dialog box displays for  the same Contact with the same **Regarding** line.

   While scheduling a follow-up is an optional step, we are certain you recognize the importance of keeping the lines of communication open with your Contacts.

6. If you would like to attach a related file (or a shortcut to a file) to the history, use the **Attach…** button to browse to and select the desired file.

   Perhaps a signed contract or a resume? Attached **Files** are copied to the \Attachments folder. Attached **Shortcuts** create a link to the selected file on your PC or network.

7. Click **OK**.

   The activity is now cleared from the list and recorded to the **History** tab. If you scheduled a follow-up, it will be displayed in the **Activities** tab.

☞ When you clear an activity, you do more than just remove it from displaying in the Activities list. The fact that the activity was completed, along with the **Result** you chose, is recorded in the **History** tab for that Contact. This History information can be incorporated into reports and used to help you analyze your work patterns and efficiency.

Practice: Clearing Stuff

What to do	How to do it/Comments
1. View all activities on the **Task List**. Clear the Meeting scheduled for **Bill Willis** scheduled for 6/30. • Change the completed time and date to today and now (if necessary). • Schedule a follow-up call with him for next Tuesday.	Click the Task List icon. Click in the check mark column to the left of the activity. Select the current date and time from the **Date:** and **Time:** controls. Click **F**ollow-Up Activity…. Be sure to change the **Activity type:** to **Call**.
2. Look up **Bill's** record and observe the **Activities** and the **History** tabs.	In Task List view, you can click Bill's hyperlinked/underlined name to quickly take you to his record. ACT! cleared the meeting, recorded it in the **History** tab, and added the call to the **Activities** tab.
3. Display the August 2010 calendar.	
4. You forgot to clear the To-Do to "Customer Thank You" for **Jonathan Jenkins** on 8/26. Add Details: "Brought along new customer packet."	In Calendar view, click the check box to the left of the activity. If necessary, put a check in the **Add Details to Histor**y and type notes in the Details section. Click **OK**.

Scheduling Your Day | 115

What to do	How to do it/Comments
5. Look up Jonathan's record and observe the **Activities** and the **History** tabs.	In the Calendar, right-click the To-Do with Jonathan and select **Go to Contact.**
6. While you are on Jonathan's record, clear the Contract Negotiations meeting as "Not Held.". That meeting was cancelled since Jonathan signed the contract without changes. Notice how the activity is recorded in **History** tab.	Click in the checkmark column to the left of the meeting to clear it. Select the Result **Not held** from the result list. ☞ *If you double-click the activity by mistake and the **Schedule Activity** dialog box displays, click **Cancel**.*

Recording an Unscheduled Activity to History

Aren't there times when instead of scheduling a call you just decide (out of the blue) to give someone a call? Or perhaps someone calls you to inquire about a product or service. Since you did not schedule the call, there is no activity to clear, and thus no History of the call will be recorded. You could schedule the activity, then immediately clear it, but that gets old really fast. There is a better and quicker way… simply record the call directly into History.

Procedure: To record a History entry

1. Look up the Contact you want to record History for.

2. **Contacts, New History…**,

    or right-click anywhere on the Contact layout and choose **Record History…**,

    or press **[Ctrl+H]**.

3. Change the activity **Type:**, if necessary.

    Changing to "Other" will offer Result options relating to E-mail, Fax, or Letter.

4. Specify the **Result:**.

    The activity Type determines what results are available.

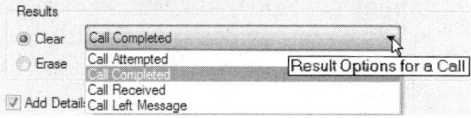

5. Specify **D**ate:, **T***i*me: and **D**u**ration:** if appropriate.

    You may be recording this the day after it occurred. It can be helpful to indicate the date (and maybe time) when it actually happened.

6. Enter something in the **R**egarding: area.

    Remember, you are recording something you have done, not something you need to do.

7. If you would like to attach a related file (or a shortcut to a file) to the history, use the **Attach…** button to browse to and select the desired file.

    Perhaps they sent you a spreadsheet file you wish to associate with this history item. Remember, attached **Files** are copied to the \Attachments folder. Attached **Shortcuts** create a link to a file on your PC or network.

8. Type any pertinent **De**tails. Details should be considered the same as notes.

    Click in the box and type as much as you like in this area. It scrolls forever if need be!

9. Schedule a **Follow-up…** activity, if desired.

    The **Follow-up…** button is located at the bottom of the History dialog box.

10. Click **OK**.

    A history is added to the **History** tab for the Contact.

Practice: Making History	
What to do	*How to do it/Comments*
1. Look up the record for **Benny Lender**.	**L**ookup, **F**irst Name…, type **ben**, and click **OK**.
2. Record the fact that he called to say that our line of credit was approved.	Hot dog!!!!!!. Press **[Ctrl+H]**. The default **T**ype: is **Call**. **[Tab]** to the **R**egarding: box and type **Our line of credit was approved**. Click **Call Received** in the **R**esult: area. Click **OK**.
3. Verify the item in the **History** tab.	Click the **History** tab, if necessary.

Recording History to Multiple Contacts

Sometimes you meet with several people at the same time, and the results of the meeting would be the same on all Contact's records. Consequently, you want the same results to display in everyone's **History** tab…you just don't want to type it more than once!

Scheduling Your Day

Procedure: To record a history entry for multiple Contacts

1. In **List View**, enable **Tag Mode** and select all Contacts for whom you wish to record the same history.

   To enable Tag Mode, display the List View and click the **Tag Mode** checkbox. When you click a row you tag it or un-tag it.

2. Press **[Ctrl+H]**.

   The names of all of the tagged Contacts display in the top of the Record History dialog box.

3. Fill in the Record History as you normally would, click **OK**.

   The same history is recorded on all referenced Contacts.

Practice: Director's Association Meeting

What to do	How to do it/Comments
1. There was a Guild of Influencers meeting (they all have an ID/Status of Influencer). Everyone but Annette Sharkey was there. Record in history for the others that "Members Voted to Raise Dues".	**Lookup**, **ID/Status**, enter "Influencer," and click **OK**. Make sure the **Tag Mode** check box is checked. Untag the first name in the list and select Annette Sharkey. Click **Omit Selected**. Now click **Tag All** to select the remaining names. Press **[Ctrl+H]**. In **Regarding:** type "Guild of Influencers members voted to raise dues." Change **Type** to **Meeting**. Click **OK**.
2. Click the Contacts button to switch to the **Detail View** and verify that the history was recorded on each Influencers **History** tab.	
3. Meant to make a note that Annette wasn't at the meeting. In the **History** tab, double-click the history you just entered, add "Annette was not at the meeting" to the Details section, and click **OK**. What happened?	When a note or history is shared by multiple Contacts, then if you change anything on one, shouldn't it change on all? (Now that is a nice feature.) Select to "Save my changes for all…." Verify that the same phrase was added to the other Contacts' histories.

Filtering History

As you review the history tab, there may be times when you want to limit the history types that display here (e.g. filter out Field Changes or Contacts Deleted).

Click the drop-down and unselect the history types that you no longer wish to view on the tab. Custom activity type histories are also available for filtering. Select or clear the entire history category or choose selected history types only.

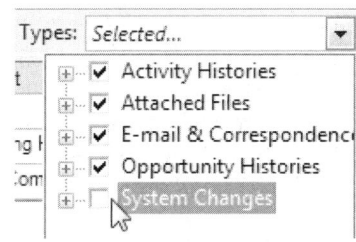

Taking Notes

While the Contact layout provides many fields to record various bits of information, there will invariably be something you want to record for which there is no field. You might want to record details about how a contact likes to do business, for example.

Procedure: To add a Note to a Contact record

1. Display the Contact that you want to enter a note for.

   Use lookup or browse to display the Contact record.

2. Display the **Notes** tab.

   The **Notes** list displays.

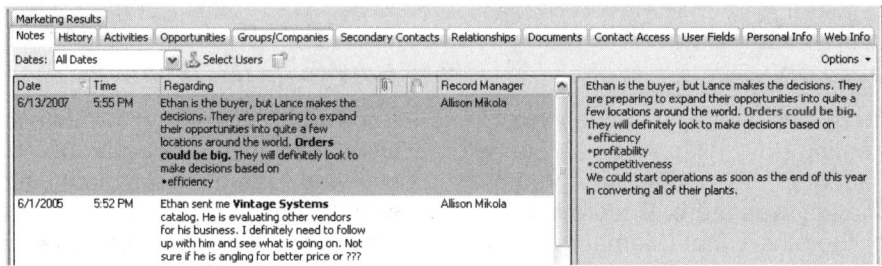

3. Click the **Insert Note** icon at the top of the list,

   An **Insert Note** dialog box displays. The date, time, and Record Manager are entered for you.

   or press **[F9]**.

4. Type the Note.
   - Notes can be as long as you like.
   - You can cut and paste into a note…including graphics.
   - Notes are stored with rich text formatting, which means you can format your notes with *font face*, size, color, and **_attributes_**.
   - You can add bullets.
   - You can check spelling.
   - You can mark the note Private to keep others from seeing it.

   URLs are hyperlinked while in the Note dialog box.

   URLs are hyperlinked while in the Note dialog box.

5. If you would like to attach a related file (or a shortcut to a file), use the **Attach…** button to browse to and select the desired file.

   Attached **Files** are *copied* to the \Attachments folder. Attached **Shortcuts** add a shortcut (link) to a file on your PC or Network.

Scheduling Your Day | 119

6. If desired, link (and display) the same note to other Contacts by clicking on the **Contact...** button.

7. Click **OK**.   The text of the note displays in the **Regarding** column and in the Note Preview pane at the right.

Viewing and Editing Notes

Each time you create a note for a Contact, it displays at the top of the Notes tab, making the most recent entries the most readily accessible. The note also displays the Date and Time it was entered as well as the name of the user (Record Manager) that entered it.

When you select a note, the Regarding contents also displays in the split-panel Note Preview area, allowing you to continue viewing the contents of a specific note while scrolling through the entire notes listing.

To edit a note, double-click it to open it into the Edit Note dialog box.

 *If you have linked the note to several Contacts, when you click **OK**, ACT! will ask you if you want to make the same changes to all Contacts associated with the note.*

The **Note Preview** area allows you to select and copy text without the need to open the note in editing mode. In addition, any hyperlinked text (pointing to a Web site or a document) in this area, when clicked, will open the file in a new window.

 You can disable the Note Preview area by clicking on the Options button at the top right of the Notes tab. Uncheck Show Preview.

Practice: **Making a Note**	
What to do	**How to do it/Comments**
1. Look up the record for **Ethan Campbell**.	**Lookup**, **Co**n**tact...**, type **Ethan Campbell**, and click **OK**.
2. Select the first note on Ethan's record and notice how it displays in the note Preview area. Notice that you can select, right-click, and copy text in the Preview area.	*[Edit Shared Note dialog box screenshot: "This note has been changed and is shared by two or more contacts. Select an option to save your changes." Options: Save my changes for all contacts associated with this note / Save my changes as a new note for this contact. OK / Cancel]*

What to do	How to do it/Comments
3. Add a new note for Ethan. **Travels to Europe every summer.**	Click the **Notes** icon or press **[F9]**. Type the note.
4. Spell check your note.	Click the **Check Spelling** icon.
5. Make **Europe** bold.	Select "Europe" and click the Bold icon.
6. Change the word "summer" to red and italic. Close the note.	Double-click the word "summer". Click the Font Color icon and select a red color. While "summer" is still selected, click the Italic icon. Click **OK** to finish your changes.
7. Edit the note to indicate he is interested in carrying our full line.	Double-click the note to open it in edit mode.
8. Make "full line" bold, green, and italic.	Select the words "full line" and change the color. While it is still selected, click the Bold and the Italic icons.
9. Close the note.	Click **OK**.
10. Look up Chris Huffman's record. On the **Notes** tab, select the 2/13/2005 note.	**Lookup**, **My Record**. Select the note on Chris' record.
11. Click the hyperlink in the Notes preview pane to open the referenced Web site.	The link displays the ACT! Add-on Solutions Web site.

History vs. Notes

If you ran into Kristi Elmendorf at the club, and she told you about a new product idea she was thinking about, should you record the results of that meeting in a Note or with a History?

Notes are great for recording general information about a Contact, their preferences, how they like to handle invoicing, what they think about their competition, etc. Notes are, by their nature, quite general. They are great places for recording facts for which your database has no specific fields.

History, on the other hand, can be created for phone calls made, phone calls attempted, letters written, and meetings completed (among other things). As a result, history works well for reporting the result of your activities…your contacts with the Contact.

Certain history types (Calls, Meetings, and Letters) also cause some of the ACT! system fields to be automatically populated. For example, when you clear a scheduled Call (or Record History for a Call), the date displayed in the "Last Reach" field is changed to reflect the date that the "Call Completed" history is created. In addition, the name of the user who made the change is recorded in the "Last Edited By" field.

Last Edited	Last Edited by
5/6/2010	Chris Huffman
Last Reach	Last E-mail
4/9/2009	1/10/2006
Last Meeting	Last Letter
4/9/2009	

Because of this, you can perform lookups based on the most recent dates that certain activity types were completed.

- When you clear an activity, both the corresponding system field (if appropriate) and the **Edit Date** field are updated.
- When you enter a history (using [Ctrl+H] or right-click, <u>R</u>ecord History…), the corresponding system field (if there is one) as well as the Edit Date field is updated.
- While there is neither a "Last Note" nor a "Last To-do" system field, the **Edit Date** and **Last Edited By** fields are updated when you enter a Note or clear a To-Do.

☞ *If you want to look up every Contact you have met with over a specific time period, it would be impossible to do if all you enter into the database is notes. A Note doesn't indicate how you gathered the information…was it a meeting or did you just speak with them on the phone? Using the Record History feature allows you to record the nature of the interaction as well as its details.*

Practice: Really…I Talked with Them Last Month	
What to do	**How to do it/Comments**
1. Look up Tommy Morgan and view the system fields (displayed below "Last Results" on the ACTDemo layout.	The System fields could be anywhere. If you don't see them, try the **Contact Access** tab.
2. When was the date of Last Reach?	Apparently you had some phone communication with Tommy in May of 2004. Well, that's too long!
3. What was the call about?	Display the **History** tab and observe the History entry for the completed call.
4. Use the history feature to record your "Chance *meeting* at the club" and enter some notes about your conversation in the Details section of the History dialog box.	[Ctrl+H] to open the History dialog box. Change the **Activity type** from **Call** to **Meeting**. In the **<u>R</u>egarding:** field, type "Chance meeting at the club." Type your notes in the **De<u>t</u>ails:** section. Click **OK**.
5. Did the system field dates change?	Yes!!! Both the Last Meeting and the Edit Date now have today's date entered in them.

Deleting a Note or History

To remove an item from the **Notes** or **History** tab, first select it by clicking on it, then right-click on the selected item and choose **Delete Selected…** Click **Yes** to confirm the deletion.

You can select more than one item and delete all the selected items at once. To select a range of items, click the first one then hold the **[Shift]** key and click the last one. All the Note or History items between the two items will be selected. To select several individual items, click the first one, the hold down the **[Ctrl]** key and click the next desired item. As long as you hold **[Ctrl]** each item on which you click will either be selected or deselected.

 This option to delete (or even modify) notes or history may have been disabled by your database administrator. In addition, you may be only allowed to delete notes and history that you have created.

Rolling Over Your Activities

Sometimes our calendar just gets away from us, and we don't get all of our stuff done on time. As long as unfinished tasks remain on your schedule, they are associated with the day on which they were originally assigned, and it is easy to lose track of them.

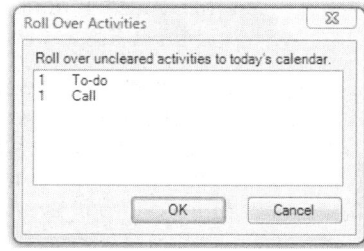

- If you wish, you can "roll over" these missed tasks so they always show up on the current day's calendar.
- You can choose which activity types you want to roll over.

Procedure: To cause activities to roll over

1. **Tools, Preferences…**. The **Preferences** dialog box displays.
2. Click the **Calendar & Scheduling** tab.

   Click the **Scheduling Preferences** button.

3. Select the Activity type you wish to enable roll over for.

   Click the **Automatically roll over to today** option check-box.

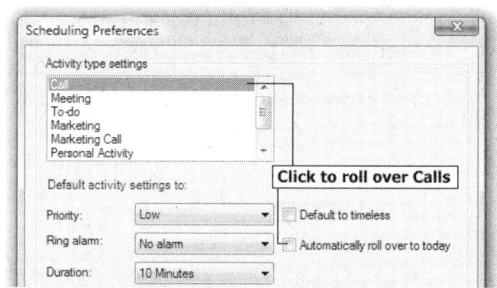

4. Click the *next* **Activity type settings** and select the "Default activity settings" for that type.

It is not likely that you will select to roll over meetings or vacations. If they didn't happen at the designated time, they usually don't roll over to the following day. (Although I guess that could be like accruing vacation days.)

Scheduling Your Day | 123

 While you are in Preferences, you may also want to set the default for your Calls and To-do's to Timeless (who wants to schedule calls for 10:05 and 10:15, etc.). You can always select a time (as for a conference call), but by default they are created with a Timeless designation.

5. Click **OK, OK**.

 *Be careful about using this feature only as a reminder. You might be rolling over less important task/calls and mixing them with the really important ones that are scheduled for today. If you are concerned about forgetting tasks, as an alternate to rolling over your activities, try filtering your Task List to **Past**. As long as you are clearing your activities as you go, you can always get a quick synopsis of what you are behind with.*

The next time you log on, if you have activities to roll over, ACT! will list the number and type and ask you to confirm the roll over. Click Cancel if you don't want the activities to be transferred to today.

Practice: Roll Over

What to do	How to do it/Comments
1. Display the **Task List** view. Observe the dates for the listed activities. Several are overdue.	Click the Task List icon. If necessary, display the filter options. Make sure that **Dates:** is set to **All dates**.
2. Turn roll over on for your To-do's, but not Calls or Meetings. ☞ *Meetings rarely roll over!*	**T**ools, **P**references..., on the **Calendar & Scheduling** tab, click **S**cheduling Preferences..., click **To-do** in the list at the top of the dialog box, and check to **Automatically roll over to today**. Click **OK, OK**.
3. Reopen the **ACT2012Demo** database.	**F**ile, **O**pen/Share Database..., select **ACT2012Demo**, and click **O**pen Database.
4. Confirm the roll-over activities.	Click **OK** to bring the overdue activities to today's calendar.
5. Observe your Task List.	The overdue To-do's are now due today.

Sage ACT! Scratchpad

The Sage ACT! **Scratchpad** is your virtual yellow sticky notepad to help you quickly capture ideas, reminders, phone numbers, etc. Prioritize and check off items once completed, print the list to take it with you, or export the items to your ACT! database. And because it runs as a separate small program outside of ACT!, you can use it with or without opening ACT!.

☞ *Scratchpad is not supported in a Citrix environment.*

Procedure: To work with your Scratchpad

1. Double-click Sage ACT! Scratchpad shortcut on your desktop,

   or click **Start, Programs, Sage ACT!, Sage ACT! Scratchpad**,

   or inside of ACT!, click **Tools, Sage ACT! Scratchpad.**

2. Click in a blank area and enter an item.

3. Press **[Enter]** to end the entry and move to the next line to create a new one.

   Use the Bold or Italicize icon to format your entries as desired.

4. Arrange the items in any order you like by using the **Up** and **Down** arrows on the toolbar.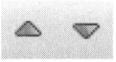

   You can also drage the items to their new location.

5. To mark an item as complete, click the item's check box or select the item and click the **Mark Item Complete** icon.

6. To delete a single item, select the row and click the **Delete** icon (x) on the toolbar.

   To clear the entire list, click on the **Clear Sage ACT! Scratchpad** icon. Click **Yes** to delete all items

7. To print the list, click the **Print** icon.

   The list is printed with checkmarks, formatting, and grid lines.

Scheduling Your Day | 125

Transfer a Scratchpad item to ACT!

If you have an item that you want to transfer to your ACT! database as a Note or History or as a scheduled Activity, then you don't need to retype everything.

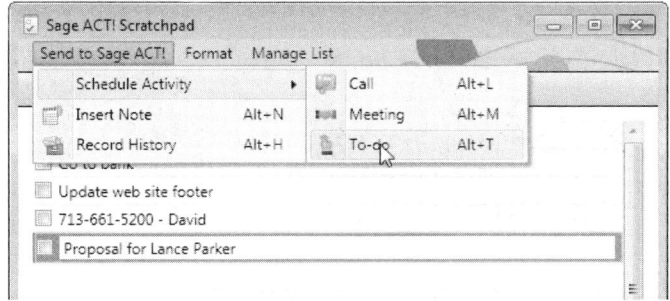

Procedure: To schedule an activity, insert a note, or record a history

1. Open ACT!.

2. Back in Scratchpad, select the item you want to transfer to ACT!.

3. Click **Send to Sage ACT!** and select either **Schedule Activity**, or **Insert Note** or **Record History**.

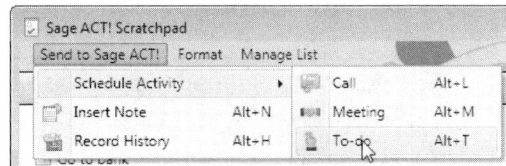

4. In the ACT! dialog that displays, type the Last Name, First Name in the Contact (or Schedule With) box to assign the item to a contact in your database (use the drop-down to help you narrow your selection).

   The Regarding will be filled in with the text from the Item.

5. Make changes as necessary in the Schedule Activity, Insert Note, or Record history dialog.

6. Click **OK**.

7. Back in Scratchpad, delete the item if desired.

Practice: Using Scratchpad

What to do	How to do it/Comments
1. Display Scratchpad.	In ACT!, click **Tools, Sage ACT! Scratchpad.**
2. Enter the top five items that you plan to accomplish this week.	
3. Arrange them in the order that you want to accomplish them.	Drag them or use the arrows to arrange the list.
4. Compete a few items.	Put a checkmark beside one or two of the items.
5. Send one of them remaining items to Chris Huffman's record as a history item.	Select the item. **Send to Sage ACT!, Record History.** In the Contacts field type Huffman or use the drop-down and select **My Record** at the bottom of the list. Note that the Regarding matches the text from Scratchpad. Click **OK**.
6. Back in Scratchpad, delete the item you just transferred.	Select the item and click the **Delete** icon.
7. Exit Scratchpad and then re-open. Is your list still there?	

Review: Scheduling Your Day

1. Schedule a call to Bruce Baker next week to see if he wants to discuss the TechONE systems for his company.
2. Clear the call that is scheduled with Mackenzie Jensen to confirm the shipment. Use whichever view you like to clear it.
3. You sent roses to your employee Melissa Pearce in appreciation for all the work. Record it in history on Melissa's record.
4. Add phone numbers to your Task List display.
5. Check out who we've written notes for this week.

Advanced Scheduling

Since keeping track of our schedules is sometimes not that straightforward, we will review all of the advanced scheduling options that ACT! offers. You will:

☑ Review the General and Advanced Scheduling options.

☑ Understand the intricacies of scheduling recurring activities.

☑ Sync your ACT! Calendar and Contacts with Outlook or Google

Scheduling

In the previous section, we focused on very basic scheduling and clearing of activities. However, much of our scheduling these days seems to be anything but basic. You can choose other options in the Scheduling dialog box. Let's review them now.

Scheduling for Other ACT! Users

When you share an ACT! database with other users on a network, you may find yourself in the enviable position of assigning tasks to the other ACT! users. Each activity in the Task List and Calendar is scheduled for one user or the other. In effect, each user of your database has a personal Task List and Calendar.

ACT! allows one user of a shared database to create activities for another user. However, it is up to you (the user) to grant scheduling rights to other users.

Procedure: To grant scheduling rights to other users

1. **Schedule, Grant Calendar Access…**.   The **Calendar Access** dialog box displays.

    All users (other than yourself) are listed. Every user can view every other user's calendars (can't change that). Managers and Administrators already have access to both **View and Schedule** for all users in the database. Permission to schedule an activity on your behalf can only be modified for Standard and Restricted users.

     Browse users can't schedule anything.

    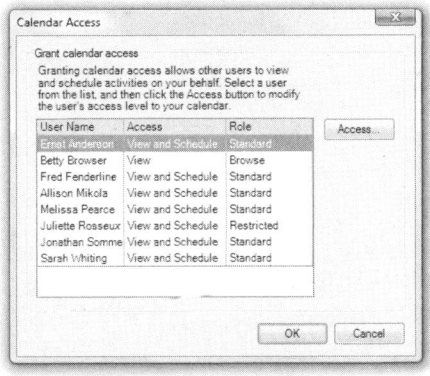

2. Select the user you wish to grant scheduling rights to your calendar. Click **Access…**.   The **Edit Access** dialog box displays.

    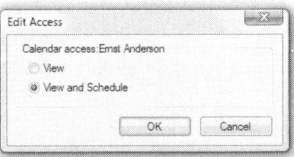

3. Choose **View and Schedule** and click **OK**.   It probably goes without saying if you choose **View**, the selected user can view your calendar but not schedule activities for you.

4. Repeat steps 2 and 3 for other users for whom you wish to grant/restrict scheduling access, click **OK**.   The modified users are now be able to schedule activities for you (or not).

Advanced Scheduling 129

Once you have been granted scheduling access to another user's calendar, you can begin to load up their calendar for them (be careful, you know what they say about power corrupting…).

Procedure: To schedule an activity for someone else in your company

1. Look up the Contact you want to schedule the activity with.

   Example: To set up lunch with Betty Jones for a fellow employee named Allison, look up Betty, *not* Allison.

2. Create the activity as you normally would.

3. Click the **Schedule For…** button at the bottom of the Schedule Activity dialog box.

   The **Schedule For** dialog box displays with your name as the user for whom the activity is scheduled.

4. From the **Schedule this activity for:** list, choose the user you want to assign this activity for. Remember, unless they grant you the right to schedule for them, you may not see their name in the list.

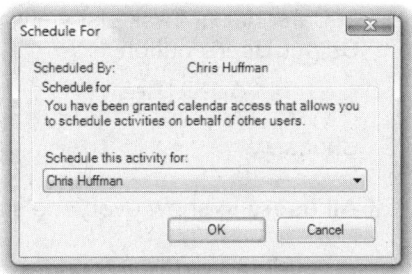

5. Click **OK** when you are done.

   The activity displays on the designated user's calendar.

 If you have been assigned an Administrator or Manager security role, you already have the right to schedule for other users. They don't need to grant you access.

Practice: Getting the Monkey Off Your Back	
What to do	**How to do it/Comments**
1. Wow, you've got so much to do this week. Let's delegate a few things.	
2. There are at least two activities we could ask others to handle for us… • Ask Melissa (your Assistant) to call Sandy Ryan to schedule your next meeting date. • Select any activity that you like on the Task List and reassign to Allison Mikola.	Look up Sandy Ryan. Click the **Schedule Call** icon on the toolbar. In the **Regarding** box, type "Schedule a meeting." Click the **Schedule For** button and select Melissa from the user list. Finish scheduling the activity. Display the Task List view. Double-click an activity to edit it. Click **Schedule For…** and change user from Chris Huffman to Allison Mikola. Click **OK**.

130 Sage ACT!

What to do	How to do it/Comments
3. What happened to the activity?	It was removed from your list since it isn't scheduled for you any more.

Displaying Multiple Users in Your Calendar or Task List

If you share a database with other ACT! users, you may find it useful to see their activities in the Calendar view, as well as your own. Usually ACT! shows only your own activities in the Calendar or Task List views, but you can easily display other users' schedules as well.

Procedure: To filter the Calendar or Task List for a user

1. In Calendar or Task List view, click the **Select Users** button.

2. Choose…

   All users to show everyone's activities,

   or **Selected users** to hand-pick the display.

3. Click **OK**.

Click any name to select it; click a selected name to unselect it.

 ACT! remembers your User list selections until you change them to something else.

Any activity scheduled for another user displays that user's name in square brackets to the left of the activity text. The List Pane to the right of the calendar displays the selected day activities grouped by the names of filtered users on "header" buttons. Clicking one of these buttons displays the activities for that user. The logged-on user will always be displayed at the top of the list.

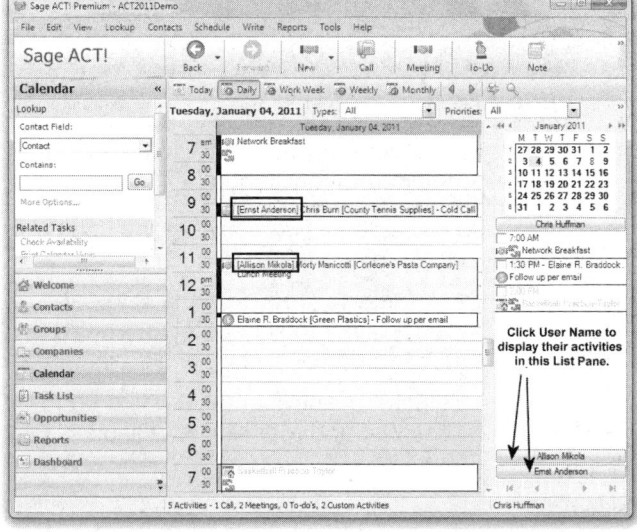

Advanced Scheduling | 131

 When filtering your Calendar view by users, if your selections include more than 10 users, you will see an information dialog box letting you know that as you add more users, it may be difficult to read the calendar.

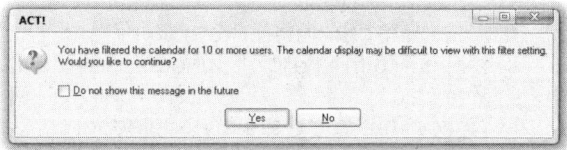

Adding "Scheduled For" to Task List View

The Task List (as well as the **Activities** tab) allows you to add the **Scheduled For** column to display the user for whom the activity is scheduled. Right-click in the view and select **Customi_z_e Columns...** from the shortcut menu. Select **Scheduled For** from the **Available Fields** list and click the "arrow button" to add it to the **Show as columns in this order** list. You can use the **Move Up** or **Move Down** buttons to change the column order if you wish.

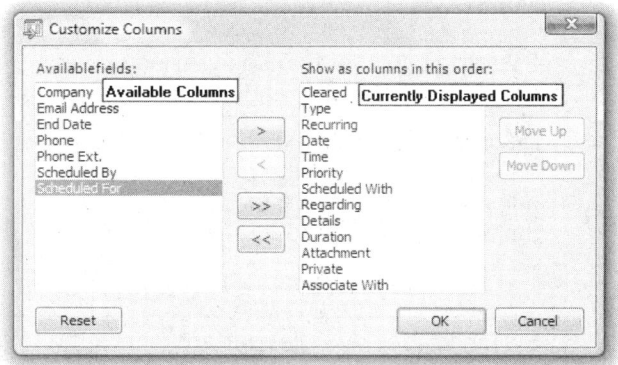

You might wish to add other fields to the Task List view while you are here (Company and Phone, maybe). You might also want to remove columns you don't want to see (such as Priority, if you don't use that feature).

ACT! remembers your changes from session to session, so feel free to customize.

Practice: Viewing Other Users' Stuff

What to do	How to do it/Comments
1. Filter the Task List view to display only Allison Mikola's activities.	In Task List view, click the **Select Users** button in the Filter area. Your user name (Chris) should already be highlighted. Select Allison Mikola's name, and then click your name (Chris) to clear it. Click **OK**.
2. How many activities are on Allison's list of tasks?	A few.

What to do	How to do it/Comments
3. Add the **Scheduled For** column and move it to the right of Scheduled With. Notice that some are scheduled for Allison, one is scheduled with Allison only, and she is one of several Contacts scheduled to attend three meetings.	Right-click in the view and select **Customize Columns....** Select **Scheduled For** and click the **Add** button. The field is added to the bottom of the list. Click it and click **Move Up** until it displays right below Scheduled With. Click **OK**.
4. View the Monthly Calendar. Filtering the Task List does not automatically filter any of the Calendar views. Filter the calendar to display Allison, Chris, Ernst, Juliette, and Sarah.	Display the Calendar View. Click the Monthly button, if necessary. Right-click, **Filter Calendar...**, or click the **Select Users** button and make sure all five names are highlighted, and click **OK**.
5. Display next month's calendar. Click on any Friday, observe the activities in the calendar, and observe the List Pane to the right of the calendar. ☞ *The logon user name displays first.*	In the Calendar, activities for users other than yourself display the user's name in square brackets (**[ ]**) followed by activity information. In the List Pane, you will see "user headers" that organize the list by user name.
6. Switch to Weekly Calendar and check the filter.	The same filter is used for all Calendar views.
7. Change the filter back to display only Chris Huffman.	In the **Select Users** dialog box unselect the other users by clicking on them again.
8. Return to the Task List view and filter the Task List to only display *your* activities for Today (since all you can handle is what is on your plate for today...not so overwhelming anymore).	In the **Select Users** dialog box, click Chris to add, and click Allison to unselect the name. Only Chris' name should be highlighted. Click **OK**. Filter the dates to show **Today**. Click **OK**.

Advanced Scheduling | 133

Scheduling for Multiple Contacts

If "one-on-one" meetings are a rarity for you (it's all about committees nowadays, isn't it?), ACT! is ready to oblige. You can schedule an activity for multiple Contacts, just by adding them to the list.

Procedure: To schedule an activity for multiple Contacts

1. Look up the first Contact and create the activity. Don't click **OK** yet.

   Create the activity (page 89) as you would for the one Contact: set type, date, time, duration, regarding, etc.

2. Click the **Contacts▼** button and choose **Select Contacts....**

   The **Contacts▼** button appears to the right of the **Schedule With:** box in the **Schedule Activity** dialog box. The **Select Contacts** dialog box displays:

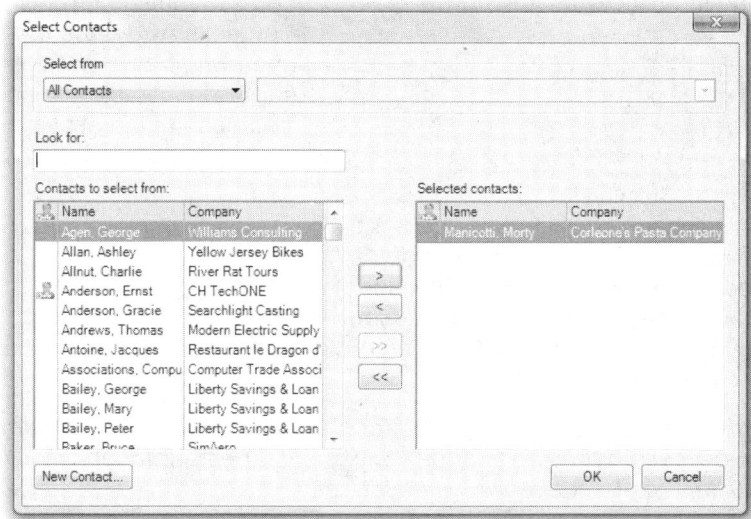

3. Locate the first additional Contact, select the name, and click the **Add** button (or double-click the name).

   The name is added to the **Selected Contacts:** list on the right of the dialog box.

   ☞ *You can locate the name more quickly by typing the last name in the **Look for:** box.*

   Repeat until you have added all desired Contacts to the list, and click **OK**.

4. If you wish to schedule a separate activity for each selected Contact, click **Options** (at the top right of the dialog box) and select **Create separate activity for each contact**.

   For example, create separate activities for follow-up calls to an event. Otherwise, clearing a multi-Contact call activity for one of the Contacts will clear it for all of them.

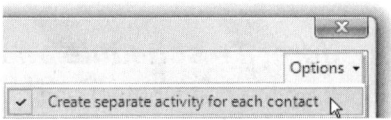

When an activity is scheduled for multiple Contacts, you will see their names (and companies) in the **Schedule With** dialog box, displayed in alphabetical order.

 *The box is not large enough to display more than two or three names at a time, but you can display the **Select Contacts** dialog box to see the entire list (step 2 in this procedure).*

5. Complete the activity as you normally would.

   The scheduled activity displays in each Contact's **Activities** tab. Then, depending upon whether or not you checked **Create separate...** in step 4, one or multiple instances of the activity will display in the Calendar and Task List views.

If an activity is scheduled with more than one Contact, a plus sign will appear in front of the name. In the Calendar view, you can right-click and choose **Go to Contact** to display the associated Contact(s) in List View. In the Task List view, you can click the hyperlinked Contact name to display the associated Contact(s) in List View.

```
Scheduled with multiple contacts
+Ernst Anderson    USA Sales Meeting
Julie Britton      Follow-up to First Order
```

 If multiple contacts are scheduled for an activity, the names are arranged in alphabetical order by last name. Only the first name (alphabetically) will display on the Calendar, Task List, Activities tab, etc.

Let's go back to the **Select Contacts** dialog box for a minute. It contains a number of useful options:

- If you performed a lookup to display everyone you wanted for the particular activity, you can choose **Current lookup** from the **Select from** list at the top left of the dialog box to display a list of only those Contacts in the lookup. You can then click the **Add All** button (**>>**) to add the entire lookup to your list.

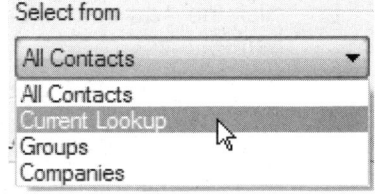

Advanced Scheduling

- In the header, click the column header named **Name** or **Company**, and you will sort the list by that column in ascending order. If several Contacts from a specific company will attend, it's easier to select them if you sort by Company.

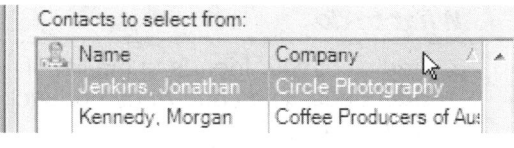

- When you type in the **Look for:** box, the sorted column will be searched, so, if the list is sorted by name, type the last name of the Contact you want to find. If you want to search for a company, sort by the **Company** column and type the company name in the **Look for:** box.

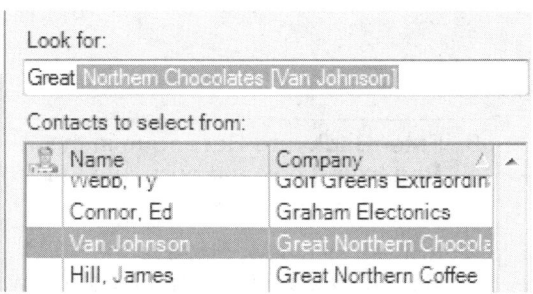

- When you schedule a multiple-contact activity, by default you create only one activity. When the activity is complete, you need only to clear it once to clear it for all Contacts. This works well for meetings where all of the Contacts in the list attend.

If you click **Options**, **Create separate activity for each contact** (at the top left of the **Schedule Activity** dialog box), you create a series of separate activities, each of which have to be cleared individually. This works well for activities such as follow-up calls to each Contact after a marketing campaign or trade show, where you want to clear each call as it is completed.

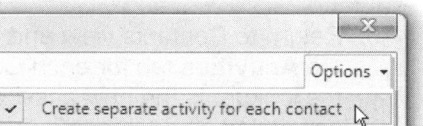

☞ *You can shortcut the process of scheduling for multiple Contacts by using the List View. First, do a lookup to display the list. Now enable **Tag Mode** (click the checkbox at the top of the List View) and tag all of the Contacts you wish to include in your activity. Schedule the activity as you normally would (click the toolbar icon or select from the **S̲chedule** menu). All of the tagged records are included in the Schedule With box. Set the remaining options as you normally would.*

Practice: A Party

What to do	How to do it/Comments
1. Look up ID/Status of Friend. Schedule a meeting for next Monday at 6:00PM for three hours with **Morty Manicotti**. Leave the activity displayed.	**L̲ookup**, **I̲D/Status** of "friend." Double-click Morty's name, click the **Schedule Meeting** icon, and schedule this as you would any activity.

136 | Sage ACT!

What to do	How to do it/Comments
2. Add all of your friends to the list of attendees. Then add Andy Federici to the list.	Click the **Contacts** ▼ button and choose **Select Contacts....** In the **Select from** area, change from "All Contacts" to "Current Lookup." Click the >> (**Add All**) button. Change the **Select from** back to "All Contacts." In the **Look for:** area type **fe**, (Andy's name should be highlighted), click **Add**, and then **OK**.
3. Enter **Backyard Barbeque** in the **Regarding** box and complete the activity.	Type **Backyard Barbeque** in the **Regarding:** box and click **OK**.
4. In Task List view, observe the **Scheduled With** column for the new activity.	The first name (alphabetically) will display on the Task List as a link.
5. Use the **+<name>** link in the Task List to look up the scheduled Contacts.	Click the link and List View displays with all of your Contacts for the Barbeque.
6. Return to Contacts view and observe the **Activities** tab for each Contact in the lookup. Is the new activity scheduled on each one?	Of course it is… You don't trust us?

Availability (Premium Only)

If you are using ACT! Premium, the Schedule Activity dialog box displays an additional tab. The **Availability** tab allows you to…

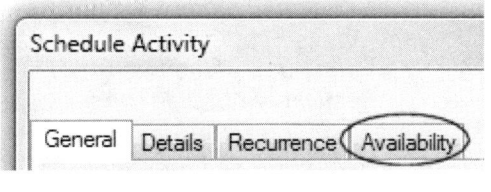

- Check your fellow ACT! users' availability at the time you wish to schedule the activities (assumes they are using ACT! to schedule their day), and then
- Add the activity to each selected ACT! user's calendar and create an ACT! invitation for those *users* (team members).

The **Availability** tab reads the ACT! calendar (not the Microsoft Outlook Calendar) to determine each user's schedule. This feature is not to be confused with Scheduling an Activity on behalf of another user (page 129). It is also different from checking the "Send invitation e-mail" which creates a Meeting Request in Outlook (page 178) for all included users. The Availability tab is only used when you are scheduling for multiple team members.

Advanced Scheduling | 137

Procedure: To invite other users to an activity

1. Create the activity as you normally would.

   Set the time, date, regarding etc. as you would with any other activity.

2. Display the **Availability** tab.

   If you are using ACT! Premium, the **Availability** tab appears.

   The **Availability** tab initially displays your name and indicates the scheduled activity time (between the two vertical bars). *Nobody has been invited to this activity yet, but it looks like Chris has a conflict at 8:00.*

   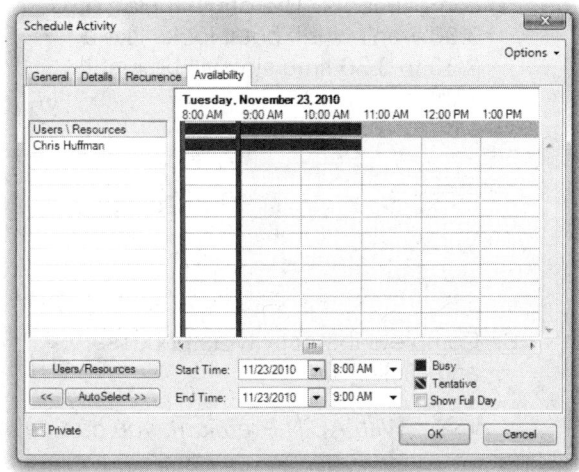

   You can change the scheduled time and date from the **Start Time:** and **End Time:** controls at the bottom of the tab area or by clicking and dragging on the grid area.

3. Click **Users/Resources**. On the left is a list of available ACT! users. On the right is (or soon will be) a list of those users you wish to invite.

   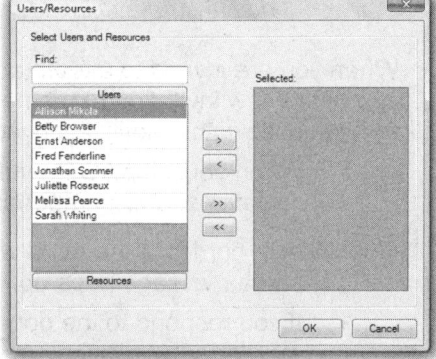

4. Select the first invitee and click the **Add** button. Repeat with the next until the **Selected** list includes all of your invitees.

   You can also add **Resources** to your activity (Meeting Rooms, equipment etc.). Click the **Resources** button to display a list. (To define resources, choose **S**chedule, **Manag**e, **Resources**....)

5. Click **OK**.

   The **Availability** tab appears. All invitees are now listed on the left. If their calendars contain any conflicts with your activities, you will see them on the grid.

In this example, it looks like everyone is busy until 2:00PM. Conference Room 1 is free at that time as well. While Juliette is available the rest of the afternoon, both Allison and Chris have prior commitments. The original plan of 3:30 won't work, but it looks like a 2:30 to 3:30 time slot will be just right.

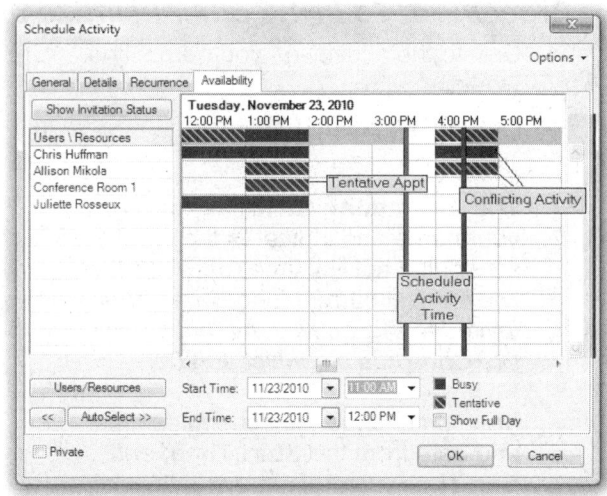

6. Complete the activity as necessary, and click **OK**.

The activity is now scheduled in your calendar, and the users you chose have been invited.

☞ *With ACT! Premium, you can define resources (**Schedule**, **Manage**, **R**esources…), and then include them in your activities, by "inviting" the resource as you would another user. In doing this, you are allowing ACT! to track and display the availability of these valuable resources (along with your coworkers).*

When you are invited to a team activity, ACT! notifies you of the new invitation(s) the next time you log on to the database with a notification icon…not an e-mail.

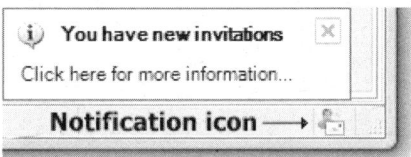

- When you start ACT!, and you have new invitations, an icon appears in the bottom right corner of the ACT! window and a message pops up.
- If you respond to the pop-up message (by clicking anywhere in the message box), the Invitations list appears.
- Use the **Go to Calendar** button to display the selected day in your calendar (in the background) so you can check your schedule.
- Use the **Open Activity** button to open the selected Activity to see who else (Show All…) has been invited or to see more of the Details.

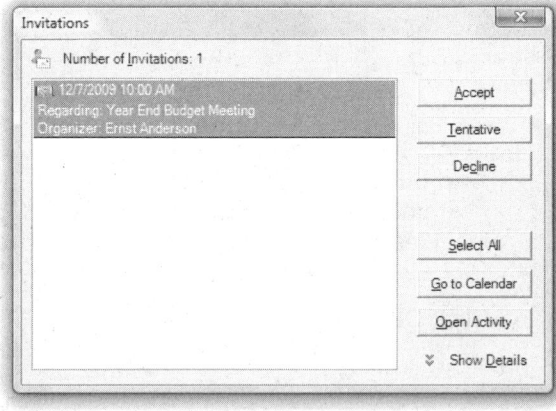

Advanced Scheduling | 139

- **Show Details**, if necessary, to see the basic details of the selected activity.

 If you ignore (close), the invitation notice, you can redisplay the invitation list any time by clicking the Notification Icon displayed in the lower-right corner of ACT!'s window.

Responding to an ACT! Invitation (Premium Only)

When you notice an invitation notification, it's only polite to respond. After all, you don't want to end up the subject of a Dear Abby column, do you?

Procedure: To respond to an invitation

1. Display the **Invitations** dialog box, if necessary.

    When the Invitations icon displays in the lower-right corner of the ACT! window, click the notification icon to display the Invitations window.

2. Select the first invitation by clicking on it. (You can select multiple ones.)

    To select more than one invitation, click the first one, then hold **[Ctrl]**, and click the next, and the next and …

3. Click either **Accept**, **Tentative**, or **Decline**.

    If you choose Accept, the activity is placed on your calendar. If you choose Tentative, the activity is placed on the calendar with diagonal stripes indicating tentative acceptance. If you Decline, the activity is removed from your calendar. Regardless of your choice, the invitation is removed from the **Invitations** list.

If you tentatively accepted a meeting, it appears on your Daily and Work Week calendars with diagonal stripes in the color block to the left of the activity. When viewed in the **Availability** tab, the stripes appear as well. When you accept a meeting, the stripes are replaced by a solid bar.

If you issued the invitation to the scheduled activity, and you want to see how the participants have responded, open the activity, and display the **Availability** tab to view the status of your invitations.

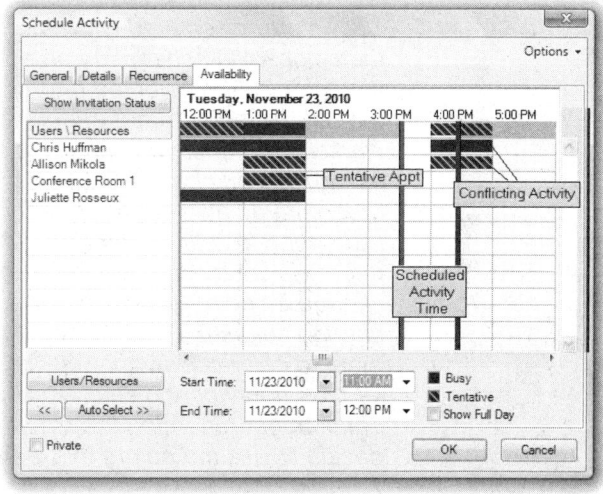

140 Sage ACT!

Practice: RSVP

What to do	How to do it/Comments
1. Chris has an Invitation pending for a Year End Budget Meeting. Accept the invitation.	In the lower-right corner of the ACT! window, click the notification icon to display the Invitations window. Click **Accept**.

Activity Colors

We have already observed that different priorities are associated with different colors. However, when scheduling any activity, you can manually change the color by clicking the **Color:** button (on the **General** tab) and clicking the color you want.

 Changes in activity colors are effective for your PC only. If you want others to use the same color scheme for Priorities, then the colors have to be changed on each workstation.

- You might like to **manually** assign different colors to different activity types. For example, prospecting calls are in (cold) blue, follow-up calls are in (warm) orange, closing the deal calls are in (money) green, etc.

- Each employee may want to choose a color as their signature color for their activities. That way when you view all users on the shared Calendar or Task List, you can quickly tell by the color of the activity who it belongs to. Unfortunately, you run out of viewable colors if you have more than 10 to 15 employees.

- By clicking the **Define Custom Colors>>** button, you can select from a pretty much unlimited choice of shades and add them to the **C̲ustom colors:**

     *Colors are associated with Priorities. Changing the color while scheduling an activity overrides the color for the selected priority. It becomes the new default for that priority (only on your workstation) until you change it again. For example: You change the color of an activity to green. If you also set the priority of that item to High, then from that point on, activities whose priority is set to High will be green (until **you** change it again). In other words, you can change colors manually each time you create them to color-code your activities, **or** you can let the priority option color-code them for you. Think about renaming the Priorities if you decide to use the colors this way.*

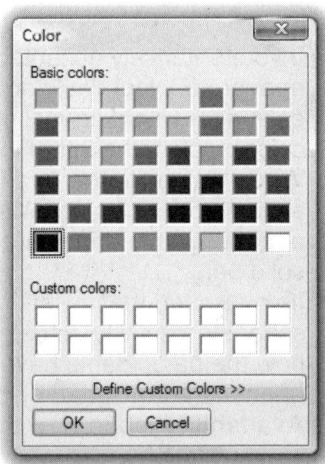

Advanced Scheduling | 141

Alarms

When your activities are scheduled for a particular time, you can set an alarm to remind you of them. No matter what you're doing in Windows, an alarm flashes to alert you to the imminent activity.

- For an alarm to go off, ACT! needs to be running, but it can be minimized or running in the background behind other applications you may be using.
- If an alarm is missed because your computer is shut down (or it's on but ACT! is not running), the alarm displays as soon as you open the database in ACT!.

Procedure: To set an alarm

1. Schedule the activity for which you want to set an alarm. Set activity options as you normally would.

   Perform this task as you normally would (page 89). You can set alarms for any activity type.

2. From the **Ring Alarm:** drop-down list, select a lead time.

   Your selection determines how far in advance of the scheduled activity time the alarm will go off.

   Ring Alarm:
   No alarm
   0 minutes
   5 minutes
   10 minutes
   15 minutes
   30 minutes
   1 hour
   1 day
   5 days
   30 days

3. Adjust the lead time, if appropriate.

   If none of the lead time options are what you want, type the lead time in the **Ring Alarm:** box. Example: to set a lead time of 10 days, type **10 days**.

4. Click **OK**.

   The alarm sounds at the specified time before the activity is scheduled. If the activity is set to Timeless, the alarm will sound the specified amount of time before midnight.

Practice: Using Alarms

What to do	How to do it/Comments
1. Look up the record for **Hayleigh Frieda**.	**L**ookup, **L**ast Name..., type **fri**, and click **OK**.
2. Schedule a meeting for today. Set the time of the meeting for about 15 minutes from now. The meeting should last 6 hours. (Don't click OK yet.)	Choose the Schedule Meeting icon. 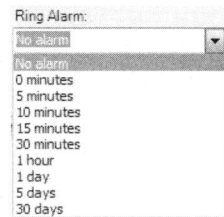 Enter a time that's 15 minutes from now. 6 hours is not an option in **D**uration: so you'll have to type it.

What to do	*How to do it/Comments*
3. The reason for the meeting? **Long Range Planning** Set the alarm to go off 5 minutes before the meeting so you won't be late.	In the **Regarding:** section, type "Long Range Planning." Change the **Ring Alarm** to **5 minutes** before the activity start time.
4. Make the activity show as a full-day banner in the Calendar. While you're at it, change the color of the activity to green (we're serious about growing) and add Details of "Bring your calculator." Now, click **OK**.	Click the **Use Banner** check box and click in **Color:** to change the color to green. Click the **Details** tab to add the note. Click **OK**.
5. View the activity in the Monthly Calendar. Do you see the banner?	Click the Calendar view icon, then click the Monthly button, if necessary.

 Now that you've scheduled the call, the alarm should go off in about 10 minutes. When the alarm goes off, we'll stop and take a look at the various ways to respond. Turn to the exercise on page 143 when you see the alarm. For now, let's continue our discussions about alarms.

Responding to an Alarm

When an alarm goes off in ACT!, the **Alarms** dialog box appears. Each alarm displays all sorts of helpful information: the activity type that the alarm represents, the Date, Time, Contact name, Phone number, and Regarding description of the activity. To see even more details for a selected alarm, click the **Show Details** button, if necessary. In the Activity Details portion, you can see the Location and activity Details. It also displays how much time is left before the activity is due (or calculates how many days that this activity is overdue…Yikes).

If you have more than one alarm going off, they appear in chronological order in the **Alarms** window. You can deal with one alarm at a time, or select them all and handle them all at once.

Advanced Scheduling | 143

When you see an alarm, respond in one of the following ways:

Select All Click this when you're short on time and want to handle multiple alarms quickly. A highlight appears over all alarms and the command you choose next affects them all.

Snooze... The **Snooze Alarm** dialog box appears in which you may set the alarm to go off again at a later time. Select the amount of time to delay (from 5 minutes to 1 week), and click **OK**.

Clear Alarm Turns off the alarm for today only, but leaves the activity on your calendar.

Clear Activity... Displays the Clear Activity dialog box for the associated activity. From here, you can tell ACT! whether or not the activity was completed, or if you at least tried to complete it. See the section on Clearing Activities (page 112).

Reschedule... Displays the **Schedule Activity** dialog box. From there, you can make changes to the date, time, or any other option.

Go To Goes to the highlighted Contact(s) so that you can get more information before you complete the activity.

Hide Details/Show Details Collapse or display the **Activity Details** section at the bottom of the Alarms dialog box.

*Notice that you can minimize this **Alarms** window while you handle the alarms, one at a time.*

Practice: Responding to an Alarm

What to do	How to do it/Comments
1. When the alarm for the **Hayleigh** meeting goes off, view the **Alarms** dialog box.	Click **Show Details** button, if necessary, to display the Activity Information at the bottom of the Alarms dialog box.
2. Snooze the alarm for 5 minutes.	Click **Snooze...**, choose **5 Minutes**, and click **OK**. The alarm goes away, but it will be back.
3. When the alarm goes off again, clear it.	Don't clear the activity, just the alarm. Click **Clear Alarm**.
4. When you clear the alarm (not the activity), does the activity still appear on the Contacts' **Activities** tab?	The activity stays there until you clear it. Clearing an alarm is not the same as clearing an activity. If you don't get around to clearing the activity today, the alarm will go off again tomorrow.
5. When it comes up tomorrow, you can clear the activity.	

Don't overdo a good thing. Alarms should be used for important activities... 10 minutes before an important conference call, 7 days before an anniversary date to remind you to buy a gift, at 5:15 every Tuesday so you can make it home in time to take your son to piano lessons. If you put an alarm on everything, then the emphasis an alarm provides gets lost...no activity is any more important or time-sensitive than the others. Get in the habit of checking the Calendar or Task List to see what's up for the day. Change the Task List Date filter to Past to see what is overdue. Besides, alarms take up system resources, always checking to see if it is time to ring yet.

Public vs. Private Activities

If you share an ACT! database, other users can view the activities you have scheduled with Public Contacts.

- If you don't want everybody knowing what you're up to, you can mark any activity as private.
- Private activities display in *your* Task List and Calendar views as normal (except with the Private icon displayed to the side).
- Private activities *will not* display in other users' Task List view.
- However, your private activities *will* display in the appropriate time slot on other users Calendars (if your name is included in their filter), indicating you are not available. Only the word "private" displays next to your name. The particulars of the activity (who the appointment is with or what it is regarding) are not shown.
- When a Private activity is cleared, it carries its "Private" status with it to the **History** tab by default. (If you didn't want anyone to see what you planned, you probably don't want others to see what you did.)

 If the Contact Access for a record is marked as Private, then the associated activities will also be Private. If you are using a Premium version of ACT!, you can assign Limited Access to a Contact, so that if users can't see the Contact, they can't see any associated activities either...except on the Calendar. If another user doesn't have the right to view a Contact's record (and activities), then the Calendar will display the activity in the appropriate time slot with only the word "private" next to "Scheduled For" name...similar to the way a Private activity is handled.

Procedure: To specify an activity as private

1. While scheduling an activity, click the **Private** checkbox at the bottom of the dialog box.   That's it, just click the checkbox. Did you think it would be complicated?

2. Complete the activity as you normally would.   This activity is not viewable by anyone but you.

Advanced Scheduling

Attachments

Some Activities are more complex than others. They may require much more detailed information than you can fit in the Regarding box (maximum of 256 characters by the way). Of course, there is the **Details** tab where you can type pretty much unlimited text, but what if you have a supporting file, like a PowerPoint presentation, or a Microsoft Excel spreadsheet, or a scanned image that you will need when you perform the scheduled task?

Procedure: To attach a file to an activity

1. Schedule the activity as you normally would. Display the **Details** tab.

   The **Attachment:** box is at the bottom of the tab.

2. Click the **Attach...** button.

   The **Attach File** dialog box displays.

3. Select File... or Shortcut...

   Attached **Files** are copied to the \Attachments folder. Attached **Shortcuts** create a link to a file on your PC or network.

    Your database administrator may have disabled the ability to attach files in the database.

4. Locate and select the file you wish to attach. Click **Open**.

   The filename now appears in the **Attachment:** box and the **Attach...** button says **Remove.**

5. Click **OK**.

    *When an Activity with an attachment displays in a list view (**Task List** or **Activities** tab), an icon displays in the Attachments column (the attachment column heading has the same icon).*

   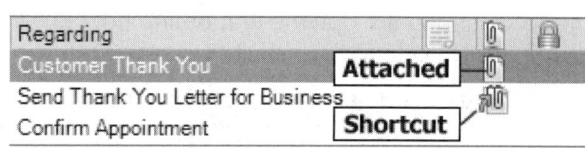

   Single-clicking the icon will open the file. If the icon appears with a paperclip, then the attachment is a shortcut to the file on your PC or network. Otherwise the file is maintained on your PC in the \Attachments folder.

Scheduling Recurring Activities

Some activities repeat over and over. You might wish to schedule a weekly staff meeting. Perhaps you want to call a Contact once a month to assess their needs. Maybe there is someone you want to close a deal with and you want to bug them twice a week until they give up and agree with you. Regardless of the reason, if you wish to repeat an activity at regular intervals, ACT! will oblige.

Procedure: To schedule a recurring activity

1. Look up the Contact the recurring activity concerns.

   If you meet with the same person each week, look up that record.

2. Display one of the **Schedule Activity** dialog boxes.

   Any activity type can be recurring.

3. Set up the first activity as you would any single activity. The recurring activities will have the same settings and options. Only the dates change.

   Choose the initial date, time, and duration. Fill out the regarding line and set options (like alarms, colors, etc.), as necessary.

4. Click the **Recurrence** tab.

   The **Recurrence** options display.

5. Choose whether the activity repeats **Daily**, **Weekly**, **Monthly**, or **Yearly**. The default of course is **On<u>c</u>e** (no recurrence).

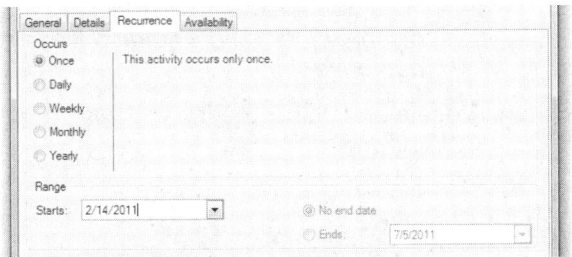

6. Choose the options that define how often and for how long the activity will repeat.

   We will discuss these options next.

7. When you have completed choosing any other options for the activity, click **OK**.

   ACT! creates an identical activity for each of the recurrence dates you specified.

Each recurrence type - **Daily**, **Wee<u>k</u>ly**, **<u>M</u>onthly**, or **<u>Y</u>early** - has its own set of options.

<u>Daily</u>   In the **Eve<u>r</u>y:** box, specify how many days there will be *between* each activity. Or choose **Every <u>w</u>eekday** to schedule Monday through Friday In the **Starts:** box, specify the date the first occurrence will be (if it's not already correct). If the recurrence will go on forever, specify **No end d<u>a</u>te** otherwise, select the **<u>E</u>nds:** option and select the last date the activity is to occur.
Example: If you specify **Every 2 days**, the activity will occur every other day until the date specified in the **<u>E</u>nds:** box is reached.

Advanced Scheduling | 149

What to do	How to do it/Comments
7. OK, if you don't make the next one Andy will give up on you. So reschedule the next lunch *only* for the 1:00 to 2:00 time slot. What happens when you click **OK**?	Double-click the activity. Change the **Start Time:** to 1:00 and click **OK**. When you change one instance of a recurring meeting, ACT! warns you.
8. Change only this occurrence.	Click the **Edit this occurrence** button. The remaining meetings remain unaffected. Notice that the meeting is now separated from the remaining "recurring" meetings.

Syncing Your Calendar and Contacts with ACT!

ACT! really is your business software hub. It works beautifully with Hoovers online services to perform research on your contacts or with Swiftpage to send mass e-mails to your clients and prospects. It seamlessly links to your web browser to display linked web pages, with Word to write letters, proposals and quotes, with Excel to export or import data, and with Outlook to write e-mail or to link incoming messages to your database. I mean really… how many other software packages do you own that can integrate with so many other software packages?

You can even sync your ACT! Calendar and Contacts with either Outlook's or Google's Calendar and Contacts… regardless of where the data is created or updated.

Why sync your Calendar and/or Contacts to another software?

- What if you work in a company where management uses the Outlook calendar for scheduling corporate meetings and activities and you and your sales staff use ACT!…you smile and say "No Problem!"
- Do you have a smart phone that can sync to Outlook or Google? If you sync your ACT! Contacts and Calendar to either Outlook, (most phones have Outlook sync built in) or Google (which can wirelessly sync to almost any device), then your smart phone, iPad or other tablet will always be updated as well.
- What if you want to have your Calendar (and Contacts) in the cloud where you can access it wherever you have an Internet connection? The Google connection may just be what you are looking for.
- Need to share your Calendar with someone else who doesn't use ACT!? You could sync your ACT! Calendar to Google and then share that online calendar with specific people or the public (or you could use the "Add a friend's calendar" option to display their calendar with your own).

Calendar Synching with Outlook

When you schedule something in ACT! or Outlook, syncing the calendars creates a corresponding activity in the other system. So here is how it works.

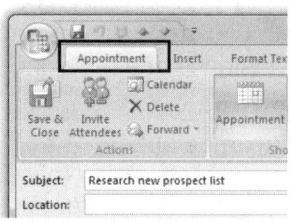

In Outlook, when you schedule something for yourself on the calendar, it is an "Appointment" (at left). If you invite someone else to the appointment, it becomes a "Meeting" (as in Meeting Request displayed at the right).

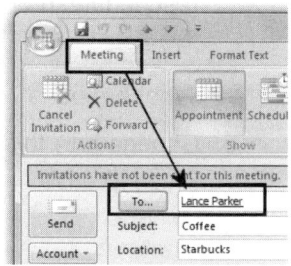

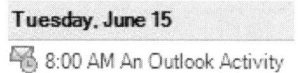

These Appointments or Meetings created in Outlook will sync to your ACT! calendar as an Outlook "Appointment" (activity type) and displays in ACT! with an icon designating its origin.

If you schedule the activity in ACT!, meetings scheduled with your own My Record sync to the Outlook as an Appointment. Meetings scheduled with another contact in ACT! sync to Outlook as a Meeting with the contact in the **To...** area.

All other activity types (Personal, Vacation, Calls, or custom activity types) scheduled in ACT! will sync to Outlook as "Appointments" (no **To...** area). In Outlook, you can double-click the Appointment to view the details for more information on who the activity was scheduled with in ACT!, along with the Company name, phone number and other address type information from the ACT! record.

You can add attendees to the appointment in either ACT! or Outlook. Calendars that are synced are always up to date, regardless of where activities were created or modified.

Procedure: To set up calendar sync to Outlook

1. **Tools, Preferences...**, click the **E-mail and Outlook Sync** tab.

   Click the **Outlook Synchronization Preferences...** button at the bottom right.

2. If necessary, click the **Select...** or **Change...** button to select and log in to your database.

   > *Users can only synch from one instance of Outlook to one ACT! database.*

3. Be sure that the **Enable Calendar Synchronization** with Outlook is checked.

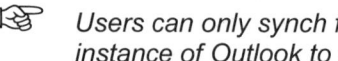

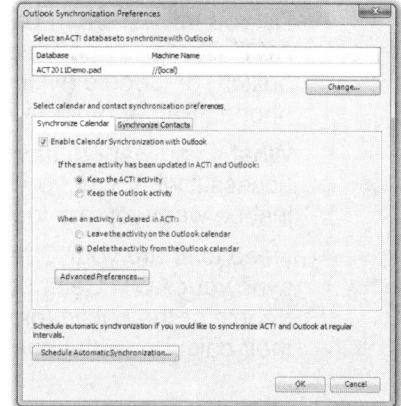

Advanced Scheduling 151

4. If the activity gets changed in both applications, which one should win? When you clear the Activity in ACT, what do you want to do with it in Outlook?

5. Click the **Advanced Preferences...** button to determine what activity types will be synced with Outlook. By default, Appointments and Meetings are the only types that are synched.

   However, Vacations are good to include on the Outlook calendar. In addition, if you have created custom activity types, such as Trade Show, you will want to include them as well.

6. Select the time frame of activities that should be included in the sync.

   Specify which application should ring alarms that have been set.

   Click **OK**.

7. Click **Schedule Automatic Synchronization** button to set an automated task.

8. Select a frequency. Perhaps..
   **Hourly
   Starting at 8:00 AM
   Ending at 5:00 PM
   Then every 4 hours**

   You can schedule Auto-synch as frequently as one minute, but to limit performance impact, a minimum 10-minute scheduling interval is recommended. I use every 4 hours.

   Click **OK**.

9. Click **OK** to close the Outlook Sync Preferences window...

10. Click **Yes** to sync, or **No** to wait until later time.

11. Click **OK** once again to close the Preferences dialog.

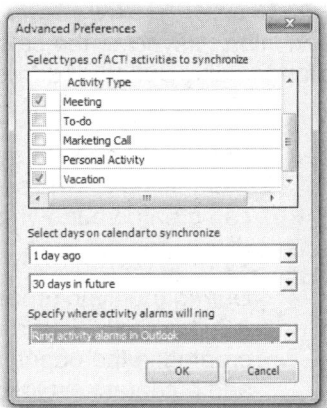

The default is to include all selected activity types from yesterday to 14 days into the future.

The default is to ring alarms in both applications... but that seems a bit much.

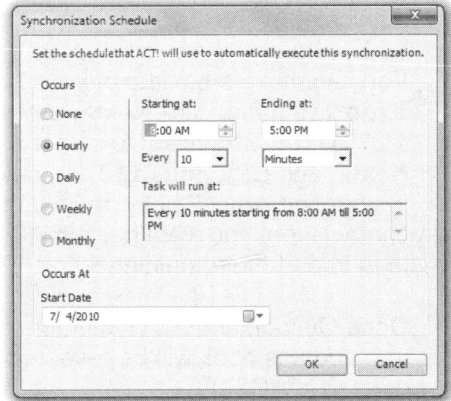

or continue to the next procedure to set up Contacts sync.

 The automatic sync runs even with Outlook and ACT! closed.

Sage ACT!

Contact Syncing with Outlook

In addition to syncing the calendar, you can also sync your contacts between your ACT! database and Outlook Address Book.

- **All** contacts in your Outlook Address Book can optionally be synced to ACT!
- You can choose to sync all of your ACT! Contacts to Outlook or only a portion of them using a sync set. One or more of the default sync sets can be selected or you can create your own sync set. Secondary contacts do not sync to Outlook.
- Sync sets only apply to your ACT! contacts (not your calendar).
- During the sync process, ACT! will use the e-mail address to try to link the records in ACT! in Outlook. If a corresponding contact is not found, a new Contact will be created in the opposite address book. (So be sure to add an e-mail address if you add a contact in Outlook.)

Important Note - Prior to Syncing Your Contacts: While you can create a sync set to limit which ACT! contacts are synced to Outlook, if you choose to sync your Outlook contacts, they will ALL be synced to ACT!. So let's consider the ramifications.

If you don't have an existing ACT! database, it is a great way to populate ACT! with contacts. However, if you have been keeping contacts in both ACT! and Outlook and you opt to sync Outlook contacts to ACT!, the first sync can duplicate some records (ACT! can interpret and merge some... but computers are very literal and will only recognize some records as actual duplicates.)

You can make a backup of your Outlook contacts (Click **File, Import and Export...**, select **Export to a file**, click **Next>**, select **Microsoft Excel**, and click **Next>**, select **Contacts** and click **Next>**, **Browse...** to select a folder location and give the file a name, click **OK** and **Next>**, and click **Finish**.) Then delete all of the contacts in your Outlook Address book prior to your first sync. Finally, review the Excel file that you just exported. If there are any contacts that you want back in ACT and Outlook, delete the ones that you don't want and then import the remaining list.

Once Outlook and ACT! contacts are syncing, any changes, additions, deletions made to one address book will be reflected in the other (e.g. delete a contact in Outlook and it will be deleted in ACT!.)

Procedure: To set up contact sync to Outlook

1. **Tools, Preferences...,** click the E-mail and Outlook Sync tab. Click the Outlook Synchronization Preferences... button at the bottom right.

Only users with an Administrator role can create contact sync sets, though each user can set up their own sync preferences.

Advanced Scheduling | 153

2. If necessary, click the **Change…** button to select and log in to your database.

   ☞ *Users can only synch from one instance of Outlook to one ACT! database.*

3. Click on the **Synchronize Contacts** tab.

   Be sure that the Enable Contact Synchronization with Outlook is checked.

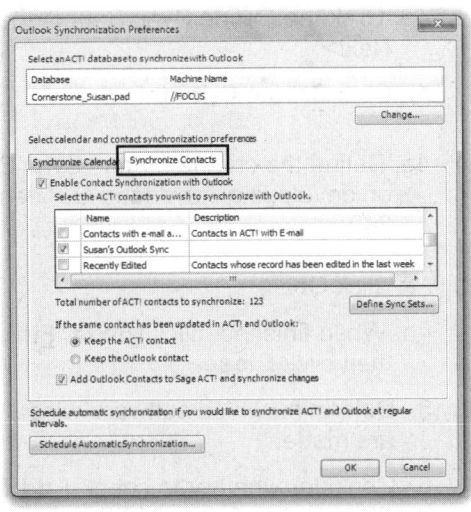

4. Select one or more of the default sync sets (the **Total number of ACT! contacts to synchronize** will display below the grid as you check any sync options).

   Default sync sets: All Contacts, Last Added, Last Edited, Customers, and/or Friends/Family

   ☞ *See the next procedure for more information on defining custom sync sets for your contact syncs.*

4a. Or create a custom sync set….

   Click the **Define Sync Sets…** button.

   Sync sets are based on field values. So you will want to think about which contacts in your database you want to sync and what field you could use to control the sync set. It could be based on multiple values in the ID/Status field. It could be based on a custom field that you create, such as the Sales Rep field. You must be as Administrator to do this.

4b. Click **Create New Sync** Set.

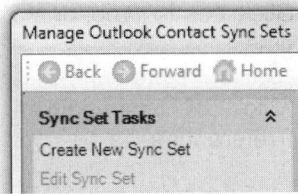

4c. Give the Sync Set a name and click **Next>**.

   Use something like "Susan's Outlook Sync".

4d. Double-click the user to select it and move it to the right-hand pane, and then click **Next>**.

Sage ACT!

4e. Click the Define Sync Set criteria and click **Next>**.

4f. Click **Create Criteria**. The Sync Set Criteria dialog opens.

4g. Define the criteria for this Sync Set. For help on developing Advanced Queries, see page 249.

Example: Sales Rep Contains Chris or ID/Status Contains Employee or ID/Status Contains Vendor.

Click **OK**.

4h. When finished, click **Next>**, **Finish**, and then click **Close**.

5. Determine which software wins if changes are made. Which will you keep... changes from ACT! or Outlook?

6. Consider whether to check **Add Outlook Contacts to Sage ACT! and synchronize changes**. Review the Important Note starting on page 152.

7. If you have not yet set up automatic synchronization, do so now. Click the **Schedule Automatic Synchronization** button to set an automated task.

   The synchronization schedule that you set up applies to both the Calendar and the Contacts sync. You cannot set up separate schedules.

   Select a frequency. Perhaps..
   **Hourly
   Starting at 8:00 AM
   Ending at 5:00 PM
   Then every 4 hours**

   You can, however, turn off one or both of the options if you don't want to synchronize one of them.

   Click **OK**.

8. Click **OK** to close the Outlook Sync Preferences window... or continue to the next procedure to set up Contacts sync.

9. Click **Yes** to sync, or **No** to wait until later time.

   ☞ *The automatic sync runs even with Outlook and/or ACT! closed.*

10. Click **OK** once again to close the Preferences dialog.

☞ *To remove the ACT! contacts that you just synced to Outlook, uncheck the sync set and sync again. However, there is no way to remove any Outlook contacts that were synced to ACT!.*

Advanced Scheduling | 155

Practice: Updating the Calendars in Outlook

What to do	How to do it/Comments
1. If you use Outlook, set up ACT! using the previous procedure. You may want to **Change…** to the ACT2012Demo database for testing this option. Only sync the next weeks activities.	Don't forget that all contacts in Outlook will sync to your ACT database (you cannot limit this). Try the Friends and Family sync set to keep the number of contacts low.
2. Play a little to see how it works. When you are finished, go back into **Tools, Preferences** and uncheck the sync set to remove the contacts from Outlook.	If you plan to use this sync option, you would also need to **Change…** the database back to your company database.

Manually syncing ACT! and Outlook

So what if you have made some last-minute changes and need to run out the door, but you want to update the contacts and calendars. You can wait for the timing of the automatic sync or you can manually update quickly.

Procedure: To manually sync Outlook and ACT! Calendars

1. In you are in ACT!, click **Tools, Synchronize with Outlook**, and select one of the options.

   If the option is grayed out, it means that you have not yet selected or created a sync set.

2. If you are in Outlook, click the appropriate icon on the toolbar.

☞ *This will not affect or override the automatic calendar update schedule. To edit the schedule, return to Tools, Preferences.*

Synching your Google Calendar and Contacts with ACT!

Do you have a Google account? If so, then you have access to a huge, and growing, list of free services. I became much more active in using my account when I got my Droid phone (though it works the same way with an iPhone, iPad, BlackBerry, or any other type of smart phone.)

I set up my Gmail account to wirelessly receive e-mail on my phone. I just configured my Gmail account to check mail using my POP3 info. So my e-mail appears in Outlook, in Gmail and on my phone. (I don't use my actual gmail.com address for sending e-mail, just as a transport agent.)

But more importantly, I wanted my ACT! contacts and calendar automatically synced to my phone wirelessly on a regular basis… with no monthly charge. Hmm. That Google account is looking even better. Previously, I used a 3rd party application called CompanionLink to sync my ACT contacts and calendar to Google. And I really like the options that it offers. However, ACT! now provides a built-in way to sync that data.

 Since both the Outlook and the Google syncs are two-way Calendar syncs (you cannot change this), to avoid duplicate Calendar and Contact data, it is recommended that you choose one supported application (Outlook or Google) to integrate with ACT!.

Calendar Integration with Google

When you schedule something in ACT! or Google, syncing the calendars creates a corresponding activity in the other system.

Google only has two activity types: **Event** and **Task**. So during the syncing process, ACT! To-Dos or timeless activities will be synced to the Google Calendar as Tasks and all other ACT! activity types will sync as an Event.

If you have selected to sync your calendars two-way, then an Event scheduled in the Google Calendar will display in the ACT! calendar as an Appointment and will display the Appointment icon.

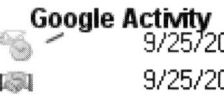

If you edited the Google Event and added Guests, then it will sync as a Meeting to the ACT! calendar with the associated Contact record. A Task or "All Day" Event (which is timeless in Google) will sync as a To-Do on the ACT! Calendar.

 If you have been syncing your ACT Calendar to Google using another product, you will most likely find duplicates after the first sync. After deleting the duplicates, your Calendar syncs should not create any additional duplicates.

Advanced Scheduling | 157

Contacts Integration with Google
In addition to syncing the calendar, you can also sync your contacts between your ACT! database and Google Contacts.

- **All** contacts in your Google Contacts can optionally be synced to ACT!
- You can choose to sync all of your ACT! Contacts to Google or only a portion of them using a sync set. One or more of the default sync sets can be selected or you can create your own sync set. Secondary contacts do not sync to Google
- Sync sets only apply to your ACT! contacts (not your calendar).
- During the sync process, ACT! will use the e-mail address to try to link the records in ACT! to Google. If a corresponding contact is not found, a new Contact will be created in the opposite address book. (So be sure to add an e-mail address if you add a contact in Google.) If there is a match, a synchronization link is established. If a change is made to the linked contact in either application, the change will sync to the other. However, Contacts deleted in Google are not deleted in ACT!. You must also delete the contact in ACT!, if desired.
- While ACT! uses address fields, such as Address 1, Address 2, City, State, Zip and Country, Google has one address field that contains all the contact's address information. Consequently, when a new Google contact is synced to your ACT! database, all data in the Google Address field appears in the ACT! Address 1 field.

Procedure: To setup calendar and contact sync with Google

1. **Tools, Integrate with Google, Google Integration Preferences**.

    Or right-click the Sage ACT! Integration Service icon in your system tray. Point to Integrate with Google, and then click Preferences.

2. Click the **Select...** (or **Change...**) button to identify the ACT! database you want to sync to your Google account.

    Users can only synch from one instance of Outlook to one ACT! database.

2a. Click the **Browse...** button to select the database (if necessary). Enter your User name and any necessary Password and click **OK**.

    It should automatically use the current database.

3. Click the **Register...** button. Click **Yes** if you have an account. Click **No** to link to the Google Web site to set up an account.

    You must have a [name]@gmail.com account already established. You cannot use a corporate domain, even if it is hosted by Google. It must be an account from the gmail.com domain. You can only link to one Google account.

Sage ACT!

3a. Enter your Google username and password, if necessary. Click the **Grant access** button.

You may not be prompted for username and password if you are already signed in to your Google account.

4. On the **Synchronize Calendar** tab, click the **Enable Calendar Synchronization with Google** option.

5. If the activity gets changed in both applications, which one should win? When you clear the Activity in ACT, what do you want to do with it in Google?

Usually you don't change the same activity in BOTH applications, but if you do, which app should win?

6. Click the **Advanced Preferences...** button to determine what activity types will be synced with Google. By default, Appointments and Meetings are the only types that are synched.

   Vacations are a good type to include on the Google calendar. In addition, if you have created custom activity types, such as Trade Show, you will want to include them as well.

6a. Select the time frame of activities that should be included in the sync.

   Specify which application should ring alarms that have been set.

   Click **OK**.

My preference is to set the time frame from "1 day ago" to "1 year in future."

The default is to ring alarms in both applications... but that seems a bit much.

7. On the **Synchronize Contacts** tab, click the **Enable Contact Synchronization with Google** option.

8. Select one or more of the default sync sets (the **Total number of ACT! contacts to synchronize** will display below the grid as you check any sync options).

Default sync sets: All Contacts, Last Added, Last Edited, Customers, and/or Friends/Family

 See the next procedure for more information on defining custom sync sets for your contact syncs.

Advanced Scheduling | 159

8a. Or create a custom sync set....

    Click the **Define Sync Sets...** button.

Sync sets are based on field values. So you will want to think about which contacts in your database you want to sync and what field you could use to control the sync set. It could be based on multiple values in the ID/Status field. It could be based on a custom field that you create, such as the Sales Rep field. You must be as Administrator to do this.

8b. Click **Create New Sync** Set.

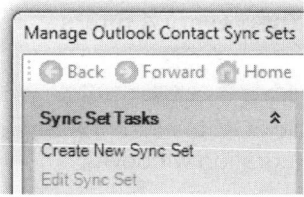

8c. Give the Sync Set a name and click **Next>**.

Use something like "Susan's Outlook Sync".

8d. Double-click the user to select it and move it to the right-hand pane, and then click **Next>**.

8e. Click the Define Sync Set criteria and click **Next>**.

8f. Click **Create Criteria**.

The Sync Set Criteria dialog opens.

8g. Define the criteria for this Sync Set. For help on developing Advanced Queries, see page 249.

    Click **OK**.

Example: Sales Rep Contains Chris or ID/Status Contains Employee or ID/Status Contains Vendor. You must be as Administrator to do this.

8h. When finished, click **Next>**, **Finish**, and then click **Close**.

9. Determine which software wins if changes are made.

Which will you keep... changes from ACT! or Google?

10. Consider whether to check **Add Google Contacts to Sage ACT! and synchronize changes.**

Review the Important Note starting on page 152.

The Record History tab is discussed on page 189.

Sage ACT!

11. If you have not yet set up automatic synchronization, do so now. Click the **Schedule Automatic Synchronization** button to set an automated task.

    Select a frequency. Perhaps..
    Hourly
    Starting at 8:00 AM
    Ending at 5:00 PM
    Then every 4 hours

    Click **OK**.

12. Click **OK** to close the Schedule Google Integration window...

10. Click **Yes** to sync, or **No** to wait until later time.

11. Click **OK** once again to close the Preferences dialog.

If you set a schedule to automatically integrate with Google, integration will run at the scheduled time. Or, you can run Google integration at any time.

The synchronization schedule that you set up applies to the Calendar, Contacts and History sync. You cannot set up separate schedules.

You can, however, uncheck any entity that you don't want to sync.

☞ *The automatic sync runs even with Google and ACT! closed.*

Advanced Scheduling | 161

Manually syncing ACT! and Google

So what if you have made some last-minute changes and need to run out the door, but you want to update the contacts and calendars. You can wait for the timing of the automatic sync or you can manually update quickly.

Procedure: To manually sync Google and ACT! Calendars

1. In ACT!, click **Tools, Integrate with Google**, and select one of the options. If the option is grayed out, it means that you have not enabled the option.

☞ *This will not affect or override the automatic calendar update schedule. To edit the schedule, return to Tools, Integrate with Google, Google Integration Preferences.*

Practice: Updating the Calendars in Google	
What to do	**How to do it/Comments**
1. If you use Google, set up ACT! using the previous procedure. You may want to **Change…** to the ACT2012Demo database for testing this option. Only sync the next weeks activities.	Don't forget that all contacts in Google will sync to your ACT database (you cannot limit this). Try the Friends and Family sync set to keep the number of contacts low.
2. Play a little to see how it works.	If you plan to use this sync option, you would also need to **Change…** the database back to your company database.

To disable Google Integration

To disable Google Integration, click **Tools, Integrate with Google, Google Integration Preferences** and uncheck the options at the top of each tab that represents the entity you want to discontinue syncing. Click **OK**.

Syncing Your Contacts and Calendar Using Sage ACT! Connect

Sage ACT! Connect is a subscription-based service that allows you to sync your ACT! calendar and contacts with two different platforms:

- your smart phone (BlackBerry, Windows Mobile, and Android devices, tablets like the iPad), and
- a web-based portal that can be accessed with any supported web browser (Internet Explorer, Firefox, Google Chrome, and even Safari).

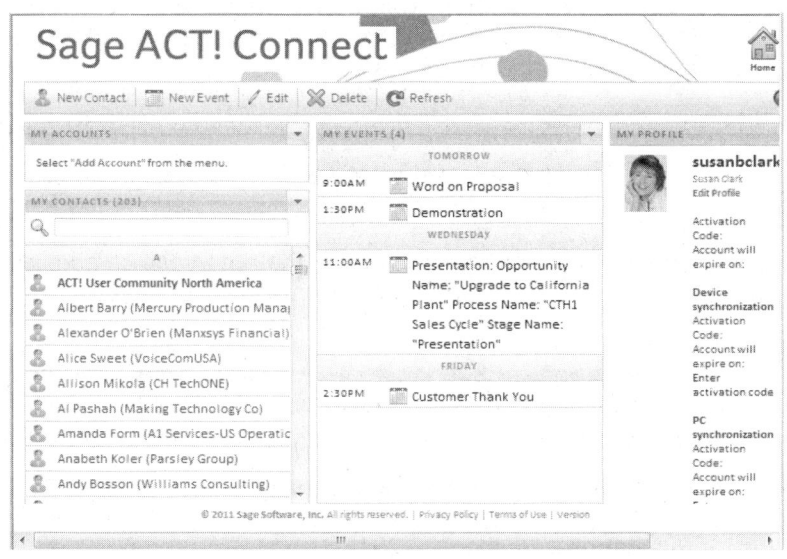

You can define one-way or two-way automated sync for one or both platforms that allows you to view, add, and edit your ACT! contact details, notes, history, meetings, and activities. Your data is secure, since Sage ACT! Connect utilizes 128-bit encryption, plus secure, physical protection for unauthorized entry and catastrophic events.

Procedures: To set up Sage Connected Services for ACT! [2]

1. In the Navbar, click the **Connections** button.

2. Under Sage ACT! Connect, click the link to start the trial.

    If you already have a Sage E-marketing for ACT! account, you can use it as your Sage Connected Services for ACT! account.

3. Click the **Try** or **Buy** button and fill out the form with your contact information.

    You will receive an e-mail with a link to creating your account online and your activation code.

---

[2] Requires additional subscription.

Advanced Scheduling | 163

4. Create your Sage ACT! Connect account online.

    Go to https://www.sageactconnect.com and click the "**Click here to Sign-up**" link. Create a Username and password. Enter your e-mail address and Activation Code, along with the Country and Time Zone. Click to agree with the Terms & Conditions and Privacy Policy and click **Submit**.

5. After your account is set up, login to https://www.sageactconnect.com

6. On the Home page, under My Phone, click **Add phone** to setup your mobile device.

    If you currently synchronize your mobile device with other products, make sure you have synchronized and disabled the other products before continuing with the installation.

7. On the Home page, under My Desktop, download and install the **Sage ACT! Connect PC client** on the computer hosting Sage ACT! Connect.

    You can download to the server and configure it to sync more than one user in the company if you like.

8. After installation, setup the preferences for each user.

    Right-click the Sage ACT! Connect icon in the System Tray and select Manage Users/Preferences.

9. In the Select User dialog, click the **Add a user** link.

10. By default the current database and user will be selected. Use the Change… button to change databases or modify the user name and password as necessary and click Next>.

    Sage Connect will verify your logon credentials

11. Enter your User name and Password that you created for your Sage ACT! Connect Account and click Next>.

12. Click the **Edit Preferences…** button to select which contacts to sync and to set up your sync schedule.

13. To the right of Contacts click the **Edit** link.

14. Click the Advanced button and then click **Change Sync Set** . Enter your query criteria for which contacts will sync from your ACT database to Sage ACT Connect.

    You will need to keep your contacts to 2,000 or less contacts.

15. Indicate the number of Notes and Histories that you want to send. You might also want to uncheck some of the history types. Click I usually click "select/unselect all" and then just check the history types that I want to sync (Appointment Completed, Call Completed, Meeting held, etc).

16. Under Synchronization at the left, click **Sync Action** and select between Two-way and One-way sync.

17. Under Synchronization at the left, click **Schedule** and select how often you want to sync.

18. Click **OK**.

19. Either **Add More Users** or click **Done**.

20. Click **Close** to exit the Select User dialog and start the syncing.

Using Your Sage ACT! Connect Account

Once your account is set up and has synced, your Contacts and Calendar will be right at your fingertips.

Let's look at some of the ways you can access your **Calendar** data online.

- Click the drop-down button on the **My Events** bar to add a new event, or filter the time frame for which events to display. You can also Import your Google Calendar
- To add an Event, click the **New Event** icon on the toolbar.
- Point to any appointment to see Location and time.
- Double-click the Event to view the Notes section to see who the activity is scheduled with, along with the contact's phone number s.
- To view your events using a Calendar View, click the **Calendar** button at the upper right. Select the Day, Week or Month view.
- To create an event, double-click on the time-slot and define the details of your event.
- Click the Today button to display Today's calendar in Day View.

Advanced Scheduling | 165

Let's look at some of the ways you can access your **Contact info** online.

- On the **My Contacts** header bar, click the drop-down at the right to Add a new contact, to sort your contact list by First Name or Last Name, or to import your Google or Yahoo contacts.
- To add a contact, click the **New Contact** icon on the toolbar.
- Enter any text in the **My Contacts** search box to lookup a contact. The results will include contacts that contain your text reference… even in the Notes, History or Activities area.
- Point to the contact to see a pop-up of Name, Title, Company and phone numbers.
- Double-click any contact to edit or view additional details.

Adding Photos of Your Facebook Friends

You can connect the photos in your Facebook account with your Sage ACT! Connect contacts.

Procedure: To add Facebook Pictures

1. In your Sage ACT! Connect online account, click the drop-down button on the **My Accounts** bar and select **Add Account**.

2. Click the **Facebook** link to share photos based on e-mail address (this link will not add any contacts to your online portal or ACT! database… only photos).

3. Click the **Setup** button to **Allow** access.

4. Click the drop-down button on the **My Contacts** bar and select **Import Facebook Pictures…**

   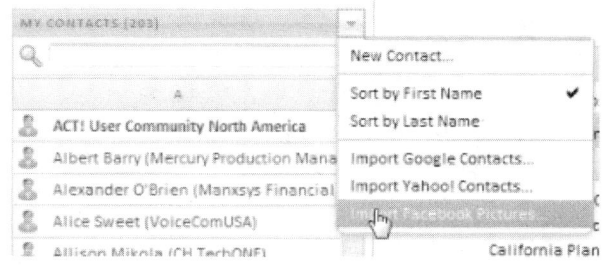

166 | Sage ACT!

Practice: Syncing to Sage ACT! Connect

What to do	How to do it/Comments
1. Setup your Sage ACT! Connect account using the instructions above. Start with setting up to sync your Contacts and Calendar to the portal. Then if you like, you can use Sage ACT! Connect to sync to your phone.	
2. Play a little to see how it works.	

Sync Product Differences

One of the differences between the ACT! Syncs to Outlook, Google or Sage ACT Connect and several third party sync applications is how the Regarding is handled. If you schedule a meeting with Lance Parker and in the regarding you enter "Product Demonstration", it's easy to see everything you need on the ACT! calendar. However, when it is transferred to an outside calendar, all you see is "Product Demonstration" with no indication of who it is with. You have to open the meeting to view the contact information in the Details.

The third party syncing products modify the Regarding line when it syncs it to any application outside of ACT! to display as something like: "Meeting-Lance Parker-Product Demonstration", so that you can easily see the details with just a glance at the non-ACT! calendar or device.

For this and other reasons, I still like the CompanionLink option and you can read more about why on my blog at:
http://cornerstonesolutions.com/tips/syncing-my-android-phone-with-act

Don't recognize the QR codes at the right? Read more about them on page xii at the beginning of this QuickStudy guide.

 There is an excellent 3rd party ACT! to iPad sync application that you might also want to consider. It actually creates a separate ACT! application on the iPad and does NOT sync to the built-in Calendar and Contacts. The advantage is you can schedule activities for a specific contact, as well as create history while on the road and then sync your activities back to ACT!. Check out http://www.itractapp.com/ to find out more.

Working Via E-mail & Letters

To understand the different ways you can use ACT! to communicate with your clients and prospects, you will:

- ☑ Set up ACT! to work with your e-mail and word processing programs.

- ☑ Practice sending basic messages.

- ☑ See how you can take advantage of the ACT! icons in your Outlook Inbox

- ☑ Create, print, and attach messages (e-mails and letters) to Contact records.

- ☑ Learn the basics of designing and using mail-merge templates.

- ☑ Understand how to use the ACT! Word Processor and E-mail Inbox, if you will be using these alternatives.

ACT! Can Help You Communicate

Written communications with business contacts can be one of the most important aspects of business and, yet, one of the easiest to neglect. A personal note after a sales meeting can be a highly effective way of keeping your name in your client's mind, but the time it takes to write a quick e-mail or address and write a note can sometimes be more than you think you can spare. Fortunately, you are an ACT! user. ACT! can make the tedious work of sending e-mail and writing letters almost effortless.

ACT!'s E-Mail Integration

ACT! can integrate with your existing e-mail system so that you can easily send and receive messages directly from ACT!, record history of that contact, attach e-mail contents to a record, create a new ACT! record from an e-mail, e-mail merge announcements to your contacts and prospects (in color and with graphics, if you like), and so much more.

ACT!'s E-marketing Feature

ACT! has also developed a partnership with Swiftpage™ to provide their E-marketing services. To use this feature of ACT!, you need to create an online account for your company and a userid for yourself. The E-marketing feature allows you to

- merge e-mail messages to your current lookup, have them sent through Swiftpage servers, and review reports of who viewed the messages,
- schedule drip marketing campaigns, and
- create online surveys and Web forms.

The E-marketing feature requires additional subscription and is therefore not covered in the Everyday course.

Setting Up Your E-mail System in ACT!

ACT! supports Microsoft Outlook (starting with version 2002(XP), Outlook Express (starting with version 5.5), Lotus Notes (starting with version 6.5), Eudora® Pro (starting with version 5.2), and the ACT! Internet mail client.

Since Gmail is a web-based solution and ACT! is a desktop solution, Gmail **cannot** be set up inside of ACT to work as the connected e-mail provider. The built-in ACT! Internet mail client does not allow configuration of specific ports other than the default Outgoing Server Port 25 and Incoming Server Port 110 and (sadly) Gmail requires other designated ports in order to work. If you like, you can set up your Outlook or Outlook Express e-mail software to access your Gmail account and then you could connect one of those apps to ACT!.

Working Via E-mail & Letters

 Just be careful. If you have already set up your Gmail account to work with your company account (e.g. clark@cornerstonesoutions.com), then also adding your Gmail account to Outlook would double your Inbox (it would be picking up e-mail from your ISP and then picking it up again from the Gmail account that also accessed the same ISP). So only connect your Gmail account to Outlook if you are not using it for a company domain account.

While you cannot set up your Gmail account to work from within ACT!, you can record history of all incoming and all outgoing e-mails.

If you normally use another e-mail (like GroupWise®), you don't have to go out and buy another software to use ACT! and e-mail. All you need is Internet access and a POP3 account. The ACT! Internet mail client is a built-in SMTP/POP3 e-mail client that you can use to send and receive e-mail.

 However, if you use an e-mail software other than Outlook or the ACT! built-in e-mail client, some of the ACT! e-mail features are not available. For example, using other e-mail systems with ACT! limits your messages and mail merges to plain text (no html) and a history of E-mail Sent may not be created with Lotus Notes.

Although you may have already set up an e-mail system when you installed ACT!, let's look at the next section to see how to configure it.

Procedure: To set up and configure your e-mail system

1. <u>T</u>ools, Pre<u>f</u>erences…, click the **E-mail & Outlook Sync** tab.

   You could also use **Help, Setup Assistant** to configure your e-mail.

2. Click the **E-mail S<u>y</u>stem Setup…** button. Click **<u>N</u>ext>** at the Welcome screen.

   Only e-mail software currently installed on your PC will display as available options.

3. Select the e-mail systems you want to use with ACT! – Put a check next to your e-mail system.

   Click **<u>N</u>ext>**.

   - ☑ Microsoft Outlook (recommended)
   - ☐ Outlook Express
   - ☐ Internet Mail

    There is an option at the bottom of the dialog to restore your e-mail from a .zip file if you used ACT! e-mail (not Outlook) on a different PC.

4. If you selected Microsoft Outlook for your E-mail System, skip to step 4c. If you selected Internet Mail, continue to step 4a. If you selected Outlook Express, skip to step 4b. If you selected Lotus Notes or Eudora, then click Finish.

4a. If you selected Internet Mail, click **Add** to fill in information about accessing your e-mail account. Your Internet Service Provider can give you the instructions necessary for adding your e-mail account.

4b. **E-mail – Editor** Click the **Edit Signatures...** button to create one or more signatures for your e-mails.

> *Give each signature a descriptive name.*

Then, select your default signature from the drop-down.

Click **Next>** and **Finish**.

If you chose Outlook Express or Internet Mail, an extra tab is added to the **Preferences** dialog.

Click the **ACT! E-mail Editor** tab and make any changes.

Then, click **OK** to save and to exit **Preferences**.

Click **Add**, enter a descriptive name. Enter text in **Edit Signature:**, as desired. Click **OK**

> *Leave a blank line in front of your signature to separate it from the rest of your message.*

If you exited Preferences in the last step, go to **Tools, Preferences** again.

You are finished setting up your e-mail. Skip to page 191 to learn how the ACT! E-mail Editor interfaces with your selected e-mail software.

4c. **E-mail – Outlook Address Books**
If you selected Microsoft Outlook, you will be prompted to set up the ACT! address book with Outlook.

You may add up to three databases.

If your database is not displayed, click **Add...**.

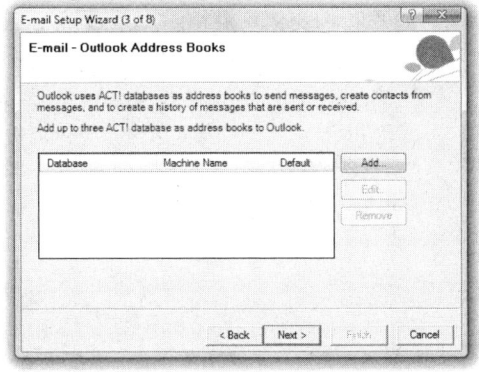

Add/Edit Address Book
Browse to select your ACT! database and click **Open**.

Enter your **User name:** and **Password**.

Click **OK**.

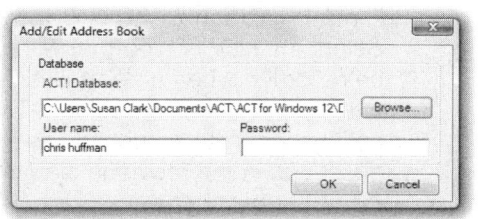

When you have finished adding your ACT! database(s) as Outlook Address Books, click **Next >**.

If you add more than one database, be sure to check the one that is your Default database.

E-mail-Editor
Select an e-mail editor.

Microsoft Outlook (recommended)

or

ACT! E-mail Editor.

ACT! E-mail Editor is chosen only if you selected an e-mail client in addition to Outlook.

If you selected multiple e-mail editors, choose your default e-mail client and create a signature for use with the ACT! E-mail Editor.

Click **Next>**.

E-mail – Record History
Select the history type that will (by default) be recorded when an e-mail is sent.

 This is a default only. You will be able to change the history type on-the-fly for each e-mail that you send.

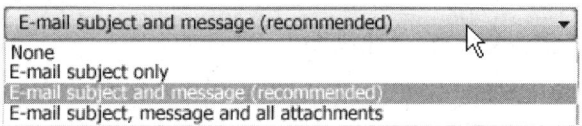

- **None** would not record any history to the Contact's record by default. You can always select to record history of any e-mail that you are about to send.
- **E-mail subject only** records the Date, Time, Subject, and Sender to the Contact's **History** tab.
- **E-mail subject and message (recommended)** records the text of the message in addition to the information captured by the Subject only option. This option allows you to instantly view the text of the message and will be synced to remote users. (Your signature text is also included with the message.)
- **E-mail subject, message and all attachments** saves a copy of the e-mail to the \Attachments folder and places a shortcut to the e-mail in the Contact's **History** tab. This is the only option that will also include any associated attachments. This option may not be available if the Administrator has disabled e-mail attachments in the Tools, Preferences, Admin tab.

Click **Next>**.

E-mail – Attach to ACT! Contacts

Select the history type that will always be recorded when an e-mail is attached from within Outlook. The options work the same way as described in the previous dialog box. **E-mail subject and message (recommended)** is the default choice.

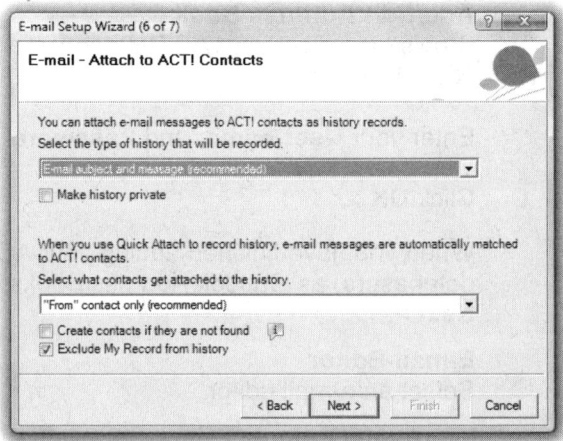

☞ *Keep in mind that this "recommended" option will not include any associated attachments. If you receive a lot of these that are important to keep, then you may want to change this option to **E-mail subject, message and all attachments**. This option may not be availabe if the Administrator has disabled e-mail attachments in the database.*

The next option on this screen determines how ACT! will save e-mails when the **Quick Attach** button is used in Outlook.

Do you want the selected message to be attached to only the "From" contact, to the "From" and "To" contacts listed, to the "From" and "CC" recipients, or attach the message to All Contacts?

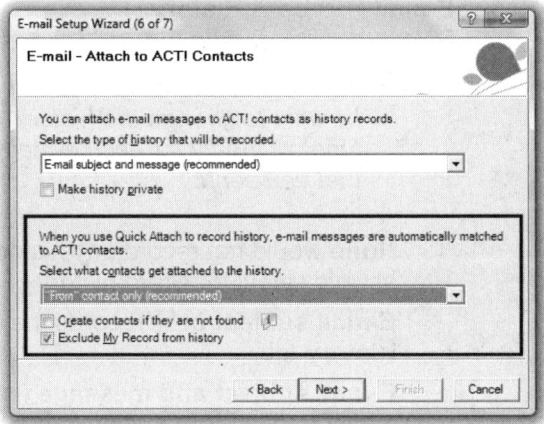

Working Via E-mail & Letters

Finally, you have two checkboxes at the bottom of the screen.

When using the Quick Attach feature, do you want ACT! to **Create contacts if they are not found**?

Checking the **Exclude My Record from history** option is a good choice if you are cc'd a lot on messages.

Click **Next>**.

E-mail – Activity Invitation
When you accept a Meeting Request in your Outlook Inbox, an ACT! Activity can also be copied to your ACT! Calendar. Select which calendar will have the alarm: ACT!, Outlook or both.

In the second option, determine if you want ACT! to "Automatically create…" or display the Schedule Activity dialog so that you can edit the activity before placing it on your ACT! calendar or ignore the Outlook invitation and not add any activity to the ACT! calendar.

> *You could set this option to None if you plan to sync the ACT! and Outlook calendars.*

Put a check in the final option to "Create contacts if they are not found", if desired.

If you select to have ACT! create contacts when the e-mail address is not found, keep in mind that you will need to look up the newly created record to complete the contact information. Only the contact name and e-mail address are filled in for the new record and any "required" fields are ignored. If additional address/phone info is included in the e-mail, it will NOT automatically be included on the contact's record. You must manually enter that information.

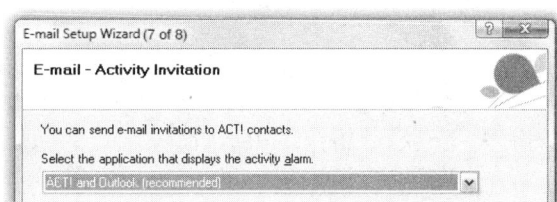

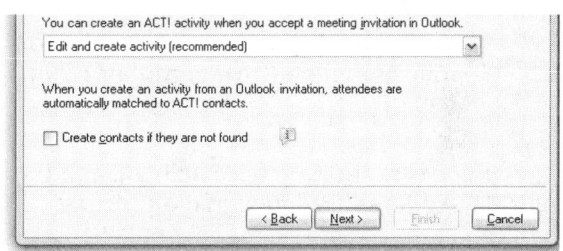

ACT! can only create a contact with a name and e-mail address. No other fields will be filled in when you use this option.

Click Next> and Finish.
Click **OK** to exit **Preferences**.

> *If you use Microsoft Outlook Express 6, you may receive a virus protection error message each time you send or receive e-mail using ACT!. Disable the message in Outlook Express by clicking **Tools**, **Options…**, clicking the **Security** tab, clear the **Warn me when other applications try to send mail as me**, and clicking OK.*

Sage ACT!

ACT!'s Integration with Outlook

If you selected to use **Microsoft Outlook** during e-mail setup (page 169), ACT! will open an Outlook new e-mail message window when you send an e-mail, perform an e-mail merge, or even when you elect to send the letter you've been working on by e-mail.

☞ *If you are using an e-mail program other than Outlook, you will be using ACT! as your e-mail editor, and you can skip to page 191.*

Sending E-mail from the Contact

You can easily send a new e-mail message starting from the Contact record in ACT!. You can also select from any template you have created to send a pre-written and formatted e-mail.

Procedure: To send an e-mail from an ACT! Contact record

1. Look up the Contact you want to send the message to.

    Verify that an e-mail address has been entered for the Contact.

2. Click the **Write E-mail Message** icon,

    The ACT! E-mail application window opens and then the **New Message** window displays.

    or choose **Write**, **E-mail Message** or **E-mail Message (from template)** from the menu,

    The message is addressed to the current contact. To change to, or add, another recipient, click the **To...** (or **Cc...**) button and select from your Contact List.

    or click the Contact's actual **E-mail Address** field to start the process,

    or right-click **Write**, **E-mail**.

3. Continue addressing, selecting options, and entering the message.

4. At the end of your message, enter your signature, if necessary.

     *You can type it manually, or select **Insert**, **Signature**.*

5. Change the ACT! History option, if necessary before sending.

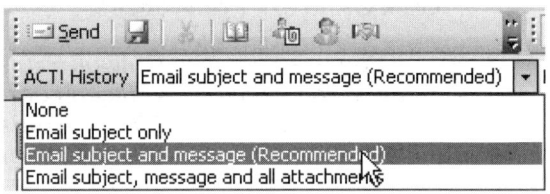

Working Via E-mail & Letters | 175

 If you are using Outlook 2007 or later, in the new message window, click the Add-Ins tab, change the Record History option in the Custom Toolbars group.

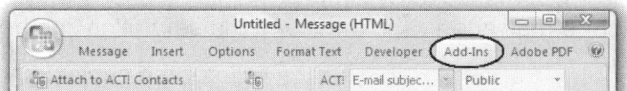

6. When you are finished click **Send**. A history is recorded in ACT. If you are using Outlook, it can take a few seconds for the history to be recorded.

Practice: Sending an E-mail from the Contact

What to do	How to do it/Comments
1. There are no valid e-mail addresses in the sample database. Look up your real name if you entered it in the first Review exercise or enter it now.	If your name is not in the ACT2012Demo database, input it now along with your real e-mail address. ☞ *If you are in your own database and not the demo, you should know that you cannot send an e-mail to your own "My Record" in ACT!*
2. Use the **Write E-mail Message** icon to start an e-mail with a subject of: **Interested in a Speaking Gig?** Message of: **I need a speaker of your stature for our annual conference. Could we talk?** Insert your signature.	Click the **Write E-mail Message** icon to start the process. The **New Message** window displays. Notice that this message has a salutation line and does not include your default signature. Enter the subject and message as described. At the bottom of the message click **Insert, Signature**.
3. Change the history to **E-mail subject and message**, if necessary Now send it.	Change the history as indicated. Click **Send**.
4. Display the **History** tab, if necessary, and notice how the e-mail was recorded.	The subject followed by the complete text of the message was recorded in the **History** tab. ☞ *If you are using Outlook, history can take a few seconds to be recorded.*

Sage ACT!

What to do	How to do it/Comments
5. Send another e-mail message by simply clicking on your e-mail address in the Contact record. Use a subject of: **Offer** Message of: **Is $20,000 plus expenses agreeable?** Change the history to **E-mail subject, messages and all attachments** Now send it.	This message only contains your signature (no salutation line here). Enter the subject and message as described. Change the history as indicated. Click **Send**.
6. View the entry in the **History** tab.	Double-click the history attachment icon to open and view the message in an e-mail window.

Sending E-mail from Outlook

You can also send an e-mail straight from Outlook and have it record the history of the e-mail on the contact's record… even if ACT! isn't open.

Procedure: To send an e-mail from Outlook (some things to know)

1. Click the **New** icon in Outlook. This procedure assumes that you have set up an ACT! Address Book in E-mail Preferences (page 169).

2. In the **To…** area, you can …
   - Manually enter an e-mail address, or
   - Type a person's name exactly as it appears in your ACT! database, or
   - Click the **To…** button to access the ACT! database to look up the names. In the **Type Name…** or the **Search:** box, type the Contact's first and last name as it appears in your database.

   After clicking To…, click the drop-down arrow to switch to another address book.

   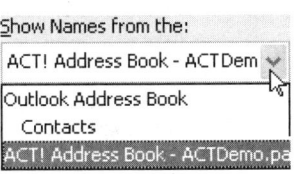

   As you type the name, the list scrolls to that spot in the database. Double-click a name to select it and place it in the **To->** box (or click the Cc -> or Bcc -> to add the selected name to that area). Repeat as necessary for other Contacts, and then click **OK**.

3. Continue with the e-mail as you normally would.

Working Via E-mail & Letters | 177

4. Click the drop-down arrow to select the type of history that should be created for this Outlook message.

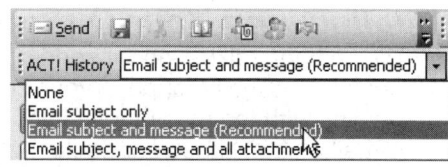

5. Click **Send**

If Outlook can locate the e-mail address in the assigned ACT! Address Book, a history will be recorded for that Contact in ACT!. History can take up to 15 seconds to appear in the History tab.

 If you are using Office 2007 or later, in the new message window, click the Add-Ins tab, change the Record History option in the Custom Toolbars group.

Skip this exercise if you are not using Outlook.

Practice: Creating an E-mail from Outlook

What to do	How to do it/Comments
1. In Outlook, start a new message.	Open Outlook and click **New**.
2. Start an e-mail to Lance Parker. Enter a Subject: TWO Component Text: The TWO Component has been configured and is ready for installation. Change the ACT! history to "E-mail Subject, Message and All Attachments".	Click on the **To:** button. If you have added the ACT2012Demo database to your e-mail preferences, then you can start typing "lance" in the "Type Name or Select from List:" box. When Lance's name is highlighted, click the **To->** button and click **OK**. Notice that this message uses your default Outlook signature. Enter the subject and message as described. Change the ACT! History option and click **Send**.
3. View the results on Lance's History tab.	It may take up to a minute for an Outlook history to display in ACT!.

Dealing with Your Outlook Inbox

We've been talking about sending e-mails. It's time to look at the communications that we receive... usually found in your Outlook Inbox. ACT! can help you be more productive dealing with the messages in your Inbox... whether you are dealing with meeting requests or e-mails...ACT! has your back.

Adding an Outlook Meeting Request to Your Calendar

We already discussed this option back in Scheduling, but Meeting Requests are about your Inbox as well, so in case you missed it... When you open and accept a Meeting Request in your Outlook Inbox, the activity is automatically added to your Outlook Calendar. ACT! can add that same meeting to your ACT! calendar...scheduled with all contacts included on the Meeting Request.

Procedure: To add an Outlook Meeting Request to your ACT! Calendar

1. Open the Meeting Request in Outlook and Accept the invitation.

    The meeting is added to your Outlook calendar.

     Accepting a meeting on your PDA will also copy the activity to your ACT! calendar.

2. When ACT!'s **Schedule Activity** dialog displays, verify that ACT! has selected the correct contact(s) in the **Scheduled With:** area.

    ACT! adds all contacts included in the Meeting Request message to the Scheduled With: area. If ACT! can't locate a contact's e-mail address in your default database, then the Activity will be scheduled with your My Record. You can manually add/remove anyone by clicking the **Contacts** drop-down (to the right of the names) and choosing **Select Contacts...**.

3. Complete any details of the activity that you like and click **OK**.

    A copy of the meeting invitation is also added to your ACT! calendar. If you are syncing the calendars, it will not duplicate.

 As we mentioned, this is a difficult one to try out, since it requires that someone send you a Meeting Request in Outlook... and besides that, most likely the meeting will be added to your REAL database... not the ACT! demo database.

Creating a Contact from an E-mail

When you receive an e-mail message from a new prospect inquiring about your services, ACT! makes it easy to quickly create an ACT! Contact in your database starting from the current e-mail. It will even check for duplicates (by Company, Contact, and Phone) before adding the new Contact.

Procedure: To create a Contact record from an e-mail message

1. Open the e-mail that you want to create a Contact for and scroll so that you can see their signature address information.

   This step is not really necessary…you can actually start with step 2. However, you may find it helpful in step 4 to have the e-mail open where you can see the contact's information.

2. In **Outlook:** Click the **Create ACT! Contact** icon at the top of the open e-mail. (In Outlook 2007 click the Add-Ins tab to find the icon.)

   Only the **Name** and the **E-Mail:** are automatically copied from the currently selected e-mail.

   In **ACT! E-mail:**, click **Actions**, **Create Contact from Sender…**.

3. Outlook users can select the ACT! database (from the defined Address books).

   If you are using the ACT! e-mail interface, the Contact will be added to the open ACT! database.

   The name listed in From is placed in the **Co<u>n</u>tact:** field.

    If the name in From is rick@bfbg.com, then the e-mail address is used for the Contact name.

3a. **Outlook users only:** If the selected e-mail contains multiple e-mail address:
1.) Select the database,
2.) Select which ones to create new Contacts for, and
3.) Click **OK**.

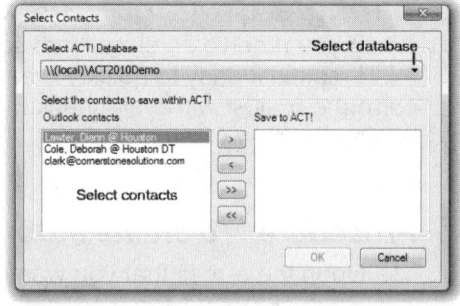

4. Enter any additional information. If you scrolled in the e-mail so that you could see the signature, it is easier to view all of the Contact information. Don't forget the Business Address tab.

5. Click **OK**.

6. Look up the Contact in ACT! and add information as necessary.

If you selected multiple contacts in the previous step, you will not be given the option to fill in additional Contact information. Go to ACT! to finish the record.

The contact information is added to the currently open ACT! database.

Like…ID/Status, Referred By, or Limited Access for starters.

Practice: Adding a Contact from an E-mail	
What to do	**How to do it/Comments**
1. In your Inbox, locate an e-mail that you will create a new Contact record from and add the Contact to the ACT2012Demo database.	If you are using Outlook, click the **Create ACT! Contact** icon. If you are using the ACT! E-mail window, right-click the e-mail and select **Create Contact from Sender**….
2. Look up the Contact to verify that the Contact was entered in the ACT2012Demo database.	Cool…there it is.

Attaching an E-mail to a Contact

When you receive an e-mail from one of your contacts that contains information that might be important to save, ACT! makes it easy to attach that e-mail to the Contact's record. There are three ways to attach an e-mail to ACT!

- Using the Quick Attach feature
- Using the Attach to ACT! icon

Working Via E-mail & Letters

Using the Quick Attach Feature

Quick Attach attaches the selected e-mail message(s) in your Outlook Inbox to an existing ACT! contact in the default database. ACT! matches the contact using the e-mail address in the From area of the selected e-mail(s).

 Quick Attach preferences can be set to create contacts for messages that do not have a match (page 173).

Procedure: To use Quick Attach to attach an e-mail to a Contact

1. Select one or more messages in your Outlook Inbox.

    Click the first message and, if desired, **[Ctrl]**+click any additional messages.

2. Click the **Quick Attach** icon.

    The e-mail is quickly attached to the Contact record in the default database whose e-mail address matches the From e-mail address.

3. Note the icon that briefly displays in the System tray indicating that it is attaching the selected message(s).

    Double-click (or right-click, Show Progress) to display the **Attach To ACT! Contacts Progress** dialog. Once it is attached, you can delete it from your Inbox.

    A dialog box will display a message that says "Messages will be quick attached to ACT! contacts". Click **OK**.

    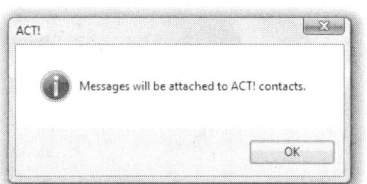

 If an address is "Bill Wonderful [info@captainsoi.com]" (where three users share the same "info@" e-mail), then ACT! will first search for the e-mail address, and then search for the Contact name. If there is a problem attaching a message, the Quick Attach icon will display in the System tray with a red X.

Practice: Attaching a Contact from an E-mail

What to do	How to do it/Comments
1. Attach the same e-mail that you just used to create a new Contact in ACT! to the Contact you created.	Select the e-mail in your Outlook Inbox, click the Quick Attach icon. Click **OK**.
2. Select another e-mail in your Inbox (that you know the contact is not in the ACT2012Demo database) and click the **Quick Attach** icon.	ACT! will attempt to locate the record for attaching the message. Depending on your preferences, ACT! may create the contact in ACT! and attach the message. If you see an error message in the System tray, the contact was not created and thus the e-mail was not attached.
3. Did ACT! create a new contact in ACT!?	Note the fields that were filled in.

Setting Your Quick Attach Preferences

Let's look at the preferences that are set for Quick Attach on your PC. The criteria that Quick Attach uses for attaching e-mails are defined in Setup Assistant (although you can also modify under Tools, Preferences, E-mail tab).

Procedure: To modify Quick Attach preferences

1. **Help, Setup Assistant...**, click **Next>** until you are at **E-mail – Attach to ACT! Contacts**.

   The Quick Attach options are displayed in the bottom half of the dialog.

2. Use the drop-down to choose which contacts are selected from the e-mail for attaching.

   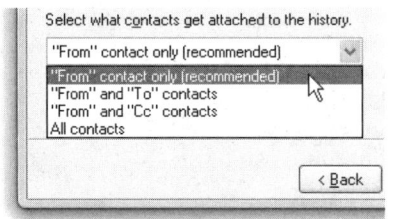

   From (the default) attaches only to the contact found in the e-mail From.

   From and To attaches to all contacts found in the From and To address sections of the e-mail. (Be sure to check the **Exclude My Record from history** if you don't want every e-mail attached to your History tab.)

   From and CC attaches to contacts found in From and CC.

   All Contacts is self explanatory.

3. Select **Create contacts** if they are not found option.

   - If this option is checked, when Quick Attach does not find the e-mail address in your default ACT! database, it creates a new contact with the e-mail address and Contact name only and then attaches the e-mail.
   - If the option is NOT checked, messages that cannot be attached are temporarily saved in the **Attach to ACT! Contact Progress** log so that you can manually attach them (see procedure above).

   This option applies to Quick Attach only, not manual attach.

   ☞ *If a new contact is created by this option, you should look up the newly created contact to add details such as Company name, phone number, etc. Quick Attach does not notify you of which e-mails were attached to existing contacts and which e-mails were attached to newly created contacts. Consequently, you may want to keep this option unchecked.*

4. Select **Exclude My Record from history** option.

   This option is important to consider if you selected anything other than **From** in Step 2 above. Otherwise, ACT! would attach all incoming e-mails not only to the "From" contact, but also to your record as well.

5. Click **Next>** until you can click **Finish**.

Working Via E-mail & Letters | 183

Practice: Check Your Quick Attach Preferences

What to do	How to do it/Comments
1. Review your Quick Attach preferences.	**Help, Setup Assistant…**, click **Next>** until you are at **E-mail – Attach to ACT! Contacts**.
2. Return to Outlook and select another e-mail in your Inbox (where you know the contact is not in the ACT2012Demo database) and click the Quick Attach icon.	You should see the red X on the Quick Attach icon in the system tray, indicating that the message was not attached.

Handling Unattached Messages

Occasionally, Quick Attach may be unsuccessful in attaching a selected message. If you have unchecked the option to create new records, and a contact is not found, then you will receive an error message indicating that there was a problem. Perhaps your ACT! database password has changed, and you forgot to update it in the E-mail Preferences, or perhaps the network is down and your PC can't access the database on the company server.
Whatever the reason, Quick Attach holds the e-mails for a specified period of time so that you can manually attach them when you are ready.

Procedure: To handle problem Quick Attach messages

1. Double-click the **Attach Error** icon with the red X in the system tray. Displays the **Attach To ACT! Contacts Progress** dialog box.

2. Click the **Not Attached Messages** tab.

   Progress tab shows recent messages attached in ACT!.

   Not Attached Messages tab is described in the next step.

   Advanced tab defines the number of days that the successful and unsuccessful messages are saved for later viewing and/or handling.

3. Select the problem message and click an icon on the toolbar.

   Retry Quick Attach... Perhaps you lost your network connection or had a password change or added the contact's Personal e-mail.

   Attach to ACT! Contact... Displays the **Attach E-mail to Contacts** dialog.

   Attach to New Contact... Displays the New Contact dialog to create a new Contact from the e-mail.

   Remove deletes the selected e-mail message from the list.

4. The **Advanced** tab allows you to specify the number of days that data is maintained about the e-mails.

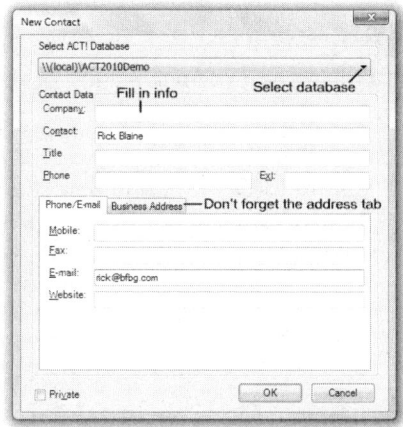

If you do not delete or manually attach the e-mails in the **Not Attached Messages** tab in the specified time period, then ACT! will cease to hold them and they will be deleted from the ACT! log.

Practice: Handling Problem E-mails

What to do	How to do it/Comments
1. Determine which of the e-mails are causing problems with attaching.	Double-click the Attach Error icon with the red X in the system tray. Click the **Not Attached Messages** tab.
2. Select the problem e-mail that you just attempted to attach using Quick Attach in the previous exercise.	Note that you can see the contents of the selected message in the preview pane. No point in clicking **Retry**, as it wasn't a password or network issue. No point in clicking **Attach to ACT!** since the contact is not in ACT!.
3. Create a new Contact in ACT! from the selected e-mail.	Click **Attach to New ACT! Contact...** and fill out the New Contact dialog and click **OK** and **OK**. The Contact will be created in ACT! and the e-mail will be attached. The e-mail will then be automatically removed from the Not Attached Messages list.

Working Via E-mail & Letters | 185

What to do	How to do it/Comments
4. Handle any additional problem messages and close the window.	Remove any messages that you don't want to resolve. When no other problem messages are found, the Quick Attach icon disappears from the System tray.

Using the Attach to ACT! Icon

While Quick Attach is the fastest option for attaching your message(s), sometimes you may want to maintain more control over how the message is added to the ACT! database.

This method allows you to attach the selected e-mail message to the ACT! contact that you specify, even if the contact is in another database. For example, a member of your staff forwards some directions from a client about the project. If you click Quick Attach, it will attach to the staff member's record. Use the Attach to ACT! icon to select the appropriate client's record in your database.

Procedure: To manually attach an e-mail to a Contact

1. Select or open your message in Outlook and click the **Attach to ACT! Contact(s)** icon.   You can also click **Actions**, **Attach**, **Attach to Contact…**.

   If using **ACT! E-mail**, right-click the e-mail you want to attach and select **Attach, Attach to Contact…**.

2. If ACT! finds the e-mail address in your database, the Contact name will be displayed in the right pane. If the address is not found, but the Contact name is found, then that Contact will be displayed in the right pane as a suggestion.

   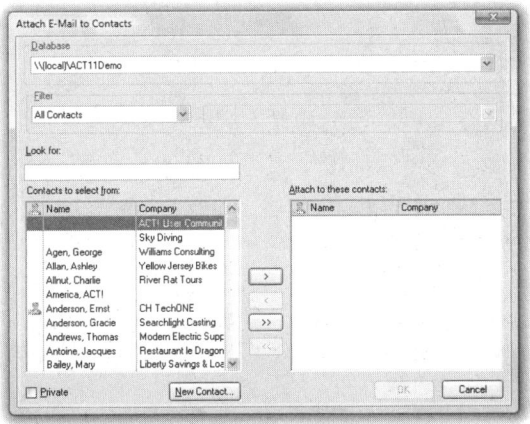

   a. If necessary, change the default database at the top of the dialog.

   b. If the contact used a different e-mail and was not found, in the **Look for:** box try typing the **[last name], [first name]** of the contact to quickly locate the Contact in the list. If found, select the Contact and click **Add** or double-click the correct name.

   c. If the contact does not exist in the selected database, you can click **New Contact…**.

3. Click **OK**.

 *The history of the attachment to an ACT! Contact can take a few seconds to display (click **[F5]** to refresh the view if you like). You can view the attached e-mail in the **History** tab. If you delete the e-mail from your Inbox, it will still display on the **History** tab of the Contact's record. The type of history that will be recorded is defined in the E-mail Setup Wizard in Tools, Preferences.*

Practice: Attaching an E-mail to a Contact	
What to do	**How to do it/Comments**
1. Select another e-mail in your Outlook Inbox and attach it to ACT!.	In Outlook: Select the e-mail. Click the **Attach to ACT! Contact(s)** icon. Select the Contact or click the **New Contact…** button at the bottom of the dialog. After you have created the Contact, **Add** them, and click **OK**.
	In ACT! E-Mail: Select the e-mail. **Attach, Attach to Contact…**.
2. Back in ACT!, locate the attached e-mail and open it.	Open the **History** tab and locate the attached e-mail message. (Remember it can take a few seconds for the history to be recorded in ACT!.) Double-click the history entry to open the message.

Working Via E-mail & Letters | 187

Creating an Activity from an E-Mail

When you receive an e-mail message from a client that requires a follow-up, you can quickly create an activity **in your currently open ACT! database**. You can do this in Outlook, as well as in the ACT! E-mail program.

Procedure: To create an activity from an e-mail message

1. Select the e-mail message in your Inbox and click the **Create ACT! Activity** icon,

    or, if you are using the ACT! E-mail client, you can right-click the e-mail and select **Create Activity from Message...** or use the menu to select **Actions**, **Create Activity from Message...**.

    A Schedule Activity dialog box displays. If ACT! could locate the Contact in your database, their name will display in the **With:** area. Otherwise the activity will be scheduled with your My Record.

    The default activity type is Meeting. The Regarding line is filled in with the same text as the e-mail's subject line. The default Start Date and Time will be the date and time of the original e-mail.

     *ACT! must be open in order to schedule an activity from the e-mail. If you are not logged in to the database that you have defined as the default one to Outlook, then ACT! will first verify that you want to schedule the activity in the currently open ACT! database (or you can click **Cancel** and open the correct database before scheduling).*

2. Schedule and modify the activity details as desired.

    If you are not in your default database, you will see a warning.

3. Click **OK**.

    The activity is scheduled.

Practice: Create an Activity from an E-mail

What to do	How to do it/Comments
1. Use one of the e-mails that you just used to create a Contact in the database, and create a follow-up activity.	In Outlook, select the e-mail and click the **Create ACT! Activity** icon. If you are using the ACT! E-mail window, right-click the e-mail and select **Create Activity from Message...**.
2. Modify the activity details as necessary.	Notice that the Activity Type: is Meeting and that Regarding is taken from the e-mail. Modify as necessary and click **OK**.
3. Note that the e-mail message is included in the Details tab of the activity.	Since you have all you need in ACT!, you can safely delete the e-mail from your Inbox.

Sage ACT!

Sending Contact Information as a vCard

If you would like to send a referral to someone, you can easily send one or more of your ACT! contacts as vCards so that the recipient can add them to their own Address Book.

The vCard includes Company, Contact, Title, Phone, Mobile, Business Address and any Home Address or Home Phone that was included in your ACT! database. Of course, it also includes the e-mail address.

☞ *Contacts sent as vCards can be added to Address Books in Outlook, Lotus Notes, Apple, Blackberry, Windows Mobile®, iPhone™ and both LinkedIn and Facebook.*

Procedure: To send ACT! Contact information as a vCard

1. Look up the contact whose information you want to send.

    If you want to send multiple contacts, select them in Contacts: List View.

2. **Contacts, Send vCard**

    or **Right-click, Send vCard**

    All selected contacts are included as vCards in a new message window.

3. Complete the e-mail and click **Send**.

    Enter e-mail address for the intended recipient, add subject line, etc.

☞ *Only Managers and Administrators can send vCards.*

Practice: Sending a vCard	
What to do	**How to do it/Comments**
1. Look up Lance Parker and send his vCard to yourself.	Type "lance p" in the Lookup pane at the left and click **Go**. Right-click the layout background and select **Send vCard**. Address the e-mail to yourself and **Send**.
2. When the e-mail returns to your Inbox, you can add Lance to your Outlook Address Book. Open the message, double-click the attachment, click **Open**, and the click **Save and Close**.	But… do you really need Lance's info in Outlook?

 OK, so here is a GREAT TIP. As an alternative, you can also quickly include basic contact information in an e-mail. Look up the contact in ACT!. With nothing selected, press [Ctrl+C] to copy the contact information to the windows Clipboard. In the e-mail message window (or in Word), press [Ctrl+V] to paste in the information. The name, title, company, phone, fax, address and e-mail are pasted. This is also a good option if you are a Standard user without rights to export using vCard.

Working Via E-mail & Letters

Recording Gmail History

You can record history of Gmail messages that you send and receive to ACT! contacts with a matching e-mail address.

If you have ever used the ACT!/Outlook connection, it is important to understand some of the differences.

- An e-mail sent from Outlook is recorded to ACT! history almost instantaneously. Gmail history recording is processed in batches.
- In Outlook, you can decided on a case-by-case basis **IF** you want to record a history of the e-mail send and how (subject and message or subject, message and attachments, etc). Gmail history is an all or nothing decision. If you set up the Gmail Integration to record history of an e-mail send, then either **ALL** e-mails sent will be recorded in ACT! or you can select that none will be recorded. Only the default history type you select when setting up the integration will be used.
- In Outlook, you can selectively attach incoming messages to any Contact in ACT! If you set up the Gmail Integration to attach e-mail from the Gmail Inbox, then either **ALL** e-mails found in the Inbox (not moved to other folders) will be attached to the appropriate records in ACT! using the default history type or you can select that none will be attached.
- In Outlook, if your try to record a history for an e-mail where that address is not found in your ACT! database, then you will see the **Attach Error** icon in your System Tray. That feature is only for Outlook messages. The Gmail Integration will not notify you of any failures to record incoming or outgoing e-mails.

My primary e-mail system is Outlook, so my preference is not to record a history of any e-mails found in my Gmail Inbox. I can do that from Outlook. However, I have setup my Google Integration to record all of my outgoing Gmail messages. That way, when I am on the road and I respond to an e-mail from any of my Gmail-connected devices (my phone or my iPad or even just from my online Gmail account), I have a record that I replied with the ACT! contact record.

Procedure: To setup Google Integration to record Gmail history!

1. **Tools, Integrate with Google, Google Integration Preferences**.

   Or right-click the Sage ACT! Integration Service icon in your system tray. Point to **Integrate with Google**, and then click **Preferences**.

2. In the **Record History** tab, click **Enable Gmail History Recording**.

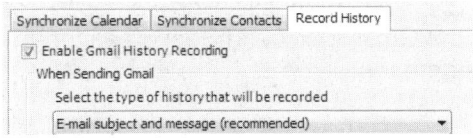

3. Select the type of history from the drop-down menu that will be recorded **When Sending Gmail**.

   See my preferences at the right.

4. Select the type of history from the drop-down menu that will be recorded **When Receiving Gmail**.

   If you receive the same e-mails in Outlook, then select None for this option. Otherwise your e-mail record history will be duplicated. Plus do you really want to record ALL incoming e-mails in ACT!?

   ☞ *If you don't maintain ACT! Contact records for senders of your junk mail or newsletters, then these would not be recorded anyway.*

5. To not have histories of e-mails recorded to your ACT! contact record, click the **Exclude My Record** from history check box.

   Exclude My Record means that e-mails where your e-mail address is included in the To or CC area along with others would be excluded from attaching to your own record. However, the message will be recorded on the other Contacts' records.

6. For initial setup only, select the start date for recording history from Gmail to ACT! Contact records.

   After you select this date and click **OK** to save the preferences, this date selection option is no longer available (and thus you cannot change it) unless you select a different ACT! database.

7. Click **OK** to complete and save your Preferences selections.

8. Answer **Yes** or **No** to launch the sync integration.

If you have set your Google Integration Preferences to perform automatic syncing, then any Record History options that you have set here will be updated at the same time. (If you need to review how to set up the automatic preferences, see page 160.)

Manually syncing Gmail History to ACT!!

Gmail history is synced in batches. Whether you have set up automated syncing or have chosen to manually sync Contacts, Calendar and Record History separately, ACT! searches the Gmail Inbox and Sent areas for any new e-mails since the last sync and then records them.

Working Via E-mail & Letters

Procedure: To manually Record History for Gmail

1. In ACT!, click **Tools, Integrate with Google, Record History**.

   If the option is grayed out, it means that you have not yet set up the Record History option in Google Integration Preferences.

 *This will not affect or override any automatic calendar update schedule you might have set. To edit the schedule, return to **Tools, Integrate with Google, Google Integration Preferences**.*

Understanding the ACT! E-mail Window

If you use Microsoft Office for all of your applications, then you can skip to the next chapter. If you are using another e-mail program (such as Lotus Notes, ACT! or Outlook Express), then read on for a few pages.

ACT!'s E-mail Window displays as a separate program. While the List View, Groups, Companies, Task List, Calendar and Opportunity List views open into windows inside the ACT! program, ACT! E-mail opens into its own window with its own button on the Windows Task Bar.

When you open **ACT! E-mail**, the Inbox displays as it would in any e-mail software. The E-mail window is divided into three panes: the Folder List, the Message Headers list and the Preview Pane. The Status Bar at the bottom of the window indicates the total number of messages and those that remain unread in the selected folder.

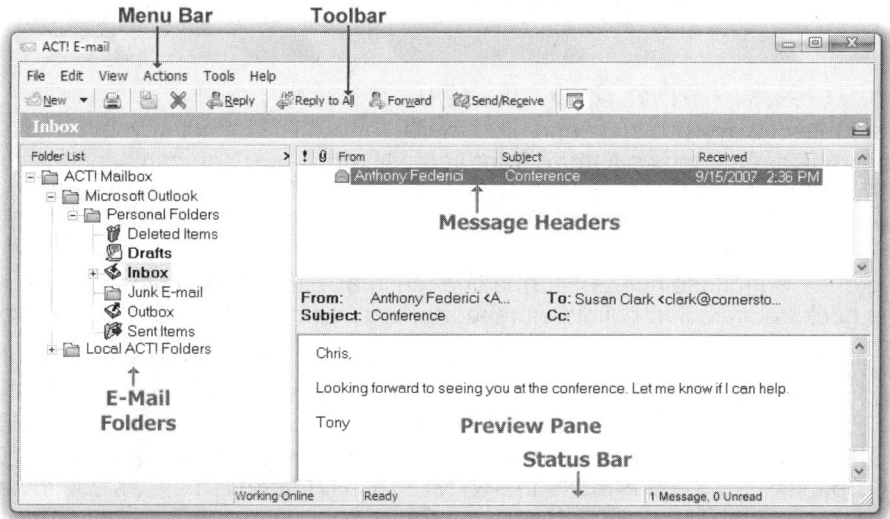

If you have set up another e-mail software to work with ACT!, your default Inbox messages appear to be duplicated here. However, this is just an overlay view of your default e-mail software. If you delete an e-mail here, it is deleted in your regular Inbox.

While it is true that you can perform almost all standard e-mail functions (read, print, create new, move, delete, reply or reply to all, forward, along with a few other amazing features) from this window, you might want to minimize this window and continue to work in your regular e-mail software. Think of the ACT! E-mail window as a link between your ACT! Contacts and your default e-mail software. Just minimize it and let it do its work of linking. There are a few things that you can only do in this window, so let's play with it a while.

Reading Your E-mail

This is so straightforward, it's almost too obvious to include in the book, however, we wanted to be sure you understand the Preview Pane options.

Procedure: To read your e-mail from the ACT! E-mail Window

1. **View**, **E-mail** or click the **E-mail** button. The **ACT! E-mail** window opens and displays the messages from your default e-mail system.

2. Select a message to view it in the Preview Pane or double-click it to open it in its own window. To hide the Preview Pane, click **View**, **Preview Pane** or click the **Toggle Preview Pane** icon.

☞ *You can change the size of the Preview Pane by placing the mouse pointer over the middle splitter bar. When the pointer displays as a double-headed arrow, drag the bar up or down.*

Sending E-mail from ACT! E-mail

There are lots of ways you can send an e-mail to an ACT! Contact in your database and have that action recorded as **E-mail Sent** in the **History** tab. You can send the message using several methods from the ACT! Detail View, from the ACT! E-mail window, and from Outlook.

To send e-mails that use rich-text formatting (such as different font types, styles and colors, different background color, bullets, numbering, alignment, hyperlinks, etc.), you must…

- Select Internet Mail or Microsoft Outlook as your e-mail system to use with ACT! (**Tools, Preferences, E-mail** tab). Outlook Express, Lotus Notes, and Eudora can only send plain-text messages from ACT!.
- If you are using Internet Mail, set your Tools, Preferences…, E-mail tab, Composing Options… to **Send e-mails in:** HTML. The HTML option allows you to send out the rich-text formatted templates from Internet Mail.

Since you've been looking at the ACT! E-mail window, let's start with that view first.

Procedure: To send an e-mail from the ACT! E-mail window

1. In the ACT! e-mail window…

   click the **New** icon on the toolbar, or

   press **[Ctrl+N]**, or

   File, **New**, **Mail Message** or **Mail Message (from template)…** .

   Start from the ACT! e-mail window.

   When you create a message, the New Message window displays. If you entered a signature during the ACT! E-mail setup, it displays in the message pane.

   If you select the **Mail Message (from Template)…** option, the ACT! Mail Merge Wizard displays.

 *If you selected more than one e-mail in the E-mail System Setup (e.g., Outlook and Outlook Express), then you can change the e-mail package that will send the e-mail by choosing it in the **From:** drop-down list.*

2. **To...** Type the last name of the person you wish to send the e-mail to in the **To…** area,

   or click the **To...** button to view the Address book to select additional recipients from **All Contacts**, **Current Lookup**, **Groups**, or **Companies**,

   or click the **To...** to enter a name in the **Bcc** area,

   or just enter a valid e-mail address.

   If the Contact is in your ACT! database, their e-mail address will be used and a history is recorded.

   If there is more than one person with the same name, a dialog box will display allowing you to select the correct Contact.

   If you enter an e-mail address belonging to one of your Contacts, a history is still created. Cool!

3. **[Tab]** to or click in the **Subject:** and fill in the text for the subject line.

4. **[Tab]** to or click in the text area of the e-mail to type your message.

5. Format your message as desired.

   You can change the font face, size, color … add bullets … hyperlinks … even pictures.

6. **S̲pelling, Check D̲ocument** or press **[F7]**.

   Don't forget to spell check.

7. Click an Attachment icon to attach
   a **Contact** record,
     a **Group** of Contacts,
       a **Company** of Contacts,
         or a **File**.

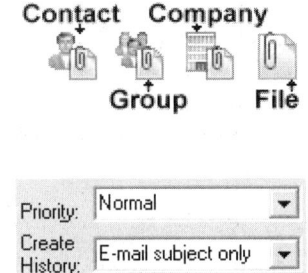

8. Change as desired, the
   Priorit̲y: option or
     Create Histor̲y: option or
       Make private option or
         Ret̲urn receipt option.

9. Click **S̲end** or press **[Ctrl+Enter]**.

   Depending on the **Create History** option you select, a history of **E-mail Sent** is placed in the Contact's **History** tab and the **Last E-mail** system field is updated.

☞ *To speed up sending e-mails during the day, leave the ACT! E-mail window minimized. If you close the window, and then later send another e-mail, it has to start up and load all the messages found in your default e-mail Inbox all over again. Remember, just think of the ACT! E-mail window as a link between your ACT! Contacts and your default e-mail software…it needs to run in the background.*

Send/Receive Button

Your system is probably already set up to automatically send any e-mail that is waiting in the Outbox and to check for any incoming e-mail at specified time intervals. If you are using Internet Mail or Outlook Express, the Send/Receive button on the top of the **ACT! E-mail** window performs an immediate Send/Receive when you are connected (instead of waiting for the next timed Send/Receive).

If you are using Microsoft Outlook, clicking the **Send/Receive** button in the ACT! E-Mail window does not perform a true send and receive. It only refreshes the display of message headers in the ACT! E-mail Inbox, making sure that the same e-mails that display in your Outlook Inbox, also display in the ACT! E-mail Inbox. To execute an actual Send/Receive command in this scenario, you must click the **Send/Receive** button in Outlook.

Working Via E-mail & Letters

Practice: Using the ACT! E-mail Window

What to do	How to do it/Comments
1. Open the ACT! E-mail window, if you haven't already.	**View**, **E-mail** or click the **E-mail** button.
2. Send an e-mail to your personal e-mail address with a **Subject:** of: New Marketing Idea Enter a message about a new marketing idea you've been thinking about. Select the **Subject only** history option.	Click the **New** icon on the toolbar. (If you entered your signature in the last practice, it will display in the message pane.) Type your e-mail address in the **To...** area. Change the **Create History:** option to record history (whichever method you like). Fill out the rest of the e-mail and click **Send**.
3. Where was the history created? **[Alt+Tab]** back to ACT! or click the ACT! button on the Windows Task Bar and locate the history.	In the first Review exercise, we asked you to create a record with your information in it. If you filled in an ACT! Contact record including your e-mail address, this e-mail is recorded to your Contact's **History** tab. If you didn't, the history was recorded on the "My Record" (Chris Huffman) Contact.
4. Don't exit the ACT! E-mail window. Just minimize it.	If you plan on sending additional e-mails through ACT!, you should always minimize the ACT! E-mail window.

 *If you reply to an e-mail from the ACT! E-mail window, your signature is not automatically added. After you have completed your reply text, you can insert the signature you entered (in **Tools**, **Preferences**, **E-mail** tab, **Composing Options...**, **Signatures...**) by clicking on **Insert**, **Signature**.*

Choosing a Word Processor

During the installation of ACT!, the Setup Assistant prompted you to select your default word processor: the ACT! word processor or Microsoft Word. The ACT! word processor is specifically designed for and integrated with your ACT! software and has many nice features. However, if you are using the Microsoft Office suite of products, you will probably want to select Word.

Sage ACT!

Procedure: To choose a word processor

1. **Tools, Preferences....**

2. Click the **Communication** tab.

   The **Preferences** dialog box appears.

   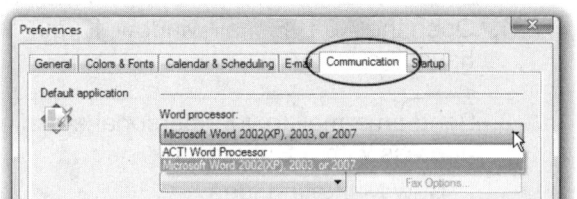

3. Select the **Word processor:** from the drop-down list.

   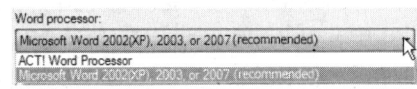

   A list of word processors supported by ACT! appears.

    Other than its own Word Processor, ACT! supports Microsoft Word starting with version 2002 (XP) to the current version.

4. Click **OK**.

 While ACT! can work quite well with Word (provided you have one of the appropriate versions), unless you need the power that this high-end word processor provides (such as advanced use of tables, columns, or graphics), you might want to try using the ACT! word processor. We think you will find it easy, fast, and reliable. You can learn more about the ACT! word processor starting on page 214.

New Menu Item in Word

If Microsoft Word is also installed on your PC, then you will find a new menu option on the standard Word menu bar ... **ACT!**.

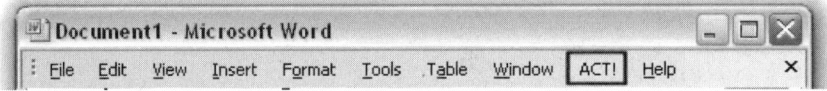

 If you are using Word 2007, the ACT! menu command is under the Add-Ins tab.

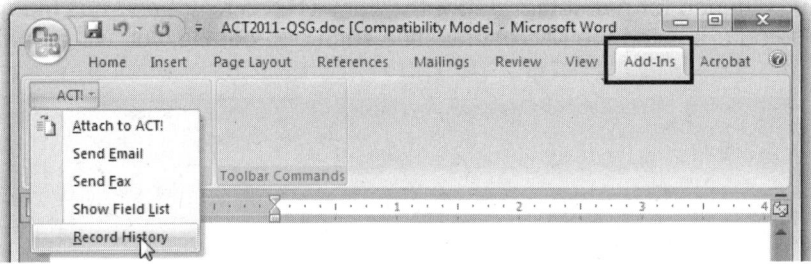

Working Via E-mail & Letters

The menu command options are:

- **Attach to ACT!** – saves a copy of the currently displayed document into the **\Attachments** folder and attaches a shortcut to the Contact(s) you select. This menu option is also available in Microsoft Excel. It is a great tool for attaching documents and spreadsheets that you have received through e-mail. However, if you have already saved the document to another location, when you click **ACT!**, **Attach to ACT!**, you will be asked if you would like to switch to working with the copy of the new document that has just been saved in the \Attachments (supplemental file system) folder.

    > *ACT! will not delete the copy of the existing document. You now have two documents on your system. After answering **Yes** to work with the new copy, you should delete the old copy.*

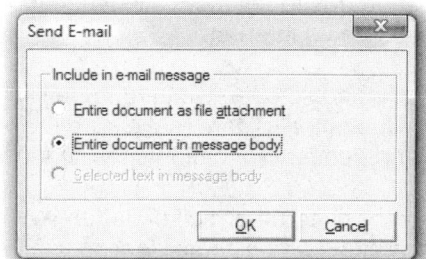

- **Send E-mail** – sends the currently displayed document as an attachment or as the e-mail message body to the selected Contact.
- **Send Fax** – faxes the currently displayed document to a Contact. Faxing from ACT! requires that you have faxing software installed on your PC.
- **Show Field List** – displays the **Show Mail Merge Fields** dialog box for creating Mail Merge templates.
- **Record History** – records a history of the document in the contact's history tab. Optionally it also saves the merged document as an attachment in the history tab. It creates a history without having to print the document.

Practice: Using Microsoft Word

What to do	How to do it/Comments
1. Verify which word processor ACT! is using.	**Tools**, **Preferences**.... Click the **Communication** tab, select **Microsoft Word 2002 (XP)**, **2003**, **2007**, or **2010** if it is available on your PC. Click **OK**.

> *If you don't plan to use Word on your PC, then you will want to skip to page 214 to learn more about ACT!'s built-in word processor and e-mail.*

Mail-merge Templates

Single e-mails are nice, but more and more, mass mailings are a common marketing tool. You can create loads of mail-merge templates with ACT!. Whether you will mail-merge them to e-mail or to the printer, the template is created in exactly the same way…using your default word processor.

You send the same e-mail or letter over and over to different Contacts in your database (such as an introduction) or to a large number of people all at once (to notify them of a new product offering or perhaps to tell them all something that is of common interest.)

You could open with a phrase like "Dear Valued Customer." Then, make sure the letter contains no gender or location specific terms.

However, an e-mail or letter like this does not make your customer feel special! And if they don't feel special... well....

```
    Generic Industrial Products
         Anytown, NH 10000

Dear Valued Customer,

We wanted you to know just how much we appreciate your business,
and hope you are finding our product(s) and service(s) adequate or
better.

On a personal note I really enjoyed our last visit. I hope the next time I
visit your neck of the woods I hope you will have time to visit. Please
call me if I can be of any service in any way. It is people like you that
make my business what it is.

Thank you

George Generic
```

Creating a Mail-merge Template

ACT! can create highly customized e-mails or letters that you can use to send to an individual contact or to a group of contacts. In each of these cases, however, you have to create the body of the letter yourself.

- A **template is a pre-defined message**. In addition to text, it contains special "place holders" that read data from the current Contact record(s) and from your My Record to make the e-mail or letter personal (names, addresses, dates, etc.).
- When you use an ACT! template to create a new e-mail, letter, memo, or fax cover page, information like **Name and Address is placed where the "place holders" were in the template**.
- Once the template is created, you can merge it with the Contact records you wish to send the e-mail or letter to. Each Contact has a separate message created for them.
- Whether you mail merge to paper or e-mail, the default word processor is used to create the merge template.
- The more information you keep on your Contacts, the more personal you can make your messages.

Working Via E-mail & Letters | 199

Practice: Understanding Mail-Merge Templates

What to do	How to do it/Comments
1. Look up Lance Parker	In the Lookup pane at the left, type "lance p" and click Go.
2. Click Wr**i**te, **L**etter ☞ *If you are in the ACT2012Demo database, the letter template has been modified to include the company logo. You can do the same for the templates in your company database.*	Your default word processor displays with the start of a letter… an inside address, a salutation and a signature.
3. Notice that the inside address picked up Lance's address information. The signature is pulled from the My Record.	If you changed your title on your My Record to Supreme Commander, then that would be title displayed in the Letter signature. If your My Record does not have an e-mail or phone number listed, then they won't appear on merged templates either, so be sure to keep all of the information on your My Record up to date.
4. Let's look at the letter template to see what it looks like before it is merged.	**Wr**i**te**, **Edit T**emplate…, choose "letter" and click **Open**.
5. Notice the mail-merge placeholders for the contact's address. Notice that the signature fields are all prefixed with the word My:. Close the template without saving.	
6. Check out the Fax Cover using Lance's record.	**Wr**i**te, F**ax Cover Page
7. Note how all the information is pulled from Lance's record and from Chris' record.	
8. Start an e-mail message to Lance.	Click **Wr**i**te, E-mail Message**.
9. A new message window displays in Outlook.	No template is used. If you have a signature in Outlook, then that signature is used. If not, then you will see a blank message window that is addressed to Lance.
10. Close the e-mail without sending.	Click on the **Close** button. Click **No** to save changes.

What to do	How to do it/Comments
11. ACT2012Demo has an "EmailBody" template that can be used as a base for creating mail-merge templates for mass e-mails. Click **Write, Other Document (from template)**, select the EmailBody template and click Open.	It opens in your default word processor, but this is what it will look like when merged to e-mail. The default EmailBody template in your ACT! database is usually blank. If you like this one, you can copy it to the \Templates folder for your ACT! database.

The easiest way to create a new mail-merge template is to modify one that has already been created.

Procedure: To create a new template from an existing template

1. Choose **Write, Edit Template...** from the menu.

   The **Open** dialog box appears.

    *ACT! displays the contents of the **Template** folder automatically. These are not documents; they are template files.*

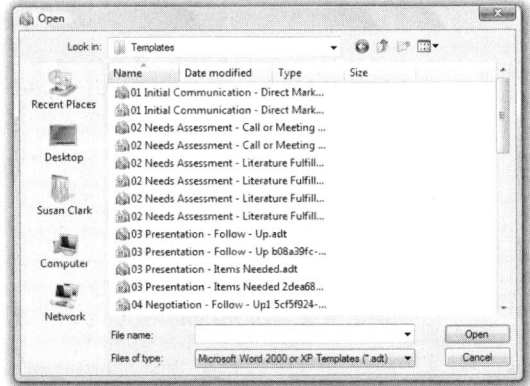

2. Select the template that is closest in style and content to what you want to use and click **Open**.

   If you are creating a letter, select the **"letter"** template. If you are creating an e-mail, select the **"emailbody"** template.

When you open the template in edit mode, you will notice the **Add Mail Merge Fields** dialog box. Depending upon the word processor that you are using, it may look slightly different from the one portrayed at the right.

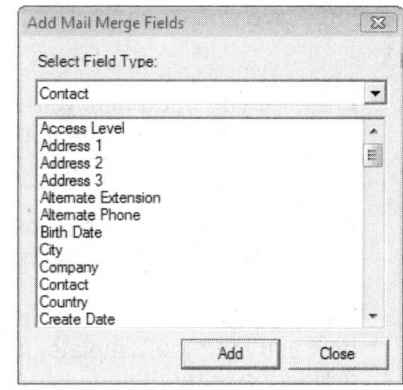

Ignore this box for a few minutes. If it gets in your way, click the **Close** button. You can re-display it (In Microsoft Word it is **ACT!**, **Show Fields List…**). In the ACT! word processor **View**, **Mail-Merge Fields**.

3. **File**, **Save As…**, type a new name for the template, and click **Save**.

    Unless you want to modify the original template, always save with a new name.

    ☞ *Do this BEFORE you edit your new template so you don't accidentally overwrite the basic template.*

4. Edit the template as desired, adding mail-merge fields, tables, formatted text, hyperlinks, graphics, etc..

    You can copy and paste from another document if you have created something similar.

5. Insert field place holders, as necessary, by positioning the insertion point in the message. Select the appropriate **Field type**,

    If you do not see the **Add Mail Merge Fields** dialog box…

    In Word, **ACT!**, **Show Fields List…**.

    In Word 2007, click the Add-Ins tab, from the Menu Commands group, select ACT!, and click **Show Fields List…**.

    - **Contact**-inserts a place holder for data from the Contact's record.
    - **Label**-inserts the field label only.
    - **My Record**-inserts a place holder for data from the current 'My Record' (allowing other users to use the same template).

    In the ACT! word processor, click **View**, **Mail-Merge Fields**.

6. Select the field to insert and click **Add**.

    A place holder displays where the actual data will be when the mail merge is run.

7. Be sure to include a signature using the My Record merge fields.

    If you are the only user of your database, then you can just type in your signature as you want it to appear in the e-mail or letter.

8. Save and close the file.   You are now ready to merge the template
                                                with one or many Contact records.

 *If you need help with some of your writing, you can use or edit the sample templates in the **Templates** folder. There are sample templates for birthday, anniversary, order confirmation, follow-up, prospecting, special offers, and more.*

OK, now that you see how basic mail-merge templates are created, let's create one that we can use to respond to prospects who have contacted us through our Web site.

The only difference in creating a mail-merge template for letters or a template for e-mails is how you start the template. If you include the contact's address at the top left, it would be used for a letter. If you just start with the salutation, it would be used for an e-mail.

Practice: Creating a Mail-Merge Template

What to do	How to do it/Comments
1. Edit the "**emailbody**" document template. When the word processor displays, click its maximize button.	**Write**, **Edit Template...**, choose **emailbody**, and click **Open**.
2. Save the template as **Web Response**. *(You should always do this **before** you make any changes to the original template.)*	**File**, **Save As...** (don't choose **File**, **Save** or click the Save button), type **Web Response**, and click **Save**.
3. Observe the **Mail Merge Fields** dialog box. (When using Word…if it blocks your view of the message, move it so it doesn't.)	Point to the title bar of the box, hold down the left mouse button, and drag the box to a different spot.
4. Type the following on a line beneath the salutation: **Thank you**, followed by a space.	You're going to insert a field after the space.
5. Insert the **Salutation** field for the contact and then a comma and a space. **Thank you, <Salutation>,**	In the **Add Mail Merge Fields** dialog box, scroll down in the list and select **Salutation**. Click **Add**. Be sure to click on the template, if necessary.

Working Via E-mail & Letters | 203

What to do	How to do it/Comments
6. Type the following: **for visiting our Web site and requesting more information. Enclosed is a sample of our CH TechONE system, which speaks for itself about our quality and commitment to outstanding products.** **People all over** and add a space.	Press the **[Spacebar]** after the word "over." You're going to insert another field at the end of the sentence.
7. Insert the **City** field for the contact and add a space.	Scroll up in the **Add Mail Merge Fields** dialog box list, select **City**, and click **Add**.
8. Finish the letter with the following: **are enjoying our products. Please feel free to call me with any questions or concerns at** Have ACT! put in the phone number of the current "My Record."	With your cursor in place at the end of the sentence, change the **Field Type:** to My Record and select the **Phone** field. Click **Add**.
9. Type a period after the My Record phone field. Save the template.	Click the Save button or choose **File**, **Save** to save the changes you just made.
10. Exit the word processor.	

Merging the E-mail Template

When your template is complete, you are ready to merge. You can merge it with the current Contact's information or with an entire lookup. You can also choose to include attachments with your e-mail merges.

It is always a good idea to test the template with one or two Contacts (before a large merge), just to see if you missed any spaces or placed any fields where they should not be.

Procedure: To merge a template

1. Perform a lookup that displays the Contact(s) you wish to receive your letter.

2. Choose **Write**, **E-mail Message (from template)** to send to a single Contact, or…
   Choose **Write**, **Mail Merge….** to send to multiple Contacts.

   If you are sending to a single Contact, you are finished.

   If you select Mail Merge, the **Wizard** starts.

3. The first window may appear as a Welcome page. Check the box **Check to hide in the future** and click **Next**.

4. **Select Output** – You can merge directly to the **Printer**, send the letter as an **E-mail** (*you must have e-mail set up to work with ACT! for this to work*), or even **Fax** it to all of the Contacts in your lookup (*each Contact must have a valid fax number and you must have a fax modem and appropriate fax software for this to work*). If you are testing your merge, or if you want to review it before you actually send or print, choose **Word Processor**.

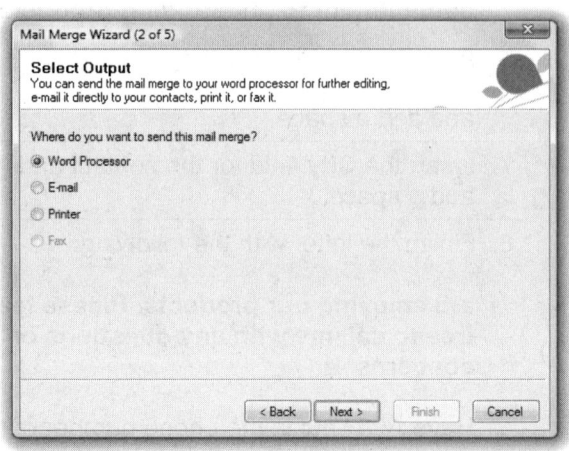

   Click **Next>**.

5. **Select Template** – Click **Browse…** to locate the template to use in the Mail Merge. Select a template and click **Open**.

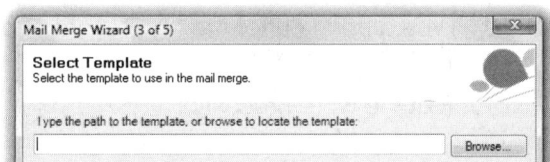

   Click **Next>**.

   ☞ *By default, the last template used in a mail merge displays here.*

6. In Select Contact…, select the Contacts for the e-mail merge.

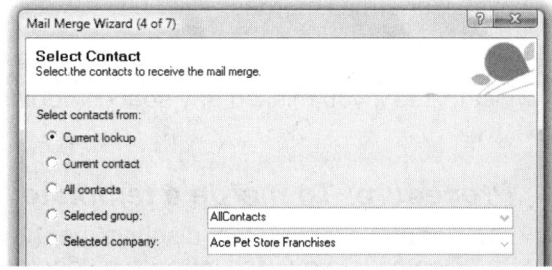

   ☞ *Use the **Current contact** if you are testing the template.*

   Click **Next>**.

7. If you chose **E-mail...**

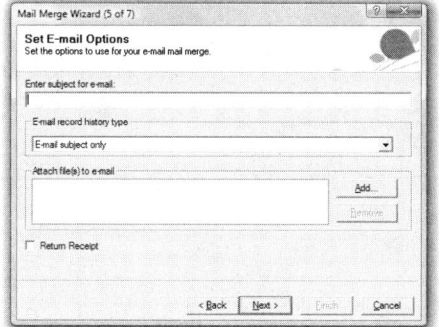

Enter a **Subject** for e-mail:

Select how you would like record the history (None, Subject only, Subject + Message, or Attach to Contact(s)),

Add... attachments and check the **Return receipt**, as desired.

Click **Next>**.

8. **Set Options for Missing E-mail Addresses** –You can select from four options. However, we like the third option. It sends your e-mails and then creates a new lookup of Contacts without an e-mail address so that you can write a letter or call to get an e-mail address for future mailings.

Click **Next>**.

If you chose **Printer**

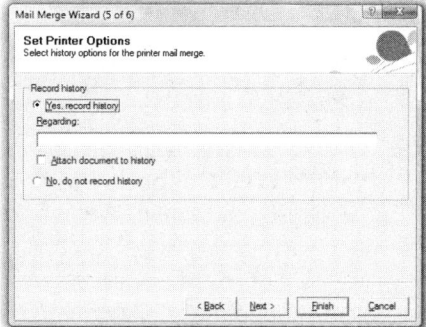

Enter what you would like to display in the **History** tab under **Regarding:** or select **No, do not record history**.

Attaching a document is probably not as valid for mail merges from templates that you use all the time.

Click **Next>** and go to step 8.

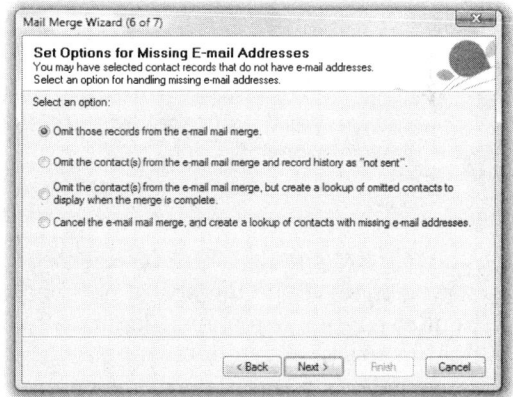

9. Completing the **ACT! Mail Merge Wizard** – provides a **Summary of tasks** completed. Click **Finish**.

You will see what is being merged, where the output is, and which template you selected.

☞ *If you output to a printer or e-mail, the messages are printed or e-mailed, and a history is created for each Contact in the lookup. If you chose word processor, the documents display in the word processor. One document is created for each Contact in the lookup. A section break is placed between each letter. If all is as it should be, you can print from the word-processor menu.*

Practice: Caution, Merging Letters Ahead

What to do	How to do it/Comments
1. Look up all Contacts who were referred by the "Web site."	Right-click the **Referred By** field and select **Lookup Referred By**. Enter the "Web site" and click **OK**.
2. Test the **Web Response** template on one of the contacts in the list.	**Write, E-mail Message (from template)**, select the "Web Response" template and click **Open**.
☞ Since there are no valid e-mails in the database, let's mail-merge the template to the Word Processor so you can see the results.	
3. Merge the **Web Response** template with the active lookup and display it in the word processor.	**Write, Mail Merge...**, and click **Next>** at the Welcome screen, choose **Word Processor**, click **Next>**, use the **Browse...** button to select the **Web Response** letter you just created (if you didn't do the previous exercise, select any template), click **Next>**, choose **Current Lookup**, and click **Next>**, click **Finish**.
4. View the results in your word processor.	Scroll down to view all messages. Notice how the inserted fields display the correct information for each Contact in the body of the letter.
5. Exit the word processor without saving your changes.	**File, Exit**, or click the **Close** button on the title bar. If you're prompted to save, click **No**.

Sending an E-mail to Group or Company Members

Although we are in the age of personalization, sometimes you just need to send a quick e-mail to everyone in a specific group (your breakfast networking group for example) to let them know of an agenda change.

Procedure: To e-mail Group or Company members

1. Display the Groups or Companies view. — Click either the Groups or Companies button on the Navbar.

2. Select the Group (or Company) you wish to send an e-mail to.

Working Via E-mail & Letters | 207

3. **Write, E-mail Message** or **E-mail Message (from template)**.

   A new message window appears with all of the member e-mail addresses displayed in the **To:** area.

4. You may need to manually delete the names of users who don't have e-mails associated with their names.

   It's easy to see which ones don't have e-mail addresses (they aren't underlined). If you don't delete the names, the e-mail may not be sent.

5. Fill out the e-mail as usual and click **Send**.

   History will be recorded on each Contact's record (except for those that you deleted).

Creating Letters, Memos, and Fax Cover Pages

Even though creating a letter is the same as creating an e-mail template, let's review very quickly. We will divide this process into two steps: creating and printing the letter.

Procedure: To create a letter

1. Display the Contact you want to send a letter to.

2. Choose **Write**, **Letter** from the menu, or click the **Write Letter** toolbar icon.

   A document window opens in your selected word processor with the date, name, address, and other relevant information entered and formatted for you.

3. Type the body of the letter where prompted with *Type body of letter here...*.

4. Click **File**, **Print...** (and attach),

   or **File**, **Send**, **E-mail** (ACT WP)
   or **ACT!**, **Send E-mail** (Word WP),
   or **ACT!**, **Attach to ACT!** (Word WP).

   For Word 2007, click the **Office Button** and select **Print** or
   On the **Add-Ins** tab, in the **Menu Commands** group, click **ACT!** and select **Attach** or **Send**.

 *To return to the ACT! database window, you can close or minimize the word-processing window. If you are using Microsoft Word as your word processor, you could just click the ACT! button on the Windows task bar (which leaves the word processor open for fast access when you create a new document) or press **[Alt+Tab]** to switch back and forth between the ACT! database window and Word.*

Click here to return to ACT!

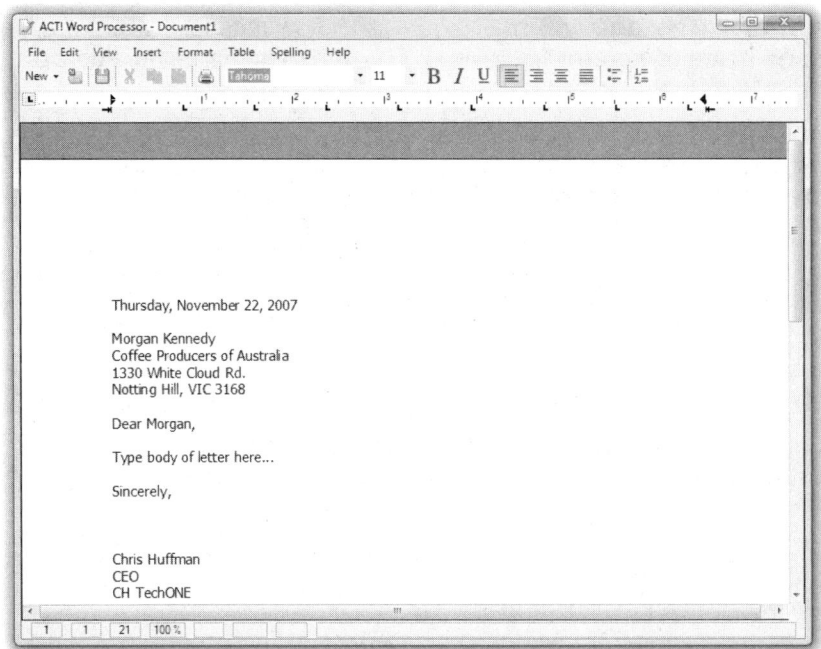

Practice: Letters and Fax Cover Sheets

What to do	How to do it/Comments
1. Look up **Kristi Cameron**.	Choose **Lookup**, **Contact…**, type **Kristi c**, and click **OK**.
2. Create a letter for Kristi.	Choose **Write**, **Letter**, or click the Letter icon on the toolbar.
3. Type the body of the letter shown below.	Delete the phrase **Type body of letter here…** before beginning.

In less than 6 months, American Dreams could reach your goal of reduced expenses while exceeding your plans to become "green" by the end of the year. Can we meet with you next week to discuss the new component in our TechONE system?

4. Spell check the letter, if you like, **and leave it displayed**.	

Working Via E-mail & Letters

Printing Documents

The process of printing from a word-processor is not tough. Click on the Print icon (or choose it from the menu). However, when you print a document that started with ACT!, something else happens after you send the document to the printer. You will be asked if you would like to record a history that you printed the document (and why shouldn't you?), as well as attach the document to the Contact. Attaching the document is a great feature. If your contact calls and refers to a document you sent them, it will be no more than a few clicks away for you or anyone on your team (in case you're not there)!

Procedure: To print a document

1. **File, Print...**

   Select your printer and print options.

   Click **OK**.

2. Enter a descriptive phrase in **Regarding:**.

    *Type a few words that describe the document contents. This description will display in the Regarding column on the Contact's **History** tab.*

   "**No**, **do not record history**" is a good option if you are re-printing the document.

   The document is sent to your printer and the **Create History** dialog box appears.

3. Check **Attach document to history** to attach a link to the document on the **History** tab of the Contact's record.

   This option allows quick access for you (or others in your company) to open the document for review or modifications later. If you have remote sync users, it may also be possible to sync these attachments. (We'll talk about sync later.)

   You would probably NOT check this option for something like a Fax Cover or a standard mail-merge letter (no need to save).

    If you opt to Attach the file to history, ACT! automatically gives your file a name and saves it to the \Attachments folder. The file name is a combination of the template name, the date, the time, and the contact name.

4. Select **Yes** if you wish to print an envelope.

5. Click **OK**.

6. If you opt to print an envelope, another **Print** dialog displays.

    Select the appropriate envelope size (10 is what most companies use). Click **Print**.

    Choose the output and change the filter, if necessary, to Current Contact. (You will need to know how your printer handles envelopes.)

    Click **OK**.

The Print envelope box will appear after clicking **OK**.

Don't be discouraged if preview is not available. Envelopes come in standard sizes. All you have to know is which one you have.

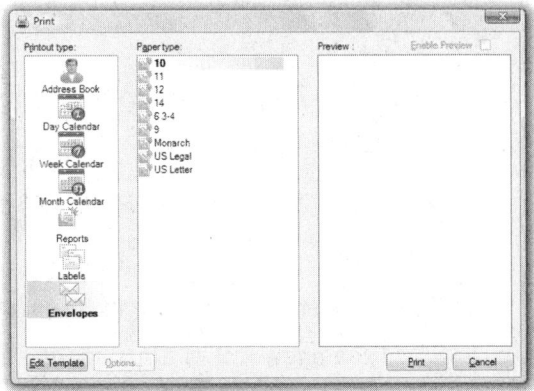

 Some printers go off-line and wait for you to manually feed the envelope. Others may feed from an envelope tray.

Editing the Attached Document

When you attach a document, it appears on the **History** tab with a special icon and displays the information you previously typed for the Regarding and Details.

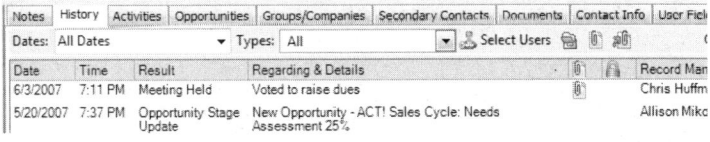

- If you single-click the Attachment or Shortcut icon, the document will open for editing.

- If you double-click the row, the Edit History dialog box displays. From here you can click the Attachment link to open the file for editing. After reviewing and then closing the file, the Edit History dialog box will still display for you to add Details of why and when you edited the attached file.

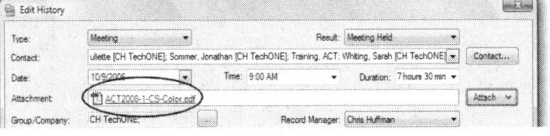

Working Via E-mail & Letters

Practice: Printing Kristi's Letter

What to do	How to do it/Comments
1. Print the letter.	If you didn't create a custom letter for Kristi in the previous exercise, just click **Write**, **Letter**, choose **File**, **Print...**, and click **OK**.
2. Create a history of the letter for this Contact noting that it was a **Promo for new TechONE Component**. Attach the document to the **History** tab. Do not print an envelope.	In the **Create History** dialog box, type **Promo for new TechONE Component**. Make sure there's a check in the **Attach document to history** check box and that the option for Printing an envelope is set to **No**. Click **OK**.
3. Notice the name of your document. Close the word-processor window.	The new document that was attached to the **History** tab is named with the name of the template (Letter) - the date + some random numbers – and the Contact's name. It was saved to the \Attachments folder. **File**, **Exit**, or click the **Close** button on the word-processor title bar.
4. View Kristi Cameron's **History** tab.	You should see the attachment icon with the **Letter Sent** history.
5. Double-click the Attachment icon to review the letter and add an additional comment to the history.	Double-click the icon for the **Promo for new TechONE Component** attachment.
6. Review the document. Make changes if you like, and then save and close the file.	
7. The **Edit History** dialog box was hiding behind the word processor. Add a note to the **Details:** section and close the **Edit History** dialog box.	Choose **File**, **Exit**, or click the **Close** button on the title bar.
8. Notice that the details that you added display below the **Promo for new TechONE Component** regarding line.	

Envelopes and Mailing Labels

Once you have completed a mail merge, it is always a good idea to immediately print the envelopes or mailing labels. That way, the order of the labels (or envelopes) printed will exactly match the printout order of the merged letters. Whether you are printing one or many, the process is the same.

Procedure: To create envelopes or mailing labels

1. Perform a lookup that displays the Contact(s) for whom you want to generate envelopes or mailing labels.

   If you have just completed a document mail merge, your lookup is probably still displayed.

2. Choose **File, Print...** ,

   or press [Ctrl+P].

   The **Print** dialog box appears. Note the **Printout Type:** list on the left.

3. Under the Printout Type: choose **Envelopes or Labels**.

   A list of envelope or mailing label sizes appears from which you may choose.

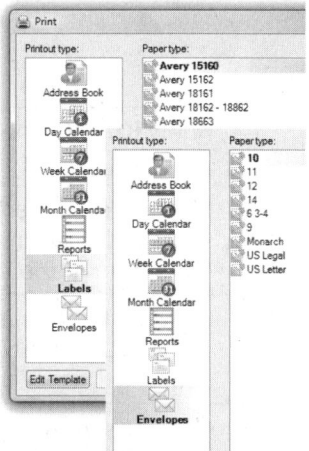

4. Choose the desired envelope size or label number.

   Select one of the choices in the list. To customize a label or envelope, or create your own, click the **Edit Template** button.

5. Click **Print**.

   A **Define Filters** dialog box appears.

6. Choose the Contact(s) to **Create report for**.

   Current Contact creates one envelope/label for the current Contact.

   Current Lookup prints all Contacts in the current lookup.

   All Contacts prints the entire database.

Working Via E-mail & Letters

7. If you want to be included in the mailing, verify that there is no check in **Exclude 'My Record'**.

8. If necessary, click the drop-down arrow and choose a **Send the report output to:** option.

☞ *Changing the Use data managed by option may change the outcome of the list of labels or envelopes. This option is also more relevant to printing reports.*

This option only affects the printing if your My Record is actually in the current lookup.

Preview displays the printout in Print Preview so you can review it before printing.
Printer sends the job directly to your printer without displaying it first.

☞ *There are other output options here, but they probably wouldn't be used for labels or envelopes. We'll talk more about the options in the Report section.*

9. If you selected **Labels**, the **Position** tab displays where you can specify the starting row and column, thus allowing you to print partial sheets of labels.

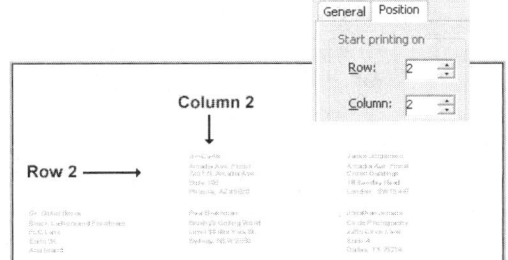

10. Click **OK**.

Practice: Creating an Envelope	
What to do	**How to do it/Comments**
1. Let's print Avery 5160 labels (3 across and 10 down) for the Web Response letters we just merged. We have one partially used sheet of labels with the first 5 labels missing.	**File**, **Print…**, click **Labels**, click Avery 15160, and click **Print**. Verify that **Preview** is the report output option selected, select the **Current Lookup**, click the **Position** tab, enter 2 for the Row and 3 for the Column, and click **OK**. No wasted sheets of labels here. Close Print Preview.
2. Print an envelope for **Kristi Cameron**.	Use any method you like to look up Kristi.
3. Create and *preview* (don't print) an envelope. Use the number 10 size.	**File**, **Print…**, choose **Envelopes**, confirm that **#10** is selected, and click **Print**. Choose **Current Contact** and **Preview**. Click **OK**.
4. Whose return address is on the envelope? Why?	Once again, we illustrate the importance of the My Record.
5. Close the Preview window.	Click the **Close** button.

ACT! Word Processor

The ACT! Word Processor is fully capable of meeting the majority of your word-processing needs, but if you need to use Microsoft Word because it is required by your company, you can use it instead. Naturally, you must have Word installed on your computer in order for ACT! to use it.

The ACT! Word Processing window has its own Menu, Toolbar, and Ruler at the top of the window and Status Bar at the bottom. While ACT! cannot format text into columns (who uses columns anymore anyway, when you can use tables) or provide the ability to do elaborate formatting of an inserted graphic, it can provide many of the same features found in Microsoft Word, like formatting text, inserting tables, and checking spelling.

Practice: Using the ACT! Word Processor

What to do	How to do it/Comments
1. Change to using the ACT! Word Processor.	**Tools**, **Preferences**.... Click the **Communication** tab, select **ACT! Word Processor**, and click **OK**.
2. Select **Write**, **Letter** to open the ACT! Word Processor window.	So that you can follow along with the descriptions.

ACT! Toolbar

A **Toolbar** displays at the top of the ACT! Word Processing window. Like toolbars in most programs, it allows you (with a single click) to create new documents, open existing documents, save the current document, cut, copy and paste text and print. It also contains formatting options for font style, font size, and attributes such as Bold, Italic, and Underline. If you are looking for even more formatting options, try using the menu command of **Format**, **Font** you can also specify Strikeout text, double-underlining, superscript (or subscript), font color or even a background color for your text.

There are four paragraph alignment buttons: Left, Right, Centered, and Justified. The **Format**, **Paragraph**... menu command also allow you to change line spacing, as well as apply Left, Right, or First line (hanging) indents.

At the end of the toolbar are the Bullets and Numbering icons. Bulleted List applies a bullet to an indented paragraph. The Numbers icon applies sequential numbers to selected paragraphs. Pressing **[Enter]** at the end of that paragraph creates a new bulleted or numbered paragraph. Additional bullet characters or number formats, and associated formatting, are available in the **Format**, **Bullets and Numbering**, **Attributes**... dialog box.

☞ *Toolbar display is controlled by **View**, **Toolbar**.*

Working Via E-mail & Letters | 215

Ruler

The **Ruler** visually displays the current tab settings, which are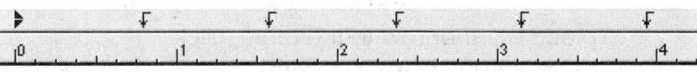
set to every half inch by default. To change the tab setting for a specific paragraph in the document, use the mouse to drag any tab off of the Ruler or to its new location on the Ruler.

You can also control the tab measurements and tab alignments from the **Tabs** dialog box (**Format**, **Ta<u>b</u>…**). The **Right most tab** option places a right-aligned tab at the right page margin.

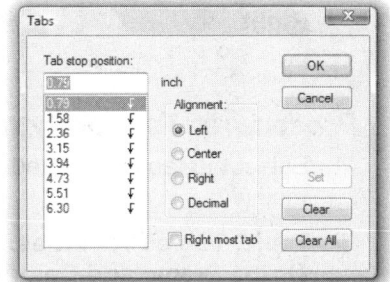

 Right-click any paragraph to add font, paragraph, or tab formatting.

Status Bar

The **Status Bar** at the bottom of the word processor window displays the location of the insertion point by page number, line number, horizontal character spacing. It also displays the current page zoom level (controlled by **V**iew, **Z**oom…).

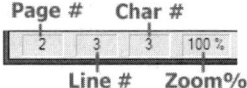

Tables

Including a table in your document or template is easy. ACT! provides lots of formatting options as well.

 When we start to talk about mail-merge fields in a few moments, you will be glad to know that you can place the mail-merge fields inside a table to help you keep your data evenly spaced in the document.

Procedure: To insert a table

1. **<u>T</u>able, <u>I</u>nsert, <u>T</u>able…**.

   Select the number of columns and rows to start with.

2. Click **OK**.

Procedure: To insert rows or columns

1. To add another row to the table, click **Table**, **Insert**, **Above** or **Below**.

   To add another column to an existing table, click **Table**, **Insert**, **To the Left** or **To the Right**.

 *You can also right-click inside any cell and select **Insert Columns** or **Insert Rows**.*

Procedure: To modify the table properties

1. Select the table rows and/or columns to modify.

2. **Table, Table Properties…**.
   On the **Frame and Color** tab…

   To add visible lines to the selected cells, select the **Line width:** and then click the **Frame** edges.

   To change the **Background** color of the cell(s), select from one of the drop-down options or click **Other…**.

   To define **Cell Margins:**, enter text distances.

 *You can also right-click (inside the table) and select **Table Properties…**.*

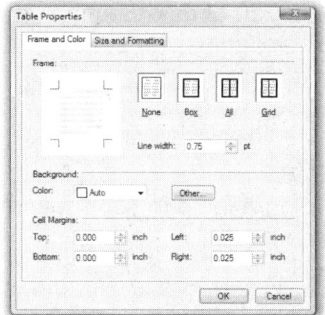

3. On the Size and Formatting tab…

   Set the **Cell Height** as desired.

   Change the **Vertical Alignment** from Top to Center or Bottom.

   Determine in **Options:** if you want to "Allow rows to break across pages" or flip to the next page, if the entire row doesn't completely fit on the end of the current page.

4. Click **OK**.

Working Via E-mail & Letters

Graphics

The ACT! Word Processor can provide some very basic capabilities with graphics. You can insert graphics into your templates, however they must already be the correct size (you cannot resize graphics inside the ACT! Word Processor).

Procedure: To insert a graphic

1. Position your cursor where you wish to insert the graphic.

   If necessary, **[Tab]** or **[Spacebar]** over to the location where you want your graphic to be placed.

2. Select **Insert, Image**.

   Then select **Fixed Position…**,

   or **Character Position…**.

   Fixed Position… will be fixed at the location of your cursor and cannot be moved unless deleted. You can say it is anchored in that location. Once it is in that location, text wraps around the graphic.

   Character Position… can be moved up and down or left and right on the page by inserting or removing text in front of the graphic or changing the alignment of the line that holds the graphic. Text will not wrap around graphics placed with this command.

☞ *If you will be using this template in an e-mail merge, you should use the Character Position option.*

Practice: Creating an ACT! Word Processor Template	
What to do	**How to do it/Comments**
1. Create a new empty template.	**Write, New Letter/E-mail Template.**
2. Create the document on the next page which we will merge and e-mail to some prospects. Name it **Everyone Needs ONE**.	Use a different font color for the titles. When you insert a Web site link, you must select it and click **Insert, Hyperlink…**, enter the full http:// Web address, and click **OK** for the hyperlink to work when it is e-mailed.
3. Try merging the template with a Contact's record.	**Write, Other Document** (from template)…, click Everyone Needs One, and click **Open**.

Sage ACT!

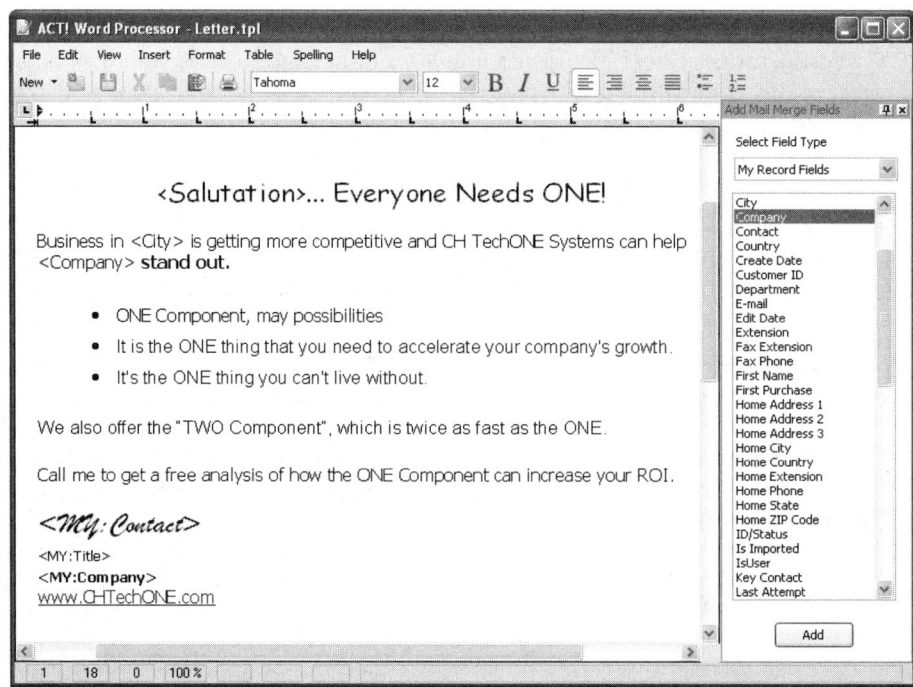

Review: Getting It on Paper

1. Look up Contacts in our database that have May birthdays. Send them the Birthday letter from all of us at CH TechONE using the template named:
   Keeping in touch –birthday
2. Edit the **"Letter"** template (save it as **Customer Discount Offer**) to contain only the following paragraph as the body of the letter:

   As a valued customer of CH TechONE since *(insert the "First Purchase" field here)*, **we would like to offer you a discount on your next component purchase. Call our office at** *(insert your My Record phone number here)* **for more details.**
3. Look up all Contacts where the Customer ID is a non-empty field.
4. Merge the **Customer Discount Offer** (or **03 Presentation - follow –up**) template with the current lookup. You can preview it on the screen (if you don't want to print).

Sage E-marketing For ACT![3]

To understand how you might maintain your relationships with your clients and prospects using effective, yet inexpensive, e-mail marketing, you will:

- ☑ Get to know the features of Sage E-marketing For ACT! and understand the difference between your default e-mail package (such as Outlook) and E-marketing

- ☑ Set up a free, trial E-marketing account.

- ☑ Create and modify a basic template that you can then send out of ACT!.

- ☑ Understand how you can download and read the results of your E-marketing efforts, as well as check online reports for a summary view.

- ☑ Review the options that are offered on the E-marketing tab

---

[3] Requires additional subscription.

Sage E-marketing For ACT! Features

The Sage E-marketing For ACT! solution gives you online tools that work directly with the contacts in your ACT! database to:

- create, send, and track e-mail,
- schedule drip marketing campaigns, and
- create online surveys and Web forms.

You don't have to upload or manage your list of contacts in two places like you do with other third-party solutions – you can send out your messages straight from your current lookup in ACT!... or bring the answers from surveys and Web forms back into the contact's fields in your ACT! database.

ACT! has developed a partnership with Swiftpage™ to provide their E-marketing services. To use this feature of ACT!, you will need to create an online account for your company and a UserID for yourself. When you create your E-marketing account, you can try out the top-tier "Team" service level account at no charge for 60 days. That means you can sign up other users on your company account as well. Each user can then try all of the cool advanced features like Call List, advanced surveys, and using the Send As option (which allows the "marketing" person to send out messages "as" a sales rep (using the rep's e-mail address) and when recipients reply to the message, it goes back to the sales rep... not the marketing person). During the trial period, each user is limited to 50 e-mails per day. However, if that number is too limiting, you can upgrade your send limit at any time by selecting a monthly base package and defining your own "Send Limit" in multiples of 1,000.

At the end of that 60-day trial period, you can select which service level works for you and your company. (You can check out the current pricing for all of your monthly paid options at www.swiftpage.com.)

How Is E-marketing Different from Outlook?

So you may be asking yourself, when should I be using Outlook and when should I be using Sage E-marketing for ACT!?

You can make your decision based on these factors:

- **Number of records in the lookup:** If you have only one or only a few e-mails to send, then sending e-mails using ACT!'s regular **Write, E-mail Message (from template)** or **Write, Mail Merge** is perfect. If you have 30-50 contacts (or more), then you will probably want to use the E-marketing feature. Consider these reasons:
- **Outlook Limit:** If you are e-mail merging to Outlook, there is a limit of around 200 that can be sent before problems can occur...depending on your PC's RAM, the size of the e-mail, and other factors. If your lists are larger, you will need to break them into smaller sends... or you could just use the E-marketing feature.

- **ISP E-mail Limit:** Your ISP (Internet Service Provider) may have a limit on the number of e-mails that you can send in one day. There is no limit on the number of e-mails that you can send in one day through Swiftpage servers (depending on your service level plan, of course). Using E-marketing can end your days of breaking your lists into smaller e-mail groups because of this limitation.
- **Productivity:** Your workstation is pretty much unavailable while it is sending out hundreds or thousands of e-mails through your own e-mail software, but sending thousands of e-mails through the E-marketing feature only takes a few minutes.
- **Templates:** If you want to utilize ready-to-go templates and an online template editor, rather than building your own, then try out the templates you get with Sage E-marketing for ACT!.
- **Anti-Spam Blacklisting:** As part of your service, Swiftpage will inspect all your e-mails to be sure you don't violate any federal e-mail regulations. They are constantly working to ensure that the servers that you would be using are not finding their way onto any blacklists. You can't get that type of protection by doing it yourself.
- **Tracking:** If you want to track who is opening and clicking on links in your e-mail then you need to use the E-marketing tool.

View Some Tracking Examples

This last reason…tracking… can provide some pretty amazing benefits. Let's see how e-mails sent using Swiftpage appear in a contact's history. (You can download and update e-mail results on a daily basis on each contact's history tab… with the click of a button.)

Chris Huffman used the E-mail Marketing feature to promote a seminar to 11 contacts in the database. Swiftpage generated a score for each e-mail that was sent, based on the number of times each recipient opened the e-mail and the number of links that were clicked in the e-mail.

Practice: Reviewing Some E-marketing Scores

What to do	How to do it/Comments
1. Look up all contacts in the database that have been sent e-mail using the E-marketing feature. Chris put "Swiftpage" in **User 10** to identify which ones should receive the e-mail blast.	On the **User Fields** tab, right-click the **User 10** field and select **Lookup User 10**. Enter "Swiftpage" and click **OK**.
2. Switch to Detail View so that you can view the History tab on each record.	Click on the **Detail View** tab in the toolbar. Click on the **History** tab of the first record.

What to do	How to do it/Comments
3. Mark Scott filled out a Web form created using an E-marketing feature. His information was imported into ACT! on 12/29/2008.	Chris is using the Survey feature on their Web site like a form so that prospects can request information. This allows Chris to easily add contacts to her database.
4. The first e-mail was sent in July. You can see the score assigned to the e-mail, the number of times the e-mail was opened, the number of links clicked, the Subject line of the e-mail, the merge template that was used, and the E-marketing UserID that sent the e-mail.	E-marketing generates a score for each e-mail that you send, based on the response to that e-mail. "000" indicates that the e-mail was not opened. Other scores are calculated based on the number of times the e-mail was opened and the number of links that were clicked. Notice that Melissa Pearce (mpearce) is sending out some of the e-mails as well.
5. You can see that some users have better scores than others.	Also note that some contacts opened one e-mail, but not the other.

Pretty amazing information, huh? Can you imagine the potential in your own business for understanding your clients and prospects interests? If they are interested enough to click on an e-mail link to find out more… then you have a warm prospect …maybe even a hot one (as opposed to spending your time calling on contacts who didn't open or click).

So worst case, you can have a free E-marketing account that will send up to 50 e-mails a day straight out of ACT!, allow you to import the results of those e-mails back into ACT!, plus you can create up to 3 Drip Marketing campaigns, as well as create and use some basic surveys to collect contact data.

You have options to grow way beyond that, but in the interim… what have you got to lose?

Creating an E-marketing Account

To use E-marketing, you need Internet access and a Swiftpage account.

Procedure: To create an E-marketing Account

1. Click the **Sage E-marketing for ACT!** icon on the toolbar, or on the Navbar, click the Connections button and click the setup links under the **Sage E-marketing for ACT!** panel.

   If the E-marketing window opens and is ready to send a selected e-mail, then an account may have already been setup for the database you are working with.

2. Click **OK** at the intro screen indicating E-marketing features.

3. Click "I need a Swiftpage Account" and click **Submit** to set up your new account.

   If you are already a Swiftpage user, you can associate your account with the current database by selecting the first option and filling in your account information.

4. Provide an **Account** name (usually something that reflects your company name), a **UserID** (something that reflects your name), a **User Password** for yourself, and an **Account Password** for the company account.

   If you are the administrator of the Swiftpage account, then you can keep the passwords the same. Otherwise you should probably create separate passwords.

   Click **Next**.

5. Fill out the complete contact information legally required to send E-marketing e-mail and click **Submit**.

6. Click **OK** to confirm that you understand that a verification e-mail has been sent to the e-mail address that you listed.

7. Click **OK** at the Congratulations! Window.

8. If you are the database Administrator, click **Submit** to "Add fields to use all E-marketing features."

   ☞ *You cannot add fields to a remote sync database. Log into the master database and access your E-Marketing account and add there.*

   Six fields are added to the database (Marketing Results Contact Grade, Marketing Results Contact Rank, Marketing Results Favorites, Marketing Results Image, Marketing Results Lookup, and Swiftpage Import Status).

9. When complete, the E-marketing dialog displays, ready to send your first e-mail.

10. Click **Close** for now.

11. Check your Inbox for the e-mail which verifies your new Swiftpage account. Open it and click on the link to complete the verification.

12. Select "I Accept This Agreement" and click **Continue**.

    After you have read the End Customer Agreement of course.

13. Either click **Purchase** or just close the window to continue on our 60-day trail, with a max of 50 e-mail sends/day. — The Download option is there for earlier versions of ACT!.
14. Close the Internet window.

Practice: Creating Your E-marketing Account	
What to do	**How to do it/Comments**
1. OK, what are you waiting for. Go sign up for your free trial using the instructions above.	If you were introduced to the product by a Certified Consultant, be sure to give them credit in the Reseller section. (It would only be polite to give them credit.) Or let them know that I sent you… Cornerstone Solutions, Inc.

Creating E-mail Templates

Once you have created your account, you can create plain text or elaborate HTML e-mail templates with a simple online editor (or you can import your own HTML templates). Swiftpage provides quite a few sample templates for you to choose from to use in starting your own library of custom templates. The template names that are prefixed by "zzz_" are part of the Global library and are Read Only... but they are there for you to use as a starting place for your own templates.

Creating your first basic Swiftpage e-mail template

Start by creating a really basic blank template (no graphics, etc.).

Procedure: To create your first plain template

1. Click the **Sage E-marketing** icon or click **Write, Sage E-marketing for ACT!, E-mail Marketing**. — The E-marketing window opens.
   Note: You could also login to your account from www.swiftpage.com.

2. Click the **Select Template** button and select:

   zzz_Template Blank – 1 Col No Header No Border

   Click **OK**.

   Or select any template you like to start with.

3. Click the **Edit Template** button.

4. Enter a new (shorter) name, such as **Plain** and click the **Copy** button.

5. Click the **Edit Template** button.

Since this is a Read Only template (signified by the zzz), you need to copy it to your Active Library.

You should now see the new name of the template at the top left.

Practice: Starting Your First Template	
What to do	**How to do it/Comments**
1. Let's base our new template on the… zzz_Template Blank – 1 Col No Header No Border Give it a new name of **"Blank"**.	Click the **Sage E-marketing** icon, then **Select Template** button, select template and click **OK**. Click **Edit Template**. Enter the new name of Blank and click the **Copy** button. Click the **Edit Template** button.
2. Notice the mail-merge field [[SpePersonalMessage]].	Mail-merge fields are enclosed in double square brackets [[field]].
3. Leave the message displayed.	

Basic Template Editor Window

The **Swiftpage Basic Template Editor** window is divided into two sections. The selected template displays at the right of the screen. The command buttons that you will need to modify the template are at the left, grouped by vertical tabs.

- At the top of the screen, under the Save button, you will see the name of the template that you currently have in edit mode.

- The **Content Editor** tab contains the commands to edit your text, images, and PDF file options.

- The **Customize Template** tab displays the commands that allow you to set column width, change the background color of the template, add horizontal lines, add or delete a window, move a window or lock a window in position.

- When you are finished with editing (or viewing) the current template, you will either **Save** your changes or **Exit** the current editing session.

Sage ACT!

What is [[SpePersonalMessage]] ?

This mail merge field allows you to add an additional personal message to the template before sending (without having to go to the e-mail editor and change the text each time). This special field merges your text from the "Personal Message" section of the Sage E-marketing dialog. You can merge a Personal Message to the current contact or merge the same Personal Message to everyone in the lookup.

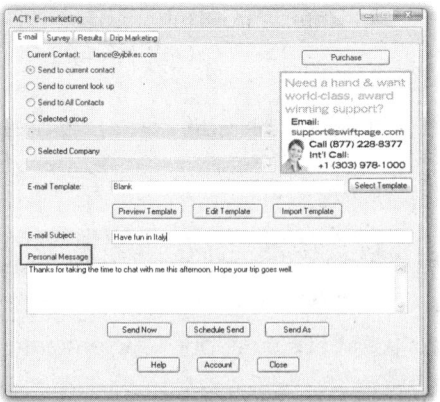

Practice: Save the Template

What to do	How to do it/Comments
1. OK, now you can click the **Save** button. Then click the **Exit** button in the middle of the screen.	We just left it open so you could see the interface while we were talking about it.

Sending the Template

With only a few clicks, you can send the message that you created to the current contact or everyone in your lookup. E-mails sent through E-marketing are delivered through Swiftpage servers (not through your own or through Outlook) delivering your message at lightning speed with no send limit restrictions.

Procedure: To send a template from Safe E-marketing for ACT!

1. In ACT!, look up the contact(s) who should receive the e-mail message.	Always start with a lookup.
2. Click the **Sage E-marketing for ACT!** icon on the toolbar, or click **Write, Sage E-marketing for ACT!, E-mail Marketing**.	The E-marketing window opens.
3. Select to **Send to current contact** or **current look up** or **All Contacts** or **Selected group** or **Selected Company**.	The default is to send to the current contact.
4. Click **Select Template** to select your e-mail template for merging.	The last template that you used (or edited) is selected by default.

Sage E-marketing For ACT! | 227

5. Enter an **E-mail Subject**:
6. Enter a **Personal Message** if desired.

   If the selected template has the SpePersonalMessage mail-merge field, you can enter text in this area. If not, then it will be grayed out in this window.

7. Click a send option:
   Send Now to send immediately

   The **Send As** option is only available if you have the Team Service Level.

   Schedule Send to specify a date and time.

   Send As to send the template using another team members signature and return address.

8. **"SwiftNotify"** can be used on mail-merges of 14 or fewer contacts. It will send a notification e-mail to your e-mail whenever the recipient opens your e-mail.

   Copy to Yourself will include a BCC to your e-mail.

   Click **Yes** to confirm that you want to send this e-mail and record the history to ACT!.

9. Click **OK** to acknowledge that your E-mail Blast has been sent.

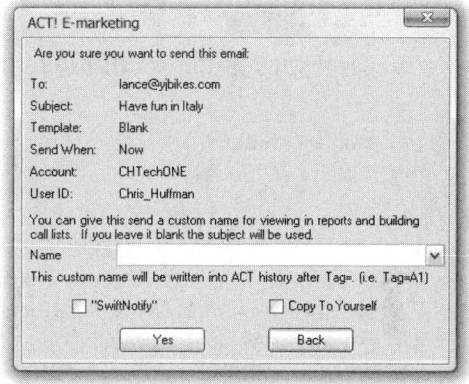

Practice: Sending Your First Template

What to do	How to do it/Comments
1. In ACT!, look up (or enter) your name in the database. Be sure your own e-mail address is correct on the record.	
2. Send yourself the **Blank** template that you just created. Enter a subject and some text in the Personal Message area and send the message.	Click the **Sage E-marketing** icon. Click the **Select Template** button and select the **Blank** template if necessary. Enter the E-mail Subject, and a Personal Message and click **Send Now**.
3. Open and review the message in your Inbox when it arrives.	

Sage ACT!

Creating a New Template Using Your Base

Now that you have a good basic template, let's make a copy of it so that we can modify and add more text.

Procedure: To copy your base template to a new template

1. Click the **Sage E-marketing** icon. The Sage E-marketing window opens.

2. Select the template that you want to base the new template on.

3. Click **Edit Template**.

4. Click **Save As**

5. Give the template a new name and click **Save** (bottom of the screen). You may need to scroll to see the Save button below the new template name.

6. Click the **Continue Editing** button. Verify that your new template name displays at the top of the screen.

7. Edit as desired.

What are SwiftWindows?

When you are in the Swiftpage Template Editor window, as you move your cursor over the e-mail message, you will notice the green border boxes that display. These are called SwiftWindows.

When a SwiftWindow is selected, it will have a blue border indicating that it is ready to be edited. You may only need one SwiftWindow for your message. However, SwiftWindows are also used if you want to add more than one graphic or pdf or if you want to add columns in your templates.

- You can have up to 23 Swift Windows in your template.
- You can have unlimited text per window.
- You can have only one image per window.
- You can have only one PDF hosted per window.

For example, the template displayed here has 3 SwiftWindows. One for the body of the message. One for the signature block, and one for the tagline (which uses a graphic for a product logo). Your template may have more or less, depending upon the complexity of your e-mail design.

Editing text

You can edit only one SwiftWindow at a time. When you click on a SwiftWindow to select it for editing, it will turn from green to blue.

The contents of each SwiftWindow is controlled by the Content Editor tab at the left. In this tab, you can...

- Use **Text Options** to add or edit the text in the selected SwiftWindow.
- Use **Image Options** to add or replace an image, remove the logo, change the position of an existing image or link an image to a survey or Webpage in the selected SwiftWindow.
- Use **PDF Options** to upload a PDF file and then link the download of that file to existing text or image in the selected SwiftWindow.

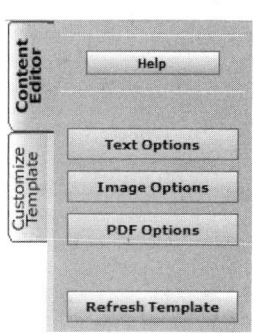

Procedure: To edit a Swiftpage template

1. Display your template in the Template Editor window.

   Click the **Sage E-marketing** icon on the toolbar. Select the desired template and click **Edit Template**.

2. Click the SwiftWindow that you want to edit.

   The active window border will display as blue.

3. Click the **Text Options** button.

4. Click the **Edit Text** button.

5. Enter text and format as desired... similar to the way that you would format a Word document.

   Add a few hard returns at the end, if you like, so that the SPAM/unsubscribe info is not immediately under your signature.

6. To enter mail-merge fields, place the insertion point in the text and then select from the **Mail Merge** drop-down. The field will be added to the template with square braces surrounding it (e.g. [[Country]]).

   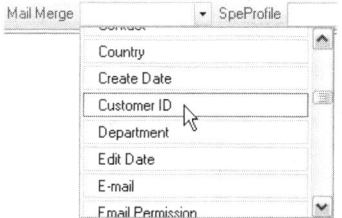

   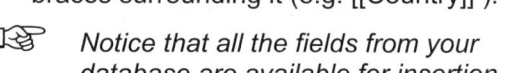 *Notice that all the fields from your database are available for insertion.*

    Don't put a comma after the [[Salutation]] or [[First Name]] field. That way if you do not have a first name (because someone signed up on your Web site, but did not include a name), your mail-merge message will just start with a blank line (which is hardly noticeable) instead of a comma on a line by itself at the top of the screen.

Saving your SwiftWindow edit

When you have finished making the text changes that you want in the SwiftWindow, you should submit your changes. Swiftpage saves the changes to the current SwiftWindow.

Procedure: To save your current changes in the SwiftWindow

1. When you are finished with your window edits, at the bottom of the window, click the **Check Spelling** button. Complete the spell check as you would in any program.

2. Click the Submit button.

☞ *Clicking the **Save** button at the top of the screen will NOT save your SwiftWindow edits. You MUST click the **Submit** button at the bottom of the screen first.*

Saving your template changes

You can continue to make other changes to the template, but before you click the **Exit** button or close the Internet Explorer window, you should click the **Save** button at the top of the window to save all of the changes you made in the current editing session.

Procedure: To save your template changes

1. Once you have clicked the **Submit** button to complete your current edit, click the **Save** button at the top left of the screen. If you are editing the current SwiftWindow, you must click the **Submit** button at the bottom of the screen before you click the **Save** button in the next step… otherwise your changes to the current window will be lost.

2. Click the **Continue Editing** button if you want to make additional changes to the current template, or click the **Exit** button to complete your changes and display your Local Templates list to start on your next template.

☞ *If you do not **Exit** from your changes, the template will not be available to send, to add to a Drip Marketing campaign, or to publish or distribute to someone else.*

Practice: Adding More to Your Template

What to do	How to do it/Comments
1. Create a new template based on the Blank one you were using and save it as **Web Response**.	Click the **Sage E-marketing** icon. Click **Select Template** icon, select the template and click **OK**. Click the **Edit Template** button. At the top of the screen, click **Save As**. Enter name, Web Response and click **Save**. Click the **Continue Editing** button.

What to do	How to do it/Comments
2. Edit the top SwiftWindow.	Select the top window by clicing on it. The outline should be blue. On the **Content Editor** tab, click the **Text Options** button, and click the **Edit Text** button.
3. Delete the field: [[SpePersonalMessage]]	Backspace over it.
4. Type the following on a line beneath the salutation: **Thank you**, followed by a space.	You're going to insert a field after the space.
5. Insert the **First Name** field for the contact and then a comma and a space. **Thank you, [[First Name]]**,	From the **Mail Merge** drop-down, select **First Name**. You could select Salutation, but using the First Name field will make this template work better as an autoresponder later (Web forms always ask for your First Name, not your Salutation).
6. Type the following: **for visiting our Web site and requesting more information. Enclosed is a sample of our CH TechONE system, which speaks for itself about our quality and commitment to outstanding products.** **People all over** and add a space.	Press the **[Spacebar]** after the word "over." You're going to insert another field at the end of the sentence.
7. Insert the **City** field for the contact and add a space.	Select City from the **Mail Merge** drop-down list and then add a space.
8. Finish the letter with: **are enjoying our products. Please feel free to call me with any questions or concerns at** Add the phone number of the current profile user.	With your cursor in place at the end of the sentence, click the drop-down for the SpeProfile mail-merge fields and select SpeProfile_OwnersPhone.
9. Type a period after the phone field. Save your edits.	Click **Submit** at the bottom of the window. (Scroll if you can't see it.)
10. Leave the template displayed.	

Add a signature

To add a signature to your template, you could just copy and paste your own signature from Outlook into this window, but if more than one user in your company will be using the Swiftpage account, you may want to create a generic signature using SpeProfile mail-merge fields that will fill in the correct information of the sender.

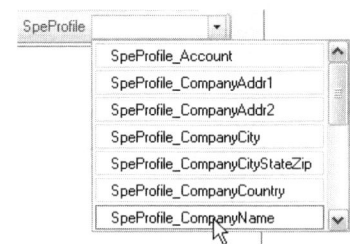

A global signature might look like this:

[[SpeProfile_OwnerName]]
[[SpeProfile_OwnersTitle]]

[[SpeProfile_CompanyName]]
[[SpeProfile_CompanyWebAddr]]
[[SpeProfile_OwnersPhone]]
[[SpeProfile_OwnersEmail]]

Practice: Adding a signature

What to do	How to do it/Comments
1. Add your signature to the bottom SwiftWindow.	Click on the blank SwiftWindow below the one you just edited to make it active. Click the **Edit Text** button. Add your signature.
2. Save the template.	Click **Submit**. Then click **Save** and **Exit**.
3. Now send this template to yourself (be sure you have a value in your City field).	In ACT!, look up your record. You might check to be sure that there are values in the City field. Then click the **Sage E-marketing for ACT!** icon on the toolbar. Select the Web Response template if necessary. Fill in a Subject and click **Send Now**.

Getting Results

Keeping track of the results is one of the cooler features of the E-marketing service. When you first send an e-mail, a history entry is added to your ACT! record will look something like this:

Score=000 Tag= Status=NoResult Clicks=00 Opens=00, IC090615103636; Subject: Have fun in Italy; Template: Blank; UserID: Chris_Huffman; Inx: 0;

Sage E-marketing For ACT!   233

Starting the next day after you send the e-mail, you can download any updates to that history entry on the contact's tab with only a couple of clicks (by following the procedure below). If the contact did not open the e-mail, then the history entry will not change. However, If the recipient did open and click, then that same history entry will be updated to look something like this:

> Score=050 Tag= Status=Opened Medium Clicks=01 Opens=01, IC090615103636; Subject: Have fun in Italy; Template: Blank; UserID: Chris_Huffman; Inx: 0;

Scoring

Swiftpage generates a score for each e-mail that you send, based on the response to that e-mail. If the contact does not appear to have opened the e-mail, then that e-mail is scored as "000". By default, when the e-mail is first opened, it gets a score of 10. For each subsequent open, 4 points are added. If the contact clicks on any link in the e-mail to find out more, the first click adds 40 points to the score and each subsequent click adds 25. These daily scores are calculated, updated, and ready for download each day after midnight. After downloading, you can view the scores on the History tab of each contact that received the e-mail through Swiftpage.

So how does Swiftpage know that someone opened the e-mail? The answer has to do with whether or not the e-mail needed to go to the server to get a graphic to display or to navigate to a link that you specified in your e-mail.

When the recipient opens the e-mail and any included graphics look like this, then unless they right-click to download the picture (from a Swiftpage server), then it may not be possible to tell if the recipient opened the 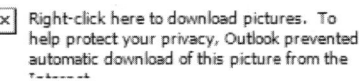 e-mail. Many times the recipient will actually open and read the e-mail in their Inbox (even though they don't see the graphics) or on their PDA. So open scores are sometimes misleading.

Procedure: To download results onto your ACT! Contact Records

1. Click the Sage E-marketing for ACT! icon. The Sage E-marketing window opens.

2. Click the **Results** tab.

3. If results display, click **Toggle All** and then **Submit**. All updated results from the past 24 hours will be imported into the History record of appropriate contact records.

4. Click **Yes** to confirm the number of updates and continue.

5. Click **OK** to acknowledge that updates were retrieved.

Sage ACT!

6. Click **Reports** to view an online summary of your e-mail blasts.

7. Select from E-mail Blasts Sent or Individual E-mails Sent and click **View Report**.

8. View Summary and Detailed Reports as desired. Close the window when finished.

You can also view detailed and graphical reports online, detailing opens, clicks, bounces, suppressions, forwards, and more…

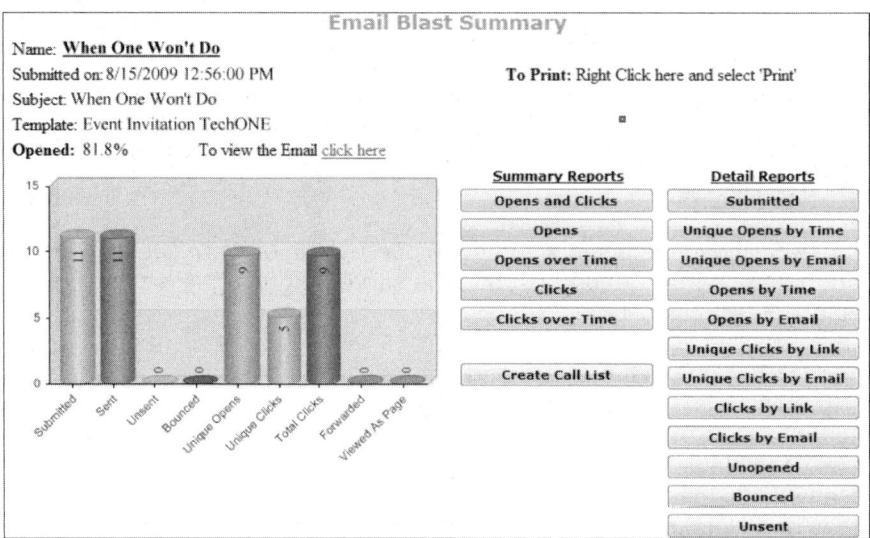

Procedure: To view online Summary Results

1. Click the Sage E-marketing for ACT! icon.

The E-marketing window opens.

2. Click the **Results** tab.

3. Click **Reports** to view an online summary of your e-mail blasts.

An e-mail blast is just another word for campaign.

4. Select from E-mail Blasts Sent or Individual E-mails Sent and click **View Report**.

5. View Summary and Detailed Reports as desired. Close the window when finished.

Sage E-marketing For ACT! | 235

Marketing Results Tab

The Marketing Results tab is displayed regardless of your service level with Swiftpage. Inside the tab you will see three sub-tab panes. The right-hand **Resources** pane provides links to valuable resources to help you be more successful in your E-marketing efforts. The left and middle panes are controlled by the five toggles in the middle of the screen. Click on the left arrow of the toggle to view the selected offering in the left pane. Click on the right arrow of the toggle to view the results in the middle pane.

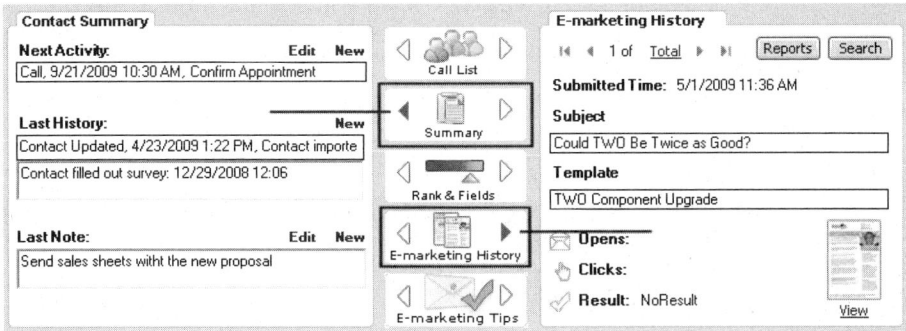

- **Call List** – Identifies contacts with the highest score by e-mail or e-mail campaign.
- **Summary** – Shows the next planned activity for the current contact, along with the most recent history recorded and the last note entered…all in one view. You can also schedule a new activity or add a new note or history to the current contact from this view.
- **Rank & Fields** – Allows you to assign an alpha/numeric rank to each of your contacts and then perform a lookup of all As or Bs… or all contacts with a grade greater than 50 (A100 is the highest rank.) At the bottom of the pane is a Change Fields button which allows you to select up to four fields from your database to view in this panel. This is a nice feature if you have lots of fields in other tabs and you want to view just a few here to help you evaluate your contact.
- **E-marketing History** – Displays the history of each Swiftpage e-mail sent to the current contact, indicating the Subject line, the template used, number of times it was opened, and the number of times that links were clicked. It also indicates the high-level rank of Hot, Warm or Cold (how Hot, Warm, or Cold is determined can be modified by the user). The Reports button opens your Swiftpage account to the E-mail Reports page where you can view the overall results of your campaigns.
- **E-marketing Tips** – Gives you tips to writing and delivering e-mails that are opened by your contacts.

Sage ACT!

Practice: **Playing with the Marketing Results Tab**	
What to do	**How to do it/Comments**
1. Let's look up all the contacts who have received e-mail through the Swiftpage servers again (using the **User 10** field.	On the **User Fields** tab, right-click the **User 10** field and select **Lookup User 10**. Enter swiftpage and click **OK**.
2. Switch to Detail View so that you can view the Marketing Results tab on each record.	Click on the **Detail View** tab in the toolbar. Click on the **Marketing Results** tab of the first record.
3. Play with the options.	

Call Lists

Call Lists allow you to quickly identify your most interested prospects using a ranked list so you know who to reach out to first. While scores are displayed on each contact's History tab in ACT!, if you are sending out very many e-mails, it can be difficult to determine who to follow up with first. The Call List feature performs a lookup of the hot prospects for any e-mail or campaign based on e-mail scores. The Call List is only available during the trial period and/or to Pro or Team service level users. You can find out more about this feature in the Training tab on www.swiftpage.com.

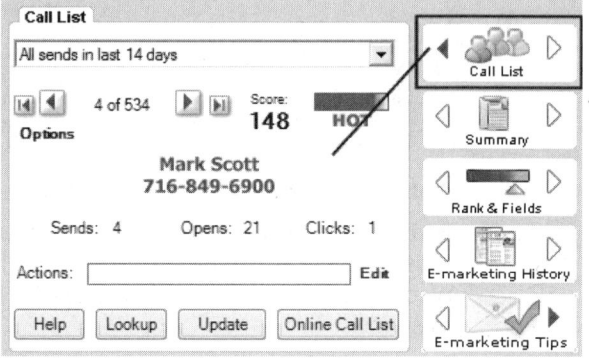

What is Drip Marketing?

Well, the "drip" in drip marketing is borrowed from the agricultural world where plants receive measured drips of water over a long period of time to keep the plants hydrated. So the point of a drip marketing campaign is to plan a steady drip of messages (not a flood followed by a drought) that nourish your customers and/or prospects.

Drip Marketing allows you to create a series of marketing messages that are automatically sent to selected contacts on a pre-determined time sequence (think Activity Series with automation). While drip campaigns can be assigned in mass, you can also assign them one at a time as you enter a new name into your system.

If you opt to sign up for the more advanced service level, you can create conditional responses to the e-mails (if someone opens the e-mail, do this... if someone clicks on any link in the e-mail, do this... if someone doesn't open the e-mail, do this..., if after syncing my

Sage E-marketing For ACT! | 237

databases to the campaign there is a field in my database that has a specific value... do this). So what can Swiftpage do based on responses ....

- automatically create Call Lists based on responses to previous e-mails.
- automatically send a list of selected contacts to your postcard, direct mail, or fax provider along with specific instructions.
- automatically send a list of selected contacts, a script, and an on-line survey to your Call Center provider for follow-up.
- transfer selected contacts to another Drip Marketing campaign (you could transfer people who signed up to attend the conference you are promoting to a reminder drip campaign).
- pause the campaign until someone reviews and gives the go-ahead to continue (you can check to see if there are enough people enrolled, or if you need to cancel a class).

Building a Drip Marketing campaign (while a little beyond the scope of this User Guide) is done in four steps.
1. Create the templates (using the procedure starting on page 228).
2. Create a campaign (similar to creating an Activity Series) that indicates which templates should be sent, at what intervals (see the next procedure).
3. Launch the campaign.
4. Add contacts to the campaign.

 Not sure what to write? Go to www.DripMarketingLetters.com for suggestions or view this online tutorial on the 7 Ways to Use Drip Marketing (www.DripMarketingLetters.com/ph-7drips).

Procedure: To create a new Drip Marketing campaign (basic steps)

1. Click the Sage E-marketing for ACT! icon. The Sage E-marketing window opens.

2. Click the **Drip Marketing** tab. If no campaigns exist, click **OK** to acknowledge that.

3. Click **Campaign Manager**.

4. Click the **New Campaign...** button.

5. Enter a **Name:** for your new campaign.

6. Enter a **Description** if desired.

7. Select the **Send As** option. You cannot mix Record Managers within a single campaign.

8. Select the source that holds the e-mail addresses you will be using. You will probably be selecting ACT!.

9. Select one of the **Campaign types**.

   Anchor Date – Usually used for Event type of marketing... something that happens on a specific date and you want to send out templates before and after that "anchor date."

   Calendar – Can be used for seasonal campaigns, such as valentine greetings on February 14th. Or perhaps everyone in the campaign gets a reminder to turn in their time cards on the 15th and the 30th.

   Duration – Used for sending sequential templates. At any given time, some people in the campaign are receiving the 3rd e-mail, while others are receiving the 5th.

10. Click **Next>>**.

11. Click one of the icons at the left to start the first stage. Name the stage, select the template, fill out the remaining options and click **Add Stage>>**.

12. When you have finished adding the stages, click **Campaign Manager** at the top of the screen.

13. Click **Launch**.

    Contacts can only be added to campaigns that have been launched.

14. Close the Internet window.

    You are ready to add contacts.

Follow-up is so important. This is a great way to set it and forget it.

Procedure: To add a contact to a Drip Marketing campaign

1. Create a lookup in ACT! that you want to add to your campaign.

2. Click the **Sage E-marketing** icon. The Sage E-marketing window opens.

3. Click on the **Drip Marketing** tab.

4. Click on the Drip Campaign you want to add the contacts to.

   If your campaign is not displayed, click Show Status for **All**.

5. Click Sync Contacts.

6. Select Add or Remove Contacts and click Next.

7. Select from Current contact or Lookup and click **Add Contacts**.

   You might use **Remove** if a contact asked to be removed from the list… or if they were on a prospecting drip and you closed the deal with them.

8. Click **Yes** to confirm and then **OK**.

Surveys and Web Forms

You can use your account to create online surveys that ask almost any type of question: Fill in the Blank, Yes/No, Checkbox, Multiple Choice, etc.). The surveys are hosted on Swiftpage servers, and you can send an e-mail to the current lookup in ACT! that contains a link to the survey (you could also post the link on your Web site if you like). When a contact clicks Submit, they see a generic thank you page. If you like, you can add an autoresponder to the Submit button that automatically sends a more personal e-mail response to the person who completed the survey. You can also have the person automatically added to one of your Drip Marketing campaigns.

You can elect to have the survey responses e-mailed to you one at a time, have a daily summary of responses sent, or you can view all current responses in the online editor where you can export the survey responses in a .CSV format.

If you upgrade to the Pro or Team service level, you can also have:
- a custom landing page (instead of the generic thank you page), or
- a custom survey background that is designed to match the theme of your Web site, or
- the ability to bring the responses back into ACT! to create a new contact records (List Builder), or
- the ability to update any record in ACT! with updated field information (List Updater).

Building a survey is a little beyond the scope of this User Guide… but can be accomplished in only a few steps. You can learn more about creating List Builder or List Updater Surveys in the Training tab on www.swiftpage.com or by searching the Support – Knowledge Base. The basic steps would be…

Procedure: To create a survey (basic steps)

1. Click the **Sage E-marketing** icon. The Sage E-marketing window opens.

2. Click the **Survey** tab.

3. Click the **Survey Editor** button.

4. Click **Survey Management**. Located at the top of the page.

5. Click the **New** button.

6. Enter a **New Survey Name**:

7. Select a **Copy Questions From:** option. **Sample** = Name and two questions

   ☞ *This is just a starting place. You can edit your choices. The "Sample" is a survey starting place. The "SPList" options are more like online Web forms.*

   SPListBuilder = First Name, Last Name, E-mail, Company Name and Phone.

   SPListBuilderLong = adds Title, Mobile, Fax, Address info and Website.

8. Click **Submit**.

9. Click the **Survey Design** button. Located at the top of the page.

10. Click **Add Questions** to add your questions/fields to display. Click **Submit** to save the question.

11. Click **Edit** to change a question, change the order, make a field required, enter a default answer (you have to edit the specific question), or hide the field. Click **Submit** to save your changes.

    For example, you might include "Referred By" as a question, change the default answer of "Our Web Site", and then hide the field. When the data is imported, "Our Web Site" will display in the Referred By field in your database.

12. Click **Title and Instructions** and enter the values.

    Instructions will display immediately below the Title.

13. Click **Background Page** to select your custom background.

    This option is available only at higher service levels.

14. Click **Display Settings** to indicate the Background and Font Face, Size and Color for the survey.

15. To change the result options, click **Survey Result Options** at the top of the page.

    Select your options and click **Submit**.

    Autoresponder – sends an e-mail acknowledgement when the user clicks Submit.

    Autoresponder-DM Autoloader - identifies drip marketing campaign the contact should be added to.

    ACT! Database Update – select which survey type you are creating. List builder is more of a Web form, where List Updater is more of a address update service.

    Survey Landing Page – identify the Web landing page that displays when the user clicks Submit.

16. The next few screens are determined by the options you selected above.

    The options available are determined by your service level.

17. The **Survey Responses** button will display all results so far.

    You could check to send results to date to your e-mail address.

18. Close the Internet window when finished.

After the survey is created, you need to
- add it to your Website (you can find the link to use by clicking the **Survey Management** button at the top of the page) or
- create an e-mail that contains the link to the survey.

Procedure: To create a survey cover e-mail

1. Click the **Sage E-marketing** icon.

   Or if you are still in the Internet window from the previous procedure, you can click the **My Swiftpage** button and click **Template Editor.**

2. Select a template and click **Edit Template**.

3. Click **Save As** to save the template with a new name (if necessary), give it a name and click **Submit** and **Show Current Template**.

   You might create a template called Survey Cover.

4. Select the SwiftWindow that contains the body text.

   A selected SwiftWindow should have a blue outline.

5. Click the **Content Editor** tab at the left.

Sage ACT!

6. Click the **Text Options** button.

7. Click the **Edit Text** button and create the text of your e-mail as you normally would.

8. Enter a phrase like "Let us know what you think." or "Take our survey."

    This is the phrase that the recipient will click to open the survey.

9. When finished click **Submit**.

10. Select the SwiftWindow again. Click **Link to Survey**.

    The SwiftWindow with your phrase should have a blue outline.

11. Type (or copy and paste) the text that you want to be hyperlinked to the survey that you have created.

    Enter only the text that you want to be hyperlinked (e.g. you could use only the word "survey").

12. Select the survey from the drop-down list.

    This is the survey that will be linked to the text.

13. Click **Submit**.

14. Click the hyperlink to verify that the correct survey is attached.

15. Close the Template Editor Window. You are ready to send.

    Review the procedure on page 226 for sending out to your lookup.

E-marketing and Swiftpage Help

This is a very full-featured product (much more than we can cover here). If you want to know more about it, check out the E-marketing QuickStudy Guide for ACT! at www.MarketingWithYourDatabase.com.

At checkout use the coupon code of "quick20" to get 20% off your copy of the book.

Advanced Lookups

To be able to slice and dice the ACT! database for more advanced data mining, you will:

- ☑ Create and run Lookup By Example queries.

- ☑ Build, save, and run Advanced Queries.

- ☑ Understand Group Query conditions.

- ☑ Delete unused queries.

Activity Data Mining

In addition to recording notes and history entries, ACT! also keeps track of *every* change you make on a Contact's record...any field changes, any changes made to scheduled activities, or any opportunities modified. ACT! even keeps track of those times that you go back to edit a note.

Since ACT! keeps track of it, you can perform a lookup for Contacts that either have or have not been modified within a specified date range. You can even specify the types of changes you want to include in your lookup. You could look up any Contact whose opportunities have changed in the last 30 days, any Contact that had a note entered (or edited) in the last quarter, any Contact whose record wasn't touched since the start of 2006 (as shown in this example).

Procedure: To lookup contact activity

1. **Lookup, Contact Activity**....

2. Select **Not Changed** or **Changed**.

    Changed displays all Contacts that have had some change made to their record since the specified date. **Not Changed** displays the list of lost prospects or unhappy customers... just kidding...but it might be close.

3. Select the **Since Date** to specify when to start looking for changes.

    Only items changed or not changed since this date are included.

4. Select the areas of the Contact record you want to search for changes (or lack thereof).

    See an explanation of the **Search In** criteria on the next page.

5. Click **OK**.

    After a brief pause while ACT! thinks about it, a list of Contacts that fit your criteria displays. Regardless of what view you were in, the Contacts are displayed in List View.

Advanced Lookups 245

Search In Criteria

Contact fields checks for changes to any field in the Contact record.

Notes locates all Contact records that contain one or more notes that were entered or edited during the specified time period.

Opportunities searches for changes made to any opportunity.

Histories searches for new or changed history entries. The default is to search all qualifying history items, but you can choose only specific history types by clicking the drop-down button and leaving only those types you want to search for checked. For example, you could search for all Contacts who called you (so you can follow-up as necessary) since last Tuesday (assuming that is, you have recorded any history for them). This feature will even search for Custom History types.

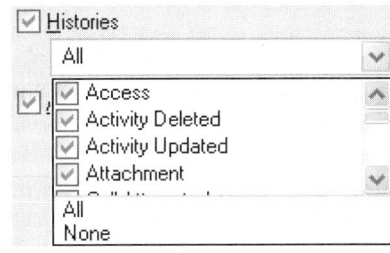

Activities searches all uncleared activities. Requesting a search on any of the activities, will search for an activity that was edited or entered. You can find cleared activities using the Histories option.

Practice: Who Has Been Slipping Through the Cracks?	
What to do	**How to do it/Comments**
1. Find all Contacts where no changes have been made to any of their *fields* since 8/1/2006.	**Lookup**, **Contact Activity…**, select **Not Changed**, change the beginning date to 8/1/2006. Clear all options except for **Contact fields**, and click **OK**.

Queries

We've done some basic lookups in our database, but ultimately you will want to perform much more complicated searches. The Lookup menu is great for quick searches, but is a little cumbersome for lookups involving several criteria.

Example: You want to look up only those records where the ID/Status is Prospect *and* the state is Texas *and* the E-mail address contains an e-mail address. You could look up **Prospect** in the **ID/Status** field, and then look up **Texas** in the **State** field, and then look up contacts with E-mail addresses. If you remember to select the **Narrow lookup** each time and execute the lookups in the right order, you eventually get to the specified records. But, how many separate operations does it take? This technique is a bit tedious.

Lookup By Example

Lookup By Example lets you specify multiple criteria for your lookup at one time. You don't have to remember to narrow or add each condition to your lookup.

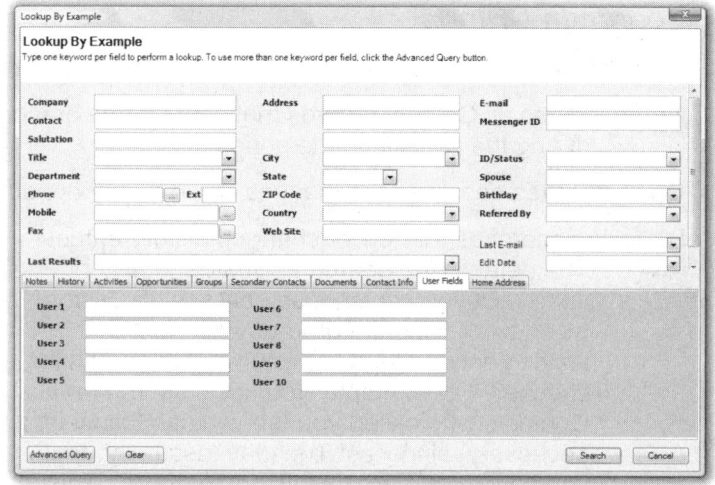

You can use wildcards to specify unknown characters in your criteria.

- The wildcard character is a percent sign (**%**). Use the percent sign to represent letters that vary in your example.

  ☞ *In previous versions of ACT! you may have used an asterisk * instead of the percent sign %. Asterisks don't work in newer versions of ACT!*

- An underscore (**_**) matches any one character. (e.g.,, C_O finds CEO or COO)

Example: To find all records where the company name begins with the word **Texas**, you would enter…

Texas

In this example, ACT! will only look at the beginning of the field.

To find all records that use the word Texas anywhere in their Company name, you would enter…

%Texas

The wildcard at the beginning of the example tells ACT! you want any record that "contains" the word **Texas** (e.g., South Texas Oil or Bank of Texas).

Procedure: To use Lookup By Example

1. Display the Contacts, Groups, or the Companies Detail View. By Example is available in all three views.

2. **L**ookup, By E**x**ample. An empty copy of the current Contact, Company, or Group displays in a separate window.

Advanced Lookups

3. Type your values in the appropriate fields.

   If you are searching for text that may not be the first thing found in the field or the field is not a multi-select field (drop-down field with check boxes at the left of each item), then you may want to use wildcards characters "%" or "_".

   If you wish to use a different layout to do this, switch layouts before you display Lookup By Example.

   To search for multiple values in a single field, you must use Advanced Queries (next section).

    "_" is used to represent a single character.

4. Click the **Search** button at the bottom right of the Lookup window.

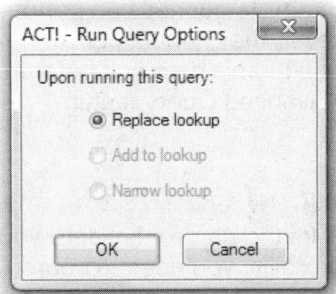

5. Click **Replace lookup**, **Add to lookup**, or **Narrow lookup** as needed.

6. Click **OK**.

   The lookup is performed for all of the specified criteria. You are returned to the List View with the new lookup in place.

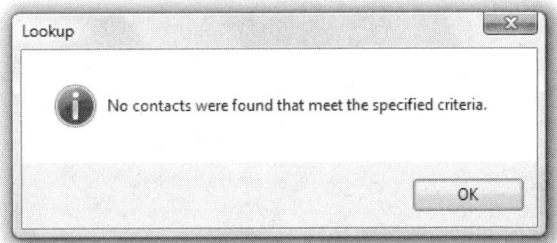

 If you specify criteria that do not fit any records in your database, ACT! lets you know. No lookup will be performed, and you must start from scratch (bummer, huh?).

Practice: Lookup By Example

What to do	How to do it/Comments
1. Use Lookup By Example to display all Prospects where the company name contains the word "record".	**Lookup**, **By Example**, in the ID/Status field enter **Prospect** and in the Company field, enter **record**. Click **Search**, **Replace Lookup**, **OK**.
2. How many contacts are in the lookup?	0

Sage ACT!

What to do	How to do it/Comments
3. Create the lookup again, this time using a wildcard.	**Lookup**, **By Example**, in the ID/Status field, type (or select) **Prospect**, and in the Company field type **%record**. Click **Search**, **Replace Lookup**, **OK**. You should have 4 contacts in the recording business.

By Example queries can perform lookups on Group and Company records as well. However, they cannot perform "either/or" queries or searches on ranges of values, like all dates after this date and before that date. For more complicated searches, you need to use the Advanced Query feature.

Advanced Queries

Don't let the name intimidate you. Advanced queries are not difficult to create and offer all the flexibility you need to search the database. Instead of displaying a blank layout for defining your query criteria, the Advanced Query window is used to create the query one step at a time, where each line you enter is a query condition.

For example, can you read this query?

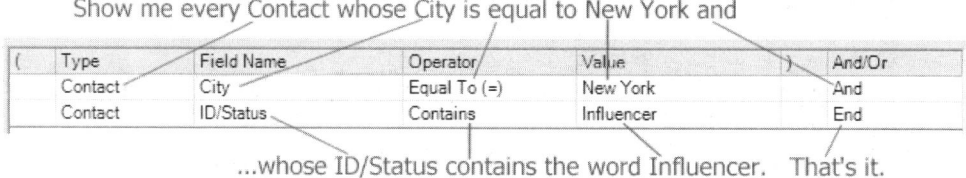

That was easy, wasn't it! An added bonus is that you can save an Advanced Query and use it over and over… AND many features in ACT! are based on creating an Advanced Query.

Advanced Lookups | 249

Procedure: To create an Advanced Query

1. **Lookup, Advanced, Advanced Query….**
   Search For displays **Contact**, but Advanced Queries can also be created for Companies, Groups, or Opportunities (page 287).

2. Select the **Type:** (Company, Contact, Group, or Opportunity), **Field Name:**, **Operator:**, and (if appropriate) enter the **Value:** for the first criteria.
   Select each option (except for the value in most cases) from the drop-down lists.

3. Click **Add to list**.
   The first criterion is added to your list of criteria.

(	Type	Field Name	Operator	Value	)	And/Or
	Contact	City	Equal To (=)	new york		End

4. Click **Preview** to check your results so far.
   When you click Preview, the result of the query displays in the Preview pane at the bottom of the window.

5. Repeat steps 2 - 4 for the next criteria, and the next and the next ….
   Once all of your criteria are specified, you may notice an **And** in the **And/Or** column for each row (other than the last).

6. Set your **And/Or** options as necessary.
   An "**And**" indicates that the current rows criteria and the next must both be true for a record to match. An "**Or**" indicates that either the current row or the next can match.

7. Group your criteria as necessary.
   You group criteria by enclosing them in parentheses. When you group two or more criteria, you cause the Advanced Query to evaluate them as a group.

8. Once the query is structured the way you want it, click **Preview** one last time.
   Don't run the query, since that closes the window and if you haven't saved it, you will lose all your work.

9. If the preview shows you the expected result, choose **File**, **Save** (if you want to rerun the query later).
   Contact queries are saved with a .QRY file extension. Always save the query before running it if you expect to use it again.

10. Click **OK** to run the query.

☞ *If you would like to modify one of the query criteria that you have added (because of a spelling mistake or to change an operator from Equal To (=) to Contains), then select the row and click the **Edit...** button.*

Once in the Advanced Query window, you will find a wonderful set of tools with which to define your queries.

Each element is defined by its column heading...

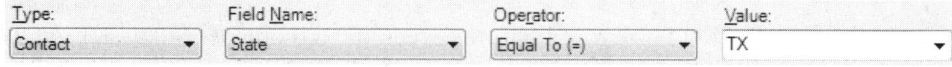

Type: Which type will you be querying... You can search for Contacts by using contact or opportunity type criteria. If you are creating a query for a Company or Group, no types are available. You can only use group criteria to search for Groups, and company criteria to search for Companies, not the contacts that belong to those entities.

Field Name: What is the name of the field you wish to query? The available list is determined by your "Type" selection. There are different fields for Contact than there are for Opportunity.

Operator: What comparison would you like to perform? See the options available next.

Value: What would you like to look for in the specified field?

Operator Options

The Advanced Query window provides a selection of operators. These determine the type of comparison that will take place.

The available **operators** are listed here along with some examples of how you might use them.

Contains – The Value you specify can appear anywhere in the field. Used with character field queries only. *Example:* "Address 1" Contains Sunset to locate all contacts with an address on a street named Sunset.

Contains Data – There is something in the field. (This does not require a Value.) Used with character, numeric, and date field queries. *Example:* "E-mail" Contains Data would look up all contacts where something was entered in the e-mail address field.

Does Not Contain – The query excludes records that contain the specified value. Used with character-type field queries only. *Example:* "E-mail" Does Not Contain @ would help you locate records where invalid data was stored in the E-mail address field.

Advanced Lookups | 251

Does Not Contain Data – The field is empty. (This does not require a Value.) Used with character, numeric, and date field queries. *Example:* "E-mail" Does Not Contains Data would look up all contacts without an e-mail address.

Equal To (=) – The Value you type must match the field exactly. Used with character, numeric, and date field queries. *Example:* "State" Equal To (=) Texas locates all records that did not use the 2 character abbreviation of TX.

Not Equal To (!=) – The Value you type must not equal the Value in the field. Used with character, numeric, and date field queries. *Example:* "ID/Status" Not Equal To (!=) Employee to make sure that no employees are included in the results.

Starts With – The Value you type must be at the very beginning of the field. Used with character-type field queries only. *Example:* "Company" Starts With Exxon would locate all contacts from Exxon USA, Exxon Mobil, Exxon Chemical, etc.

Ends With – The Value you type must be at the very end of the field. Used with character-type field queries only. *Example:* "Company" Ends With Inc to locate all companies that are incorporated (unless someone entered a period after Inc.).

Greater Than – The number in the field must be greater than the Value you type. Used with character or numeric queries. *Example:* "Revenue" Greater Than 1000000 would return all companies with revenue greater than a million.

Greater Than or Equal To – The number or text in the field must be greater than or the same as the Value you type. (Use the On or After operator if you want to query a date field.) *Example:* "Opportunity -Probability of Close" Greater Than or Equal to 75 to help you locate deals ready to close.

Less Than – The number in the field must be less than the Value you type. Used with character or numeric queries. *Example:* "Number of Employees" Less than 50 to help you locate smaller companies.

Less Than or Equal to – The number or text in the field must be less than or the same as the Value you type. (Use the On or Before operator if you want to query a date field.) *Example:* "Zip Code" Less Than or Equal to 77499. This could be used in conjunction with Greater Than or Equal To for specifying a range of Zip Codes.

On or After – The date in the field is the same as or later than the date you enter for Value. Used with date field queries only. *Example:* "Create Date" On or After 1/1/2007. This is often used in conjunction with On or Before for locating contacts created during a specific time period. (This operator is similar to Greater Than or Equal To which can only be used for character or numeric fields.)

On or Before – The date in the field is the same as or earlier than the date you enter for Value. Used with date field queries only. Example: "Edit Date" On or Before 12/31/2009 would show all contacts who had not been edited since 12/31/2009.

Older Than [days] –The date in the field is older than the specified number of days from today. Example: "Edit Date" Older Than [days] 365 would find all contacts who haven't been edited in the last year. Similar to On or Before except that this query would always be updating. The On or Before operator compares the date against a fixed time or field.

After Next [days] – The date in the field is more than the specified number of days from today. *Example:* "Contract Renewal Date" After Next [days] 365 would locate all contacts whose renewals weren't expiring for another year.

Within Last [days] – Allows you to specify a range of days before today, with the specified number of days entered in Value. *Example:* "Edit Date" Within Last [days] 365 would look up all contacts that had been modified in the last year. Older Than [days] would be used to look up those contacts **not** modified.

Within Next [days] – Allows you to specify a range of days after today, with the specified number of days entered in Value. Used with date field queries only. *Example:* "Contract Date" Within Next [days] 90 would look up all contacts whose contracts were expiring in the next 90 days.

Day Equals [number] – Enter a number between 1-31 to search date fields for a specific date. *Example:* "Equipment Maintenance Date" Date Day Equals [number] 20 would select all contacts whose equipment needs to be serviced on the 20th of each month.

Month Equals [number] – Allows you to search the specified date field for a specific month using the numbers 1-12. *Example:* "Birth Date" Month Equals [number] 7 would display all contacts with a July birthday. This would be an alternate to Lookup, Annual Event.

Year Equals [number] – Allows you to enter a four-digit year [YYYY] for a date field search. *Example:* "Birth Date" Year Equals [number] 1943 would create a lookup of everyone turning 65 this year.

So the process of building a query is to create a "row" by filling out a set of options (Type, Field, Operator, etc.) and adding it to the list. With a little practice, you can use the Advanced Query window to create very complex queries. You will probably find it best to build the query one or two sets of conditions at a time, testing and saving it as you go.

Advanced Lookups

Practice: Building an Advanced Query

What to do	How to do it/Comments
1. Let's create a query to lookup all prospects in Scottsdale. Build the query one row at a time. Start with finding all Contacts that live in **Scottsdale**. Then preview your query. How many records are displayed?	**Lookup**, **Ad**v**anced**, **Advanced Query…** Choose **City** from the Field list, **Equal to (=)** from the Operator list, select **Scottsdale** from the value column, and click **Add to list**. Click **Preview**. The count of records appears below and to the left of the preview pane.
You could also start this query from the basic Lookup menu. Right-click the City field and select Lookup City. Enter Scottsdale, but instead of clicking **OK**, click **Go to Advanced Query**. This starts the first row of your Advanced Query.	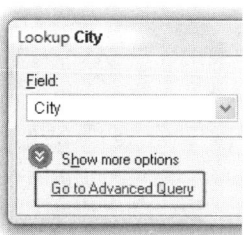
2. Add a condition to narrow the query to all Contacts with an **ID/Status** of **Prospect**. Preview the query.	Choose **ID/Status** from the Field list, **Contains** from the Operator list, and either type or select **Prospect** from the value column, click **Add to list**. Click **Preview**.
3. Save the query. Name it **Scottsdale Area Prospects**.	**F**ile, **S**ave, type name, and click **S**ave.
Your query should look like this. Notice the **And** that was placed in the **And/Or** column. Both the City condition and the ID/Status condition must be true in order for a record to fit this query.	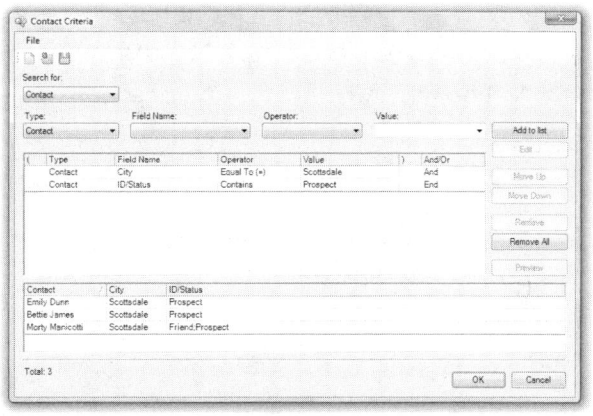

Sage ACT!

What to do	How to do it/Comments
4. Now let's try expanding the query by adding Phoenix. The result should be Contacts from Scottsdale or Phoenix who are Prospects. Preview the query.	Choose **City** from the Field list, **Equal To (=)** from the Operator list, either type or select **Phoenix** from the value column, and click **Add to list**. Click **Preview**.
5. No records match? What's wrong with this picture?	Read the lines of the query as if they were a sentence. "City equals Scottsdale *and* ID/Status contains Prospect *and* city equals Phoenix. How can someone live in both Scottsdale *and* Phoenix?
6. Save the query, we will fix it in the next exercise.	**File**, **Save** or click the Save button on the toolbar.
7. Close the query window without running the query.	Click **Cancel**.

And/Or

When you have multiple criteria (or rows) in a query, it is important for you to understand **And** and **Or** and how they affect queries. When one row is connected to the next with an **And**, both conditions must be true in order for a record to fit the query. If you use **Or**, either condition can be true, and the record will fit. Once a query has been saved, you can reopen it and modify it.

Procedure: To open a saved query

1. **Lookup, Advanced, Advanced Query....** The empty Advanced Query window opens.

2. **File, Open....**

3. Select the query file you wish to open, and click **Open**. The query is now displayed in the Advanced Query window.

Advanced Lookups | 255

Practice: Open and Modify Your Query

What to do	How to do it/Comments
1. Open your saved query (or open the query file named **Scottsdale Area Prospects2.qry** in the \Attachments folder).	**Lookup**, **Ad**v**anced**, **Advanced Query…**, **File**, **Open…**, navigate to the Attachments folder, select **Scottsdale Area Prospects2.qry**, and click **Open**.
2. The query will read better if we put the two City rows together. Move the Phoenix row up one.	Click the "Phoenix" row, and click the **Move Up** button.
3. Change the query so it looks for Scottsdale **Or** Phoenix.	Click the **And/Or** field at the end of the **Scottsdale** row, display the drop-down list and choose **Or**.

(	Type	Field Name	Operator	Value	)	And/Or
	Contact	City	Equal To (=)	Scottsdale		Or
	Contact	City	Equal To (=)	Phoenix		And
	Contact	ID/Status	Contains	Prospect		End

What to do	How to do it/Comments
4. Preview the query.	Click **Preview**. You got both cities, but you have all sorts of ID/Status entries (not just Prospects).
5. What do you think the problem is? You can see from the Preview that the Scottsdale list contains Contacts whose ID/Status did not contain Prospect.	Computers read from left to right… top to bottom. They perform each command in sequence. So the computer interpreted your request to mean that you want to see… • Any Contacts whose City = Scottsdale, • Or any Contact whose city = Phoenix and whose ID/Status contains Prospect.
6. Save your query and close it.	Click the **Save** icon, and then click **Cancel**.

Grouping

When you group two or more conditions in a query, you cause ACT! to evaluate all of the conditions in the group *as* a group. In our current example, each row is evaluated in the order in which they are listed, therefore the And condition joins only the second and third conditions. So we get everyone from Scottsdale regardless of their ID/Status, and only those records from Phoenix where the ID/Status contains Prospect.

What we really want is all records from Scottsdale or Phoenix (either one) where the ID/Status (for either city) contains Prospect. A subtle difference, yes, but a difference nonetheless.

Procedure: To group criteria in a query

1. Arrange your query with elements you wish to group together.

   Use the **Move Up** and **Move Down** buttons to arrange the rows in groups.

2. In the **(** column at the start of each group, select the **"("** from the drop-down list.

   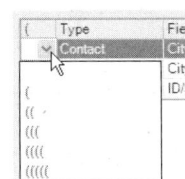

   The left parenthesis "(" defines the start of two or more grouped criterion.

3. In the **)** column at the end of each group, select the **")"** from the drop-down list.

   The **)** defines the end of a group of two or more criteria.

More complex queries might have grouped criteria nested inside a larger group. This requires the nesting of parentheses. This is why the drop-down lists include **((, (((,)),)))** etc. Use these to nest groups as necessary.

If you build the query a little at a time, these parentheses will start to make more sense to you. It's similar to those math formulas you used to do in high school.

$$4 \times 3 + 2 = 14 \quad \text{but} \quad 4 \times (3 + 2) = 20$$

Practice: **Grouping the Cities**	
What to do	**How to do it/Comments**
1. Open your saved query (or open the query file named **Scottsdale Area Prospects3.qry** in the \Attachments folder.	**L**ookup, Ad**v**anced, Advanced **Q**uery..., **F**ile, **O**pen..., browse to the \Attachments folder, select **Scottsdale Area Prospects3.qry**, and click **O**pen.

Advanced Lookups

What to do	How to do it/Comments
2. Group the two city conditions.	Click the **(** column at the start of the first row and select **(**, click the **)** column at the end of the second row and select **)**.

(	Type	Field Name	Operator	Value	)	And/Or
(	Contact	City	Equal To (=)	Scottsdale		Or
(	Contact	City	Equal To (=)	Phoenix	)	And
	Contact	ID/Status	Contains	Prospect		End

The query criterion now looks like this. Note the parentheses that "enclose" the first two rows.

What to do	How to do it/Comments
3. Preview your query. Are the results correct now?	Click **Preview**. Now that's more like it! Contacts from Scottsdale or Phoenix and every one of them has **Prospect** in their **ID/Status** field. Glad you trusted us now?
4. Save and run the query.	Click the Save button. Click **OK**, **OK**.

Deleting Query Files

There are several ways of deleting query files when you no longer need them. You can use a Browser window, the Windows Explorer, or you can delete them from within ACT!.

Procedure: To delete a query file in ACT!

1. **Lookup, Advanced, Advanced Query...**
   The Advanced Query window displays.

2. **File, Open**
   or
   click the Open toolbar button.
   A list of saved queries displays in the **Open** dialog box.

3. Select the file you wish to delete, press **[Delete]**, and confirm the deletion.
   You cannot mark multiple files using this method. If you have many files to deal with, we recommend that you use the Windows Explorer.

4. Click **Cancel** when you are done and click the **Cancel** button for the Query window.

 You can also right-click a file in the Open dialog box and choose **Delete** from the shortcut menu.

Practice: Deleting Unnecessary Queries

What to do	How to do it/Comments
1. Delete any saved queries you no longer want. Keep **Scottsdale Area Prospects4.qry** for the review at the end of the chapter.	**L**ookup, Ad**v**anced, Advanced **Q**uery…, **F**ile, **O**pen…, or click the **Open** toolbar button. Select each file you wish to delete in turn, press **[Delete]**, and confirm the deletion. Click **Cancel** when done. Click the **Cancel** button to close the Advanced Lookup window and return to the database.

Review: Queries

1. Open the query named **Scottsdale Area Prospects4.qry** (stored in the \Attachments folder) into the Advanced Query window.
2. This query displays Contacts that are Prospects from two cities. Modify the query so it includes Contacts (from the two cities) that are also Customers (instead of Prospect). Hint: Customers may be anywhere in the ID/Status field. You may need to group some conditions.
3. When you are done and the query is working as desired, delete the query file (or don't…we're easy).

Groups & Companies

Groups and Companies are a great way to categorize your Contacts. To learn to effectively use these two features, you will:

- ☑ Practice creating and adding members to a Group or Company record.

- ☑ Understand how Subgroups and Divisions are created and used.

- ☑ Learn how to differentiate between the two.

- ☑ Discover how membership is defined.

- ☑ Update linked Contact records with new data.

- ☑ Create notes for different Group or Company records.

- ☑ Associate activities with Group or Company records.

Groups

Groups are a powerful feature of ACT! used to collect Contacts...allowing you to organize, catalog, classify, subdivide, pigeonhole, and otherwise make sense out of groups of Contacts, and the information that is stored with them. The **Groups** feature helps you sift through and display only the Contacts that belong to the selected Group.

- You can create a Group at any time for any reason.
- A Group is like a saved lookup of Contact records and can contain any number of Contacts.
- Membership in a Group can be based on a query or can be manually assigned (it is possible to manually add people who have nothing in common but their love of Basset Hounds... unless your database has a custom field named **Dog Preference**).
- Groups can have Subgroups to help you further categorize your database (e.g., Prospects could have subgroups of Hot Leads, Potential, and Cold).
- And the best thing is that any Contact can be a member of any number of Groups.

Don't think of Groups as permanent things. You can create and delete Groups without any fear of affecting the Contact records.

Displaying a Group Lookup

Once any group is created, you can display the group members in **Contacts** or **List View** (similar to a Lookup). Only the Contacts that are members of the group are displayed.

Procedure: To view a Group (or Subgroup)

1. From the Navbar, click the **Groups** button.

    Click **Detail View**, if necessary, so that the Group tree view displays.

2. Right-click the desired Group and select **Create Lookup**.

    If you are looking for a Subgroup, you may need to expand the list by clicking on the + sign.

3. Choose **Lookup, All Contacts** from the menu (or click "View All Contacts" in the Related Tasks pane) to redisplay your total list of Contacts in the database.

☞ You can also click **View Groups/Companies** in the Related Tasks pane at the left, select the Group and click **OK**.

Groups & Companies | 261

Practice: Viewing a Group

What to do	How to do it/Comments
1. In Contacts view, display the **Customers** Group.	Click **Groups** in the Navbar. Right-click the "Customers" group and select **Create Lookup**.
2. How many records are displayed?	All "Customers" are immediately displayed in List View.
3. While still in the List View, replace this list with **Hot Opportunities** (a subgroup of Prospects).	Click **Groups** in the Navbar. Right-click the "Hot Deals" group and select **Create Lookup**.
4. Now return to displaying all Contact records.	Choose **Lookup**, **All Contacts**. All records are displayed.

Manually Adding a Contact to a Group

So you can see that Groups can be a handy quick lookup. In addition, Contacts are not limited to only one Group. They can belong to as many as you like.

A Contact is added to a Group in one of two ways:

- **Static** members are manually added or removed. You can add a single Contact or multiple Contacts to the Group using the current lookup or using Contacts that already belong to another Group. When a Contact is assigned to a Group manually, the Group name displays on the Contact's record in the **Groups/Companies** tab.

- **Dynamic** members are automatically added or removed based on a query that you create for the Group. For example, if part of the query criteria says that the Contact must live in NY to be included in the Group, when the person moves to NJ, they are removed from membership automatically. When a Contact is assigned to a Group by a query, the Group name will NOT display on the Contact's record in the **Groups/Companies** tab. However, you can verify a Contact's membership by clicking the **Display Dynamic Groups Membership** button.

     Queries let you specify much more complex criteria. Review the Advanced Queries chapter in this QuickStudy Guide for more help.

Sage ACT!

Procedure: To manually add/remove Group members in Contacts view

1. Look up a Contact and display the **Groups/Companies** tab.
2. Click the **Add/Remove Groups** button.

   Add/Remove Groups

   or right-click (on the Contact Detail background) and choose **Add Contact to Group...**.

Look up the Contact you wish to add to a Group.

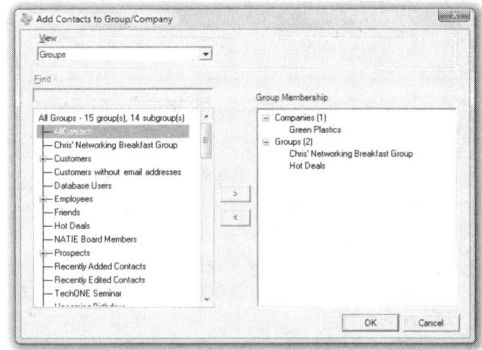

3. To add membership, select a Group in the left pane and click the **Add** button in the center (or double-click the Group name).

   >

   To remove membership, select the Group in the right pane and click the **Remove** button.

   <

4. Click **OK**.

If a Subgroup is not displayed, click the parent Group's name to display the dependent list.

You can also double-click names to move them into the opposite pane.

Practice: Manually Adding and Removing Membership

What to do	How to do it/Comments
1. Look up Steve Reese.	**Lookup**, **Last Name**, enter Reese, and click **OK**.
2. He has just joined the NATIE Board. Add him to the Group.	Either right-click the layout background and select **Add Contact to Group...**, or click **Add/Remove Groups** button on the top of the **Groups/Companies** tab. Double-click NATIE Board Members and click **OK**.
3. Has the Group name been added to the **Groups/Companies** tab?	Yes, since you manually added his record to the Group, it displays on the tab.

What to do	How to do it/Comments
4. Steve replaced Louis Hill on the Board. Remove Louis' name from the Board membership.	Look up Louis Hill. Display the **Groups/ Companies** tab and click the **Add/Remove Groups** button. In the right-pane, double-click the NATIE Group to remove him from membership. Click **OK**.

Before we discuss how to populate a group **dynamically**, let's look at the **Companies** function.

Companies

Groups and Companies are a lot like twins. They look alike, they act alike, they play alike, they even play together, but once you get to know them (like all twins), there are some subtle differences.

Companies have all of the features and benefits of Groups, with some added functionality. Their difference is in their focus. While Groups are primarily used to collect names to be used as a lookup, Companies are used to provide an overall view of the combined notes, history, activities, and opportunities. (Yes, you can see a combined view of notes in Groups as well, but we are talking focus here. As Mr. Miyagi would say…Focus.)

So if you want to maintain a lookup of Terri's Group of West Coast prospects, you might create a **Group**. However, if you want to maintain an overall view of one of your larger clients to see which sales reps are calling on which Contacts at the account, what activities are scheduled with anyone associated with this company, or which opportunities are pending for this national corporation, you might create a **Company**.

That's the focus part. What about the subtle differences? A Group record starts with a group description and one address block. A Company record starts with fields that help you maintain basic company data (e.g., phone, fax, toll-free, Web site, three sets of addresses, industry category, revenue, etc.).

The major functionality difference between Groups and Companies is the ability to create a "Company Link." While you can add any Contact to any Company record, if you **link** the Contact, you get a few extra benefits that we can try out.

So let's take the bullet points we used for Groups and review them for the **Companies** feature.

- You can create a Company at any time for any reason.
- A Company is like a saved lookup of Contact records and can contain any number of Contacts.
- Membership in a Company can be based on a query or can be manually assigned (like all companies associated with a specific project).
- Companies can have Divisions to help you further categorize your database.

- And the best thing is that any Contact can be a member of any number of Companies (as well as Groups).

☞ *Don't think of Companies as permanent things. You can create and delete Companies without any fear of affecting the Contact records.*

Practice: Groups vs. Companies

What to do	How to do it/Comments
1. Click the **Groups** icon in the Navbar. Observe the Group names listed in the tree display and the tabs available.	It doesn't make any difference which Group you are viewing, we just want to display the Groups: Detail View.
2. Now click the **Companies** icon in the Navbar. Note you have the same tree type display and the same basic **tabs**.	Both Groups and Companies have **Contacts**, **Notes**, **History**, **Activities**, **Opportunities**, and **Documents** tabs.
3. Notice the difference in the number of fields on the top detail pane between the two features.	Click the **Groups** icon…now the **Companies** icon.
4. Notice the number of addresses in the Companies vs. Groups.	There are three addresses for Companies and one for Groups.
5. Look up Ed Connor. His company, Graham Electronics belongs to a holding company we are tracking called Widget Corporation. Add him to that Company record.	Right-click the layout background and select **Add Contact to Company…**, or view the **Groups/ Companies** tab, change the "Show membership for:" to **Companies and Divisions**, and then click the **Add/Remove Companies** button. Double-click Widget Corporation in the left pane and click **OK**.
6. Wow, déjà vu. That was the same as adding Group membership. Has the company been added to the **Groups/Companies** tab?	Yes! Notice that you may need to switch the "Show membership for:" option between **Companies and Divisions** and **Groups and Subgroups** to display the memberships you have assigned. They do play well together.

Since you now understand similarities between these siblings, the remainder of the chapter will describe features that are common to both and that can be accomplished using practically the same menu commands.

Groups & Companies

Creating and Populating a Group or Company

Now that we have briefly looked at Groups and Companies, let's create a new one. ACT! makes it very easy (isn't everything easy in ACT!). All you have to do is display the feature window (Groups or Companies), click the **New** icon, and enter a name. Voila, your new Group or Company is created.

Procedure: To create a Group or Company

1. Click the appropriate icon on the Navbar or **V**iew, **G**roups or **Co**mpanies.

   Click either the **Groups** or **Companies** icon on the Navbar at the left.

2. Press **[Insert]** on the keyboard,

   or click the **New** icon,

   or right-click the layout background and select **New**....

   A blank record displays, ready for you to enter the new name.

3. Type a name for your **Group** or **Company**.

   Keep the name brief. If you plan to create a query to populate the Group, why not enter the query criteria that you will use in the **Description** area.

4. Fill in any remaining fields, as desired.

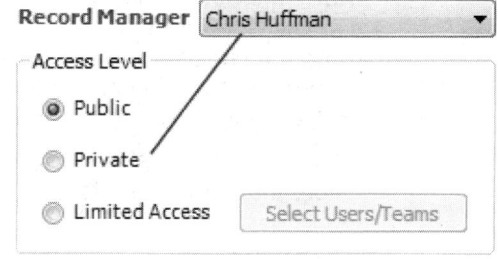

Group (or Company) Access: Public, Private, or Limited Access: All records by default are marked as **Public** (view the Group Info or Company Info tab). If you share the database with other users in your company, you can opt to change this field to Private for certain records. After a Group or Company is marked as **Private**, only the listed "Record Manager" can see it. Not even the Administrator can see it unless they log on to the database as that Record Manager. This also affects the total number of Groups (or Companies) displayed in the record counter. Your private records are included in your count, but not in anyone else's count.

 *If you are using ACT! Premium, you have a third level of Group or Company Access...Limited Access. The Limited Access feature allows you to select a user(s) or a defined team of users that can access the current record. Only users with Administrator or Manager roles can create Teams. If you would like to assign Limited Access as a default on all new Contacts, you can do that in **Tools, Preferences**, **Startup** tab, click **Record Creation Options...**, define the options and click **OK** and **OK**.*

Practice: Creating a Group

What to do	How to do it/Comments
1. Display the Groups window. Observe the existing Groups.	Click the **Groups** button on the Navbar. Several Groups have already been defined.
2. Create a new Group named **Tennis**. The description should read **People who play Tennis**.(We'll add names in a minute.)	Press **[Insert]**, type the **Group name**, press **[Tab]** or click in the **Description** box, type the description.
3. Display the Companies window. Observe the existing Companies.	Choose **View**, **Companies** or click the **Companies** button on the Navbar. Several Companies have been defined.
4. Create a new Company named **A1 Services**.	Press **[Insert]** and type the Company name. You don't need to enter any additional information.
5. Our European sales team handles all A1 Services work. If you are using ACT! Premium, assign Limited Access to the new company to the European team.	On the Company Info tab, select Limited Access and click Select Users/Teams. Click on the Teams tab and double-click Europe to assign access. Click **OK**.

After your Group/Company is created, remember, you can add Contact(s) in several ways:

- **Static** members are manually added or removed. You've seen how easy it is to add a single Contact. You can also add multiple Contacts to the Group or Company using the current lookup or using Contacts that already belong to another Group or Company. When a Contact is assigned to a Group or Company manually, the Group or Company name will display on the Contact's Groups/Companies tab.
- **Dynamic** members are automatically added or removed based on an Advanced Query that you create for the Group or Company.

Companies have a third way of adding Contacts...linking.

- A Contact can be **linked** to one Company through the Contact's company name (i.e., since a Contact only has one company name on their record, they can only be "linked" to one Company record with the same name (down to the periods). When Contacts are linked to a Company, the company name displays as a hyperlink.

Groups & Companies | 267

Adding Multiple Contacts to a Group or Company

When you first create them, Groups and Companies are like empty containers that need to be filled. You can add several things to Groups or Companies, but the most common thing is Contacts.

Procedure: To add multiple Contacts to a Group or Company

1. Look up Contacts, if appropriate.

2. Click the **Groups** or **Companies** button in the Navbar or choose **View**, **Groups** or **Companies**.

3. Click the name of the Group or Company for which you want to add the Contacts.

   You may need to click the + to the left of a name to display the Subgroup or Division names.

4. Click the **Add/Remove Contacts** button on the toolbar,

   The **Add/Remove Contacts** dialog box appears.

   or click the **Contacts** tab and click the **Add/Remove Contacts...** button.

   You cannot define **Linked** Contacts from this dialog box.

To manually add or remove multiple members (Static):

5. Click the **Contacts...** button. Select from **All Contacts, Current Lookup, Groups,** or **Companies**.

   Choose **Current lookup** to display Contacts in the current lookup. Choose **Groups** or **Companies** if you wish to select Contacts associated with an existing entity.

6. Click a specific Contact and click the **Add** button,

   To add one Contact at a time, you can type their name in the **Look for:** box to quickly search the list (last name, first name).

   or click the **Add All** button **>>** to add the entire lookup,

   You can also click **<<** to **Remove All** to start over with membership.

   or select a name under **Selected Contacts:** and click **Remove**.

7. Repeat until all desired Contacts have been added and click **OK**.

   Your Group or Company now contains some static members.

OR... to define a query to automatically add/remove members (Dynamic):

Sage ACT!

5. Click the **Edit Criteria...** button. Create a query that defines which Contacts will be included in the Group or Company and click **OK**.

   The Criteria window displays and it looks like the Advanced Query window (because it is). Review the Advanced Query chapter to refresh your memory on building queries.

6. Click **OK**.

   The number of contacts in the group displays in the Status bar at the bottom of the screen.

Manually adding members is appropriate for cases where there really is no way to look up the Contacts in the database using any of the fields. It is a little harder to maintain Groups and Companies using this method, since it is easy to forget to add someone to (or remove them from) the Group (or Company). However, sometimes there really isn't another way (active members of your breakfast group).

Dynamically adding members using a query is the preferred method. While it may take a minute or two to define the query criteria, it is great for housekeeping. Change someone's ID/Status from Prospect to Customer, and they are immediately moved out of the Prospect Group and into the Customer Group.

Practice: Populating Your Groups and Companies

What to do	How to do it/Comments
1. Let's create a lookup of everyone who has the word "tennis" in their record.	**Lookup**, **Keyword Search**.... Type "tennis" in the Search for area. Change "Record type:" to **Contacts**, if necessary. Verify that every option is checked in the Look in area. Click **Find Now**. Click **Create Lookup**.
2. These tennis buddies should be added to the Tennis Group you created in the previous exercise.	Click the **Groups** button in the Navbar to display the available Groups. Select the Tennis Group. Click **Add/Remove Contacts** Click the **Contacts...** button. Change **Select from:** to the **Current lookup** option. Click **Add All >>**.
3. Wait, Chris Burn doesn't play tennis...he just works there. Remove him from the **Selected Contacts:**.	With the **Select Contacts** dialog box still displayed, click Chris Burn's name under Selected Contacts: and click the **Remove** button.

Groups & Companies | 269

What to do	How to do it/Comments
4. Can you add Gracie Anderson to the **Selected Contacts:** while you are still here?	Change the **Select from** to **All Contacts**. In the **Look for:** area, type **ander**. When you see her name, double-click it.
5. Click **OK** to close the **Select Contacts:** dialog box. (Notice that you can see some of the names displayed in the Static Members section.) Click **OK** to close the **Add/Remove Contacts** dialog box. Display the **Contacts** *tab* for the **Tennis** Group (at the bottom of **Group** view) to view the members of this Group.	Click **OK** to close the window. Note that you can see the number of contacts belonging to this group at the bottom of the window.

Now let's define membership using a simple query. This time let's add the Contacts to a Company, instead of a Group. The process is the same; it's just the container type that is different.

What to do	How to do it/Comments
6. Let's add Contacts to the **A1 Services** (which you created in a previous practice session) using a simple query.	Display the **Companies** view. Select the A1 Services Company record. Click the **Add/Remove Contacts** icon. Click the **Edit Criteria...** button.
7. There is A1 Services, A1 Services of UK, and A1 Services-US Operations. All of them belong to the A1 Services Company record. So the query might say…Add all Contacts where the company name contains the words "A1 Services."	In the query window **Field Name:**, select **Company**. In **Operator:**, select **Contains**. In **Value:**, enter "A1 Services." Don't forget to click the **Add to list** button. Preview the results to see if it looks reasonable. Click **OK** and **OK**.

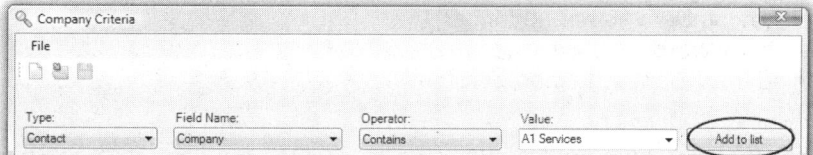

What to do	How to do it/Comments
8. See who was added to the Company membership.	Click the **Contacts** tab, if necessary, to display the Contacts automatically added to the Company.

What to do	How to do it/Comments
9. Display Amanda's record in Detail View. Click the **Groups/ Companies** tab. Change the **Show membership for:** to **Companies and Divisions**.	Click Amanda's name to display her record. Click the **Groups/ Companies** tab to view membership for **Companies and Divisions**.
10. **A1 Services** does not display. Why?	When a Contact is added to a Company or Group using a query, then the Company or Group name will NOT automatically display on the Contact's **Groups/Companies** tab. Only Contacts manually added to Groups or Companies are listed on the **Groups/Companies** tab.
11. Click the **Show Dynamic Membership** button to verify Amanda's membership.	OK, she is there. Close the Membership box.
12. Display the A1 Services Company record (works the same way as displaying Groups.)	Click the **Companies…** button in the Navbar, right-click the A1 Services Company record and select **Create Lookup**. Yep, they are all there as well.
13. Unfortunately Andy Harrison (A1 Services) has decided to go out on his own. His new company name is Andy's Services. Change his Contact record to reflect that change and then save the changes.	Double-click Andy Harrison's record to display it in Detail View. Change the company name to: **Andy's Services** Click the Save icon on the toolbar.
14. View A1 Services once again to see if Andy's Services still maintains membership. Since the company name no longer contains the words "A1 Services," it is removed from Company membership.	Click the **Companies…** button. Select the A1 Services and click the **Contacts** tab. He's gone.

 Queries work great for Groups or Companies that have a consistent value in a field. However, you can't always use queries. Groups like Male or Female are difficult to automate. Groups of Contacts that belong to your Wednesday morning networking breakfast are also difficult to create queries for. For these types of Groups, you have to manually add the Contact (page 262).

Using Criteria for Your Groups

We just created a simple criteria for a Company in the last practice session. However, once you get the hang of creating Groups that use Criteria (aka Advanced Queries), you can start to keep track of amazing things in your database. Usually Groups that are created using queries have more than one criteria (otherwise you would just use a lookup). Think about some of these for groups…

Customers with e-mail addresses (so you can market to them). As you add contacts to the database that have an e-mail address, the list is automatically updated. You don't have to worry if your staff is keeping this group up-to-date.

| Contact | ID/Status | Contains | Customer | And |
| Contact | E-mail | Contains Data | Nothing | End |

Customers without e-mail addresses (so you have a list that you can work on to update). As you add e-mail addresses, the name is immediately removed from the list.

| Contact | ID/Status | Contains | Customer | And |
| Contact | E-mail | Does Not Contain Data | Nothing | End |

Allison's Customers W/O Recent Contact (query of all customers where Allison is assigned to their account and they haven't been contacted in the last 6 months). As contact is made, their names are removed from the list and as time passes, other contacts may be added to the list if Allison is not keeping up with her contact relationships.

Contact	ID/Status	Contains	Customer		And
Contact	Sales Rep	Contains	Allison		And
Contact	Edit Date	Older Than [days]		183	End

Customers-Purchased Service-TX (contacts who have purchased Service Contracts in TX). You can mix Opportunity and Contact in the same query.

Opportunity	Status	Contains	Won	And
Opportunity	Product Name	Contains	Service	And
Contact	State	Equal To (=)	TX	End

Customers Active 5 Yr (contacts who made their first purchase more than 5 years ago and still were making purchases last year).

| Contact | First Purchase | Older Than [days] | 1825 | And |
| Contact | Last Yrs Purchases | Greater Than or Equal To | 3000 | End |

Hopefully these examples have you thinking about some groups that you can create to better segment your database. You may need to create some fields in your database to help better utilize this feature. Basing your Group memberships on fields can be quite powerful. Just by changing the ID/Status from Prospect to Customer, ACT! would immediately update all Groups that used that field as a criteria.

Linking Contacts and Companies

In the previous exercise, we took companies with very similar names (A1 Services) and grouped them under one **Company** record. If you have several companies that you want to group into one Company record, and they all have the same name, then you might want to *link* them to the Company record. Linking a Contact provides a couple of handy benefits:

- Linking creates a direct hyperlink from the Contact record to the Company record.
- The link ensures that all future notes and history are permanently shared with the Company record (unless you specify otherwise) and that new activities and opportunities will always be associated with the Company. Consequently, if the Contact changes companies, all linked objects will still display on the original Company record. If the Contact is deleted, only the shared notes and history will remain with the linked Company (the activities and opportunities will be deleted with the Contact).
- Default Basic Company information (Company name, Address 1, Address 2, Address 3, City, State, ZIP Code, Country, and Web Site) can be instantaneously updated for all linked Contact records. However, any Contact field can be linked to any compatible Company field... so that keeping up-to-date information in two places (without double entry) is a snap.

> *A Contact can be a member of several Companies, but each Contact can only be linked to one Company.*

Create a Company from a Contact

You could manually create a new Company (see page 265), however, if you have a Contact with complete address information and you were planning on linking anyway, it is easier to create the new Company record from the Contact's record.

Procedure: To create a Company record from a Contact

1. Display the Contact for creating the Company record.

2. Click **Contacts**, **Create Company from Contact**.

    The Company Detail window displays with the company, address, and Web site fields completed. The original Contact record is linked to the Company record and listed on the **Contacts** tab.

3. Complete additional info.

    Assign Company Access if desired.

> *If the Company record already exists, you will be prompted to link to the existing Company record instead.*

Procedure: To link a Contact to an existing Company record

1. In **Contacts: Detail View**, click the browse button to the right of the Company name field.
2. Select the Company.
3. Click **OK**.

The **Link to Company** dialog box displays. If the Company name (or something similar) exists, it will be highlighted.

If the wrong company name was highlighted, select the correct one.

If the Company has not yet been created, then **Cancel** and create it.

All *future* activities and opportunities will be **associated** with the linked Company record. Only users who have rights to see the Contact will be able to see the linked activities or opportunities.

All *future* notes and history will be **shared** with and displayed on the Company record as Public, regardless of the security setting on the Contact record that owns the note or history.

So if another user doesn't have access to the Contact, but they have access to the Company, they could see a linked note or history that belongs to the inaccessible Contact. Consequently, if your Contacts have Limited Access, then you will probably want to assign Limited Access to the associated Companies (or Groups) as well.

Link...Associate...What's the Difference?

If you are assigning Private or Limited Access to any of your Contacts, you should understand how ACT! works to protect the data that belongs to that Contact. (If all of your Contacts are public, you can skip this topic.)

- Any note, history, or activity instantly inherits the security access (Public, Private, or Limited Access) of the Contact that owns it.

    > However, opportunities do not inherit the Contact's security access. They have their own security.

- So...if a Contact has been marked as **Private**, then only the Record Manager of that specific record can view the Contact or data that belongs to the Contact. This also affects areas like the Task List or the Calendar.

    > Although a private activity will still display on all Calendar time slots with the word "private".   [Chris Huffman] private

- OR...if a Contact has been assigned **Limited Access** for only three users, then only those three users can see the notes, history, or activities created for that Contact.

Let's look at scenarios where a Contact is **linked** to a Company record, or you decide to manually share an item (note, history, activity) to a Group or Company record.

- Activities created for a *linked* Contact are automatically "associated" with the Company record. Their security is maintained. If you don't have access to see the Contact, you will not see their activities displayed on a Company record.
- Any note or history created for a *linked* Contact is automatically "shared" with the Company record by default. The security for *linked* (shared) notes or history is not maintained.
- Consequently, if the linked Company record is public, then a shared note or history will be viewable regardless of the security assigned to the Contact. It will display on the Company record even if you don't have rights to see the Contact record it belongs to.

So let's look at some potential ramifications of this…

- Clearing any activity creates a history. If the Contact is *linked*, then the history of that activity will be shared with the Company record and thus viewable if the Company record does not use the same security settings as the Contacts that belong to it.

It is important that you understand and are comfortable with the ramifications of how your notes and history will display with linked Companies. If you are concerned about the security implications, you can disable the automatic linking of a note or history….one item at a time or as a preference for all future notes and history. Assigning Limited Access to the associated Company records would also handle this problem.

- **Global Setting:** A Manager or Administrator can modify the default Global setting for the database so that it is not set to automatically share notes or histories of linked Contacts. (**Tools, Preferences, Admin** tab, **Company Preferences…**, uncheck "Share new…" click **OK**, **OK**.) Notes or history can then be manually shared, if necessary.

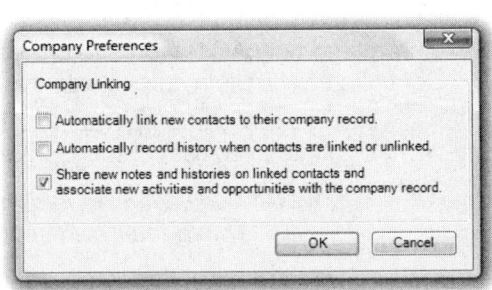

- **Manually:** You can avoid sharing a new note or history publicly on a linked Company record by removing the link from any specific note (or history) or by marking it as Private before you click OK.

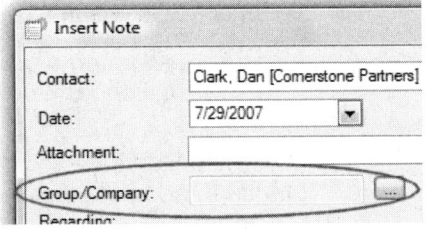

Create a Contact from a Company

Not only can you create a Company record from a Contact record, but you can also create a Contact record from a Company record.

Procedure: To create a Contact record from a Company record

1. Display the Company record.

2. Click **Companies, Create Contact from Company** — The Contact record is created and automatically linked to the Company record.

3. Fill in the contact's name and other information.

 If you have another Contact record already filled in, you can also right-click, Duplicate Contact to create a new Contact for the same company. You will need to click the Browse… button to the right of the company name to link the Contact to a Company record. Use whichever method you like.

Disabling a Company Link

If a linked Contact accepts a position with another company, you will need to disable the current link. Once disabled, you can enter a new company name for the Contact. The great news is that all notes, history, and activities that were created while the Contact was linked to the original company are still associated with (and are displayed on) that Company record…even though the contact now works for a new employer.

Procedure: To disable a Company link

1. In **Contacts: Detail View**, click the browse button to the right of the Company name field. — Displays the **Disable Company Link** warning message.

2. Click **OK**. — Copies of shared notes and history will remain with the Company. Associations with activities will continue to display under the original Company record as long as the Contact is not deleted. You can manually create associations.

Practice: Linking

What to do	How to do it/Comments
1. Create a Company record for Great Northern Coffee using James Hill's Contact record.	**Lookup**, **Company...**, Great Northern, and click **OK**. Use James's record to create the Company record. **Contacts**, **Create Company from Contact**.
2. Add the other two Great Northern Coffee Contacts, but don't link Van. Van Johnson is with Great Northern *Chocolates*. Try linking his record and notice how ACT! does not automatically highlight any Company record and the **OK** button is not enabled. You can't link to a Company that has not been created... unless you want to change Van's company name.	Click the **Contacts** button in the Navbar to display the "1 of 4" lookup in Detail View. Notice that the company name on James's record is hyperlinked. Click the **Forward** arrow to move to the next Contact. Click the **Browse...** button to the right of the company name. Notice that since the Company field name and the Company record name were the same, ACT! selected it for you. Click **OK**. Link all but Van.
3. Click the company hyperlink to display the Company record. Display the **Contacts** tab to view the member names. Click the **Add/Remove Contacts...** button to verify the **Linked contacts** are displayed. Then cancel out of the Add/Remove dialog box.	Clicking on the hyperlink takes you to the Company record, displayed in Detail View.
4. What if Great Northern Chocolates was really the same company, just a different subsidiary? Manually add any Great Northern Chocolates records to Great Northern Coffee. In the Company record, click the **Add/Remove Contacts** button to verify membership.	**Lookup**, **Company**, great northern chocolates, and click **OK**. Right-click and select **Add Contact to Company...**, double-click Great Northern Coffee, and click **OK**. Click on the Great Northern Coffee Company record again. Van now displays with the rest of the Great Northern Company without having to change his company name.

Pushing Company Changes Back to Contacts

When companies change their corporate address, it is sometimes tedious to change all of the associated address information. If your Contacts are linked to a Company record, you can quickly change all of the linked Contacts' address information. ACT! starts with nine fields, by default, which are linked from the Company record to the Contact record. However, you can define as many linking fields as you like. We'll discuss more about defining them in the "Database Design and Layout" chapter (page 337).

The default fields that will be updated are: Company, Address 1, Address 2, Address 3, City, State, ZIP Code, Country, and Web Site. You can check to see which fields have been defined by clicking on **Companies**, **View Linked Fields**.

Procedure: To push changes from a Company record to linked Contacts

1. In the Company record, make appropriate field changes and…

    click the **Save** icon,

    or **Companies, Update Linked Contacts,**

    or click the **Update Linked Contacts** icon.

2. Answer **Yes** to update the linked Contacts.

ACT! needs to know when you are finished. If you forget to click the Save icon, ACT! will automatically save your work as soon as you try to move off of the record. You can also update the linked Contacts without making any changes to the Company record using the menu command.

The Contacts are immediately updated.

 Since this feature updates all linked Contacts, you should be careful with it. Even those who work in different states will be updated with the new information, if the address fields are linked.

Practice: Distributing Changes

What to do	How to do it/Comments
1. Display all Contacts belonging to the Great Northern record.	Click the **Companies…** button, right-click the Great Northern company you created in the previous exercise and click **OK**.

278 Sage ACT!

What to do	How to do it/Comments
2. Notice that three of the four Contacts have the same address, and the fourth one has no address. Update all Contacts linked to Great Northern Coffee from the Company record. Their new address is: **One Hill Blvd** **St. Paul, MN 55125**	Click the **Companies** button in the Navbar. Double-click **Great Northern Coffee** to display it in Detail View. Make the change to the address and ZIP. Click the **Save** icon. Answer **Yes** to update the linked Contacts.
3. Return to the Contacts to verify the address changes for the linked Contacts and that an address was not added to Van. *Don't link Van yet. We have other plans for him.*	Right-click the Great Northern Coffee name in the tree view and select **Create Lookup**. While Van is a member of the Great Northern Coffee Company record, he is not *linked* to the Company record. Therefore, his address information was not updated.

Pulling Changes from the Company Record

Sometimes you just want to be sure that a Contact has the most up-to-date Company information. While you are on the Contact's record, you can refresh the data from its linked Company record. All linking fields will be updated to match the Company data.

Procedure: To pull changes from a Company record to linked Contacts

1. While viewing a Contact with a linked Company record, click **Contacts, Update Lin<u>k</u>ed Contact**.

   Data is pulled from the Company record to update the Contact record.

    If you want to verify which fields are linked and would be updated, you can select ***Companies****,* ***View Linked Fields****. Linking fields are defined under* ***Tools****,* ***Define Fields****.*

Groups & Companies

Practice: Pulling Changes

What to do	How to do it/Comments
1. Look up Van Johnson's record.	**Lookup**, **Co**n**tact**, **van jo**, and click **OK**.
2. His record is not linked to any Company record. Go ahead and link it to Great Northern Coffee (the company you created in a previous exercise).	Click the **Browse…** button to the right of the Company name, select Great Northern Coffee, and click **OK**. Notice that the Company name was updated, but no address information was added to the Contact.
3. View the linked fields defined for this database and notice that we have defined three additional linking fields: Customer ID, ID/Status, and Phone. Van doesn't have a Customer ID, which makes sense if his ID/Status is Prospect.	**Companies**, **View Linked** **F**ields. Click **Close** when you are finished.
4. Update Van's contact information with the linked Company data.	You need to save the change to the record before you can do this. Click the **Save** icon. Then click **C**ontacts, **Update Lin**k**ed Contact**.
5. Notice the Address update.	
6. Change the ID/Status on the Company record to Customer and enter a Customer ID. Update all linked Contacts.	Click the company link on Van's record to display the Great Northern Coffee Company record. Change the ID/Status to Customer and add a Customer ID of US-10705. Click the **Save** icon and confirm the change.
7. Verify the change on Van's record.	Display the Contacts tab for the Great Northern Coffee company and click on Van's name.

Convert a Group to a Company

If you are a long-time ACT! user, you may already have set up Groups to represent companies in a previous version. With the addition of the Companies concept, you can convert those Groups into Companies. However, you can't convert a Company back to a Group.

Procedure: To convert a Group to a Company

1. Click **Groups** button on the Navbar and select the Group name to convert.
2. **Groups, Conver̲t to Company...**,   A wizard appears.

   or right-click, Conver̲t to Company....
3. Click **N̲ext>** to move through the wizard.
4. Map the fields, if necessary.   If you created additional **Group** fields, you will need to create the same fields in **Companies** in order to transfer the data upon conversion.

Divisions and Subgroups

Divisions and Subgroups are all about ownership.

- **Divisions** are subsets of Companies. They might be used for Departments within the company or for other companies that belong to or are associated with the parent Company.
- **Subgroups** help you divide a Group into smaller, more meaningful chunks.
- You can have up to 15 levels of Divisions or Subgroups. Each level is indented under its parent in the tree view.

Procedure: To create a Subgroup or Division

1. Select the Group or Company that will be the owner.   While either in the Companies or Groups view, select the parent record.
2. Click the icons on the toolbar,

   or right-click the name and select **New Division** or **New Subgroup**.
3. Enter any name that you like.   If you plan to create a query that will add Contacts, why not enter the query criteria that you will use in the **Description** area.

Groups & Companies | 281

4. Enter other data as desired.
5. Add Contacts to the Subgroup or Division as necessary.

Add Limited Access as desired.
See the procedure on page 267.

 Membership in a Subgroup (or Division), does not automatically create membership in the parent Group or Company. Membership in each Subgroup/Division is independent of all other Groups/Companies. If you want Contacts to be members of a parent Group or Company as well, you must add them manually or using a query.

Practice: **Making a Subgroup**	
What to do	*How to do it/Comments*
1. Select the Employees Group.	Click the **Groups** button on the Navbar. Click the **Employees** Group.
2. View the Subgroups for International Employees.	AsiaPac and European Employee groups have already been created.
3. Create an additional Subgroup for the **Friends** Group called **Friends-Arizona** (always a good list for a quick party invite).	Click the Friends group first to make it the active group. Click the **New Subgroup** icon. Enter the name of **Friends-Arizona** and click **Save** so that you can see the hierarchy.
4. If you feel adventuresome, populate the Friends-Arizona Group using a query.	Click **Add/Remove Contacts…**, **Edit Criteria…** The query that would select Contacts with an ID/Status that contains "Friend" and state = AZ.

What's the Up Button?

You may see a Hierarchy field with an Up button to its right somewhere on a layout. This feature was primarily used in previous versions of ACT! to help view and navigate through Group and Company ownership relationships. (If you are currently displaying a Subgroup, clicking the **Up** button displays the parent Group. If viewing the parent Group, the Subgroups display below. Double-click any Subgroup or Division displayed to display its information in Detail View.) The tree view is much more efficient now.

Move or Promote a Division

If a Division or Company changes ownership, it is easy to move the Company to another owner or to promote a Division to a Company.

Procedure: To move or promote a Company or Division

1. Display the Company or Division that you wish to move or promote.
2. **Groups, Companies, Move Company...**,

   or right-click, select **Move...**.
3. Select the option.
4. Click **OK**.

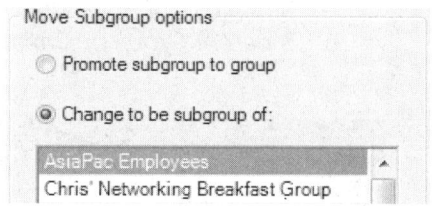

☞ *You could also just drag the Subgroup or Division to another location.*

Practice: Merger	
What to do	**How to do it/Comments**
1. Mercury Production was bought out by Widget Corp. Make Mercury Production a Division of Widget.	In Companies view, right-click Mercury Production and select **Move...**. Select Widget Corporation and click **OK**. (Or just drag it down there.) Notice that the Company link for Albert Barry is maintained.

Cumulative Views of Notes, History, etc.

One of the advantages to adding Contacts to Company membership is the ability to provide a management view of the associated Contacts and their combined notes, history, activities, and opportunities.

Company Note or History

You can also create a note or history specifically for a Company (or Group) record that does not have to be associated with any Contact in the database.

Procedure: To create a Company note or history

1. Display the Company record in Detail View.   Click the **Companies** button.

Groups & Companies | 283

2. Display the **Notes** (or **History**) tab. Notes for individual members of the Company are displayed here. If a note belongs to a Contact record, a column identifies the Contact name.

3. Click the **Insert Note** icon.   If you are displaying the **History** tab, you can click the **Record History** icon.

4. Type the note as you would for any record. This note belongs to the Company record...not to any individual.

Practice: Check the Cumulative View

What to do	How to do it/Comments
1. Look at the notes on Lance Parker's record.	**Lookup**, **Co**n**tact**, Lance Parker, click **OK**. Display and view the **Notes**, **History**, and **Opportunities** tabs.
2. Now, view the cumulative notes for the Yellow Jersey Bikes **Company** record.	Click the linked company name to quickly display the Yellow Jersey **Company** record.
3. You should see Lance's note displayed again, along with notes and history for other Contacts at Verge Records. Notice that some of the notes do not display a Contact name.	View the entries for the different Contacts on the **Notes** tab. View the **History** and the **Opportunities** tabs, noting the Contact for each entry. On the **Activities** tab you can see scheduled appointments for all member Contacts.
4. Make a note on the "Yellow Jersey" Company record that "They have a new VP Sales who is making some great changes that could benefit CH TechONE."	Click the **Insert Note** icon and enter the note at left. Notice that no Contact name is associated with the note.

Manually Sharing Items with a Company (or Group)

Actually a Contact doesn't even need to belong to the Company record for a note or history to be displayed here. For example, what if you met with a consultant who was temporarily working with your client and you discussed information on a mutual project for the client. You can link any note, history, activity, or opportunity with a Company record....even if the Contact (the consultant in this example) doesn't belong to the company.

Procedure: To manually share a note or history with a Company

1. Start to create a note, history or opportunity as usual.

2. Click the **Browse...** button next to the **Share With**: field.

   Activities are "Associate With:"

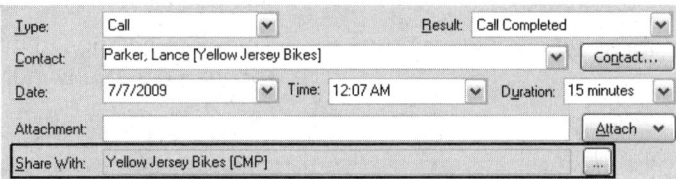

3. Confirm (if necessary) that you understand that sharing a note, history or opportunity makes it public.

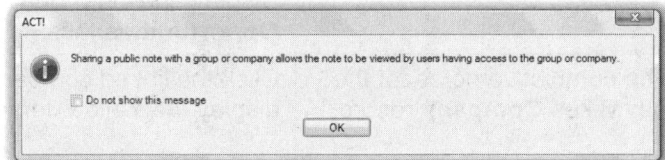

 Reason for this warning was discussed on page 273.

4. Select one or more Companies or Groups and click **OK**, **OK**.

 If the Contact is linked to, or is a member of, the Company record, then all created items (notes, history, or activities) will automatically be displayed with the Company record.

Procedure: To manually associate an activity with a Company

1. Start to create the activity item as usual.

    If you would like to link a pre-existing item to a Company (or Group), double-click the item to edit and add the link.

2. Click the **Browse...** button next to the **Associate With**: field.

3. Select one or more Companies or Groups and click **OK**, **OK**.

Groups & Companies | 285

Procedure: To manually associate an opportunity with a Company

1. Create or edit the opportunity.
2. Right-click the Association panel select **Add/Remove Groups or Companies…**
3. Select one or more Companies or Groups and click **OK**.

 You can also right-click the background of the Opportunity view.

Practice: *Notes for the Company Record Only*

What to do	How to do it/Comments
1. Look up Benny Lender. He called to say that Great Northern Coffee had received their line of credit for the merger they had been working on.	Look up Benny.
2. Create a history for this call on Benny's record and associate this history with the Company record for Great Northern Coffee.	Press **[Ctrl+H]** to record a call. Change the Result to **Call Received**. Click the browse button for Group/Company, click **OK** to acknowledge the warning, click the **Companies/Divisions** tab, double-click **Great Northern Coffee**, and click **OK**. Fill in the **Regarding** "Line of credit for merger received" and click **OK**.
3. Display the Company record for **Great Northern Coffee** again and view the **History** tab.	Click the **Companies** icon in the Navbar. Click **Great Northern Coffee** to display the Detail View. Notice the history entry for Benny, but also notice that he does not display in the **Contacts** tab.

Changing Companies

When a client leaves one company and moves on to another, what happens to the their notes, history, and activities? If they were linked or associated to a Company record, then their *linked* notes, history, and activities continue to display with the original Company record….regardless of the Contact's new company name or new link status.

If the Contact is deleted, then the activities and opportunities will also be deleted. However, the shared notes and history stay with the linked Company record and the Contact name changes to blank.

While Opportunities may display on the Contact's record, they are independent of the Contact and will not be deleted if the Contact is deleted. Only the association to the Contact is deleted.

Practice: Leaving Your History Behind

What to do	How to do it/Comments
1. Drew McLintock is currently linked to Verge Records. Enter a note on his record that he approved our budget.	Look up Drew. Insert a note on his record. Notice that since his Contact record is linked to the Verge Company record that the note is automatically associated with the Company record.
2. Disconnect Drew's Record from Verge. He went to work with Swing Software (which is also a Company in our database). Connect him to that Company record.	Click the **Browse...** button to the right of the Company field and answer **OK** to disconnect. Click the **Browse...** button again to display the list of Company record names. Select Swing Software and click **OK**.
3. Display the Verge Records Company record and view the note that Drew left behind.	Click **Companies**. Click Verge Records and display the **Notes** tab. Notice the note left behind by Drew, even though he no longer displays in the **Contacts** tab.

Filtering Tabs

The Detail View for both Companies and Groups can be filtered. You control what displays here through the filter settings.

Most of the filters are fairly obvious. The **Dates:** filter can narrow the display to only recent activity if you like. The **Select Users** filter can help you track the activities of some of your Sales Reps. The **Types:** filter allows you to narrow your vision to specific types of history or activities. The combinations are mind-boggling. (Well, they boggle our minds anyway.)

The **Show For:** is probably the only one that needs a little explanation.

- **Company** (or **Group**) will narrow the display to items that were entered directly in the record and not connected with any Contact record. Items connected to a Contact's name are excluded.
- **Company Contacts** (or **Group Contacts**) will narrow the display to items that were entered on a member Contact record or where the item was specifically Associated With the Company (or Group) record. Company (or Group) items are excluded.
- **All** will display both Company-specific (or Group-specific) items, as well as items connected to a Contact name.

*You can also click the **Options** button, select **Customize Columns...**, and modify what fields are displayed in any of the list view tabs.*

Lookup Companies or Groups

Just as in the Contacts, you can also perform lookups for Companies or Groups.

- **Lookup, Name...** or **City...** or **ID/Status...** etc.
- Right-click any field to get a field-specific Lookup dialog box.
- To look up a Company name, use the Lookup pane in the Navbar.
- **Lookup, Keyword Search...**, change the **Record type:** (if necessary) click **Include contacts** to search only Contacts belonging to a specific group or company.
- From the Companies or Groups Detail View, click **Lookup, By Example...**.
- **Lookup, Advanced Query...**
- To lookup a contact while in this view, click **Lookup, Contacts**, select a field.

If more than one Group or Company matches your criteria, the results are displayed in List View. Just as in Contacts: List View, the List View for Companies or Groups will be displayed in columns and the column headers can be customized. In fact, almost anything you could do in Contacts: List View (see page 35), you can also do in Companies: List View or Groups: List View.

Practice: Company Record Lookups

What to do	How to do it/Comments
1. Look up all Company records that are headquartered in Arizona.	Click the **Companies** button. **Lookup, State**, enter AZ, and click **OK**. Notice this is a *Companies:* List View, not a *Contacts:* List View. No contact names are displayed in this list.
2. Return to Detail View to display all contacts.	Click **Detail View** to return to the detail view (which will display all records).

Advanced Queries for Companies and Groups

You can also use the Advanced Query feature to accomplish more complicated lookups. (Review Advanced Queries starting on page 249). Advanced queries for Companies will only display the Company records that match your criteria, not the Contacts belonging to those Companies. The same is true for Group Advanced Queries.

Procedure: To create an Advanced Query for Companies or Groups

1. **Lookup**, Advanced **Query**

2. Select the **Field Name:**, **Operator:**, and (if appropriate) enter the **Value:** for the first criteria.

   There are no options for Type: when you search for Company or Group.

3. Click **Add to list**.

   The first criterion is added to your list of criteria.

(	Type	Field Name	Operator	Value	)	And/Or
	Company	Any State Field	Equal To (=)	TX		End

4. Repeat steps 2 - 3 for the each criteria.

   Once all of your criteria are specified.

5. Set your **And/Or** options as necessary.

   An "**And**" indicates that concurrent rows must both be true. An "**Or**" indicates either the current row or the next can match.

6. Group criteria as necessary.

7. **OK**

   Saved Company queries have an extension of .CRY. Group queries have an extension of .GRY. (Contact = QRY and Opportunity = .ORY)

 *If you would like to modify one of the query criteria that you have added (because of a spelling mistake or to change an operator from Equal To (=) to Contains), then select the row and click the **Edit...** button.*

Practice: Advanced Company Queries

What to do	How to do it/Comments
1. Look up all Company Records that are our Customers where Chris Huffman is the Record Manager.	Click the **Companies** button. **Lookup**, **Advanced Query**. Create a query to locate all Company records where the ID/Status contains Customer and the Record Manager contains Chris Huffman.

(	Type	Field Name	Operator	Value	)	And/Or
	Company	ID/Status	Contains	Customer		And
	Company	Record Manager	Contains	Chris Huffman		End

Opportunities

It's important to keep track of the opportunities available to your company. To understand this valuable tool, you will:

- ☑ Create new and track existing opportunities.

- ☑ Edit and update opportunities as the deal progresses.

- ☑ Learn to quickly create Quotes from opportunities.

- ☑ Manage the Opportunity List view to filter and display selected opportunities.

- ☑ Export from the Opportunity List view to Microsoft Excel.

Creating Opportunities

You've already seen how ACT! keeps track of names and numbers, and even notes and history, to keep you in the know. But what if you want to know about pending deals? What if you want to review deals you clinched in the past, including wonderful details like when the deal closed or (better yet) how much the deal was worth?

This is what the **Opportunities** feature is all about. Not only can you track everything we've already mentioned, but you can also estimate the probability of success, note your competition, and generate reports and graphs that put it all on paper, you can even export the opportunities to Microsoft Excel where ACT! creates a list, a pivot chart, and a pivot table. Who really knows what a "pivot" is... but once you've seen it, you're off the farm, baby, and you're never going back.

An **Opportunity** can be created as a stand-alone record, much like a Contact record, or a Group or Company record. For example, if you've just heard about a potential Opportunity and you don't know much about it yet, you can create a new Opportunity that isn't associated with any Contact, Company, or Group. However, it is likely that most of your opportunities will be associated with one or more Contacts, Groups, or Companies. If associated with a Contact, it will display on the Contact's record in the Opportunities tab.

Procedure: To create a new opportunity

1. Start the new Opportunity from the view (Contacts, Groups, Companies, or Opportunities) that reflects the primary association.

    Look up the record (Contact or Company or Group) that will be associated with the Opportunity.

    If the Opportunity will be associated with a Contact, look up the Contact(s) associated with the opportunity. If you don't know the Contacts yet, you can look up a Company in Companies view to start the process. Or you can just display the Opportunities view and start ... without any associations.

2. Click the drop-down arrow on the Global toolbar's **New...** button, and select Opportunity...,

    The **Opportunity** Detail View displays.

    or click the **New Opportunity** button on the Opportunity tab header,

    or you could also press **[Ctrl+F11]** to start the new opportunity.

3. Enter an **Opportunity Name:**.

    Use a descriptive name that would distinguish this opportunity from others with the same Contact.

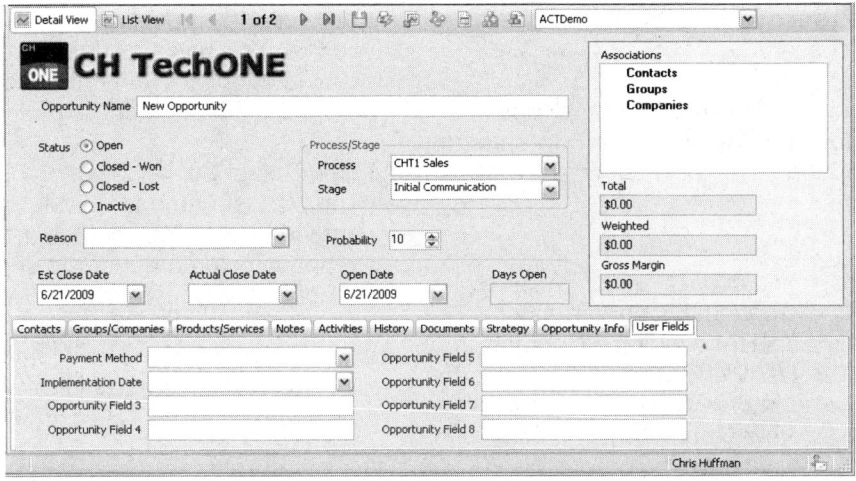

4.	Select a **Process**.	On new ACT! databases, three sales processes are available to choose from: **ACT! Sales Cycle**, **New Technology Process**, and **Promotional Sales Cycle**. You can also create your own sales processes for different parts of your business.
5.	Select a **Stage**.	Select the stage that most closely matches where you are in the sales process. When you select a Stage, the Probability % associated with the Stage displays in the Probability field.
6.	If necessary, change the **Probability** % that you will win this deal.	You can override the default suggested by the Stage you selected.
7.	Enter or select an **Est. Close Date**.	Enter the date that you believe the client will make a final decision on this opportunity. Today's date appears by default.

8. Add associated Contact records if necessary.

    Click the **Contacts** tab and click **Add/Remove Contacts...** to enter any additional Contacts associated with the deal.

    ☞ *You could also have started creating this opportunity by selecting multiple Contacts in List View, then right-clicking the selected Contacts and selecting **New Opportunity....** All selected Contacts would have been added to the Contact list.*

    You can add as many associated Contacts as you like. You can view the contacts associated with the opportunity in the Associations pane and/or on the Contacts tab.

    In the Select Contacts dialog box, enter the person's last name to quickly scroll to their name in the list. You can also click on the Company column header to sort the list by Company name. Then, type the name of the company to quickly display all names associated with a specific company. Double-click the names to add to the Opportunity (or select and click the **Add** button). Click **OK**.

    Keep in mind that if any associated *Contact* is Private or has Limited Access, then other users will only be able to see the associated Contact names they have Access to.

9. Add any associated **Companies** or **Groups**.

    Click **Groups/Companies** tab. Change the Show for: as necessary and then click the Add/Remove button.

    You can associate an Opportunity with any number of Groups, Subgroups, Companies, or Divisions participating in the deal. The Opportunity will display on each Group's or Company's detail view.

10. On the **Products/Services** tab, click **Add...** button.

    Select a **Name** from the drop-down list, or select an **Item #**, or just type any product text or name that you like.

    As you type the first few letters of the product **Name** or **Item #**, ACT! fills in any pre-defined products. The product or service does not need to be in a list. You can type anything you like here.

    Entering a new ad hoc product or service name does not automatically add it to the list.

    ☞ *If you manually entered a product (and did not select a product or service from the drop-down list), enter an Item #, associated Cost, and selling Price if desired.*

11. Enter **Quantity**.

    You may use the decimal place in Quantity to indicate service hours (e.g., 1.5 hours).

12. The Cost and Price are automatically entered if you selected a product from the drop-down list.

    You can also enter these items.

Opportunities | 293

13. Offering a discount? Either…
    - enter a revised selling price in the **Adjusted Price** column, or
    - enter a % in the **Discount** column.

When you enter an Adjusted Price, the Discount % is calculated and displayed.

If you enter a Discount %, the Adjusted Price is calculated and displayed.

 *To discount the whole order, add a product named **Discount** and in the **Price** field, type the discount amount for the order with a – (minus).*

 *You may need to click **Display Fields…** to see all of the product fields that are available for your database. You can also arrange the order of these fields. Your selections are unique to your logon and workstation.*

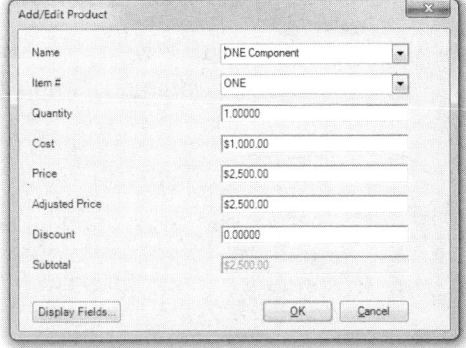

14. Click **OK** to save your Product addition.

15. Click **Add** to include more products or services.

You can fill out every field in Products or maybe you only want to enter a Price that would reflect a total project estimate.

Double-click any product line item to edit it.

16. On the **Notes** tab, enter any additional information that you want to associate with this opportunity.

17. On the **User Fields** tab (or any other tabs with fields), enter any additional information desired.

You can customize any of the eight Opportunity Fields in the **User Fields** tab.

18. Fill in other fields found regarding this Opportunity (ex: on the **Opportunity Info** tab).
    - Record how you got the lead in the **Referred By:** field.
    - Revise the **Open Date:** if necessary.
    - Enter names of any **Competitor** on this opportunity.

The **Open Date:** field is used to calculate the **Days Open**. If you reopen an opportunity, the Open date resets to the current date.

19. On the **Opportunity Access** tab, change the security to Private or Limited Access.

    Change the **Record Manager:** to the appropriate sales rep, if necessary.

20. To schedule a follow-up activity, click on the **Contacts** tab. Select the contact(s) to be included and click the **Follow-Up...** button to schedule an activity.

    Enter a **Start Date** and **Time** and click **OK**.

21. Click **OK**.

Limited Access is only available in the Premium edition.

If you are an Assistant inputting the opportunity data, you may need to change the **Record Manager** for this opportunity.

You can also click the **Schedule Follow-up Activity** hyperlink in the Related Tasks pane.

The default follow-up activity is a phone call. The **Regarding** line reflects the **Opportunity Name,** the Process Name: and the current **Stage Name**.

 The currency type that is used in opportunities was defined when you created the database. Once the database is created, there is no way to change it.. unless you create a new database with the appropriate currency and then export the original database to the new one.

Practice: Creating Opportunities

What to do	How to do it/Comments
1. We just received an inquiry call from Lance Parker. Look him up.	**Lookup**, **Last Name**, type **Parker** and click **OK**.
2. Create a new opportunity.	Right-click the layout background and select **New Opportunity....**
3. Enter the opportunity information displayed below.	

```
Name:            YJBikes-Oregon Facility
Stage:           2. Needs Assessment
Est Close Date:  end of next month
Product Name:    TechONE System
Quantity:        1
Discount:        15%    (Volume Discount)
Referred by:     Andy Federici
```

 *Notice the Total and Weighted Total figures in the window. **Weighted Total** is the Probability % times the Total.*

What to do	How to do it/Comments
4. He also wants to purchase… Service Contract	Click **Add** to add a product line. ☞ *Note the Weighted and Total figures in the window.*
5. Add… Customization Cost: $1,000 Price: $1,750	Click **Add** to create a new product line. Customization is not part of our product list, but you can enter it anyway.
6. On the User Fields tab, use the drop-down list to add a payment method of PO in the User Fields area…otherwise, just type it in. Enter an Implementation Date for two months from today.	
7. Click the **Strategy** tab and notice the fields that were created for this database.	You can create fields like this for your own database to track different aspects of your own opportunities.
8. Schedule a follow-up call for next Monday.	On the Contacts tab, click the **Follow Up…** button to schedule the call. Notice the Regarding line.
9. Finish the opportunity and return to Lance's record to view the Opportunities tab.	Click **OK**. Click Lance's name on the Contacts tab to display his record in Contacts: Detail View.

Opportunities tab

The **Opportunities** tab in Contacts: Detail View displays the default fields in a list view. So, if you don't care about the Weighted Total and would rather see the Estimated Close Date instead, remember, it is just a list view. You can right-click inside the tab and select **Customize Columns…**, or you can click the **Options** button on the **Opportunities** tab header to change your view at any time.

Sage ACT!

Updating an Opportunity

As you work on opportunities, you can open and update them at any time to make changes such as selecting a different **Stage** or altering the **Probability.**

Procedure: To edit an opportunity

1. Double-click an existing opportunity to open it for editing.
2. Enter changes as necessary.
3. Click **OK**.

 *Opportunity history is created when you create a new opportunity, change the status or stage of the opportunity, change the estimated close date, or complete and close the sale. The history of the opportunity changes are listed on the **History** tab and print on the Summary Report.*

Practice: Adding Another Product

What to do	How to do it/Comments
1. We're adding training to our product offerings. Add this to our product list. Name Training Item# Train Cost $125.00 Price: $250.00	Click the **Opportunities** button on the Navbar. Click **Opportunities**, **Manage Product List…**. Click **Add**. Enter the information and click **OK**.
2. Dorothy Gale called to get more information about our training program for her TechONE System installation (currently in the Presentation stage). She has four people to train.	**Lookup**, **Contacts**, **Last Name**, Gale, and click **OK**. Double-click the opportunity displayed on her **Opportunities** tab. On the **Products/Services** tab, click **Add** to insert a new product line. Select the training that you just created, change the **Quantity** to 4, and click **OK**.
3. Change the **Est Close Date:** to next week.	
4. Save the Opportunity.	Psych… no need to save…that's automatic in ACT!… or you could click the Save icon.

Creating a Quote

With just the click of a button (really...one click), you can easily and quickly produce a quote from ACT!, combining information from the Contact's record and product information from the opportunity. You could be saving countless hours of your time each week, while presenting a professional image to your customers. In addition, since you can save and attach the quote, it takes only a few clicks for anyone on your team to look up the Contact and display any previous quotes.

If you like, ACT! can prompt you for a quote number before printing. When you create a quote, you are prompted for a "Quote Number" (this feature does not provide a sequential number for your quotes). You can enter any alpha or numeric characters, (e.g., perhaps a combination of a customer or sales rep or region identifier, a dash, and the current date (e.g., ABC-20101223).

 Even though you may have selected the ACT! Word Processor as your default word processor, you must have Microsoft Excel 2002(XP) or more recent version and Microsoft Word 2002(XP) or more recent version installed to generate opportunity quotes.

Procedure: To add a prompt for the quote number

1. **T**ools, Pre**f**erences....   This preference must be added to the PC of anyone who will generate quotes.

2. On the **General** tab, click **Quote Preferences...** button.

3. Select **Prompt for quote number when generating**.   This feature will not provide a sequential number for your quotes.

4. Enter a **Quote prefix** if desired. Remember, this is a PC-specific (not database-specific) preference.   You might use a prefix of "A" as a quick indicator that the quote came from ACT! instead of your accounting software. Or use it to identify which sales rep or office generated the quote.

5. Click **OK**, **OK**.

Procedure: To create a quote from the Opportunity window

1. Create or edit an opportunity.   A Contact must be associated with the Opportunity in order to create a quote.

2. Click the **Create Quote** hyperlink in the Related tasks pane at the left.   Or click the **Create Quote** icon on the View toolbar.

3. Enter a Quote Number, if prompted, and click **OK**.

    If you set quote preferences to prompt you for a quote number, enter any alphanumeric text here.

4. Modify as necessary. Double-click in the grid (spreadsheet area) to add Shipping & Handling charges. Replace 0.000% with your local tax rate percentage, and the Taxes are automatically calculated and included in the Total.

    The Word document contains an embedded Excel spreadsheet to handle the calculations of this quote.

    Taxes are calculated on the Sub Total and **do not** include any Shipping & Handling charges.

5. Click outside of the embedded spreadsheet.

    Word requires that you click outside of the spreadsheet before saving or printing it.

6. **F**ile, **P**rint…, and click **OK**.

7. Fill in the **Regarding**. If your preferences are set so ACT! prompts you for a Quote Number, the number you provided is automatically added to the Regarding line for you.

    Click **Attach document to history** if you want to keep a copy of the Quote in the **\Attachments** folder for quick retrieval.

    Click **OK**.

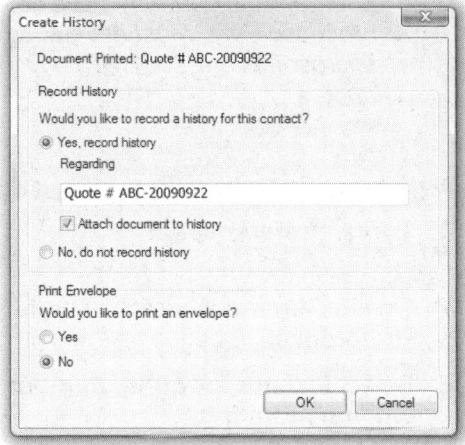

8. Close the quote document.

    If you attached the file, you don't need to save it.

9. If you printed the file, a notation has been recorded on the **Contact's History** tab. If you clicked the Attach option in step 7, a shortcut to the saved Quote will display with the history.

 *To print a quote for an existing open Opportunity from the Opportunity List view, select the open Opportunity and then click the **Quote** button on the toolbar.*

Opportunities | 299

Practice: Preparing a Quote

What to do	How to do it/Comments
1. Change your preferences to prompt you for a Quote Number.	**T**ools, Pre**f**erences…, click the **Quote Preferences…** button, and select **Prompt for quote number when generating**. Enter a prefix if you like. Click **OK**, **OK**.
2. Dorothy Gale wants us to send her a quote so that she can send it to her accounting department for payment. So, create one!	Look up Ms. Gale, if necessary. Double-click the opportunity found in her **Opportunities** tab to open it for editing. Click the **Create Quote…** icon. Add any Quote Number that you like and click **OK**.
3. Wow…fast and accurate. Print it and choose to attach it to her record.	**F**ile, **P**rint…, and click **OK**. Notice that ACT! filled in the Quote Number for you in the Regarding line. Click **Attach document to history** and click **OK**. Close the Word document without saving it and click **OK** on the Opportunity dialog box.
4. Better change the **Stage** to the next one in the process.	Change the stage to Negotiation.
5. View the **History** tab to see how ACT! recorded and saved the quote.	It doesn't display in **Opportunities** view. Remember, all quotes belong to a Contact, and therefore will display in the **History** tab of the Contact's record.

Closing the Deal

The day will come when the deal closes successfully or (gulp!) bites the dust. You can close a deal from the **Opportunity** dialog box or from the **Opportunities** tab.

Procedure: To close an opportunity

1. Locate the Opportunity to close in the Opportunities: List View or in the Opportunities tab of a specific Contact.

    Lookup the Opportunity name or the Contact that is associated with the Opportunity record.

2. Double-click and change **Status** to **Closed**-**Won** (or **Lost**).

    The **Actual Close Date** is filled in with today's date. If Won is selected, the Probability field changes to 100%.

3. Enter a **R**eason.

    This is a brief phrase about why the deal was won or lost.

4. If necessary, click the **Notes** or **History** tab and enter more information.

Practice: **The Check is in the Mail**	
What to do	*How to do it/Comments*
1. Dorothy called and the check is in the mail. Close the deal and note that she really admired our Quality Service team.	Look up Dorothy Gale, if necessary. On the **Opportunities** tab, double-click the opportunity and change the Status to **Closed - Won**. Enter the **Reason:** (you can manually enter a reason if the one you want isn't in the drop-down list).
2. Back on Dorothy's record, note how the Opportunity Status changes to **Closed-Won** on the **Opportunities** tab.	On the Contacts tab, click Dorothy's name to display her record. Click the **Opportunities** tab to see that the Status changed to **Closed – Won**.

Opportunity Management

We've been focusing on entering and tracking the stages of single opportunities. Hopefully, you have more than one deal pending and would like to see an overview of all your opportunities. ACT! provides a means to filter and view all of your opportunities to your heart's content. If the deals need to be on paper...no biggie. What? You want the list in Microsoft Excel? It's only a single click away.

Opportunity List View

You can view all of your opportunities in the Opportunities: List View. The filter options are located at the top of the Opportunities: List View window. As you change filter options, the Opportunities list changes to display only the options you selected. The number of opportunities in the list, their Weighted Total value, and their Grand Total display on the status bar. The Weighted Total is the sum of calculations based on the opportunity total times the probability of each opportunity. The Grand Total is the sum of all opportunities in the list, regardless of status or stage. The filters at the top are...

- **Dates:** Allows you to narrow the list of opportunities by Date. (Dates used for this filter are Est. Close Date for Open or Inactive opportunities and Close Date for Closed opportunities). You can select from custom filters like **Current Quarter**, or you can manually enter a **Custom...** From - To date range.
- **Status:** Allows you to select only Open, only Won, only Inactive, only Lost, or any variation of those options.
- **Process:** Allows you to display opportunities that are following a specific process. One of the advantages of having multiple Processes is that you can view your opportunities by Process and thus view your opportunities by product lines.

Opportunities | 301

- **Stage:** If you have selected a specific Process, you can narrow your search even more by selecting only one (or two or three) stages from that specific process. The default is All.
- **Probability:** Allows you to search for a single value or a greater or less than probability. It is not an equal to. If you want to display everything greater than or equal to 50% probability…enter 49. When you enter the number, press **[Enter]** or **[Tab]** out of the field to begin the search.
- **Total:** Allows you to only view the higher-dollar volume deals (or the lower volume ones, if you like).
- **Select Users** button: Allows you to filter the list for selected users (identified by the **Record Manager** on each opportunity). By default, the list only displays your opportunities.
- **Reset** button: Resets all filters to All. The Selected Users option is filtered to your name.
- **Options** button: Allows you to include or exclude your **Private** opportunities. It also has an option to **Customize** the column display if you would like to modify the current default.

Notice that the names in the Contact column appear as hyperlinks. If you click a Contact hyperlink, the associated Contact record(s) will display. To return to the Opportunities: List View, click the **Opportunities** button on the Navbar. As always, you can click the column headings to sort the list for the selected field.

If multiple Contacts were selected for an opportunity, only the first Contact's name (alphabetically) displays followed by an ellipsis. If you point to the opportunity, a pop-up will display all associated Contact names. If the Contacts are from more than one Company, the Company name will also display an ellipsis.

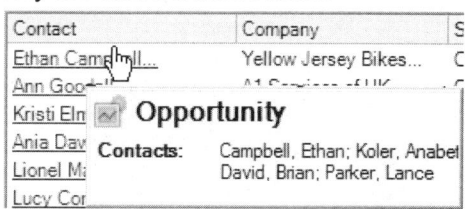

 You can enable or disable the pop-ups for opportunities by clicking the Options button and selecting Show Pop-ups.

Procedure: To filter the Opportunity List view.

1. Click **Opportunities** on Navbar.

2. Always start by clicking **Reset** to verify that you are viewing a complete list.   Resets filters back to All and Selected Users to your name.

3. Select the filter options you want to use.   See a description of the options above.

Sage ACT!

4. Click the **Create Contact Lookup** icon or right-click, **Create Lookup**. Once your list is filtered, you can create a lookup of all Contacts whose opportunities met your filter parameters. Work that list!

 You can do several things with right-click in the Opportunities: List View. Right-click the list to view your options.

To create and print a quote for an existing opportunity, select an open Opportunity, and then click the **Create Quote** button on the toolbar. Then, click Print.

Practice: Displaying Your Opportunities

What to do	How to do it/Comments
1. Display your opportunities in List view.	Click **Opportunities** button on the Navbar. Click the **List View** button.
2. Play with the filters.	Click **Reset** to display the default list.
3. Notice how clicking on a contact name displays the Contact record in Detail View.	To lookup contacts for a specific opportunity, click the Contact name hyperlink.
4. Return to the Opportunities: List View and look up all Contacts associated with the filtered opportunities.	Click the **Opportunities** button in the Navbar. The list will be using the same filters. Click the **Create Contact Lookup** icon.

 If you are a Premium user, note that you can limit the access to any Opportunity. Access can be restricted by User of by Team.

Lookup Opportunities

If filtering and sorting (by clicking on the column headers) still does not help you get to the opportunities you need to work with, then you can use the Lookup menu command. The Lookup menu offers the commands that are used most frequently, but you can look for data in any Opportunity field.

If you are looking up or creating an Advanced Query Opportunity Status, you will need to use numbers instead of words. Use 0 for Open, 1 for Closed Won, 2 for Closed Lost or 3 for Inactive.

Opportunities | 303

Procedure: To look up an opportunity by field value

1. Right-click any field in the Opportunities: Detail View and select Lookup <fieldname>.

2. Enter the search criteria.

You can also use the Lookup menu to **Lookup, Stage…** or **Product…** or other fields.

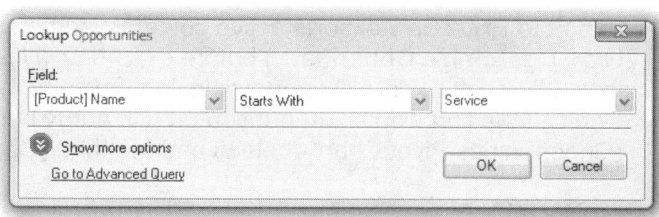

3. Click **OK**.

Opportunities that meet your lookup criteria are displayed.

4. Click **Create Contact Lookup** icon to view the associated Contacts in List View.

☞ *You could right-click the **Days Open** field to look up **Days Open**, **Greater than: 180 (days)** or all opportunities that contain a specific product.*

Practice: Opportunity Lookup

What to do	How to do it/Comments
1. Find all Opportunities that have included a Service Contract from us.	In Opportunities view, click **Lookup, Product…**, change the operator from **Starts With** to **Contains**, enter a value of **Service**. Click **OK**.
2. Narrow the lookup to opportunities where the Record Manager is Chris.	**Lookup, Record Manager…** and enter "Chris Huffman". Don't forget to select the field to change the option to **Narrow Lookup**. Click **OK**. ☞ *Lookup, Previous applies to lookups based on Contact fields… not Companies, Groups, or Opportunities fields.*
3. Lookup contacts associated with these opportunities.	Click **Create Contact Lookup** icon. Now we could contact them about an upgrade to our Service Plan.

Export to Microsoft Excel

Once you have your opportunities displayed in Opportunities: List View (either by filtering or by Lookups), you can export your list to Microsoft Excel. While this may seem supremely unexciting, it's actually pretty neat.

Export to Excel only exports active columns, so be sure to customize the column view (right-click, **Customize Columns...**) before exporting. When you click the **Export to Excel** icon, Microsoft Excel will open displaying the same opportunities you listed in ACT!. Don't let the first worksheet put you off (it's pretty boring). It's the second worksheet (Opportunities Pivot Chart - below) and the third (Opportunities Pivot) that you will love!

A pivot table is a marvelous Excel device that allows you to summarize a list in just about any way you can imagine. In this case, the list is located on the first worksheet of the workbook (Opportunities). The third sheet shows the data from the list rearranged and summarized, and the second sheet is a graphical representation of that summary.

The standard report takes the detailed list on the first worksheet and "pivots" it around to summarize the list, providing the opportunity count, sum of the total, and sum of the weighted total of all opportunities for each Record Manager.

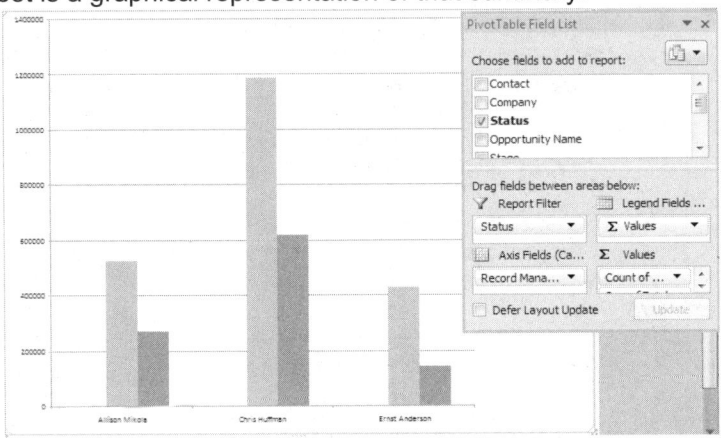

So, try exporting the data to Microsoft Excel and enjoy the results (without much work on your part at all).

Procedure: To export the Opportunity List to Microsoft Excel

1. In Opportunities: List View, filter or look up the opportunities to export.

   Neither Restricted nor Browse users can export to Microsoft Excel. Some Standard users may be restricted from exporting to Excel.

2. Right-click, **Customize Columns** to include fields to export.

   Only the first product in the opportunity is exported.

3. Click **Export to Excel** icon or right-click the list and select **Export to Excel**.

Opportunities | 305

4. Three worksheet tabs are created:

   Opportunities worksheet repeats the display (and totals) that you see in the Opportunity List View.

   Opportunities Pivot Chart worksheet displays in chart form the pivot report on the third worksheet.

   Opportunities Pivot worksheet displays the pivot report itself. This is the table that generates the chart.

On the Opportunities Pivot Chart page, the **Status** filters the chart by All, Inactive, Lost, Open, or Won opportunities (depending on what you exported).

The **Record Manager** filters which users will display in the chart. The list is limited to the names that you exported.

The **PivotTable Field List** displays a list of fields that were exported to Excel, allowing you to further slice and dice your data.

The really amazing thing about pivot reports/charts is their interactivity. In the pivot report, you will observe grey "markers" that represent the fields that make up the report. You can drag these markers around and place them in different locations to summarize the report differently. For example, if you drag the Status marker to the right of the Record Manager marker, the report further breaks down each Record Manager's opportunities by their status.

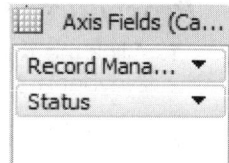

 In Excel 2007 and later, you can also drag the fields to summarize the report differently. As in the example above, you would drag the Status "marker" from the Report Filter pane to below the Record Manager in the Axis Fields pane.

 As you work with the Pivot Chart, remember that **[Ctrl+Z]** will undo the last action, in case you insert something that didn't do what you thought it would do.

The pivot report is an great analysis tool with tremendous flexibility. Don't be afraid to experiment with it. Remember, you are working with copies of the original data, so even if you mess it up "big time", you can always return to ACT! and create a brand-new report. So don't be afraid; play all you like.

Practice: Export to Excel	
What to do	**How to do it/Comments**
1. Reset the Opportunity List to remove all filters.	Click the **Opportunities** button on the Navbar, and click **List View** button on the View Toolbar to display your opportunities. Click the **Reset** button.
2. Add opportunities for all users to the display.	Click the **Select Users** button and change the option to **All users**, **OK**.

What to do	How to do it/Comments
3. Export to Excel.	Click the **Export to Excel** icon on the toolbar.
4. View all three worksheets.	Notice that the columns displayed in ACT! are the same columns that were exported to Excel.
5. Close Excel.	

Opportunity Reports

What if you don't need to filter, sort, rearrange, or torture the Opportunity List? ACT! provides some really great standard Opportunity reports for ...well... reporting on your opportunities. ACT! has over 30 different opportunity reports and graphs available in the **Reports** view. Just choose the report you want, make a few decisions about the data and how you want to see it, and presto! All your good work appears in a neat, concise report. If the person who wants to view the report doesn't have ACT! on their computer, you can even print it out to a .pdf file for easy viewing.

Procedure: To run an Opportunity report

1. Click the **Reports** button on the Navbar at the left. Select a report.	Lookups are not used to create or filter most Opportunity reports. (Opportunity reports start with Gross margin, Lost, Opportunities, Pipeline, or Sales.)
2. Select output type.	**Preview** displays the report in print preview. **Rich-Text File** creates a Rich-Text Format file that can be edited in most word processors. **HTML File** creates an HTML file suitable for publishing to the Web. **PDF File** creates file that anyone with Adobe Reader can view. **Text File** creates a plain text file with no formatting. **Printer** sends the report directly to your printer. **E-mail** transmits the report via an e-mail message.
3. Select the Status types to include in the report.	Open, Closed – Won, Closed – Lost, Inactive, or all of them.

Opportunities

4. Select a **Date Range** or select **Custom…** to define your own start and end dates.

   Date Range is based on the Est. Close Date for Open and Inactive opportunities and on the Close Date on for Closed opportunities.

5. Select the users whose opportunities should be included in the report.

   Only active users are available in the list.

6. Click **OK**.

   Some Opportunities Reports may have additional tabs for filtering. Select the options as necessary.

☞ *Opportunities without contacts will not appear on reports.*

Practice: *Playing with Opportunity Reports*

What to do	How to do it/Comments
1. Generate a Sales Analysis by Record Manager opportunity report for all types of opportunities for the current month. Preview it on the screen.	Choose **Reports**, **Opportunity Reports**, **Sales Analysis by Record Manager**. Be sure that all types of opportunities are checked. Change the **Date Range:** to **Current Month**. Click **OK**.
2. View the page in Actual Size.	Click the **Actual Size** tool to make the report larger.
3. Review the statistics that are displayed for each Record Manager. Close the report.	Click **Close**.

Opportunity Pipeline

Sometimes we focus so closely on closing the deal that we forget about prospecting...or filling the pipeline. The idea is that we won't win every deal that we open (we wish). Over time, you start to develop your own ratio (e.g., you have to have at least five potential deals for every deal that you close). To verify that you are on track and not focusing too much on one stage of the deal, you can display the Sales Pipeline to see how many opportunities you have at each stage of the deal. Be sure you have enough numbers in the top of the funnel to help you meet the results you need at the bottom.

The Opportunity Pipeline is a visual representation of the number of open opportunities at each stage in your sales development process. Each section of the pipeline represents a stage in your sales development cycle.

Procedure: To display the Opportunity Pipeline report

1. **Opportunities, Opportunity Pipeline…**,

    or click the **Opportunity Pipeline** icon in the Opportunity List view.

    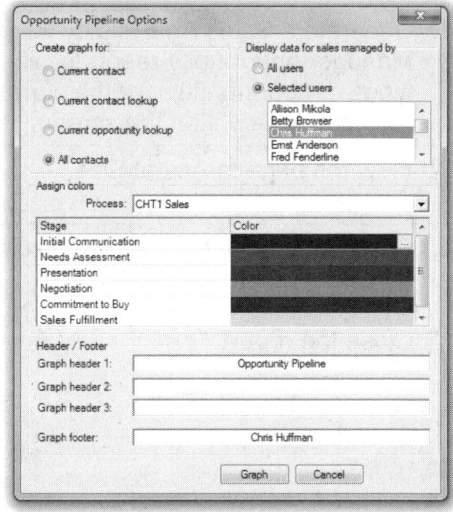

2. Select any options. (You could start with a lookup of all Contacts in TX, and then run reports based on the **Current contact lookup** to display opportunities in that state.) You could also display only opportunities managed by **Selected users**.

3. Select the **Process** you want to display.

    Change the Graph header and footer fields as you like.

    If necessary, select a color for each stage by clicking the browse (...) button in the Color column.

4. Click **Graph**.

Notice that the stages listed here match the stages we've been working with.

 The size of each section is fixed and not based on the number of opportunities at each stage.

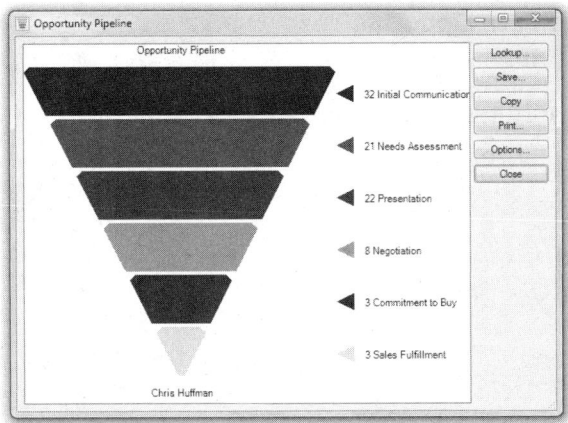

5. To view the specific opportunities that make up a specific stage, click the color bar.

The Opportunity Pipeline dialog box closes and the opportunities that make up the stage you clicked will be displayed in the Opportunity List view.

6. To view other stages, display the pipeline again.

Practice: Opportunity Pipeline	
What to do	**How to do it/Comments**
1. What does Allison Mikola's pipeline look like?	In Opportunities: List View, click the **Opportunity Pipeline** icon. Make Allison Mikola the selected user and click **Graph**.
2. Get a list of her contacts who are in the Negotiation phase.	Click the Negotiation wedge. Click the Create Contact Lookup icon to display the list of contacts.

Opportunity Graph

Sometimes you may want a longer range view of potential deals. ACT! can display your opportunities in a graph.

Procedure: To display the Opportunity Forecast Graph

1. In Opportunities view, **Opportunities Opportunity Graph...**,

    or click the **Opportunity Graph** icon.

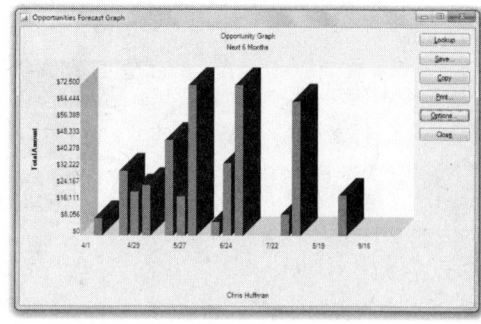

2. Select any options.

    The **Graph** tab allows you to change from a line to a bar graph, colors, etc.

3. Click **Graph**.

    Better start planning for October!

Practice: Opportunity Graph	
What to do	**How to do it/Comments**
1. What do our prospects look like for the next quarter?	In Opportunities: List View, click the **Opportunity Graph** icon. Change the **Dates to Graph**. Probably better adjust for probability.
2. Create a Lookup of those opportunities.	Click the **Lookup** button on the graph.

Viewing Dashboards & Reports

To learn to work with an overview of our data, we will...

- ☑ View the default Dashboards that come with ACT!.

- ☑ Understand how the ACT! Report writer generates reports from the ACT! database.

- ☑ Review the anatomy of an ACT! report

Using Dashboards

ACT! Dashboards give you the input necessary to "drive" your business using graphically-oriented panels. Each panel is designed to offer an at-a-glance overview of key performance indicators in your business.

If you are using the Premium version of ACT!, Dashboards can also provide a view of opportunities and activities for all (or selected) users of the database, thus providing a company-wide performance snapshot.

Displaying Dashboard Views

Five Dashboards (Default, Activities, Administrative, Contacts, and Opportunities) ship with ACT!, but more can be created. Each Dashboard window can display summary lists, charts, or gauges. From within each Dashboard, you can

- quickly display the records that make up the components,
- easily create new calls, meetings, or to-do's, or add details to existing opportunities,
- identify how you're tracking toward your goals using benchmarks and summary information, and
- copy any Dashboard component or the entire ACT! Dashboard to any application including Microsoft® Office applications, for use in e-mails, reports, presentations, and more.

Procedure: To view a Dashboard

1. Click the **Dashboard** button in the Navbar at the left.

   The Dashboard view displays.

2. To change to a different view, click the Dashboard Layout drop-down on the View Toolbar.

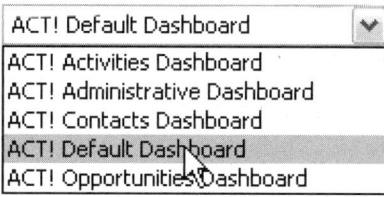

 Dashboards will not include data that you don't have access to (Private or Limited Access data).

Viewing Dashboards & Reports | 313

Practice: Viewing a Dashboard

What to do	How to do it/Comments
1. Display the **Dashboard** view.	Click the **Dashboard** button on the Navbar.
2. Which Dashboard view is currently displayed?	The view name displays on the current View Toolbar. Five views: Default, Activities, Administrative, Contacts, and Opportunities.
3. Quickly view each of the Dashboard options, and then display the ACT! Default Dashboard.	Click the Layout drop-down on the View Toolbar and select a view. After reviewing each of the options, select the ACT! Default Dashboard.

Working in the Dashboard Views

The ACT! Default Dashboard contains six panels, representing the different component types that can be placed in your dashboards. Let's review each of the panels to see:

- the purpose of the panel,
- what options are available when using the Filter button,
- what options are available with mouse over, right-click, click, or double-click

My Schedule At-a-Glance displays your scheduled activities for the day sorted by time with timeless activities displayed first. The listings include the activity type, time, and Contact name and Company (if not scheduled with your My Record). If you have more activities than can display in the panel, a small **More** button will appear in the lower-right corner of the panel. When clicked, the Daily Calendar view will appear with all activities listed.

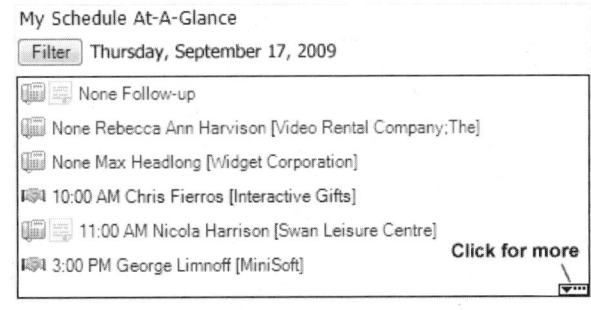

Filter: You can filter this component for any or all Activity Types (including custom ones). You can also limit the display by Priorities and a few other Options (Show Private or Show Cleared Tasks). If you are using the Premium version, you can also filter which users to include in the list. Activities scheduled for other users will display their name in [square brackets] immediately after the time.

Right-click: Use the right-click mouse button to view **Show Contacts** for any selected activity. The pop-up pane will display the Contact, Company, Phone, Title and ID/Status of records associated with the selected activity. You can also right-click to **Schedule** additional activities, **Create Lookup**, **Go to Contact**, **Clear**, **Erase, Send Activity E-mail, Reschedule....** Oh, just go right-click in that panel and see all the cool things you can do in this component. You might especially like the option to **Copy to Clipboard**. This option copies the **My Schedule at a Glance** to the clipboard so that you can paste this view into another program (as a graphic).

Mouse Over: Use your mouse to hover over any activity to display a calendar pop-up providing you with the Regarding and other pertinent details on that particular activity.

Call
Regarding: What do we need to move ahead on...
With: David Yale [Yale Computer Company]; Will Blake [Parsley Group];
Date: Friday, April 15
Time: 1:30 PM
Duration: 1 hour
Details: Remind him of their desire to go to...
Location: Conference Call

Click: You can click dashboard elements to see the records that were used to create the element.

Double-Click: Finally, as you might expect, you can double-click any activity to modify the details.

Practice: My Schedule

What to do	How to do it/Comments
1. While in your **Dashboard**, use right-click to schedule a reminder for yourself to book your airfare to Las Vegas.	Right-click anywhere in the My Schedule At-A-Glance pane and select **Schedule, Call....** Schedule as you normally would.
2. Point to an activity to display the Calendar pop-up.	
3. Double-click any activity and change it to tomorrow.	It should remove it from today's list.
4. Clear one of the activities on your schedule.	Right-click one of the activities and select **Clear Activity.**
5. Filter the display to show Cleared Activities.	Click the **Filter** button and place a check in **"Show Cleared Tasks"**. Click **OK**.
6. Right-click the cleared activity and select **Go To Contact**.	The Contact will display in Detail View.
7. Return to the Dashboard.	Click the **Dashboard** button in the Navbar.

OK, so now you have seen the basics of how to move around in a panel in the dashboard, we'll focus the rest of this section on the purpose of the various panels in the different dashboards.

Viewing Dashboards & Reports | 315

My Activities (or "Activities by User" if you are using ACT! Premium) - See how your time is allocated using this panel, with a complete view of all activities in a bar chart. A Manager or Administrator can edit this view to change the Display Type to a Pie Chart or List View.

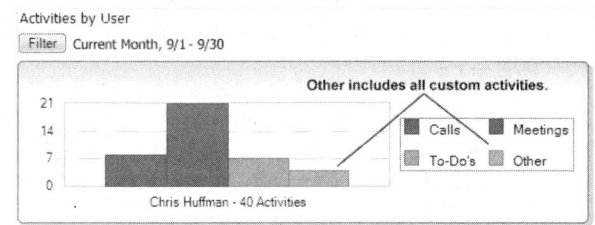

Practice: *My Activities (or "Activities by User")*

What to do	How to do it/Comments
1. Filter the pane to display this week's activities.	Click on the Filter button. Change the **Dates:** option to Current Week. If you are using ACT! Premium, select an additional user to display, and click **OK**.
2. Point to several of the columns to observe the mouse-over function.	If you are using the Premium version, each user's activities will display their own count of activities.
3. Display the filtered list in Task List view.	Click one of the elements (a column or the legend) to display the same filtered list in Task List view.
4. Return to the Dashboard.	Click the **Dashboard** button in the Navbar at the left.

Opportunities Pipeline by Stage – This panel allows you to focus on an overview for the company of how sales opportunities are tracking by stage in a graphical pie chart. The values listed with each opportunity are the Total amounts (not Weighted Totals). A Manager or Administrator can edit this view to change the Display Type to a Bar Chart or List View, as well as display the Weighted Total at the bottom of the chart.

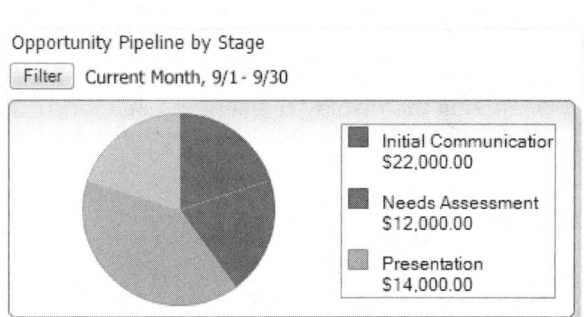

☞ *The legend may not have enough room to display the entire list of stages. Note in the example above there are four slices of pie and only three stages displayed in the legend.*

Practice: Opportunities Pipeline by Stage

What to do	How to do it/Comments
1. On the Opportunity Pipeline panel, how many opportunities are in each slice of the pie?	Mouse over each slice of the pie to see how many opportunities are included.
2. Display the same filtered opportunities in List View.	Click anywhere on the pie or legend to display the same filtered list in Opportunities: List View.
3. Return to the Dashboard.	Click Dashboard button at the left.

Contact History Count by History Type - While the previous panel focused on what you are planning on doing, this panel focuses on what you have accomplished. If you have the Premium version, you can also view the contributions of other users in ACT!. The Filter button controls how many days of history will display. A Manager or Administrator can edit this view to change the Display Type to a List View or other chart type.

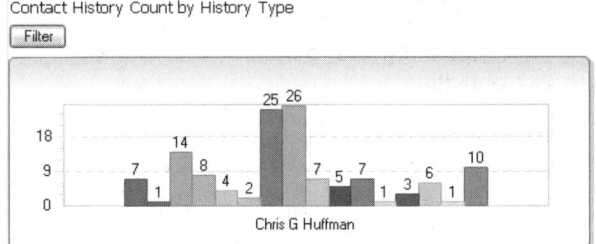

Practice: Contact History by History Type

What to do	How to do it/Comments
1. Change the number of days to display.	Click the **Filter** button. Change the **Days since creation:** to a different number of days.
If you are an ACT! Premium user, limit the display of users to Chris and Allison.	If you are a Premium version user, click the **Selected users:** option. Select Allison and Chris. Click **OK**.

Viewing Dashboards & Reports | 317

Top 10 Opportunities – Use this pane to quickly view a list of top opportunities by Total for your company. Click any of the columns in the list to sort it. You could use the filter to remove lower-level stages from this view (or filter by Probability), so that large-dollar opportunities with only a 10% chance of closing don't display over a medium-dollar opportunity with an 80% chance of closing.

Practice: Top 10 Opportunities

What to do	How to do it/Comments
1. Change the Estimated Close Date of one of the opportunities to next month.	Double-click any opportunity and change the **Est. Close Date**, enter the new Close Date. Click the Dashboard button on the Navbar to return.
2. Sort the list by Company.	Click on the Company column header.
3. Add another field to the display.	Right-click the panel and select **Customize Columns…**. Double-click an available field and click **OK**.

Closed Sales to Date - View all closed sales to date for the selected time period. The gauge is a great way to track how well you are meeting your sales goals. If you are using the Premium version of ACT!, the legend at the right displays the users whose opportunities are included in the gauge. A Manager or Administrator can edit this panel to add company targets and breakpoints to help you identify your progress. Point to different elements of the gauge to display pop-ups. If you have set a target, you can point to it (triangle) to display your company's designated target amount. Hover over the needle (pointer) to show the dollar amount of your total closed sales to date. Hover over the gauge to show the number of closed opportunities (and the number of users they belong to, if you have Premium).

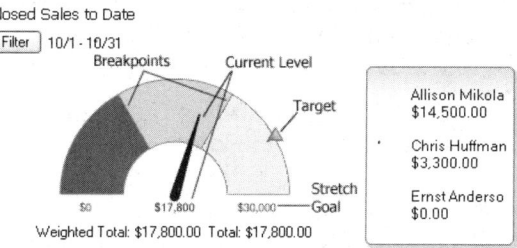

☞ *You can copy the entire Dashboard view using the menu command (in ACT!)* ***Edit***, ***Copy***. *It is then ready to paste as a graphic into any other application.*

Practice: Closed Sales to Date

What to do	How to do it/Comments
1. How many opportunities have been closed?	Point to the gauge and note the information in the pop-up.
2. In the Top 10 Opportunities pain, clear one of Chris Huffman's opportunities for today. (Note the Company name and Total before clearing it.)	Double-click any opportunity and close the deal. Click the Dashboard button on the Navbar to return.
3. Is the opportunity still in the Top 10? Are there still 10 opportunities displayed?	The Top 10 displays (by default) only open opportunities. When one is cleared, another will take its place if it is available.
4. Now, how many opportunities have been closed?	Point to the gauge once again and note the information in the pop-up. ☞ You may need to click the Refresh icon at the top of the screen to refresh the gauge.
5. Copy the Closed Sales to Date panel and paste it into a Word document. Then, you can close the new document without saving the changes.	Right-click the gauge and select **Copy to Clipboard**. Open a Word document (or any other application you like) and click **Edit, Paste**. Cool.

Other Dashboards

The **ACT! Activities Dashboard** puts the most frequently used activity panels in the same pane.

The **ACT! Administrative Dashboard** contains three panels that help you stay on top of how your users are using ACT!. Are they logging in? Are they keeping up with syncing?

The **ACT! Contacts Dashboard** shows how many contacts have recently been added to the database by Record Manager, how many have been edited during a specific time period, and what types of activities you have been up to.

The **ACT! Opportunities Dashboard** puts all of the opportunity panels on one screen so that you can see the larger picture for your opportunities.

ACT! Reports

ACT! does a wonderful job of tracking contact information and helping you keep in touch with your contacts. We looked at some visual reports in Dashboards, but ACT! can also produce detailed printed reports about your activities that can help you get a handle on how you spend your time, who you have talked with, and when. You can print a report that lists all you know about a contact or just print a list of phone numbers. The pre-defined reports in ACT! are pretty complete and impressive. As with everything in ACT!, you can create your own reports or further customize the existing ones.

The Reports view in ACT! displays a **Report List** of all available reports for the current database. Let's start with running and understanding the basics of a report. Then we can talk about how to add your favorite ones to this top pane.

Running a pre-defined report is simple. You need only tell ACT!
- which Contacts you want to include,
- which report you want to use, and
- where to send the report (printer, fax, e-mail, PDF, etc.).

Procedure: To generate an ACT! report

1. You will usually start with a lookup or query to filter what records will display in the report. If you don't create a lookup first, the report is run on the entire database.

2. Click the **Reports** button in the Navbar. The **Report List** of all reports for the current database displays.

    You can also select reports from the **Reports** menu.

    You can add the column Last Modified field to the Favorite Report and Report List views.

3. Double-click the report you want from to run (or right-click, **Run Report**).

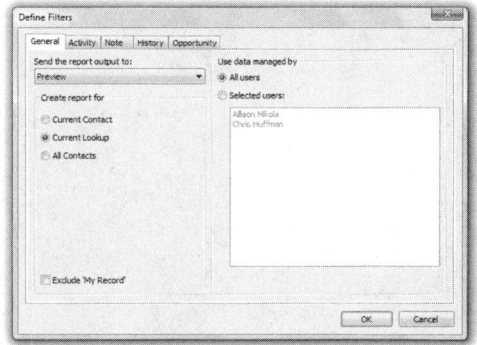

4. If necessary, click the drop-down arrow for **Send the report output to** and choose an option.

    Preview displays the report in print preview.

    Rich-Text File creates a Rich Text Format file that can be edited by most word processors.

    HTML File creates an HTML file suitable for posting to the Internet.

    PDF File saves the completed report to a file that can be printed by anyone who has Adobe® Reader®.

    Text File creates a text file that can be edited by most word processors.

    Printer sends the report directly to your printer.

    Fax or **E-mail** transmits the report via either method (if your PC is capable).

5. Choose a **Create report for** option.

    ☞ *Click the **Exclude 'My Record'** check box if you don't want to include information about you in the report.*

    Click **Current Contact** to include data only for the person displayed in the Detail View.

    Click **Current Lookup** to include data for the records in the current lookup.

    Click **All Contacts** to include everybody in the database.

6. Click one of the **Activity, Note, History, Opportunity** tabs.

    If the selected report design does not include **Activities**, **Notes**, **History**, or **Opportunities** subreports, these options are unavailable. Don't let this bother you. You can't filter something you don't have.

Viewing Dashboards & Reports | 321

7. On each tab, click the desired check boxes to include/ exclude items from the report.

   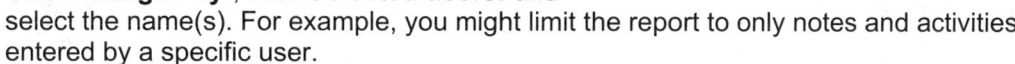

   Select from a predefined **Date range:** drop-down list to filter the item display in the report.

   Click **Custom...** to enter a start and end date for the filter.

   To limit the report to data input by specific users of your shared database, choose **Use data managed by:**, click **Selected users:** and select the name(s). For example, you might limit the report to only notes and activities entered by a specific user.

   > 👉 Only users marked Active (defined under Tools, Define Users) will display in the **Use data managed by:** list.

8. Click **OK**.

Practice: Generating a Report	
What to do	**How to do it/Comments**
1. Generate a **Phone List** of contacts in our database with an ID/Status of Customer. View the report on the screen.	**Lookup, ID/Status, Customer, OK**. Click the **Reports** button in the Navbar. Double-click the **Phone List**, verify that the report output is set to Preview and the Current Lookup is selected, and click **OK**.
2. Leave the report preview displayed on the screen.	

Sage ACT!

The Anatomy of an ACT! Report

Each time you run a report, ACT! collects the most up-to-date data available. While you can send your report directly to a printer, you may find it useful to preview it before you print. When print preview first displays, the first page of the report appears in full-page view

You cannot edit a report once it has been generated (like you can with a document in the word processor).

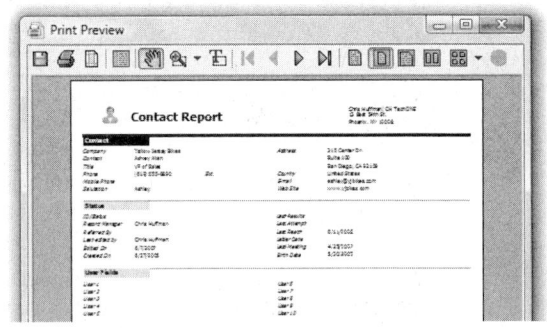

☞ *Well…technically you could edit it if you printed it to an HTML, Rich-Text, or Text file.*

Procedure: To view reports in Print Preview

1. Click the **Actual Size** icon to increase the display to a more readable size.

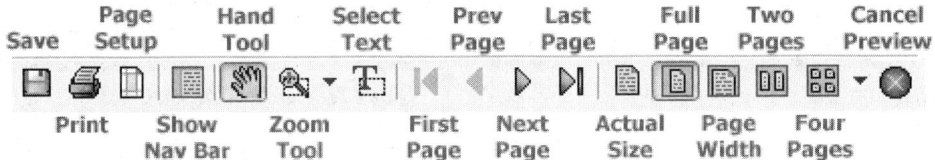

2. Click the **Next Page** browse button or press **[PageDn]**. — The next page appears on the screen in whatever magnification you are currently viewing.

3. Try some of the other icons for the Print Preview window. — The Select Text tool allows you to copy text from the report to paste into another application.

If the preview shows what you want, you are ready to print your report. Click the **Print** button on the print preview toolbar to display the **Print** dialog box. From there, you can choose from the output print options and send the report on to the printer.

Practice: Using the Report Feature	
What to do	**How to do it/Comments**
1. A **Phone List** report should be on your screen.	If not, choose **Reports**, **Phone List**, **Preview**, and click **OK**.
2. Display report in **Actual Size**.	Easier to read, isn't it?

Viewing Dashboards & Reports | 323

What to do	*How to do it/Comments*
3. View the last page.	Click the **Next Page** button, or press **[PageDn]** to navigate to the last page.
4. Return to the first page.	Click the **First Page** icon.
5. Close the Report window.	Click the **Close** button.
6. Generate and preview a Contact Report for Colleen McCarthy. Be sure that all activities are displayed. Notice the default filters and date range in each tab.	Look up Colleen McCarthy, choose **Reports, Contact Report**, select **Current contact**, and verify that **Preview** is selected for **Send output to**. View the options on the other tabs and click **OK**.
7. Zoom in to read her activities.	Click the **Actual Size** icon. Scroll to view the data.
8. Close the report preview.	Click the **Close** button.
9. Generate an E-mail List of everyone in the database. Notice that there are no tabs for selecting filter options for History, Notes, etc.	In the **Report List** view, double-click the E-mail List report. Select **All Contacts**, and verify that Send the report output to is **Preview**. There aren't any tabs for the additional items because the report was not designed to display them. Click **OK**.
10. Does the My Record name (Chris Huffman) appear in the list?	Click the **Actual Size** icon and scroll to locate it in the list. (The list is sorted by Last Name, so look for Huffman in the second column of the report.) Chris is not in the list.
11. Close the report and generate it again. This time, include the data from the My Record.	Click the **Close** button, choose **Reports, Phone List**, select **All Contacts**, select **Preview**, if necessary, clear **the Exclude 'My Record'** check box, and click **OK**.
12. Is Chris Huffman in the list now? Close the report.	Yes!
13. Look up all Contacts that have something in the Referred By field and then display the Source of Referrals Report. Why perform the lookup? Otherwise every Contact is in the final report.	Right-click the Referred By field, select **Lookup Referred By**, change the operator from **Starts With** to **Contains Data** and click **OK**. Choose **Source of Referrals** from the Report List and click **OK**.
14. Close the Report window.	Click **Close**.

Favorite Reports

A panel at the top is available to display your **Favorite Reports** (so you don't have to remember the exact name of the reports you want to run).

Favorite Reports selections...
- are log-on user-specific. Each person on your team can choose their own favorite reports to display in this area.
- can have their own Description, unique to each logon user, like "Run month-end query before running this report" or "Run this report every Monday for Chris." Descriptions are not shared with other users.
- are maintained by database, so if you have multiple databases, you can select your favorites for each database.

Procedure: To add an ACT! report to the Favorite Reports pane

1. Click **Reports** in the Navbar.
2. In the **Report List**, check the desired report in the Favorite Reports column.

   A copy of the report name appears in the **Favorite Reports** pane.
3. Right-click a report and select **Edit Properties**.

   You can edit the properties in the Favorite Reports or Report List pane.
4. Modify the description to a more descriptive name or to remind you what query you should run before generating the report.

   You are the only one who will see the description.
5. Click **OK**.

   The new description displays in the top and the bottom panes.

Practice: Adding to Your Report Favorites	
What to do	**How to do it/Comments**
1. Select a report to add to the Report Favorites.	Put a checkmark beside one of the reports.
2. Modify the Description to remind yourself to perform a look up first.	Right-click the report that you just made a favorite and select **Edit Properties**. Enter a new description and click **OK**. Admire your handiwork.

Customizing ACT!

Database Design & Layouts

To be able to view the data you want in the exact way you want it, you will:

- ☑ Create a new customized database.
- ☑ Add and format fields.
- ☑ Manage drop-down lists.
- ☑ Create a new layout.
- ☑ Create custom tabs.
- ☑ Edit field entry order.

Sage ACT!

Creating a New Database

Creating a new database is not something you do every day. In fact, most users do it only once. In this QuickStudy Guide, you have worked with a sample database we created for your use. Now that you are ready to go forth into the world of Contact and Customer Management, you need to know how to create your own ACT! database.

When a new database is created in ACT!, it is created with a single record already in it. This is the My Record we talked about earlier. The contents of the My Record are important because ACT! uses it in reports and document templates to enter things about you, like company name, address, phone, etc. The My Record also defines you as a user in a multi-user database.

As you start to create your own database, keep in mind these things:

- The ACT! software must be on the machine (server) that will hold the database.
- You must be physically at the computer that will hold the database when you create it. You *cannot* perform this procedure across the network.
- However, you can make changes across the network.

☞ *Check out my 10 Steps to a Guaranteed Successful CRM Implementation.*
cornerstonesolutions.com/articles/10StepsCRMImplementation.pdf

Procedure: To create a new database

1. Go to the computer that will host the database.

   ☞ *You cannot perform this procedure across the network. You must be physically at the computer that will hold the database.*

2. **File**, **New Database...** from the menu,

   or press **[Ctrl+N]**.

   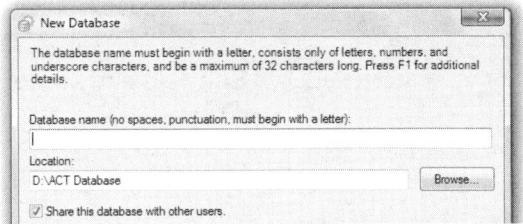

3. Enter a **Database name** for the database (no spaces or punctuation).

   The new database displays with one record. This user has been automatically assigned an Administrator role.

Database Design & Layouts | 329

4. Enter a new **Location:** (you can **Browse…** if you need to) however, you can only create a new database on a local drive (not on a network drive).

   Select the default **Currency:** for the database.

   Check **Share this database with other users**, if desired.

   Enter a **User name:**.

   Enter a **Password:**, if desired.
5. Click **OK**.

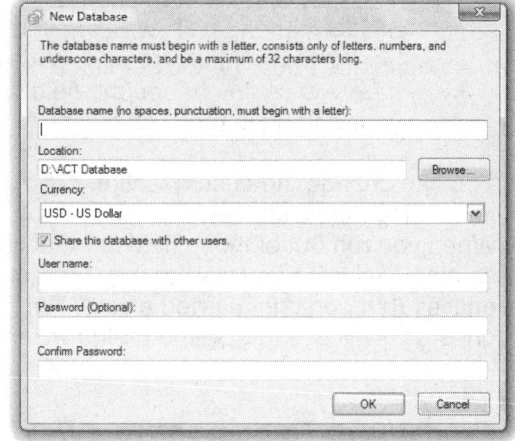

ACT! can only have one database open at a time. When you create a new database, ACT! closes the open database before it begins creating the new one. Don't confuse database windows with word-processing windows. You can have several documents related to the same database open in word-processing windows, but only one database can be open at any time.

> *You can create a new database for yourself now or later.*
> *However, the following customization exercises assume*
> *you are still using the ACT2012Demo database.*

Customizing Fields

You may have noticed the **User** fields available to you in the Contacts: Detail View on the **User Fields** tab. These fields are just begging to be customized to your needs.

You may want to customize a field for several reasons:

- You should give each field a *specific name* so that, as you enter data, you always put the same kind of information into the same field. (Hmmm Did you put the customer # in User 1 or User 2 on all those other records? Well, let's just name the field so you don't have to remember which one you want to use.)
- Fields can be customized to hold a variety of specialized data types and can display drop-downs of pre-defined answers to ease data entry. They can be forced to display uppercase characters only, initial capital letters, or Web site addresses, to name a few. You also can require that the field contain dates or numbers only. Perhaps you only want a Yes/No field.

- You may also want to *change the size of the field*, so that if you need to type in a lot of information, ACT! will give you enough space. On the other hand, if you want User 3 to be "Mailing List?", and all you want to enter is "E-mail", "Mail" or "Remove," then you could change the field size from 50 characters to 6 characters to make your database more efficient.

You can change the customization options for almost any field in your database. Most often, you change the User fields (because you're the user, and that's what they are there for). When you run out of those fields to modify, you can start adding new fields. You can create as many fields as you like for the Contacts, Companies, Groups, Opportunities or Products entities (but don't get carried away). Whether you are editing existing fields or creating new ones, you will use the Define Fields wizard.

Procedure: To customize a field

1. **Tools**, **Define Fields**....

2. Select the record type to **View fields for:** creating, editing or deleting.

   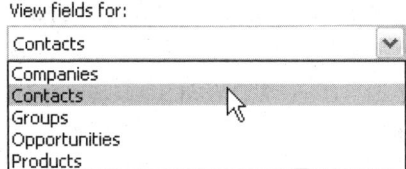

   ACT! has five record types that you can create fields for: Contacts, Companies, Groups, Opportunities, and Products. You can modify specific fields in all the record types as well as add fields to each type. Since the process of adding and modifying fields is the same for all five types, we will concentrate on describing field attributes for the Contact record type.

3. Either select an existing field and click **Edit field** (or double-click field to start the process),

   or click **Create new field**.

   Options are described below.

4. Change the options for the field.

5. Click **Finish** and then **Close**.

6. Click **Yes** or **No** to modify layout.

☞ Once you have set all of the desired attributes and clicked **Close**, be patient. On larger databases, processing changes can take some time. Whenever possible, we recommend setting up the fields before entering data into your database.

Database Design & Layouts

Field Attributes

You can assign a myriad of attributes to your field, but not all attributes are available for all types of fields. For example, Character fields will not prompt you for the number of decimal places. A Memo field can't have a drop-down list, nor will it ask you for a field format or a maximum number of characters.

Over the next few pages, we will give you a brief overview of all potential attributes (organized by the order that they appear in the Define Fields Wizard screens).

Enter field name and type

Let's focus on each of the Wizard screens separately as we modify the database design. First, you will be asked to define the field name, type, and behavior.

Field name: - What name do you want the field to have (**User 1** is just a bit too generic, don't you think?). Keep it short. Spaces are allowed. However, you may not include any special characters except an ampersand (&), a dash (-), or an underscore (_). That means no periods either. Even a forward slash is not allowed (yes, we know it is in "ID/Status," but it was grandfathered into the new structure).

Field data type: - What kind of data is permitted in this field? A wide variety of choices are available in this drop-down list. Choose the one that is most suitable for your uses. When trying to rename User fields 1-10, be aware that these 10 fields have some restrictions on available field types. If you don't see the field type you want, then create a new field.

 Changing a field's data type in an existing database can result in the loss of data. Some changes are not even possible. For example, you cannot change a Character field to a Phone field (for your own protection). Back up your database first if you plan on making changes.

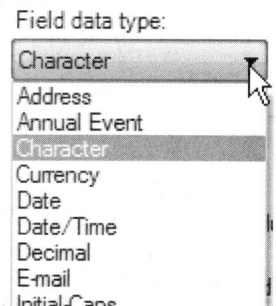

Address field designation automatically creates all of the fields necessary for an address. For example, create a new field named "Physical" with a data type of Address. When you click Finish, ACT! creates seven fields: Physical Address 1, Physical Address 2, Physical Address 3, Physical City, Physical Country, Physical State, and Physical ZIP Code. The Address fields display in the list as Character fields. However, by defining the fields at the beginning as Address, it enables the new address fields to be a part of the **Lookup, Other Fields, Any <address type>** queries.

 When you name the field, do not include the word "Address" in the name that you assign (like Physical Address) or you will have a field named: Physical Address Address 1.

Annual Event is a date field that recurs annually. The field displays a drop-down calendar for date selection. However, you can only perform searches on this field based on the month and day (ignoring the year). This is ideal for birthdays, anniversaries, contract renewal dates, etc.

Character allows you to type any combination of characters and numbers that you like. All character-based fields (Character, Initial Capitals, Lowercase, Uppercase, or URL) have a maximum of 450 characters. However, if the end user needs to type that much, you should create the field as a Memo field type, since Character fields do not wrap in the field display.

Currency displays a dollar sign and the defined number of decimal places in the **To the right:** option. Reports created in ACT! can use this field type to create Summary (Total, Average, Minimum, and Maximum) calculations. Use the Number field type if you want to display whole numbers without a dollar sign. Use the Decimal field type to display more than two numbers to the right of a decimal point.

Date fields are formatted according to the settings in the Windows® Regional Settings (found in Control Panel). The field contains a drop-down date selector.

Date/Time fields are formatted according to the settings in the Windows Regional Settings (found in Control Panel). The field contains a drop-down date selector. Both date and time display in the field.

Decimal allows a maximum of 30 digits (more than a trillion) to be divided between places to the right and left of the decimal point. Commas and decimal points don't count as part of the number you assign, but they will display. Reports created in ACT! can use this field type for Summary (Total, Average, Minimum, Maximum) calculations.
E-mail allows you to assign alternate e-mail address fields that will hyperlink to a New Message window in your defined e-mail client.

Initial-Caps make the first character of each word a capital letter and each succeeding letter lowercase…regardless of how the user inputs the data. This field type is great for use with simple fields (such as those requiring a one-word answer) so that all answers maintain the same format. However it can also cause problems. For example, if you made the Contact field an "Initial Capitals" field, then "Jane de laVega CPA" would become "Jane De Lavega Cpa."

Lowercase would make any text entered...well...all lowercase. As in all character-based fields, numbers are allowed.

Memo is a field type that allows virtually unlimited data entry. However, this notes-style field cannot contain formatted text (bold, underline, etc.) or drop-down lists.

Number is a whole number (no decimal places) with a maximum of 10 digits (almost a billion). Commas don't count as part of the number of digits you assign, but they will display according to your Windows Regional Settings. Any alpha characters in this field are ignored. Reports created in ACT! can use this field type to create Summary (Total, Average, Minimum, and Maximum) calculations.

Phone fields automatically format numbers entered as a phone number (with dashes and parentheses) according to the country selected upon installation of the ACT! program. The end user can select the proper country code formatting by clicking on the Browse... button to the right of any phone field. When a Phone type field is created, a companion Ext field is also created automatically. Contents are included in the **Lookup**, **Other Fields**, **Any Phone Field** query.

> *Don't like the (parentheses) in the phone format? You can create your own default format in the Contacts: Detail View (not Define Fields). Click the **Browse...** button to the right of the Phone field. Click the **Edit Formats...** button. Click **Add**. For an alternate US format, enter: %%%-%%%-%%%%. Make it the default (for all phone fields) if you like and click **OK**, **OK**. It only affects future input...it does not reformat existing phone numbers. It also changes the default for all database users.*

Picture allows you to maintain a unique graphic with each record. Supported formats are .bmp, .gif, .jpg, .png, .ico, .emf, or .wma. The width and height (as well as the aspect ratio) of the graphic are static and are determined by the layout designer (all pictures must be about the same size in order to display well).

Time is formatted according to the time settings in the Windows Regional Settings. The field contains a drop-down time selector.

Uppercase is handy for fields that will contain alphanumeric characters, like customer codes (which may be a combination of characters and numbers, but you want all characters entered as uppercase). Many International ZIP Codes contain alpha characters, which makes this type of field ideal for the Uppercase field type.

URL Address makes any Web address entered an active link that when clicked opens the specified Web page in your default Web browser window.

Yes/No is really a check-box field. If the check box is selected, it has a "Yes" or "True" value. If the check box is cleared, it has a "No" or "False" value. For purposes of importing, a 1 would convert to a check (or Yes) and a 0 would convert to a blank (or No).

Customize field behaviors

Allow Blank - Need we say more? While this is a great option to remind you to fill in really important fields, it can also be irritating when used in practice...use it sparingly and only clear it if you want to be nagged.

Generate History - Generate history fields cause a history entry to be created when the field is modified. If you apply this attribute to a field, and then make a change to the field, a **Field Changed** entry is created on the **History** tab. The Regarding area will record which field was changed, the previous value in the field, the new value entered into the field, the date on which it was changed, and the Record Manager who changed it. We have already seen two fields like this...do you remember? Last Results and ID/Status.

☞ *When adding a new Contact, the Generate History feature will not activate until the record is saved for the first time (either by clicking on the Save icon or moving off of the record).*

Primary Field - The contents of primary fields are duplicated when you choose **Contacts**, **Duplicat*e* Contact...** from the Contacts: Detail View menu. Fields can be also duplicated from the Companies or Groups Detail Views when creating a new Company or Group. Use this option for any field you wish to be carried over to a new Contact (or Company or Group) record.

☞ *The default primary Contact fields are Company, Address 1, Address 2, Address 3, City, State, ZIP, Country, Phone, Fax, and Web site. You might change ID/Status to a Primary field.*

Use drop-down list allows you to attach a pre-defined drop-down list to a specific field. Drop-down lists ensure consistency when entering data into fields. If this option is enabled, a drop-down arrow displays at the right of the field. The ability to select multiple drop-down items is controlled by an option in the next wizard screen.

☞ *Drop-down lists should be defined before you define new fields.*

One-to-Many Tables

ACT! does not have the built-in capability to add one-to-many tables to the database (e.g. each certification training course taken by your contacts, each job listing you are working on by contact, etc.) However, there is a third-party product that will help you accomplish this. If you would like to know more: http://bit.ly/ToplineDesigner

Database Design & Layouts | 335

Customize field and list behavior
If you put a check by **Use Drop-down list**, then this wizard screen displays next.

> **Limit to List** - Field entry is limited to those values found in the drop-down list.

Customize field and list behavior

☑ Limit to List - Allows users to select values from the drop-down list only
☐ Allow Multi-select - The user can select multiple values from the list
☐ Show Descriptions - Displays description text along with list values
☑ Enable Type-ahead - As user types, list values are displayed based on the entered value

> **Allow Multi-select** – Allows users to check multiple values from the list. Checking this option also changes how data in this field is searched. The default lookup on any field is a "starts with" type of lookup. If "Allow Multi-select" is enabled, the lookup will change to a "contains" anywhere in the field.

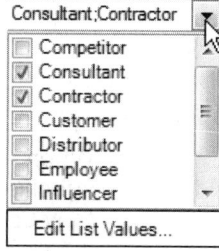

> **Show Descriptions** – Displays a description of an item in the drop-down list, but does not store any text from the description in the field. For example, if your State drop-down list has a value of MI, it would be handy to see a description to let you know if it stands for Michigan, Mississippi, or Minnesota. However, even if the drop-down has a description, it will only display if you click this option.

> **Enable Type-ahead** – As a user starts to type, the field value is suggested if the entered value matches the initial characters of any values in the drop-down list.

Customize field behavior
Depending on the field data type you selected, this screen may display different options (or even skipped if you entered a format of Address, Date, Date/Time, E-mail, Memo, Phone, Picture, or Time).

> **Default value:** - Any data specified for this attribute automatically appears in the field when you create a new record. You might specify a default value if most new records should have the same information in this field (such as a default State if all your jobs are in TX...if you get one in neighboring LA, you can change it in the record). For Yes/No fields, you can set a default of Yes or No. You can even set default values for numeric types of fields. Only Date, Memo, Phone, or Picture fields cannot contain default values.

Customize field behavior
Specify formats or rules for entering data in the field.

Default value (optional):

Field format (optional):

Field length:
64

☐ Link to company field:
Note: Fields can only be linked to other fields of a compatible data type.

Field format: - Allows you to specify how the data entered in the field is to be automatically formatted. This attribute is only available for Character, Initial Capitals, Lowercase, and Uppercase data types. You cannot define a format for numeric, date, or memo fields. Field format is used when you need your data to have a very specific layout (like a Social Security Number, for example which would be ###-##-####).

Using special symbols will control what type of data can be used and where:

This code:	Represents this type of character:
#	Numeric (no letters or symbols)
@	Alphabetic (no numbers)
%	Alphanumeric (data entry anarchy!)

When you specify a field format, you may only enter the types of characters specified by the field format. If you type more characters than the format specifies, they do not appear (e.g., the Number of characters is set to 50, but your field format is %%%%, so only four characters can be entered). You may also specify default characters like letters, numbers, parentheses, or dashes.

Example:	Code:	Meaning:
LL-123	@@-####	Two alpha characters and three numeric characters. The dash is entered for you.
A34-(ABC)	%%%-(@@@)	Three alpha or numeric characters and three alpha-only characters. The dash and the parentheses are entered for you.

☞ *To enter any of the three place holder symbols as actual symbols in the field, precede them by a backslash (\) character. For example, \#### would display the # symbol, and then allow the entry of three numeric characters.*

Field length: - How many characters can be entered into this field? The default is 50, but the maximum length of a character field type is 450 characters. Be realistic. Be sure to designate only the number of characters that you need. For example, if you have a field that uses E for East and W for West, and those are the only options for the field, then change the number of characters to 1. The user may not exceed the number of characters specified by this attribute. Remember, Character fields do not wrap in the field display. So, if the end user needs to type that much, create the field as a Memo field type (which doesn't ask for Field Length, because it is infinite).

Number of decimal places to the left of the decimal separator: - Currency and Decimal (not Number) use this option to determine the maximum number of numeric characters that the user can enter. For example, if the field will be used to represent a percentage or someone's age, then the maximum number will never be more the three (e.g., 100).

Database Design & Layouts

To the right: - This companion option determines the number of places after the decimal point. If the field is defined with 1 and the user inputs 4.56, then the number will be rounded off and the red data entry error icon will display to the right of the field, letting the user know that they entered too many digits in the field. To accept the rounding, the user just needs to click in the field again.

Link to company field: - ACT! databases have nine default linking fields (Company, Address 1, 2, and 3, City, State, Zip, Country, and Web Site). This option will link (or unlink) the current Contact field to any field of compatible data type and field length in the Company table (don't even consider linking a Character field to a Date field). Fields can only be linked once and some data entry rules are ignored, such as limit to list (especially if the Drop-down lists are not the same). All linked fields on the Contact record can be updated to match the values on the linked Company record.

> ☞ *The Link to company field option will not display when you are first creating a new field. It will only display after you finish defining the field, and you return to edit it.*

There is another screen in the Define Fields wizard concerning Triggers. Let's practice creating a few fields, and then we will come back to that option.

Practice: Field Attributes

What to do	How to do it/Comments
1. In the ACT2012Demo database, display the **Define Fields** dialog box for the **User 1** field.	**T**ools, **D**efine Fields.... Scroll to and double-click the **User 1** field.
2. Change **User 1** to **Sales Rep**. Leave it as a Character field. It should generate a history when it is changed. We want to know when any new salesman took over the account. It should also be a Primary field so that when a Contact is duplicated, the sales rep name is also copied to the new Contact. The field length should probably be a maximum of 45 characters.	Make sure **User 1** is the selected field. In the **Fie**l**d name:** text box, delete the "User 1" text and type the new field name. Add a check to Generate History and Primary Field. Using a drop-down list would be a great idea, but we don't have one created yet. Click **N**ext>. Change the **Field length:** from 64 to 45 and click **N**ext> and **Finish**. Click **Y**es if a message displays warning about a potential data loss. There's nothing in User 1 yet, so there can't be data loss yet.

What to do	How to do it/Comments
3. Change **User 2** to **No of Employees**. Change the **data type** to Number (we don't need decimal places). It would seem logical to make this one a Primary Field as well.	Scroll in the field list to double-click the **User 2** field and change the name. You can't use the # sign in a field name. Click the drop-down for **data type** and select **Number**. Answer **Yes** to verify that you understand there may be a loss of data. Place a check in the Primary Field option and click **Next>**.
4. Edit the field you just created (No of Employees) and link it to the Company field named "Number of Employees."	Put a checkmark in "Link to company field: and select "Number of Employees" from the drop-down, click **Next>**, and **Finish**.
5. We need to add a Yes/No field to our database named **Newsletter?** (to determine whether or not the Contact receives our newsletter). You cannot change one of the pre-defined **User #** fields to a Yes/No field, so let's create a new one.	Click **Create new field**. Enter a **Field name:** of "Newsletter." (Can't use a character like "?" in any field name.) Change the **Field data type:** to **Yes/No**. Click **Next>**, make the **Default value:** "No." Don't link to a company field. Click **Next>** and click **Finish**.
6. Close the Define Fields box. Don't modify the layout yet.	Click **Close**. Click **No** when prompted to modify the layout.
7. Click the **User Fields** tab and notice that the Field Label Names did not change. Also notice that our **Newsletter** field is nowhere to be found.	New fields added to the database do not automatically appear on the layout. You must manually add them. We will add the new field and make the Field Label name changes in the Layout editor in a few minutes.

8. Look up these Contacts and enter their Sales Rep and # Employees. You will have to enter a new sales rep on Mr. Finlay's record.

Contact	Sales Rep/User 1	# Emp/User 2
James Finlay	Fred Fenderline	250
Sandy Ryan	Allison Mikola	27
Mary Nara	Allison Mikola	17

What to do	How to do it/Comments
9. View the **History** tab for Sandy Ryan, to see how the Sales Rep history was recorded. Notice how the history is recorded a little differently on Mr. Finlay's record, where the Sales Rep field data was replaced by Fred Fenderline.	Changes are saved to a Contact record as soon as you change to another record. The change in the Sales Rep field will not record to the **History** tab until you move off the record and then back to it. Finlay's history record shows that the Sales Rep was changed from Sarah Whiting to Fred Fenderline.
10. Look up Ace Pet Store Franchises and notice that none of the Contacts has information on No of Employees.	Right-click the Company field and look up "ace". There are five Contacts in the database, and they are all linked to a Company record.
11. Display the Ace Pet Store Franchises Company record.	Click on the linked Company name on the Contact's records.
12. Display the Company Info tab and enter "17" in the "# of Employees" field and update the linked Contacts. Verify which fields will be updated.	Click on the Company Info tab and enter the number of employees. Click **Companies**, **Update Linked Contacts**. Click the **View Linked Fields** to verify that the Number of Employees will update and then click **Close**. Click **Yes** to update the Contacts.
☞ *You can usually click **Save**, and the dialog box appears. However, since you just created the Company/Contact link for this field, the field update may not be triggered until you exit and restart ACT!*	
13. Display all of the Ace-linked Contact records and verify that the number of employees were added to each record.	Click the **Create Lookup from Company** icon on the toolbar.

Set field triggers

The **Set field triggers** screen lets ACT! run an Activity Series or program when the field is entered, exited, or changed. This option contains three choices: Launch on change, Launch on entering, and Launch on leaving.

Example: When you enter the field, you want to automatically display an Excel rate sheet.

Set field triggers

Set a trigger on the field to automatically schedule an activity series, launch a program, or launch a web site when entering, exiting, or changing information in the field.

When changing a field, launch
None

When entering a field, launch
Programs   J:\Client\Pricing.xls

When leaving a field, launch
None

Sage ACT!

Procedure: To create a trigger for a field

1. Display the **Define Fields** dialog box for the desired field. — See page 330.

2. Define options as desired, pressing **Next>** until you reach the **Set field triggers** screen.

3. Select what you will launch (a Program or an Activity Series) for the specified event (change, enter, or exit). — Depending on whether you want the event to occur before or after you enter your ACT! data. Change includes changing from blank to a value.

4. Enter the path and name of the program's executable file, or a specific file to launch, or specify the program script you wish to run. — You may use the Browse button to locate the executable file, the file, or program.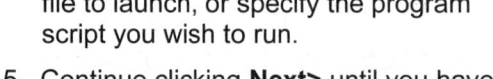

5. Continue clicking **Next>** until you have finished selecting options for the field. — The database is updated and your trigger now runs when you enter, exit, or change the field.

Say you wish to launch Excel and open a worksheet file called **PriceList.xls**. Your command might look like this:

J:\Attachments\PriceList.xls

You could use the Browse button, change the **Files of type:** to All Files (*.*), and locate the file you want to display.

Manage Drop-down Lists

Using drop-down lists can speed the process of entering data, especially in those fields where a limited number of choices are possible. When a list has been attached to a field, the end user sees a downward pointing arrow at the right of the field. ACT! provides preset lists for several fields.

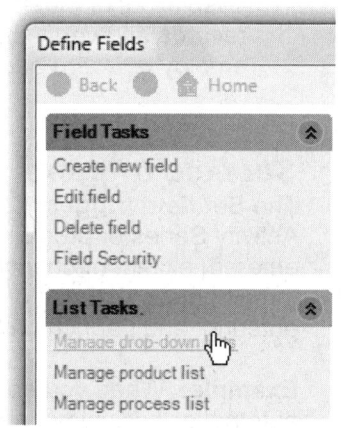

- Drop-down lists can be developed for Character, Currency, Number, and Decimal fields.
- Drop-down lists cannot be created for Date, Memo, Phone, Picture, or Yes/No fields.
- You can share any custom drop-down list among multiple fields.
- Changes made to the drop-down list in one field are reflected in all shared drop-down lists.

Procedure: To create a drop-down list

1. **T**ools, **D**efine Fields....

2. Click **Manage drop-down lists**. Under the **List Tasks** area at the left.

3. Click **Create drop-down list**.

4. Enter a name for the list.

5. Select the type of field this drop-down will be associated with.

6. Enter an optional Description (e.g., list the field names you will link to this drop-down list).

7. To allow end users to make changes to the drop-down list, put a check in **Allow users to edit items in this list**.

    If you don't check **Allow users...**, then additions or deletions must be made through the Define Fields menu command (by a Manager or Administrator) and would require all users to be locked out of the database while changes are made.

8. To update the list with whatever users type in the field, put a check in **A**u**tomatically add new items to drop-down**.

    Au**tomatically add...** can be handy for adding new cities to the drop-down, but it can also add misspelled cities to the list.

    Click **N**ext>.

9. To create your own list...
    To add an item, click **Add**. Type the Value and click in or **[Tab]** to the Description area to enter one, if desired.

    Descriptions are useful for helping the end user understand the code (e.g., is MS Mississippi or Missouri?).

    To delete an item, select it and click **De**l**ete**.

    You must enable **Show Descriptions** in the Field Definition to display descriptions.

10. Click **Finish** to apply the changes. Click **Home** to return to **Define Fields** dialog box.

    Click **Close** to finish defining fields.

 *When you link a drop-down list to a field, you can further define the list behavior in the Define Fields dialog box. Options for **Limit to List**, **Allow Multi-select**, **Show Descriptions**, and **Type-ahead** are defined when you create a field.*

Sage ACT!

Practice: Define and Attach Some Drop-downs

What to do	How to do it/Comments
1. Create a drop-down list for the Sales Rep field with the following names: **Fred Fenderline** **Europe** **Allison Mikola** **USA** **Betty Browser** **AsiaPac** Allow users to edit items in the list without locking other users out of the database. Don't automatically add names.	In the Define Fields wizard (**Tools**, **Define Fields…**), click **Manage drop-down lists**. Click **Create drop-down list**. Name the list "Sales Rep" and create as a Character type. Check **Allow users…** options. Remove the check from **Automatically add…**. Click **Next>**. Click **Add** and enter the sales rep name and description for the three sales reps at the left. Click **Finish**.
2. Link this list to the Sales Rep field. After linking the field, apply the options to limit to list, allow the selection of multiple sales reps (team selling). Show descriptions in case someone isn't sure who handles which region. Leave Enable Type-ahead checked.	Click **Home** to return to the **Create, edit or delete fields** screen. Double-click the Sales Rep field to edit the field. Put a check in the **Use drop-down list** option and select the "Sales Rep" list that you just created. Click **Next>**. Add and remove checks per the instructions at the left. Click **Finish**.
3. Return to Detail View and enter a Sales Rep (User 1) for several Contacts. Try entering multiple values.	Click **Close** and then **No** to modify layouts. Click **Contacts**, if necessary, to display the **Detail View**. Display the **User Fields** tab.

Creating Drop-down Lists for Importing

When you need to create a new list, and the list is long, you will find the process faster if you create a text file containing the list information and import it into your drop-down list.

To be able to import the list, you must enclose each item in your text file in quotes, with a comma separating the value and the description, and a hard return (meaning you press **[Enter]**) between lines.

You can create a text file in almost any word processor, but the easiest place to do it is in the Windows Notepad. (Every Windows computer has this simple text editor usually found in Start, Programs, Accessories, Notepad.)

Database Design & Layouts | 343

Procedure: To create a text file for importing to a drop-down list

1. Open Windows Notepad.   **Start**, **All Programs**, **Accessories**, **Notepad**.

2. In a text document, type the first entry surrounded by quotes, type a comma (,), then type the description inside quotes. Press **[Enter]**.
   "Travis Clark","South"
   "Elizabeth Kohler","West"
   "Rob Johnson","Central"

   Each line becomes another entry. (*If you do not wish to type a description, you may omit the comma as well.*)

3. When the list is complete, save the file as a text file. Text files have a **.TXT** file extension.

   If you are using Notepad, it saves the file as a text file by default. If you are using your word processor, you must tell it to save as a text file.

4. Close the file.   Remember where you saved it. You will need this information later.

Importing the Drop-down List

When you create a drop-down list, if you **Allow users to edit items in this list** then most things that have to do with drop-downs (editing, adding, and deleting items) can be performed without displaying the **Define Fields** dialog box. However, **Limit to List**, **Allow Multi-select**, **Show Descriptions**, and **Type-ahead** are controlled only from the Define Fields dialog box.

Procedure: To import a delimited text file to a drop-down list

1. **Tools Define Fields…**.
   Click **Manage drop-down lists**.

2. Click **Create drop-down list** (or select an existing list and click **Edit drop-down list…**). Enter the name, select the type, type a description, and click **Next>**.

3. On the Enter drop-down list values screen, click Import drop-down list items.

344 | Sage ACT!

4. An **Import List Items** dialog box displays.

     A **Browse...** button, displayed at the right of the text box, can help you find your text file.

    Include descriptions imports the descriptions (if any) to the second column of the list.

    Append imported items: option adds to any existing list items.

5. Click **Import**.
6. Click **Finish** to apply the changes. Click **Home** to return to **Define Fields** dialog box.
7. Click **Close** to finish defining fields.

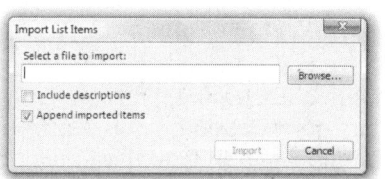

If you don't check **Append imported items**, the import replaces any existing values.

Practice: Do You Have an Import License?

What to do	How to do it/Comments
1. We need to add the Canadian province abbreviations to our database. A text file of Canadian province abbreviations is attached to Chris Huffman's **Documents** tab. Open it to see what it looks like. Save a copy to your desktop.	**Lookup**, **My Record**. Click the **Documents** tab. Double-click the **Canadian Provinces for Importing.txt** file so that you can review the list to see how it was created. **File**, **Save As...** change the location to Desktop (click the Desktop item at the left) and click **Save**. Exit Notepad.
2. Import the Canadian provinces and their descriptions file into the **States** drop-down list. After you import the file, but before you exit the Define Fields dialog box, look at the next step.	**Tools**, **Define Fields...**, and click **Manage drop-down lists**. Double-click the **States** drop-down list to edit it. Click **Next>** to display the **...values** screen. Click **Import drop-down list items** at the left. Click **Browse...** to locate the file you just saved on your desktop and click **Open**. Be sure to check **Include descriptions** and **Append imported items**. Click **Import** (they import to the bottom of the lists, but will resort alphabetically when you save the list) **Finish Home**. Don't click **Close** yet.

Database Design & Layouts 345

What to do	How to do it/Comments
3. Notice that the Home State field uses the **States** drop-down list as well, so it will also display the Canadian province abbreviations.	Double-click Home State and verify that the **Use drop-down list:** is checked and that the shared list is **States**.
4. Click **Finish** and **Close** to apply the changes.	
5. Click in the State field and enter the abbreviation for Manitoba.	Scroll to Manitoba and select the MB abbreviation.
6. Notice that the Canadian provinces are also available in the Home State field.	

Minor Changes to the Drop-down List

If you need to make minor additions or changes to your drop-downs, there is an easier way. (You don't mind if we show you the easier way, do you?)

Procedure: To modify a drop-down list

1. Click the drop-down arrow (in the field that contains the list you wish to modify) and click **Edit List Values…**.

    If the list has been defined to **Allow users to edit items in this list**, a list displays containing the items in that field's list, plus several command buttons.

2. To modify an existing item, click the value in the list and make your changes.

    Modify the Description the same way.

3. To add a new item, click the **Add** button. A new line is added to the bottom of the list.

    Enter a new value and (if you wish) a description.

    The list is sorted alphabetically when you exit the Edit List dialog box.

    You could also click the Value column to view the final sort before you click **OK**.

4. To delete an item, single-click the value and click the **Delete** button.

5. Click **OK**.

☞ If **Allow Editing** was not checked for a specific field, then you cannot edit the list this way (it's not allowed!). So a user with an Administrator or Manager role would have to edit a drop-down list by displaying the **Define Fields** dialog box (which means all users have to exit the database) and editing the list using the **Manage drop-down lists** option.

Sage ACT!

Practice: Modifying Drop-Downs

What to do	How to do it/Comments
1. "Banff" is not in our list of default cities. We will probably be adding a few Contacts for this beautiful Canadian city, so let's add it to the drop-down list.	On any Contact in the database, you can add a city to the drop-down without affecting the current selection. So, click the drop-down arrow in the City field and click **Edit List Values**…. Click **Add**… and enter "Banff" as a **Value** box. In **Description**, enter "Canada." Click **OK**. Click **No**.
2. Look up UR Powerful. UR will be living in Banff for the summer. So in the Home Address, enter… Fairmont Banff Springs Banff, Alberta Canada T0L 0C0	Since the database is sharing drop-downs, the Home City also shows the Banff city name. You will notice that AB is the abbreviation for Alberta.
3. Use the drop-down list to display the list of cities. Where is the Banff description of Canada?	When we defined the fields, we opted not to **Show descriptions** for the City field. After all, what can you say about cities?

Editing the Database Structure

If Allow Editing is not checked, you have to make changes to your drop-downs using the Tools, Define Fields command. If you are in a multi-user database, everyone logged into the database must exit before you can make changes to the structure. When you try to access the Define Fields dialog box, and other users are logged into the database, you will see the Lock Database dialog box, indicating which users are currently logged into the database.

The polite thing to do would be to call them to ask if they could exit ACT! for a few minutes while you make a few necessary changes to the database. However, sometimes they are not at their desk. In fact, they left the building two hours ago… they must have left ACT! open at their desk. Instead of trotting over to their work area, you can issue the comment here to close the ACT! database on their PC.

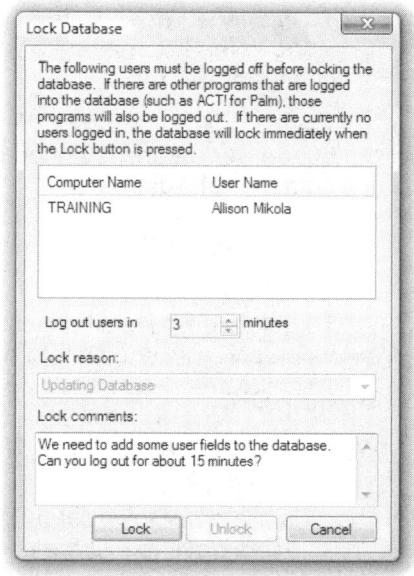

Database Design & Layouts | 347

Enter some **Loc<u>k</u> comments:** to display a message on user's workstations indicating why you are shutting down the database. Clicking on the **Lock** button displays your message and indicates that the Administrator (you) is preparing to close the database and that they have three minutes to complete whatever it is they are doing before ACT! shuts down. The users who are logged out by the system will still have ACT! open on their screen, but with no database displayed. When all users have been logged out, the Define Fields dialog box displays, and you can make your changes.

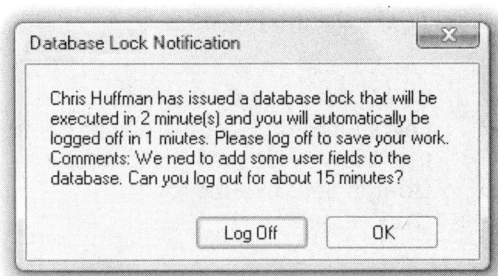

Field Security

While Contact Access restricts which users can see which records, Field Security allows you to control access to specific fields. Most fields in your database can have…

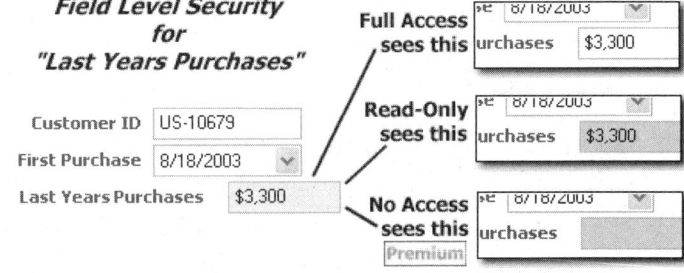

- **Full Access** – The default permission for all fields for all users. When applied to a specific field, it allows a user to view, add, edit, or remove information in that field without restriction.
- **Read-Only Access** – Lets you restrict specific users and/or teams from editing or deleting a field while allowing them to view the contents. The field contains a grey background if you have Read-Only Access. This permission could allow you to restrict editing access for all but one or two users on your staff – those who are responsible for updating the data.
- **No Access (Premium Only)** – Allows you to restrict which users can even see specific fields. If you have No Access, then the field appears empty with a grey background. You might assign this permission to fields related to personal or financial data (such as credit card or salary information). It is only available in the Premium version.

☞ *Some fields in the Contacts, Groups, or Companies tables are restricted and cannot have security applied: Company, Contact, City, State, ZIP Code, Phone, E-mail, ID/Status, Salutation, Groups Name or Company Name. Opportunity fields will support the "Read Only" access level, but not the "No Access" level.*

Procedure: To add Field Security

1. **Tools Define Fields**....

   Only users with Administrator or Manager roles can assign Field Security.

2. Select the table that contains the fields for Field Security by changing the "View fields for:" to Contacts, Companies, Groups, or Opportunities.

   Security is on a field-by-field basis.

   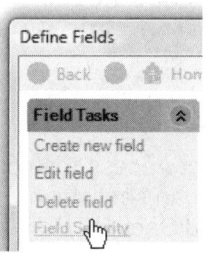 *You cannot assign field-level security to any Product fields. In addition, neither Groups "Group Name" nor Companies "Company Name" can be set to anything but Full Access.*

3. Select the field you want to restrict access to and click **Field Security** in the "Field Tasks" area at the upper left.

4. Assign the "Default Permission:" for the field. Select from **Full Access**, **Read Only**, (or **No Access** if you are a Premium user). You can assign user or team permission to override the default.

   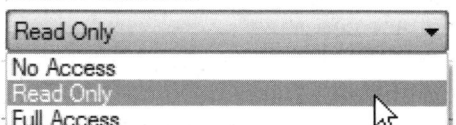

   The default permission is applied to all users.

5. Click **Yes** to assign default permission for all users.

6. First, select either the **Users** or the **Teams** tab.

   (The function is only available in the Premium version.) Teams can be a much more efficient way of assigning field-level access. As your company changes, simply add, replace, or delete users assigned to a team, and permissions are updated for all fields immediately.

7. Click **Edit**....

   A complete list of users (or teams) displays.

Database Design & Layouts | 349

8. Select each user (or team) and define their Access Level: from the drop-down list. When finished, click **OK**.

9. To change a single user's access back to the Default Permission, select the user and click **Reset**.

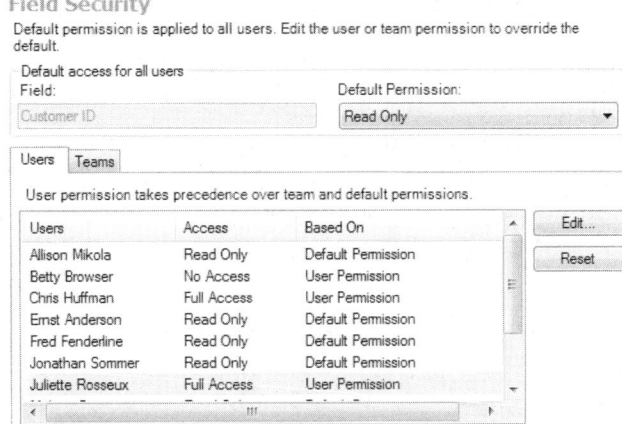

10. Click **Finish**.

Fields that have Field Security permissions assigned display a Private icon to the left of their name.

☞ *If a user does not have permission to view the contents of a field (No Access), then the field name will not be available for queries, importing or exporting, or for displaying in any list view. Company Fields and Contact fields (even though linked) do not share access levels and therefore may not be updated if user doesn't have full access.*

Practice: Changing Field Security

What to do	How to do it/Comments
1. Change the layout to ACTDemo layout so that you can see the Last Years Purchases field.	Click the **Layout** button in the lower left corner and select ACTDemo from the drop-down menu.
2. Look up Company Yellow Jersey and update their Last Years Purchases from $3,300 to $5,200.	Can't do it. Chris's rights are set to Read Only.
3. View the Field Security of Last Yrs Purchases field.	**Tools**, **Define Fields…**, select the "Last Yrs Purchases" field. Notice the Private icon to the left of the field name. Click **Field Security** in the Field Tasks area.
4. What is the Default Permission for the field?	Read Only.

What to do	How to do it/Comments
5. Even Chris is Read Only on that one.	Even the Administrator for the database can have Read Only permission when they are using the database on a daily basis (of course the Administrator can always change their own permission if they like).
6. View the Field Security for "Customer ID."	Click **Finish** to exit from the Last Yrs Purchases field security. Select Customer ID and click **Field Security**.
7. What two users have exceptions?	Chris and Juliette. Because Juliette is in Finance, she is the one responsible for maintaining the Customer IDs.
8. If you have Premium, are there any Teams that have exceptions?	Click the Teams tab. No exceptions.
9. Notice that even though it is linked to Customer ID in the Companies table, the Customer ID in Companies has no Field Security applied.	Change the "View fields for:" from Contacts to Companies. Verify that Customer ID does not have the Private icon to the left of its name, yet it is linked to the Contact Customer ID field.
10. Apply the same Field Level Security to Customer ID in the Companies table. Then return to "View fields for:" Contacts.	
11. For Contacts, change the "User 3" field to "Credit Rating" and then assign Field Security of Read-Only by default. Give Juliette full access.	Click **Finish** to return to Define Fields. Double-click the User 3 field and rename it to "Credit Rating." Click **Finish**. While the field is still selected, click **Field Security**. Change from **Full Access** to **Read Only** and click **Yes** to verify the changes. Click Juliette's name and click **Edit…** Change her access to **Full Access** and click **OK**. Click **Finish**.
12. If you have Premium, go back and change the security for Last Yrs Purchases for Chris to No View.	Select Last Yrs Purchases and click **Field Security**. Click Chris' name and click **Edit…**. Change to **No Access**. Click **OK**, **Finish**.
13. Notice that User 3 (Credit rating) is grayed out (unless you are logged in as Juliette).	Click **Close** to finish the Define Fields session and view User 3 on the User Fields layout.

Database Design & Layouts | 351

What to do	How to do it/Comments
14. Look up the Yellow Jersey company again and view Last Yrs Purchases. If you have the Premium version, the field is blank.	If you are logged on as Chris Huffman, the security has been set to **No Access**, so Chris can no longer see the data in that field.

Creating New Fields for Other Entities

In addition to defining fields for Contacts, you can also create new fields for Companies, Groups, Opportunities, or Products. Creating the fields for these other entities works exactly the same as it does for creating fields in Contacts. You just select: **Tools, Define Fields**, select the feature that you want to create fields for and continue with your design work (see page 330 to refresh your memory).

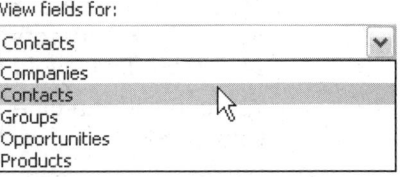

☞ When defining fields for Products, you cannot define a required field (cannot uncheck "Allow Blank"). Also, even though you can duplicate a Product (like you can a Contact or an Opportunity), you cannot identify a field as a Primary field…all fields are copied over to the duplicated product record.

Practice: Adding Other Fields

What to do	How to do it/Comments
1. Add a character field to Opportunities: Hot Button.	**Tools, Define Fields…**, change **View fields for:** to **Opportunities**. Click **Create new field** at the left. Change the field name to Hot Button. Finish the wizard with defaults. Click **No** when asked about adding the field to the database.
2. Open any Opportunity and double-click one of the product lines to notice that the Quantity field has too many zeros. Change it to zero decimal places. Then review the Products tab again.	**Tools, Define Fields…**, change **View fields for:** to **Products**. Double-click the Quantity field, click **Next>** and change the number of decimal places to the right to 0 and click **Finish**.

Defining and Modifying Layouts

ACT! comes with several pre-defined Contact, Company, and Group layouts. Layouts allow you to display the information stored in your ACT! database in different ways.

Simply put, a **layout** controls which bits of information are displayed, and where and how they are displayed on your screen (the same data, just arranged differently). As we add *new* fields to the database, you will not be able to see or enter data into the fields until you add them to your layout.

Each Contact Layout consists of static information that displays in the top portion of the screen and the tabs at the bottom.

- You can create new or modify existing layouts.
- All layouts have **Notes, History, Activities, Opportunities, Groups/Companies, Secondary Contacts**, and **Documents** tabs, but the rest of the tabs are a part of each individual layout that can be modified.
- You can select a different layout using the Layout button at the lower-left of the screen.
- Different layouts can be designed for the Contacts: Detail View, the Groups: Detail View and the Companies: Detail View.

Designing Layouts

To modify an existing or create a new layout, display the Design Layouts screen.

Procedure: To display the Design Layouts screen

1. Display the layout that most closely matches what you want.

   It's easier to modify an existing layout than to start from scratch.

2. Choose **Tools**, **Design Layouts** and select the layout type (**Contact**, **Group**, or **Company**).

   The most recently selected layout displays in Layout Designer view. Opportunity views cannot be modified.

The Layout Designer window has its own **Toolbar** for controlling **Field & Text Properties** as well as **Layout** properties. The **Splitter** bar divides the top **Detail Panel** from the **Tab Panels** below. The **Toolbox** at the left contains the tools for placing objects (fields, pictures, boxes, lines, text, etc.) on the layout. Notice the difference between a **Field Label** and a **Field**.

Database Design & Layouts | 353

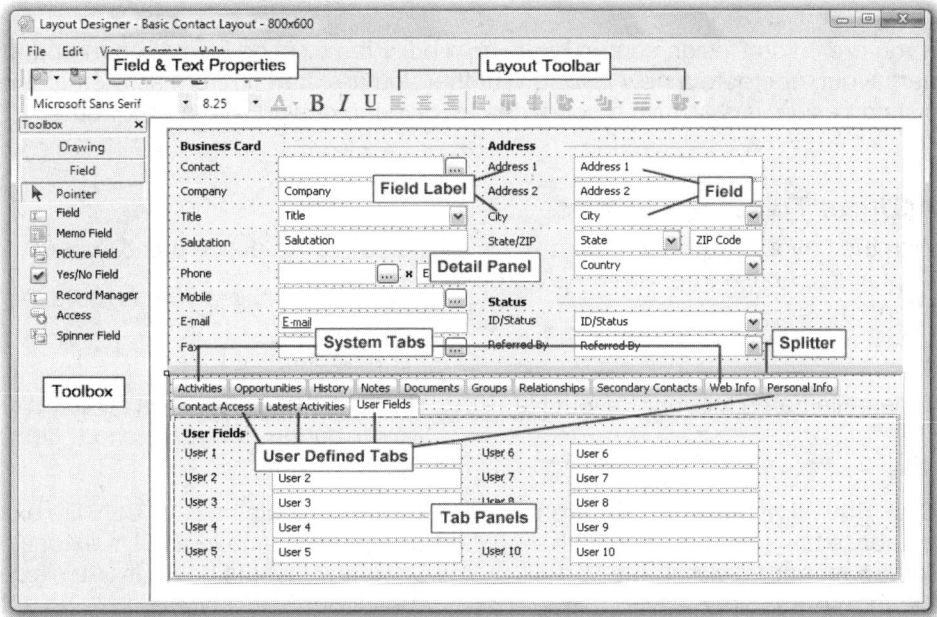

You can't edit any of the **System Tabs** (Activities, Opportunities, History, Notes, Documents, Groups, Relationships, Secondary Contacts, or Web Info). You can, however, choose to hide any of them from the end user or change the order of their display. However, you can edit, remove, or add to the **User Defined Tabs**.

Practice: Design Layouts

What to do	How to do it/Comments
1. Display the Contact Details view. Make sure **Contact Layout 800x600** is the current layout.	If necessary, click the **Contacts** button on the Navbar. Click the Layout button to verify that **Basic Contact Layout 800x600** is selected (if not, then select it).
2. Switch to Layout Designer view.	**T**ools, Design **L**ayouts, **C**ontact.
3. Observe the Design screen.	Everything is there, but instead of displaying Contact information, this screen displays the names of the Contact fields.
4. Leave the Design screen displayed.	

Saving Layouts

Once you are in the Design screen, you can modify the existing layout, open and modify another layout, or create a new layout. Whether you are starting from scratch or modifying an existing design, it is always a good idea to save the design with a new name.

Procedure: To save a layout

1. With the Layout Designer screen displayed, choose **File**, **Save As...** from the menu.

    The **Save As** dialog box displays:

    ☞ *ACT! saves your layouts to the default **Layouts** folder of the currently open database.*

2. Type a file name for your Layout file.

    This is the name that will be listed on the Layout button, so type a short, descriptive name.

3. Click **Save**. Layouts for the current database are stored as files in the **[databasename]-database files\Layouts** folder.

    Contact layouts have a .CLY file extension. Group layouts have a .GLY extension, Company layouts have an .ALY extension, and Opportunity layouts have an .OLY extension.

4. As you make additional changes to your new layout, click the **Save** icon.

    To close the Layout Designer view, click the **Close** button.

 *In case you get a little crazy and design a dozen new layouts, you can delete those you don't need. Open the Windows Explorer and delete the necessary .CLY, .GLY, or .ALY files from the **[databasename]-database files\Layouts** folder.*

Practice: A New Layout	
What to do	**How to do it/Comments**
1. You should still be displaying **Basic Contact Layout 800x600** in Design view. Save the Layout as: **CH TechONE**.	**File**, **Save As...**, CH TechONE, and click **Save**.
2. Leave the Layout Designer screen displayed.	

Database Design & Layouts

The Tool Palette

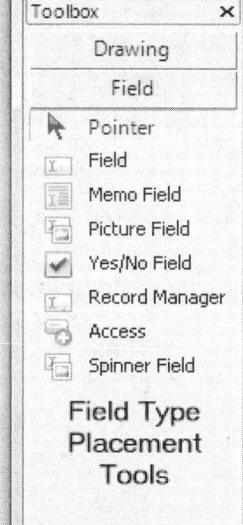

Field Type Placement Tools

The Design screen has its own toolbars at the top of the screen for formatting and a Toolbox at the left for adding objects to the layout.

The Toolbox is divided into two tabs. The **Field** tab contains the tools for placing the different types of fields (that have been created for the current database) on your layout.

If you click the **Drawing** tab at the top, you will see the tools for placing additional text, images, rectangles/lines, or ellipses/ circles on the layout.

To return to the **Field** tab display, click its name at the bottom of the Toolbox.

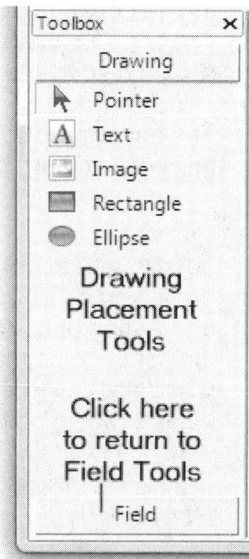

Drawing Placement Tools

Click here to return to Field Tools

Formatting Toolbar

While the Toolbox icons are used to add objects to the layout, the Formatting toolbar is used to change their appearance.

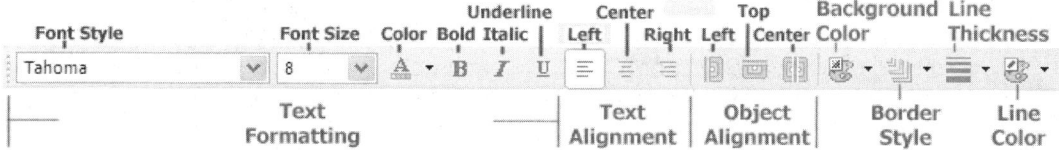

The **Formatting Toolbar** contains…

- **Text formatting icons** – change the font style, size, color, and appearance (bold, italic, underline) of any text objects (fields, labels, or text boxes).
- **Text alignment icons** – align the text within a single object (a field or a label or a text box) to a left, center, or right alignment (e.g. right-aligned number fields).
- **Object alignment icons** – line up selected objects (like fields or labels) so that they are all evenly lined up at the left (or at the top or by their centers).
- **Background Color icon** – changes the fill color of selected objects.
- **Border Style icon** – applies a border of 3D, Single, or None to the selected object.
- **Line Thickness icon** – changes the line thickness of Drawing Objects such as Rectangle or Ellipse objects (not fields).
- **Line Color icon** – changes the line color of Drawing Objects such as Rectangle or Ellipse objects (not fields).

While you can use the Formatting toolbar or right-click to apply most of the commonly used properties to your fields and labels, you can also view the complete properties available by pressing **[F4]** to display the **Properties** window.

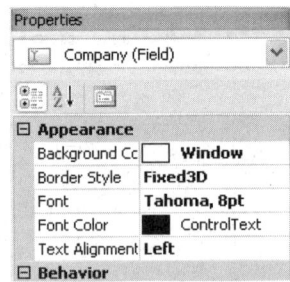

The associated properties display for the selected object. Field properties differ from label or text or tab properties.

Modifying Layouts

While you can start from scratch to create a new layout design, it is usually easier to modify an existing one. You may want to reposition the fields or change their size. You must select the fields or their labels in order to size or move them on the Layout screen. These fields and labels are called **objects**. You can select one or many objects at a time. If you select several objects, any modifications you make are made to all of the selected objects.

Procedure: To select one or more objects

1. To select a single item, click the item you wish to select.

   Click any object. A selected object displays square **handles** around its perimeter.

   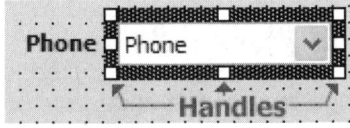

2. To select additional objects, press and hold down the **[Shift]** or **[Ctrl]** key and click the next, and the next, and the next....

   As long as you hold **[Shift]** (or **[Ctrl]**), you add each object you click. (If you click an object that has already been selected, you unselect it.)

 To select multiple objects at once, you can click the background and drag around all the fields and labels that you want to select. This selects all objects that the rectangle (that you just drew) touches.

Procedure: To size a layout object

1. Select the desired object(s).

   If you select multiple objects, you may size them all at once.

2. Place the mouse pointer on a selection handle.

Database Design & Layouts

3. When the mouse pointer displays as a double-headed arrow, drag the handle to change the size of the object.   ↔   If you selected multiple objects, they size proportionately.

Practice: Making the Fields Smaller

What to do	How to do it/Comments
1. You should still be in the Layout Designer View in your new CH TechOne layout. Maximize the Layout Designer window.	Click on the Maximize button in the upper-right corner or double-click the window title bar.
2. We need to shorten the length of the two fields that we created earlier.	In Layout Designer view, if you did not change the field names for User 1 and 2, just use those fields in this practice.
3. Drag over the two fields we created to select them all. Don't select the labels to the left. ☞ Start by clicking on the background between the top of the tab and Sales Rep.	
4. Make them about 1-inch wide. Position the mouse pointer on the center right handle of any selected box and drag left until the boxes are the correct size.	
5. De-select the objects.	Click an open area of the Layout Designer screen. The handles disappear.
6. The No of Employees should probably be the smallest, since it is only two or three characters.	Click No of Employees field (not the label). Drag it to a smaller size.
7. Save and close your layout.	Choose **File**, **Save** from the menu, or click the Save toolbar button. Click the Close button for the window.
8. Yikes! What happened to your changes?	No worries. You are still in the Basic Contact Layout – 800x600. Click the **Layout** button to change to your newly created layout.

Renaming the Field Labels

As you create *new* fields for the database, when you place them on the layout, the label will match the field name (although you can modify the label text if you like). However, if you modify any fields (such as **User 1** through **User 10** fields or any other fields that you have created), you will need to change the labels to match their new field names.

Procedure: To modify field labels

1. While in Layout Designer mode, double-click the label to be edited.

    The background of the label turns white. Click again to place the insertion point.

2. Select the current label text and type a new one.

3. Change the width of the label to accommodate the new text.

Practice: Creating Meaningful Label Names

What to do	How to do it/Comments
1. Change the **User 1** label to: **Sales Rep**	Back in Layout Designer view (**Tools**, **Design Layouts**, **C**ontact), click the **User Fields** tab to make it active. Double-click the User 1 label (not the field). Select and replace the text with the words "Sales Rep." Click outside of the label to complete the change.
2. Change the **User 2** label to: **No of Employees**	Double-click the User 2 label. Replace the text with the words "No of Employees." Click outside the label to complete the change.
3. The label is not quite large enough to display the new text "No of Employees." Make the label large enough to display the complete text.	Select the label. Position the mouse pointer on the center left side of the label. When the mouse displays as a two-headed arrow, drag to the left until you can view the entire label text.

Moving Objects

The layout of the screen may not work for you. Perhaps you want to move the address fields to a tab on the bottom or move the Alternate and Home phones to the top panel. Maybe you would like to move the State and the ZIP fields to the same line to allow room for more fields.

Procedure: To move an object on the tab

1. Select the object(s). — If you select multiple objects, you can move them all at once.

2. To move the selected objects to a different tab pane (or from a bottom tab pane to the top detail pane) click **Edit**, **Cut**.

   Click the pane that will receive the object (to make that pane active), and click **Edit**, **Paste**.

   — When you click **Edit**, **Paste**, the selected objects are moved to the middle of the active pane.

   If you are just moving the field within the same pane, go to the next step.

3. Point to the selected object(s). — If you have selected multiple objects, point to any of the selected objects.

4. Click and drag the object to a new position. — If you have selected multiple objects, they move as one.

☞ You can also use the arrow keys on the keyboard to move selected objects with much greater control.

Remember, the field box and the label text that usually appears to its left are two separate items. If you want to keep them together as you move them, be sure to select them both first.

Practice: Moving Around

What to do	How to do it/Comments
1. We need to make room for moving the Sales Rep field to the top panel. Delete the Status label and horizontal line that displays above the ID/Status field.	While still in Layout Designer view, start at the right of the horizontal line and drag to the left until the Status label is also included in the selection. Be sure to include only the two items as you drag. Click the **[Delete]** button.
2. Move the Sales Rep field from the bottom tab pane to the top pane above the ID/Status field.	Select both the Sales Rep field and its label in the **User Fields** tab. Drag the field to its new location over the ID/Status field. Use the arrow keys (if necessary) to adjust the positioning, but don't worry about making it perfect. We'll line up everything in the next section.
3. Save your layout.	Choose **File**, **Save** from the menu, or click the Save toolbar button.

Aligning Objects

If your fields or labels are not lined up with one another, you can have ACT! line them up into neat, straight lines with perfect vertical or horizontal spacing. Select the objects and…

- Click one of the toolbar alignment icons.
- Right-click and select an alignment option.
- Use one of the **Format**, **Align** menu options.
- Use the **Format**, **Horizontal Spacing** or **Vertical Spacing** options to make the spacing between your fields equidistant…or to remove all spacing between your fields to simulate a spreadsheet type of look. For smaller increment fine tuning, you can select multiple objects and click **Format**, **Grid**, **Align to Grid**.
- Use the arrow keys to nudge the alignment.
- Use the **Properties** window ([F4]) to individually control the Location of objects by changing the X (pixels from the left of the screen) and Y (pixels from the top of the panel) coordinates.
- Use the mouse to drag fields and labels to their new location. Their placement will be more precise if **Format**, **Grid**, **Snap to Grid** is checked.

Procedure: To align fields or text objects

1. Drag over the objects to be aligned.

   The first selected object displays clear, square handles around its perimeter.

2. **[Shift+click]** additional objects that you want aligned. You can also **[Shift+click]** any object to remove it from the selected group.

   The object with the black handles determines the alignment for the rest of the selected objects.

3. Single-click the object you want to act as the primary object.

   When you select multiple objects, one has black handles, and the rest have clear handles. The object with the black handles is the primary object of the group. If you perform an alignment on the group, for example, the other objects align to the primary object.

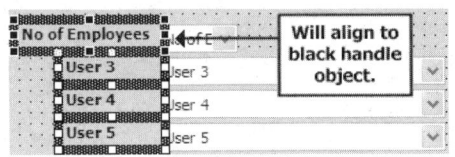

4. Click one of the Alignment icons,

   or right-click one of the objects and choose an align option,

   or choose **Format**, **Align...** to display the **Align** options.

   You can also align by Right, Middle (a horizontal or row alignment), and Bottoms.

   ☞ *When you right-click a field to select an alignment option, it makes that field the primary field, so you could skip step 3.*

Database Design & Layouts | 361

5. Select the desired alignment option. Remember, all selected objects align on the primary object (the one with the black handles).

 *If you select several objects and then realize that you chose the wrong primary object, single-click the object you want to be the primary (this object should already be selected). The black handles display on that object, and the rest remain selected. Of course there is **Edit**, **Undo**.*

Practice: Laying Out Your Layout

What to do	How to do it/Comments
1. The Address labels and the Sales Rep label aren't lined up. Line them up. Since we had to make the No of Employees label larger, line up the labels on the **User Fields** tab as well.	In Layout Designer view, start at the top and drag over the Address 1 label down to the Referred by label. Click **Address 1** to make all of the labels align to that label. Click the **Align Left** icon on the toolbar. Drag over the labels on the **User Fields** tab. Make No of Emp the primary field and click the **Align Left** icon.
2. Now make sure that the **Sales Rep** and **Phone** fields and labels are lined up horizontally.	Start at the right of the Sales Rep field and drag left until the Phone label is also included in the selection. Be sure to include only the current row as you drag. Click the Phone field (to make it the primary). Click the **Align Tops** icon. Click the background to view the new alignment.
	Phone — Phone ▾ × Exten ▾ Sales Rep — Sales Rep ▾ Mobile — Mobile Phone ▾ ID/Status — ID/Status
3. The Phone and Sales Rep labels seem too high. Let's redo that same alignment and select the **Align Middles** option. **Hint:** Align Middles is not one of the icons on the toolbar.	Select the same fields once again. Don't worry about which one has the black squares. Right-click the Phone field and select **Align Middles**. Click the background and view the results. *When you right-click a field to select an alignment option, it makes that field the primary field.*
4. Save your layout.	Choose **File**, **Save** from the menu, or click the Save toolbar button.

Adding New Fields to Your Layout

As you add fields to your database, they will not automatically appear on any of the existing layouts. You must manually add new fields and their labels to any layout where you wish them to appear. For this, you use the one of the buttons in the Toolbox.

Procedure: To add new fields to your layout

1. In the Toolbox, click the Field type you wish to place on the layout (e.g., the **Field** button).

   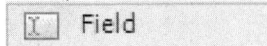

   The button appears to be pressed in when it is active. You could also place a Memo, Picture, Yes/No, Record Manager or Access field.

2. Position your mouse pointer where you want the top left corner of the field to be. Click and *hold* the left mouse button. Drag the mouse pointer down and to the right until the field is the size you want it to be. Release the mouse button.

   You use the mouse to draw the field box.

   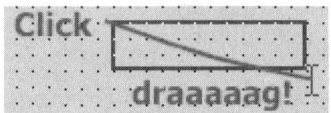

3. The **Select Fields** dialog box displays with a list of fields in the database that

   * match the field type button you clicked in Step 1 and
   * have not yet been placed on the layout.

   If you created a Yes/No field named "Club Member," that field name only displays when you use the **Yes/No Field** button to insert a field on the layout. The same also applies to any Picture or Memo fields that you create, as well as to the Record Manager field. You must click on the associated Toolbox Field icon to display the list of available fields to place on the layout.

   The new field is placed at the position and size you specified. The **Fields** dialog box displays.

   ☞ *Fields can only be placed once on any layout.*

Database Design & Layouts

4. Select the field you wish to be displayed in the control you just created (by control, we mean the box you just drew).

   Choose whether to **Include a label**.

5. Click **New Field** to create a new database field that you can add to the layout.

6. Click **Add**.

   The box you drew now displays the name of the field that it contains. If you chose to add a label, it displays to the left of the box.

7. If you wish to add more fields to your layout, click the **Field** tool again and start all over.

If you leave the **Include a label** check box checked, a field name is placed as a label to the left of the field box. When you use the layout, the field object displays the contents of the field, while the label displays the name of the field.

This handy option allows you to jump immediately to the **Define Fields** option to create a new field you just thought about....without closing the Layout Designer window. You may return to Define Fields later to modify the field options (e.g., number of characters or drop-down behaviors).

If you want to add multiple fields to the layout at the same time, before clicking **Add**, **[Ctrl+click]** on each field in the **Select Field** dialog box. Each selected field is added below the previously added field. Each added field is the same size as your original.

When you add a field to the layout, it is removed from the list of available fields.

☞ *You cannot add the same field to the layout twice.*

Practice: Adding Fields

What to do	How to do it/Comments
1. Let's add the **Newsletter** field that we created in the practice on page 338 to our new layout. Place it where the Sales Rep/User 1 field used to be on the **User Fields** tab.	In Layout Designer view (**Tools**, **Design Layouts**), if you didn't create the field in the earlier practice, we can do it on the fly. Click the **Yes/No Field** button. Click and drag to place the field above the No of Employees field. When you release the mouse button, the **Select Field** dialog box appears. (If **Newsletter** is not an available field, click **New Field** and add it.) Click the **Newsletter** field and click **Add**.

Sage ACT!

What to do	How to do it/Comments
2. Observe the layout. The label doesn't line up on the left. Fix it.	Click on the background to deselect the field, then click on the label to select it. Make the label larger (if necessary). Select the labels in the column and align them all on the left with the **No of Employees** label. The label for the Newsletter field is right-aligned text. You will also need to click the **Left** text-align button.
3. Line up the Newsletter field and label with the User 6 field and label to the right. Make other alignment changes as necessary. Save and close your layout.	Drag horizontally over **User 6** and **Newsletter** fields. Right-click **User 6** and select **Align Middles**. Line up the **Newsletter** check box with **No of Employees** if necessary. Click the **Save** icon. Click the **Close** button.
4. Mark a few Contacts to receive our newsletter.	Easy to mark!

Layout Tabs

All Contact layouts have nine system tabs defined (**Notes**, **History**, **Activities**, **Opportunities**, **Groups/Companies**, **Secondary Contacts**, **Relationships**, **Documents**, and **Web Info**). The Company, Group and Opportunity layouts have similar system tabs. You cannot modify or combine System tabs. (For example, you cannot combine the Notes and History tabs and you can only have one Products/Services tab on any layout.)

However, you can modify any remaining tabs that contain user fields. As you add more objects to your layout, you may find you want to rename or add your own tabs to the layout to better organize the data. You may also decide to hide some of the system (or user-defined) tabs that don't apply to how you will use ACT! in your company.

Procedure: To create a new tab or rename an existing tab

1. From the Layout Designer screen (**Tools**, **Design Layouts**, layout type), choose **Edit**, **Tabs** from the menu.

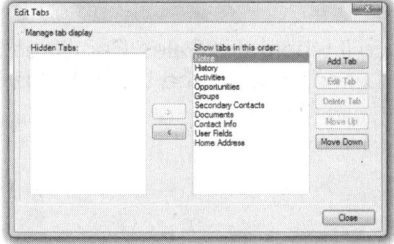

Database Design & Layouts

2. **Add Tab** button adds a new tab (to the bottom of the list and thus to the far right in the tab display).

    Edit Tab allows you to give one of the user-field tabs (not System tabs) another name.

    Dele̱te Tab deletes the selected user-defined tab. Any fields that were on the deleted tab can now be placed on other tabs.

    Move U̱p or **Move Ḏown** buttons change the tab order for the selected tab.

3. Click **C̱lose** to return to the Layout Designer screen.

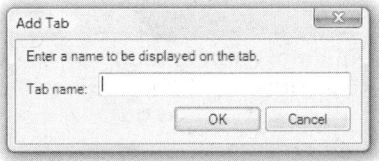

While the system tabs cannot be deleted, they can be hidden from view.

The **Remove** arrow (in the middle of the dialog box) hides the selected system tab from the end user view.

You can display the **Edit Tabs** dialog box any time to add, rename, delete, or change the tab order.

Practice: A New Tab

What to do	How to do it/Comments
1. Create a new tab for your layout named: **Address**. Move it to the right of the **Secondary Contacts** tab.	In Layout Designer view, **Edit**, **Ṯabs...**, click **Add Tab**, type **Address**, and click **OK**. Select the **Address** tab and click the **Move U̱p** button until it is below Secondary Contacts. Click **Close**.
2. Move all of the address fields on the top tab to the new **Address** tab.	Click the new **Address** tab to make it active. Drag over the address fields and their labels and drag them to the bottom Address pane. Use the Arrow keys on the keyboard to help you move them to the right location on the tab.
3. Let's add a memo field called **Directions** to the right of the address fields on the **Address** tab.	This is a new field that has not yet been created for this database. Click the **Memo Field** button in the Toolbox and draw a large square to the right of the address fields. Click **New Field** in the Select Field dialog box. For the Field name: enter **Directions**. Click **Finish**. Click **Directions** and click **Add**. Use the Arrow keys to reposition the field.
4. Save and close the layout.	Click the **Save** icon. Click the **Close** button.

What to do	How to do it/Comments
5. Try entering some text on how to get to the client site into the Directions field.	You could go on and on. If you enter more text than can display in the current Directions field window, the scroll bar at the right will activate, allowing you to scroll through the entire entry.

Adding Other Objects

You may wish to add *more* objects to your layout like Text (your company name or an inspirational message), an Image (such as your logo), a Rectangle (which can also be used to place a line), or an Ellipse.

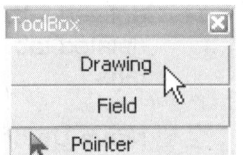

Procedure: To add text to your layout

1. In the Toolbox, click the **Drawing** tab, and then click the **Text** button.

2. Point to where you want your text to begin, and drag a box the approximate size you want for your text. Release the mouse button and the text box appears.

   Don't be too concerned about the size of the box. You can always adjust it later.

3. Double-click inside the text box. Select the default text to delete it. Then type the desired text.

   As you type, extra text wraps to the next line, and the box grows vertically to contain the text.

4. Format the text box as desired.

Practice: Add a Layout Title

What to do	How to do it/Comments
1. Back in Layout Designer view, add our company name to the top part of the layout where the address fields were. Enter the text: **CH TechONE**	In Layout Designer (**Tools**, **Design Layouts**, **Contact**), click the **Drawing** tab in the Toolbox and then click the **Text** button. Click and drag a box in the blank area on the top of the layout. When you release the mouse button, double-click inside the label, select, and replace the existing text with **CH TechONE**.
2. Observe the new text.	Supremely unexciting isn't it? Don't worry; we'll dress it up shortly.

Database Design & Layouts

What to do	How to do it/Comments
3. How would you return to adding fields?	Click the **Field** tab displayed at the bottom of the Toolbox.
4. Save your changes, but leave the layout displayed.	

Formatting

You can control the look of your layouts with a variety of options including font style, size, and color, and the background color. Formatting can serve to make your layouts easier to read and use. Formatting also makes your layouts look really, really cool!

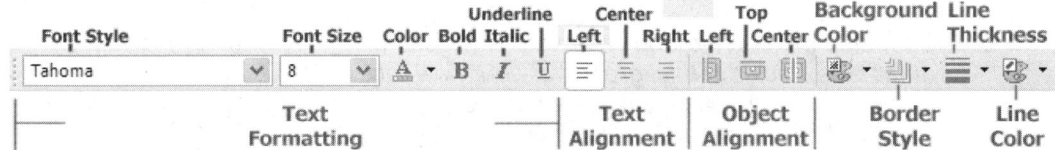

Procedure: To apply a format to a part of the layout

1. Select the object(s) you wish to format. You may apply the same format(s) to multiple objects.

2. Choose the format option to apply.

3. Apply any additional formats while the object is still selected. The format buttons are identified above.

 You can also right-click any object and select **Edit Properties** to display a shortcut menu for the current object's properties or press **[F4]** to display the **Properties** window.

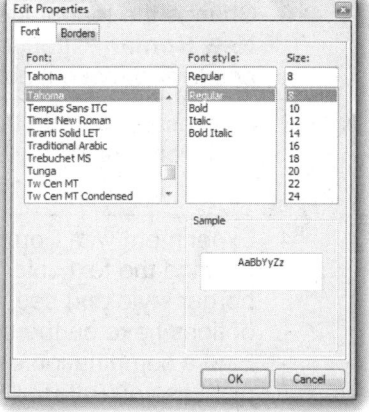

Changing Background Tab Color

If you added a tab to your layout, the default background color is a light grey.

Procedure: To change background color

1. From the Layout Designer screen (**Tools**, **Design Layouts**), click in the tab whose background color you want to change.

2. Click the drop-down arrow of the Background Color icon and select a new color.

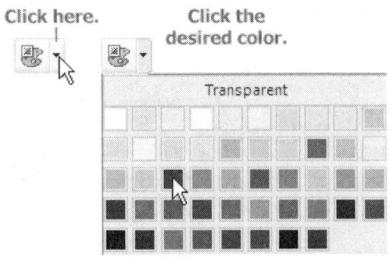

Click here. Click the desired color.

 To match the background color currently used on other tabs, click the background of your new tab, and press **[F4]** to display the **Properties** window. Replace the current word (Control) with RGB values.

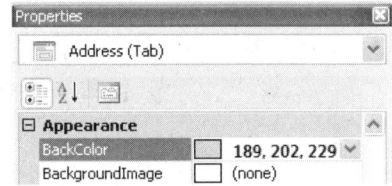

Practice: Formatting Practice

What to do	How to do it/Comments
1. While still in the Layout Designer view of your new layout, select the "**CH TechONE**" text you created in the previous practice session.	Click the text (handles appear around it to indicate that it's selected).
2. Change the font of the text to **Times New Roman**. Change the size to **18** points and make it bold and italic.	On the toolbar at the top of the screen, choose the font name, choose **18** from the Font Size list, and click the **Bold** and **Italic** icons.
3. If necessary, resize the box so the text all fits on one line.	When you add text to a box, or change the size of the text, the box does not automatically grow to accommodate the changes.
4. Experiment with Formatting icons. Change the text color, fill color, or border style and see what effect these options have on the selected object. Find a combination of options that pleases you (after all, you're the one with taste here).	☞ You can also right-click any object to display its **Properties** dialog box.

Database Design & Layouts

What to do	How to do it/Comments
5. Change the Background color of the Address layout to your choice.	Click the background of the **Address** tab. Press **[F4]** to display the **Properties** toolbar at the right. Click the drop-down arrow to the right of the **BackColor** option. Select a color. Press **[F4]** again to close the toolbar. ☞ *If you want to use the same color as the other tabs, just type in 242,242,242 (the RGB values used on the other tabs).*
6. Save and close your layout and admire your work.	Click the **Save** icon. Click the **Close** button.

Make Same Width or Height

Sometimes when you have added an object to the layout, you would like it to be exactly the same height and width as another object.

Procedure: To make same width or height

1. Select two or more objects.

2. Click the primary object to make its handles black.

    The primary object is the one that you want to model the others after.

3. **Format, Make Same Size**, and then select **from Width, Height, or Both**.

Practice: Sizing Practice

What to do	How to do it/Comments
1. While still in the Layout Designer view of your new layout, make all the phone numbers the same width as the Phone field.	Select all the phone fields (even on the Personal Info tab if you like). Click the Phone field (in the top pane) to make it the primary item. **Format, Make Same Size, Width**.
2. Save and close your layout and admire your work.	Click the **Save** icon. Click the Close button.

Testing Your Layouts

Normally, you move from field to field in ACT! by pressing the **[Tab]** key (**[Shift+Tab]** moves you backwards). Layouts should have a logical order of data entry, so that when you type something into a field, you can press the **[Tab]** key to move to the next logical field. ACT! also allows you to use the **[Enter]** key to quickly jump to some of the most commonly used fields. While there is a default field entry order, as you add or move fields on the layout, you may need to modify the sequence, to put them back in the proper order.

Practice: Testing Entry Order

What to do	How to do it/Comments
1. In Detail View, start in the Company field, use the **[Tab]** key to move from field to field. Observe how the focus proceeds from field to field in your layout.	As you continue moving through the layout, you can tell that it needs some work. We need to change some of the tab order.
2. Leave the layout displayed.	

Field Entry Order

Fortunately, you can easily control the order in which fields are selected when you press **[Tab]** or when you press **[Enter]**.

Procedure: To set the field entry order

1. **T**ools, Design **L**ayouts, **C**ontact or **G**roup or C**o**mpany.

   You need to be in Layout Designer view to change the order.

2. **V**iew, **T**ab Stops, Show **T**ab Stops or **V**iew, **E**nter Stops.

   The field entry order displays to the right of each field as a red number box if you are setting **[Tab]** stops and green if you are setting **[Enter]** stops.

   ☞ The Toolbox and Formatting toolbar are disabled while in this view.

3. To clear a number from the field, click the field (not the number).

   ☞ If you have many changes to the field entry order, you may find it easier to clear the existing order. To start from scratch, click **View**, **Tab Stops**, **C**lear. Then, click the fields in a logical sequence to define the field entry order.

   Each time you click a field without a number, the next number in sequence is added. To set a specific number to a field, right-click the field, enter a number in the **Set Index** dialog box and click **OK**.

4. To save your changes, click **View**, **Tab Stops**, Show **T**ab Stops.

   If you click the **Close** button of the window, you will be prompted to save your changes, and the Layout Designer window will close.

Database Design & Layouts

 While you are assigning tab stops, if you expect the next available number to be 14, but the system enters 16, that means that 14 and 15 have been assigned elsewhere on the layout.

There are three things to remember when setting field entry order:

- If you have a field that is only occasionally used (like Department), you can eliminate it from the field entry order to speed up data entry by simply removing the field number. If no number appears beside the field, it's not part of the tab order.
- If you click a field that already has a field entry sequence number, you remove that number. ACT! always uses the next number in sequence when you click a blank field.
- The starting field entry sequence number on each layout tab (in the bottom panel) will be the same number. If the starting tab number of the User Fields tab is 25, then it will also be the starting number on each of the other layout tabs in the bottom panel.

Practice: Clearing and Setting Field Entry Order

What to do	How to do it/Comments
1. Back in Layout Designer view, display the field entry order, if necessary.	**T**ools, Design **L**ayouts, **C**ontact **V**iew, **T**ab Stops, Show **T**ab Stops.
2. Observe the numbers. **Sales Rep** is out of sequence.	
3. OK, let's start from scratch. Clear the field entry order.	**V**iew, **T**ab Stops, **C**lear.
4. Experiment with defining a new field entry order manually. Entry order should reflect the most logical order to *enter* data, and not necessarily the order in which they appear (*although the two usually coincide*).	Click each field in sequence to add the next available number.
5. Now modify the Enter stop sequence to include **Company**, **Phone**, **ID/Status**, and **Sales Rep**.	Click **V**iew, **T**ab Stops, Show **T**ab Stops to close the **Tab stop** view. **V**iew, **E**nter Stops, Show **E**nter Stops to display the current Enter stops. Modify the sequence by clicking on the fields.
6. Test your **[Tab]** order after closing (and saving) your layout.	Click **V**iew, **E**nter Stops, Show **E**nter Stops to exit Enter Stops View. Then click the **Close** button and then **Y**es (to save). Press **[Tab]** to move from field to field.

Sage ACT!

What to do	How to do it/Comments
7. Test your **[Enter]** order.	Try pressing **[Enter]** to move around the layout.

☞ *If you prefer to use **[Enter]** instead of **[Tab]** to move from field to field in the layout, just reset the order to match the sequence of the tab stops.*

Customizing the Product View

In addition to customizing the Contact views, you can also easily customize the Companies, Groups, or Opportunities views... using the same techniques that we've already been using.

There are a few additional Layout Controls in Opportunities Layout Designer View (Process and Stage, Status, Probability, and Associate With), but other than not, your design options are the same.

While you can't modify the Products layout to appear the same on each workstation, end users can identify which fields will display and in what order they will be shown. By simply clicking the **Display Fields...** button, you can modify how the fields display in the Add/Edit Product dialog (it uses the Customize Columns dialog).

☞ *Changes to the Products view are workstation-specific.*

Practice: Modifying the Opportunity Layout View

What to do	How to do it/Comments
1. If you created the "Hot Button" field in one of the previous exercises, add it to the Opportunities Layout, to the bottom-right of the Strategy tab.	**Tools**, **Design L̲ayouts...**, **Opportunity**. Display the **Strategy** tab. Click the Fields tab and place the Hot Button field at the lower right. Complete and save your design.
2. Modify the Products dialog to remove Item # and Cost from the display (we don't really use those fields).	Display any Opportunity in **Detail View**. Click the **Products/Services** tab. Double-click a product line to display it in Add/Edit Product view. Click the **Display Fields...** button. Double-click the fields in the right-hand pane and click **OK**, **OK**.
3. View your changes.	

Feature Customizations

To enhance your use of ACT! by customizing some of its great features, you will:

- ☑ Add an option to the Menu, a Toolbar or enable it as a shortcut Keystroke.

- ☑ Create custom Web Info links

- ☑ Learn to create and use new Activity types.

- ☑ Map ACT! fields into an Excel document.

- ☑ Create Events that will display on all users' calendars.

- ☑ Customize some of the Opportunity features to better support your sales efforts.

Customizing Menus and Toolbars

Now that the fields have been designed, and the layouts are arranged, let's make a few tweaks to the menus and toolbars on each user's workstations.

While changes to the database design and layouts are shared throughout the enterprise, modifications to the menu and toolbar are PC-specific (you have to go through the same procedure on each PC). There are three ways to execute a command that you create:

- You can add it to a menu.
- You can create a toolbar button.
- You can create a keyboard shortcut.

The **Global** toolbar is located below the menu bar. It has large buttons for commands used most frequently in every ACT! view. The global toolbar cannot be relocated or undocked from its location. You cannot customize the global toolbar.

The **View** toolbar is located at the top of each view and displays commands (tools) for tasks related to the view. You can modify the view toolbar by adding or rearranging your favorite tools. You can remove tools that you rarely use. You can also create custom toolbars.

Procedure: To customize the toolbar or menu display

1. <u>T</u>ools, <u>C</u>ustomize, <u>M</u>enus and Toolbars….

   Toolbars: Allows you to add **New**, **Delete**, **Rename**, display, or hide a **Toolbar**.

   Commands: Allows you to drag a menu **Command** to the menu bar, to a different menu location, or to the toolbar as an icon.

   Options: Toggle **Options** to display Full or Short menus, as well as Tooltips.

   Keyboard: Assign a **Keyboard** shortcut key to any command.

   Custom Commands: Create a Custom Command to add to any Toolbar, Menu, or Keyboard shortcut.

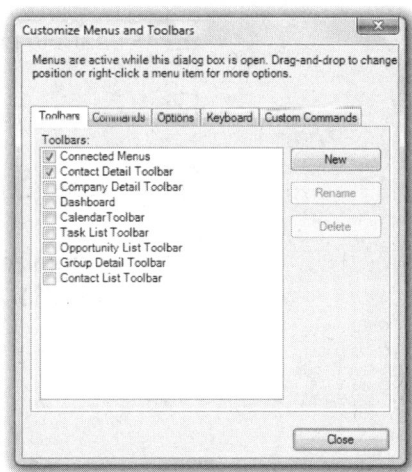

Feature Customizations | 375

2. Click on the **Commands** tab to display the menu options.

   Note that **Categories:** replicate the menu commands (File, Edit, View…) in alphabetical order… with a few extra thrown in.

   Right-click the toolbar icon and select **Default Style** to display the icon only.

3. Select a Category (a menu command), then drag any command from the **Commands:** area to a menu or toolbar location.

   When the mouse displays as a vertical bar, you can release the mouse button to drop the icon at that location.

4. Right-click the command that you just placed, and select a style:

   Default Style displays the icon only on the toolbar or text only on the menu.

   The other options are self explanatory.

   Begin Group places a vertical separator bar to the left of the toolbar icon or to the top of a menu command.

5. While this dialog is displayed, you can also edit any of commands on the menu bar.

6. Click **Close**.

While this dialog box is displayed, you can click on any menu command at the top of the screen and move a menu command or right-click and delete the command.

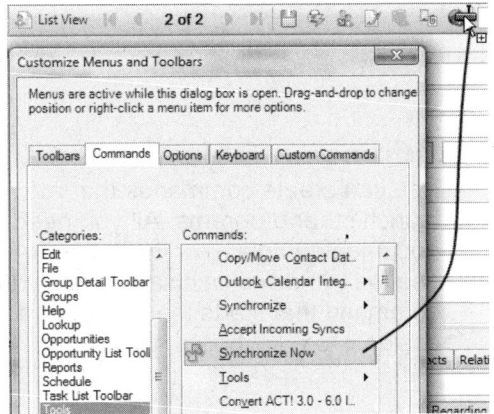

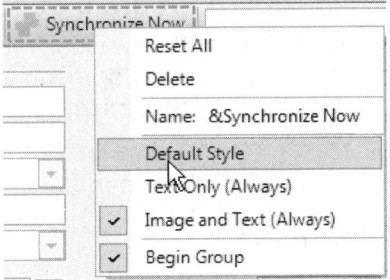

 Note that you can also right-click any command to Delete it or rename it. The ampersand should be placed in front of the letter that you want underlined and used with the Alt key for issuing commands.

Practice: Add View, Refresh to the toolbar

What to do	How to do it/Comments
1. Add the Refresh command to the toolbar. Display the icon only.	**Tools, Customize, Menus and Toolbars....** Click the **Commands** tab. Think about where that command is currently displayed in ACT!... it is on the View menu. So in the Categories: column, select View. Select the Refresh command at the right. Drag it to the desired location on the View Toolbar (remember, you can't add commands to the Global Toolbar.) Right-click the command and select **Default Style**. Click **Close**.

Adding an Object to the Menu/Toolbar/Keystroke

You can create commands that run ACT! reports, open document templates, and even launch other programs. All you need to do is to specify the path to the report template, document template, or the program's executable file. For example, if you frequently need to use the Windows calculator while you are working in ACT!, you can create a custom command that starts the program, and then add the command to the toolbar or the menu, or assign it to a keyboard shortcut.

Procedure: To create a custom command

1. Display the ACT! view where you want to modify the toolbar or menu and select **Tools, Customize, Menus and Toolbars...**

    Toolbar icons and menus are unique to ACT! views (Contacts, Groups, Calendar, etc.) If you make a menu command change, you may want to make it in more than one view.

2. Click **Custom Commands** tab.

3. Click **New**.

4. Enter a **Command name:** and **Tooltip Text:**. (Usually they will be the same.)

    The Command name is what displays in the menu. The Tooltip text displays when the mouse hovers over the icon on the toolbar.

5. Use the **Browse...** button to locate the command that you will use and click **Open**.

    If necessary, change the file type from **Executable Files (*.exe)** to **All files (*.*)**.

    By default, the browse button will search for commands to allow you to launch another program or applet from within ACT!.

    However, you can also add a file (such as a specific Word or Excel document, or ACT! template).

Feature Customizations | 377

6. Click the **Icon...** button to browse for a graphic file with an .ico extension.

7. Click **Add Command**.

8. Click the **Commands** tab.

9. Click **Custom Commands** under the Categories: column.

10. Drag your custom command to the View Toolbar and/or to the menu location of your choosing.

11. Right-click the command that you just placed, and select a style **Default Style**.

Most commands come with their own icon, but you can also assign a custom icon to your command if you have any.

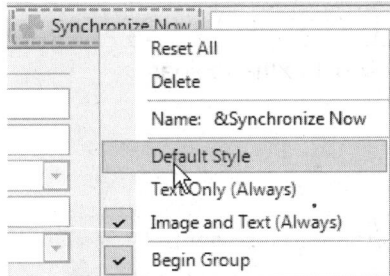

Let's do a quick exercise together to see how you might use this feature in ACT!. Let's say you print the same "Keeping in Touch-Birthday" template multiple times every day. It would be great to be able to add that template to the Write menu, to the toolbar, or to a keyboard shortcut. Well, you can.

Practice: **At Your Fingertips**	
What to do	**How to do it/Comments**
1. Start the Customize Menus and Toolbars process. First, create a new command.	**T**ools, **C**ustomize, **M**enus and Toolbars.... Click the **Custom Commands** tab and click **New**.
2. Make the command merge a Template. Name both the **Command name:** and the **Tooltip text:** **Birthday** Browse to the \Template folder to find file named: **Keeping in Touch-Birthday**.	Enter the Command name and the Tooltip text as indicated. Click the **Browse...** button, change the **Files of type:** to All files (*.*) then navigate to the \Documents and Settings\All Users \Shared Documents\ACT \ACT Data\Databases \ACT2012Demo-database files \Templates folder. Find the **Keeping in Touch-Birthday**. There should be two. Select the first one (with the .adt extension if you see it) if you are using Word. If you use the ACT! Word Processor, select the second one (with the .tpl extension) and click **Open**.

Sage ACT!

What to do	How to do it/Comments
If you are using Windows Vista and Windows 7, the path would be Users\Public\Public Documents\ACT\ACT Data\Databases\ACT2012Demo-database files\Templates	
3. Add the Command to the Custom Commands.	Click **Add Command**.
4. Add it to the toolbar.	Click the **Commands** tab. Select the **Custom Commands** from the Categories: column. Birthday displays in the Commands: column. Drag it to the toolbar; drop it where you want it to display.
5. Add it to the menu.	Now drag the Birthday command to the Write menu. When the Write menu displays, drag the icon to the location on the menu where it should display. Click **OK**. Click **Close**.
6. Test the two methods of generating the Birthday template (toolbar icon and menu item).	Notice the Tooltip when pointing to the icon on the toolbar.

 *If you have access to icon libraries or custom icons, you can also assign a custom icon to your command. Click the **Icon** button, locate and select the icon file. When you assign this command to a toolbar button, it displays the icon you selected.*

Resetting Toolbars, Menus, and the Keyboard

Somewhere along the line, you may find yourself wanting to put a toolbar, menu, or shortcut key list back to its original configuration. You can go to each item and delete the commands you added, but what if you can't remember what you did exactly? Fear not! To return a menu, toolbar, or shortcut back to normal, all you have to do is reset it.

Procedure: To reset toolbars, menus and shortcuts

1. Click **Tools, Customize, Reset Menus and Toolbars**.

2. Click **OK** to restore the defaults for toolbars, menu, and keyboard shortcut customizations. | This does not delete the Custom Commands that you have created. It returns *all* menu, toolbar, and keyboard shortcut options to their ACT! defaults.

Feature Customizations | 379

Practice: Clean Up Your Room

What to do	How to do it/Comments
1. Delete the custom commands.	**Tools**, **Customize**, **Menus and Toolbars…**. Click the **Custom Commands** tab, select the command we just created, and click **Delete**, **OK**. Click **Close**.
2. Reset your menu, toolbar and keyboard shortcuts.	**Tools**, **Customize**, **Reset Menus and Toolbars**. Click **OK**.

Modifying the Navbar

Not planning on using the Welcome page or the Dashboard feature and want to remove it from the Navbar at the left? Easy to do.

Procedure: To reset toolbars, menus and shortcuts

1. Click on the drop-down arrow at the lower right-corner of the Navbar.

2. Select **Navbar Options**.

3. Uncheck options that you don't want to see in the Navbar.

4. Use the **Move Up** and **Move Down** buttons as desired.

Creating Custom Web Info Links

The Web Info tab (found on the Contacts or Companies Detail View) contains some great links for browsing the Internet using pieces of data from the Contact or Company record. You can also add some of your own links if you like. However, it does require that you understand how the Website expects to receive search parameters.

Procedure: To create custom Web info links

1. In Detail View, display the **Web Info** tab.

2. Click **Edit Links**. Edit Links displays at the top of the tab.

3. Click **Add**. A new line displays at the bottom of the current link list.

4. In the **Site Name** column, enter a name for your link.

5. In the **URL** column, type or past the Web site address.
6. Click **Advanced Edit**...
7. Select a field at the right and click **Add**.   You can select other fields as well.
8. **OK, OK**

☞ *Perform a search as you normally would and notice the parameters in the search string to see if you could replace some of those parameters with the contents of an ACT! field.*

Practice: *Creating Some Web Links*

What to do	How to do it/Comments
1. Launch an Internet Explorer window and go to www.mapquest.com	Do this outside of ACT!.
2. Enter any valid address.	Try your home address.
3. Click in the Address Bar and copy the new Web address.	http://www.mapquest.com/maps?addressInput=315+Gateway+Center+Dr.%0ASan+Diego%2C+CA+92102
4. Create a MapQuest Link	In the Web Info tab, click **Edit Links**, click **Add**, type MapQuest in the Site Name. Paste the URL from MapQuest. Click **Advanced Edit**. Replace the actual field values (like CA) with fields (State) from the list at the right. **OK, OK**.
5. Test it on Lance Parker.	Look up Lance. Click the MapQuest link on the Web Info tab.
6. While on Lance's record, on the Personal Info tab, enter "yjbikes" in the Twitter field.	
7. Create a Web link for Twitter using the Twitter field found in the ACT! database.	In the Web Info tab, click **Edit Links**, click **Add**, type Twitter in the Site Name. The URL should look like this: http://twitter.com/ Click **Advanced Edit**. Scroll to the Twitter field at the right and click **Add**. (This field was added to the database.) Click **OK, OK**.
8. See what Lance is tweeting.	Click Twitter on the Web Info tab.

Feature Customizations | 381

Priorities

When you are scheduling any activity in ACT!, you can specify a **Priority:** of **High**, **Medium**, or **Low**.

- Setting a priority for an activity causes that activity to appear in a particular color on the ACT! Task List or Calendar views. Normally, Low priority activities appear in grey or black, Medium in blue, and High in red.
- The Task List and Calendar views can be filtered to display only specified levels of Priority.
- The Task List can be sorted and printed by Priority assignment.

Like many options available to you in ACT!, use of the Priority feature is a matter of personal choice. Some users are happy to allow the default (Low) to be assigned to all activities, while others like to segregate activities by their importance. Play with it and see what works best for you.

Customizing Priorities

At first glance, it would appear that there are only three priorities (Low, Medium, and High). Actually there are two more: **Medium High** (purple) and **Medium Low** (Aqua).

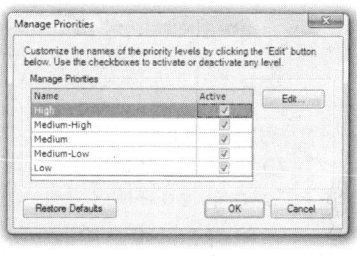

These two additional priorities (for the terminally detail-oriented) are turned off by default. If you need them, they are there for you, and (and this is the best part if you really, really want to take your schedule and wrap it around your little finger), you can change the names of the priorities to suit your needs.

 However, keep in mind that the priority assigned to an open activity will not display once the activity is cleared and placed in history.

Procedure: To Activate or Deactivate an existing Priority

1. Click **Schedule, Manage, Priorities…**.

   Only users assigned a Manager or Administrator role can make these changes.

2. Check any priorities you wish to activate and clear those you wish to deactivate.

3. Click **OK**.

   The next time you schedule an activity, only priorities you checked will be available.

Sage ACT!

Procedure: To edit a Priority name

1. Click **Schedule, Manage, Priorities…**.

   This feature can only be accessed by users assigned to a Manager or Administrator role.

   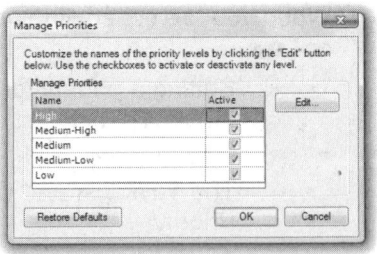

2. Click the priority you wish to edit and click **Edit…**.

   The **Edit Priority Name** dialog box displays.

3. Type the new name for the priority. Click **OK**.

   The priority name changes in the Manage Priorities list.

4. Repeat until all priorities have been renamed to suit you. Click **OK**.

   A dialog box lets you know what is about to happen. Namely, all existing Activities that used the original priority names will now use the new ones.

5. Click **Yes** to complete the process. ACT! changes the priority on all existing activities to match the new value(s).

   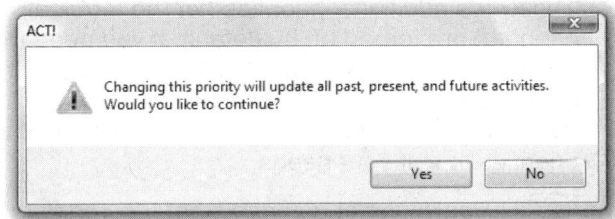

☞ *Deactivating a priority you have used in your scheduled activities will have no effect on those activities. They will continue to display the selected priority (as long as you select All), even though it will not be available to assign to future activities.*

Feature Customizations | 383

Practice: How Important Is It?

What to do	How to do it/Comments
1. Schedule a meeting with Sean Duffy for Next Tuesday at 3:00 PM regarding **Photo shoot for our new TechONE Component systems**. Make it a Medium-High Priority.	First enable the Medium-High Priority. Click **Schedule**, **Manage**, **Priorities**…. Put a check next to Medium-High (and Medium-Low if you like), and click **OK**. Then **Lookup**, **Last Name**… type **duf**, and click **OK**. Click the Schedule Meeting icon on the toolbar and set the meeting time and **Priority**. Enter the suggested **Regarding** and click **OK**.
2. Display the **Activities** tab, if necessary, and observe the new activity.	It's a different color than usual, isn't it?
3. Display the **Task List** view and filter All Activities to show only **High** and **Medium High** Priorities.	Display the **Task List** view. In the **Priorities:** clear **Medium**, **Medium-Low**, and **Low**.
4. Display all Priorities.	

Creating New Activity Types

ACT! comes with five basic activity types: Call, Meeting, To-Do, Personal Activity, and Vacation. However, you can create additional activity types. For example, if your business markets through trade shows, you might want to create a "Trade Show" activity type. You can also use this valuable feature to better manage your sales force by creating activity types that differentiate between Prospecting Calls and Maintenance Calls. The possibilities are endless.

Procedure: To create a custom activity type

1. Click **Schedule**, **Manage**, **Activity Types**….

    Don't create new Activity Types lightly. Once created, they cannot be deleted, only edited or deactivated. Only users with Administrator or Manager roles have the authority to create a custom Activity Type.

   Think it through carefully, and create only those you need.

   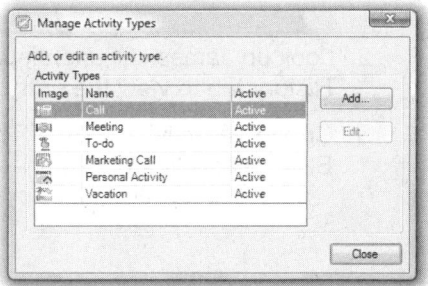

2. Click the **Add…** button.

384 | Sage ACT!

3. **Name:** the activity type.

   If you have access to icon files, you can use the **Browse…** button to select an **Icon:** for your new activity type.

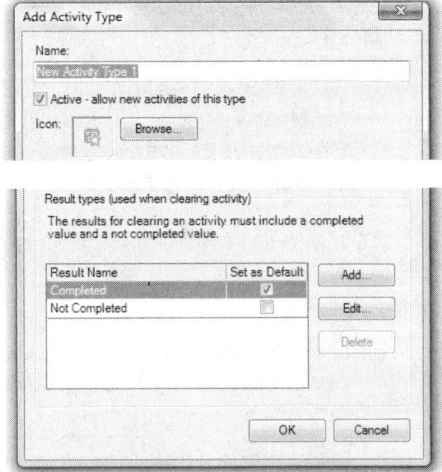

4. Select a Result, click **Edit…**, and modify the **Result name:** to include the new Activity Type name, and click **OK**.

   To add a new result, click **Add…**, type the new Result Name, and click **OK**.

 *If the Activity Type is "Focus Group," change **Completed** to **Focus Group Completed**. If you leave the default result name, all you will see in **History** is **Completed** with no indication of what type of activity was completed (or originally scheduled).*

5. Click **OK**.   The Activity is available to all users.

Practice: Using Custom Activity Types	
What to do	**How to do it/Comments**
1. Filter the Task List to display the Marketing Call activity type only. Clear the activity for James Hill.	Click the **Task List** icon on the Navbar. In the Type: drop-down, clear all but Marketing Call activity types. Put a check in the activity for James Hill to clear the activity.
2. Look up James Hill and display the History tab to view the entry.	Look up James and view the history entry for this cleared activity.
3. Create an Activity Type of Trade Show. Be sure to edit the results.	Follow the procedure outlined above to create a new Activity Type. Remember, while you can edit them, you can't delete these once they are created…so add carefully.

Feature Customizations | 385

What to do	How to do it/Comments
4. Schedule a Trade Show with Chocolate Trade Associations for February of next year (Their members are big users of the TechONE systems.)	Look up Chocolate Trade. **Schedule**, **Other**, **Trade Show**. Complete the activity information and click **OK**.
5. We scheduled the other Trade Shows as meetings. Change a few of them to your new Activity Type.	If you scheduled all of your trade shows this way, you could filter the Task List to view all upcoming Trade Shows.

Events

An Event is a notification that displays on all users' calendars. You can define either one-time events (Trade Shows, Conferences, or Company Picnics) or recurring events (Holidays or Employee Birthdays).

Events do not display in the **Task List** view, are not considered when checking scheduling conflicts, and do not transfer to Outlook if you are copying your calendars between ACT! and Outlook. In addition, Events are not included in ACT! reports.

Procedure: To manage Events

1. Click **Schedule, Manage, Events**....

    You must have Administrator or Manager role to create Events.

2. If any events have been defined for this database, they display in the **Currently scheduled events:** list.

   Click **Add**.... The **Add Event** dialog box displays.

   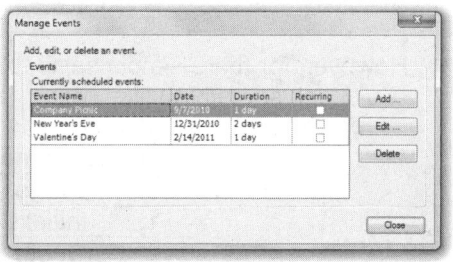

3. In the **Add Event** dialog box, give an **Event Name:**, a **Date:**, and a **Duration:**. Then choose the appropriate option from the **Occurs** section, and click **OK**.

   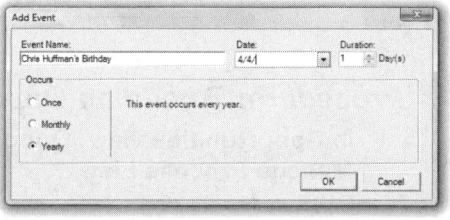

4. The event is now added to your list. Click **Close** when you are done.

   Repeat steps 2 and 3 for any other events you wish to add.

Practice: Creating Events

What to do	How to do it/Comments
1. Create an event for your Birthday and then check the Calendar for the specified date.	**Schedule**, **Manage**, **Events…**, click **Add…**, type "My Birthday" in the **Event Name:** box, select the **Date:**, choose **Yearly**, and click **OK** and **Close**.

Creating a Custom Opportunity Process

Your business may offer products or services that would have completely different sales cycles. Some product sales may have a quick turnaround and require only minimal follow-up. More complicated offerings may require additional steps to close the deal. You would most likely have a different way of following up on each of these opportunities.

For many opportunities, the **ACT! Sales Cycle** (or New Technology Process, or Promotional Sales Cycle) process works reasonably well. For example, the ACT! Sales Cycle is made up of six stages that a sales rep might go through to close a deal:

Process Name: ACT! Sales Cycle

#	Stage	Prob %
1.	Initial Communication	10%
2.	Needs Assessment	25%
3.	Presentation	40%
4.	Negotiation	65%
5.	Commitment to Buy	80%
6.	Sales Fulfillment	90%

However, for more simple sales, the sales process might be only two to three stages. It could look something like this:

Process Name: Phone Sale

#	Stage	Prob %
1.	Initial Communication	10%
2.	Quote Sent	50%
3.	Commitment to Buy	90%

Procedure: To add an Opportunity Process

1. In **Opportunities** view, **Opportunities**, **Manage Process List…**.	Click the **Opportunities** button on the Navbar. You must have an Administrator or Manager role to add or edit Processes.
2. Click **Create New Opportunity Process**.	

Feature Customizations | 387

3. Enter a process name (replacing New Process1) and optional description and click **Next>**.

   Enter opportunity process name and description

   Opportunity process:
   New Process1

   Description (optional):

   ☑ Active

4. Double-click **New Stage 1** and replace it with your first stage name.

   Keep the stage name short.

5. Enter a **Description** to better explain the stage.

   [Tab] to the field and enter a longer description to help your sales staff correctly identify what stage the opportunity is in.

6. Assign an associated probability with the current stage.

   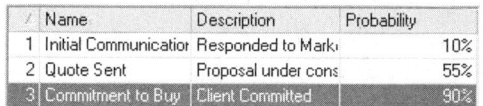

   Customize stages for Phone Sales

/	Name	Description	Probability
1	Initial Communicatior	Responded to Mark<	10%
2	Quote Sent	Proposal under cons	55%
3	Commitment to Buy	Client Committed	90%

7. Click **Add**. Repeat steps 4-6 for each new stage.

8. Click **Finish** and **Close**.

☞ To edit an existing process, click **Opportunities**, **Manage Process List...**, and double-click the process name.

Practice: Adding a Process

What to do	How to do it/Comments
1. Create a new process: **Phone Sale** with a description of: **No face-to-face presentation required**. Click **Next>**.	You must have an Administrator or Manager role to complete this exercise. Click the **Opportunities** button on the Navbar. **Opportunities**, **Manage Process List...**. Click **Create New Opportunity Process**. Enter the process name and description.

2. Enter the following stages:
 	
  #   Name   Description   Probability
  1. Initial Communication   Responded to marketing efforts   10%
  2. Quote Sent   Proposal under consideration   55%
  3. Commitment to Buy Client committed 90%	

Sage ACT!

What to do	How to do it/Comments
3. Finish and close the Process List window.	*Customize stages for Phone Sales* Name Description Probability 1 Initial Communication Responded to Mark 10% 2 Quote Sent Proposal under cons 55% 3 Commitment to Buy Client Committed 90%
4. Look up Yale Computer Company and create an opportunity for a "Service Contract". Using the "Phone Sale" process, select a stage of "Quote Sent". Enter an estimated close date for the end of this month.	**Lookup**, **Company**, Yale, and click **OK**. Click the **New Opportunity** icon. You don't have to enter an Opportunity name. You can just use the default. Change the Process to "Phone Sale." Select the second stage. Enter an Est. Close Date for the end of the month. Select Service Contract from the Product listings and click **OK**.

Creating Defined Product Lists

Products typed in the Name field of a New Opportunity are not automatically added to the list for other opportunities. If you want to make the product available for all opportunities, you must add it to the product list.

Procedure: To add an item to the opportunity product list

1. In Opportunities view, **Opportunities, Manage Product List…**.	Click the **Opportunities** button on the Navbar. You must have an Administrator or Manager role to add or edit Processes.
2. Click **Add**.	
3. Type the Name, Item Number, Cost, and Price of the product you are adding.	You can also import data into the Product list.
4. Click **OK**.	

Editing the Quote Template

You may want to make some minor edits to the template to more closely reflect your corporate image. Perhaps you would like to change the logo or add text at the bottom of the document about early or late payment. Before making any changes, make a backup of the template!

The opportunity quote template contains Microsoft Word formatting and an embedded Microsoft Excel table. You can edit and save changes to the Microsoft Word portion of the template, but any changes made to the embedded Microsoft Excel table are not saved…but there is a way around that.

Procedure: To edit "Quote.adt" template

1. Make a copy of the "Quote.adt" template for safekeeping.

    Before making changes, make a backup of the template! Really...this is important.

   Use Windows Explorer to copy this file from the **\[databasename]-database files\Templates** folder into the **\Backup** folder.

2. Click **Write, Edit Template...**.

3. Select Quote.adt and click **Open**.

4. Add text by placing the cursor where you want, and then begin typing. You can format the text as you type.

   Add mail-merge fields by selecting each from the **Add Mail Merge Fields** list, and then clicking **Add**.

   Delete fields by selecting the text, and then pressing **[Delete]**.

   To reopen the **Add Mail Merge Fields** box, on the Microsoft Word menu, click **ACT!, Show Field List**.

   If you replace the graphic with your corporate logo, you may want to right-click it, select **Format Picture...**, change Layout option to "In front of text," and click **OK**.

   If your quote numbers are long, drag the column divider to the left.

5. At the bottom of the quote, add comments about payment options or other marketing messages as desired.

   You can remove the "Office Use Only:" if you like.

   You could add text reflecting your charges for late payment or discounts for early payment. You could also include some marketing statement like "Check our Web page for daily specials."

6. Click **Save**.

   Do not change the name of the opportunity quote template (you may not be able to generate an opportunity quote if you do).

 Remember, don't make any changes to the embedded Excel file here.

Procedure: To add tax rate to the embedded Microsoft Excel template

1. Open Excel.

2. Make a copy of the Quote.xlt template for safekeeping.

    Really...this is important.

   Use Windows Explorer to copy this file from the **\[databasename]-database files\Templates** folder into the **\Backup** folder.

3. **File, Open...** change the **Files of type:** to Templates (*.xlt).

4. Display your **My Documents** (or **Documents**) folder. Then navigate to your…

   \[databasename]-database files\Templates folder

   Select **Quote.xlt** and click **Open**.

   Your files may be on the network somewhere.

5. Change the 0.000% value to your current tax rate.

   The cell should be around D29.

6. If your taxing authority requires that you charge tax on Shipping & handling, modify cell E29 to…

   =D29*(E27+E28)

   Be very careful when making other changes, as they could cause the embedded Excel template to stop working.

7. Save and close Microsoft Excel.

   *These changes will be automatically reflected inside the Word document the next time you click the **Quote…** button.*

Practice: Changing the Quote Template

What to do	How to do it/Comments
1. Add your local tax rate to the default quote template using the procedure just outlined.	The ACT2012Demo template is in: C:\Documents and Settings\All Users\Shared Documents\ACT \ACT Data\Databases \ACT2012Demo-database files\ Templates *If you are using Windows Vista or 7, look for the ACT2012Demo files in \Public\Public Documents\ACT\... etc.*
2. After you have made your changes to the **Quote.adt** and/or the **Quote.xlt** files, select and open any opportunity for editing. Click the **Quote…** button to admire your work.	

Activity Series & Smart Tasks

To help automate your workflow, you will:

- ☑ Learn to create Activity Series that lead you through each step of your more complicated work flows.

- ☑ See how Smart Tasks can automate some of your activities and e-mails based on pre-defined criteria.

- ☑ Understand the difference between manually assigning and automating the Smart Tasks.

Activity Series

You call a hot lead on Monday…you want to follow up the call with a letter on Wednesday…and another call on Friday. (That's the spirit; don't give them a moment's rest!) Normally, this would involve scheduling three separate activities. If this is a common scenario for you, you might want to create (and schedule) an **Activity Series**.

An Activity Series is … well… a series of activities. This pre-planned series of activities (all of them) is given a name and saved. When you are ready, you can schedule all the activities included in the saved Activity Series with one or many Contacts using only a few keystrokes.

The scheduled activities are based on an anchor date that you select when you schedule the Activity Series for a Contact. The date is used to define a starting point for scheduling … both before and after the anchor date. You can schedule each activity any number of days, weeks, or months before and/or after the anchor date. So, the anchor date might be the day a particular event takes place (like a conference or meeting), and you could schedule both pre-conference and post-conference activities. Or the anchor date might be the starting date for a series of activities that would follow (like a marketing campaign).

Procedure: To create an activity series

1. Click **Schedule, Manage, Activity Series Templates…**.

    The first **Activity Series Template Creation Wizard** dialog box displays.

2. Make sure **Create a new activity series** is the selected option (that is unless you want to edit an existing activity series).

    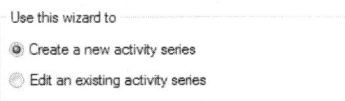

    Click **Next>**.

3. Give the series a **Name:**. The name can be just about anything but should be descriptive of the series. Add a longer description if you like.

    Choose whether this activity will be Public (all users can access it) or Private (for your use only).

    Click **Next>**.

Activity Series & Smart Tasks | 393

4. This is where the series is designed. You can add new (or edit existing) activities to your series.

   To create a new activity, click **Add...** to display the **Add Activity** dialog box.

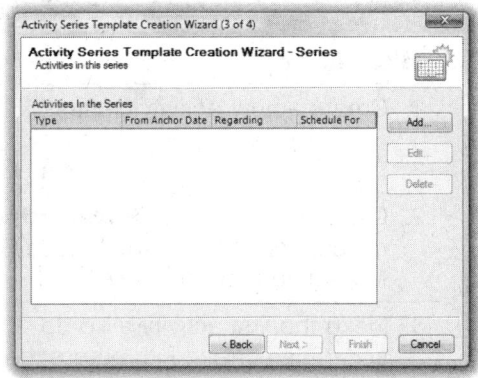

5. Select the **Activity Type:**.

   Complete the **Starts:** criteria indicating **Before Anchor Date** or **After Anchor Date** and specify the **Duration:**, if necessary.

   Enter a **Regarding:** line. You may want to consider prefacing the Regarding comments with something like "AS-TS:" (Activity Series-Trade Show:) so that you can differentiate between regularly scheduled activities and ones that are part of an Activity Series.

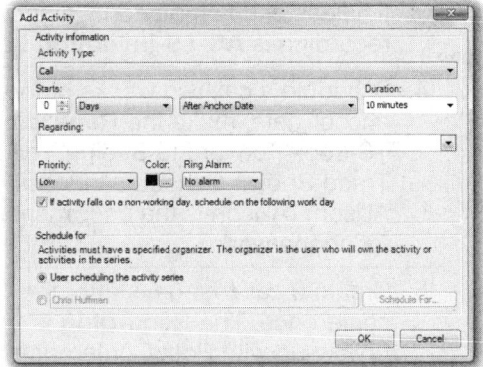

This makes it possible to assign a To-do that involves document production to a user who is in charge of that department in your organization. If an activity is not specifically assigned, then whichever user schedules the Activity Series is assigned to complete the activities for the Contact.

The second dialog box displays with the new activity.

☞ *There are three activity series already created for you that ship with ACT! (Confirm Information Change, Key Customer Communication Series and New Project Series), but you can create your own.*

Sage ACT!

Practice: Create a Series

What to do	How to do it/Comments
1. Create a new Activity Series.	**S**chedule, Mana**g**e, Activity **S**eries Templates…. Confirm **Create new activity series** is the selected option, and click **N**ext>.
2. Call the new series **TS Marketing**. The description should read "Trade Show Marketing and Follow-Up."	Enter the name of the series in the **Name:** box. Type the description in the **Description** box. Click **N**ext>.
3. Make the first activity a To-do scheduled one month before the anchor date. Set the duration to timeless and leave priority alone. The regarding is **AS-TS-Invitation Letter**.	Click **Add…** Change **Activity Type:** to **To-do**. Set **Starts:** to 1 Month, Before Anchor Date. Enter the suggested Regarding text (indicating that it is part of an Activity Series for a Trade Show). Click **OK**.
4. Schedule a call two weeks before the anchor date, make the **Regarding** "AS-TS-Look Forward to Seeing You at the Trade Show." Schedule this activity for Allison. (Allison is the user responsible for phone work.)	Click **Add…**. Change **Activity Type:** to **Call**, and set **Starts:** to 2 Weeks, Before Anchor Date. Enter the suggested regarding line. Click the second option at the bottom left of the dialog box and use the **Schedule For…** button to select Allison Mikola. Click **OK** and **OK**.
5. Create a call four days after the conference. The **Regarding** is "AS-TS-Follow-up with Post Conference Sales." Allow the activity to be assigned to the user scheduling the activity series.	Click **Add…**. Set **Starts:** to 4, Days, After Anchor Date and **Duration** to 0 minutes. Type AS-TS-Follow-up with Post Conference Sales in the **Regarding:** box. Click **OK**.
6. That's all. Don't schedule it for now.	**N**ext>, click **No, schedule later**, and then click **Finish**.

Scheduling an Activity Series

Scheduling an Activity Series for one or multiple users is a snap. You can schedule them manually, or you can define a field in your database to automatically schedule a particular Activity Series when you enter, exit, or change data in the field.

Activity Series & Smart Tasks | 395

Procedure: To schedule an activity series

1. Look up the Contact(s) you will schedule the Activity Series for.

   By default, the activities are scheduled with the current Contact.

2. Click **Schedule Series of Activities** in the Related tasks pane at the left, or from the menu, click **Schedule, Activity Series**.

   The "Schedule Series of Activities" option does not display in Related tasks if you are in Contact List View.

3. Choose the Activity Series from the **Activity series template:** drop-down list.

   Select the date from the **Series anchor date:** pop-up calendar.

   Note: If you wish to add more Contacts (e.g., from the current lookup), choose **Contacts▼, Select Contacts…** and add them to the list of selected Contacts. Click **OK** to return.

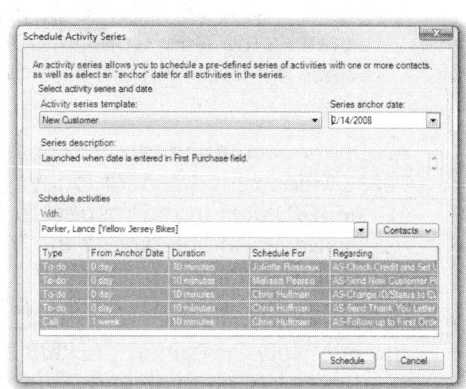

4. Click **Schedule** to activate the series for the current or selected Contacts.

   All of the activities in the series are scheduled with the selected Contact(s).

 Activities in an Activity Series are linked to each other. If you edit the date of one activity that is part of a series, then you will be prompted to update the rest of the series accordingly or only the current activity.

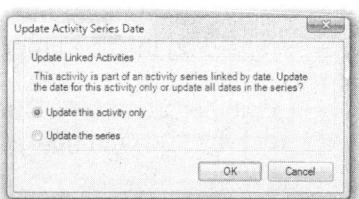

Practice: Using a Series

What to do	How to do it/Comments
1. We have a trade show coming up next November. Schedule the **Trade Show Marketing and Follow-Up** for Ashley Allan. Set the anchor date to the second Monday in November.	Look up Ashley Allan. Click **Schedule Series of Activities** from the Related Tasks pane and select **TS Marketing** (or choose another from the list). Click the second Monday in November from the **Series anchor date:** pop-up calendar and click **Schedule**.
2. Observe Ms. Allan's Activities list. Are the activities scheduled?	All of the activities are scheduled in their appropriate relationship to the anchor date.

What to do	How to do it/Comments
3. James Finlay is a new customer for the company. He made his first purchase today. Change the First Purchase date field to today and **[Tab]** or click out of the field. Notice that ACT! will prompt you to schedule the **New Customer** Activity Series when exiting the field. Schedule it.	Look up James Finlay. Enter today's date in the First Purchase field (you must be displaying the ACTDemo layout to see this field). Then click or **[Tab]** out of the field. The **New Customer** Activity Series window is launched and waiting for your response. Click **Schedule**. You can assign any Activity Series that you create to a Trigger in a field. See "Database Design & Layout" to learn how to do this.
4. On the **Activities** tab, you have four activities scheduled for today. Change the ID/Status from Prospect to Customer and then clear the "AS-Change ID/Status…" activity. Clear the Thank You letter activity as well.	Change the values in the ID/Status field. Uncheck Prospect and check Customer. Then mark the AS-Change ID/Status to Customer activity as completed. You can clear the **Add Details to History** option. Clear the Thank you letter as well.
5. The "New Customer" packets aren't in from the printer yet, and you won't be able to send one out for another two weeks. Notice the date for the follow-up call regarding the first order. Edit the "Send New Customer Packet" activity and change the date to a week later.	Double-click the "AS-Send New Customer Packet" activity to edit it. Change the date to the following week and click **OK**. Select to **Update the series** since you don't want to have a follow-up call for something that hasn't been sent yet. Click **OK**.
6. Notice that the remaining activities have all been rescheduled for a week later.	

What are Smart Tasks?

Smart Tasks are like virtual assistants that can automatically send e-mails on your behalf or schedule a single or multiple activities based on certain criteria. For example, you could create a Smart Task that would scan all of the contacts that you are responsible for and schedule an activity for any contact that you have not called in the past 90 days.

Which records?: Smart Tasks can be assigned to a single Contact or Opportunity record, the current lookup, or all contacts or opportunities in the database .

When?: Any Smart Tasks can be manually triggered (like an Activity Series), or they can be automatically scheduled to run at predetermined intervals.

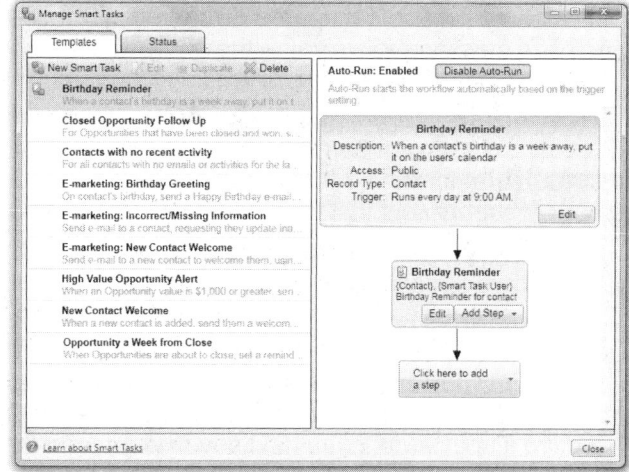

There are a few predefined Smart Tasks that ship with ACT! that can help you take care of common tasks. But you can use the easy visual designer to create as many Smart Tasks for you and your team as you like.

The predefined Smart Tasks templates are:

- **Birthday Reminder** – When enabled, ACT! searches the database each weekday at 9am to locate any Contact whose "Birth Date" is within the next seven days, and then automatically schedules a "Birthday Reminder" To-Do for the User that enabled this Smart Task.

- **Closed Opportunity Follow Up** – When enabled, ACT! searches the database each weekday at 9am to locate any Closed Opportunity with a Close Date of Today, waits seven days and then automatically schedules a Follow-Up call with the contacts associated to the opportunity.

- **Contacts With No Recent Activity** – When enabled, ACT! searches the database each weekday at 9am to locate any contact who has not been contacted by e-mail, phone or in person within the last 90 days and automatically schedules a "Follow up with…" To-Do .

- **E-marketing: Birthday Greeting** – When run manually against the current contact or lookup, the E-marketing feature immediately sends a personalized birthday message (it is not scheduled for their actual birthday). You must have a subscription to a Sage E-marketing for ACT! account for this to work.

Sage ACT!

- **E-marketing: Incorrect/Missing Information** – When run manually against the current contact or lookup, the E-marketing feature immediately sends a personalized message that includes the contact's basic contact information and asks the recipient to correct or supply missing information. You must have a subscription to a Sage E-marketing for ACT! account for this to work.
- **E-marketing: New Contact Welcome** - When run manually against the current contact or lookup, the E-marketing feature immediately sends a personalized message to welcome the contact to the company. You must have a subscription to a Sage E-marketing for ACT! account for this to work.
- **High Value Opportunity Alert** - When enabled, ACT! searches the database each weekday at 9am to locate any opportunity created within the last day whose value is greater than 1,000 and sends an e-mail to the Opportunity's Record Manager to let them know that they have a "High Value Opportunity Alert".
- **New Contact Welcome** – When enabled, ACT! searches the database each weekday at 9am to locate any contact created within the last day and automatically schedules an e-mail to be sent from Outlook (no other e-mail is supported) thanking the contact for their information. The e-mail will request permission before sending.
- **Opportunity A Week From Close** –When enabled, ACT! searches the database each weekday at 9am to locate all Open Opportunities were the Estimated Close Date is within the next seven days, and then automatically schedules a "Follow up on…" To-Do for the Opportunity's Record Manager.

Creating a Smart Task

You can easily create your own Smart Task. Start by creating the Type:

- Will it be run against a **Contact** or an **Opportunity** record?
- Will it be run **manually** or will it be **automated**?

Then you just add the steps that you want to accomplish with this Smart Task. Let's start by learning to create a simple manual Smart Task.

Procedure: To create a manual Smart Task

1. Click **S̲chedule, Manage Smart Tasks**.

   You can also click the **Manage Smart Tasks** link in the Related Tasks area of the Contact or Opportunity records.

2. Click the **New Smart Task** button on the toolbar.

3. Give the Smart Task a name.

4. Enter an optional description.

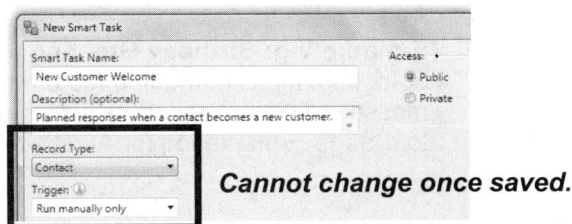

Cannot change once saved.

Activity Series & Smart Tasks | 399

5. Select the **Record Type:** (Contact or Opportunity).

    This selection determines what query type you can create if you select the Trigger to "Run at scheduled time"

6. Select the **Trigger:** type of "Run manually only".

    To see more about how to create a query to Run at scheduled time, review the procedure on page 409.

7. Click **OK**.

    Important: Once you click OK, you **CANNOT** change the Record Type or Trigger method.

 You cannot design a Smart Task in the ACT! web platform, but you can run ones that have already been created.

Practice: Creating a Manual Smart task	
What to do	**How to do it/Comments**
1. Create a new manual Smart Task named "New Customer Welcome".	**Schedule, Manage Smart Tasks**. Click **New Smart Task** button. Enter the name, description, keep the record type of Contact, and choose to run manually. Click **OK**.

Adding Steps to the Smart Task

You can add one or more steps to your Smart Task. Unlike the Activity Series where all stages are added at once to the Contact's record, Smart Tasks only display the current step in the sequence. The next step will appear when you have marked the current one as completed.

Procedure: To add a step to the Smart Task

1. In the **Manage Smart Tasks** dialog, be sure the desired Smart Task is selected.

    This is a continuation of the previous procedure.

2. Click the add step button and select the type of step you want to create.

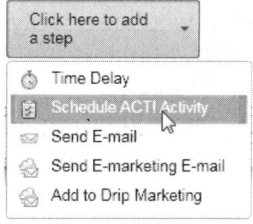

2a. **Schedule ACT! Activity:**

Enter the **Step Na̲me:** to display in the Pending Smart Task dialog (more on this later).

Put a check in **Automatically sc̲hedule...** unless you want to be prompted to launch this task.

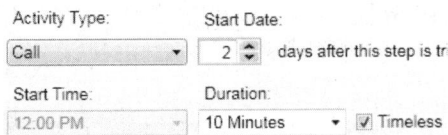

Consider prefacing the **Step Name:** with the **step number** if you are creating a multi-step Smart Task (so you can keep track of where you are in the automated task).

Select the **Activity Ty̲pe:**, the number of days to delay the **Start D̲ate, Start T̲ime, D̲uration**, etc. (See, you don't need the Time Delay for an Activity step.)

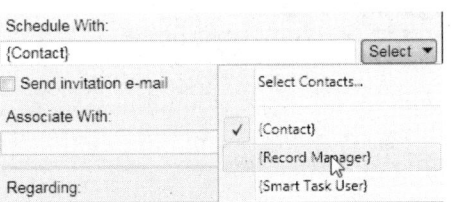

Select who to **Schedule With:**. The default is to schedule it with the current {Contact}, but you can also use the **Select** button to schedule with the {Record Manager} {Record's Contact List} (if you are displaying Opportunities) or the {Smart Task User} who runs the task.

For example, you might create a conference call and **Schedule With**: the Contact and the Record Manager and **Schedule For** the sales manager in your company

Enter the activity **Regarding**. Consider prefacing the regarding text with "[Smart Task name]-step number" to make it clear it was created from a Smart Task and where you are in the process.

Select who the activity should be **Scheduled For:** from the drop down.

Select from the {Smart Task User} who runs the Smart Task or a specific user in the company.

Click the **Details** tab to add any necessary information. **OK**

OR...

Activity Series & Smart Tasks | 401

2b. **Time Delay:** Used before the "Send E-mail" or "Send E-marketing E-mail" step to delay sending. Set the number. Change to Days or Months (can't think of any reason to use Minutes or Hours). Then click **OK**.

OR…

2c. **Send E-mail:**
Enter the **Step Name:** to display in the Pending Smart Task dialog (more on this later).

Automatically schedule… I prefer to leave it unchecked so I am prompted to view before sending the e-mail. It allows me to add additional notes to the e-mail before sending or cancel the send.

Click the Contacts button to select {Contact} to send **To:** the selected contacts.

You might send a **CC:** to the contact's {Record Manager} or to the {Smart Task User} who launched the Smart Task.

Enter the desired **Subject:** line for the e-mail.

Preface the Step Name regarding text with "[Smart Task name]-step number".

Browse… to select any **Attachments:** you want to include.

Enter the desired **Message:.** Don't forget to include a full signature.

The e-mail will be sent through Outlook, but will not use your default signature. It will be sent **From** the user that launched the Smart Task.

Note: Mail merge fields cannot be included in the message.

Click **More Options** and select the **History Type:** for this e-mail.

Put checks in the remaining options only if desired (I hate receiving Read Receipt e-mails).

Click **OK**.

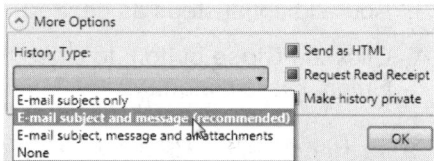

The Send as HTML option will accept some HTML code, but you will want to thoroughly test before sending to a real client.

OR...

2d. **Send E-marketing E-mail:**
   Enter the **Step Na̲me:** to display in the Pending Smart Task dialog (more on this later).

   Click the **Select Template** button to choose a template for mail merging with the current contact or lookup.

   Enter the desired **E-mail Subject:** line for the e-mail.

   Enter a **Personal Message** if you like and the template allows.

   Click **OK**.

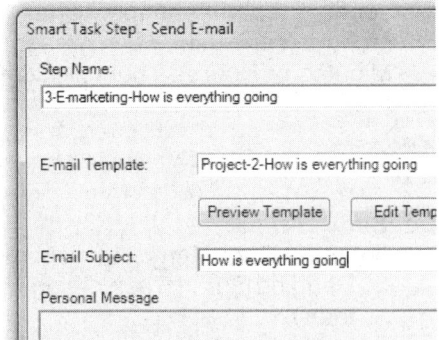

Consider prefacing the name with "**[Smart Task name]-step number**" along with your regular regarding text.

 If this step is included in the Smart Task, then the ACT! user who runs it must have their own Sage E-Marketing Account with the selected E-mail Template in their account.

OR...

2e. **Add to Drip Marketing:**
   Enter the **Step Na̲me:**

   Use the drop-down to **Select a Drip Marketing Campaign** (See E-marketing chapter.)

   Click the **Manage Drip Marketing Campaigns** to go to the Campaign Manager view.

   Click **OK**.

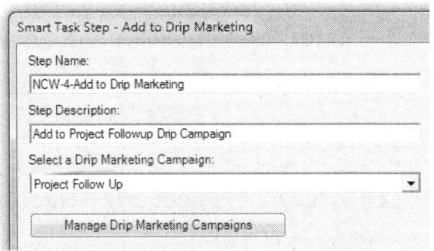

Consider prefacing the name with "**[Smart Task name]-step number**" along with regular regarding text.

3. Add additional steps as desired.
4. Click the **Close** button to close the Manage Smart Tasks dialog.

 *The **Add to Drip Marketing** or **Send E-marketing E-mail** options require a Sage E-marketing for ACT! subscription for the current ACT! user.*

Activity Series & Smart Tasks | 403

The E-marketing E-mails can include mail-merge fields from your database and may contain graphical elements. The basic **Send E-mail** option may not include any mail-merge fields (including [Salutation]) and should primarily be considered a text only document. In addition, the **Send E-mail** option is the only one that can be sent to someone other than the contact, can include a CC: and/or an Attachment.

Practice: Adding Steps

What to do	How to do it/Comments
1. Add "steps" to the **"New Customer Welcome"** Smart Task you just created. Add a reminder to call the customer to thank them. Automatically schedule.	Click to add a step. Select **Schedule ACT! Activity**. Name it "NCW-1-Call to welcome customer". Be sure that "Automatically schedule…" is checked. Change the Activity Type to Call and start date for 0 days and timeless. Schedule with the {Contact} only. Make the Regarding, the same as the Step Name. Click **OK**.
2. Add a To-Do to remind yourself to send them a hand-written note. Do not automatically schedule.	Since you put a check in the first task to automatically schedule, don't put one here so you can see the difference when you run the Smart Task. Use a Step Name of "NCW-2-Send hand-written note of thanks". Use the same text for the Regarding.
3. Wait 1 minute and add an e-mail that includes your phone and e-mail. Don't forget to include your full e-mail signature. Click the More Options button and be sure to add a history of the send.	Add a step for a Time Delay. Normally 1 minute is way too short, but we are just playing here. Then add another step for Send E-mail. Enter a Step Name of "NCW-3-Email Contact Information". ☞ *You cannot use mail merge fields in the e-mail.*
4. You can add an E-marketing E-mail step if you have an account.	
5. Click **Close** when finished.	

Manually running a Smart Task

Now that you have a Smart Task created, it is time to run it.

☞ *Any filter defined for the selected Smart Task is ignored when it is run manually.*

Procedure: To run a Smart Task

1. Create a lookup of the Contact(s) or Opportunity(s) for the Smart Task.

2. Click **Schedule, Run Smart Task…**

    or right-click the layout and select Run Smart Task

3. Select a Smart Task to run.

    If you are displaying contacts, only Smart Tasks created with a Record Type of Contact will display. If you are displaying Opportunities, only Smart Tasks created with a Record Type of Opportunities will display.

4. Select from **Selected records, Current Lookup,** or **All Contacts**.

    If you are in Contact Detail view, the current contact is the selected record. If you are in Contact List view, the can tag the records you want to apply the Smart Task to.

5. Click **Run**.

6. Click **OK** to acknowledge that the Smart Task has been started.

    You can also click "Do not show this message again" to bypass this message in the future.

7. If the first step was not checked to automatically run, then the Pending Smart Task Steps dialog will display for you to select and Run the next step. Select the task and click **Run**.

    It the step is an e-mail, you can click the **Preview** button to make any necessary changes before clicking **Send**. Once you have clicked **Preview** the task is removed from the Pending status and the next task is triggered.

☞ *If the Smart Task contains multiple steps, only the first step will display. No future steps will be scheduled until the previous step is cleared.*

Activity Series & Smart Tasks

Practice: Run with it

What to do	How to do it/Comments
1. Lookup your own contact information in the database (or add it if necessary). Run the New Customer Welcome on your contact record.	Lookup your name. Click **Schedule, Run Smart Task...**, select New Customer Welcome and click **Run**. Notice that the first task is scheduled immediately, but you don't see future tasks.
2. Clear the first task (to call the new customer).	On the Activity tab (or in the Calendar), clear the activity.
3. In the Pending Smart Task Steps dialog that displays, select the next To-Do step and add it to the Activity tab. ☞ *Remember we didn't make this one automatic.*	Notice that the Pending Smart Task Steps dialog displays to prompt you to add the second task (which is a To-Do) to your calendar. Notice how it displays in the dialog. Select the activity and click **Run** to add it to the Activity tab.
4. Clear this second task.	It will be a minute before the third Send E-mail step is initiated.

Pending Smart Task Steps

You can use the Pending Smart Task Steps dialog box to Preview, Run or Delete Smart Task steps that have been assigned to you.

Procedure: To handle pending Smart Task steps

1. Click **S**chedule, Show **P**ending Smart Task Steps....

2. Select the step you want to **Preview** or **Run**.

   Show Details determines whether you can see the Contact (or Opportunity) name and the Smart Task that launched the step.

   Click the **View Status of all Smart Tasks** hyperlink to display the Status tab in the Manage Smart Tasks dialog.

   You can **Preview** an e-mail to add more, or verify existing, information before sending. You can also preview an Activity to change any details, regarding, etc. before scheduling the activity with the contact.

   If you select **Run**, any selected e-mail will be immediately sent and recorded in history. An activity will be immediately scheduled with the appropriate contact(s).

*If you click Preview for an e-mail step, you MUST send or save it to drafts, or the step will be cancelled. The same is true of activities. If you click Preview, click **OK** to complete the changes. If you click Cancel on the Activity, (even if you didn't make changes), the activity step will not be created and the Smart Task will be cancelled for the selected record.*

Don't have time to review and deal with the pending steps at the moment?

You can snooze this dialog by selecting the next time you want to be reminded to run or preview the pending steps from the drop-down.

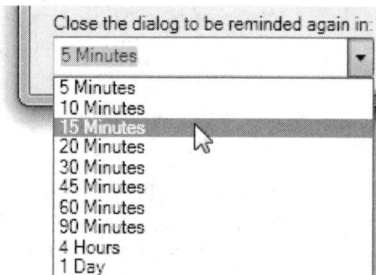

3. Click **Close**.

 You can only select and deal with one step at a time. Each step runs automatically and is then cleared from the queue.

Practice: **Pending**	
What to do	**How to do it/Comments**
1. We've been waiting for the next step to launch. Click on **Schedule, Show Pending Smart Task Steps** to see what displays.	

Status of Smart Tasks

Regardless of how many Smart Tasks you have scheduled, it is always good to keep track of where you are. The Status tab displays a list of Smart Tasks by Contact or Opportunity Record.

The Status tab displays which Smart Tasks are Completed, Cancelled, Paused, In Progress, or In Progress – Awaiting User. Since the next step in the Smart Task will not be executed until the current step is completed… reviewing the status of Smart Tasks on a regular basis is a good idea. (You can quickly see if anyone is holding up the process.)

From this dialog you can Pause, Resume, or Cancel the Smart Task, but you cannot view which steps are pending, cannot complete any individual step or go to the Record with the pending task to see any additional information about the task (like who are we waiting on). Click the **Show Pending Smart Tasks Steps Dialog** hyperlink at the top of the window to clear any pending tasks.

Activity Series & Smart Tasks | 407

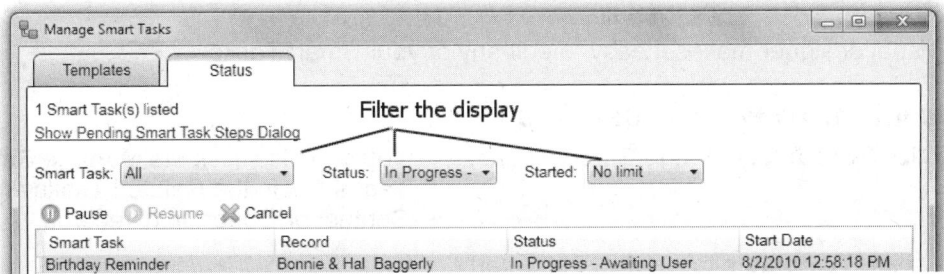

Procedure: To view the status of all Smart Tasks

1. Click **Schedule, Manage Smart Tasks**. You can also click the **Manage Smart Tasks** link in the Related Tasks area of the Contact or Opportunity records.

2. Click the **Status** tab at the top.

3. Use any of the three filter tabs at the top to narrow the list of Smart Tasks.

4. Click the **Show Pending Smart Tasks Steps Dialog** hyperlink at the top of the window if you want to handle some of the pending tasks that are displayed. You can also clear any of the Activity tasks from your Task list or Calendar views.

5. Click the **Close** button.

Practice: Smart Task Status	
What to do	How to do it/Comments
1. View the status of all Smart Tasks.	Click **Schedule Manage Smart Tasks** and click the **Status** tab. This tab only displays contacts by Campaign. Specific steps are not listed. Notice the filters at the top of the view.
2. Close all Smart Task windows. Check your Inbox to see if the e-mail arrived. Check your History tab to see the history that was entered for the Smart Task E-mail send.	

Editing a Smart Task

The visual designer makes it easy to edit any of your Smart Tasks

Procedure: To edit a Smart Task

1. Click **Schedule, Manage Smart Tasks**.

   You can also click the **Manage Smart Tasks** link in the Related Tasks area of the Contact or Opportunity records.

2. On the **Templates** tab, select the Smart Tasks template.

3. Click the **Edit** button of the step you wish to modify or click **Add Step** to create additional steps in the Smart Task.

4. When you have finished with each step, click **Close** to complete the changes.

 If you edit a Smart Tasks template, the changes will not take effect until the next time the Smart Task is run by each user. If the Auto-Run is enabled, then the changes will not take effect until the next time the Smart Task is triggered to run. If you want the changes to be available immediately, you must notify all possible users that if Auto-Run is enabled, Auto-Run must be disabled. After disabling Auto-Run, each user can click Enable Auto-Run to restore Auto-Run for the Smart Task.

Practice: Editing

What to do	How to do it/Comments
1. Edit the New Customer Welcome Smart Task. Notice what options you can change.	**Schedule, Manage Smart Tasks** Select the NCW task and click **Edit**. Review options and then close the dialog.

How Does A Smart Task Run Automatically?

A good understanding of Advanced Queries (see page 249) is important if you want to trigger the Smart Task to run against the database on a scheduled basis. When Auto-Run is enabled, at the time you specified, the Smart Task is run for all records that meet the criteria.

For a Smart Task to run automatically,

- ACT! must be open,
- there must be a trigger that specifies **when** the Smart Task is run and
- criteria has been created to specify **which** records (contacts or opportunities) the Smart Task should be run against.

Activity Series & Smart Tasks | 409

Procedure: To create an automatic Smart Task

1. Click **Schedule, Manage Smart Tasks**.

   You can also click the **Manage Smart Tasks** link in the Related Tasks area of the Contact or Opportunity records.

2. Click the **New Smart Task** button on the toolbar.

3. Give the Smart Task a name.

   ☞ *It is a good idea to add a date to the end of the name since you will probably use the option Run Only Once (see #12 below).*

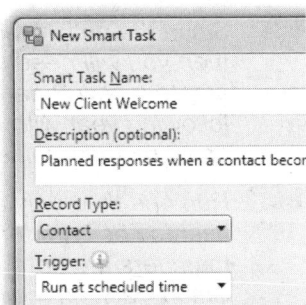

4. Enter an optional description.

5. Select the **Record Type:** (Contact or Opportunity).

   This selection determines what query type you can create if you select the Trigger to "Run at scheduled time"

6. Select the **Trigger:** type "Run at a scheduled time".

7. Select from **Daily**, **Weekly** or **Monthly**.

8. Choose either Every # days or Every weekday.

   Unless you do a lot of work on the weekends, "Every weekday" probably works.

9. Set the time of day that you want the Smart Task to run.

   The default is 9am, but you can change it to a time when you are more likely to have ACT! open on your PC.

10. Click the **Edit Criteria…** button and create your Smart Task criteria. For more information on creating criteria, see the procedures starting on page 249.

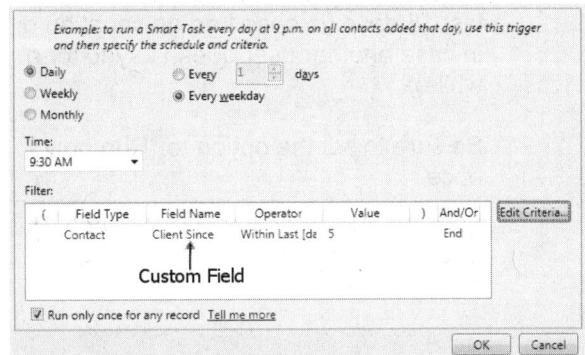

11. Click **OK** and click **OK**.

    Important: Once you click OK, you **CANNOT** edit or change the Record Type or Trigger method. However, you can return to modify the criteria.

12. Put a check in the **Run only once for any record** option.

    ☞ *It is only available for Smart Tasks that use Criteria.*

    ☞ *Since the option will run only once, then you will need to copy and create a new Smart Task for the following year with a new name to continue the reminders.*

    ☞ *Run one time only applies for same user, so be sure that multiple team members are not running the same Smart Task on their workstation.*

    This option prevents a Smart Task from being run against a record multiple times.

    For example, if the criteria chooses all records created in the past 5 days (to allow it to continue to pick up contacts synced from remotes… ones that were added while you were out…, etc.), it will only add the Smart Task once to any record if this option is checked.

13. Add one or more steps as discussed starting on page 399.

14. When finished, click the **Close** button.

Practice: Creating an automatic Smart Task

What to do	How to do it/Comments
1. You cannot edit an existing manual task to make it automated. Create a New Task to run Daily on every weekday at 9:30 am.	
2. Create a criteria for Create Date is with last 15 days (in case I go on vacation or in case another user doesn't sync for a while). Be sure to set the option to "Run only once…"	In reality, I would not use this criteria. We have a field in our database called "Client Since" so that I can keep track of when they actually became a client. This would be a better date field to use. But this is just practice.
3. You can add steps if you like or not. This is just for practice.	

Activity Series & Smart Tasks | 411

Enabling a Smart Task
Before enabling a Smart Task against your entire database, it might be a good idea to test it by manually running it against a few internal records. If it works as you expected, then you can enable it to run automatically.

Procedure: To create enable an automatic Smart Task

1. Click **Schedule, Manage Smart Tasks**.   You can also click the **Manage Smart Tasks** link in the Related Tasks area of the Contact or Opportunity records.

2. Select the Smart Task at the left.

3. Click **Enable Auto-Run** at the upper right.

           [Enable Auto-Run]

4. The **Pending Smart Task Steps** dialog may display if you have any pending tasks. It may not have any tasks related to the current Smart Task.   To disable auto-run, do the same procedure again. The button is a toggle.

☞ *Enable Auto-Run enables the Smart Task for the current workstation.*

Smart Tasks vs Activity Series

Features	Activity Series	Smart Tasks
How Do They Run?		
Manually run on current contact or lookup	X	X
Automatically run based on criteria		X
Trigger activity on field change (see Define Fields)	X	
Trigger activity based on an anchor date (before or after)	X	
Trigger activity to begin on completion of a previous step		X
Preview steps before they are scheduled/send	X	X
Preview all future steps	X	
Can complete steps out of sequence	X	
What Will They Do?		
Schedule For Specific or Launching User (not for Record Manager)	X	X
Schedule Activity "With" Contact and Record Manager (not For)		X
Automated e-mails (can view before launching) and record in history		X
Create and send Sage E-marketing e-mails		X
Convert scheduled date to work day from a weekend, if necessary	X	
Admin Stuff		
Create, Edit, or Delete Templates	X	X
Copy from one database to the next – Sorry – neither one	☹	☹
Copy existing Smart Task to facilitate creating similar tasks		X

X = Works

Criteria for when to use Activity Series

- You need to see the complete list of tasks to be accomplished (not just the next one) or you may need to accomplish list items out of sequence.
- Your tasks are based on an Anchor Date (tasks to accomplish before the Trade Show and tasks afterwards... unless you want to add to a Sage E-Marketing Anchor Date Campaign
- You want to launch a series of tasks when a field is changed in the database.

Criteria for when to use Smart Tasks

- You want to automatically send an E-mail or schedule an activity based on the results of a query that is run on a scheduled basis.
- You want to schedule for or include the Record Manager (not available in Activity Series).

Activity Series & Smart Tasks | 413

Keep These Suggestions in Mind

- The simpler, the better.
- Name and number your Smart Task steps.
- Have one person in control of all Smart Tasks
    - Review Smart Task Status regularly
    - Review Pending Smart Task Steps regularly
    - Don't shut down your PC for long periods
- If you run on the server, ACT! must remain open, and have Outlook installed (Outlook Express doesn't work) if e-mails are included in the Smart Task, and have its own Sage E-Marketing account if necessary.
- Watch for potential log jams by others, since the next activity will not display until the current one is completed.
    - If for another user, check to automatically schedule.
    - The Awaiting User is only activities assigned to you. You would have to log in as another user to see if they had any Smart Tasks awaiting their completion.
- Consider running everything in Manual mode.

Drip Marketing vs. Smart Tasks

The Sage E-Marketing Drip Marketing feature (see page 236) is designed to create a series of marketing messages that are automatically sent to selected contacts on a pre-determined time sequence (think Activity Series with automation). In many ways, Smart Tasks can duplicate that process, but on a smaller, more individual scale. Check out the following grid to see some of the differences between the three options.

Features	Sage Drip Marketing	Smart Tasks	Activity Series
"Duration" Campaign (see page 238)	X	X	X
Anchor Date or Calendar Campaigns (see page 238)	X		~
Include Mail Merge Fields	X		
Automatically E-mail	X	X	☹
Automatically send letters, postcards, make calls	X		
Filter a specific step/stage by previous response	X		
Filter a specific step by field criteria	X		
Add contacts to Drip Marketing Campaign by Group	M		
Add contacts to Drip Marketing Campaign by criteria		X	
Review e-mail before executing (but not SPE)		~X	M
Remove contacts from campaign	M	M	M

X = Works   M = Manual process   ~ = Can work, but more difficult

Using Smart Tasks for Service Contract renewals is a great use of this feature. If you have a field in your database for Contract Expiration, you could set a query to run 45 days prior to expiration to fire off a series of client follow-up tasks.

Designing Dashboard & Reports

To understand and better manage your business through reporting, you will:

- ☑ Examine the Report Designer window.

- ☑ Create and modify report templates.

- ☑ Place fields on the report, add and size report sections, and add subreports.

- ☑ Learn to define report filters.

- ☑ Practice previewing and printing custom reports.

Creating Your Own Dashboards

Users with a Manager or Administrator role have the ability to customize individual Dashboard components or create totally new Dashboards. In addition to customizing the existing components that we just reviewed, Managers or Administrators can add or remove components, change titles or legends, and use drag-and-drop functionality with the Dashboard Designer for easy customization of any existing Dashboards or creation of new Dashboard components. If you are using ACT! Premium, you can also set default filters to view all (or selected) users' data for further analysis.

 Regardless of the number of Dashboards that you create, they will be available to all users of the database.

Dashboards are designed (and edited) using a step-by-step wizard that offers a **Preview** button at each stage to help you create the view that you need. Let's start by creating a new Dashboard. Then, editing existing ones will be a snap.

 If you don't allow enough room on the layout, components may not be able to show full data without user interaction.

Procedure: To create your own Dashboard from scratch

1. Click the **New Dashboard** hyperlink in the Related Tasks pane at the left.

   You must have an Administrator or Manager role to complete this task. New Dashboards start with a default two-column, three-row, blank table-grid.

2. **File**, **Save**, enter a new Dashboard name, and click **Save**.

   The default display is optimized for an 800 x 600 screen resolutions with six cells (two columns by three rows).

3. **File**, **Layout Settings…**, select the optimum screen resolution size for the users in your company, and click **OK**.

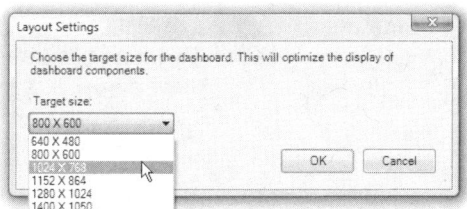

4. Use the **Format** menu to **Insert** or **Delete** cells, columns, or rows in your Dashboard view.

Designing Dashboards & Reports | 417

5. To add a component to one of the cells, you can right-click and select **Add Component** or drag one of the components from the Activities, Opportunities, or Custom groups under the Toolbox at the left.

   Once you have selected an Activity or Opportunity component, a dialog box displays where you can start a wizard to help you design your panel. You will need to double-click Custom components to modify their settings. Settings for Custom components are discussed at the end of this procedure.

6. Click the **Select Display Type** as your first component task.

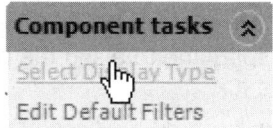

☞ *The Component tasks available at the left will vary depending on the component type you selected.*

7. **Select Display Type** - (Display types will vary depending on the component type selected.)

   Select from the types available. Change the Filter bar placement (Above or Below Display), if you like. Click the **Preview…** button to see your progress.

   Click **Next>**.

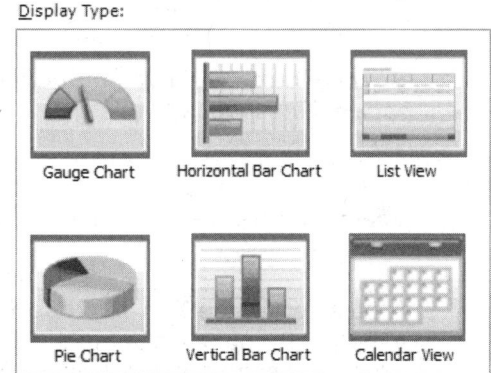

8. **Edit Default Filters** - Specify your default filters and click **Next>**.

   These options will be used as your defaults. They can always be changed by the individual user using the **Filter** button.

9. **Edit Header/Footer** - Change the default header text and font style as desired. Add a footer if you like and click **Next>**.

   Don't forget to click **Preview…** to check your display.

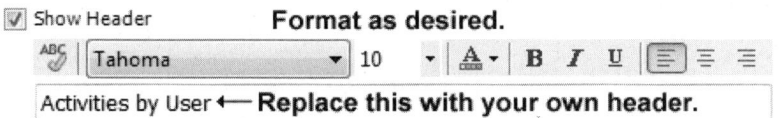

10. **Change Legend** - Change the location of the Legend (or remove its display) and click **Next>**.

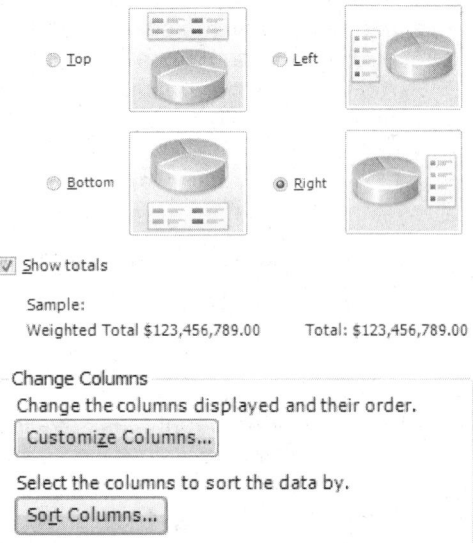

11. **Change Totals** - Indicate if you want to display the totals in the panel and click **Next>**.

12. **Change Columns** – If you selected a List View display type, you can choose the default column display and sort options.

13. **Specify Target** – Click the **Show target option**, if desired, add a target, and click **Next>**.

    Activities and Opportunities targets are in units (number of activities or opportunities as in 100 cold calls/month). Closed Sales targets are set with dollar values.

14. **Scale/Limits** – Select your scale, if desired.

    Use this option to scale opportunity sales display from billions, millions, thousands, hundreds, etc., so that the axis numbers are not so large.

    If you selected the **Top 10 Opportunities** component, you can change the default for selecting the top 10 from Total to Weighted value.

    The Gauge display type in the **Closed Sales to Date** component, allows additional settings in the Scale/Limits screen. The **Maximum:** might be the stretch goal for either the company or the user. The **Minimum:** can be set to 0 or some other threshold.

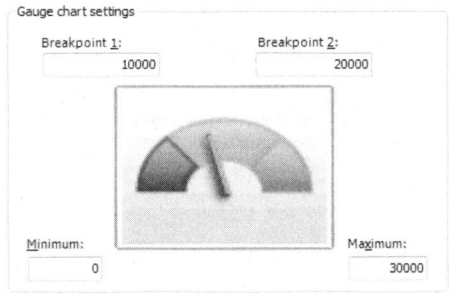

Designing Dashboards & Reports | 419

Breakpoint 1 could be set to display the minimum acceptable sales. **Breakpoint 2** might indicate the level at which bonuses might apply.

You can use the chart settings to indicate whatever works for your company. The current sales will be reflected by the needle. The **Target** triangle is set in the **Specify Targets** section.

 Consider adding the same component multiple times to show different views. If you are using ACT! Premium, one panel might display Allison's Closed Sales and another display Ernst's. You could also create regional dashboards to display opportunities by East or West team members, etc.

Custom Components

There are several custom components that ship with ACT! that you can add to any of your dashboards.

Procedure: To add a Custom Component to your Dashboard

1. When creating or editing a dashboard, click on the **Custom** slider bar in the **Toolbox** at the left.

   Keep in mind that Custom Components are not clickable like the Activities or Opportunities components.

2. Drag the **Data Chart** component to the desired pane.

3. Double-click the component.

   The Data Chart Designer displays.

4. Choose a template.

5. Check to **Show Data as Chart** if you prefer graphic output.

   Otherwise, the display will be in list view format.

   Select the Chart Type.

   The same chart types are available here as are for the Activities and Opportunities components.

   Indicate if you want to show a Legend or Point Labels. Check to display the chart in 3D.

   Usually you will select Legend or Point Labels... both might be redundant.

6. Enter a Header and a Footer for the Chart.

   By default, the Header will be the same as the chosen template.

7. The **Preview Data** button displays the Filter Criteria that is available for the end-user.

8. Click **OK** to save the changes.

Sage ACT!

Practice: Create Your Own Dashboard

What to do	How to do it/Comments
1. Create a new dashboard, named "My Dashboard".	In Dashboard view, click the **New Dashboard** button. Click **File**, **Save**, enter My Dashboard, and click **Save**.
2. Add a My Schedule At-A-Glance component.	Drag the "My Schedule At-A-Glance" component into the upper-left cell.
3. Change the default filter to display only Meetings.	Click **Next>** or click **Default Filters**. From the **Types:** drop-down list, click None, and then click Meeting.
4. Change the Header to "My Meetings At-A-Glance".	Click the **Edit Header/Footer** Component task and edit the Header text.
5. Save your changes for this cell so that you can add another.	Click **Finish**. Answer **Yes** to acknowledge that your filter changes will affect all users. Click **Close**.
6. In the cell to the right of the one you just created, let's add a My Activities (or an Activities by User) component.	Drag the **Activities** component into the upper-right pane.
7. Create this view to display tomorrow's activities in a List View.	Use **Select Display Type** to choose the List View display type and click **Next>**. Change the **Dates:** filter to display **Tomorrow** and click **Next>**.
8. Change the Header to Tomorrow's Activities.	Change the default header to the suggested title and click **Next>**.
9. Have ACT! display the totals.	Click the **Show totals** option and click **Next>**.
10. Add Phone to the list of displayed columns.	Click **Customize Columns…** Double-click Phone from the Available fields option and move it up.
11. Save your changes.	Click **Finish**, **Yes** and **Close**.
12. Make the second row a single, wide cell.	Click in the second row of the Dashboard. Click **Format**, **Delete**, **Cell at End of the Row**.
13. Add the My Opportunities (or Opportunity by User) component to the second row.	Drag the component to that row.

Designing Dashboards & Reports | 421

What to do	*How to do it/Comments*
14. Make this panel a Vertical Bar Chart display, filtered to display opportunities that are estimated to close this month. Only display opportunities that are in the Presentation stage or higher.	Click **Select Display Type** and select the Vertical Bar Chart. Click **Next>**. Click the **Stage** drop-down option and remove the check marks from the first two stages. The default **Dates:** is probably already set to the current month. Click **Next>**.
15. Change the title to "Hot Opportunities".	Change the header and click **Next>**.
16. Enter a target of two opportunities for each stage of the opportunity.	Click **Specify Targets** Component task. Click the **Show target** option and enter a target number of 2.
17. Save your changes.	Click **Finish**, **Yes**, and **Close**.
18. View your handiwork.	**File**, **Save** and **File**, **Exit**. You will need to change the Dashboard view to the one you just created.
19. Delete the bottom row of the dashboard and view your work.	Click the **Edit Current Dashboard** icon. Click **Format**, **Delete**, **Row at the Bottom**. Click **Finish**. Click **Close**, **File**, **Save**, and then **File Exit**.
20. On the **ACT! Contacts Dashboard**, replace one of the components with the Custom Component of **Contacts by Country**.	On the **ACT! Contacts Dashboard**, click the **Edit Current Dashboard** icon. Delete a component, drag the **Data Chart** component (under Custom slider bar) to the desired pane. Double-click the new component to select the template and modify the options. Save and view.

Alternative Dashboards

 If you find you are having problems with developing dashboards that give you the information that you need, you might look at this add-on product to help you develop more advanced dashboards.
http://bit.ly/ToplineDash

Report Templates

Report templates can be designed based on Contact, Company, Group, Product, or Opportunity information and can include calculated values such as totals and averages of numeric data. Report templates are not only used for reports, but they are also used for envelopes and labels.

Reports can sort, organize, group, and otherwise make sense of large amounts of data. Report templates are easy to create once you understand the Report Design screen.

- If ACT! already has a report template that suits your needs, you should use it.
- If ACT! has a report template that almost meets you needs, you can modify it.
- If none of the report templates provided by ACT! suit your needs, you can create your own.
- Once saved, new reports are added to the Reports view.

ACT! provides a wide variety of these templates, and you may find that they suit all of your needs initially. Eventually, however, you may want to modify a template or create one for a purpose not thought of by the creators of ACT!.

 The following procedures and practice sessions are based on a Contact report. However, you can transfer any of the skills learned to one of the other report types (Companies, Groups, Opportunities, or Products).

Procedure: To create a new report template

1. Click the **New Report Template** in the Related Tasks pane, or click **Reports**, **New Template...**.

2. Select one of the **Report Types:**, at the left.

    Select from Contact, Company, Group, Opportunity, or Product.

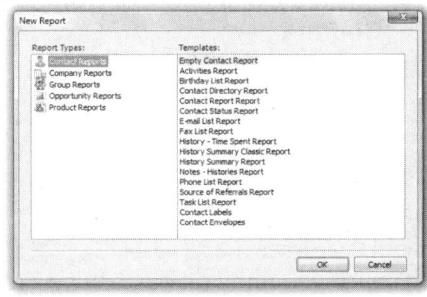

3. Then select one of the basic **Templates:** designs at the right that most closely matches what you need or select the Empty Report.

    This creates a starting template with some basic fields already placed on the report or displays a blank template for you to start from scratch with.

4. Click **OK**.

    ACT! displays the design view for a new, blank report template.

Designing Dashboards & Reports | 423

Practice: A New Report Template

What to do	How to do it/Comments
1. Before we start the report template, **Lookup**, **All Contacts**.	You should always create a lookup prior to creating a report so that you have data to test the report with.
2. Create a new report template for a Contact report using the "Empty Contact Report" design.	**Reports**, **New Template...**, select one of the **Report Types:** (like **Contact Reports**), and then select the **Empty Contact Report** design to start. Click **OK**.
3. Observe the template in the Report Designer window.	
4. Leave the report displayed.	

The Report Designer Screen

The Report Designer screen is initially divided into five sections: the **Report Header** section, the **Page Header** section, the **Detail** section, the **Page Footer** section, and the **Report Footer** section. A label displays at the top left of each section.

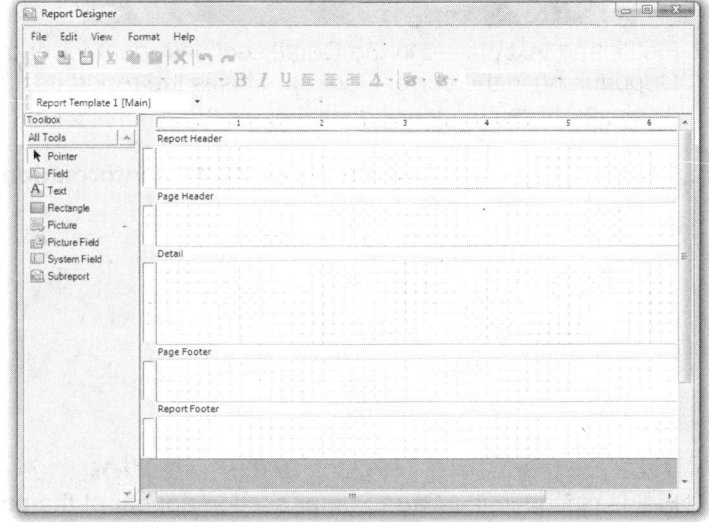

To create a report, you place text and fields on the Report Designer screen. The section where you place your text or fields determines the position of data on the printed page.

The Report and Page Header Sections

Fields and text placed in the **Report** Header section appear once at the beginning of the report. Objects placed in the **Page** Header section appear at the top of every page. Any data you wish to display at the top of every page in the printout should go in the Page Header section.

Some examples of header information might be:

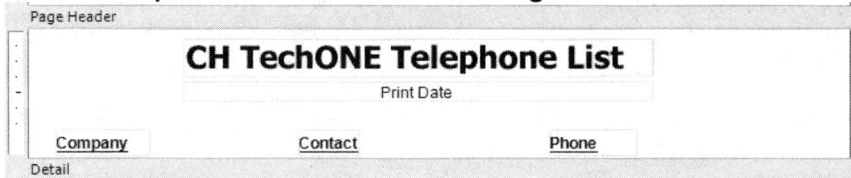

- The title of your report
- The date the report was generated
- Column headers

The Detail Section

Fields and text placed in the Detail section repeat for each Contact (or Group or Company or Opportunity) in the current lookup. This is the report itself. Any field in the database can be displayed here.

Some examples of Contact Detail Section information might be:

- Company name
- Contact name
- Phone number

The Report and Page Footer Sections

Fields placed in the **Page** Footer section appear at the bottom of each page in the printout.

Some examples of Page Footer information might be:

- Date and/or time the report was generated
- Page number

Designing Dashboards & Reports | 425

Fields placed in the *Report* Footer appear on the last page of the printout. This is usually a good place for Summary fields.

Beyond these obvious differences, there are many similarities between the Report Designer and the Layout Designer screen (the screen for designing the layout of Contact record information, remember?).

- Fields and text are added to a report in the same way as they are added to a layout (pages 362 and 366).
- Fields and text are formatted in a report the same way as they are in a layout (page 367).

In other words, if you know how to add objects and format a layout, you know how to do the same in a report template.

Adding Report Objects

You start designing your reports by placing the fields you want your report to contain in the appropriate section.

Procedure: To place fields in your report

1. Start in Report Designer view.   **Reports**, **New Template...** or **Edit Template…**, select a template, and click **Open**. Be sure to Save As to give the report a new name if you are designing a new report.

2. Click the Field tool.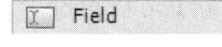

3. Use the mouse to draw the field to the approximate size, shape, and position you want.   When you release the mouse after drawing the field on the report, the **Select Field** dialog box displays.

4. **Select a record type:**
   The drop-down list at the top of the dialog box lets you select a record type (based on the type of report you are creating). Once selected, it displays the corresponding list of available fields.

   The record type of **Contact** provides a list of fields that relate to the Contact record. The **Contact Note** type provides fields that relate to the **Notes** tab, the **Secondary Contact** type contains fields displayed on its associated tab, etc.

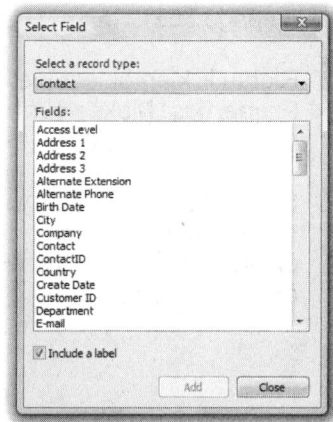

*Just because you can insert a field from the record type of **Contact Note** in the Detail section, doesn't mean it will work. Insert only fields that are consistent with the type of report you are building. If you want to insert some Contact Note or Contact Opportunity fields, then you will need to add a subreport to contain those fields.*

5. Once you've selected the record type, click on the field you wish to add to the report.

6. Choose whether to **Include a label**. A check box at the bottom left of the dialog box is supplied for this.

7. Click **A̲dd**.

    You can place a single field multiple times within the same report.

   The field displays on the layout at the location you just created with the mouse.

8. You can click additional fields and click **A̲dd** to place them on the report below your original field. These fields match the original in size and horizontal position.

9. Click **Close** when you're done.

 *You may have noticed the **My Record** record type in the drop-down list. When this box is selected, the fields you add to the report display the information from your My Record only. Use this option only in the Header or Footer of the report where you wish your name or other information about you to appear.*

Formatting

Formatting reports is done the same way as formatting layouts. If necessary, view those procedures (starting on page 356).

Right-click an object (field or label or graphic) and select **Properties.** Make your formatting changes and click **OK**.

Select multiple objects to update at the same time using the **Properties** dialog box. You can also press **[F4]** to display the **Properties** window for complete control of any selected object.

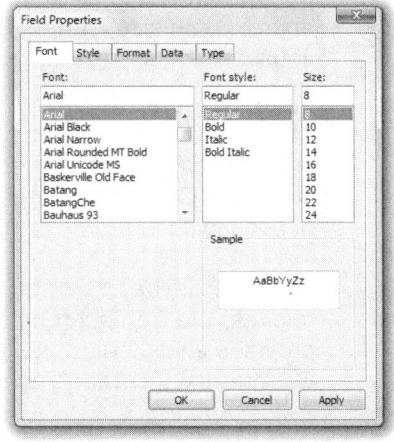

Designing Dashboards & Reports | 427

Practice: Creating a Custom Phone List

What to do	How to do it/Comments
1. In the Page Header section, add a text label that reads: **CH TechONE Telephone List**. Make the text **Bold** and **18 points**. Resize the label (if necessary) to display all of the text.	We started a new report template in an exercise on page 423. You should still be in Report Designer. In the Toolbox, click the Text tool, drag a box in the top left corner of the Page Header section (between the words Page Header and Detail). Click outside of the box, then double-click inside the text box and enter **CH TechONE Telephone List**. Click the report background and then click the box again to select it (handles should appear around the box). Click the Bold icon and change the type size to **18** using the toolbar. If necessary, enlarge the text box by pointing to the right handle (the mouse pointer becomes a two-headed arrow), and drag to the right until all the text is visible.
2. At the top right of the Page Header section, add the **Contact** and **Phone** fields from the My Record. Do not add field labels.	Click the Field button, and drag the first field at the top right of the Page Header form. Clear the check from the **Include a label** check box. From the **Select a record type:** select **My Record**. Click **Contact**, click **Add**, scroll to select **Phone** and click **Add**. Click **Close**.
3. Add a "Print Date" field just below the report title and line it up on the left side with the title.	Print Date is a System field. Click the **System Field** button, drag a box below your report title, select **Print Date** (clear **Include a label**) and click **Add** and **Close**. Drag over the two objects to select them. **Format**, **Align**, **Left**.
4. Save the report to the default folder and call it **CHT1 Phone List**.	**File**, **Save As...**, type the file name, and click **Save**. Your report should look roughly like the example above.
5. Print Preview to view the report so far. Then close the Preview window.	**File**, **Print Preview**. Click the **Actual Size** icon on the toolbar to more clearly see your report. Click the **Close** button.

428 Sage ACT!

What to do	How to do it/Comments
6. To the Detail section of your report, add the following fields. **Contact** **Phone** **Mobile Phone** **Home Phone** Include the field labels for these fields.	Click the Field button and drag the first field in the Detail section (between Detail and Page Footer, about an inch from the left margin). Leave the check in the **Include a label** check box. Select **Contact**, click **Add**, and repeat with **Phone**, **Mobile Phone**, and **Home Phone**. **Close**.

Detail section contains:
- Contact [C:Contact]
- Phone [C:Phone]
- Mobile Phone [C:Mobile Phone]
- Home Phone [C:Home Phone]

Is it a Field or a Label?

With so many record types from which to choose, it is possible to become confused as to the source of the fields on your reports. Fields are enclosed in [square brackets], and the field name is preceded with a code. There are equivalent codes for Groups, Companies, and Opportunities.

C: = a field from the Contact table [C:Contact]

My: = a field from My Record (your personal information) [My:Contact]

SC: = a Secondary Contact [SC:Contact]

CA: = an Activity field [CA:Regarding]

CH: = a History field [CH:Regarding]

CN: = a Note field [CN:Regarding]

CO: = a Contact Opportunity field [CO:Opportunity Name]

System fields (like Print Date) have no indicator.

Text and Field Labels also display without any special indicators.

Designing Dashboards & Reports | 429

Sizing Sections

You may need to remove extra space in report sections. Or, you may need to expand them to allow for more field placements.

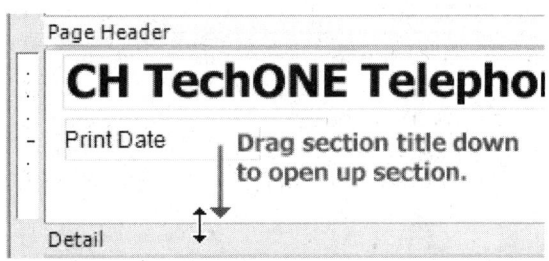

For each field you place in the Detail section of a report, that data will be repeated for each Contact included in the report. In addition, any extra vertical space in the Detail section of the Report Designer screen reflects the space each record will take up on the printed page.

- If the Detail section is 1.5 inches high, each Contact record will take up 1.5 inches of space on the page.
- If the Page Header section is two inches high, including fields, text, etc., then the header will take up the first two inches of every printed page.
- The space in the Page Footer section takes up as much space on each page as displayed in the Design screen.

It is likely, therefore, that you must change the size of sections from time to time (actually, most of the time) to suit your needs. Fortunately, this is easy.

Procedure: To size a report section

1. Place the mouse pointer over the bottom of the section until it becomes a two-headed arrow.

   Section sizes are controlled by the separator line at the bottom of each section.

2. Click and hold the left mouse button and drag the bottom of the section up or down as needed.

   You cannot make a section smaller than its current contents or the lowest field.

 You have probably already noticed the horizontal "grid" lines that run across each report section. Any item you place on a report automatically fits between these lines.

Practice: Sizing and Dressing Your Report

What to do	How to do it/Comments
1. Make the Page Header larger so that we can add column labels in this section.	We want column headers at the top of every page. Drag the separator line at the bottom of the Page Header section (top of the Detail).

430 | Sage ACT!

What to do	How to do it/Comments
2. Drag the field *labels* up to the **Page Header** section and arrange them as column headings. Arrange the fields below each label and size accordingly.	Click each field or label to select it and drag to the desired location. Try to make your report look like the illustration below.

What to do	How to do it/Comments
3. Save your report.	Click the **Save** button.
4. Print Preview your **Telephone List** report.	**F**ile, Print Pre**v**iew.
5. Observe the problems with the layout.	The labels at the top of each column do not align with the data in the column. There is waaaaaaay too much space between the Contacts.
6. Close **Print Preview**.	Click the **C**lose button.
7. Line up the column headers.	Drag over the labels (Contact, Phone, Mobile, etc.) to select them. Click **F**ormat, **A**lign, To**p**. While the labels are still selected, use the arrow keys to move the labels up just enough to allow for a horizontal line placed beneath them.
8. Use the Rectangle tool to create a horizontal line in the Page Header section below the column labels. ☞ *A line is just a skinny rectangle.*	Click the Rectangle tool in the Toolbox. Click in the ruler section at the left and start to drag a thin line across the Page Header below the column headings. If you start in the ruler at the left, the line will automatically display the entire width of the report.

Designing Dashboards & Reports

What to do	*How to do it/Comments*
9. Select each of the column labels and its corresponding field and left-align them.	You cannot drag over these fields because the line is in the way. Click the Contact field and **[Shift+click]** the Contact column label, **F**ormat, **A**lign, **L**eft. Repeat for each of the phone numbers. ☞ Remember, alignment is determined by the object with the black handles.
10. Line up the fields (horizontally) in the Detail section and place them at the top of the section.	Drag over the fields (Contact, Phone, Mobile, etc.) to select them. Click **F**ormat, **A**lign, **Top**. While the labels are still selected, use the arrow keys to move the fields up to the top of the Detail section.
11. Size the **Detail** section so it uses as little space as possible.	Drag the bottom of the Detail section up as far as it will go.
12. Add a page number to the **Page Footer** section with a label of "Page:" and close up any remaining space.	Click the System Field tool and drag a control in the Page Footer below the Detail section and about an inch from the left margin, click Page Number, click **A**dd, and then **C**lose Drag the **Footer** section title up as far as it will go.
13. Preview the report. Does it look a little better? However, it is not sorted by last name.	**F**ile, **Print Pre**v**iew**.

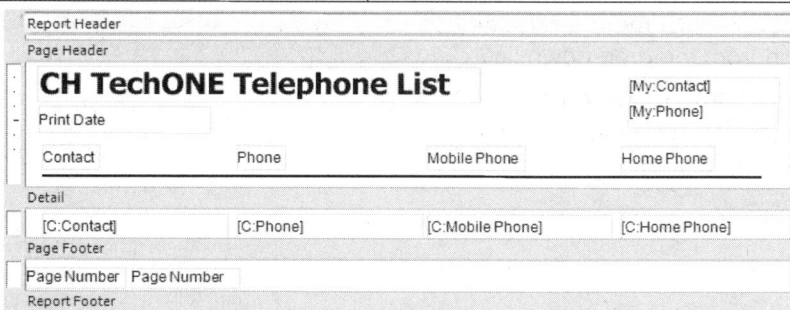

14. Close **Print Preview** and make any adjustments (like closing up empty space in the Report Header and Footer). Save and close the report.	**F**ile, **C**lose, **Y**es. The report should look similar to the example below.

Using Group By for Sorting or Subtotals

Contact reports are sorted alphabetically by Company name (the default unless you have selected a different sort order by clicking on a column in List View). If you would like to modify the sort order, you can add a section that will group (and thus sort) the report by any field that you select. For example, in the report we have been working on, the list is sorted by Company name, even though the Company field is not included in the report. A **Group by** section can help us rearrange our phone list in alphabetical order by the Contact's name.

Sections can also be added to allow for calculations by group. For example, if we grouped the same list by State, you might want to display a total for how many Contacts are in each state.

Procedure: To create a new section in a report for sorting the output

1. While editing a report template, double-click any section header to display the **Define Sections** dialog box or choose **Edit**, **Define Sections...**,

    or right-click and select **Define Sections...**.

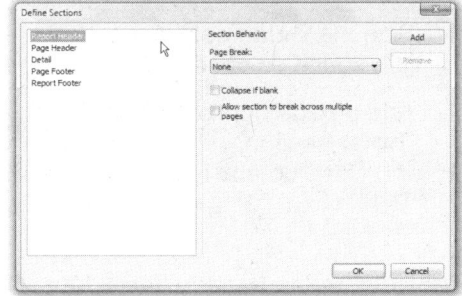

2. Click the **Add...** button.
3. **Select a record type:** for the new section from the drop-down list.
4. Click the **Field to Group By**. Your selection will determine the sort order of the report.

    Click **OK**.

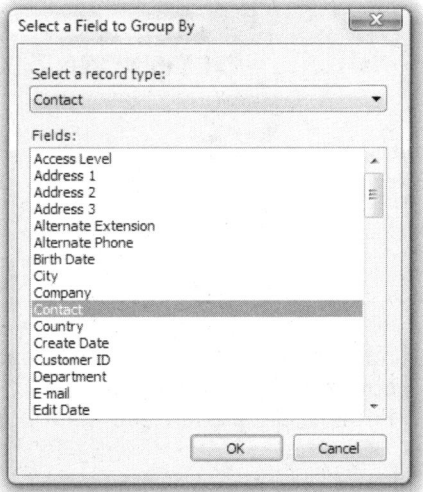

Designing Dashboards & Reports | 433

5. In the Define Sections dialog box, click the **Section** you added, and define the Sorting: behavior. (See the option descriptions below.)

   Sorting allows you to select from Ascending (usually used for character fields) or Descending (usually used for numeric or Date fields).

6. Then click the **Section - Header** that you created and define the Section Behavior.

   Add a Page Break if desired. Allow the section to **Collapse if blank** (which is a good idea). Also **Allow section to break across multiple pages**, if desired.

7. Define the desired behavior for the **Section – Footer**.

8. Add more sections if you wish, and click **OK** when done.

   The report displays with the new section added. Both a Section Header and Section Footer are added for each new section that you define.

9. Be sure to close up any unused section headers or footers.

   So the additional blank space will not appear in the report.

Section Behavior

Each report section can also have options set for it that control how the section reacts when the report is printed.

Page Break: Several options allow you to place a page break Before (or at the beginning of) the specified report section. You can also select After, Before and After, Page Before and Page After.

Collapse if blank does not display fields or any associated titles if the fields are blank.

Allow section to break across multiple pages allows a section to wrap to another page instead of moving the entire section to the next page.

Once you master sections, a wide variety of reports are possible. With a little practice, you can create some amazingly detailed reports.

☞ *We won't pretend that the Report Designer is easy to understand. The best way to understand sections and how they relate to each other is to practice. If you make a mistake, try again. So, let's try adding a simple section.*

In this next practice, we will begin to look at sections. We will start by using the simple **Group by:** option to sort the report by Contact name. This section can also contain totals.

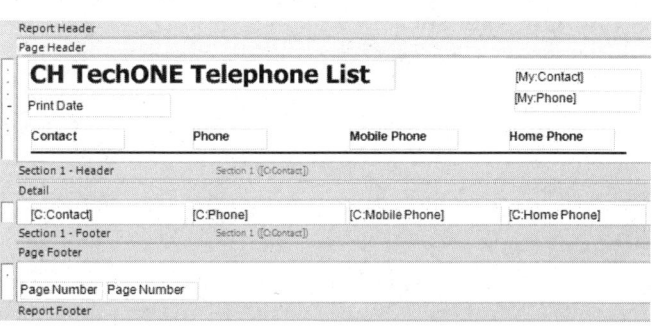

Practice: Sorting by Last Name

What to do	How to do it/Comments
1. Make the Phone Report sort by Contact name.	Choose **Reports**, **Edit Report Template...** select **CHT1 Phone List**, and click **Open**.
	Double-click one of the section bars to display the **Define Sections** dialog box. Click **Add**. Leave the record type as Contact. In the Fields area, select **Contact** and click **OK**. Click **Section** 1 and notice that the default sort order is Ascending. That works for this list. Click the **Section 1 – Header** and notice the **Section Behavior** options. Click **OK**.
2. **Print Preview** to verify that your sort options work. Save your work so far.	**File**, **Print Preview**, review the list to verify the sort, then click **Close**. Save your work.
3. Close up the **Section 1 – Header** and **Section 1 – Footer** and preview the report again.	The section was added for sorting purposes only. We don't need to move any data into the header or footer sections. However, we need to close up the sections so the report doesn't display a header and footer around each name.

Summary Fields

ACT! provides several ways to summarize the data in your database. You can generate a Count of specific fields (this counts all fields – not unique fields). You can also calculate a Total, Average, Minimum, or Maximum for a specific field as long as the field is defined as a number-based or date-based field.

Procedure: To place summary fields in your report

1. While editing a report template... use the **Field** tool to place the field you want to summarize in a Header or Footer section.	This is probably the second time you have placed the field on the report... only this time if will be a summary of that field.

Designing Dashboards & Reports | 435

2. Once placed, double-click the field to display its **Field Properties**.

3. Click the **Data** tab.

4. Click **Summary** Field Type.

5. Select the type of calculation you would like to perform.

   ☞ *Not all calculation types may be available for the field you have selected. For example, you can only **Count** character fields.*

6. Click **OK**.

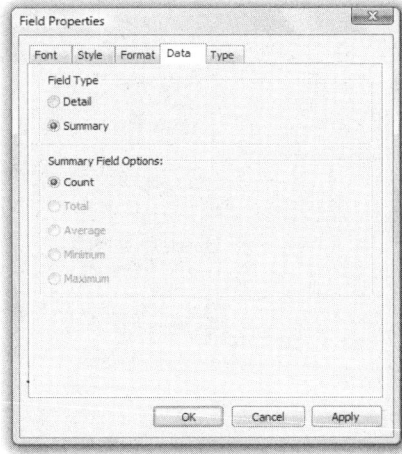

7. Modify the label to reflect its new value (e.g., "Total Contacts").

   Double-click the label to edit it.

Practice: How Many Are There?

What to do	How to do it/Comments
1. Let's add a summary field to the end of the report to see how many Contacts are in the list. You have to pick a field for the summary. Why not use the Create Date as the field to summarize?	If necessary, expand the Report Footer to allow for a new field. Use the Field tool to place the **Create Date** field in the Report Footer section. Double-click the field to edit the Field Properties. Click the **Data** tab. Click the **Summary** Field Type. Count is already selected. Click **OK**. Double-click the label to change the text to read: "Total Contacts =." Adjust the fields so that they display properly. Make the label right-aligned and the field left-aligned.
☞ *You could use Contact, however, you could have a record in the lookup that contains a company name and no contact name, so the summary field would not display the intended answer. However, every record has a Create Date.*	
2. Print Preview the report.	

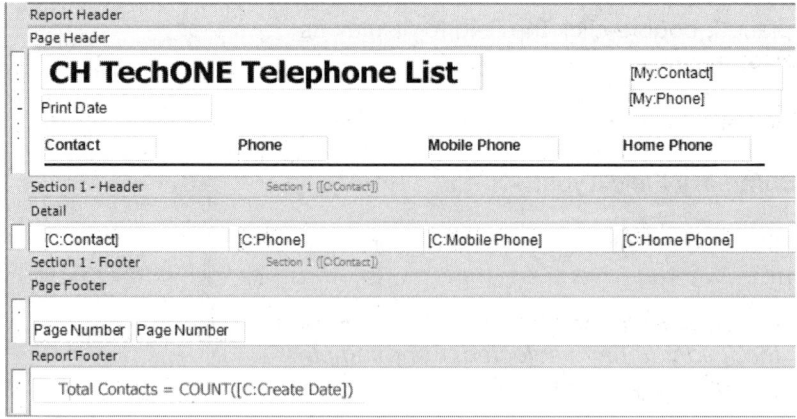

Subreports

If you would like your custom report to include data from one of the **system tabs** that displays its information in list views of columns and rows (such as Notes or Opportunities or Secondary Contacts... but not the User Fields tab), you will need to add a **subreport**. For example, to display a list of Opportunities for each Contact in your report, you can create a subreport that contains whatever Opportunity information you would like to display. If you would like to display all notes for each Contact in your report, you can add another subreport to display those as well. The date filtering for the notes will be handled at printing time.

So while regular fields are displayed in **sections** (like the Detail section), data from the Notes, History, Activities, Documents, Opportunities, Groups/Companies, and/or Secondary Contacts list view tabs are displayed in **subreports**. You can also use subreports if you are creating a Group report and want to display records from the **Contacts** tab (or any of its other list view tabs).

While you can right-click to display the most commonly used properties for most objects, you can also view the complete properties available for change by pressing **[F4]** to display the **Properties** window. Properties for fields will differ from properties available for labels and text, as well as properties available for sections and subreports. As you begin to design more complicated reports, you will want to become more familiar with using this dialog box. Explanations for any selected Property option is displayed at the bottom of the Property window.

Procedure: To insert a subreport

1. Open the existing report template in edit view or create a new report and place regular fields as desired.

Designing Dashboards & Reports | 437

2. If necessary, insert the field "ContactID" into the Detail section.

    If you are creating a new report, or if you are modifying a report that never had a subreport, then you need to add a unique linking field.

Click the Field tool and drag a place holder in the Detail section. Clear **Include a label**, select the **ContactID**, click **Add** and then **Close**.

 If you are developing a Company or Group report, the linking field would be CompanyID or GroupID. For an Opportunity report, it would be OpportunityID.

 The linking field is necessary to be sure that the right subreport data is linked to the right Contact. It does not need to display.

3. To make the ContactID field invisible, press **[F4]** to display the **Properties** window. Change the Visible property to False. Press **[F4]** again to close the **Properties** window.

The Visible option is the last one in the Appearance section. Select **False** from the drop-down list.

4. In Report Designer view, drag open the Detail section enough to allow space for a subreport.

5. Click the **Subreport** field tool in the Toolbox, click at the left margin of the window (not in the ruler), and drag to the right margin to define the subreport's width. The height of the subreport is not relevant. It will expand as necessary.

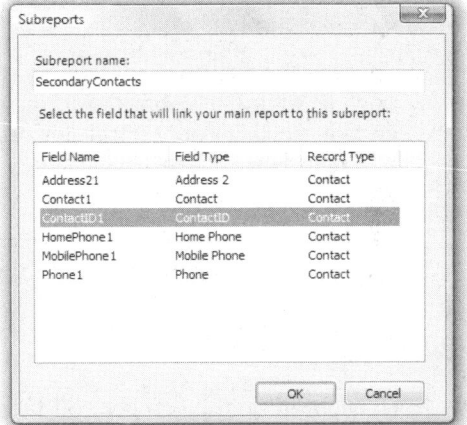

6. Enter a descriptive **Subreport name:**.

Usually the subreport name should be the same as the tab name.

7. Select **ContactID1** for the linking field (if this is a Contact report) and click **OK**.

If this is a Contact-based report (instead of Company, Group, or Opportunity-based), then ContactID1 would be the link to the tab information. If this field is not available, go back to step 2.

8. While selected, use the arrow key to move it to the left margin.

Press the left arrow until the Subreport is at the left margin.

9. Double-click the subreport container you just created.

The empty report displays. Notice the name of the subreport (the one that you assigned in step 5) is displayed above the Toolbox at the left.

10. Expand the new Detail section so there is room for you to place fields in the subreport.

Place your mouse pointer on the bottom of the Detail section (the line between the Detail header and the Page Footer) and drag down.

11. Use the **Field** tool to drag a new field in the Detail section.

    Select a record type: for this subreport. Then select a field and click **Add**. Continue adding any fields you want for the current record type. Click **Close** when finished.

If this subreport is for **Secondary Contacts**, then only place fields belonging to the Secondary Contact record type in this Detail section. Do not mix tab information. If you wish to display **Notes** as well, you will need to add a different subreport for Notes.

12. Format and rearrange the fields and labels as desired. Close up any extra space in the sections.

13. Display the **Properties** window (**[F4]**) and click the Detail header to make that section active. Verify that both **Visible** and **Can Shrink** are set to **Yes**.

Sections that are not visible will display with a lightly shaded background. If the section's **Visible** property is set to **No**, it will not display in the final report.

14. Return to the [Main] report design by clicking on the drop-down list above the Toolbox.

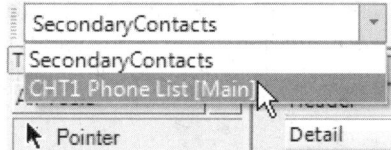

15. To tighten up the display so that extra space is removed for Contacts without data, single-click the Subreport object to select it. In the **Properties** window, change **Can Shrink** to Yes and change **HideOnEmpty Subreport** to **No**.

If you don't change HideOnEmptySubreport to No, then only those Contacts with data in the subreport will display. For example, if you include a subreport for Secondary Contacts and the Contact doesn't have any Secondary Contacts, then the main Contact will not be included in the report.

Click the Detail header and change its properties for **Can Shrink** to **Yes**.

16. Add more subreports (linked to ContactID) as desired.

Designing Dashboards & Reports

Practice: Adding Subreports

What to do	How to do it/Comments
1. Let's add a Subreport to our phone list for Secondary Contacts and *their* phone numbers.	You should still be editing the CHT1 Phone List report, or you can edit the report named "Phone List."
2. In Report Designer view, drag open the Detail section to make space for the subreport.	Drag the bottom of the Detail section down to provide more space.
3. Insert the field "ContactID" into the Detail section (right below the Company field). Make it invisible.	Click the Field tool in the Toolbox and drag to place the field inside the Detail section. Select **ContactID** from the Select Field dialog box, clear **Include a label** and click **Add** and **Close**. Press **[F4]** to display the **Properties** window. Change the **Visible** property to **False**. Press **[F4]** again to close the **Properties** window.
4. Insert a subreport below the fields in the Detail section (covering up the invisible ContactID field you just placed).	Click the **Subreport** field tool in the Toolbox and click at the left margin of the window (not in the ruler) and drag to the right margin to define the subreport's width. The height of the subreport is not relevant. It will expand as necessary. The Subreports dialog box displays.
	Detail: [C:Contact] [C:Phone] [C:Mobile Phone] [C:Home Phone]
5. Give the Subreport a name of "Secondary Contacts" and link it to **ContactID1**.	Enter a descriptive **Subreport name:**. Select **ContactID** for the linking field and click **OK**.
6. Edit the subreport and add the fields Contact and Phone for the Secondary Contacts that belong to our primary Contact record.	Double-click the subreport container you just created. Expand the new Detail section so there is room for placing fields in the subreport. Use the **Field** tool to drag a new field in the detail section. Select a record type: of **Secondary Contact**. Select the **Contact** field. Uncheck **Include a label** and click **Add**. Scroll to click **Phone**, click **Add**, and click **Close**.

What to do	How to do it/Comments
7. Arrange the fields side by side, line them up, and close up the blank Detail space.	Place the fields side by side. Select both and select **Format**, **Align**, **Top**. Use the **[UpArrow]** on the keyboard to move the fields to the top of the section. Use the mouse to drag the bottom of the Detail section up to close up the blank space.
8. Make sure the Details section will be visible when the report displays.	Press **[F4]** to display the **Properties** window. Click the Detail header to make that section active. Verify that both **Visible** and **Can Shrink** are set to Yes.
9. Return to the [Main] report design to Print Preview the report.	Click the drop-down above the Toolbox. **File**, **Print Preview**
10. Tighten up the display so that extra space is removed for Contacts without data. Print Preview again.	Single-click the subreport object. In the **Properties** window, change **Can Shrink** to Yes. Click the Detail header and in the **Properties** window, change **Can Shrink** to Yes.
11. Yikes...some of the Contacts are missing now. The Contacts without Secondary Contacts are no longer displaying. Fix it and Print Preview again. Leave the report displayed in Design view.	Select the Detail section and change the property for HideOnEmptySubreport to No.

Designing Dashboards & Reports | 441

 OK, if you want to align the Contact phone numbers with the Secondary Contact phone numbers, use the Property window to determine the Left property on the Phone field. In the Secondary Contact subreport, change the Left property of the phone to match.

Report Filters

When you Print Preview, ACT! uses the current report filter settings (often the same thing as the current lookup). If you are working with a large database, previewing a report with no filter in place can take a very long time.

- You are most likely familiar with filtering reports, as you are asked to apply a filter every time you print any report. You can define a *default* filter for any report, and then change it, if necessary, when you run the report.
- Report filters define which records print in a report and, when applicable, what date ranges are selected for dated items like notes, history, activities, or opportunities.

Procedure: To define a default filter for a report

1. Display the Report in Designer view and choose **Edit**, **Define Filters**,

    or right-click and select **Define Filters**....

    The **Define Filters** dialog box displays (have you two already met?).

2. Specify the desired **Send the report output to:** and Create report for options.

    You can choose to print only the current lookup or all Contacts. You can default the report to Preview instead of sending it directly to the printer.

3. Check whether you want to include/exclude your My Record from the report.

4. If you want to include date-specific data or wish to eliminate certain types of information from the report, display the appropriate tab of the dialog box.

    Click the **Activity**, **Note**, **History** or **Opportunity** tab.

    You can choose what types of data to include. You may also limit the data by specific date ranges.

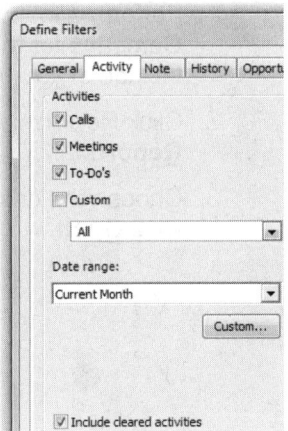

5. You can also limit each type of data to only that data managed by a selected user.

6. When you have set all of the desired filter options, click **OK**, and save your report.

You have just defined the default filter setting for this report.

Practice: A Report Filter	
What to do	**How to do it/Comments**
1. Display the **Define Filters** dialog box for your report.	In Report Designer view, right-click the report and select **Define Filters**.
2. Set the report to print the current lookup only. The report should assume you wish to Print Preview. Be sure to uncheck "Exclude My Record."	Select the **Current Lookup** and **Preview** options, and click **OK**.
3. Save and close the report.	

Using Custom Reports

Once your report is created and saved, you can use it to create reports for the current lookup.

Procedure: To generate a custom report

1. Perform a lookup or display a Group or Company for the Contacts you wish to include in your report.	A report can print all Contact records or just the current lookup or Group or Company.
2. Click **Reports, Other Contact Reports...**.	The **Open** dialog box displays with a list of all available report templates.
3. Choose the desired report template and click **Open**.	The **Define Filters** dialog box displays (it should look familiar).

Designing Dashboards & Reports | 443

The **General** tab allows you to choose basic output options such as whether to use all contacts, current lookup, or current contact only. You can also choose where the report will go (to the printer, preview, or to a file).

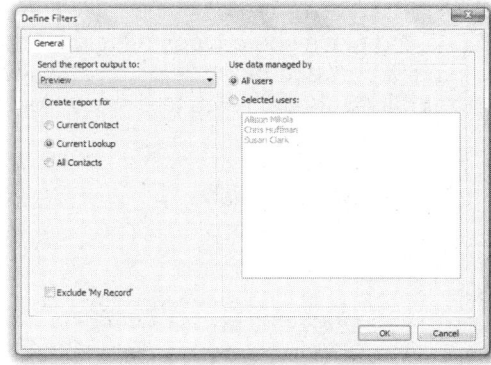

4. Click one of the **Activity**, **Note**, **History**, **Opportunity** tabs for more filtering options.

5. Click **OK**.   ACT! generates the report to your specifications.

Practice: Generating a Custom Report

What to do	How to do it/Comments
1. If necessary, display the Contacts view.	
2. Look up all Contacts in AZ.	**Lookup**, **State**, enter **AZ**, and click **OK**.
3. Generate the **CHT1 Phone List** report using the current lookup. Observe the filter options (Current lookup and Preview) are already set for you.	**Reports**, **Other Contact Reports...**, choose the **CHT1 Phone List** report template, and click **Open**. After viewing the default filters, click **OK**.
4. Observe the preview.	It displays only the records in the current lookup.
5. Close **Print Preview**.	Click **Close**.

Using Scripting in Your Reports

You can use some simple Visual Basic scripting to spice up your reports. You don't have to know Visual Basic to accomplish these few examples. You just have to be a little adventurous and understand how to replace the sample field names with the actual names in your report. Try these out. What have you got to lose?

Removing Blank Space Between Fields

As you place some types of fields on your reports or labels, you may want to take out the space between those fields…you know…scrunch them together. For example, do you want the City Sate Zip fields to display like this…?

```
Houston        ,        TX        77277
San Francisco  ,        CA        94104
```

or like this:

```
Houston, TX    77277
San Francisco, CA    94104
```

This procedure is not for the faint of heart, but it is very satisfying to see it work. The overview of the process is: Place the fields on the report (even though they won't scrunch together). Then, hide the fields. Finally, add a Custom System field to the report that uses a script to combine the fields in a nice tight format.

Procedure: To remove extra space between fields

1. Display the report in Report Designer view. If you want to modify a label or envelope, click **File**, **Print**, change the **Printout type:**, select the template and click **Edit Template**.

2. Place the fields on the report as you normally would.

3. Press **[F4]** to display the **Properties** window.

4. Click the first field for scrunching (e.g., [C:City]). Notice (and write down) its Object Name (found at the top of the **Properties** window).

5. Change its Visible status to **False**.   Click in the Visible option to make it active. Select **False** from the drop-down menu.

   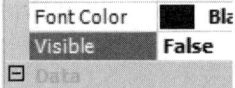

Designing Dashboards & Reports | 445

6. Drag the original field size to make it tiny and move it to the far right of (and above) where you will add the custom label. Use the **Properties** window, if you like, to change the width and height of each field to ".1".

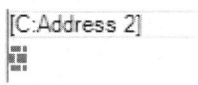

7. Repeat steps 4-6 for each field that you want to scrunch together.

8. Click the **System Field** button on the toolbox, and draw the field on the layout where you want the compressed text to display. Make it wide enough to display the combined fields.

9. Uncheck **Include a label**. Select **Custom** and click **Add**, **Close**.

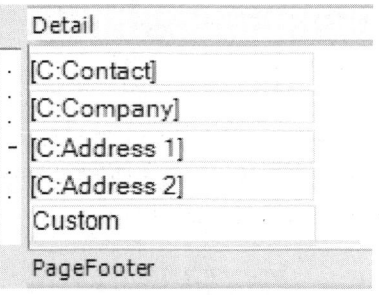

10. Select the "Custom" field that you just created.

    In the Data area of the **Properties** window, enter the **Expression**….

Use the Field Object Names that you wrote in step 4. Include the Object Names in square brackets.

([City1] & ", " & [State1] & " " & [ZIPCode1])

> ☞ *This expression says: Take the value in the field object named [City1], add a comma and a space, add the value from the [State1] object, add a couple of spaces, and finally add the value found in the [ZIPCode1] field object.*

10. Right-click on the background of the section containing the Custom field you just placed and select **Edit Report Scripts**….

This dialog box can be used to program instructions for any Custom field contained in the section you just right-clicked (not the Header or Footer section). Don't freak out…it's not too bad…keep reading.

Enter something like the script at the right. It says, if the City field is blank, go ahead and make the Custom1 field we just entered equal to the City1 field, add a comma and a space, add the State1 field, then add a space, and add the ZipCode1 field. If the City field contains data, do the same thing.

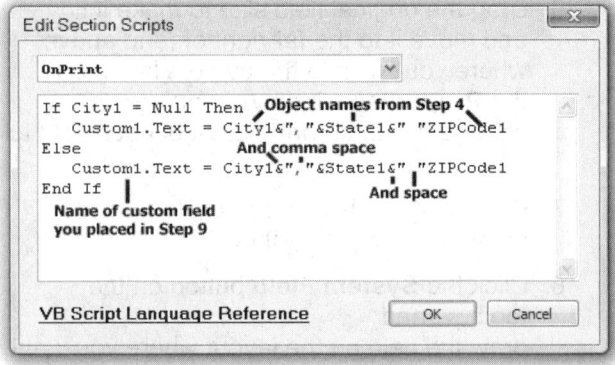

11. Preview your changes. If everything looks good, save your changes with a new name. **File**, **Save As**.

Using Checkmarks for Yes/No Fields in Reports

Yes/No fields (like Key Contact in the ACT2012Demo database) are an easy, quick way to enter data in a record. However, if you add one of these fields to a report, it will display like this:

Key Contact: True

instead of this...

Key Contact: ☑

You can replace those "True" values with a check. The overview of the process is that you place the Yes/No field on the report. Then, hide the field. Finally, add a Custom System field to the report that uses a script to replace True values with a check and False values with a blank.

Procedure: To add a check instead of "True" on your report

1. Click **Reports**, **Edit Template…**, select the report and click **Open**. Open the report you want to modify in Report Designer view.

2. Click on the **Field** button and drag one of your Yes/No type of fields onto the report.

3. Press **[F4]** to display the **Properties** window and determine the object name of the Yes/No field (not the label). This will be our <fieldname>.

Designing Dashboards & Reports | 447

4. Drag the field (not the label) to the right (and slightly below) where you will add the custom check field. Then change the field size to make it tiny.

   Use the **Properties** window, if you like, to change the width and height of the field to ".1".

5. Change its Visible status to **False** by clicking in the Visible option to make it active and selecting **False** from the drop-down menu.

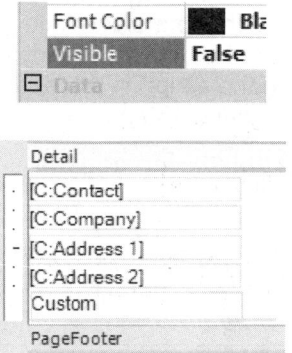

6. Click the **System Field** button on the toolbox, and draw the field on the layout where you want the checkmark to display.

7. Uncheck **Include a label**. Select **Custom** and click **Add**, **Close**.

8. Change the font for this field to "Wingdings."

   Since it no longer displays the word True or False, you can make it a smaller width.

9. While the Custom field is selected, note its Object name in the **Properties** window. This will be our <customname>.

   Now you have two names to remember - the <fieldname> of the actual field (e.g., KeyContact1) and the <customname> (e.g., Custom5).

10. Right-click on the background of the section containing the Custom field you just placed and select **Edit Report Scripts**….

    Be sure to right-click in the Detail section, not one of the Header or Footer sections.

    ☞ You may see some scripting already entered in the OnPrint window. We'll just add ours to the bottom.

11. Enter the following script. Add a blank line between any existing scripts and this new one.

    The script says….If the Yes/No field = True, then display ☑, else display ☐.

    ☞ Replace <fieldname> and <customname> with the actual object names.
    ```
    If <fieldname> = -1 Then
        <customname>.Text = chr(254)
    Else
        <customname>.Text = chr(168)
    End If
    ```

    ☞ An example where we substituted the field names.
    ```
    If KeyContact1 = -1 Then
        Custom5.Text = chr(254)
    Else
        Custom5.Text = chr(168)
    End If
    ```

12. Click **OK**.

13. Click **File**, **Print Preview**, make adjustments, and save the report.

If you don't have the Wingdings font, or you want to make a different character selection, you can use Word to help you find the right character code. In Word, click **Insert**, **Symbol…**, select the **Font:**, select a character, notice the **Character code:**. Change the font of the field to the one you selected here and use the three-digit character code shown here in the script. In the example above, we used 254 = ☑ and 168 = ☐.

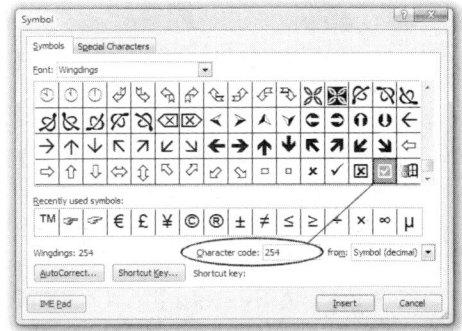

You might want to use 252 = ✓ and 32 =   instead.

Practice: **Converting a Yes/No Field**	
What to do	**How to do it/Comments**
1. Add the Key Contact field to the "Contact Report."	The Contact Report comes with ACT! containing all standard fields. Key Contact was added to the database, so it is not on the report.
2. Change the display of the field to a check.	Use the previous procedure.

Make Your Label Choose Home or Business on Print

Do you have clients that give you their business address, but prefer that you send all correspondence to their Home (or other) address? These were really hard to deal with…until now.

If you have been following our previous examples of how to enter simple VB Script in the ACT! Report Writer, you will like this last example of having the ACT! software print the preferred address on the label (without having to print the labels twice).

The overview of the process is: Add a field called "Preferred Mailing Address." Place that field on the label (or envelope). Then, place all of the address fields for both Home and Work on the label. Hide all of the fields. Next, add a Custom System field for each address line in the label. Finally, create a script to replace True values with a check and False values with a blank.

Designing Dashboards & Reports | 449

Procedure: To modify a label to choose address at printing

1. Add a "Preferred Mailing Address" field with a drop-down list (including "Work" and "Home") to your database.

   You can use other values if you like or have added other Address fields to your database. Default the field to "Work."

2. Click **File**, **Print**…, select a "Printout type:" of **Labels** or **Envelopes**, then select a "Paper type:" template that matches the size you will use.

   Select Avery 15160 for the labels that are 3 across and 10 down.

3. Click the **Edit Template** button at the bottom left.

4. **File**, **Save As**…, give the template a new name, and click **OK**.

5. **Edit, Select All**, and press **[Delete]**.

   Start clean.

6. Press **[F4]** to display the **Property Window**.

7. Place the **Contact** and **Company** fields on the label as you normally would.

   Use the **Field** tool to place them on the first two lines of the label.

8. Place your newly created "Preferred Mailing Address" field on the label and note the Object name in the **Properties** window.

   In our case, it was "AddPref1."

9. Place all the address fields you plan to use for both the Work and Home on the label.

   As they near the end of the label, they start to add on top of each other. Don't worry that they don't fit.

   ☞ *If you won't use Address 3 or Country, no need to add them.*

10. Select all of the address fields you just added and change their Visible Property to False.

11. Change both their Height and Width properties to .01.

    Now they are all tiny and stacked on top of each other in the lower left corner of the label where they won't get in the way.

    Change their Left property to 2.4 and their Top property to 1.9.

12. Add a System field to represent Address line 1. Click the System tool and drag a box for the third line in the address. Select **Custom** from the pop-up dialog box. Uncheck "Include a label" and click **Add** and **Close**. Notice the name.

    Probably "Custom1".

13. Add another System field to represent the City, State Zip line of the label.
14. Right-click on the background and select **Edit Report Scripts...**.
15. Delete all of the text in the box. Your new script should look something like this. You may need to use the drop-down box in the **Properties** window name section to verify the exact names of your address fields to compare to the sample script.

Custom2.

If the **OnPrint** does not display, click **Cancel** and right-click somewhere else.

Start clean on this one as well. Basically the script says if the preference is marked with Home, then print the home address. Otherwise (if it is blank or contains some other value), print the main address.

```
If AddPref1 = "Home" then
    Custom1.Text = HomeAddress11&" "&HomeAddress21
Else
    Custom1.Text = Address11&" "Address21
End If

If AddPref1 = "Home" then
    Custom2.Text = HomeCity1&" "&HomeState1&" "&HomeZIPCode1
Else
    Custom2.Text = City1&" "&State1&" "&ZIPCode1
End If
```

16. Click **OK** to save the script.
17. Click **File**, **Print Preview**, make adjustments, and save the label.

Practice: Printing a Preferred Address Label

What to do	How to do it/Comments
1. Add the Preferred Mailing Address field to the ACT2012Demo database.	Or you could use the Extension field if you just want to play.
2. Look up Friends and add Home or Work to your new field. (Only add Home if there is a Home Address.)	
3. Create a label and test it on your friends lookup.	Use the preceding procedure.

Administering ACT!

Setting Up

To setup the server and all workstations, you will:

- ☑ Understand your help resources
- ☑ Set up a multi-user database.
- ☑ Prepare the server for database installation

Sage ACT!

Using Available Documentation

Good documentation can be your friend in this job. Fortunately for you, you have two good sources right at your fingertips...this User's Guide (we could be biased about that) and the ACT! Knowledge Base ...the ACT Administrator's best friend.

Using the ACT! Knowledge Base

The Knowledge Base on the Internet is a great way to find your own solutions to your ACT! questions. Most problems that users experience and their solutions are documented in the Knowledge Base.

Procedure: To use the ACT! Knowledge Base

1. Start your Internet browser.
2. Go to: http://kb.sagesoftwareonline.com/ — This is the Sage ACT! Technical Support Web site.
3. Enter your error message or a keyword in the **Search text** area and click **Search**. — For example, if you are interested in synchronization, type a keyword like: synchronize or synchronization

Practice: Using the Knowledge Base

What to do	How to do it/Comments
1. Open the ACT! Knowledgebase.	http://kb.sagesoftwareonline.com/
2. Search the Knowledgebase to find suggestions for sharing a database.	
3. See what you can find on security levels.	

Enabling Your Database for Multiple Users

ACT! can be set up on a network so that other users can access the same database at the same time. You only need to do a few things to prepare for this type of setup.

- Move the database onto a networked drive to which ACT! users have access.
- Enable the database for sharing.
- Decide security roles to assign and add logon user names to the database.
- Change the Tools Preferences on each logon user's PC to enable ACT! to find the database.

☞ *All users in a multi-user environment must be using the same version of ACT! to access the same database.*

Setting Up | 455

Examining Structure

By default the ACT! program installs to: C:\Program Files\ACT\ACT for Windows or C:\Program Files (x86)\ACT\ACT for Windows

 This installation structure allows you to run an older version of ACT! (versions 6 or earlier) while still running ACT! 2012. However, you cannot run versions 2005 through 2011 on the same PC.

File Structure

When you are in ACT! and you choose **File, Open/Share Database** you see only one filename for each database, but there are actually a few other files working in the background for each database.

ACT! is designed on a SQL database engine. While there are some relational elements built into the database design (each contact can have multiple notes and history, multiple activities, multiple secondary contacts, multiple sales opportunities, multiple attached files in the Documents tab, and multiple group or company associations), the structure is currently fixed and you may not add additional relational tables without a third-party add-on product.

So let's look at the files that make up this database. An ACT! database is made up of 3 main files, which have the same filename with different file extensions.

Extension	Data	Description
.ADF	ACT! Database File	The database file maintains all of the contact and associated data.
.ALF	ACT! Log File	The Log file keeps track of changes that have been synchronized or are awaiting synchronization.
.PAD	Pointer to ACT! Database	The PAD file is a pointer file which describes the path and filename of the database it is associated with. The PAD file can reside anywhere. You can open the database that a PAD file is associated with by double-clicking on the PAD file.

 *If a previous version of ACT! was installed on your PC, then the database files will be found in the **\ACT for Windows #\Databases** folder. It's a legacy thing.*

Directory Structure

There are also multiple supporting files, including the layouts, dashboard, word processing, and reporting templates, etc. As you create new databases, a subset of directories is created for each database in order to maintain all associated files together in one location. The default location for a new database is in the user's...

\My Documents\ACT\ACT Data\Databases
    or
 \Users\Public\Public Documents\ACT\ACT Data\ Databases

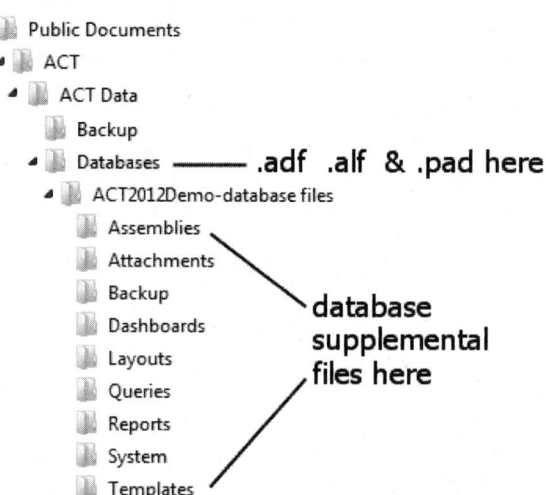

folder of the current computer. The default folder structure is displayed above. Notice that the 3 files that make up the actual database are maintained in the default \Databases folder and that all of the associated supplemental files are maintained under the \<databasename>-database files folder.

You can, however, choose a different starting location when you first create or restore the database. For example, you might want to create a folder named \ACT and create or restore all databases to that folder. You can see from the folder structure at the right that the 3 files that make up the actual database are maintained in the folder that you created and that all of the associated supplemental files are kept under the \<databasename>-database files folder.

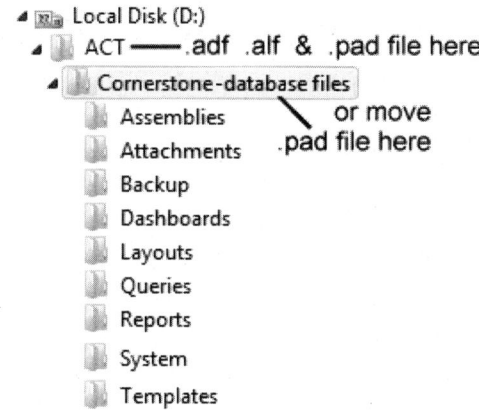

You could also move the .pad file to the shared **database files** folder and take advantage of the security that ACT! sets up.

Setting Up | 457

Moving the Database to the Server

If you have been designing the database on your own workstation (instead of the server), you will need to move the database to a location on the server shared by others in your organization.

Unfortunately, you can't use Windows Explorer to copy or move the database to the new location. You will get an annoying error about the files being used by another person or program. (All Microsoft® SQL Server® databases work this way. Sigh!)

You will need to use the ACT! **Back Up** and **Restore** commands to transfer your custom designed database to its new location. (Gee…if we named this section "Restore Your Database"…you might have skipped right over it.)

 It is not required that a shared database be on a "server". The database can be on any workstation on the network where the users have Read and Write access to the folder where the database resides. However, as your database gets larger, and more users are logging in, you will find that a computer running Windows Server® 2003 Server (or greater) provides much better performance and stability.

Procedure: To transfer a database from one PC to another

1. Backup the database you want to transfer.

   If you need help, the details for this procedure are on page 489.

2. Go to the computer that will host the database.

   ACT! must be installed on the computer.

    You cannot perform this procedure across the network. You must be physically at the computer that will hold the database.

3. Verify that you are logged on to the computer with Administrator rights.

   We're not logging in to ACT! right now. We are talking about logging on to the computer as an administrator.

4. If necessary, create a folder on the server to hold the database and associated files. Copy the backup (.zip) file to the folder.

   You might create a folder called
   \ACT
   to hold the database files and subfolders.

5. Open ACT!.

   ACT! must be installed on the PC that holds the database.

6. Click **File**, **Restore**, **Database…**, select **Restore as**, click **OK**. **Browse…** to the backup you created in step 1 above, click **Open**, and then click **OK** to start the process.

   If you are transferring the database to a server so that multiple users can share the database, you must perform the "Restore As" step while logged on to the actual server. If you need help with the options in the restore process, details for this procedure are on page 492.

7. Enter the new name for the database.

   Browse to the location you created in step 4.

   Check the **Share the database** option.

   Enter a **User name:** for the ACT! database that has been assigned to an Administrator role. Enter any associated **Password:** and click **OK**.

8. Click **OK** to acknowledge the successful completion of Restore.

9. Open the restored database.

   File, Open/Share Database... click the file and click **Open Database**. If prompted, enter a valid **User name:** and any associated **Password:**, and click **OK**.

Enable Share for an Existing Database

If the database is on a computer that others can access, you can enable sharing of that database. Enabling the sharing of ACT! supplemental files not only sets the folder permissions in Windows Explorer, but also allows the users to share the layouts, templates, reports, etc., that were created to go with the database. Shared folders display with a hand holding the folder. In Windows Vista and Windows 7, an icon with multiple heads indicates shared permission.

 This procedure does not assign network user permissions to the parent folder where the database is stored (e.g., D:\ACT folder). Your network administrator needs to add or limit access to that parent folder, which holds the three files that make up the ACT! database. However, do not have the administrator assign security rights to the "[databasename]-database files" subfolder…let ACT! handle that part using the following procedure.

Procedure: To enable share on an existing database

1. Go to the computer that is hosting the database.

   You cannot perform this procedure across the network. You must be physically on the computer that holds the database.

Setting Up | 459

2. Log on to ACT! as a user with an Administrator role.

    *You could also click the "Share" button at the left of the database name in the **Open/Share Database Dialog**.*

3. Point to **Tools, Database Maintenance**.

   If there is no checkmark to the left of **Share Database**, then click that menu option to place one there.

   If there is already a check on **Share Database**, then the database has already been shared…escape out of the menus.

4. Click **OK** to acknowledge that the files associated with the database will be shared.

Opening the Shared Database

Once the database has been restored to the server, and **Share Database** has been enabled, multiple users on your network can open the same database. On the workstation, click **File, Open/Share Database…** click "**The database I want is not listed**" hyperlink and browse to the network folder that holds the database. Select the database and click **Open Database**. Each user should log on with their assigned name (and password if appropriate).

 All users in a multi-user environment must be using the same version of ACT! to access the same database.

Sage ACT!

Pre-Install Checklist

Some of the procedures in the checklist may seem unnecessary, but if you want a trouble-free installation, you will want to be sure that you follow most of them. It only takes one failed install to make you realize the truth of Benjamin Franklin's advice of "an ounce of prevention is worth a pound of cure."

Make sure workstation/server meet Minimum System Requirements.
Really… review this list.
http://www.act.com/Products-and-Services/system/2012

But pay particular attention to these items:

- If you are using Office (Word, Outlook, etc), it must be Office 2003 or greater (Office 2000 will not work with ACT!).
- Make sure that all service packs have been applied to Windows and Office.
- Verify that there is 2 GB of free space on the C:\.
- Each PC should have a minimum 1GB of RAM, but the more the better.
- Ensure that File and Printer sharing is an installed service (this is most likely only a potential problem on a server where a printer has not been set up).
- Verify that you have Local Administrator Rights for installing the software. You don't need it to run the software, but you need the rights for installing.
- Delete all temp files on the machine (excessive temp files are the biggest cause for failed ACT! mail merges). Click **Start, Run**, %temp% **OK**   It is safe to delete all files found this way.

Database Security

If you will not be the only user of your database, then you should understand how to set up your database to allow others in your company to share the ACT! database. In this section we will,

- ☑ Create new and assign security levels for users.

- ☑ Learn how Teams play a role in security (if you are using the Premium version of ACT!).

- ☑ Understand how to create rules for adding passwords to the database and the implications of the requirements.

Database Security

You should treat your database of clients and prospects as if it is your number one business asset... wait...it is!

Data in your ACT! database is secured in the following ways:
- If you don't know a logon user name, you can't get into the database.
- Optional passwords can be simple or can be required to follow complex rules set by your database Administrator.
- Roles and permissions are assigned to each user, determining what ACT! features any user has access to...whether they can delete records, back up the database, sync to a PDA, etc.
- Limited Access (Premium version only) restricts access to Contacts, Companies, Groups, or Opportunities by user name or Team membership.
- Field Security (Premium version only) can be assigned to almost any field in the database, restricting which users can edit which fields. Three levels of access can be defined for a field: Full Access, Read-Only, and No Access. The rights are assigned by field by user or teams of users.

Understanding Security Roles

ACT! includes five levels of security called **roles**. Your security role determines which features you can access and the functions you can perform.

When you first create a database, you are automatically assigned an Administrator role. As you add users to the database, you will be prompted to assign a security role to each new logon name. While you can view a more thorough listing of the permissions granted by each security role in the Appendix on page 528, you can get a quick overview of each role below.

- **Administrator** role provides access to all functionality in ACT! except that, like other ACT! users, they cannot view, edit, or delete records marked as Private if the Record Manager is someone else.
- **Manager** role can perform almost all functions with the exception of deleting or restoring a database and creating any logon users. However, they can import/export data, modify the database structure and layouts, create and manage Teams, set up synchronization, delete data owned by other users, and schedule activities for any user in the database (even when access has not been granted).
- **Standard** role is the most common role assigned. Standard users can perform almost all contact and customer management functions in the database. However, they cannot perform any administrative or database functions, including importing data. They cannot schedule activities for other users without specifically being granted calendar access. Finally, they cannot delete data (records, notes, history, activities, etc.) owned by other users.

Database Security | 463

- **Restricted** role can create Contacts, Opportunities, and Activities, but cannot create Groups or Companies or assign membership. While they cannot create or edit any word-processing or report templates, they can run them. They cannot delete anything from the database (even data they have created).
- **Browse** role can view or look up any data they have access to. They can also view other user's calendars. They cannot create or edit anything, including activities, notes, or history. They cannot write a letter or send e-mail from the ACT! database. They can print reports.

 *You can verify your own security level by mousing over your log-on name in the ACT! Status Bar. You can also click **Help**, **About ACT!**. Click the **Database Information...** button. Your **Security Role:** is listed in **Database User Information:**.*

Custom Permissions for Manager or Standard Roles

Additionally, **custom permissions** can be added to or removed **from Manager or Standard roles** (you cannot define custom permissions for any other roles). The options are:

- **Accounting Link Tasks** – use of an Accounting/back-office link. This custom permission determines if the user can access the ACT! Link for Peachtree, Sage MAS 90, BusinessWorks, Sage MAS 90 links, or other accounting software.
- **Handheld Device Sync** – synchronization of ACT! with handheld devices. This permission determines if they can sync their PDA with the ACT! database.
- **Remote Administration** – database back-up, restore, and check and repair on a remote database. This permission is designed for remote sync users. It allows them to back-up, restore, and check and repair their database… tasks that are usually limited to Administrators. However, it could be valuable to allow the remote user to perform maintenance.
- **Export to Excel** – exporting data in a list view to Excel. While Standard users cannot, by default, export any data, this custom permission allows them to export any current list view to Excel. This custom permission option is only available for Standard users.
- **Delete records** – deletion of Contacts, Companies, Groups, activity series, notes, history, opportunities, and Secondary Contacts that the user owns. Removing this default custom permission ensures that nothing gets deleted from the database without someone's (whoever has rights) approval. This custom permission option is only available for Standard users.
- **Manage Sync Subscription List** – allows (or prevents) a user of a remote database to receive additional Contact records (outside of those defined by the Sync Set for that remote database) by manually selecting from a list of all Contacts in the database.

Creating New Users

An ACT! database located on a network can be shared by many users. This has many advantages, among which are shared access to common information and ease of maintenance. In order for users to share Contacts while maintaining a separate calendar of their own activities, a record of who created new opportunities, some private Contacts, etc., then the users must be defined.

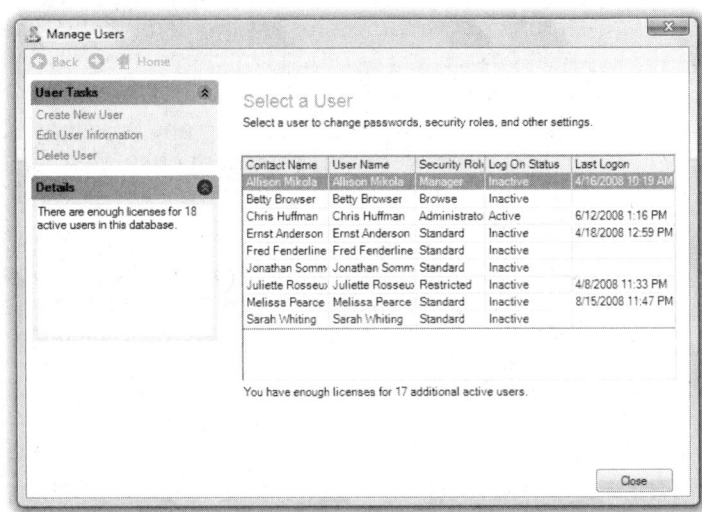

Procedure: To add and manage logon users

1. Enter the new user as a Contact record first.

   You can use the Duplicate command to copy a fellow employee's company name, address, and phone number information. A real time-saver.

2. Click **Tools, Manage Users...**.

   ☞ *You must be an Administrator, and you cannot do this in a remote database.*

   A list of current user's displays on the right side of the dialog box.

3. Under User Tasks at the left, click **Create New User**.

4. Click **Create User from Contact**.

   Click **Next>**.

   If you forgot to create a Contact record before starting this process, when you click **Next>**, go to step 6.

5. In the **Look for:** text box, start typing the letters of the user's last name to quickly scroll to it.

   When the new user's name is highlighted, click **Next>**.

6. Type a different logon **User Name:** (if necessary).

   This is their logon name for this database. You can use their actual name or create an abbreviated ID.

Database Security | 465

7. Choose a **Security Role:**.

    Roles are briefly defined on page 462, but you can find more information on page 528 in the Appendix.

8. Enter and confirm a password, if desired.

    If you do not specify a password, none will be required for entry into the database for this user name (unless you have set a Password Policy – we'll cover that next).

9. Set any options desired.
    - **User must change password…** - forces the user to change (or add) a password the next time they log on.
    - **User cannot change…** - prevents the user from changing their password using the **F**ile, **Set Passwor**d… option.
    - **Password never expires** – overrides any global Password Policy settings about changing passwords.
    - Click **N**ext>.

    If you check "User must change password at next log on," you do not need to assign a password, but the user will be prompted to set one when they log on for the first time.

    Setting any of these options will take precedence over Password Policy settings. For example, if you select the "User must change…" option, then the user must change their password the next time they log on, even if the number of days between log ons is less than the number of days identified in the Password Policy. If you set the "Password never expires" option for a user, then regardless of the settings in the Password Policy, the password will not have to be changed.

10. Verify that current Logon Access is set to **Active**.

    Click **N**ext>.

    Active access allows the selected user to access the current database. Inactive users can no longer log on to the database. Inactive status also frees a license to allow access by another user.

11. Add (or remove) permissions as desired.

    Click **N**ext>.

    You can only modify permissions for Manager and Standard roles. Explanations of the permissions can be reviewed on page 463.

12. Click **Add** to select the Team Name(s) that the user will be associated with.

    Click **F**inish.

    Teams are only available in the Premium version of ACT!. They are discussed in the next few pages.

13. Repeat for each user you wish to define.

    Click **C**lose.

    Each user is assigned their own My Record.

*Once you have defined more than one logon user, users are asked to log in when they open this database. They need to know their **User name** exactly as it appears in the user list and their password (if any). While user names are not case-sensitive, passwords are.*

Practice: Adding Users

What to do	How to do it/Comments
1. Create a user for a Contact that is already in our database: Cecilia Carter. Cecilia should have Standard rights, but allow her to sync her Palm and perform database backups.	**Tools**, **Manage Users...**, click **Create New User**, click **Create User from Contact**, and click **Next>**. In the Look for area, type "cart" and click **Next>**. Keep the same security role and click **Next>**. Keep the record as **Active** and click **Next>**. Double-click "Remote Administration" and "Handheld Device Sync" and click **Next>**. Finally, click **Finish**.

2. While you are in the Manage Users dialog, notice that you can see the **Last Logon** dates for each user.

Contact Name	User Name	Security Role	Log On Status	Last Lo
Chris Huffman	Chris Huffman	Administrator	Active	7/5/201
Melissa Pearce	Melissa Pearce	Standard	Active	8/15/20
Ernst Anderson	Ernst Anderson	Standard	Active	4/18/20
Allison Mikola	Allison Mikola	Manager	Active	4/16/20

Making Users Inactive

For a number of reasons, you may need to change a user's status to inactive. For example, you can inactivate one user, freeing up a license to allow access by another. You may also want to temporarily inactivate a user for security reasons, and then reactivate the user at a later time.

Procedure: To inactivate a user

1. Click **Tools, Manage Users....** You must be a user with an Administrator role.

2. Double-click the user you wish to inactivate. You can also select the user and click **Edit User Information**.

3. Click **Next>** to advance to the **Specify Access** screen.

Database Security | 467

4. Click **Inactive** under Logon Access.   To reactivate the user, repeat and click **Active**.

5. Click **Finish** and then **Close**.

 If you like you can click Delete User. Just be sure to Reassign their Contacts and History items to another user. This will also reassign all notes, history, activities and opportunities to the other user.

Password Management

Passwords are used to further control access to your ACT! database. They are not required to use the database, but are easy to implement.

- An Administrator can set global password options for all users in the database.
- An Administrator can define individual password requirements for each user name that can override some of the global requirements.
- Even if no password options have been set, a user can opt to add their own password.

Defining a Global Password Policy

To help protect your valuable Contact information from unauthorized access, Administrators can define a Password Policy which applies to all users of the database. The policy can control the length, the complexity, the expiration options, and reuse of a password.

The Policy can be defined using these options…

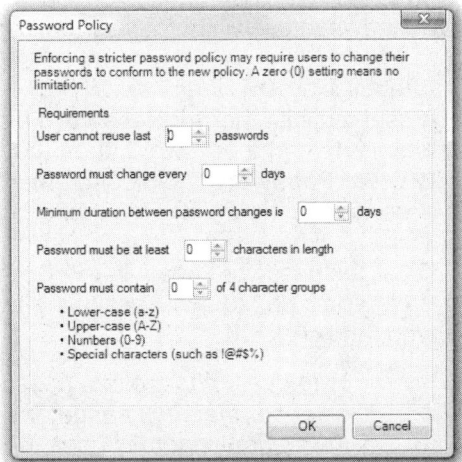

- **User cannot reuse last __ passwords** – indicates the number of previous passwords that cannot be reused. The maximum is 9. A setting of 0 indicates that a password may be reused.

- **Password must change every __ days** – indicates how frequently a user must change their password. Once a year is the longest time allowed. If the option is set to 0, then the user never needs to change their password. Administrators can override this option by setting the "Password never expires" and/or "User cannot change password" options on individual records.

- **Minimum duration between password changes is __ days** – indicates the minimum number of days a password must be in use before a user is allowed to change it. A year is the longest time, but if the option is set to 0, the user can change their mind about their password the second they click **OK**.

- **Password must be at least ___ characters in length** – indicates the minimum number of characters for a password. The maximum can be set to 25 (now, that would take a long time to log on). If the setting is 0, then the user can determine their own length. If you set it to 1, then it is the same as requiring a password for all users. The value that you set for this option must be equal to or greater than the value in the next option concerning character groups. (After all…if a password must contain two character groups, then you have to input at least two characters.)

- **Password must contain ___ of 4 character groups** – determines the complexity of the password, such as requiring a combination of lowercase, uppercase, numeric, or special characters. A setting of 1 is effectively the same as 0, since any password you could type would have at least one character group.

Procedure: To define a global Password Policy

1. **Tools, Password Policy**....

2. Change the requirements, as desired. The explanation of each option is described above.

3. Click **OK**.

When a Password Policy is implemented or changed, all users will be prompted to enter a password the next time they log on to the database (unless their password already complies with the new policy).

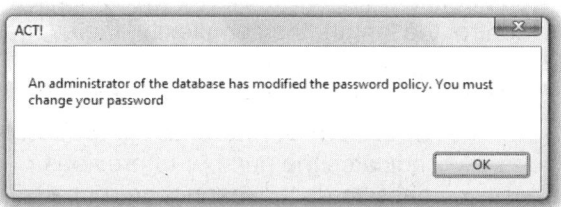

After clicking **OK**, the user will be presented with the **Set Password** dialog box. If the user has never had a password, then they should leave the **Current Password:** blank and enter the **New Password:** according to the Policy Requirements listed.

Enter the password again in the **Confirm New Password:** box to avoid assigning a password with a typo, and click **OK**.

> *With every change of a password, ACT! warns the end user that the change affects handheld links, the Outlook address book, or other third-party applications. When you change your password in ACT!, you will need to update your passwords in the Palm linking software, the one you entered for the Outlook Address Book, and the one for ACT! Scheduler.*

Database Security | 469

Practice: Define a Global Password Policy

What to do	How to do it/Comments
1. Define a Password Policy for the ACT2012Demo database that requires a password that is a minimum of six characters coming from three character groups.	Practice with this on the ACT2012Demo database before implementing in your own database. It is always a good idea to **File**, **Backup Database…** prior to implementing this policy. **Tools**, **Password Policy**…. Change "Password must be at least…" to 6 and change the last option to 3. Click **OK**.
2. Log off the ACT! Database	**File**, **Close**.
3. Log back on as Chris Huffman.	**File** and click the **1 ACT2012Demo.pad** (above the Exit option). Click **OK** to acknowledge the Password Policy change. Unless you have set up a password previously for Chris, the **Current Password:** is blank. Enter a **New Password** (and retype it in the Confirm area) conforming to the new Password Policy requirements. Click **OK** to acknowledge that you might need to update other links.
4. **IMPORTANT:** Remove the Password Policy from the database and then remove Chris' password! (So you can log on later to do more exercises.) Really, this is important… don't skip this step or you may not remember how to get back into the ACT2012Demo database.	**Tools**, **Password Policy…**, starting with the bottom option, change all options back to 0, and click **OK**. **Tools**, **Manage Users**, double-click Chris Huffman, click the **Reset Password** button, and clear the "User must change password at next log on" option. Click **Finish**, then **OK**, and finally **Close**.

Setting a Password for Yourself

If you are the only user of your database, you may not want to go to the trouble of using a password. However, should your laptop ever get lost, would you want your client list falling into the hands of just anyone? You may add a password to your database anytime you decide that you want to password-protect your data.

If you are the Administrator of your database, you may want to add a password for a different reason. There are a few ACT! menu commands that only a user with an Administrator role can execute, such as deleting a database or adding users to your database. If several users in your company can access the data, you may want to limit what each user has the ability to do. Consequently, all users that have been assigned to the Administrator security role should probably have a password.

Procedure: To add a password to your logon name

1. Click **File**, **Set Password**....

2. If you do not currently have a password, start by entering your **New Password:** and then click **Confirm New Password:** As you type, your password will display as ***.

     A Password Policy may have been set for your database that requires your password to meet certain criteria (minimum number of characters, include different characters, etc.).

3. Click **OK** to confirm. Your password has changed.

 *If you want to remove your password, use the same procedure as above, except type your current password in the **Current Password:** area and leave the **New Password:** and **Confirm New Password:** areas blank. Click **OK**, and your password is replaced with a blank password.*

There is an option that allows ACT! to **Remember password** as you log on. Hello… then what is the point of a password! Either remove the password or clear this option.

 Actually, in multi-user environments, some users leave it checked to make it easier to log on from their own PC, while others on the network would have to know the password in order to log on as them.

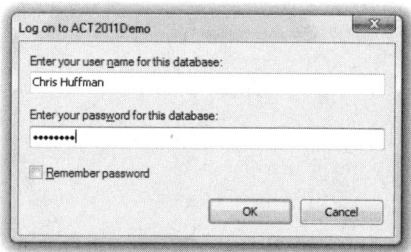

Database Security | 471

Team Management (Premium Only)

Growth is a wonderful thing, but sometimes it has its downside. As your company expands and the number of Contacts in your database grows, you may want to divide the database into smaller chunks to make it more usable.

- Some users may find dealing with large numbers of Contacts rather cumbersome and only wish to view their own Contacts' records.
- Or perhaps your sales staff works in clearly defined geographical areas or vertical market territories, they want to access only Contacts that fall within those territories.
- Some sales groups are very competitive (no... really!). They may want to restrict access to their Contacts (or their Opportunities) to members of their team only.

One possible solution is for each user to mark their Contacts as Private, but then the other members of their sales team would not be able to see them (remember we're talking teamwork here). And what about Managers? They will probably want to see what's happening with all Sales teams. Fortunately, ACT! has a way to keep everyone happy.

 ACT! Premium provides a Limited Access feature which allows you to assign a Contact, Company, Group or Opportunity record to a specific User, Users, or Team of Users, thus limiting which users can view which Contacts in the database.

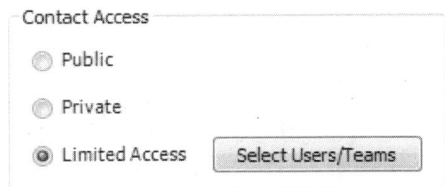

So, while **Roles** define which features in ACT! each user can access (deleting, backing up, importing, etc.), **Teams** are used to define which Contacts (and their associated notes, history, activities, Secondary Contacts, and documents) or Opportunities or Companies or Groups any user can view.

A **Team** then, is a collection of users who have access to the same Contacts. While you can **Limit Access** to specific users, it is much easier to manage the Limited Access feature by using Teams. For example, you could create a Team for the West Coast made up of the West Coast sales reps, the inside sales staff, the VP Sales and the Record Manager for the Contact. We can add the Limited Access by Team to all of the Contacts in our database who are in California, Oregon, and Washington. The East Coast Team would consist of the East Coast sales staff, the VP, and the Record Manager. In this way, the sales teams could only see their own region, but the VP could see both coasts (and you can't even do that from Pikes Peak on a really clear day). When a West Coast Team member gets transferred to the East Coast, and you bring in the replacement, just change out the Team membership and...Wham!...all Contacts on the West Coast are now immediately accessible to the new sales rep, and the transferred user can see the East Coast Contacts, without touching all the records.

Since users can belong to more than one Team, and Contacts can be viewed by multiple Teams, the possibilities for controlling access to Contacts are unlimited.

Sage ACT!

Procedure: To create a Team (Premium Only)

1. Click **Tools, Manage Teams...**.

    You must have a Manager or Administrator role to manage Teams.

2. Under Team Tasks, click **Create Team**.

3. Enter a Team name: and optional Team description:.

   Enter Team Information
   Team name:

   Team description (Optional):

4. Double-click names in the **Available users:** column to add them to the Team.

5. Click **Finish** and **Close**.

   You are returned to **Select a Team**, the starting page for managing Teams. You can close this window.

 You can only do this exercise if you are using the Premium version

Practice: Creating Teams

What to do	How to do it/Comments
1. Create a Team for "AsiaPac" that includes Betty Browser and Jonathan Sommer.	**Tools, Manage Teams...**, click **Create Team**, enter AsiaPac, double-click Betty and Jonathan, and click **Finish** and **Close**.

Limiting Contact Access (Premium Only)

Now that your Teams are set up, you can easily limit access to Contacts in your database. You can add access to one record at a time or to multiple Contacts. Let's start with adding team membership to one Contact.

Procedure: To limit Contact access by Team membership for a Contact

1. On the Contact's record, display the tab with the Contact Access field.   Usually the **Contact Access** tab.

2. Select **Limited Access**.

3. Click **Select Users/Teams** button.

4. Click the **Teams** tab to display available Teams.

Database Security | 473

5. Double-click an available Team at the left to grant access to this Contact.

   You have just limited who can view this Contact to the members of the selected Team (plus users with an Administrator role).

6. Click the **Users** tab to add any ad hoc members.

   For example, one sales rep on the East Coast also calls on this Contact.

7. Click **OK**.

Practice: Limiting Access by Teams	
What to do	**How to do it/Comments**
1. Add AsiaPac team access to Ania Dawson. ☞ *You can only do this exercise if you are using the Premium version.*	Look up Ania Dawson. Click the **Contact Access** tab. Select **Limited Access** and click the **Select Users/Teams** button. Click the **Teams** tab and double-click the AsiaPac team name. Click **OK**.

Assigning Limited Access to a Lookup (Premium Only)

Assigning Limited Access to your entire database (or to a large lookup) one record at a time could get tedious. Fortunately, you can assign access to multiple records (Contacts, Companies, Groups or Opportunities) with a few clicks.

Adding Limited Access to selected Contacts is handled with one of two commands: **Create New Access List** or **Add Users/Teams**. It is important to note the difference between the two commands.

- **Create New Access List** overwrites (removes) any existing user or Teams from the selected Contacts and assigns the new Limited Access rights that you specify.
- **Add Users/Teams** adds the specified users or Teams to all selected Contacts who already have an Limited Access assigned.

Consequently, to make sure that you are not overwriting any previously assigned Limited Access, it is always handy to view the Access Level for your lookup before issuing one of the commands.

Procedure: To display Access Level for your Lookup

1. In Contacts: List View, right-click the column headers and **select Customize Columns**.

2. Double-click **Access Level** field in the Available fields: list to add it to the columns to display.

3. **Move Up** as desired.
4. Click **OK**.

 Access Levels will display as Public, Private, or Limited. The specific user or Team names will not display in this column.

Procedure: To assign new Contact Access to selected users

1. Look up the Contacts to whom you wish to assign user or Team access.
2. In List View, display the Access Level column. — See the procedure above.
3. Verify that all selected Contacts are either Public (or Private) or that it is OK to replace their current Access Level. — Log-on users must remain Public. If any users display in the list, select them and click **Omit Selected** before trying to apply new Limited Access to the Contacts.
4. Remove any Limited Access Contacts from the lookup by selecting the Contact(s) and clicking **Omit Selected**. — Unless it is OK to overwrite the existing access.
5. With your final list displayed in List View, click **Tag All**. — Or manually select the Contacts to be affected by the command.
6. Click **Contacts, Edit Contact Access, Create New Access List...**, — You must have more than one Contact selected.

   or right-click and select **Edit Contact Access, Create New Access List...**.
7. Add Users and/or Teams, as desired, for the current lookup.
8. Click **OK**.
9. Click **Yes** to verify that you understand that this command overwrites the previous access list for the selected Contacts.
10. If one or more Contact records could not be changed, a message appears. Click **OK**. — If an ACT! user was in the list, it could not be changed. All ACT! users must maintain Public access.

 If any of the selected Contacts had been assigned Limited Access, the access list is overwritten. If the selected Contacts are Public or Private, the access level is changed to Limited Access, and the new access list is assigned to them.

Database Security | 475

Procedure: To add Teams/Users to selected Contacts

1. Look up the Contacts to whom you wish to add User or Team access.

2. In List View, display their Access Level. — See the procedure above.

3. Verify that all selected Contacts have Limited Access. — You can't add to something that doesn't exist. If the Contact displays as Public access, you have to define Limited Access first and then you can add to the list.

    To remove a Contact from the lookup (ones with Public or Private access), select the Contact, and click **Omit Selected**.

4. With your final list displayed in List View, click **Tag All**. — Or manually select the Contacts to be affected by the command.

5. **Click Contacts, Edit Contact Access, Add Users/Teams…**,

    or right-click and select Edit Contact Access, Add Users/Teams….

6. Add Users and/or Teams as desired for the current lookup.

7. Click **OK**.

8. Click **Yes** to verify that you understand that this command only works with Contacts that have existing Limited Access.

9. If one or more Contact records could not be changed, a message appears. Click **OK**.

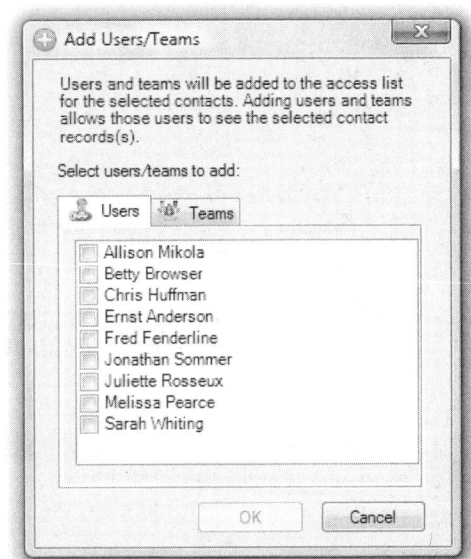

☞ You can only do this exercise if you are using the Premium version.

Practice: *Adding Team Access to a Lookup*

What to do	How to do it/Comments
1. Look up all Contacts in Australia.	On any Contact's record, right-click the Country field and select **Lookup Country**. Enter Australia. Click **OK**.

Sage ACT!

What to do	How to do it/Comments
2. Display the **Access Level** field in the Contacts: List View.	Customize the columns to display the Access Level. If you assigned access in a previous exercise to Ania Dawson, you should see that her record has Limited access. The rest display as Public access.
3. Assign the **AsiaPac** Team (that you created in a previous exercise) to this lookup.	Select Ania's record and click **Omit Selected**. Click **Tag All** to select the rest. Right-click, **Edit Contact Access**, **Create New Access List...**, click the **Teams** tab, double-click **AsiaPac**, and click **OK**, **Yes**, **OK**.
4. Notice that Access Level did not change for CH TechONE employees that are users.	
5. Select three of the Contacts and add the **Europe** Team to their access.	Click **Untag All**, enable **Tag Mode**, if necessary, select any three Contacts, right-click, select **Edit Contact Access**, **Add Users/Teams...**, click the **Teams** tab, click **Europe**, click **OK** and **Yes**.

 *To remove selected users or Teams from all selected users, click **Contacts**, **Edit Contact Access**, **Remove Users/Teams**..., select the user or team to remove, and click **OK**, **Yes**.*

*To remove Limited Access from all selected users and return them to Public status, click **Contacts**, **Edit Contact Access**, **Make Contact Public**, **Yes**.*

Lookup Contacts by Access (Premium Only)

Sometimes it would be helpful to review a list of all Contacts that the "Europe" team has access to.

Procedure: To look up Contacts by access

1. Click **Lookup**, **Advanced**, **Contact by Access**.	This query can be in Contacts or Opportunities view.
2. Select from **Contacts** or **Opportunities** for your **Search for** parameters.	You can identify Contacts or Opportunities that have security applied.
3. Select from the **That are:** security options.	You can select from Limited Access, Public, Private, or <Any Access>.

Database Security | 477

4. Specify the **And accessible to:** parameter.

   User: Indicates Contacts specifically given access to a record. If they can view the Contact or Opportunity through their Team membership only, then they will not be found in this lookup.

   Team: Displays current Teams.

5. You can also specify (or further narrow your search) by Record Manager.

6. Specify if you want to **Include users** in your results.

7. Click **OK**.

You can select a specific user or a Team of users. You can also select <Any User> or <Any Team> if you want to focus on one of the other variables in this lookup.

Right-click a Team name, select **Show Team Members** to confirm the membership.

This option is grayed out if Limited Access is selected (since users are Public).

Practice: **Lookup Private**	
What to do	*How to do it/Comments*
1. Locate private Contacts for Chris Huffman.	**L**ookup, Ad**v**anced, **C**ontact by Access, change to **Private Contacts**, and click **OK**.

 These are Contacts that are only private to Chris. If you want to see what Contacts Allison has marked as private, you must sign on with her logon credentials.

"Managers" Team

One team that is created by default in all ACT! databases: "Managers" (though it doesn't display in the Manage teams dialog). All users assigned to a Manager role are automatically added to the "Managers" team. In older versions (2005, 2006, or 2007) of ACT!, the "Managers" team was automatically added to all records with Limited Access. Consequently any user with a Manager role could view all Contacts and could **not** be restricted by Limited Access assignments.

While the "Managers" team is no longer automatically added to records with Limited Access, if your database was converted from an older version, you may want to remove the "Managers" team from all Limited Access records.

 *To remove the Managers team access, **L**ookup, Ad**v**anced, **C**ontact by Access. Search for Limited Access Contacts and click **OK**. Use **[Ctrl+A]** to select all Contacts in the resulting list. Click **Contacts**, Edit **C**ontact Access, **R**emove Users/Teams. Select the **Teams** tab. Click **Managers** and click **OK**. Answer **Yes** to continue.*

Field Security

While Contact Access (Public or Limited Access) determines which users can see which records, Field Security controls access to specific fields. The available settings for each field are…

- **Full Access** is the default permission for all fields for all users.
- **Read-Only** access in the basic version of ACT! allows you to mark a field as Read-Only (viewing, but no editing or deleting contents) for all users of the database. In the Premium version, you can specify Read-Only access for individual users (and/or teams) for a specific field.
- **No Access** is only available in the Premium version. It restricts specific users and/or teams from seeing any data in fields configured with this setting.

This security feature is covered more in-depth the Database Design & Layout chapter, with details on how to assign the security to fields in your database.

Review: Database Security

1. Create a new user for Jane Chan. Give her Standard rights. Make her change her password at log on. Assign her to the USA team.

2. Look up ID/Status of Vendor and change any that have Limited Access back to Public.

3. Make Betty Browser a Standard user.

4. Add Handheld device Sync rights to Fred Fenderline.

Database Maintenance

If you find yourself administering an ACT! database, you might wish to cultivate a few skills. In this section we will,

- ☑ Manage some database preferences settings.

- ☑ Learn the basics of database maintenance.

- ☑ Familiarize yourself with the built-in ACT! backup and restore utilities.

- ☑ Begin to clean up your database, dealing with duplicates and replacing old data.

Database Preferences

The Tools, Preferences dialog helps you to configure ACT! so that it more closely works the way that you do. Most of the preferences set here are *workstation* specific, not username specific. In other words, if you go to another PC and log in with your name, the preferences may not be set the same.

However, the preferences on the Admin tab affect every user and every record in the current database. The options on the Admin tab can only be accessed by a user with an Administrator role (they are grayed out for everyone else).

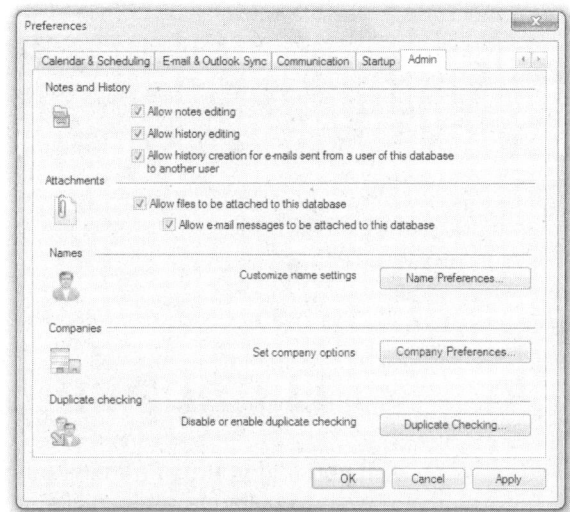

 The Names Preferences option was discussed on page 45 and the Company Preferences option was discussed on page 274.

Disabling Notes and History Editing

In some companies there is a need to ensure that no history or notes entered for any contact in the database can be changed or deleted… not even ones that you have entered yourself. It could be a regulatory issue. It could be a tracking issue (a Contact Deleted history is left on the My Record of the person who deleted a contact in the database). Whatever the reason, disabling Notes and History editing is only a click away.

Procedure: To disable notes and history editing

1. Click **Tools, Preferences…**.

2. Click the **Admin** tab (click the arrows at the top right of the dialog to display the Admin tab).

3. Under the Notes and History section, uncheck **Allow notes editing** and **Allow history editing**.

4. Click **OK**

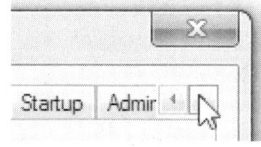

Disabling E-mail History on User Records

Many times e-mails sent from one person in your own company to another may contain contents of a more personal nature (reprimands, employee reviews, notes about who is being fired, etc). Perhaps you have members of your team that cc you on much of their client correspondence, and do you really want a copy of those e-mails on the client record AND on your record?

It is possible to restrict e-mail history from being created for user records (login users in your own company) will still allowing it for all other contacts in your database.

Procedure: To disable e-mail history on user's records

1. Click **Tools, Preferences…**.
2. Click the **Admin** tab (click the arrows at the top right of the dialog to display the Admin tab).
3. Under the Notes and History section, uncheck Allow history creation for e-mails sent from a user of this database to another user.
4. Click **OK**

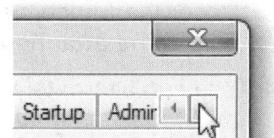

Disabling File and/or E-mail Attachments

This Preferences option disables the ability to attach files to the Documents tab as well as the History, Activities or Notes tab. However, users can still attach *Shortcuts* to files. This means that no files (Internet Explorer pages, Word files, Mail Merged documents or e-mails) can be attached to the Notes, History, Activities, or Documents tabs.

There is a sub-option that allows you to disable only the attachments of e-mail history. Disabling this option allows you to record the history of the e-mail send, but it restricts the users from using the Attach option.

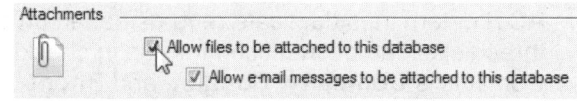

You might want to disable one of these options for several reasons.

- It **prevents the creation of duplicate files** caused by selecting the "Add Document, File" option (creates a duplicate of the selected file in the \Attachments folder under the ACT database).
- Using file shortcuts **helps to maintain your current file management structure** so that all users (even non-ACT! users) have access to files on the server.
- The \Attachments folder is a public folder that contains all files and e-mails attached to the database, including files attached to contacts with Limited Access. This folder can be searched by all users. If you alternately only use shortcuts to files in secure folder locations, then it will **help to maintain file security**.

- It **keeps synchronization file packets to a smaller size**, so the remote databases syncs are faster. However, if files are attached using the "Add Document, **Shortcut**" option, remote sync users may not have access to the files referenced by the Shortcut, unless they have VPN access to the remote folder location where the files are stored.

Procedure: To disable file attachments (but not shortcuts)

1. Click **Tools, Preferences**....

2. Click the **Admin** tab (click the arrows at the top right of the dialog to display the Admin tab).

3. Under the Attachments section, uncheck **Allow files to be attached to this database**.

4. You can alternately only uncheck Allow e-mail messages to be attached to the database.

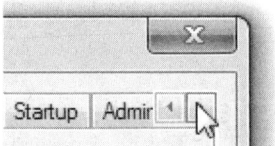

When you uncheck this option, users can still record and include the message text in the history, they just can't attach the e-mail (and its associated attachments). Consequently e-mail is not searchable from outside the database.

5. Click **OK**.

☞ *Disabling either of these options affects all users in the current database.*

Changing ACT!'s Default Duplicate Checking Criteria

ACT! determines duplicate records based on the defined Duplicate Checking criteria. Up to three fields can be identified for use in checking for duplicates. The default fields for all new Contacts is **Company**, **Contact**, and **Phone**. The default for Companies is **Company**, **Phone**, and **Record Creator**. The default for Groups is **Group Name** and **Record Creator**.

When entering new records into your ACT! database, if those fields match exactly (down to the period after Inc.), then the record is considered a duplicate, and you will receive a warning to be sure that you want to continue creating the record. Given the many different ways that you could enter a company name or even a contact name (Robert Johnson, Robert E Johnson, Robbie Johnson), the default duplicate checking criteria may not detect, and thus warn you, that you are entering a duplicate record. Using First Name and Last Name could alleviate this issue.

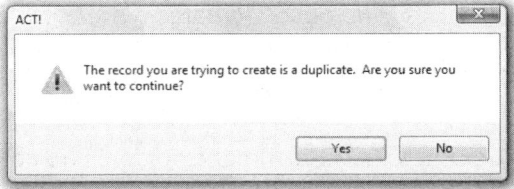

Database Maintenance

Procedure: To change the Duplicate Checking Criteria

1. Click **Tools, Preferences…**.

2. Click the **Duplicate Checking…** button at the bottom right of the dialog box.

3. Select up to three matching criteria.

   You must be a Manager or Administrator to perform this task.

   A default combination of Last Name, First Name and Phone (or City) might help ACT! catch more duplicate Contacts as they are entered.

   > ☞ *Notice that you may also select Duplicate Checking Criteria for Groups and Companies.*

4. Click **OK**.

File Locations for a Multi-user Database

Let's go back to the General tab in the Preferences dialog. To make it easier for your users to work in ACT!, you may want to make some minor changes to the way ACT! is set up on each workstation. These changes are all made in the **Preferences** dialog box. One example is to change the default File location that ACT! uses, so that users can more easily open the database on the network drive.

Procedure: To change default file locations

1. Click **Tools, Preferences…**.

2. On the General tab, in **Location:**, browse to the folder on the network where the database has been saved, and click **OK**.

   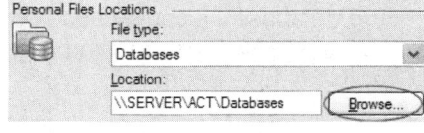

   > ☞ *It is unlikely that you will need to change the default locations for **Documents**, **Internet Links**, and **Dictionaries**. However, you may want to change the default **Backup Location** on the server from the My Documents folder to a more public location.*

3. Click **OK**.

> *After you have changed the Preferences for the user, when you click **File**, **Open/Share Database**, the database name should always be displayed.*

General Database Maintenance

While most databases seem to work forever without any issues, preventative care is always a good thing. Keeping your software up-to-date, backing up the data, and performing general maintenance are all good standard practices.

Automatic Update Notification

From time to time, ACT! releases minor updates to the program that modify your installation of the software to the latest release. For example, if you are using ACT! 2012, the version number is 13.0.xx. (You can determine your current version of the program by clicking on **Help**, **About ACT!**.) You can have ACT! search for and apply any available updates to your current version.

Updates will not change any of your personal files or settings. An ACT! update will however, do two things...

- Add fixes to the program that are likely to overcome potential problems you may encounter. Updates may also add minor functionality to the program.
- Update the open database to make it compatible with the newly updated software.

ACT! has made it easy to check for updates...it's automatic. By default, your ACT! software periodically checks for updates through the Internet and prompt you to apply the changes. Keeping this automatic notification enabled makes it easier for single users of ACT! to stay up to date.

However, if you are in a corporate environment where several users share the same database, ACT! Premium has the automatic notification disabled. (If you have upgraded your software, you may want to verify that the automatic update feature is disabled.) It makes more sense to have one person download the update (which can be quite large) when it is available from www.act.com and update all workstations on a schedule. In addition, if even one workstation applies the update, and then opens the company database (which updates the database), it could cause problems with synchronization of remote databases and PDA devices. Also, keep in mind that Restricted or Browse users may not apply software updates to their workstation.

  The updates only modify the current version of the program that you originally purchased. To upgrade to the latest version of the program (from ACT! 6 or from ACT! 2000 to ACT! 2012), you must purchase an Upgrade.

Database Maintenance | 485

Procedure: To change the update interval

1. Click **Tools, Preferences….**
2. Click the **Startup** tab.

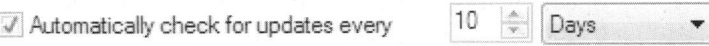

☞ *You must have a Manager or Administrator role to change these options.*

3. Select **Days**, **Weeks**, or **Months** from the drop-down list. Scroll and select the desired interval.

   Uncheck "Automatically check for updates every" if you don't want ACT! to automatically search for updates.

☞ *To manually check for an update, click **Help**, **ACT! Update…**. A message appears at the bottom right of the screen to prompt you to download any available updates or to let you know that you already have the latest version. If an update is available, you will be prompted to download.*

Practice: Check for Updates

What to do	How to do it/Comments
1. See what version of ACT! you are currently running.	**Help**, **About ACT!**.
2. See how often your PC is checking with ACT! through the Internet for updates.	**Tools**, **Preferences**, click the **Startup** tab.
3. **IMPORTANT:** If you share a database with others in your organization, skip this step. It is important that all users accessing a shared database be on the same version. Otherwise, check now to see if your PC needs updating.	**Help**, **ACT! Update…** Your database administrator will let you know when to update your ACT! software.

Back Up

Backing up your database enables you to recover quickly from equipment failures or other catastrophes (like having your laptop stolen…Yikes). It can also help you move your database to a new location or give it a new name. (In fact, it is the only way to rename your database).

ACT! comes with a built-in backup utility, which not only can back up all of your database information, but can also backup your personal supplemental files as well.

When you issue the Backup command, you have two options...

- **Database...** option includes all files that make up your database (the three files in the \Databases folder that have the same name with extensions of .ADF, .ALF, and .PAD) along with *all* files found in the \[databasename]-database files folder, including folders like \Attachments, \Dashboards, \Layouts, \Reports, and \Templates.
- **Personal Files** are the Documents, Internet Links, and spelling Dictionaries that you have created and/or modified. "Documents" are those files found in the \My Documents\ACT\ACT Data \Documents folder. The default location for "Internet Links" and "Dictionaries" is \Documents and Settings\<username>\ Application Data\ACT\ ACT Data\Netlinks and ..\Spell. However you can change the default folder locations with **Tools, Preferences**.

The default location on Windows Vista and Windows 7 for "Documents" is \Documents\ACT \ACT Data\Documents folder. The default location for "Internet Links" and "Dictionaries" is \Users\<username>\AppData\Roaming\ACT\ACT Data\ Netlinks and ..\Spell, however you can change the default folder locations with **Tools**, **Preferences**.

ACT! provides two methods to back up your ACT! database. You can manually back up your database with a menu command or you can automate the process with the ACT! Scheduler function.

 *Your company may have software that handles all of your file backups on a regular basis. However, regular backup software **will not back up a SQL Server database like ACT!**, and the software designed to handle tasks like that can be expensive. So, it is quite likely that your current backup software is NOT making backups of your ACT! database.*

Automatically Backing Up Your Database
Let's look at ACT!'s automatic method first. Manual backups are easy to do, but so easy to forget. The ACT! Scheduler can automate the task for you so that your database is backed up on a regular schedule to the location you specify.

Backups will occur in the background even while multiple people are still working in the database. In fact, the automatic backup operation is so quiet you may look at the ACT! Scheduler Task Log, or at the time stamp on the .zip file in Windows Explorer, to verify that the backup actually took place.

As you define the task in ACT! Scheduler, you will be prompted to assign a name to your backups. Each time the Scheduler performs a backup, it will append the specified name with the date and time of the backup to give it a unique name, so that no backup overwrites any

Database Maintenance | 487

previous backups. After a period of time, you may want to review the backup folder to delete selected backups (especially if you specified hourly backups) to keep the folder to a manageable size.

Procedure: To set up automatic backup

1. Click **Tools, ACT! Scheduler…**.

2. Click **Create a task**.

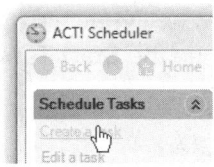

3. **Browse…** to locate your database, and click **Open**.

   Enter your **User name:** and any associated **Password:**.

   Click **Next>**.

   ACT! will verify that you have rights to back up the database.

4. In the Task: area, use the drop-down arrow to select **Database backup** and click **Next>**.

5. **In the Database Backup Options screen, click Browse… to select your preferred location.**

   If you are backing up on the server, select a location that is not in the My Documents folder. You may want to create a folder for it.

6. Enter a name for the backup file.

   When the Scheduler makes a backup, the date and time are appended to each backup file name (e.g., "ACT! ACT2012Demo 11-12-10 05:00PM.zip").

   Indicate if you want to **Include Attachments** in the backup.

   Add a password to the backup zip file if desired.

   The "Include attachments" option is only available to Administrators.

   Click **Next>**.

   Your regular backup software will have no problem backing up the \Attachments folder, but it is nice to keep all of the ACT! files together in one backup zip file.

Sage ACT!

7. In the Backup File Management screen, select the number of backup files to save and click **Next>**.

8. Set a schedule. Perhaps
   Daily
   Every weekday (M-F)
   Change the **Start Time**

9. Click **Finish**.

10. Click **Start Service** if needed and then click **Exit**.

If you have regular backup software, it is making backups of your zip files. So it is not necessary to keep more than a few days of backups.

If you are backing up your remote database, be sure to select a time when your machine is on. The operation is so silent, anytime during the day will work.

Once a task is scheduled, the ACT! Scheduler icon will display as running in the System Tray. If you see an X on the icon, the service is not started and your tasks cannot be handled by ACT!. Return to ACT! Scheduler and click Start Service.

Practice: Schedule an Automatic Backup

What to do	How to do it/Comments
1. Schedule a daily automatic backup of the ACT2012Demo for a few minutes from now.	**Tools**, **ACT! Scheduler...**, click **Create a task**, **Browse...** to locate the ACT2012Demo database and click **Open**. Enter Chris Huffman as the user name and click **Next>**. In the Task: area, use the drop-down arrow to select **Database backup** and click **Next>**. Accept the default backup location and file name, and click **Next>**. Set a Daily Schedule for a few minutes from now and click **Finish** and **Exit**.

We'll keep working and check the logs in a minute.

Manually Backing Up Your Database

If you are planning to make major changes to a database (e.g., import data, add a password policy, or change the database design), you should make a quick manual backup in case something goes wrong.

Database Maintenance | 489

Procedure: To manually back up your ACT! database

1. Click **File, Back Up, Database...**. Users with an Administrator or Manager role can back up their database. Standard users may have their roles customized to add this remote administration capability.

   The **Back Up Database** dialog box suggests a location and name for the backup file.

    The backup utility compresses the data in your database into a .zip file. This allows all data to be stored in one file to minimize the disk space needed.

2. Use the **Browse...** button to change the suggested location and file name for the backup, as desired. If you have backed up the database before, you may want to provide a different name (or location) so that the original backup file is not overwritten.

3. Determine if you want to **Include Attachments**. If you want to back up before making a field change or an import, you really don't need to include attachments in the backup file.

4. For additional security, add a check to the **Password protect file** option.

5. Click **OK**. ACT! proceeds to back up your data. Back Up progress is displayed.

    If a previous backup with the same filename exists, you will be prompted to replace it.

    Enter and confirm the password, if you checked that option, and click OK.

   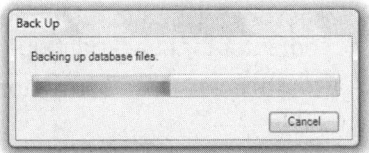

6. Click **OK** to confirm the completion of the backup.

 Your regular backup software will easily back up the \[dbasename]-files folder. However, the primary data files (the databasename.ADF and the databasename.ALF) cannot be backed up by regular backup software (SQL Server holds these files open). ACT! Scheduler can back up the database, then your backup software can make backups of the zip files.

Sage ACT!

Practice: Back Up Your New Database

What to do	How to do it/Comments
1. Even though the ACT2012Demo database is just for practice, let's back it up.	You should have the **ACT2012Demo** database open.
2. Backup the database (to the default folder).	Choose **File**, **Back Up**, **Database**..., accept the default location and filename, and click **OK**. When the backup is complete, click **OK**.
3. Use Windows Explorer to view the Backup folder. You should find two backups: one from the Scheduler and one that you made manually. How can you tell them apart?	The default location for backups is \My Documents\ACT\ACT Data\Backup. The filename with a date is the one created by Scheduler. Documents\ACT\ACT Data\Backup
4. When you see the one created by ACT! Scheduler, you should probably delete the task that makes automatic backups of the ACT2012Demo database.	**Tools**, **ACT! Scheduler**..., select the Back Up task for ACT2012Demo and click **Delete a task**. Click **Yes** to verify the deletion.

☞ *In real life, the backup process could take a great deal longer. We are aware of how boring performing backups can be, but when you are making mass changes, an ounce of protection is...well... you know.*

Restoring a Backup

The purpose of backing up your data is so that you can restore a database when it becomes necessary. When restoring a backup, you have three options:

- **Restore** – Used to restore a database to the exact same folder on the original computer that backed it up.
- **Restore as** – Used to restore a copy of the database to a new location or with a new name
- **Unpack and Restore Remote Database** – Used to restore a database that was created for synchronization.

We'll look at the first two commands here. The **Unpack and Restore Remote Database** option is for sync databases only and is covered in the synchronization chapter of this QuickStudy Guide.

The **Restore** command only restores the database to the same machine name, to the same drive and folder name, and with the same name as the original.

Database Maintenance | 491

Procedure: To restore a database backup

1. Go to the computer that will host the database.

   You must also have an Administrator role to restore a database.

    You cannot perform this procedure across the network. You must be physically at the computer that will hold the database.

2. Click **File**, **Restore**, **Database**….

   The current database will close.

3. Select **Restore** and click **OK**.

4. Use the **Browse…** button to locate and select the .zip file of your database backup and click **Open**.

   The default location **is \My Documents\ACT\ACT Data\ Backup** folder.

    Documents\ACT\ACT Data\Backup

   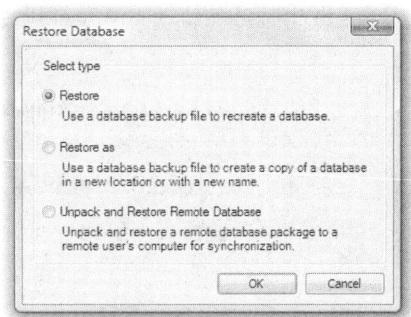

5. Click **OK**.

6. Enter a valid **user name** and any associated **password** and click **OK**.

   A user name with an Administrator role.

7. Click **Yes** to acknowledge that newer files may be overwritten by any older files in the backup file.

   This means the \Attachments folder changes or additions as well. The database and associated files will be restored.

    *If you backed up the database without attachments, when you use the **Restore** command, it will not overwrite the current \Attachments folder with a blank folder.*

8. Click **OK** to acknowledge the successful completion of Restore.

9. Open the restored database.

Restore As

The **Restore as** command is used to restore a copy of the database with a new name or to a new location. For example, if you want to restore one of your backup copies to verify some data, you would use this option so that you could give the restored copy of the database a different name (you probably don't want to overwrite your good working copy).

 *This is probably obvious, but if you backed up the database without attachments, when you use the **Restore as** command, there will be no files in the \Attachments folder for the new database.*

Sage ACT!

If you need to **move** your database from one server (or workstation) to another machine, use the **Restore as** command. Even if you set up the same exact folder structure, the **Restore** command will only restore a database to a machine with the same name that backed it up. So unless you named your new server with the same name as the old one, you will need to use the **Restore as** option.

Procedure: To use "Restore as" to move or rename a database

1. Go to the computer that will host the database.

   You must also have an Administrator role to restore a database.

2. Click **File, Restore, Database…**.

3. Select the **Restore as** option and click **OK**.

4. Use the **Browse…** button to locate and select the .zip file of your database backup and click **Open**.

   The default location is **\My Documents\ACT\ACT Data\Backup** folder.

    Documents\ ACT\ACT Data\Backup

5. Enter a **New database name** for the database.

   Enter a new **To location:** (you can **Browse…** if you need to).

   Check to **S**hare this database with other users if desired.

   Enter a **User name:** that has an Administrator role in the original database.

   Enter the associated **Password:**.

   Click **OK**.

 You cannot perform this procedure across the network. You must be physically at the computer that will hold the database.

The current database will close.

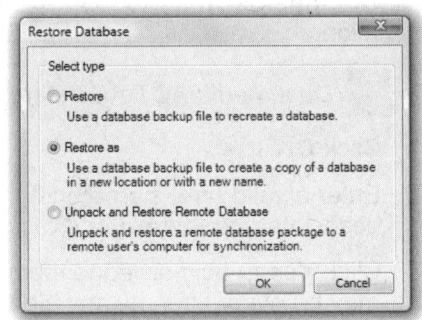

Database Maintenance | 493

6. Click **OK** to acknowledge the successful completion of Restore.
7. Open the restored database. **File**, **Open/Share Database...**, click the database, and click **Open Database**. If prompted, enter a valid **User name:**, any associated **Password:**, and click **OK**.

Practice: Restoring

What to do	How to do it/Comments
1. You should always verify that your backup system is working. Use the **Restore as** option to restore one of your backups to a new name like: ACT2012DemoRestored.	**File**, **Restore**, **Database**, select **Restore as**, click **OK**, click **Browse...** to select one of the backup files, and click **Open**, **OK**. Enter a new name for the backup (like ACT2012DemoRestored). **Browse...** to select the location. (This is the tricky part. If you had previously installed ACT! on your machine it will be: \My Documents\ACT \ACT for Win 7\Databases (or \ACT for Windows 8 ... 11). Otherwise, it will be in the \ACT Data\ Databases folder). Enter the username of Chris Huffman and click **OK**. Click **OK** to acknowledge the restore.
2. Open the restored database.	

Deleting a Database

As you work with ACT!, you may find yourself with a database you don't need. Perhaps you merged two smaller databases into one, and the smaller one is now redundant. Perhaps you restored a backup that you no longer need. You can't delete the database and associated files using normal Windows Explorer delete commands. Deleting just the ".pad" file from a Windows Explorer window will not delete all of the rest of the files. Fortunately, ACT! has a command to take care of this for you.

Sage ACT!

Procedure: To delete the current database

1. Log on to the database that you want to delete as a user with an Administrator role.

   Only a user with an Administrator role can delete a database.

2. Click **Tools, Data**b**ase Maintenance, Delete Database**.

   ☞ *Before executing this command, be sure that you do not need to copy or move any files.*

   Deleting a database includes deleting **all** files associated with that database, including the files that make up your actual database (the three files in the **\Databases** folder that have the same name with extensions of .ADF, .ALF, and .PAD) and *all* files found in the **\[databasename]-database files** folder, including files in the \Attachments folder.

3. Click **Yes** to verify that you want to delete the database.

   Be careful. You cannot undo this action. The database will then be locked.

4. Click **Yes** again to proceed with the deletion of the database.

Practice: Deleting a Database

What to do	How to do it/Comments
1. If you completed the previous exercise, you should be in the database that you restored from a backup copy. So let's delete this database. Otherwise, skip to the next page.	**Tools, Data**b**ase Maintenance, Delete Database**. Click **Yes, Yes**.
2. Open ACT2012Demo again.	**F**ile, click **2 ACT2012Demo.pad**.

Check and Repair

The **Check and Repair** operation is a good preventative measure to safeguard your data and to improve performance. It is important to the general health and speed of your database. While it should be a common practice to run this tool after you have completed changing the database structure, it should also become a fundamental procedure in a multi-user environment and be performed on a regular basis. (Yes, we know that "regular" is a relative term. It just depends on how many users you have accessing the database and how much data each one is changing/adding. Regular could be anywhere from weekly to monthly. Just pick an interval and run with it. You can always change it as your business needs require.)

You can manually perform Check and Repair with a menu command. You can also automate the process with the ACT! Scheduler function.

Database Maintenance | 495

Procedure: To check and repair the database

1. Click **Tools, Database Maintenance, Check and Repair…**.

    - **Integrity Check** inspects for errors/non-compliant field data and repairs them if possible.
    - **Reindex rebuilds** the index files that the database uses to organize your data.

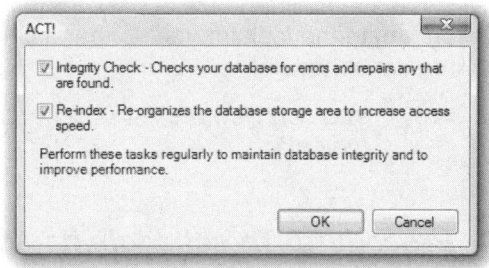

2. Click **OK**.
3. Click **OK** to verify the successful completion of **Check and repair**.

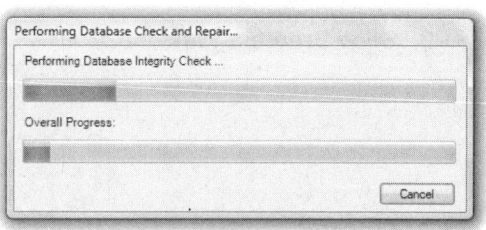

4. If errors are found, you will be prompted to lock the database so that ACT! can make the necessary repairs.

Even though you can run Check and Repair while other users are logged on to the database, if ACT! locates any errors, it can't make them unless everyone is logged out.

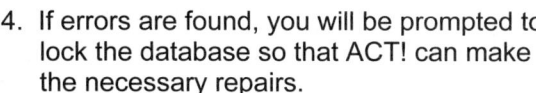

What to do	How to do it/Comments
1. Run Check and Repair on the database.	**Tools, Database Maintenance, Check and Repair…**.

Sage ACT!

Scheduling Database Maintenance

Database maintenance is easy to do, but so easy to forget. The ACT! Scheduler can automate the task for you so that a Check and Repair is performed on your database on a regular schedule.

 You can view the ACT! Scheduler Task Log to verify that the maintenance actually took place.

Procedure: To schedule database maintenance

1. Click **Tools, ACT! Scheduler**....

2. Click **Create a task**.

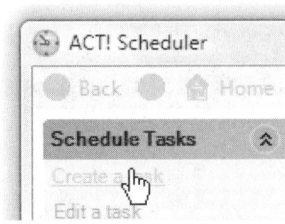

3. **Browse...** to locate your database and click **Open**.

   Enter your **User name:** and any associated **Password**.

   Click **Next>**.

   ACT! will check your user name and password and verify that you have rights to perform maintenance.

4. In the Task: area, use the drop-down arrow to select **Database maintenance** and click **Next>**.

5. In the Database Maintenance Options screen, verify that Integrity Check and Re-index are both checked and click **Next>**.

6. Set a schedule. Perhaps
   Daily
   Every weekday (M-F)
   Select a **Start Time**
   Click **Finish**.

   Be sure to select a time when your machine is on. You can not schedule a Database Maintenance task to occur within 10 minutes of a Backup.

Database Maintenance | 497

7. Click **Start Service** (if necessary) and then click **Exit**.

Once a task is scheduled, the ACT! Scheduler icon will display as running in the System Tray. If you see an X on the icon, the service is not started, and your tasks cannot be handled by ACT!. Return to ACT! Scheduler and click Start Service.

Practice: Scheduling Maintenance

What to do	How to do it/Comments
1. Schedule maintenance for the ACT2012Demo for one minute from now.	**Tools**, **ACT! Scheduler...**, click **Create a Task**, **Browse...** to locate ACT2012Demo and click **Open**. Logon name=Chris Huffman, click **Next>**, set schedule, click **Finish** and then **Exit**.

Checking the ACT! Scheduler Log

It is a good idea to check the ACT! Scheduler Log every now and then to verify that your Backups and Database Maintenance Tasks are being successfully accomplished. After all, what if someone changed a password and forgot to let the ACT! Scheduler know. It's easy to check the Scheduler's Event log.

Procedure: To check the ACT! Scheduler log

1. Click **Tools, ACT! Scheduler...**.
2. Click **View Task Log**.   The start time, type of event, result, listing of errors (among other things) is listed.
3. Click **OK** and **Exit**.

Practice: Viewing the Scheduler Task Log

What to do	How to do it/Comments
1. View the ACT! Scheduler Task Log to verify that the ACT2012Demo was backed up earlier and that Database Maintenance ran on schedule.	**Tools**, **ACT! Scheduler...**, click **View Task Log**. Purge the log if you like and then click **OK**.
2. Delete the Maintenance task that you set up in the previous practice.	Select any ACT2012Demo database tasks and click **Delete a task**. Click **Yes** to confirm.
3. Exit ACT! Scheduler.	Click **Exit**.

Importing an Excel File

Many times you will want to import data that has been exported from another program or data that you purchased from a list vendor. It may come to you as an Excel file or as a file with a .txt or .csv extension. Be sure to delete any rows before the header row (any blank or title rows) and save the file.

Procedure: To import an Excel file

1. Open your ACT! database.

2. Click **File, Back up, Database…**. This is the number one rule of importing. Back up first.

3. Select a new name and file locations if desired.

4. Click **OK**. Click **OK** to acknowledge that the backup completed.

5. **File**, **Import…** Be sure that you have exited Excel and the file is not open on your system.

6. Click **Next>** at the Welcome screen.

7. Change the File type to import:

   Excel or one of the Text options

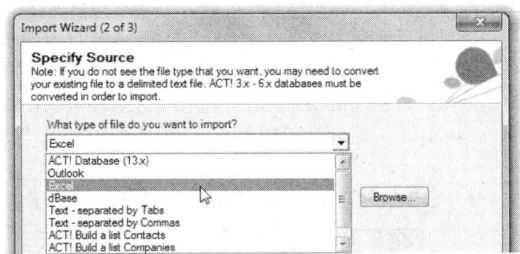

8. Click the **Browse** button.

9. Locate the file to import and click **Open**.

10. Click **Next>**. No User Name and Password are required for Excel or Text Delimited files.

11. Select the kind of records you would like to import. **Contact Records** is the default.

    Click **Next>**.

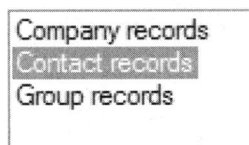

12. Select the **Custom import** option. If you *know* that the import headers exactly match the ACT! field labels then **Typical** is fine. However **Custom** only involves a few more clicks and you can easily verify all fields are mapping.

Database Maintenance

13. Usually the first record is row 1 and contains the column headers, so don't put a check in this option.

    Click **Next>**.

14. Verify that all Contact fields are mapped correctly.

    ☞ *If you have saved a previous mapping, click **Load Map**.*

    For every field on the left, there should be a linked field name on the right. ACT! will use some synonym mapping and will ignore case, spacing and common punctuation.

    If a field in the left column is not mapped, use the drop-down to select a field. If you leave it blank, the data WILL NOT BE IMPORTED.

    Scroll through the list to verify that there are no incorrect or blank fields.

15. If you are not sure about the mapping, you can click the right arrow to display a **Preview Data** column.

    This column displays values from the database so that you can see if your mapping makes sense.

If Row 1 (the first record) has the names of the columns, you don't want to import the first record. You only use it for mapping.

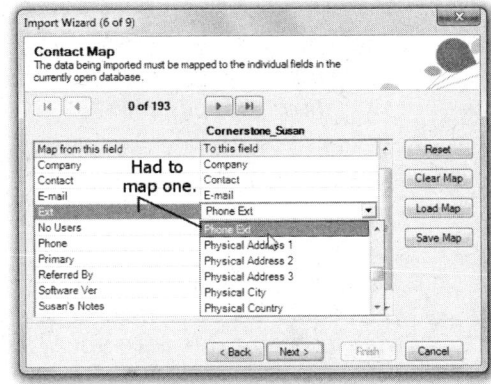

☞ *For example, ACT! is able to map "ext" to "Extension" or "Phone Ext", but may not be able to map "Employee Count" to "No of Employees". You will need to use the drop-down to locate the field name so that your data will be imported.*

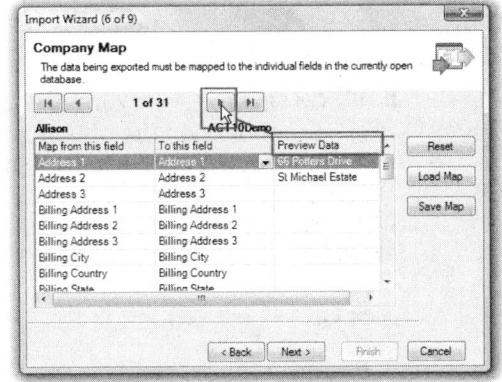

16. If you are in the master database (not a remote), and you have not yet created a field to hold the imported data, you can alternately click the <Create new ACT! field> to create and automatically map the data.

     All fields created will be Character fields, regardless of the data that is being imported.

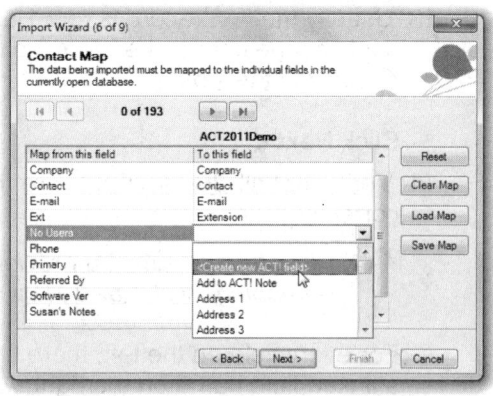

17. Once you have all of your fields mapped, you could click **Save Map** to save your work for the next text file you will import.

This is a big help if you import the same text file with the same columns every month.

    Click **Next>**.

18. After you have finished mapping the fields, click **Next>**.

19. If you clicked to create a new field, you will see an additional dialog that allows you to double-click to change the field name and field length. Click **Next>**.

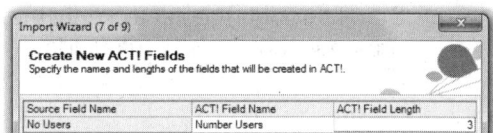

20. Click the **Contact...** button to specify your Merge Options.

     *Or **Group...** or **Company...** button depending on the option you selected in step 11.*

    Select the options that make sense for this import.

    Click **OK**.

Merge - Fills in blank fields in the record with data from the source file. If the destination field contains data, no data is imported.

Replace with newest records - Replaces the data in the record with the most recent Edit Date. (Not relevant for this import type.)

Replace with source record - Replaces the field data with the Excel data.

Do not change – Ignores data in the text file.

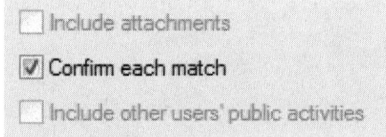

21. At the lower left, determine if you want to be prompted to **Confirm each match** by checking or unchecking.

    Click **Next>**.

22. Click **Import**.

If there is a problem, the button may not be enabled. You can click the **Details** button to determine where the mismatch has occurred and then use the **<Back** button to make corrections.

23. Click **Yes** or **No** as desired.

If you create a new field, you will be prompted to modify the layout.

24. If you need to make additional field modifications, click **Tools**, **Define Fields** and make the changes as desired.

On the Import Complete page, to view the details of imported data and any errors, click View import log.

25. Click **Finish**

26. Click **Tools, Database Maintenance, Check and Repair... OK**

Whenever you make these kinds of changes it is a good idea to perform database maintenance.

☞ *Close and reopen ACT! between each import.*

Check the database. Does all look OK. Did the number count increase to about the right amount (some of the records may have merged into existing records in the database).

If you have other import issues, you might check out this guide on importing all kinds of data into ACT!: http://www.cornerstonesolutions.com/import.html

Cleaning Up the Data

Over time, your database will need a little spring cleaning. You may find duplicate names in the database. There may be companies whose name or address information needs to be changed (on 25 records...Yikes).

Duplicates

Who knows how they get there, but almost every database will eventually contain duplicate Contacts. Sometimes you forget that you already entered the name. If you are working in a multi-user sync environment, someone might not have used the Lookup command to see if the name was already in the database before they input a new Contact. If you import names from another database or another source, you can also bring in duplicates.

ACT! has a tool that can help you locate some of these duplicates, but you will still have to find some on your own.

Sage ACT!

Procedure: To lookup duplicates

1. Click **Tools, Sca<u>n</u> for Duplicates…**.

2. Select the three matching criteria.

 ACT! determines duplicate Contact records based on the three fields listed. If all three fields do not match (down to the period after Inc.), ACT! will not display the records as duplicates.

3. Click **OK**.

Try different combinations to help you identify the duplicates (e.g., Last Name, First Name, and City).

4. Duplicates will display in the **List View**. If no duplicates were found, you will see a message to that effect.

5. If you are a user with a Manager or Administrator role, you will be asked if you would like to start combining them. Answer **Yes** or **No** as desired.

See the next procedure for more details on combining Contacts.

Tips for Dealing with Duplicates

Sometimes you just know that there are duplicates in the database, and you need to find and deal with them. You can try scanning for duplicates based on different match criteria (e.g., last name, phone, and city).

The best way we know of to easily identify your database duplicates is to display the List View. Add the Last Name and First Name fields to the right of the Contact name (see page 38 to refresh your memory). Click the Last Name column to sort alphabetically by Last Name. Start scrolling to eyeball the database and find the duplicates.

You can enable **Edit Mode** while in List View and make changes to the **Company**, **Contact**, or **Phone** fields so that they will be included in future scans for duplicates.

You may want to enable **Tag Mode** to help you mark the Contacts as duplicates. As you locate duplicates, you could add them to a Group that you create, named Duplicates, to deal with them later.

Combine Duplicate Records

You could also deal with duplicates now by using the **Copy/Move Contact Data** feature. Once you have identified the Contacts that you want to merge, you can copy or move the data from one record to the other. However, keep in mind that you can only combine two Contacts at a time.

Procedure: To copy/move Contact data

1. Log on to the database as a user with an Administrator or Manager role and locate the records you want to merge.

   Tools, **Scan for Duplicates** to locate Contacts for merging or display the Group that you created.

2. Select two Contact Records to combine by selecting the first record, then **[Ctrl+click]** the second record.

   You can only combine two records at a time…even if you have three to combine.

   Click **Next>**.

3. Click **Tools, Copy/Move Contact Data…**.

   If you forgot to select two records, you can do it now.

4. Specify Source and Target Contact Records. Determine which Contact will receive all updates.

   Select the Contact with the most data as your target.

   Click **Next>**.

5. **Copy Data from Source to Target Record**.

   Select a field in the Source record and click **Copy** to copy the data to the Target record (the one you are keeping). Scroll to view and copy each field to the target Contact.

   You can scroll to view the different values in each field. Viewing the Edit Date field might help you decide which record has the most up-to-date information.

   ☞ *You cannot copy system fields (e.g., Edit Date, the ones that are grayed out).*

   Click **Next>**

6. **Move Additional Items from Source to Target (Optional)**.

   Select the additional items to move to the target Contact (you will probably want to select all of the options).

   After the selected items are transferred to the target Contact, they are deleted from the source record.

   ☞ *Secondary Contacts may be duplicated.*

   Click **Next>**.

Sage ACT!

7. **Delete the Source Record.**

   Select **Yes** to delete the source or **No** to keep the Contact.

   Click **Next>**.

    *If you selected **Yes** to delete the source Contact, click **Yes** to confirm and continue with the deletion.*

8. Click **Finish**.

Since everything has been transferred, it should be OK to delete the source Contact. If you select **No** (to keep the Contact) then a notation is placed on that Contact's **History** tab to indicate the name of the target Contact that now contains all of the notes, history, activities, etc.

Logon users cannot be deleted.

 Neither Static (manually added) Group membership nor Relationships transfer to the target Contact, so check that before combining them.

Practice: Dealing with Duplicates

What to do	How to do it/Comments
1. Find duplicates in the demo database based on the standard Company, Contact, and Phone fields.	**Tools**, **Scan for Duplicates**. None found.
2. Try again changing the matching criteria to Last Name, First Name, and City, but don't combine yet.	We found a few. Let's look more closely at the remaining Contacts. Click **No** to combine Contacts.
3. The Barretts are not duplicates...one is Sr. and the other is Jr. Omit them from the list.	Select each name and click **Omit Selected**. The Cadbury and Dittmeier records are duplicates.
4. Notice that Dittmeier has entries in the **Notes**, **History**, and **Secondary Contacts** tabs on both of her records.	Double-click Liz's name to view her record. Notice that some of the history on the Brandee's Bakery Contact is also associated with the "Company" record for Brandee's Bakery.
5. OK, let's merge the Dittmeier records and delete the remaining one. (She left Brandee's Bakery and started her own bakery.)	**Tools**, **Copy/Move Contact Data…**, click one Liz, **[Ctrl+click]** on the second one, and click **Next>**. Make Dittmeier Delights the target Contact, and click **Next>**. Copy her Birth Date and her Key Contact status from the old record to the new one, and click **Next>**. Select all additional items, and click **Next>**. Delete the source and click **Next>**. Answer **Yes** to confirm the deletion and click **Finish**.

Database Maintenance | 505

What to do	How to do it/Comments
6. Notice that the notes moved to the remaining Contact are still associated with Brandee's Bakery. Is her birthday there?	Even though Liz changed jobs, her history with Brandee's Bakery will still display on the original Company record.
7. Combine the Cadbury Contacts, but do not delete the record with no company name.	**T**ools, Copy/Move Contact Data….
8. Notice how the items were combined on Cadbury's record. Look at the History entry on the remaining Cadbury history.	If you opt to keep a record, ACT! lets you know that the original notes, history, activities, opportunities, Secondary Contacts, and documents were transferred.

Edit, Replace

Do you have one company name spelled 25 different ways in the database? Is the city name spelled just as many wrong ways? Do you have a client that has moved and now you have to change the address line on lots of records? All of these changes can be easily handled by the ACT! Replace command.

  *To clear the contents of an existing field and make it blank, don't enter anything in the **V**alue, and click **OK**.*

Procedure: To replace field with a specific value in multiple records

1. Look up the records that need to be changed.

     *If you don't perform a lookup first, this command will update **every** Contact in the database.*

2. Click **E**dit, **R**eplace Field….

3. Select the field to **Replace contents of:** from the drop-down list.

4. Enter the **V**alue that you wish to insert on all records in the current lookup.

5. Click **OK** to apply the change to the lookup.

6. Click **Yes** to continue.

You may have to work with the Contacts in the List View using Tag mode to get to the list that you want.

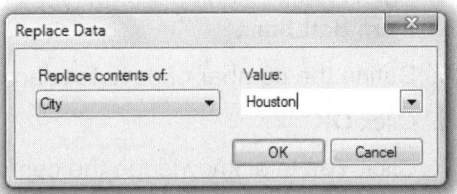

Check the Lookup status indicator at the lower left. If you didn't perform a lookup first, this change will be applied to the entire database.

Sage ACT!

Practice: Changing All At Once

What to do	How to do it/Comments
1. We received a notice that **American Dreams** has moved to… **1400 Smith Street Houston, TX 77002 Phone: 713-661-5095 No suite number.**	Look up all Contacts that belong to the Company – American Dreams. **Edit**, **Replace Field**. **Enter** the new Address 1, City, and phone number information. To remove the existing suite number for Address 2, replace Address 2 with nothing (a blank).

  Or you could create a Company record from one of the existing Contact records. Link the rest of the lookup to the Company records. Then, change the address on the Company Detail record and have it update all linked Contact records.

Remove Old Data

If you are a pack rat, you can skip this section. However, if you want to remove obsolete data from a database, you're in the right place. While it may seem desirable to keep this information forever, in a mature database, these items can offer little or no value.

The most logical data to remove is older, cleared activities. Once cleared, a copy of an activity is entered in the History tab. However, if you delete older, cleared activities, this will also remove them from the Calendar view.

Procedure: To remove old data

1. Log on to the database as a user with an Administrative role.

    Only a user with an Administrator role can remove old data.

2. Backup the database.

    File, **Back Up**, **Database**….

3. Click **Tools, Data**b**ase Maintenance, R**emove **Old Data**….

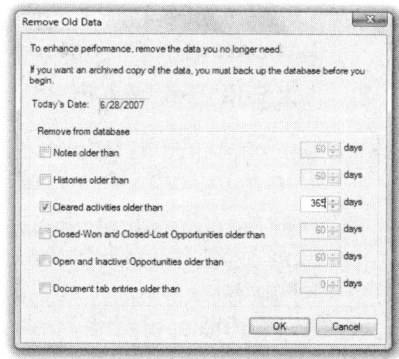

4. Put a check beside the data types to **Remove from database**.

5. Define the number of days for each item checked.

6. Click **OK**.

7. Click **Yes** to acknowledge the confirmation dialog box. Click **No** to Cancel the deletions.

8. Click **OK** to acknowledge the completion.

  It would be good to run Check and Repair after this procedure.

Synchronization

To be able to maintain up-to-date information with other ACT! users, you will:

☑   Review the concept of synchronization.

☑   Set up the final environment prior to creating the remote databases.

☑   Understand how to set up the remote user database(s).

☑   Discover how to realign territories.

Synchronizing Databases

If you are tied to your desk (and computer) all day, and/or if you are the only person in your company who needs access to your ACT! data, you don't need to synchronize, and you can close this book now (or skip to the Appendix).

If however, you have any of the following…

- remote users or an office that cannot directly access the database across a network, through Citrix® or Terminal Services, or if you have decided that the ACT! for Web version would not be appropriate, or
- users who need to have a copy of the database on their laptop as they travel around the countryside, or
- a single user who keeps copies of the database on a PC at home and on the one at work,
- …you will need to set up synchronization.

Synchronization is a method of sharing the contents of more than one database.

Synchronization is a two-way process. It will both send and receive database updates. This allows you to input different data into two or more separate databases and easily duplicate all of the data in each database. All of the databases are "synchronized" with each other.

Synchronization can be selective. You can choose to synchronize only records that belong to specified users or Teams (if you have Premium).

Synchronization is a pull process. The master database can only wait for the remotes to initiate the sync. Once synchronization has been set up, the only thing the remote user need do is issue the **Synchronize Now** command to update the master and the remote databases (or get ACT! to do it automatically).

ACT! synchronization is a background process that allows for normal use of the database during synchronization.

 There are no practice sessions for this chapter. Synchronization requires two PCs. You can perform each of the procedures as we discuss the synchronization setup. However, you will not be able to synchronize the two databases unless you actually set up the practice databases across a network. Let's take this process one step at a time.

Administrator Tasks – Setting Up the Sync Environment

As the database administrator, you will need to make a few decisions and perform a few tasks before you actually enable and set up the synchronization process.

Determine and Setup the Connection Method

Synchronization can be performed in one of three ways.

- **Network – Application Sync** – This is the only method available for syncing if you are using the basic ACT! by Sage version. This synchronization method requires an "inside a firewall" network connection (LAN, VPN, or RAS). The main **database must remain open** on the server to accept any incoming syncs.

- **Network – Sync Service** (Premium Only) – This synchronization method requires an "inside a firewall" network connection as well. However, an additional application is installed as a service to watch for incoming syncs, and thus the main database does not have to remain open on the server to accept incoming syncs. In addition, the Network Sync Service provides a mechanism for load balancing and can monitor incoming syncs for multiple databases simultaneously. This method is only available in ACT! Premium.

- **Internet – (HTTP) Sync** (Premium Only) – This synchronization method provides the ability to synchronize from "outside a firewall." It is similar to the network style database-to-database synchronization, but it is actually an IP address to IP address synchronization, via an open port. Thus, it requires a server with a static IP address that has IIS installed. Since it runs as a service, it also provides a mechanism for load balancing and can monitor incoming syncs for multiple main databases simultaneously. This method is only available in ACT! Premium. See page 518 for more information on Internet Sync.

The choice is really determined by which version of ACT! you are using and the infrastructure available to your remote users. For instance, your company may or may not have VPN (Virtual Private Network) access enabled. You may or may not have an IIS server with a static IP address for setting up Internet Sync.

Define Remote User(s)

Before you can set up synchronization with another user, that individual must be defined as a user in the database. In the Database Administration chapter, you can review how to create a new user on page 464.

Whatever security roles are assigned in the master database will also be assigned in the remote database. Keep in mind that Restricted and Browse users cannot synchronize. Consequently, you must assign remote users a Standard, Manager, or Administrator role. Standard role is the most logical choice for most users.

You will want to consider two custom permissions when defining users who will be using remote databases: **Remote Administration** and **Manage Sync Subscription List**. An added permission of Remote Administration allows the remote user (who does not have an Administrator role) to handle necessary tasks like back up, restore, and check and repair of their database. The custom permission for Manage Sync Subscription List defines whether a remote user may search a list of all Contacts in the database and manually add Contacts to the sync set (thus adding to the list of Contacts selected by the sync set).

 You may want to assign a Manager role to a remote user at the beginning. For example, you must have a Manager role to be able to import (including the import of another ACT! database or an Outlook Contacts list). You can temporarily assign Manager status to allow them to handle their imports, and then change their role to Standard. The next time they sync, their logon name is changed to a Standard role.

Restore the Database to Its Final Location

Set up the final environment for the database prior to enabling synchronization. This means that when you are ready to set up synchronization, the database has been...

      1.) installed on the server,
      2.) in a specific folder,
      3.) with a final database name,

and that none of these three items will change. If necessary, review the procedure outlined on page 457 to move the database to its final destination.

It is a best practice to only create the remote databases from your final setup environment (server machine, folder, and database name). If you later move the master database to a new server or folder or give the database a new name, changes in each remote user's Synchronization Panel (Manage Main Database Location) will need to be made to allow them to synchronize to the master.

Administrator Tasks – Creating the Sync Databases

Once you have made the decisions discussed on the previous pages and given some thought to how you will answer some of the questions for each remote user, you can set up synchronization.

Enable Synchronization

For a main database to be active and allow creation of remote databases, the database must be enabled. Enabling turns on the other synchronization tasks.

Synchronization

Procedure: To enable Synchronization

1. Click **Tools, Synchronization Panel…**.

2. Click **Enable Synchronization**. — All other options are grayed out.

3. Click **Yes** to confirm enabling synchronization. — All of the additional options in the dialog box are now enabled.

Manage Sync Sets

A **Sync Set** determines which Contacts in the main database will synchronize to a remote database. This is not a security issue.

 *Security is controlled by the **Limited Access** feature (a Premium only feature). You could sync the entire database to the remote user and only give them access to see their portion. However, regular syncing of the entire database and associated files may take longer than syncing only portions of the database.*

Sync Sets use Advanced Queries to control which Contacts will be included in a remote database when initially creating them and when later syncing them. So Sync Sets determine which Contacts the remote user *wants* to see in their database. The user may have access to see the entire database, but they only want to see the Contacts for which they are responsible.

Although you may create one Sync Set that is used by all remote databases, you may want to consider creating separate Sync Sets for each user (even if each Sync Set is exactly the same). This method gives you the most flexibility should you decide to change what one person receives vs. another after the roll out. Whichever method you use, you must create at least one Sync Set before you can create a remote database.

Procedure: To manage Sync Sets

1. Setup the sync user in the database, if necessary.

2. Click **Tools, Synchronization Panel…**.

3. Click **Manage Sync Set**.

4. Click **Create New Sync Set**. — Under Sync Set Tasks at the left.

5. Enter a **Sync Set name:** and associated **Description** and click **Next>**. — If you will create one Sync Set for all users, you could name the Sync Set "All". However creating a sync set for each user gives you the most options.

6. **Select Users** who will have access to the remote database using this Sync Set,
   - **All current and future users of this database**.
   - or **Select users**:

   and click **Next>**.

   The **All current and future users** option is good for a sync database that will be installed at a remote office. Anyone from the home office can open and review their schedule on the remote database.

   Use **Selected users:** will be the most often used choice. Select the intended user(s) of the Sync Set.

   ☞ *You can log into any remote database with a user name that has an Administrator role, so you don't need to add an Administrator user.*

7. **Select Contacts** that will be synchronized with the remote database,
   - **Synchronize all available Contacts**.
   - or **Define Sync Set criteria**.

   ☞ *If you select the first option (synchronize all), skip step 7a and go to step 8.*

   Click **Next>**.

   Synchronize all available = syncs all *available* Contacts to the remote database. If you have assigned Limited Access (ACT! Premium), then only contacts that the defined users can have access to will be synced.

   Define Sync Set criteria = uses an Advanced Query to limit the number of Contacts that are synchronized to the remote database. As Contacts are added to the database, any Contact that matches the Advanced Query criteria used by this Sync Set is sent to the remote user. The remote user may also be able to access additional records through a process called subscription.

7a. If you selected Define Sync Set criteria, then click **Create Criteria** (at the left).

   Define the criteria for this Sync Set. For help on developing Advanced Queries, see page 249.

   Click **OK** and then **Next>**.

   Sync sets control which Contacts will sync. All Opportunity, Group, and Company names will sync (if they are Private or have Limited Access then other users cannot see the data or associated items... but they can see the names.

   ☞ *Private or Limited Access. Opportunities do not inherit the security of their associations (Contacts, Companies, or Groups).*

8. Click **Finish**.

9. Return to step 4 to create additional sync sets

   or click **Home** to return to the Synchronization Task screen.

   Create additional Sync Sets, if necessary, for multiple remote users. If you like, you can use the Copy Sync Set (instead of the Create New Sync Set) to make your work go faster.

☞ *Any changes to Sync Set criteria are reflected in all remote databases that use that Sync Set the next time synchronization occurs. (Can you say that six times fast?)*

Create Remote Databases

Once Sync Sets are defined, you can create a remote database for each of your remote users. Remote databases are created only from a main database and cannot be created from another remote database. It is important to understand that you may **not** change the following options after you have created the remote database (without recreating the remote database).

Procedure: To create a remote database

1. Click **Tools, Synchronization Panel....**

2. Click **"Create Remote Database."**

3. Enter the number of databases you plan to create.

   This feature allows you to set criteria for creating up to 50 remote databases prior to actually creating them.

4. Assign the **Remote Database Name** (this will be used for the first remote created).

   Tab to change the **Location:** if desired.

   Click **Next>**.

   This is the name of the database that the remote user will open on their computer. No spaces are allowed, and the name cannot start with a number. Try the database name, an underscore, and the user name (ACTDemo_Allison).

   The default location is the \Databases folder. It is a temporary location only until you transfer the file to the new PC.

   ☞ Do **not** choose a folder location under the \[dbname]-database files folder. All files and folders under this folder structure are automatically included in newly created remote databases, including any backup files you may have placed there.

5. Select a Sync Set.

   Click **Next>**.

   You can only select one. Once the remote database is created, you cannot switch Sync Set names (though you can modify the criteria).

6. Under **Database Synchronization Options,** check or uncheck:

   Allow database supplemental files to synchronize.

   Supplemental files are files stored under the **\[name]-database files** folders. All supplemental files are initially synchronized (by default) to the remote database. This first option allows changes and additions to these files to be continually synchronized to the remotes.

☞ *If there are layouts, templates, or reports that you do not want to use (i.e., the sample letter templates that ship with ACT!), delete them now before you set up the remote database.*

Under **Attachments**, select:

Allow the database to synchronize attachments

or **Do not allow this database to synchronize attachments.**

If "Do not", then:
Include at creation, or **Do not include at creation**

Attachments are files, shortcuts, and e-mails in the \Attachments folder. This option allows you to synchronize the attachments so that anyone, at any time, may view an attached document… whether it was created by a remote user or a network user. Remote users can only access files using shortcuts if they have a network connection (VPN).

☞ *Only the attachments related to contacts selected by the Sync Set will synchronize.*

Set number of days to synchronization expiration.

Click **Next>**.

Set the number of days that can pass without the remote user synchronizing to the master. Starting at half the time selected (15 days if you selected 30), the user will receive a message reminding them to synchronize when they open their database. Then in half the days remaining (7), another reminder message displays and so on until the expiration date arrives. After that point a message is displayed each time the user logs on reminding them to sync their database.

The default is 30 days, and the maximum is 365 days.

Synchronization 515

7. Select the Sync Server Connection type.
   - Network
   - Internet

   (These options are discussed in more detail on page 509.)

   Fill in the corresponding identification information.

   Click **Next>**.

If you select a Connection Type: of **Network**, then the Machine Name (name of the server) and Port number are automatically entered for you. The default Port number is 65100 (the Port that the ACT! Network Sync Service will monitor for incoming syncs).

However, you may change the Port number to whatever your Network Administrator advises you to use.

If you select **Internet**, then you will need the URL or IP address of the IIS server that will run the sync service. See page 518 for more on Internet Sync.

8. If you elected to create one remote database, then review your settings and click **Next>**.

   If you indicated more than one remote database in step 3, then modify the **Remote Database Name** and **Sync Set** for each of the remotes.

   When you are finished, click **Next>**.

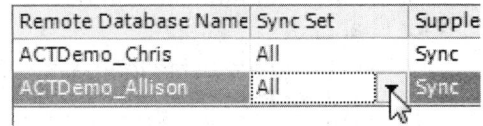

Double-click the name to change the remote name. Use the drop-down to select the correct sync set.

It is usually easier to change the sync set first (using the drop-down). Then you can easily match the name of the Remote Database Name.

9. Add a password if desired.

Provides additional security if you are sending the remote database on a CD or through an FTP site.

10. Click **Finish**.

ACT! creates the file(s) with an .RDB extension in the \Databases folder. You will be able to monitor the progress of the creation.

11. Click **Home** and **Close**.

Sage ACT!

Prepare the Remote Database(s) for Delivery

Once the remote database is created, you need to make it available to the remote computer. You can copy the .RDB database you just created to a CD, to an FTP site, or a shared folder on the network. Users can then copy the file to their computer (you can't restore a database from a CD) and restore the database so they can begin using it. Don't forget to let them know:

- any passwords you assigned when you created the remote database,
- their logon name to the database, and
- any password you may have initially assigned to their logon name.

Administrator Task – Turning On Synchronization

It's time to flip the switch. Your next step is to have ACT! watch for remote users who want to synchronize. Unfortunately, the master database can't make the remote users synchronize. All the master database can do is wait for the remote user to contact it to send and/or search for changes.

- If you are using the basic ACT! by Sage version, then you will need to set up **Application Sync**.
- If you are using ACT! by Sage Premium and plan to use Network Sync, you will need to install and start the **Network Sync Service**.
- If you are using ACT! by Sage Premium and plan to use Internet Sync, then you will need to install and set up **Internet Sync**.

Setting Up Application Sync

To set up application sync, open the master database. Click **Tools**, **Synchronize**, **Accept Incoming Syncs**. That's all there is to it. You're finished.

 *The database **must remain open on the server** to accept incoming synchronizations from remote users. If you close the database, the remote users will receive an error when they try to synchronize.*

Setting Up the Network Sync Service (Premium Only)

If you are using ACT! by Sage Premium, you don't have to leave ACT! up and running on the server in order to accept the incoming syncs. This is one of the key benefits of the Premium product. Network Sync can run as a service which means you don't even need to be logged on to the server for the syncing to take place.

 *If you will be running Network Sync, you should open ACT! and uncheck the option to Accept Incoming Syncs (click **Tools**, **Synchronize**, verify that there is no check beside the **Accept Incoming Syncs** option), so that the two methods do not fight for control.*

Synchronization | 517

Procedure: To install and set up the ACT! Network Sync Service

1. While on the server, insert the ACT! Premium CD.

2. Click Install ACT! Synchronization Services.

3. Click **ACT! Network Synchronization Service**.

    If the CD does not automatically start, browse the CD to locate and open the **ACT! Network Sync** folder. Double-click **setup.exe**.

4. If prompted, answer **Yes** to install additional Microsoft components.

5. Click **Next>** at the Welcome screen.

6. Enter your customer information as prompted. Accept the default install for **Anyone who uses...** and click **Next>**.

7. Modify the Destination Folder, if desired, and click **Next>**.

8. Accept the suggested Program Folder and click **Next>**.

9. Verify the setup information and click **Next>**.

    The Setup Status bar will display as the program installs.

10. Check **Launch ACT! Network Sync** and click **Finish**.

11. The **ACT! Network Sync Service** dialog box should display.

    If you didn't check to Launch the program, then click **Start**, **All Programs**, **ACT! Network Sync Service**, **ACT! Network Sync** before going to next step.

12. Click **Add...**.

13. Select the master database, and then click **Open**.

    Browse to a different location if your database is not displayed.

14. Modify the **Port...** field, if necessary.

    Only your Network Administrator can give you this number.

15. Click **Start Sync Service** to manually start the service and click **OK** to acknowledge that the service is running.

Sage ACT!

16. Click the **Close** button. (If you click **Exit**, you will need to click **OK** to acknowledge that you are not stopping the network service.).

    The ACT! Network Sync will run as a service in the System Tray.

17. Double-click the service in the System Tray to change any options.

     It is set by default to automatically restart any time that the server is restarted.

18. Exit the original Install window by clicking **Back**, and then **Exit**.

 You can add another database to the Sync Service if you like. If the Sync Service has already been started, you will need to stop and restart the service.

Setting Up Internet Sync (Premium Only)

If you are using ACT! Premium, and your users do not have a network connection, then you can set up an Internet Sync. The Internet (or HTTP) Sync setup requires a computer with a static IP address (obtained through your Internet Service provider) and with IIS (Internet Information Services) server (v5.0.2 or better) installed.

The IIS Server must be outside the firewall. The Internet sync will automatically configure the IIS setup to add a new virtual directory under the Default Web Site listings called ActInternetSync. If you don't understand that last sentence, it's not important. It's automatic.

 To determine if IIS is installed on the server, click Start, All Programs, Administrative Tools, and see if Internet Information Services is listed. If you can find no reference to IIS, then you need to have your network administrator install this Microsoft program.

Procedure: To install and set up Internet Sync

1. While on the server, insert the ACT! Premium CD into the CD-ROM drive.

2. Click **Install ACT! Synchronization Services**.

    If the CD does not automatically start, browse the CD to locate and open the **ACT! Internet Sync** folder. Double-click **setup.exe**.

3. Click **ACT! Internet Sync Service**.

4. If prompted, answer **Yes** to install additional Microsoft components.

5. Click **Next>** at the Welcome screen.

Synchronization 519

6. Enter your customer information as prompted. Accept the default install for **Anyone who uses…** and click **Next>**.

7. Modify the Destination Folder, if desired, and click **Next>**.

8. Accept the suggested Program Folder and click **Next>**.

9. Verify the setup information and click **Next>**.

10. Click **Finish**.

11. In Windows Explorer, locate the **SyncConfigFile.xml** file. Right-click and select **Edit**.

    The default location is C:\Program Files\ACT\ACT for Windows\ACT Internet Sync.

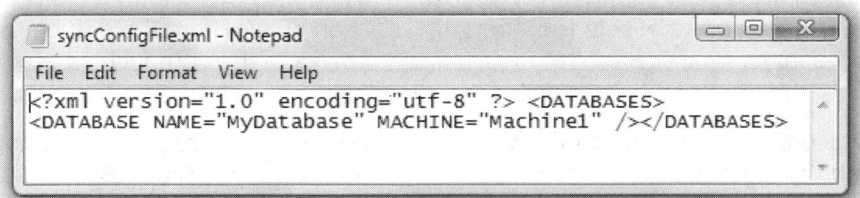

12. For the DATABASE NAME field, replace **MYDATABASE** with your specific database name. Be sure to keep the quotes.

    For the MACHINE field, replace the **Machine1** in quotes with the name of the server that holds the database. Keep the quotes.

    To add more databases, copy the text between the <DATABASES> and </DATABASES>, paste it below the existing text (but above </DATABASES>) and make changes to the database and machine name.

    Save the changes and close the file.

13. Stop and restart the IIS service.

    Start, All Programs, Administrative Tools, Internet Information Services.

    Right-click the server name and select **Restart IIS…**.

14. Exit the original Install window by clicking **Return to installation tasks**, and then **Exit**.

Sage ACT!

User Tasks – Restoring and Syncing Your Database

Once you receive the remote database ([name].RDB), you can restore it to your computer with a quick double-click. The .RDB file is a temporary file used only to transport the data to the new computer. Once restored to the remote computer, the .RDB file should be deleted.

☞ *If you receive your remote database file on a CD, copy the file to your desktop. Remote databases cannot be installed from a CD.*

Procedure: To restore a remote database

1. Double-click the remote database file that was sent (the file has an .RDB extension).

    You could also click, **File**, **Restore**, **Database…**. Select **Unpack and Restore Remote Database** and click **OK**. **Browse…** to **Select the remote database file to restore:**.

2. Click **Browse…** to change the **Restore remote database to this location:**, if necessary.

    You may change the \folder location, but you can only restore the database *to a local drive* of the computer where you are logged on.

3. Put a check in the **Share this database with other users**.

    If this is a database at a remote office that other users will access across the network, or if you plan to sync supplemental files, then it is important to enable this option.

4. Click **OK**.

    ☞ *If an existing remote database has the same name as the one you are unpacking and restoring, you will be prompted multiple times to overwrite the existing ACTIVE database.*

5. Click **OK** to acknowledge that the restore completed successfully.

6. The database will automatically open for you.

    Enter your user name and password.

7. Click **Yes** to synchronize with the main database.

    You must have an active network (LAN, VPN, or RAS) or Internet connection.

Synchronization

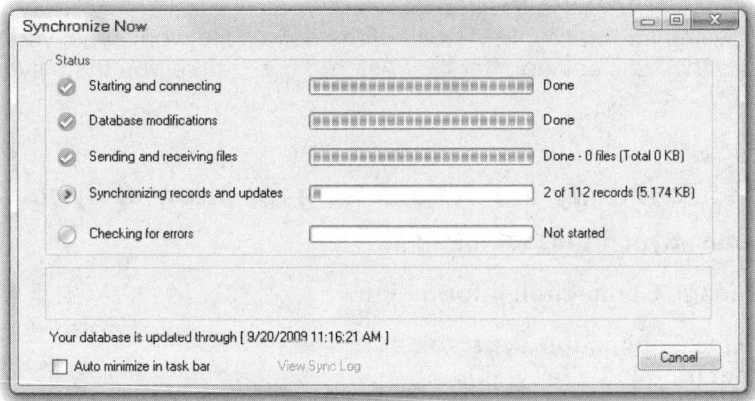

The Sync Status dialog will display to visually track the status of your sync.

8. Click **Close** to acknowledge the completion of the sync.

9. Click **V**iew, **R**efresh or press **[F5]**.

10. Delete the *.RDB file.

Click **Auto minimize** if you don't want to follow the progress.

You can click the **View Sync Log** hyperlink in the bottom of the window for more information.

This command ensures that you are seeing all changes sent to you.

It is a temporary file only used for restoring the database one time.

 This is a REALLY IMPORTANT step. RDB files can only be used once. You don't want the end-user to double-click the file and restore the file again. If the original database had data in it, the changes will be overwritten. In addition, if the original database had been synced at least once, the new database will NOT be allowed to sync.

Changes for Remote Internet Sync

If you will be using Internet sync, instead of the default Network sync, you may need to quickly modify the sync setting after it is restored and before you try to synchronize the database.

Procedure: To modify the sync setting for Internet Sync

1. Click **Tools, Synchronization Panel**....

2. Click **Manage Connection Information**.

3. Change the **Connection Type:** to **Internet (outside a firewall)**.

4. If necessary, enter the URL or IP address of the ACT! Internet Sync Server and the name of the virtual directory.

    If you are entering a URL, after http://, type the machine name and the virtual directory name.

    http://<machine>/ActInternetSync

5. Click **Finish**.

Synchronizing the Remote Database

You can synchronize your database as often as you like (since synchronization takes place in the background and does not interrupt your normal PC operations), or you can set a schedule for automatically synchronizing your data.

Procedure: To manually synchronize your database

1. Click **Tools, Synchronize Database, Synchronize Now**.

2. Minimize the Sync progress bar, if you like. Click **Close** when complete.

3. Click **View, Refresh** or press **[F5]**.

    This command ensures that you are seeing all changes sent to you.

☞ *You could also include an icon on the task bar to Synchronize the database, as well as for the View Refresh command. Review the procedure for adding icons to the toolbar on page 374.*

Synchronization | 523

Set Up a Sync Schedule with the ACT! Scheduler

You can use the ACT! Scheduler to synchronize your remote database with the master database. ACT! Scheduler runs as a service so that even if ACT! is not open on your workstation, your database will synchronize on schedule. Your PC just needs to be turned on.

Procedure: To set up automatic sync using the ACT! Scheduler

1. Click **Tools, ACT! Schedule**r....

2. Click **Create a task**.

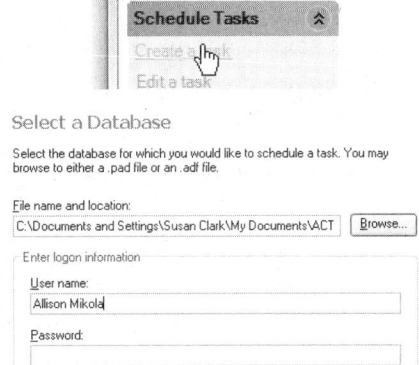

3. **Browse…** to locate your database and click **Open**.

   Enter your **User name:** and any associated **Password:**.

   Click **Next>**.

4. In the Task: area, use the drop-down arrow to select **Database synchronization** and click **Next>**.

   This option will only display if you have selected a remote database in the previous step.

5. Set your options. Perhaps…

   Hourly
   From **8:00 AM** to **5:00PM**
   Every 1 hours

   If your PC is not turned on or connected to the network during those times, then ACT! will attempt to sync at the next scheduled time.

    *If you are setting up quite a few users to sync, change the **Starting at:** time for the first person to a time like 8:10AM and for the next person at 8:15 or 8:20. This way, not every remote database is trying to sync with the master at the same time. You can also space out the starting time (have some start at 9:10 AM and set for every 2 or 3 hours).*

Sage ACT!

6. Click **Finish**, click **Start Service** if necessary, and then click **Exit**.

Once a task is scheduled, the ACT! Scheduler icon will display as running in the System Tray.

 *You can choose to sync anytime you like by clicking **Tools**, **Synchronize**, **Synchronize Now**. This will not affect the automatic sync schedule. To edit the schedule, open the ACT! Scheduler again and edit the task.*

Using the Subscription List in a Remote Database

If your remote database used a Sync Set query that only sent you a portion of the total number of Contacts that you are allowed to see, you may be able to access other Contacts in the master database (depending on your user rights). You can access a feature called Subscription List which displays all names in the master database that you are **allowed** to see. From here, you may select to have additional Contacts (not currently included in your database) synced to your remote database. For example, there may be a Contact in New York who handles national accounts, but his record did not get included in the Sync Set, because his address was outside of California.

 If Limited Access is used to restrict access to the contacts in the database, then only the contacts that you have access to will be displayed in the Subscription List. However, your user name may be restricted from accessing the subscription list using the custom permissions feature.

Procedure: To add Contacts using the subscription list

1. Click **Tools, Synchronization Panel…**.

2. Click **Manage Subscription List** at the left under **User Tasks**.

    The Contacts you have access to displays. Those specifically included in your Sync Set are indicated by a check mark in the Sync Set column.

3. Click **Add Contacts to Sync Set**.

4. In the **Look for:** text box type the first and last name of the Contact you wish to add to your Sync Set.

5. Double-click the Contact name or click the **Add** button to add them to the **Selected Contacts:** list.

    You can also remove any Contacts in the **Selected List:** by selecting them and clicking the **Remove** button.

6. Click **OK**, **Finish** and then **Close**.

    The additional Contacts will appear in your database **after your next synchronization**.

Administrator Task – Territory Realignment

The contacts included in a remote database are determined by two things: does the record meet the criteria defined in the Sync Set and the Record Manager. Even if you change the sync set for the Allison remote database to only include the database users (the minimum number of contacts possible for any remote), all contacts that list Allison as the Record Manager will remain in the remote. Each time that Allison has entered a contact in the database, she has been listed as the Record Creator and the Record Manager by default.

When you need to change what a user has access to in the remote database, you should consider the following.

- In order to remove all of the contacts that don't belong to Allison (other than her friends or family), you will need to first change the Record Manager on those records that should be reassigned.
- If you defined a Sync Set for each remote user using a query, you can modify the criteria (the Sync Set Query) to add and/or remove Contacts from the remote database at the completion of the next synchronization.
- Be sure to have the remote user click **Tools**, **Database Maintenance**, **Check and Repair** after removing Contacts from their sync set. This removes attachments belonging to the Contacts that were removed from their sync set.
- If you defined a Sync Set for each remote user using the All Contacts option and use the Limited Access feature to assign Contacts to Teams of users, simply by changing a user's Team membership, you can update the list of Contacts the remote user can view at the completion of the next synchronization. For example, let's say that a sales rep in our West Team gets transferred to the East Team. By removing the sales rep's name from the West Team and adding it to the East Team, during the next synchronization, the Contacts that belonged to the West Team are removed from the remote user's access/view and those belonging to the East Team will now display in the remote database.

Synchronization Troubleshooting

Many elements are involved in a successful synchronization. Some problems you encounter may be ACT!-related, but you may also experience network difficulties, security problems, administrative rights issues, SQL Server install dilemmas, etc. If after following these instructions for setting up your sync, you experience problems, your first line of defense should be ACT!'s Knowledge Base. The Knowledge Base is an excellent source for troubleshooting everything in ACT!. Go to: www.act.com/support

Sage ACT!

Scroll to and click on the Knowledge Center link. Then, select from the Top Issues and Frequently asked questions, or click on the Knowledge Center link again. Log on with your profile, if necessary. In the Search Text area, type "troubleshooting internet sync" or "troubleshooting network sync" or enter part of any error messages you are receiving. Follow the directions to help you narrow down your problems.

Review: The Final Exercise

1. Go through each of the Synchronization procedures (using the ACT!2011Demo database) and set up Synchronization with Allison Mikola.

2. If you have a second computer to practice with, set up the second computer as if it belonged to Allison Mikola.

3. Set up a simple Network Sync as described on pages 509 and 516.

4. You may now exit ACT!.

5. Pat yourself on the back.

Appendix

Sage ACT!

User Roles and Permissions

Your security role determines the features you have access to and the functions you can perform.

☞ You can verify your own security level by clicking **Help**, **About ACT!**. Click the **Database Info** button. Your **Security Role:** is listed in the **Database User Information:** area.

User Roles and Permissions	Admin	Mgr	Stand	Restrict	Browse
Administrative Functions					
File, Import/Export	X	X			
File, Backup, Database	X	X			
File, Restore Database	X				
File, Backup (or Restore), Personal Files	X	X	X	X	X
Contacts, Opportunities, Manage Product (or Process) List	X	X			
Contacts, Send vCard	X	X			
Schedule, Manage, Activity Series Templates (Create/Edit)	X	X	X		
Schedule, Manage, Activity Types, (or Priorities, Resources)	X	X			
Schedule, Manage, Events	X	X			
Schedule, Manage Smart Tasks (Create/Edit)	X	X	X		
Schedule, Run Smart Task	X	X	X	X	
Tools, Define Fields (including drop-down lists)	X	X			
Tools, Design Layouts	X	X			
Tools, Design Dashboards (or edit existing)	X	X			
Tools, Manage Users-Add, Remove, Inactivate	X				
Tools, Manage Teams-Create, Edit, Delete	X	X			
Tools, Password Policy	X				
Tools, Database Maintenance	X				
Check and Repair	X	X			
Lock/Unlock Database	X	X			
Remove Old Data	X				
Delete Database	X				
Share Database	X				
Tools, Convert 3.0-6.0 Items	X	X			
Tools, Scan for Duplicates	X	X	X	X	X
Tools, Copy/Move Contact Data	X	X			
Tools, Synchronization Panel	X	X			
Tools, Update Salutation Field	X	X			
Tools, Synchronize with Outlook	X	X	X		
Tools, Integrate with Google	X	X	X		
Tools, Sage ACT! Connect	X	X	X		

User Roles and Permissions

	Admin	Mgr	Stand	Restrict	Browse
Tools, Customize, Menus and Toolbars	X	X	X		
Tools, Preferences, Allow History Editing (or Notes)	X	X			
Tools, Preferences, Name Preferences	X	X			
Tools, Preferences, Duplicate Checking	X	X			
Tools, Preferences, Admin tab	X	X			
Tools, Preferences, Startup, Automatically Link to Company	X	X			
Help, Check for Updates	X	X	X		
Change Contact Access or Record Manager	X	X			

General User Activity

	Admin	Mgr	Stand	Restrict	Browse
Data					
View Data (that user has access to view)	X	X	X	X	X
Create Contacts, Opportunities, Activities	X	X	X	X	
Create Groups, Companies, Relationships	X	X	X		
Create Notes/History	X	X	X	X	
Edit My Data	X	X	X	X	
Edit History Entry (controlled by)	X	X			
Promote Secondary Contact (controlled by)	X	X			
Delete My Data	X	X	X		
Delete Data owned by other users	X	X			
Assign Group/Company Membership	X	X	X		
Export a list view to Excel	X	X	X		
Scheduling					
Create, Edit, Delete My Activities	X	X	X	X	
Schedule For (any users)	X	X			
Schedule For (when granted specific access)	X	X	X	X	
Grant Calendar Access	X	X	X	X	
Exchange Activities with Outlook	X	X	X	X	
Run Activity Series	X	X	X	X	
Delete My Activity Series	X	X	X		
Delete Activities/Activity Series owned by other users	X	X			
Templates (Report or Word or E-mail)					
Print Reports	X	X	X	X	X
Write Letter or Mail Merge	X	X	X	X	
Create, Edit templates	X	X	X		
Delete any template (through Windows Explorer)	X	X	X	X	X
Synchronize					
Modify subscription list	X	X	X		
Smart phones	X	X	X		

Converting an Older ACT! Database-Custom Conversion

Converting your ACT! database to the new version of ACT! is easy. All you have to do is open the database. If you are upgrading from a newer version of ACT! (since ACT! 2005), the database conversion takes only a few minutes, and then it is ready to use.

Procedure: To convert an ACT! 6 (aka 2004) or earlier version database

1. Run **Scan and Repair** on the older database.

   In Windows Explorer, browse to the old ACT software folder and double-click actdiag.exe.

   C:\Program Files\ACT\ or
   C:\Program Files\Symantec\ACT

   Depending on your version, click **Maintenance, Scan and Repair Database** and follow the prompts.

2. Open the database in the old version of ACT! to restore the index files that Scan and Repair removed.

   When you open the database, you will see a warning about missing files. Answer **Yes** to repair.

3. Close the old ACT! and open your new version of ACT!.

4. Click **File, Open/Share Database**.

5. Click "The database I want is not listed."

6. Change the file type from "ACT! Database (*.PAD) to "ACT! 3.x, 4.x, 5x (2000) or 6.x(2004) Databases (*.DBF)."

7. Browse to locate your old database and click **Open**.

   Any current database will close and the ACT Data Conversion Wizard will begin.

8. Click **Next>** at the Welcome screen.

9. At **Conversion Type**, select from **Standard** or **Custom**.

   To make this decision, see the next page.

10. Select your preferred option for converting attachments.

Note that the "Convert attachments as files" option will make **copies** of the files on your PC or network and place them in the \Attachments folder.

"Convert attachments as shortcuts" more closely mimics the functionality of ACT! version 6 (and previous versions). However, copies of attached files will not be synced to remote databases. Remote users must have access to the network path in order to view attached files.

11. Continue answering questions as prompted until you can click **Finish**.

Your converted database displays.

Standard vs. Custom Conversion

No matter how many or what type of custom fields you have created in your older version of ACT!, a Standard conversion will automatically convert the fields to an equivalently created field in the new version of ACT!. In other words, ACT! will create all the Contact record and Group record fields in the new database automatically and bring over your old data into the new structure.

The ONLY purpose for custom conversion is to handle any additional (or modified) fields you may have defined that fall into one of three categories...

- a phone field,
- or an address field,
- or a secondary contact field.

Additional Phone fields: If you have added another phone field to your database (in addition to the default ones that come with ACT!), you will want to select the Custom conversion options. If you do not identify any of your new phone fields at conversion, then they will be converted as character fields with no phone formatting (dashes or parentheses available). They cannot be changed to phone fields after conversion (although they will continue to display on any converted layout). In addition, one of the new lookup features is the Lookup, Other fields, Any Phone Field (or Any City Field or Secondary First Name or Secondary Phone). Consequently, if you have created a **Main Phone**, you will want to identify it so that it will be mapped to a **Main** phone in the new database. If you don't identify them at conversion, they will not be found using the "Any Phone Field" lookup.

Additional Address fields: If you created additional address fields in your database (e.g., for Physical or Billing address), then you will want to select the Custom Conversion option. The only reason for identifying address fields at conversion is so you can use the "Any" lookup. If you do not identify an address field at conversion, then it will be converted as a character field and will not be included in any of the Any address field lookups (however, it will continue to display on any converted layout).

Secondary contact fields: "2nd Contact" and "3rd Contact" were default fields in previous versions of ACT!. In newer versions, these fields (and any associated Titles and Phone numbers) are converted to Secondary Contacts and placed on a tab where you can add as many Secondary Contacts as you like...along with more detailed information like their e-mail address, address information that might be different from the primary contact, etc. If you have defined "4th Contacts" and "5th Contacts" or "Attorney" and "Accountant" in your older database, you will want to select the Custom Conversion option and identify these fields at conversion (along with any other associated Contact information), so that they can be mapped appropriately to the new Secondary Contact fields. When you map them during the conversion, any fields that were defined as "additional contact" information, will be converted to the new Secondary Contacts and then deleted (and thus will not display on any converted layouts as fields).

Other fields: All other field types will be converted automatically to an equivalently created field in the new version of ACT!. In other words, ACT! will create all the Contact record and Group record fields in the new database automatically and bring over your old data into the new structure. You don't have to create or map anything...ACT! will handle it all for you.

 If you used the Group feature in your older database to simulate Companies, you cannot map those fields to a Company record in this newer version during the conversion process. However, you can import the data into Company fields. In your older version of ACT!, export the company-specific data to a text file. After your older database has been converted to the new version, define the Company fields that you need in the new version of ACT!. Then, you can import the text file into the Company record in the new version.

If you are having trouble converting your database, you might consider this third-party product to help you find problem areas in your older database:

www.cornerstonesolutions.com/redflag.html

Appendix 533

Using the OLE DB2 Provider

OLE DB was designed by Microsoft to allow one application to access the data in another application. An OLE DB connection can be made to allow several software applications (such as Crystal Reports, Excel, Access, etc.) to read the data in your ACT! database. The 2.0 version is faster and more powerful…has more fields available for reporting. It can also be used to create new Dashboard components. Any existing OLE DB reports developed in previous versions of ACT! to report on Opportunities will not work. However, you can rewrite the reports using the new OLE DB2 provider. Let's make a connection to Excel as an example.

Procedure: To create an OLE DB2 connection to Excel

1. Open Excel.

2. Click **Data, Import External Data, Import Data…**.

     On the **Data** tab, in the Get External Data group, click **From Other Sources**.

3. Click **New Source…** button at the bottom of the window.

     Click **From Data Connection Wizard**.

4. Select **Other/advanced** and click **Next>**.

5. Select the **ACT! OLE DB Provider for Reporting 2.0** and click **Next>**.

    The 2.0 version is faster and more powerful…has more fields available for reporting.

6. Click the **Browse…** button to locate the ACT! database that you want to connect to and click **Open**.

     OLEDB honors security, so the user can only see the records to which they have rights.

    Enter your **User Name** and **Password**.

    The **Select Database and Table** screen appears. Connections are created on a per database basis.

    Click **Test Connection** and click **OK** when the connection succeeds.

    Click **OK**.

7. In the Data Connection Wizard, select a table and click **Next>**.

    Contact could help you analyze demographic data. Contact_History would help you analyze… well… history entries.

8. Enter a Description and click **Finish**.

    Example: "ACT2012Demo connection to History Table"

9. Click **Cancel** or click **Finish** and go to step 4 of the next procedure.

    This was a one-time setup.

Procedure: To use the OLE DB2 connection to Excel

1. Open Excel.

2. Click **Data, Import External Data, Import Data…**. On the **Data** tab, in the **Get External Data** group, click **Existing Connections**

3. Select the data source and click **Open**.
   For example, choose: ACT2012Demo Contact_ History.odc

4. Select the anchor cell for the imported data.

5. Either click **OK** to import the straight data or click **Create a Pivot Table report…**.

6. If you click Pivot Table, select the cell and click **Finish**.

   Drag the fields on to the Pivot Table. Pivot tables are beyond the scope of this guide. However it is worth you time to play with them. They can be quite powerful.

7. If you are using the History table, try dragging the following fields to the first row.
   Record Manager
   Types Name
   Created On

   Drag **Types Name** to the **Row** fields. Drag **Record Manager** to the **Column Fields**. Drag **Created On** to the **Data Items** area.

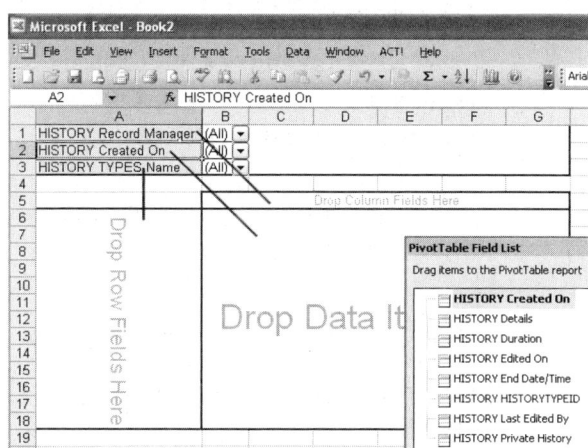

8. Click the drop-down button to the right of All to limit the selections.

9. Save the worksheet and exit Excel.

☞ *Next time you open the worksheet, click **Data, Refresh Data** (or **Data, Refresh All**) to update the ACT! information.*

Index

A

ACT! Business Info, 76
ACT! E-mail. See E-mail
ACT! Premium for Web, 6, 7
ACT! Scheduler, 487, 523
    Backup, 487
    Database Maintenance, 496
    Log, 497
    Synchronization, 523
ACT! Software Update, 484
ACT! Word Processor, 214, See Word Processor
Activities, 88
    Alarms, 141, 142
    Attaching a File, 145
    Clearing, 112
    Color, 140
    Creating from an E-mail, 186
    Details, 93
    General Tab, 128
    Granting Calendar Access, 128
    Invitations, 89, 136
    Modifying, 111
    New Types, 383
    Priorities, 381
    Public vs. Private, 144
    Recurring, 146
    Rollover, 122
    Scheduling, 89, 96
    Scheduling for Others, 128, 129, 131
    Scheduling Multiple Contacts, 133
Activity Lookup, 244
Activity Series, 392
    Creating, 392
    Using, 394
Add Columns to View, 38
Add Document, 65
Adding Fields
    Layout, 362
    Report, 425
Adding Text
    Layout, 366
Adding Users, 464
Address, 331
Address Labels, 444, 448
Administration
    Back Up, 485
    Database Maintenance, 484, 494
    Delete Database, 493
    Multi-User Database, 454
    Password, 470
    Software Updates, 484
Administrator Role, 462
Advanced Query
    Defined, 248
Alarm, 141, 142, 144
    Clear, 143
    Snooze, 143
Alerts, 81
Aligning Objects, 360
Allow Blank, 334
Allow Multi-select, 335
Alternate Contacts. See Secondary Contacts
Android, 162
Android phone, 156
Anniversary, 55
Annual Event, 55, 332
Application Sync, 516
Attach
    Disable, 482
    File, 65, 92, 114, 116, 118, 145
    Shortcut, 65, 92, 114, 116, 118, 145
Attach document to history, 209
Attach to ACT!, 172
Attach Web Page, 74
Attachments, 210
    .mht extension, 75
    Company, 194
    Contacts, 194
    E-mail, 194
    File, 194
    Group, 194
    Web Page, 74
Availability, 136

B

Back Button, 50
Back Up, 485
    Automatic, 486
    Database Files, 486
    Manual, 489
    Personal Files, 486
    Restore, 490
Background Color, 368
Basic Template Editor, 225
Birthday, 21, 55
Blackberry, 156, 162

Browse Role, 463
Browsing Records, 34
Build A List, 83
Business Info, 76

C

Calendar, 97
    Activity Series, 392
    Calendar Pop-ups, 98
    Daily, 100
    Filter, 103, 130
    Monthly, 97
    Navigating, 99
    Printing, 104
    Rollover, 122
    Scheduling Activities, 96
    Task List Comparison, 106
    Today Button, 100
    Weekly, 102
    Work Week, 101
Calendar Sharing
    Google, 156
Calendar Syncing
    Google, 149
    Outlook, 149, 150
Call Lists, 236
Calls. See Activities
CH TechONE, 19
Character, 332
Check and Repair, 494
Citrix, 6
Clear Alarm, 143
Clearing Activities, 112
Close an Opportunity, 299
Columns
    Adding, 38
Companies, 263
    Add Members, 267
    Associating Activity or Opportunity, 284, 285
    Convert a Group, 280
    Create, 265
    Create a Contact From, 272, 275
    Defining Linked Fields, 337
    Disabling a Link, 275
    Divisions, 280
    Dynamic, 266
    History, 282
    Linked, 266
    Linked Activities/Opportunities, 274
    Linked Notes/History, 274
    Linking Contacts, 272
    Lookup, 287
    Note, 282
    Preferences for Sharing Notes/Histories, 274
    Promoting Divisions, 282
    Puling Changes From Companies, 278
    Pushing Changes to Contacts, 277
    Sharing a Note, 284
    Static, 266
    View Linked Fields, 278
CompanionLink, 156, 166
Company Profile, 79
Completing Activities, 112
Contact, 18
    Attach E-mail, 180, 185
    Browsing, 34
    Create Company From, 272
    Create from a Company, 275
    Creating from an E-mail, 179
    Delete, 31
    Duplicating, 27
    Linked, 266
    Linking to Companies, 272
    Locating, 34
    New, 22
    Pulling Changes from Companies, 278
    Saving, 22
Contact Access. *See* Security, *See* Security
    Lookup By, 476
Contact Activity, 244
Contact Detail View, 35, *See* Layout
Contact Fields. See Fields
Contact Layout. See Layout
Contact Layout Design. See Layout Designer
Contact List View, 35
    Displaying Columns, 38
    Edit Mode, 57
    Sorting, 36
    Tag Mode, 57
Contact Syncing
    Google, 156
    Outlook, 152
Content Editor, 225
Copy/Move Contact Data, 503
Create History, 194, 209
Create New User, 464, 466
Create Remote Database, 513
Create Separate Activities, 134
Creating a Letter, 207

Currency, 294, 329, 332
Custom Activity Type, 383
Customize Template, 225

D

Dashboard, 312
    Breakpoint, 419
    Changing Views, 312
    Creating, 416
    Custom Components, 419
    Target, 419
Data Cleanup, 501
Database
    Add User, 464
    Back Up, 485
    Check and Repair, 494
    Conversion from Older Versions, 530
    Copy, 490
    Delete, 493
    Maintenance, 484
    Manage Users, 464
    Move, 490
    Move to a New Location, 457
    Multi-User, 454
    New Name, 492
    Opening, 9, 10
    Restore, 490
    Share, 458
Database Design Fields. See Also Fields
Database Security. See Security
Date, 332
    Annual Event, 332
Decimal, 332
Decimal Places, 336
Default File Locations, 483
Default value, 335
Define Fields. See Fields
Delete
    Contact, 31
    Database, 493
    Lookup, 31
    Note or History, 122
    Records, 57
Delete User, 467
Details, 93, 113
    History, 115
Directory Structure, 456
Disable attachments, 481
Discount, 293

Divisions, 280
Document
    Printing, 209
    Template, 198
Documents Tab, 64
    Adding Files, 65
    Adding Shortcuts, 65
    Disable attachments, 482
    Editing Files, 67
    Removing Documents, 67
Drip Marketing, 236
Droid, 156
Drop-down List, 335, 340
    Allow Editing, 345
    Importing, 342
    Lookup, 42
    Minor Changes, 345
    Multiple, 22
    Multi-select, 335
    Sharing, 341
    Show Descriptions, 335
    Using, 22, 334
Duplicate Checking Criteria, 482
Duplicates, 501
    Combining, 503
    Tips, 502
Duplicating Contact, 27, 334
Dynamic Groups, 261

E

Edit Mode, 57
Edit Replace, 505
Edit Template, 198
Editing Activities, 111
E-mail, 332
    Address Book, 170, 193
    Attach to Contact, 180, 185
    Attachments, 194, 205
    Creating a Contact, 179
    Creating a Template, 198
    Creating an Activity, 186
    Disabling user history, 481
    Folder List, 191
    Internet client, 168
    Mail Merge, 198
    Merging a Template, 203
    New, 193
    Outlook, 174
    POP3, 169

Preview Pane, 191, 192
Quick Attach, 180
Send/Receive, 194
Sending from ACT!, 174, 176
Sending from ACT! E-mail, 193
Setup, 168
Signature, 218
Signature Formatting, 170
To Group or Company Members, 206
Window, 191
E-marketing, 220
Call Lists, 236
Creating an Account, 222
Downloading History, 232
Drip Marketing, 236
Modifying Templates, 228
Results, 232
Scoring, 233
Sending, 226
Signature, 232
Surveys, 239
vs Outlook, 220
Enabling Synchronization, 510
Enter Stop, 370
Envelopes, 210, 212
Eudora Pro, 168
Events
    Defined, 385
    Managing, 385
Excel, 304
    Editing the Quote template, 388
    Importing, 498
Export to Excel, 304
Extensions, 455

F

Facebook, 72, 165
Fax, 207
    Mail Merge, 204
Field Entry Order, 370
    Displaying, 370
Field Format, 336
    Codes, 336
Field Level Security, 347
Fields, 18, 20
    Address, 331
    Allow Blank, 334
    Allow Multi-select, 335
    Annual Event, 332

Attributes, 331
Blanks, 334
Character, 332
Currency, 332
Customizing, 329
Date, 332
Decimal, 332
Decimal Places, 336
Default value, 335
Drop-down, 340
E-mail, 332
Enable type-ahead, 335
Field Format, 336
Field Level Security, 347
Field Name, 18, 331
Generate History, 334
Initial Capitals, 332
Length, 336
Limit to List, 335
Lowercase, 333
Memo, 333
Number, 333
Phone, 333
Picture, 333
Primary field, 334
Sharing Drop-down Lists, 340
Show Descriptions, 335
Time, 332, 333
Triggers, 339
Type, 331
Uppercase, 333
URL, 333
Use Drop Down List, 334
Yes/No, 333
File Locations, 483
File Structure, 456
Filenames, 455
Filter
    Calendar, 103
    Calendar Display, 130
    Calendar or Task, 130
    Printed Calendar, 95, 104
    Report, 319, 441
    Task List, 107, 130
First Name Prefixes, 45
Folders, 456
Formatting
    Layout, 367
    Reports, 426
Forward Button, 50

G

Generate History, 334
Global Toolbar, 12
Gmail
   Manually synching, 190
Gmail History, 189
Google, 72
   Calendar Sharing, 156
   Calendar Syncing, 149
   Contact Syncing, 156
   Gmail history, 189
   Manually synching, 161, 190
Google History, 189
Google Integration, 189
   Calendar and Contact, 157
   Disable, 161
Grant Calendar Access, 128
Graph, 310
Graphics, 217
Group Layout Design. See Layout Designer
Groups, 260
   Add Members, 261, 267
   Associating Activity or Opportunity, 284, 285
   Converting to a Company, 280
   Create, 265
   Criteria, 271
   Dynamic, 261, 266
   Filter Notes/History Tab, 286
   Lookup, 287
   Static, 261, 266
   Subgroups, 280
   View, 260
GroupWise, 169

H

Handles, 356
Hierarchy, 281
History
   Attachment, 210
   Details, 113
   Editing disabled, 480
   Filtering, 117
   Record for multiple contacts, 117
   Recording, 115
   Removing Files, 67
   vs Notes, 120
Hoover's, 76
   Alerts, 81
   Build A List, 83
   Importing Companies, 80
   Importing Contacts, 82
HTTP Sync, 518, 522

I

ID/Status, 20
Image, 217
Import
   .csv file, 498
   Drop-down List, 342
   Excel file, 498
   Text file, 498
Importing Companies, 80
Importing Contacts, 82
Inactive Opportunity, 299
Inactive User, 466
Initial Capitals, 332
Insert
   Contact, 22
   Note, 118
Install Checklist, 460
Install Study Guide Files, 9
Integrity Check, 495
Internet Explorer
   Attach Web Page, 74
Internet Sync, 518, 522
Invitation, 89, 95, 138, 173, *See also Meeting Request*
   Responding, 139
Invitations, 136
iPad, 6, 156, 166

K

Keystrokes, 376
   Resetting Shortcuts, 378
Keyword Search, 54
Knowledge Base, 454

L

Labels, 212
Last Name Prefixes, 45
Last Name Suffixes, 45
Layout, 16, See Layout Designer
   Changing, 16
   Default View, 12

Defined, 352
Sizing Windows, 17
Layout Designer
   Adding Fields, 362
   Adding Tabs, 364
   Adding Text, 366
   Aligning Objects, 360
   Background Color, 368
   Displaying, 352
   Editing, 352
   Field Entry Order, 370
   Formatting, 367
   Formatting Toolbar, 355
   Handles, 356
   Modifying, 356
   Moving Objects, 359
   Renaming Labels, 358
   Same Width Height, 369
   Saving, 354
   Selecting Objects, 356
   Sizing Objects, 356
   Splitter, 352
   System Tabs, 353
   Tabs, 364
   Testing Tab Order, 369
   Toolbox, 352, 355
Layout Tabs, 15
Letter, 207
   Attach document, 209
   Creating, 207
   Printing, 209
Limit to List, 335
Limited Access, 21, 144, 265, 471, 472
   Add Additional Teams/Users, 475
   Assign New, 474
   Assigning to a Lookup, 473
   Lookup By, 476
   Managers Team, 477
Link to Company Field, 337
Link vs Associate, 273
Linkedin, 73
Locating Contacts, 34
Log on, 8
Logon User, 464
Lookup, 40
   Add to, 47
   Advanced Query, 287
   Annual Events, 55
   Any fields, 54
   By Example, 246, 288
   Contact, 43
   Contact Activity, 244
   Contacts, 34
   Delete, 31
   Duplicates, 482, 502
   Modified, 244
   Narrow, 48
   Nav Bar, 39
   Not Modified, 244
   Operators, 42
   Opportunity Fields, 302
   Options, 47
   Previous, 49
   Printing, 60
   Search, 51
   Secondary Contacts, 62
   Stage, 302
   Tips, 42
Lookup Selected, 58
Lost Sale, 299
Lotus Notes, 168
Lowercase, 333

M

Mail Merge, 198
   Creating a Template, 198
   E-mail, 204
   Fax, 204
   Word Processor, 204
Manage Activity Types, 383
Manage Product List, 388
Manage Teams, 472
Manage Users, 464
Manager Role, 462
Marketing Results Tab, 235
Meeting Request, 89, 95, 173, 178
Meetings. See Activities
Memo, 207, 333
Menu, 376
   Bar, 12
   Resetting, 378
Menus and Toolbars
   Customizing, 374
Merge Duplicates, 503
Messenger ID, 21
Microsoft Outlook. See Outlook
Microsoft Word, 196
   ACT! Menu Item, 196
   Choosing, 196

Mini-calendar, 90, 110
Modifying Activities, 111
Moving Between Records, 34
Moving Objects, 359
Multi-User Database, 454
My Record, 18, 198, 426

N

Names
　Fixing Problems, 46
Nav Bar, 13
Network Sync Service, 516
New Activity Types, 383
New Contact, 22
New Database, 328
New Opportunity, 290
New Template
　Report, 422
No Access, 347
Notes, 118
　Associating with a Group/Company, 284, 285
　Editing, 119
　Editing disabled, 480
　Preview Area, 119
　Sharing with Company or Group, 283
　Spell Check, 120
　Tab, 118
　Viewing, 119
　vs. History, 120
Number, 333
Number of Characters, 336

O

OLEDB2 Connection, 533, 534
Omit Selected, 58
Opening a Database, 9, 10
Opening ACT!, 7
Opportunity, 290
　Add, 290
　Close, 299
　Currency, 294
　Customizing Tab, 295
　Discounts, 293
　Edit, 296
　Export to Excel, 304
　Graph, 310
　List View, 300
　Pipeline, 308

Probability, 291
Process, 291, 386
Product List, 388
Products, 292, 293
Quote, 297
Reports, 306
Security, 302
Stage, 291, 386
Opportunity List, 300
　Filters, 300
Other Templates, 202
Outlook, 174
　Address Book, 170
　Attach E-mail to Contact, 180, 185
　Calendar, 108
　Calendar Syncing, 149, 150
　Contact Syncing, 152
　Create an Activity, 186
　Creating a Contact, 179
　Default Address Book, 170
　Inbox, 178
　Manually synching, 155
　Meeting Request, 95, 178
　Sending E-mail, 176
　Sending from the Contact Record, 174, 176
　vs E-marketing, 220
Outlook Express, 168, 173

P

Palm, 6
Password, 8, 465
　Policy, 467
　Setting Your Own, 470
PDF, 320
Pending Smart Tasks, 405
Personal E-mail, 21
Personal Files
　Backup, 486
Phone, 333
　Format, 333
　Picture, 333
PIM, 88
Pipeline Report, 308
Plaxo, 73
Pocket PC, 6
Preferences
　File Locations, 483
　Limited Access, 30
　Names, 45

Index

Word Processor, 195
Prefixes, 45
Premium version, 7
    Advantages, 7
Primary Field, 334
Print
    Attach document, 209
    Calendar, 104
    Create History, 209
    Envelope, 209, 212
    Labels, 212
    Letter, 209
    Report, 319
Print Preview, 320, 322
Priorities, 381
    Activating, 381
    Customizing, 381
    Dectivating, 381
Private, 20, 28, 265
    Contact, 36
    Note, 118
Private vs. Public Activities, 144
Probability, 291
Process, 291, 386
Product List, 388
Products, 292, 293
Promote, 63
Properties Window, 426
Public vs. Private Activities, 144
Public/Private, 20, 265
Purge. See Remove Old Data

Q

Queries, 245
    Advanced, 248
    And/Or, 250, 254
    Defined, 245
    Deleting, 257
    Editing, 249, 288
    Grouping, 256
    Lookup By Example, 246
    Operators, 250
Quick Attach, 181
    Messages that didn't attach, 183
    Preferences, 182
QuickAttach, 172
Quote, 297
    Attach to Contact, 298
    Create, 297

Editing the template, 388
Prompt for number, 297

R

Read Only Access, 347, 478
Record, 18
    Browsing, 34
    Delete, 31
    Locating, 34
    New, 22
Record History, 115, 116
Recurring Activities, 146
Referred by, 20
Reindex, 495
Related Task Pane, 37
Related Tasks Pane, 13
Relationships, 68
Remote Database
    Restore, 520
Remove Old Data, 506
Rename
    Database, 485
Replace, 505
Report, 319
    Design, 423
    Favorites, 324
    Field Identifier, 428
    Filters, 321, 441
    Formatting, 426
    Graph, 310
    List, 319
    Opportunities, 306
    pdf, 320
    Pipeline, 308
    Print, 319
    Print Preview, 320, 322
    Running Custom Reports, 442
    Scripting, 443
    Section, 432, 434
    Sorting, 432
    Subreport, 436
Report Designer, 423
    Adding Objects, 425
    Address Labels, 448
    Checks, 446
    Close up blank space, 444
    Detail Section, 423
    Footer, 424
    Group By, 432

Header, 423
Options, 433
Sizing Sections, 429
Summary Field, 434
Yes/No Fields, 446
Report Sections
Sorting, 432
Report Template
Creating, 422
Reports
OLE DB2, 533
Reschedule Activity, 111
Reset Menus and Toolbars, 378
Restore, 490, 491
Restore As, 492
Restricted Role, 463
Roles. See Security, See Security
What is mine?, 19
Rollover, 122

S

Sage ACT! Connect, 162
   Facebook, 165
   Setting up, 162
   Using, 164
Sage Business Info Services, 77
Sales Opportunity. See Opportunity
Salutation, 20
Save
   Contacts, 22
   SwiftWindow, 230
   Template, 201, 230
Scan and Repair. See Check and Repair
Scan for Duplicates, 501
Scheduled For, 131
Scheduler. See ACT! Scheduler
Scheduling. See Activities
   Accept, 138, 139
   Activities, 89
   Call, 89
   Decline, 138, 139
   For Multiple Contacts, 133
   For Others, 128
   General Tab, 128
   Invitations, 89
   Meeting, 89
   Notification, 138
   Personal Activity, 89
   Recurring Activities, 146

   Tentative, 138, 139
   To-Do, 89
   Vacation, 89
Screen Elements
   Windows, 12
Screen Layout. See Layout
Search, 51
   Keyword Search, 54
   Special Characters, 52
Secondary Contacts, 60
   Lookup, 62
   Promote, 63
Security
   Custom Permissions, 463, 465
   Field Level, 347, 478
   Limited Access, 20, 29, 265, 471
   Limited Access by Default, 30
   Private, 28
   Public/Private, 20, 265
   Role, 19
   Roles, 462
   Roles and Permissions, 528
Security Role
   What is mine?, 19, 463
Selecting Objects, 356
Send/Receive, 194
Services, 292
Setup Assistant, 8, 169, 182
Share Database, 458
Show Descriptions, 335
Sizing Objects, 356
Sizing Windows, 17
Smart Tasks, 397
   Automating, 408
   Creating, 398
   Criteria, 408
   Editing, 408
   Enabling, 411
   Manually running, 404
   Pending, 405
   Status, 406
   Steps, 399
Snooze, 143
Sorting, 36
   Contacts List View, 36
   Report, 432
Special characters, 52
Spell check, 230
Spell Check, 120
SPEPersonalMessage, 226
Splitter, 352

Index 545

Spouse, 21
Stage, 291, 386
   Lookup, 302
Standard Role, 462
Starting ACT!, 7
Startup View, 13
Static Groups, 261
Subgroups, 280
Subreport, 436
Subscription List, 510, 524
Suffixes, 45
Summary Field, 434
Surveys, 239
Swiftpage, 168, *See* E-marketing
SwiftWindow
   Editing text, 229
   Saving, 230
   Spell check, 230
SwiftWindows, 228
Sync
   Gmail History, 190
   Google, 161
   Google Calendar, 156
   Google Contacts, 157
   Outlook, 155
   Outlook Calendar, 150
   Outlook Contacts, 152
Sync Set, 511
   Criteria, 512
Synchronizing, 508, 516
   Accept Incoming Syncs, 516
   Application Sync, 516
   Connection Methods, 509
   Create Remote Database, 513
   Define Users, 509
   Defined, 508
   Enabling, 510
   HTTP Sync, 522
   Internet Sync, 509, 518, 522
   Network Application Sync, 509
   Network Sync Service, 509, 516
   Remote Database, 513
   Restore Remote, 520
   Subscription List, 524
   Sync Now, 522
   Sync Sets, 511, 512
   Troubleshooting, 525
   VPN, 509
System Fields, 121

T

Tables, 215
Tabs. See Layout Designer
Tag Mode, 57
   Lookup, 58
   Omit, 58
Task List, 106
   Calendar Comparison, 106
   Filter, 107, 130
   Printing, 110
   Scheduled For, 131
   Viewing, 107
Task Scheduler, 487, 523
Team, 465
   Create New, 472
   Limited Access, 472
   Manage Teams, 472
Template, 198, 203, 207
   E-marketing, 224
   Report. See Report Designer
   Sending from E-marketing, 226
Template Editor
   Basic, 225
Templates
   Saving, 230
Territory Realignment, 525
Time, 332, 333
Time Delay, 401
Title bar, 12
To-dos. See Activities
Tool tip, 14
Toolbar, 12, 14, 376
   Resetting, 378
Toolbox, 352
   Defined, 355
   Displaying, 355
Treo, 6
Triggers, 339

U

Universal Search, 51
Up Button, 281
Update Notification, 484
Uppercase, 333
URL, 333
Use Drop Down List, 334
User
   Adding, 464

Delete, 467
Inactive, 466
User fields, 21
User Security Roles, 528

V

Vacation, 89
vCard, 187
Version, 7
Version Update, 484
View Linked Fields, 278
View Toolbar, 14
VPN, 509

W

Weather, 73
Web Forms, 239
Web Info
   Custom links, 379
Web Info Tab, 71
   Business Info, 76
   Links, 72
Web Page
   Attaching, 74
Web Site, 20, 71
Website, 72

Welcome Page, 12
Windows Mobile, 162
Windows Screen Elements, 12
Won Sale, 299
Word. See Microsoft Word
Word Processor
   ACT!, 214
   Choosing, 195
   Create History, 209
   Graphics, 217
   Mail Merge, 198
   Mail Merge Fields, 201
   Printing, 209
   Ruler, 215
   Tables, 215
   Template, 198
   Toolbar, 214
Write
   E-mail, 174
   E-mail from Template, 174
   Letter, 207

Y

Yahoo, 73
Yes/No, 333
   Adding to Reports, 446